Migration in Irish History, 1607–2007

Migration in Irish History, 1607–2007

Patrick Fitzgerald and Brian Lambkin
Centre for Migration Studies
Ulster American Folk Park, Omagh

First published 2008 by
PALGRAVE MACMILLAN

Palgrave Macmillan in the UK is an imprint of Macmillan Publishers Limited,
registered in England, company number 785998, of Houndmills, Basingstoke,
Hampshire RG21 6XS.

Palgrave Macmillan in the US is a division of St Martin's Press LLC,
175 Fifth Avenue, New York, NY 10010.

Palgrave Macmillan is the global academic imprint of the above companies
and has companies and representatives throughout the world.

Palgrave® and Macmillan® are registered trademarks in the United States,
the United Kingdom, Europe and other countries.

ISBN 13: 978–0–333–96241–1   hardback
ISBN 10: 0–333–96241–9   hardback
ISBN 13: 978–0–230–22256–4   paperback
ISBN 10: 0–230–22256–0   paperback

This book is printed on paper suitable for recycling and made from fully
managed and sustained forest sources. Logging, pulping and manufacturing
processes are expected to conform to the environmental regulations of the
country of origin.

A catalogue record for this book is available from the British Library.

Library of Congress Cataloging-in-Publication Data
Fitzgerald, Patrick, 1964–
    Migration in Irish history, 1607–2007 / Patrick Fitzgerald and Brian
    Lambkin.
        p. cm.
    Includes bibliographical references and index.
    ISBN 13: 978–0–333–96241–1 (hbk.)
    ISBN 10: 0–333–96241–9 (hbk.)
    ISBN 13: 978–0–230–22256–4 (pbk.)
    ISBN 10: 978–0–230–22256–0 (pbk.)
      1. Irish – Migrations. 2. Irish – Foreign countries – History.
    3. Ireland – Emigration and immigration – History. 4. Northern
    Ireland – Emigration and immigration – History. 5. Ireland – History.
    6. Northern Ireland – History. I. Lambria, B. K. (Brian K.) II. Title.
    JV7711.F575 2008
    304.809415'0903–dc22

                                                        2008020802

10   9   8   7   6   5   4   3   2   1
            3 12 11 10 09 08

reat Britain by
penham and Eastbourne

Migration in Irish History, 1607–2007

Patrick Fitzgerald and Brian Lambkin
Centre for Migration Studies
Ulster American Folk Park, Omagh

First published 2008 by
PALGRAVE MACMILLAN

Palgrave Macmillan in the UK is an imprint of Macmillan Publishers Limited,
registered in England, company number 785998, of Houndmills, Basingstoke,
Hampshire RG21 6XS.

Palgrave Macmillan in the US is a division of St Martin's Press LLC,
175 Fifth Avenue, New York, NY 10010.

Palgrave Macmillan is the global academic imprint of the above companies
and has companies and representatives throughout the world.

Palgrave® and Macmillan® are registered trademarks in the United States,
the United Kingdom, Europe and other countries.

ISBN 13: 978–0–333–96241–1   hardback
ISBN 10: 0–333–96241–9   hardback
ISBN 13: 978–0–230–22256–4   paperback
ISBN 10: 0–230–22256–0   paperback

This book is printed on paper suitable for recycling and made from fully
managed and sustained forest sources. Logging, pulping and manufacturing
processes are expected to conform to the environmental regulations of the
country of origin.

A catalogue record for this book is available from the British Library.

Library of Congress Cataloging-in-Publication Data
Fitzgerald, Patrick, 1964–
    Migration in Irish history, 1607–2007 / Patrick Fitzgerald and Brian
    Lambkin.
        p. cm.
    Includes bibliographical references and index.
    ISBN 13: 978–0–333–96241–1 (hbk.)
    ISBN 10: 0–333–96241–9 (hbk.)
    ISBN 13: 978–0–230–22256–4 (pbk.)
    ISBN 10: 978–0–230–22256–0 (pbk.)
      1. Irish – Migrations. 2. Irish – Foreign countries – History.
    3. Ireland – Emigration and immigration – History. 4. Northern
    Ireland – Emigration and immigration – History. 5. Ireland – History.
    6. Northern Ireland – History. I. Lambria, B. K. (Brian K.) II. Title.
    JV7711.F575 2008
    304.809415'0903–dc22
                                                        2008020802

10 9   8   7   6   5   4   3   2   1
                3   12 11 10 09 08

reat Britain by
penham and Eastbourne

For the Fitzgerald, Moore, Lambkin and Muhr families,
at home and abroad

> *Do-ell Érinn, indell **cor**,*
> *Cechaing noib **nemed** mbled*
> [He turned away from Ireland, he entered a *pact*,
> He crossed in ships the *sanctuary* of the whales]
> (poem in praise of St Columba by Beccán mac Luigdech, seventh century)

> *Salve regina ... ad te clamamus, **exsules** filii Hevae ...gementes et flentes in hac*
> *lacrimarum valle ... post hoc **exsilium** ...*
> [Hail, [Holy] Queen ... to thee do we cry, *banished* children of Eve
> ...mourning and weeping in this valley of tears ... after this *exile*...]
> (*Salve Regina*, prayer of petition to the Blessed Virgin Mary, eleventh century)

> As I walked through the ***wilderness*** of this world ... and behold the **City**
> shone like the sun; the streets also were paved with gold ...
> (John Bunyan, *The Pilgrim's Progress from This World to That Which Is To*
> *Come*, 1678)

Contents

List of Plates, Figures and Maps

Plates

1. *The Departure of O'Neill out of Ireland* (1958), Thomas Ryan, courtesy of the artist
2. Map of Ulster (1591), Francis Jobson, TCD MS 1209/17, The Board of Trinity College Dublin
3. *Belfast* 1613, Sketch for mural in Belfast City Hall (1951), John Luke, Collection Ulster Museum, Belfast
4. *The North Gate Bridge and Jail, Cork City* (c. 1770), Nathaniel Grogan, Crawford Municipal Art Gallery, Cork
5. *Street scene at St. Patrick's Cathedral, Dublin* (c. 1810), Private collection; formerly with John Nixon, Agnew & Sons, London
6. *Liberty Welcoming the Arrival of the Immigrants* (1800), John James Barralet, Winterthur Museum, Delaware, USA
7. *Riaghlacha agus Orduighthe* (Rules and Regulations): A Proclamation issued by the War Office, a branch of the Chief Secretary's Office in Dublin Castle (1 November 1806), National Library of Ireland
8. *The Market Square, Ennis* (c. 1820), William Turner De Land, Frost & Reed Gallery, London (sold at auction, Christie's, May 1997)
9. *Emigrants at Cork* (c. 1840), anonymous pupil of Nathaniel Grogan, UCD Delargy Centre for Irish Folklore and the National Folklore Collection
10. *Five Points, New York City* (c. 1850), Geoffrey Clements, Bettmann Picture Archive, New York
11. *Homeward Bound* (1850), Erskine Nicol, National Library of Ireland
12. *The Irish Chiefs* (1850), Dorcas McGee, John Sutton and Brendan Meegan
13. *Letter from America* (1875), James Brenan, Crawford Municipal Art Gallery, Cork
14. *Gold Diggers Receiving a Letter from Home* (c. 1860), attributed to William Strutt, Art Gallery of New South Wales, Sydney, Australia
15. *Irish Emigrants Waiting for a Train* (1864), Erskine Nicol, Sheffield Galleries and Museums Trust, UK/ The Bridgeman Art Library
16. *View of Belfast, Sydenham, Belmont and Glenmachan* (c. 1861), J. H. Connop, Belfast Harbour Commissioners
17. Aerial view of Liverpool (1859), John Isaac, Liverpool Record Office, Liverpool Libraries
18. *Listed for the Connaught Rangers* (c. 1880), Elizabeth, Lady Butler, Bury Art Gallery, Museum and Archives, Lancashire

Figures

Maps

Foreword

This book is the culmination of a very unusual project, undertaken in a very unusual place.

It has always been easier to study presence than absence. Immigration has thus traditionally received more attention than emigration, and scholarship has been concentrated in countries of reception rather than regions of departure. The work of Robert Park and his colleagues of the Chicago School in the 1920s, for instance, explored many of the questions still relevant to scholars of immigration today, summed up in two simple questions: who comes and how do they fit in? But it paid little or no attention to the countries of origin of migrants, to the concern of some migrants to retain aspects of their own culture once settled in a new place, or to the notion that the encounter between migrants and host society was a two-way process which changed both sides.

Comparatively few research projects have attempted to explore the migration process in a more holistic way: who comes, who goes, who comes back and what are the effects on them, on those left behind, on new regions of settlement and on succeeding generations? Do migrants and their descendants assimilate and ultimately vanish into the host society, as was once assumed, or do they retain aspects of their ethnic origins in the new country as well as a sense of felt membership of a diasporic or transnational community? In an increasingly mobile world, interconnected as never before by technology, travel, globalised economic patterns and shared ideas, such questions are more relevant than ever.

For centuries Europeans saw themselves as emigrants: it was our *mission civilisatrice* to bring European values to other supposedly less enlightened parts of the world. In the case of Ireland and the Irish, occupying an ambivalent and liminal position in the developing project of European expansion as well as being victims of colonial oppression themselves, it has never been easy to capture their multifaceted and complex role and presence in the history of European migration. Were they emigrants or exiles, voluntary or forced migrants, lost children of the nation or the vanguard of a colonising movement in the new world? And how unique or exceptional was the Irish experience anyway? For many, it is probable that emigration simply represented opportunity. Furthermore, the process of leaving was conditioned by a culture which, for better or worse, normalised it as something that was inevitable, if regrettable.

The past 20 years have seen a welcome growth in interest in the story of Irish migration, in Ireland and beyond. This interest has been conditioned by political realities such as the emphasis given by President Mary Robinson in the Republic to the Irish Diaspora – a term not in common use before the 1990s. In Northern Ireland the period of the Troubles saw the quiet and often unremarked departure of a generation of young people who saw little hope or future in a troubled society and faltering economy. As the rate of departure soared in the Republic in the 1980s, other commentators were angered by what they saw as a kind of sanitisation of migration. Finally, the post-Belfast Agreement period has coincided with a remarkable change in the fortunes of both parts of the island as emigration fell to an all-time low and Ireland, for the first time since the seventeenth century, became a region of immigration.

A new generation of scholars is posing interesting and fundamental questions about Irish migration. The roles of women migrants have begun to be explored after much neglect. The painstaking reconstruction of individual migrants' lives through the use of letters and other personal sources has enabled new insights to be gained. There is a new interest in the multi-stranded nature of Irish migration – the role of Protestant migrants, the stories of those who went to less obvious places such as Argentina, the experiences of people who left for reasons of religious or sexual oppression and the negative as well as positive legacies of these migrants and their descendants in other societies around the world. Research on Ireland is now focusing on the emerging multi-ethnic nature of contemporary society and is seeking to explore, *inter alia*, what we can learn from Irish experiences elsewhere and apply in Ireland itself.

This new scholarship has come from many sources. As well as the signal achievements of a number of the most prominent individual scholars, a thriving virtual community of researchers has emerged around the world, aware of and interested in each other's work and able to exchange ideas and information in ways not previously possible. The role played by Patrick O'Sullivan's Irish Diaspora email discussion forum is particularly noteworthy in this regard.

In Ireland itself, the Centre for Migration Studies at the Ulster American Folk Park in Omagh, Co. Tyrone, occupies a unique position. It is currently the only dedicated migration research centre in either part of Ireland, and its specialist library and online databases provide a unique resource. Its excellent taught MSSc in Irish Migration Studies was the first in the country and continues to grow from strength to strength, generating new scholarship with a particular focus on regional migration. It collaborates actively with migration research centres in Europe and worldwide and has worked with other scholars in Ireland. With University College Cork, it has pioneered the development of oral archives, using a life-narrative approach to explore the lives and experiences of migrants.

This book is the first to offer an integrated narrative of Irish migration from the seventeenth century to the present. The choice of a four-century span is not arbitrary. The early seventeenth century saw the Flight of the Earls and the permanent departure of a key part of the remaining leadership of Gaelic Ireland, followed by a century characterised by immigration on an unprecedented scale, with all the consequences of that immigration for Irish history to the present day. It is appropriate that the book finishes at a hopeful point in that history, when a resolution to the negative consequences of that seventeenth-century immigration is finally in sight, even as Irish emigration itself seems to be becoming a fact of history, and a new, more benign immigration changes the face of the country in challenging but exciting ways.

Piaras Mac Éinrí
Cork

Preface

This book comes out of the experience of teaching postgraduate Irish Migration Studies since 1996 at the Centre for Migration Studies at the Ulster-American Folk Park, Omagh, Co. Tyrone in association with Queen's University, Belfast. These years have seen an unprecedented growth of interest worldwide in the theme of human migration, defined simply as 'changing place of residence' or 'moving home', and now seen as a major aspect of globalisation. There has certainly been cause for growth of interest in Ireland where such a dramatic shift from net emigration to net immigration has been taking place since the late 1990s. This leads us to believe that there may be interest in what we have to say here beyond specialist students of migration or Irish studies and we have tried to bear such readers in mind. Learning from our historical experience of migration, especially emigration, should help us to make informed choices as we come to terms with its contemporary challenges, especially those of immigration (Hoerder and Knauf 1992, 10; Koivukangas 2005, 62).

Increasingly, migration is being used as a prism through which to view societies as a whole, since the migrants, who are moving in and out of them, are in relationship, both in their old and new worlds, with those who are non-mobile and settled. Focusing on the minority that migrate sheds light on the majority that do not. This is the first book to survey the theme of migration in Irish history over four centuries (1607–2007) and to examine the dynamic relationship between its three main directions: immigration (including return migration), internal migration and emigration. Our basic argument is that each can only be understood fully in relation to the other two. In this 400th anniversary year, we take the Departure, or Flight, of the Earls in 1607 as an iconic event that marks a new start both to the Plantation (immigration) project of 'Making Ireland British' and to the emigration flow that has resulted in what we now call the Irish Diaspora.

In Part I, 'Putting Migration into Irish History', we give a fuller definition of what we mean by migration, as distinct from the two other fundamental elements of demography: fertility and mortality. Although historians often treat 'movement' and 'settlement' separately, as if they were opposites, we would emphasise at the outset that we see them as integrated in migration, a *coincidentia oppositorum* or agreement of opposites, in much the same way as Joyce saw life and death integrated in the 'wake' (Ellman 1959, 543). We should also make clear that by 'Irish' migration we mean migration into, within, out of and back to the whole island of Ireland and, as appropriate, we refer to its two main parts as Northern Ireland and the Republic of Ireland. To avoid tedious repetition, we should also point out here that the fragmentary nature of the surviving historical record means that estimating the numbers migrating before regular census-taking in the middle of the nineteenth century is difficult, if not impossible, and that therefore the figures offered should be treated as rough approximations.

Also in Part I, we are concerned with explaining how our approach fits into an already well-developed historiographical framework. Preceding *Migration in Irish History* are studies of *Migration in World History* (Cohen, R. 1997; Hoerder 2002; Manning 2005; Rodriguez and Grafton 2007) and *Migration in European History* (Bade 2003; Page Moch 1992; 2003; Bade et al. 2007); and at the national level there are studies of Irish immigration (Fanning et al. 2007) and Irish emigration (Fitzpatrick 1984; Delaney 2002), particularly of the Irish diaspora (O'Sullivan 1992–7; Akenson 1993; Bielenberg 2000). There is also a study of the British Isles diaspora (Richards 2004). This framework is based on the key migration concepts of 'home', 'family' and 'diaspora'. 'Home' is taken to mean the place of residence to which an individual most closely belongs. 'Family' is taken in its broad sense to mean the social group or community to which an individual most closely belongs, from the level of the nuclear family through the local, regional, and national levels to that of the international community. 'Diaspora' is taken as a useful term for describing collectively not only those migrant members of the 'family' (however defined) who are no longer living in the 'family home', but also their descendants.

Having set the scene, we present an overview of migration in Irish history between 1607 and 2007. Migration is seen as a three-stage process of 'leaving', 'crossing' and 'arriving'; as a three-way process of immigration (including return migration), internal migration and emigration; and as a three-outcome process of segregation, integration and modulation or alternation between the two. Distinctive aspects of continuity and change in the Irish migration land-scape are highlighted: the slackening of the immigration flow, the slow tipping of the rural–urban balance as a consequence of the internal migration flow, the persistence of the emigration flow, the high proportion of females in the emigration flow and the low proportion of return migrants in the immi-gration flow.

In Part II, 'In-Within-Out-Migration, 1607–2007', a more detailed, chrono-logical survey of the four centuries is offered in chapters that deal with a half-century each. The exception is the decade of the Great Famine (1845–55), which is given its own chapter. In the course of the survey a particular migra-tion chronology emerges, marked by key dates that mostly do not conform to those of the more familiar political chronology of Irish history. For example, between 1900 and 1950 the years 1907 and 1929 are prominent; the former as the high-point of European emigration and the latter as the turning-point when Irish emigration was reoriented away from the United States and towards Britain. Rather than divide up the chapters according to such less obvious landmarks, we have found the structure of half-century blocks easier to navigate, integrate and memorise across the four-century span, helping the reader to explore the detail of shorter periods without losing sight of the bigger picture. Each chapter of Part II follows the same pattern of three sections which deal in turn with immigration, internal migration and emigration, again in the hope that this will aid exploration of the dynamic or tension between them.

In Part III, 'The World in Ireland – Ireland in the World', we are concerned with the long-term outcomes of migration over the four centuries: with Ireland as a site of diaspora for the peoples of Britain and the rest of the world, and the rest of the world as sites of diaspora for the peoples of Ireland. We return to the key migration concepts of 'home' and 'diaspora' and consider the 'family' relationship between them. A fundamental concern of all communities or 'families', whether at the level of the planet, continent, nation, region, town, parish, townland or family home, is the so-called 'Goldilocks' question: how close is our community to being 'just right', in the sense that its condition is as it should be? Whether the focus of enquiry is political, economic, religious or cultural, migration plays an important part in constituting communal conditions that are more or less near to 'just right' and so communities generally tend to keep an eye on who is moving in and who is moving out, becoming particularly concerned when it appears that too many of the 'right sort' (however defined) are leaving and too many of the 'wrong sort' are arriving.

With the common human concern for knowing whether or not 'our' community is growing, stagnating or dying goes the aim of achieving that elusive equilibrium between being an overly 'open' or 'closed' society. The terms 'open' and 'closed' reflect the two main strategies available to communities for adjusting their immigration/emigration balance: integration and segregation. So we return also to the third possibility: that of the skill or 'art' of continually 'modulating' between integration and segregation. Just as Thomas Ryan's painting *The Departure of O'Neill out of Ireland* provides an icon of Irish migration at the opening of our survey (Plate 1), so does Petra Fox's painting *Small Island* provide an icon of it, towards the close, with the island apparently 'full up' (see front cover of Ó Gráda 1995). This prompts the question of how a better understanding of our migration past might be useful in meeting the current challenges of migration.

In 2007 we heard much about how migration is transforming the world and its many nations, about how more than 200 million (one in 35 of the world's population, or 3 per cent) are now living outside the country of their birth, and about how urgently we need to strive for social cohesion. The three epigraphs to this book, in what have been the three main languages of the island, Irish, Latin and English, are reminders of the depth of our migration past and of how the idea of migration has transformed our understanding of the human condition. Catholic and Protestant alike, following St Columba (Columcille), the author of the *Salve Regina* or John Bunyan, have mostly seen themselves as 'banished' from the original Garden of Eden into the 'wilderness' of this world, 'exiles' and 'pilgrims' intent on crossing over to final 'sanctuary' in a new world 'City', where the streets are paved with gold. The idea of migration has been central not only to religion but also to the secular ideologies of the nineteenth and twentieth centuries and their projects of leaving the 'wilderness' of the present to arrive, either back in an original 'garden' of some kind, or in some kind of 'gold-paved city' in a brave 'new world'. We can see the interpenetration of the religious and the secular, for example, in the US holiday of Thanksgiving (fourth Thursday of November) for the 'Pilgrim Fathers', who were first described as such in the eighteenth century when the humble self-description of the first settlers as 'strangers and pilgrims on the earth' (Hebrews 11: 13) was fused with the patriarchal, civic piety of the phrase 'founding fathers'.

Common to both religious and secular visions of the future is a concern with crossing to an 'otherworld' and with how entry to it will be regulated. In this book we are concerned with the historical crossings that were made by secular migrants (and religious missionaries) between the different 'worlds' of this world and with how their migrations were regulated. These range from the seventeenth-century immigration from Britain to Ireland of Planters, like Sir Arthur Chichester, the internal migration from the countryside to the new towns that they built, the emigration of the Earls O'Neill and O'Donnell, and the return migration of Owen Roe O'Neill, to the twenty-first-century immigration of those arriving at Dublin and Belfast airports as economic migrants, refugees, asylum seekers and returned emigrants. Within all this criss-crossing of internal migration, emigration and immigration are also the migrations of those who are continually in a state of migrancy, in mobile homes on land or sea, on the move 'between worlds'.

Although we write as historians, we have tried to bear in mind that the broad discipline of migration studies seeks to include the insights of others, including architecture, art history, anthropology, folklore, geography, literature, sociology and socio-linguistics, and that it is about, as Patrick O'Sullivan says, 'putting the song next to the census'(1992a, xv). We have tried also to follow J. J. Lee's injunction to 'incorporate the visual' by making detailed use of paintings, drawings and photographs, maps and diagrams (2005, 218). As well as providing landmarks across the four centuries, the illustrations intimate something of the 'art' of migration, in the dual sense not only of the range of artistic representations of the migrants themselves, but also the skill or art that they exhibit in migrating. Migration is about the moving of people between places. Accordingly the Index is arranged in three sections: Subject, Personal Names and Place Names. We hope that this will not only be useful as a tool for navigating the text, but, also be seen as a reflection of the 'through-otherness' that has come, for better or worse, from migration in Irish history. We hope that by pointing to further reading, the diversity of current research directions, debates about research and indeed gaps in research, readers may be inspired to explore the field further and contribute to the ongoing research effort, particularly at the level of the localities and families with which they are most familiar, at home and abroad.

December 2007
Castletown, Omagh

Acknowledgements

Without the hard work, support and goodwill of many people in the development of our Centre for Migration Studies (CMS) this book would not have been possible, and so we have many to thank, far more than those mentioned below.

First and foremost we thank John Lynch of Queen's University, Belfast who with Patrick Fitzgerald has pioneered the teaching in Omagh of the MSSc in Irish Migration Studies, President Mary McAleese, who in her time at Queen's University was instrumental in getting the course started, and all our students, past and present, whose contributions in tutorial discussions and on memorable field trips have informed this book in many hidden ways. Their dissertations are listed at the CMS website. With the privilege of working in a specialist Irish migration library and archive we owe a special debt of gratitude to our CMS colleagues past and present, Librarian Christine McIvor, Senior Library Assistant Christine Johnston, ICT managers Joe Mullan, Des McMorrow and the late John Winters, Irish Emigration Database Collection project manager Lorraine Tennant, Patrick Brogan, Belinda Mahaffy and our resident Queen's University Research Fellow (2004–8) Johanne Devlin Trew.

The Centre is the main project of the Scotch-Irish Trust of Ulster whose Trustees and Chairman Sir Peter Froggatt and Secretary John Gilmour have been especially supportive, not least in providing a generous grant towards the cost of illustrations, as also have members of the CMS Management Committee past and present, Rosemary Adams, Valerie Adams, Leslie Clarkson, Bernard Cullen, Joe Eagleson, Russell Farrow, Tom Fraser, Keith Jeffery, Geraldine Keegan, Liam Kennedy, Dan McCall, John McKinney, Eric Montgomery, Paul Nolan, Helen Osborn, Anne Peoples, Gary Sloan, Jack Smith and John Wilson . We are grateful to our colleagues in the Ulster American Folk Park and the National Museums of Northern Ireland, the Northern Ireland Library Service, especially the Western Education and Library Board, Omagh District Council, the Public Record Office of Northern Ireland and the Department of Culture, Arts and Leisure.

In Queen's University, we would like to thank especially Jonathan Bardon, Dominic Bryan, Fiona Clark, Catherine Clinton, Sean Connolly, Peter Gray, David Hayton, Sophia Hillan, John Kirk, Patrick Maume, Mary O'Dowd, Pat Patten, Nini Rodgers and the late Peter Jupp; and in the University of Ulster, Billy Kelly, Don MacRaild, Éamonn Ó Ciardha, Emmet O'Connor, Alan Sharp and all the MA students since 1999 of Migration and the Politics of Violence, 1945–98 (POL802). Also in Northern Ireland we would like to thank Jonathan Bell, John Bradley, Peter Carr, Brenda Collins, Peter Collins, Bill Crawford, John

Cunningham, David Fitzpatrick, Len Graham, David Hammond, Roddy Hegarty, Richard Hurst, Shane McAteer, John McCabe, Claire McElhinney, Robert Heslip, Annesley Malley, Brendan and Jenny Meegan, John Moulden, Fintan Mullan, Trevor Parkhill, Vivienne Pollock, Stephen Roulston, William Roulston, Tony Scullion, Tim Smith and Brian Trainor.

If we have succeeded to some degree in transcending our narrow northern perspectives, it is thanks largely to those associated with Piaras Mac Éinrí in Migration Studies at University College Cork, Liam Coakley , Breda Gray and Caitríona Ní Laoire, and also to Andy Bielenberg, Ciara Breathnach, Nicholas Canny, Patricia Coughlan, Frank Cullen, David N. Doyle, Patrick Duffy, Máire Herbert, John McGurk, Cormac Ó Gráda, Mícheál Mac Craith, Hiram Morgan and Nollaig Ó Muraíle. Beyond Ireland we are likewise grateful to many who have been good colleagues and friends, including Don Akenson, Geoff Branigan, Katharine Brown, Bruce Elliott, Marianne Elliott, Peter Gilmore, Patrick Grant, Marjory Harper, Liam Harte, Mary Hickman, Audrey Horning, Warren Hofstra, Steve Ickringill, Bryan Lamkin, Joe Lee, Ian McKeane, Elizabeth Malcolm, Kerby Miller, Mick Moloney, Michael Montgomery, Bill Mulligan, Edmundo Murray, Brad Patterson, Jonathan Riley-Smith, Richard Straw, Tom Devine, Rory Sweetman, Phil and Molly Townsend, Ronald Wells and David Wilson. For our European and global outlook, such as it is, we owe much to our membership of the Association of European Migration Institutions (AEMI) and of the Irish Diaspora Studies scholarly network, initiated and sustained by Patrick O'Sullivan.

The length of the Bibliography alone is an indication of the breadth and depth of the field that we have drawn on, and we are indebted individually and collectively to the accumulated scholarship of all those named. In thinking about the nature of Irish migration we have found ourselves returning repeatedly to the interplay between the ideas of Kerby Miller and Don Akenson. We are especially grateful to Palgrave Macmillan's anonymous reader and Piaras Mac Éinrí, Magdalen Lambkin, Kay Muhr, Johanne Devlin Trew and Eric Walker for their close readings of the typescript and invaluable suggestions and advice. Michael Strang, Ruth Ireland and Ruth Willats at Palgrave Macmillan have been most patient and understanding in getting us into print at last. Once again we thank Piaras Mac Éinrí, not only for his Foreword but also for extending from the outset the hand of cross-border co-operation and friendship from *Ionad na hImirce, Coláiste na hOllscoile, Corcaigh* / the Irish Centre for Migration Studies, Cork.

Finally, our thanks go with love to our wives and children, Thelma, Conor and Owen, and Kay, Bréanainn, Angus and Magdalen, remembering also our parents, Joyce Fitzgerald and the late Stanley Fitzgerald, and Joan and Douglas Lambkin.

Part I
Putting Migration into Irish History

Migration is defined broadly as a permanent or semi-permanent change of residence. No restriction is placed on the distance of the move or upon the voluntary or involuntary nature of the act, and no distinction is made between external and internal migration. Thus, a move across the hall from one apartment to another is counted as just as much an act of migration as a move from Bombay, India, to Cedar Rapids, Iowa, though of course the initiation and consequences of such moves are vastly different ... No matter how short or how long, how easy or how difficult, every act of migration involves an origin, a destination, and an intervening set of obstacles.

Everett S. Lee (1966)

Introduction

We have taken the classic definition of Everett Lee as the cornerstone of our approach to migration in Irish history. It is based on the three dimensions of time, space and community. With regard to time, migration is distinguished from other movement, such as a holiday or temporary business visit, by being sustained – that is, it is permanent or semi-permanent. With regard to space, it is distinguished by the crossing of a significant boundary or border that involves a changed relationship to the physical environment. With regard to community, it is distinguished by a social transition that involves a change of status or a changed relationship to the local, regional or national community. Quite legitimately, specialists in international emigration and immigration, such as that between India and the United States, and even specialists in internal migration, have found the idea of including moves between apartments in the same block impossibly elastic, stretching the meaning of migration so far that, for their purposes, it becomes unserviceable:

> First, we will expect migration to be a *significant* movement. By this we mean that it has demographic consequences such that the move has involved a shift across a definite administrative boundary. This will mean that we will not consider as migration moving Grandad into a 'granny flat' in the same village or small town, so some quite significant moves will be omitted. However, every move to another town or across a country or district line we will include as migration.
>
> (Jackson 1986, 4; on the work of Jackson, see Delaney 2007, 4)

In this book we restrict ourselves to moves that cross the lowest-level administrative boundary which, in the case of Ireland historically, is that of the townland (Muhr 2000, 5, 11; Crawford 2003, 35). The great elasticity of the term migration, like that, for example, of 'community', makes it important to be clear about its limits if we are not to empty it of meaning altogether

(Williams 1988; Manning 2005, 3–4, 13–14; Koser 2007, 16–19). It is worth noting that Lee himself imposed limits. Missing from the quotation above is the following:

> However, not all kinds of spatial mobility are included in this definition. Excluded, for example, are the continual movements of nomads and migratory workers, for whom there is no long-term residence, and temporary moves like those to the mountains for the summer.

The exclusion of nomads and migratory workers can be seen as arbitrary, in this case for the convenience of Lee in making his self-imposed task of reassessing Ravenstein's 'laws of migration' (see Appendix II) more manageable. A major study of *Migration, Migration History, History* (Lucassen and Lucassen 1999) happily *includes* a study of Europe's 'eternal vagrants' and 'travelling groups' (Lucassen, L., 225–52). It would be very difficult to justify excluding, for example, seasonal agricultural workers from migration in Irish history. The intimate relationship between short-distance internal migration and international migration is illustrated by the well-known Irish case of the returned emigrant Michael MacGowan (Micí Mac Gabhann), who spent 17 years in America, in the steelworks of Bethelehem, the silver mines of Butte and the goldmines of the Klondike. His first experience of migration was in May 1874 at the age of eight, as a hired farm servant, moving from his home townland of Derryconor (*Doire Chonaire*, 'Conaire's oakwood') in Cloghaneely to that of Meenadrain (*Mín an Draighin*, 'the mountain grassy patch of the blackthorn') in Glenveagh, less than 20 miles away and still within the county of Donegal. He described arriving in Meenadrain:

> It wasn't the kind of landscape that I was used to at home. I missed the sea and the islands and there wasn't the same green countryside around me. I was in a mountainy desert: *charbh é an cineál radhairc é a rabh mé cleachtaithe leis fá bhaile. Cha rabh an fharraige, ná na hoileáin, ná an talamh glas céanna le feiceáil agam. Bhí mé anois istigh i bhfásach sléibhe.*

MacGowan, who knew about international migration, clearly classed this childhood experience as migration. Reflecting, in old age, on his return home that November to Derryconor, he told his interviewer: 'You'd think I'd returned from America, there was such a warm welcome given to me: *shílfea gur as Meiriceá a tháinig mé, bhí an oiread sin fáilte romham ar ais* (MacGowan 1962, 18, 23; Mac Gabhann 1996, 38, 44).

In order to make study of migration more manageable and give due recognition to important differences, it is necessary to distinguish among different types according, for example, to the distance involved, the nature of the boundary crossed or the voluntary or involuntary nature of the act (see Appendix I). In this book our primary focus is on the three types: immigration (including return migration), internal migration and emigration.

Notwithstanding these qualifications, we insist on the validity of Lee's comprehensive definition of migration and its relevance to our basic argument: that immigration (including return migration), internal migration and emigration each can only be understood fully in relation to the other two, and that each is part of a common migration process, however long or short the move: from origin, across a set of intervening obstacles, which may include administrative boundaries or borders, to destination.

Defined objectively, migration is about moving 'place of residence', but it also involves the idea of moving 'home', as is made clear by the common practice of calling those without a place of residence 'homeless'. It makes sense for social scientists grappling with large-scale movements to restrict their concern to data related to places of 'residence', but migration history needs also to deal with what is subjectively thought of as 'home', and the fact that the two do not necessarily coincide. Although international migration and internal migration are in many respects 'vastly different', as Lee acknowledges, the latter is not necessarily less stressful and challenging, as is evident from the case of Irish Travellers: 'an "outsider" group in Irish society, a negative "Other" perceived as a 'problem' that needs to be solved' (Hayes 2006, x; Mac Éinrí 2007, 232).

Sociologists, starting with the classic study by Thomas and Znaniecki, *The Polish Peasant in Europe and America* (1918–20), were quicker off the mark than historians in seeing the importance of migration, and in the 1960s were exposing the myth of the static society, which assumes that:

> by harking back to some pre-existing rural utopia, that the natural condition of man is sedentary, that movement away from the natal place is a deviant activity associated with disorganization and a threat to the established harmony of *Gemeinschaft* relationships which are implied by life within a fixed social framework
> (Jackson 1969, 3; Manning 2005, 2; Black and MacRaild 2000, 149)

The myth of the static society came under challenge from historians in the 1990s when the case was being widely advocated for 'putting migration into history'. A leading advocate was Leslie Page Moch in *Moving Europeans* (1992; 2003, 1–21), where she highlighted the distortion of our previously dominant image of a sedentary Europe – due to our overlooking of mobility – and went on to show how our understanding of history 'alters dramatically with the realization that its actors were not sedentary'. Other pioneering scholars, such as Dirk Hoerder (2002), Karl Bade (2003) and Leo Lucassen (2005), agree that migration is 'a missing piece in the standard understanding ... of the nature of historical change'. One important sign that the case for 'putting migration into history' has not only been widely accepted but acted upon is *Diasporas, Migration and Identities*, the £5.5 million, five-year trans-disciplinary, strategic research programme launched by the UK Arts and Humanities Research Council in April 2005. Once we take migration into proper account, so the argument goes, the central story that emerges is one of 'human movement, comprising primarily local and seasonal migration in the seventeenth century that subsequently shifted, then dramatically expanded by the end of the nineteenth century' (Moch 2003, 21).

In Part I we are concerned with the more specific case of 'putting migration into Irish history', dealing first with what exactly we mean by migration, then with the emergence of the discipline of migration studies and of Irish migration studies in particular, and finally with how our resulting new approach to thinking about migration as a three-stage, three-way, three-outcome process can be applied to the history of Ireland.

1
Migration and Irish Migration Studies

Ireland in Europe

The scale of the shift in Europe's migration story, driven by the twin engines of industrialisation and urbanisation, is seen most starkly in the growth of its cities in relation to its population. Between 1800 and 1900 London grew by 340 per cent to 6.5 million; Paris by 345 per cent to 2.5 million; Vienna by 490 per cent to about 2 million; and Berlin by a staggering 872 per cent also to about 2 million. In 1800, when Europe's population was about 200 million, 6 million (3 per cent) were living in its 23 major cities with populations over 100,000, but by 1900, when the population had reached 400 million, about 50 million (12 per cent) were living in 135 major cities. By 1914 there were a dozen million-plus conurbations in Europe, with London, Paris, Berlin, Vienna, St Petersburg and Istanbul having reached that status first, followed by Glasgow, Manchester, Leeds, Liverpool, Birmingham, the Ruhr, Hamburg and Moscow (Manning 2005, 169). Dublin and Belfast in 1901 had populations of 290,000 and 350,000, respectively.

A major component of this growth was internal and transnational migration within Europe (always more significant than emigration) which was highly complex according to the diversity of both the receiving and sending areas and of the causes and effects of the migration flows between them as changing cross-currents and counter-currents were driven by economic cycles of boom and bust as well as intermittent crises of famine and war. Towns and cities grew differently, as for example London and Paris, whose growth rate due to in-migration in the second half of the nineteenth century was 16 and 64 per cent respectively. While all towns had service sectors of administration and commerce, they varied greatly in the relative importance of their primary and secondary manufacturing sectors. Predominantly service towns, such as Amiens in France and Cologne in Germany, had low birth rates and grew mainly through in-migration, especially through women going into domestic service. Textile towns, such as Manchester in England, Roubaix in France and Barmen in Germany, had high birth rates (decreasing after 1870) and high in-migration, mostly from the immediate vicinity, with a very high proportion of women; and coal and steel towns, like Sheffield in England and Duisburg in Germany, had the highest volume of in-migration with high birth rates and a very high proportion of men.

Cultures of migration

The migration process did not affect all parts of a country equally of course. Therefore, as Dudley Baines (1991) has warned, the country may not be the appropriate unit of analysis because of the high degree of regional variation. It is important to bear in mind that some countries, such as Germany after unification in 1871, were particularly large and heterogeneous to the point of developing different 'cultures' of migration within them. In all the European countries, even the smallest, some regions produced relatively large numbers of migrants, while others produced relatively few, with sharp contrasts often observable down at the level of neighbouring sub-regions, and even between and within local communities. So as well as seeing the countries of western, central and northern Europe as 'core' and the southern and eastern countries as 'peripheral' in the nineteenth century, we need to be aware of both the core and periphery areas *within* the countries of western, central and northern Europe. One such example of an internal core–periphery relationship was that between Britain and Ireland, within the United Kingdom.

In the history of the migration streams between these areas lies the explanation for the take-off of mass overseas migration from Europe during the crisis years of the 1840s, when between 200,000 and 300,000 left each year. Not surprisingly, it was the countries of western, central and northern Europe which initially supplied the largest proportion of overseas migrants, especially Britain and Ireland. Of the 50 million or so Europeans who migrated overseas between 1800 and 1914 (40 million to the United States), about 10 million were from Britain (England, Scotland and Wales) and 6 million from Ireland, together accounting for over 30 per cent of the mass emigration. That said, however, overseas migration in the long nineteenth century (1815–1914) was at a rate of only 3 per 1,000 per year and migration *within* remained the dominant aspect of Europe's migration story (Baines 1991, 22).

It is understandable then that Ireland, with its migration story dominated by emigration, should receive little attention in a survey of European migration from 1650 to the present, notwithstanding the acknowledgement of its importance as a special case (Moch 2003, 120–1). The focus shifts between different areas across four main periods, but not to Ireland. Thus in the first period, between 1650 and 1750 (the 'pre-industrial' period), the focus is on the rural

English midlands, Artois in northern France, Tuscany and some parishes south of Stockholm, as well as on the German cities of western and central Europe, London, Amsterdam and the North Sea migration 'system' which linked seasonal workers from northern Germany to the western Netherlands. In the second period, between 1750 and 1815 (the 'rural industrialisation' period), the focus is on rural industrial villages in Normandy, the English midlands and today's Belgium, as well as on the industrial towns of Bordeaux, Rouen and Verviers and the migration system that connected the highlands of France with Spain. In the third period of 'urbanisation', between 1815 and 1914, the focus is on the deindustrialising countryside of Normandy and Languedoc as well as the prosperous agrarian areas of Prussia and northern France, and also the growing cities of Roubaix (France) and Duisburg and Cologne (Germany), and the links between the Polish territories of the Austro-Hungarian Empire and eastern Prussia and western Germany and the United States. Finally, in the fourth period, between 1914 and the present, the focus is on international migration, especially the movement of Belgians, Italians, Portuguese and North Africans into France, and of Poles, wartime forced labourers, post-war Turks and eastern Europeans into Germany.

Multi-level migration studies

Any survey of this kind cannot include every country, let alone region. Having offered the 'big picture' in outline, grounded in these detailed case studies, Moch (2003, 143) points to the need for further case studies and comparative research at the national, regional and local levels. As another leading migration historian points out, 'the more we know about other regions, the more partial our explanations become. But the comparative method, although difficult, is the one that yields the insights' (Baines 1991, 28; see also MacRaild 2000, 42–6). We may see the overall picture, but we can only explain it in terms of detailed and local studies because, like any other highly complex phenomenon, migration cannot be explained adequately in terms of simple patterns or relationships. This is true, for example, of the effect of immigration on a receiving economy where the outcome may be negative or positive, and not necessarily one or the other. As we have noted, regional and local studies can reveal an astonishing diversity of migration experience down to the level of families in the same small community, where the tradition of migration may be common in some and rare in others. Hence there is great value in the reconstruction of individual migration stories. Rarely, however, have individual migrants left full records of their own stories, such as *Mes mémoires* by Jeanne Bouvier, who was born into a peasant family in eastern France near Lyon in 1865, moved to Paris as a domestic servant, became a skilled dressmaker and found, when she returned to her home village in the 1890s, that she could no longer understand the local *patois* (Moch 2003, 102–3).

Through tracing such individual migration stories we may discover the network of connections between the poor uplands that exported people and the fertile plains of crowded villages, between the growing towns and their hinterlands, and between the towns and the great, labour-hungry metropolitan centres and the developing economies that lay beyond them overseas (Hoerder and Moch 1996, 3). This is not to suggest that the 'big picture' of the macro-level is nothing more than the sum of all activity at the micro-level, but it is to assert the value of both disaggregating and aggregating migration data 'so that neither large-scale change nor the migrants themselves are lost'. While our main concern is Ireland's migration story, we need to be able, as it were, to keep zooming in to the level of the individual migrants and their communities and zooming out to where we see Ireland as a region of Europe, and even further to where we see Europe as a region of a world economic system. The more we modulate or move coherently between the meso-, micro- and macro-levels, the more finely grained and comprehensive our picture of migration.

Defining migration

As we have noted, the definition of migration by Everett S. Lee, quoted as the epigraph to this Part, as movement that involves a semi-permanent or permanent change of residence is too broad for some. Moch, for example, prefers to narrow it to include only change of residence that is 'beyond a municipal boundary, be it village or town', while others prefer to exclude seasonal moves (i.e. lasting less than a year) (2003, 18). However broadly or narrowly defined, what distinguishes migration from movement in general is that it results in resettlement, and therefore, putting it at its simplest, we can say that migration is about 'moving house'. Whether or not this also means 'moving home' depends on the attitudes of those involved, which brings us to the core idea of 'migration': movement between an 'old world' and a 'new world'. As a leading sociologist of migration has pointed out:

> it is migration, albeit of a limited kind, when a child moves from cradle to bed, leaves home for his first day at school or goes courting in the next village … every such movement implies an element of disassociation from the usual and familiar world, a transition and an involvement with a new environment, a new context of physical space and – most significantly – social relationships.
>
> (Jackson 1969, 1–2)

Given this fundamental definition of a process that involves disassociation, transition and re-association, we are free to impose our own limits on the types of migration with which to concern ourselves. In this book we have limited ourselves more narrowly than Lee in that we have excluded migration within units smaller than the townland, but more broadly in that we have included seasonal migration.

Types of migration

Recent research into the history of European migration has shown that different types of migration – seasonal, temporary, rural–rural, rural–urban, urban–urban, urban–rural – have long existed alongside emigration from and immigration to Europe. It has also shown how, over time, the balance between the different directions of migration (immigration, internal migration and emigration) has varied greatly. (For further discussion of the typologies of migration, see Appendix I.)

Numbers of migrants

Having distinguished between different types of migrants it is necessary to obtain as accurate data about them as possible, which in the first instance means counting them. As we noted in the Preface, obtaining precise numbers of migrants from the surviving records is difficult if not impossible before the middle of the nineteenth century and even today, as we note in chapter 16, the accuracy of migration statistics can be questionable. Nevertheless, there has been a massive improvement in the collection of demographic data, which can be seen vividly by comparing the records of the Census (*c.* 1659) and the Poll and Hearth Taxes conserved by Sir William Petty (1623–87), for example, with the standard forms used by the enumerators of the 1841 Census (Gurrin 2002; Pender 2002; Crawford 2003, 21). Ever since the pioneering work of E. G. Ravenstein in the 1880s on Census data (see Appendix II), demographers have been concerned with the statistics of migration as one of the three components of population change, along with fertility and mortality. As Akenson warns in his *Primer*,

> Numbers are not much fun. But before one becomes engaged in the enjoyable aspects of chronicling the Irish diaspora (things such as the heroics of individual migrants, the flash of sectarian riots, the machinations of ambitious politicians) one needs to know where within the big picture the individual story is situated.
>
> (1993, 11)

Thanks to a lot of hard work by economic historians and historical geographers with fragmentary materials, we are provided with a big picture of Ireland's population in which to situate migration. In 1607 there were about

750,000 people on the island (compared with one million in 1300). By 1641 there were between 1.5 and 1.6 million, declining to 1.3 million in 1652, and rising again to 1.97 million in 1687 (Cullen 1975; Connolly 2007, 405). By 1712 there were between 2 and 2.3 million, rising to between 4.2 and 4.6 million in 1791. By 1821, the year of the first major, modern Census, there were 6.8 million, rising to 8.2 million in 1841, and then falling to 4.5 million in 1901, 4.4 million in 1911 and 4.2 million in 1926 (Houston 1992; Kennedy and Clarkson 1993, 160; Crawford 2003, 13–15). In the Census years of 2001 and 2002, the populations of Northern Ireland and the Republic of Ireland were 1.7 and 3.9 million respectively, a total of 5.6 million. In 2006 the population of the Republic of Ireland was 4.2 million (Fahey 2007, 14).

Emergence of Irish migration studies

So great has been the growth of interest in migration over the last 20 years that it has resulted in the emergence of a new academic field of study, distinct from demography (population studies), which is concerned with fertility and mortality as well as migration (Brettell and Hollifield 2000, 27–42). Such has been the volume and quality of research devoted to the theme of migration by scholars in long-established disciplines, including history, geography, politics, economics, sociology, anthropology and literary and art criticism, that we now have a 'turbulent' body of theory, consisting of a number of theoretical frameworks, by which we may better understand the whole phenomenon of migration (Hammar 1997; Castles and Miller 1998; Massey 1998; Papastergiadis 1999; Brettell and Hollifield 2000). The discipline is now known broadly as migration studies and includes the rather more specialised settlement, integration and diaspora studies. The *Journal of Ethnic and Migration Studies* was founded in the late 1990s. It is concerned mainly with exploring five basic questions: Why does migration occur? Who migrates? What are the patterns of 'old worlds' and 'new worlds' and of the flows between them? What are the effects of migration on the 'old world'? What are the effects of migration on the 'new world'? (White and Woods 1980, 1; Guinness 2002, 1). The already vast and growing literature of global migration studies has been surveyed by Cohen (1997), Hoerder (2002), Bade (2003), Manning (2005) and others.

As mentioned in the Preface, there is now a well-developed historiography into which *Migration in Irish History* can be fitted. At the global level there is *Migration in World History* (Manning 2005) and also *World Migrations in the Second Millennium* (Hoerder 2002), *Global Diasporas: an Introduction* (Cohen, R. 1997), *Migration, Migration History, History* (Lucassen and Lucassen 1999), *Migration in History: Human Migration in Comparative Perspective* (Rodriguez and Grafton 2007; see also Olson 2003; Hatton and Williamson 2005). At the European level there is *Migration in European History* (Bade 2003) and also

Moving Europeans: Migration in Western Europe since 1650 (Moch 1992; 2003) and the *Encyclopaedia of European Migration: from 1600 to the present* (Bade et al. 2007; see also Emmer and Mörner 1992, 1–11). At the national level, with a UK focus, there is *Britannia's Children: Emigration from England, Scotland, Wales and Ireland since 1600* (Richards 2004); and, with an all-Ireland focus, *Irish Emigration 1801–1921* (Fitzpatrick 1984), *Irish Emigration since 1921* (Delaney 2002), *The Irish Diaspora: A Primer* (Akenson 1993) and *The Irish Diaspora* (Bielenberg 2000). In recent years, within migration studies generally, 'diasporic' and 'transnational' approaches have been highly productive, much thought having been given in particular by Patrick O'Sullivan and Kevin Kenny to future directions in Irish migration and diaspora studies, about which there is currently lively debate (Akenson 1993; Vertovec and Cohen 1999; Kenny 2003ab; O'Sullivan 2003; Delaney, Kenny and MacRaild 2006).

The emergence of Irish migration studies was marked by the publication of the six-volume series *The Irish World-Wide* (O'Sullivan 1992–7) and *The Irish Diaspora: A Primer* (Akenson 1993), and also by the launch in 1997 of the on-line Irish Diaspora Studies Discussion List, moderated by Patrick O'Sullivan. Subsequent surveys include those by Cullen (1994), Delaney (2000), Bielenberg (2000), Gray (2002b; 2004), Hickman (2002; 2005), Walter et al. (2002), Mac Éinrí and Lambkin (2002), O'Sullivan (2003), Kenny (2003ab), and Delaney, Kenny and MacRaild (2006). We refer readers with further interest in the emergence of the multidisciplinary analytical framework of Irish migration studies to Appendix II.

To sum up our central concern here with migration in Irish history, we return to the related ideas of 'home' and 'homelessness': the relationship between those who feel themselves to be 'at home' and 'settled', and those who feel themselves to be 'homeless', either as 'pilgrims' seeking arrival in a 'new world', or as 'exiles' seeking return to an 'old world'. A powerful image of this relationship is that of the walled town or city, and Bunyan's *The Pilgrim's Progress* (1678) provides us with a paradigm illustration of how migration works in its picture of arrivals at the Celestial City:

> When he [Ignorance] was come up to the gate, he looked up to the writing that was above, and then began to knock, supposing that entrance would have been quickly administered to him; but he was asked by the men that looked over the top of the gate, Whence came you? and what would you have? ... Then they asked him for his certificate, that they might go and show it to the King. So he fumbled in his bosom for one, and found none. Then said they, Have you none? But the man answered never a word. So they told the King, but He would not come down to see him, but commanded the two shining ones, that conducted Christian and Hopeful to

the City, to go out, and take Ignorance, and bind him hand and foot, and have him away.

On arrival, pilgrims read the inscription written in letters of gold over the city gates: 'Blessed Are They That Do His Commandments, That They May Have Right To The Tree Of Life, And May Enter Through The Gates Into The City'. They request admission by knocking, and the gatekeepers respond by demanding that they produce the necessary 'certificate' as proof of conformity to the City's 'commandments' and eligibility to enter (for the frontispiece of *The Pilgrim's Progress*, see Chadwick 1995, 217; compare also the illustration of 'The Departure of Sir Henry Sidney from Dublin Castle' by John Derricke 1581, with the heads of executed Irish rebels shown above the entrance between the towers of the gatehouse, Quinn 1985, Plate VI).

As we mentioned in the Preface, a concern in every community, whether at the level of the family, townland, parish, town, city, region or nation, has been to decide what, if anything, the 'family' should write over its 'gates'; what 'commandments' or laws and regulations it should bind its members by; what restrictions it should place on their access to its 'tree of life' or resources; who its 'gatekeepers' and 'king' should be; and what kind of 'certificate', if any, it should require of migrants that arrive seeking sanctuary, residence and full citizenship.

The religious idea of transmigration to an otherworld is not possible without some grounding in the migration of this world. Thus, in picturing how admission is regulated through the gates of the Heavenly City, writers have inevitably been influenced by the 'cities' of their day (McDannell and Lang 1988, 73–6, 117–18, 189–93). We know, for instance, how migration was regulated by Columba's community on Iona in the eighth century and by Bunyan's Bedford in the seventeenth century (Lambkin 2007b; Farrar 1926; see also Clark and Souden 1987; Barry 1990; Borsay and Proudfoot 2002, 198). We also know how migration was regulated by the walled towns of Ireland:

Undesirable aliens, beggars, vagabonds or people suffering from diseases such as leprosy could easily be turned back at the gates, as could those who were not residents. This may have led to the development of the many 'Irishtowns' which appeared particularly in the seventeenth century outside gates, for example at Clonmel's West Gate and Athlone's Dublin Gate.

(Thomas 1992, 131)

In chapter 10 we refer to the gates of Cork city being shut in 1847 during the Great Famine against the arrival of the starving from the countryside. Although the walls of Ireland's towns were largely removed or allowed to fall into disrepair in the eighteenth century, they were replaced by new barriers, the latest of which are to be seen operating most clearly perhaps at our airports in International Arrivals. As well as physical barriers, such as those across the car parks of Ireland that bar entry to the caravans of Travellers, there are the less easily detectable mental barriers, which both settled communities and migrants erect in order to try to manage, or cope with, migration.

The walled town or city, with its citadel or fortress, remains a dominant image in thinking about migration, as when the European Union, in its efforts to keep non-EU goods, businesses and nationals out of its 27 member states, is referred to as 'Fortress Europe' (Loshitzky 2006). It was reported in 2007 that at least 11,521 people had died since 1988 along Europe's frontiers, among them 4,134 at sea. In the case of Ireland we need only mention Derry's walls and the role of the siege of Derry in Ulster Protestant mythology. The injunction 'to close the gates and man the walls' is often seen as 'emblematic of a closed ideological system, incapable of responding to a changing world' (MacBride 1997, 81). The distinction between communities that are 'open' and 'closed' is widely applicable, even at the level of the parish (Wrightson 1982, 171–3). We should not, however, let the 'closed' image of the walled community under siege obscure the fact that normally the gates are open, permitting migration in and out.

As well as in and out, there is also movement within the walled town, making up the three main directions of migration: immigration (including return migration), internal migration and emigration. Given the archetypal importance of St Columba in the history of Irish migration, we may reflect that the three patron saints of Ireland – Patrick, Brigid and Columba – usefully symbolise the three directions: Patrick the immigrant, arriving from Britain and making at least one return visit; Brigid (also called 'Mary of the Irish') the internal migrant, whose traditional life portrays her as a wanderer (*seachrán*) visiting virtually every part of the island; and Columba the emigrant, who left for Britain and made several return visits. The migration stories of all three follow the same linear, three-stage pattern of leaving, crossing and arriving, made circular in reverse by return. The outcome of the migration of all three can be characterised as skilful modulation between segregation and integration: the establishment of networks of monastic churches which were both separate from and well integrated into the secular life of Ireland and Britain, and in continental Europe, in what was called *comúaim n-eclasa fri túaith*, 'the sewing together of Church and State' (McCone 1990, 83). Having commended the value of 'putting migration into Irish history' and traced the emergence of Irish migration studies, in the next three chapters we look in more detail at migration as a three-stage, three-directional and three-outcome process.

2
A Three-Stage Process: Leaving, Crossing, Arriving

All processes can be thought of as a three-stage 'journey' – movement that involves leaving a point of departure and crossing to a point of arrival. Defined as movement from one place of residence to another, the migration process therefore has the same basic three-stage structure as the journey: leaving, crossing and arriving. We look now at Irish migration over the last four centuries in terms of each of these three stages.

Leaving

The act of 'leaving Ireland' seems to have been ritualised from an early period, as is evident from the poem *Do-ell Érinn* (He turned away from Ireland), in praise of the pilgrim saint Colum Cille, or Columba, who migrated from Derry to Iona in the sixth century (quoted as an epigraph to this book). The 'ritual' of leaving is also evident in the contemporary account by Sir John Davies of Hugh O'Neill's departure in September 1607:

> the Saturday before, the Earl of Tyrone was with my Lord Deputy [Chichester] at Slane ... he *took his leave* of the Lord Deputy in a *more sad and passionate manner* than he used at other times; from thence he went to Mellifont, Sir Garret Moore's house ... he *wept abundantly* when he *took his leave*, giving a *solemn farewell* to *every child* and *every servant* in the house, which made them all *marvel*, because it was not his manner to use such *compliments*.
> (CSPI, 1606–8:270 (our emphasis); Carty 1951, 31; Ó Muraíle 2007, 458; Carty 1951, 31)

This English-language account of O'Neill's departure parallels the Irish-language account of the departure of Red Hugh O'Donnell for Spain five years earlier:

> When this plan was heard by all and sundry, pitiful and sad were the great clapping of hands (*lamhchomairt*), and the violent lamentations (*golmhair-*

gneach), and the loud wailing cries (*nuallghubha ard accaointech*) which arose throughout O Domhnaill's camp the night before his departing (*an adaigh ria nimthecht dho*). There was good reason for it, if they knew it at the time, for those whom he left behind never again set eyes on him, and if they were aware of that, it would be no wonder if heavy tears of blood (*troimdhera cró*) coursed down their cheeks.

(Walsh 1948, 341)

Handclapping, violent lamentation and loud, wailing cries as part of the funeral ritual in Ireland can be traced back to the time of Columba and beyond, as can the motif of weeping tears of blood (Lambkin 1985–6, 74).

Wake

Such solemn, face-to-face leave-taking at a family gathering, accompanied by weeping (in a manner that echoes the 'mourning and weeping' of the *Salve Regina*), was the climax of a long-established custom of 'waking' departing emigrants (the same funeral ritual term that attracted Joyce for its fusion of life and death). This was a feature of emigration unique to Ireland, unparalleled apparently even in southern Italy and southern Spain which were the only other regions of Europe where traces of pre-Christian funeral customs survived into the twentieth century (Miller 1985, 556; Neville 2000; Lambkin 2007a, 154, 160; for Italy and Scotland, see Levi 1946; McLeod 1996, 37). From the late eighteenth century onwards it became known generically as the 'American Wake', even if the emigrant was going to Australia (Schrier 1958, 210). As we know it mainly from the evidence of the nineteenth century, the American Wake (also called the 'live' or 'living' wake) was an all-night party, a mixture of joy and sadness, held the night before departure, which is well described in relation to the townland of Carrownamaddy, south Roscommon (Dunnigan 2007, 28–32). The emigrant wake echoed the funeral ritual of death in the Irish countryside, as illustrated by William Willes (1815–51) in his painting *The Mock Funeral* (Crookshank and Glin 2002, 230–1). If the emigrant was going further from Ireland than Britain, the likelihood of return was considered so remote that the departure was treated as if it were an actual death.

The ritual of leave-taking began with the intending emigrant making a round of final visits to the homes of neighbours, inviting them to the 'wake' at his or her home, as in the account given by Michael MacGowan (1962, 49; Mac Gabhann 1996, 84). The bounds of the family farm or townland might also be walked to take, as it were, a mental photograph of the home place. A final visit to church on the Sunday before departure would usually be made, with ministers and priests alike keen to give advice and warnings about keeping the faith. Catholics might call at their priest's house to receive presents of prayer books, scapulars, holy pictures and medals, as well as his blessing. On the evening of the 'wake', family and friends would gather in the kitchen for food and drink, with music, dancing and singing till morning. Ministers and priests, often disapproving of such gatherings as much as they did of funeral wakes, would not usually attend before the morning and the time of departure to give a final blessing, as pictured by the *Illustrated London News*, 10 May 1851 (Griffin 1981, 40). Overnight there might have been gaiety mixed with sorrow because the pain of final physical separation was relieved somewhat by the shared belief that the emigrant was going to a 'better place', akin to 'heaven' or 'the promised land' – John Bunyan's 'City' with its streets paved with gold. However, as at a funeral, the dominant mood was one of lamentation, not celebration.

Convoy

The 'final parting' with family and local community might take place in stages, starting at the door of the family home and proceeding in 'convoy' with relatives and neighbours accompanying the emigrant to a point on the boundary of the local area. Such places as 'The Rock of the Weeping Tears' in west Clare or 'The Bridge of Tears' (*Droichead na nDeor*) in west Donegal must often have seemed to fit with the 'mourning and weeping in this valley of tears' (*gementes et flentes in hac lacrimarum valle*) referred to in the prayer *Salve Regina*. Some of the 'convoy' might continue with the emigrant to the platform of the nearest railway station or the quayside of the port. The 'last look' of departing children at their parents and their home place made the most indelible impressions of all, as illustrated in the 1904 painting by Francis Walker of Killarney emigrants at a railway station (Aalen, Whelan and Stout 1997, 216). This was also the case with the Presbyterian Thomas Mellon, members of whose own family in 1816 were waked and convoyed on their departure from Castletown, Tyrone, for Derry and Pennsylvania (Briscoe 1994, 12). Numerous songs of emigration illustrate how emigrants in their 'new world' would revisit these scenes in their mind's eye for the rest of their lives (Wright 1975, 605–31; Moulden 1994, 32).

If the circumstances of leaving were particularly traumatic, as they were in the case of the 5½-year-old Mellon (Lambkin 2002, 47–8) and even more so in the case of Michael Davitt, who was 4½ at the time of his family's eviction and emigration to England (Marley 2007, 16–17), the scenes of departure left an indelible impression. If there was a collective sense of trauma among emigrants and their descendants, it was aggregated from individual memories such as these.

Contract

As Jackson remarked, a *rite de passage* such as a wake has the function 'not merely to ritualize the transition but also to prepare and socialize the individual for the changed circumstances he will encounter' (1969, 2). The immediate social purpose of the emigrant wake, as in the case of a death, was to honour the 'departed' and to share and assuage the grief of the 'bereaved'. Not only this, it also performed important longer-term, legal, economic, religious and political functions. Like a baptism, wedding or funeral, the 'departure' was an event publicly witnessed by the community. Whatever the actual state of relations between them, the appearance presented was that of a new contractual arrangement (reminiscent of the 'pact' or *cor* made by St Columba), entered into willingly by the parties concerned. It was made clear that the emigrant had sought and obtained permission from parents or guardian, and received the blessing of the church. (We may note in passing that a feature of Hugh O'Neill's leaving was that, in spite of his 'more sad and passionate manner', he had not formally obtained the permission of the Lord Deputy, Chichester, to go abroad, and in his case this was interpreted as treason.) With appropriate permission, emigrants were released from their current domestic and communal obligations, but on the unspoken condition that they were effectively renouncing any claim to the family farm: normally it was not expected that they would ever return to make such a claim. At the same time, they were required to undertake a new set of obligations by promising to write home frequently, send money home regularly and, paradoxically, to return home eventually. The intense emotion of parting, heightened in Irish-speaking districts by the formalised weeping and lament of the 'keen' (*caoine*), served to reinforce the bond between emigrant and home and increase the likelihood of faithfulness in the performance of the new duties, especially the duty of contributing materially to the well-being of the family farm by sending home money for the rent, or for slates to replace the thatch, or for a ticket for the crossing of a younger brother or sister. Similarly, the emigrants might be more predisposed to keep faith with their church, becoming active members of it in their 'new world', and sending their children to church schools. In this way parents and priest or minister represented the interest of home and church in the success of the emigrant enterprise. Also entering into the relationship, although this is not so much written about, were the representatives of political and social organisations like the Ancient Order of Hibernians, the Masonic Order and the Orange Order, which had a vested interest in emigrants establishing or joining local branches in the 'new world' overseas (Senior 1972, 91–7; Buckley and Anderson 1988; McCaffrey 1992, 47–88; MacRaild 2002/3; 2005a; 2005b; MacRaild and Stevenson 2006).

The general pressure to remember not only father and mother but also 'Mother Church' and 'Mother Ireland' led to emigrants being encouraged to practise social solidarity with their fellows in their 'new world'. Thus the emigrant would promise, as in the concluding verse of one of the most popular emigration songs, that 'If ever friendless Irishman chances my way, with the best in the house I will greet him in welcome, at home on the green fields of America' (Moloney 2002, 9). In short, the American Wake was a powerful social mechanism for ensuring the successful operation of a communal migration strategy: the establishment of a 'community' of successful emigrants in the new world, showing social, political and religious solidarity with one another, not least by marrying within the group, and sending money back to sustain the home community in Ireland and support further chain emigration. In this way migration became embedded in the lives of communities as a self-perpetuating phenomenon (Massey 1990, 72).

Hope of return

Emigrant wakes were more common in rural areas where the traditional funeral custom of 'waking' persisted and where attachment to the land was strongest. Emotion was likely to be at its most intense in cases where emigration entailed leaving the family home empty as the last members of the family left. In such cases it was customary in some places for the emigrant to carry a burning ember from the family hearth to that of a neighbour and to leave the tongs there, in the hope of returning one day to take an ember from it back to the family home. In one poignant case in Co. Mayo (see Map 1) a man was reluctant to be the last to leave his home because he had 'four fires there' in his fireplace (Healy 1978, 115).

Other attitudes

Not all emigrant departures were such highly ritualised, communal events of course. In more anglicised and more commercialised urban areas, where a tradition of emigration was longer established and social bonds less intimate or extensive, it might be seen less in terms of disruption of communal obligations. For some, in town or country, it might be seen more in terms of the exercise of freedom of individual choice and the pursuit of economic opportunity. In such cases departure was likely to be a less emotional, less public affair. So, for example, on the eve of the Great Famine, the Ordnance Survey Memoir for the Parish of Tamlaght Finlagan, Co. Londonderry (1834–5), reported that:

> Emigration to the United States, the Canadas and New Brunswick prevails to a continually increasing extent: indeed notices of passages of ships are to be seen in every house. The favourite place seems to be Quebec or St John's [sic] in New Brunswick. The emigrants do not much regret their native land. Those who were sent out by the Fishmongers' Company felt themselves happy in having such powerful patrons among the opening difficulties of their change of state. 'To emigrate' is a pleasing idea to all, except the old men who naturally wish, as they sometimes express it, 'to lay their bones in their own country'.
>
> (Day and MacWilliams 1994, 92–3)

The differing effects of age on attitude to emigration are brought out by the singer of 'The Green Fields of America': his aged parents are heartbroken 'to think that they must die upon some foreign shore' and 'the tears down their cheeks in great drops they are rolling', whereas he asks, 'what matter to me where my bones may be buried / If in peace and contentment I may spend my life?' (Moloney 2002, 9). Notwithstanding this attitude of young emigrants, preference for death and burial in Ireland was still strong amongst Irish-Americans in the late twentieth century, as was evident from the story of the legendary Boston undertaker, Gene Sheehan, who would 'take you or your loved ones back to be buried in the old sod by Aer Lingus' (Coogan 2000, 340–3; for report of a new Ireland-based international service for those who would like to have some Irish soil placed on their funeral caskets, see Henry MacDonald, *The Observer*, 10 December 2006).

There is also the wider question of social control in conflict with the right of the individual to freedom of movement. No doubt many left with a complete absence of ritual, especially in cases where individuals needed to escape from family and local community with as little notice as possible (Fitzpatrick 1996a, 635). Nevertheless, we may see that, in the late nineteenth century at least, emigration from Ireland was strongly characterised in the minds of most by the image of the American Wake. Such is the universal nature of the emigration experience that even those who did not experience departure as a 'wake' readily identified with its presentation in popular ballads as reflecting broadly the Irish Catholic majority experience of 'leaving Ireland'.

Choice

The extent to which anyone 'leaving home' exercises a completely free choice is a moot point. Usually there are 'structuralist' as well as 'voluntarist' aspects to migration. Just as children, having reached the appropriate age, are required to leave school, so they are required to leave the parental home and establish a 'new home' elsewhere – staying on indefinitely is not normally an option. The choice for a young landless man (although not normally open to the poor) was jokingly referred to as 'the collar or the dollar' – joining the Catholic priesthood in Ireland or emigrating – and school teachers in the 1950s might warn even the elite minority of pupils taking the Leaving Certificate to get 'high marks or the boat [to England]' (Garvin 2004, 133; see also Hannan 1970).

Movement up and down the social ladder also often brings pressure to relocate, resulting in internal migration, if not emigration. In other words, if individuals do not take a conscious decision to act otherwise, they tend to follow the 'default option' set by the customary practice of their community, and in an Ireland that had become effectively an 'emigrant nursery' the default for all was emigration, at least in the sense that 'virtually every young man and woman … had to consider emigration as a serious option', although the middle classes remained less likely to emigrate than the rural and urban poor (Kenny 2000, 139; see also Hout 1989). This is illustrated by the choice of destination, where we can see patterns of chain migration at work in the late nineteenth century, some of the origins of which lie in the seventeenth century: the United States receiving emigrants more from the west of Ireland, and Upper Canada receiving them more from Ulster; Scotland receiving them mainly from the north-east, and England receiving them mainly from eastern and southern coastal regions; Australia receiving many emigrants from the south-west and north midlands, and New Zealand receiving many from Ulster and Munster. Other particular links between homeland and diaspora included Waterford with Newfoundland, Wexford, Westmeath and Longford with Argentina, Clare with Australia, Kerry with New Zealand and Derry with Philadelphia (O'Day 1996, 191). Selection of destination was also influenced structurally by relative costs. Passage to Canada, for example, was significantly cheaper than to the United States in the nineteenth century, although it should be noted that many who took this route, like the Mellon family, continued on to the United States.

Emigrants and exiles

Not surprisingly perhaps, given the difficulty of establishing the motives and intentions of individual migrants and the balance of push and pull forces acting on them, there has been a major controversy about agency in Irish migration studies, centred on the classic exposition by Miller (1985) of the distinction between the voluntary 'emigrant' and the involuntary 'exile' who is forced to leave. In response, Akenson has been concerned to refute any suggestion that the majority of Irish emigrants were 'mere passive bits of flotsam on some alleged historical tide' and to present them as 'individuals who collected information, weighed alternatives, and then took journeys to various New Worlds' (1993, 11, 273). Given the limitations of the surviving historical record, there is great difficulty in generalising about the motives and intentions of Irish migrants, when these could vary so greatly according to situation in time and place, social class, religious denomination, political affiliation and gender, as well as according to literacy and skills levels and the quality of relationships among family members. Here we are reminded of the importance of trying to recover, as far as possible, individual and family migration stories at the local level, like that of Jeanne Bouvier (page 9 above), as we discuss further in chapter 15.

Collective accommodation

David Fitzpatrick (1999, 262) offers a way of reconciling the opposition of the structuralist and voluntarist perspectives by suggesting that 'Irish emigration is best pictured not as the outcome of expulsion or selfishness, but as a collective accommodation to the chronic incapacity of Irish society to provide for each new generation'. That 'collective accommodation' we find given ritual expression in the American Wake. By the 1980s the wake had long since become a thing of the past, with political leaders like Charles Haughey happily welcoming the 'new wave' of emigrants, whom he described as 'climbing social ladders' in the 'benign tax fields' of western Europe and the United States. Many of these were ambivalent about describing themselves as emigrants in the traditional sense. Seeing themselves as 'sojourners' rather than 'settlers', they were engaged as much on a quest for self-fulfilment as escape from poverty and were highly likely to return (Corcoran 1999).

Leaving within Ireland

Tracing the tradition of the American or 'living' wake we find that it echoes not only the Irish funeral but also other occasions of 'leaving home' on long and dangerous journeys, as when going to sea or to war or on pilgrimage (Hughes 1989, 20). The emigrant's departure might alternatively be called 'the farewell supper', 'the feast of departure' or 'parting spree' (Irish *spraoi*), which suggests a parallel with the party given for a bride on leaving her home as much as a funeral wake (Schrier 1958, 86; Miller 1985, 557). Here is a reminder that the 'normal' pattern of internal migration across Europe since antiquity has involved young adults (most often but not only women) leaving the parental home to make a new home within their community's 'marriage field' – usually within a radius of about 15 miles – and men and women leaving their homes in the countryside to take up permanent residence in neighbouring towns (Scally 1984, 10; Page Moch 2003, 127, 159, n.228). Such departures, as also those for seasonal work abroad, are still usually marked by some ritual aspect, like a special meal or *deoch an dorais* (parting glass).

Leaving Ireland

Since the time of St Columba (c.521–97), the widespread practice of leaving Ireland to go on pilgrimage involved elaborate leave-taking, and this aspect of the 'waking' tradition probably accounts for the unusual behaviour of Hugh O'Neill, recorded by Sir John Davies (an immigrant from Tisbury, Wiltshire), in bidding a solemn farewell to family and friends with tears (Lambkin 2007b, 151). As the modern Irish diaspora developed, and for as long as the crossing to the 'new world' remained dangerous and the prospect of return remote, the idea that emigrants left Ireland *both* as 'exiles' taking a last tearful look back at the homeland *and* as 'pilgrims' in search of a 'promised land' resonated with Catholics and Protestants alike, schooled as they were by stories of Columba and Bunyan's Christian. To some extent it conditioned the experience of all concerned.

Crossing

Between 'leaving' and 'arrival', the 'crossing' is the middle stage of the migrant journey. What is crossed is a boundary or frontier of some kind which separates the 'old home' from the 'new home'. Bearing in mind that migration broadly defined includes 'a move across the hall from one apartment to another' as much as 'a move from Bombay, India, to Cedar Rapids, Iowa' (Lee 1966), the boundary crossed might be a corridor, road, railway line, river, mountain range or ocean – separating the country from the town, one 'end of the town' or 'side of the tracks' from another, or one country or 'world' from another.

Sea-crossing

In the long Irish tradition of migration, the stage of crossing the threshold between 'old world' and 'new world' is most powerfully associated with a sea voyage. So terrifying was the prospect of an ocean crossing to North America, let alone South Africa, Australia or New Zealand, that well into the twentieth century many Irish emigrants took with them special charms, often given as presents at the wake, such as tokens sewn into their clothing to ensure their fidelity in love and eventual safe return, special bread to keep them immune from fever on board ship and even a baby's caul to protect them from drowning (Schrier 1958, 92; for a quayside scene featuring the sale of religious objects at Queenstown, Cork, from *Illustrated London News*, 5 September 1874, see Bishop 1999, 94). Thus, as Tommy Lunny informed Henry Glassie in 1972, clay from the grave of Saint Mogue, near Bawnboy in Cavan, was carried by emigrants on the voyage to America to be cast on wild seas to still them:

> And all the emigrants ever went to America, even me sisters, they brought Saint Mogue's clay with them ... It's interesting that when they'd be going to America long ago, they'd chip a wee bit of it, like that, into the sea. And the sea would be at its roughest and it would drive the waves back.
>
> (Glassie 1982, 174)

This emigrant ritual recalls that performed by Hugh O'Neill on his 'crossing' to Europe in 1607, as described by Tadhg Ó Cianáin:

> After that they spent thirteen days at sea with excessive storm and danger-ous bad weather. It gave them great relief when they placed in the sea, trailing after the ship, a cross of gold (*cros óir bhuí*) which Ó Néill had, [and] in which there was a portion of the Cross of the Crucifixion along with many other relics (*rannchuid den Chroich Chéasta go n-iomad reiligeas oile*).
>
> (Ó Muraíle 2007, 52–3; Walsh 1916, 11; see also Akenson 2005, 171–2)

It was little wonder, then, if intending emigrants were glad of encouragement such as from singers of 'The Green Fields of America' who urged their listeners to 'pack up your sea-stores, consider no longer' (Moloney 2002, 9).

'Emigrant trade'

What we observe over the span of our four centuries is tremendous progress in the efficiency of the transportation network that facilitated the crossing of migrants, to the extent that out of earlier haphazard arrangements for ship passengers, from the middle of the eighteenth century on, we can speak of the development of the 'emigrant trade' (Truxes 1988, 127). The sailing ship (name unknown) which took Hugh O'Neill and his company from Port-namurray, near Rathmullan, Lough Swilly to France in 1607 was 80 tons, with not more than the traditional 99 on board, and the voyage took three weeks (McCavitt 2002, 93). Most ships transporting emigrants across the Atlantic from Ireland to Philadelphia in the eighteenth century were less than 150 tons. Fitted out to carry about 100 passengers (the largest number of passengers reported for any one vessel was 146), they sailed in spring or late summer, taking between six and eight weeks, and returned with holds full of newly harvested flaxseed (Wokeck 1999, 185; Hood 2003, 153–6). From the 1770s fewer emigrants were being carried in ships converted temporarily for the purpose, such as whalers, and more in specially built emigrant vessels. This trend accelerated after 1815, and by about 1830 the transition was virtually complete and crossing time had been cut to five or six weeks (Scally 1984, 16–17; Wokeck 1999, 129, 208). The sailing ship which took Thomas Mellon and his family from Derry to St John New Brunswick in 1818 was fairly typical of the 1810s and 1820s: about 300 tons, registered to carry about 160 passengers. But their voyage was untypical: delayed by bad weather, it took 12 weeks.

From sail to steam

The first crossing of the Atlantic by a steam ship was in 1838, but the main phase of transition from sail to steam was not complete until the American Civil War (1861–5). The steamship *Celtic* on which Mellon returned from New York to Ireland (Queenstown) in 1882 was 4,000 tons with 850 passengers, and the voyage took nine days (Briscoe 1995, 287). This *Celtic* was one of several 'new and splendid vessels' of the White Star Line, which, as the advertisements of the time boasted:

> reduce the passage to the shortest possible time, and afford to Passengers the highest degree of comfort hitherto attainable at sea. Average passage 8 days in Summer, 9 days in Winter. Each Vessel is constructed in seven watertight compartments. The STEERAGES are unusually spacious, well lighted, ventilated, and warmed, and Passengers of this class receive the utmost civility and attention. An unlimited supply of Cooked Provisions. Medical comforts free of

charge. Stewardesses in Steerage to attend the Women and Children. Steerage fare as low as by any other Line.

(*Armagh Guardian*, 23 April 1875, CMS IED 100127)

The main improvements brought about through the development of the specialist emigrant trade, highlighted by the advertisements, were short journey time (8–9 days); a high level of passenger safety (construction of watertight compartments); a high level of passenger comfort in steerage [emigrant] class (space, light, ventilation, warmth, food, civility from captain and crew, medical care, and care of women and children); low fares at the most competitive rates; and an extensive network of emigration agents (in this case in Queenstown, Liverpool, London and Armagh). In addition, the scheduled railway and steamship timetables were more effectively integrated than ever before.

In the eighteenth century, although levels of safety and comfort were lower, crowding on ships crossing the Atlantic was rare, except in periods of heavy demand, especially during the subsistence crises of the late 1720s and early 1770s. Living conditions, although 'cramped', were 'not unlike farmhouses at home' (Wokeck 1999, 206). Supply was usually able to meet demand, with an average of 14 vessels a year sailing in the 1770s from Ulster ports to Philadelphia. After 1800 passengers were required to purchase and prepare their own provisions, whereas in the eighteenth century ship owners provisioned even their poorest passengers, having a more direct vested interest in the health of their passengers since many were contracted to indentured service of 3–5 years on arrival. Generally, the chances of having an easy voyage were improved according to the size of the ship, the amount of space between decks, the character of the other passengers and the 'humanity' of the captain.

'Coffin-ships'

Overcrowding was often the response when demand exceeded normal supply, as during the Great Famine (1845–50), and could result in infamous cases of 'coffin-ships', such as the *Exmouth of Newcastle*, which feature largely in the literature of Irish-American nationalism in the later nineteenth century (Maume 2005, xxiv, 128; Wilson 2008). Built as a whaler in 1817, the *Exmouth* was a brig of 300 tons, registered to carry 167 passengers, which sailed from Derry to Quebec in 1847, carrying 208 men and women, 63 children under 14 and nine infants (two children being counted as one adult). It was wrecked on the coast of Islay, off the west coast of Scotland, with only three survivors (Wiggins n.d.; Lambkin 2008). Similarly, the *Carrick* was lost in April 1847 on its passage to Canada with emigrants from the Palmerston estate in Sligo (Duffy 2004, 94). By contrast, the *Jeanie Johnston*, a brig of 510 tons, built in 1847, sailed from 1848 to 1851 between Tralee, Co. Kerry and Quebec without losing a single passenger. On the route to Canada between 1845 and 1851 about 50 ships were wrecked with a loss of about 5,000 lives, a very small proportion of the thousands of crossings being made in those years to carry about one million emigrants overseas, but sufficient to make a lasting impact on popular perception of the danger (Coogan 2000, vii, 369–70).

Overcrowding could still be a problem in the age of steam: in 1904, when immigration to the United States from Europe was almost at its peak, the White Star liner *Celtic,* which had carried Thomas Mellon, arrived in New York overloaded with 283 more passengers than her available berths, amid charges of overcrowding and extortion by the crew (Fox 2003, 333). For most, seasickness was inevitable. Although the cures available were many and varied, none was effective. Emigrants were also at high risk in the eighteenth and first half of the nineteenth century, even more so than on land, from contagious disease – smallpox, dysentery and cholera. Surprisingly, perhaps, shipboard mortality rates were usually only about 2 per cent, with most deaths among infants, small children (often from measles) and the elderly. However in bad years such as 1817–18 and 1832–3, when typhus and cholera ravaged Irish emigrant ships, rates of 10 per cent were frequent and could be as high as 25 per cent or more (Fox 2003, 170–2).

Fares

In the late eighteenth and first half of the nineteenth centuries the full-fare price fluctuated around £4 (the actual cost to the merchant was about £3) with one guinea required as a down-payment and one chest normally included in the price. This was equivalent to a year's wages for the average mid-nineteenth-century labourer (Ó Gráda 1989, 15, 55). Ulster emigrants tended to travel light because 'they carried cash from the proceeds of the sale of their leases, improvements, and other assets in order to buy household and other goods after they landed' (Wokeck 1999, 203, 205; see also Scally 1984, 18, 21). From the middle of the nineteenth century, the steamers from Ireland to Liverpool usually took between 14 and 30 hours and gave priority to baggage and livestock, carrying passengers on the open deck for a fare that never exceeded 10d (Scally 1984, 19; Guinnane 1997, 109–10). Emigrants were often at their most vulnerable on the dockside in Irish ports or Liverpool, prey to unscrupulous ticket agents and others for overcharging, robbery or simply misleading information about times of sailing and quality of lodgings and vessels.

Transatlantic systems

Marianne Wokeck (1999, xxii) has described how the German system operating out of Rotterdam in the middle of the eighteenth century was adapted for transporting Irish emigrants in the last decades of the 1700s and 'established a model for the better-known mass migrations of the nineteenth and twentieth centuries', through Liverpool, Le Havre, Hamburg, Bremen, Naples and other European ports to North American ports from Quebec to New Orleans. In the transitions from sail to steam (1860s) and from steam to air (1960s) we see the same basic system of three components first analysed by Ravenstein (see Appendix II): 'push' (from old world) and 'pull' (to new world), connected by a transportation network that is capable of 'locating, inspiring, collecting, transporting and unloading large numbers of migrants year after year' (Wokeck 1999, xxiv). In the Irish case in particular, a dense transportation network, linking merchants, ship owners, captains and agents, was well established by the end of the eighteenth century. The economy of the island was dominated by the port towns from which few inhabitants were more than 50 or 60 miles distant. Compared with Germany, Irish migrants had relatively short travel times to seaports, predictable and low overland transportation costs and dependable lines of communication. Road transport improved greatly from 1815 with the development of Bianconi's cheap, timetabled services which eventually connected with the railways. The first train from Dublin to Cork was in 1849, making the journey in $5\frac{1}{2}$ hours, and on the route north to Belfast the barrier of the River Boyne was bridged in 1853. In 1849 there were 360 miles of track and in 1920, when the railway network was at its maximum, there were 3,750 miles. For many, their first trip on a train was their last in Ireland, as the railways, according to integrated time-tables, carried thousands of emigrants to the transatlantic ports, especially Queenstown (Cobh) and Derry, and the waiting steamers of the new 'ocean railway' (Fox 2003; Casserley 1974). Ocean steamships, the largest and most complex machines yet built, were effectively floating 'towns' in which steerage was the 'tenement district' where 'a patchwork quilt of nationalities and religions lived in dirty, overcrowded rooms, with questionable air and light, eating crude and monotonous food' (Fox 2003, 325). The *Titanic*, for example, was carrying 706 emigrants in steerage, of whom about 120 were Irish, including Thomas Morrow, a solitary Orangeman from Rathfriland (Molony 2000). For many emigrants this was a first taste of the culture shock of urban living that lay ahead. In addition, the political and religious baggage they brought with them meant that where Protestant and Catholic Irish emigrants found themselves quartered together, there might often be, as in the age of sail, 'faction fights and pitched battles' (Miller 1985, 258; Hughes 1989, 25).

From steam to air

The internal transition from rail to road in the 1950s was succeeded by the transition from steam to air on the transatlantic routes in the 1960s. Aer Lingus, which started in 1936, was restricted to the Liverpool service during the Second World War, but by 1948 was operating regular services to London, Liverpool, Glasgow, Manchester, the Isle of Man, Paris and Amsterdam. It introduced its first transatlantic service in 1958, carrying 15,000 passengers in the first year and 75,000 by 1963 (Weldon 2002, 168). Such was the boom in traffic that it had increased its fleet to eight long-haul aircraft by the end of the 1960s. In 1971 Boeing 747s were introduced on the transatlantic route, always the most profitable part of the operation. With the advent of Ryanair on the European aviation scene in 1985 and the development of other 'low fare/no frills' airlines the character of the migrant journey changed again. Although some fear flying as much as an ocean crossing, it is regarded generally as much more like a train journey through a long tunnel and this, together with increasingly affordable airfares, has greatly facilitated the possibility of frequent return to the 'homeland', marking well and truly 'the end of the Irish Wake' (Corcoran 1999).

'Vacillating between hope and fear'

However, the transatlantic voyage in the age of sail remains emblematic of the crossing of the liminal space or threshold that separates old and new worlds. Whereas journeys by stagecoach, river boat or train seldom strayed out of sight of familiar landmarks and the supposed safety of civilisation, the ship spent most of a much longer journey without landmarks through vast, trackless space, day after day – so different was crossing the ocean. Emigrants might suffer in turn from an intensity of homesickness, travel sickness and boredom otherwise unparalleled. The last look back at land was a key moment when thoughts of home were uppermost. Sailing from Queenstown, the last sight of Ireland was the Fastnet Rock, known as 'Ireland's Teardrop'. As one emigrant expressed it: 'Oh thou spot of earth, endeared by a thousand tender ties and fond recollections, your receding form but little knows with what sad feelings your unhappy exile bids you his last farewell' (Miller 1985, 257). Seasickness would usually give way to boredom as the rhythm of a new daily routine on board was established and passengers might find entertainment in music, dancing, games and card-playing, reassurance in religious services and solace in handicrafts, letter-writing or keeping a journal. For many, the experience of being thrown together with an assortment of fellow passengers from different religious, ethnic and social backgrounds came as a shock. As well as this, the disruption of a storm could be terrifying, and Miller (1985, 257) goes as far as to comment on how Protestant and Catholic passengers, in the different ways they reacted, exemplified 'fundamental differences in culturally determined behavior'.

Having been caught in this curious liminal, in-between state of the 'middle passage', at some point thoughts turned mainly from the stage of leaving to that of arriving and the threshold had been crossed (Scally 1984, 14). A signal moment was the first sighting of land. One emigrant remembered how 'the exciting cry of "Land!", "Land!" "Land!" ran through the ship like wild fire. Such were my feelings, vacillating between hope and fear, that I could hardly believe it' (Miller 1985, 261; cf. Hughes 1989, 28; Adams and Somerville 1993). Although anxiety may not be so acute today, thanks to the relative safety, speed and comfort of air travel, the situation of migrants remains basically one of 'vacillating between hope and fear', especially at the point of crossing between old and new worlds. It is still the case that immigrants – asylum seekers especially, but also economic migrants – are rarely guaranteed a smooth, trauma-free reception on arrival.

Arriving

If it is hard to pinpoint exactly when during a crossing the leaving stage ends and the arriving stage starts; it seems clear that the final stage of migration must be underway at least by the time the destination comes into view – as it does most dramatically on a sea voyage when land is first sighted. While the conductors of the emigrant trade in the eighteenth and nineteenth centuries might consider both the 'crossing' and the 'arriving' stages completed with safe arrival on dry land, the full process of arriving was far from complete. It might be many years, if ever, before the immigrants (as well as their new neighbours and state) might think of themselves as having finally 'arrived' (Cwerner 2001, 27–8). There was so much to get used to, do and prove before they could feel fully accepted and 'at home'. Even into the twentieth century, the 'new world' for Irish immigrants, as Akenson puts it so vividly, was 'as far from their previous experience as colonies on the moon would be for someone of our own age' (1993, 273). Some had been 'seasoned' for ocean crossings by prior migration from countryside to town within Ireland or to Britain, but others were not so prepared, such as the hundreds in 1847 who were assisted by the state to emigrate from the townland of Ballykilcline, near Strokestown, Roscommon to New York, via Dublin and Liverpool (Scally 1995). Whatever their degree of readiness, migrants naturally responded to the challenge of coming to terms with the strangeness of their new situation by trying to make best use of available resources.

Connections

For any new arrival, whether in a family group or alone, the most important resource was having a link to relatives or friends already there, able and willing to help them – in the first instance by 'redeeming' or paying off any debt they had incurred in making the crossing, and then by directing them to the areas where their precursors had gone and where there were still good opportunities. This, more than any assets the migrants might have with them in the form of goods or money, would influence the paths they followed to success or otherwise. Some would find the costs of moving on inland prohibitive, as from the ports of the Delaware and elsewhere, and so would remain in an increasingly competitive labour market, with a poorer prospect of integrating successfully into the receiving society. As the emigrant trade developed, entrepreneurs of various kinds concerned with the process of settlement took over where those concerned with oceanic transportation left off. The goal of realising the emigrant dream by finding a niche in which to earn a decent living was more difficult for those who came later into a more densely colonised marketplace; for those who had been exploited on the crossing; for those who had arrived with limited means; and for those who had only strangers to help them gain a foothold.

The same pattern of arrival that characterised the waves of German and Irish migration mainly through Philadelphia in the eighteenth century was evident in the nineteenth-century inflows from Europe to all new world destinations: the willingness of pioneers to assist financially weak relatives and compatriots; a shift from whole families moving to more single young men and women; and the systematic role of businessmen concerned with the waves of settlement that rippled out across the continent. New arrivals faced key choices, or had these made for them by default: whether to begin new settlements themselves or settle into established communities. Old world traditions could be transplanted most successfully where the new arrivals came from the same region and linguistic and religious background, and where they could cluster with adequate resources under a competent and stable leadership. Where new arrivals moved in alongside neighbours of other ethnic origins, success was more likely to be achieved through mutual interdependence and by making an early move from being 'Irish' or 'German', to being Pennsylvanians, New Yorkers, Marylanders or Carolinians collectively, contributing to a greater whole. While this move may have been difficult if not impossible for first-generation immigrants to complete, it was less so for their children and grandchildren. This was the case with Thomas Mellon, who, having arrived in Pennsylvania in 1818 at the age of five and grown up alongside Germans, was proud to describe himself in 1885 as a 'Yankee', but also as 'Scotch-Irish' (Briscoe 1994, Lambkin 2002, 37). The migration choice between segregation and integration is explored further in chapter 4.

Remittances

As promised on leaving, a traditional duty of Irish immigrants on arriving was to write home with 'consolation' in the form of both emotional and financial support, if they could, to sustain the self-perpetuating migration mechanism (Fitzpatrick 1994, vii, 19–20). Those who were newly arrived tended to enclose larger sums (bank drafts, money orders, passage tickets, as well as cash) than those who had been in America for some time (Schrier 1958, 103–6). Remittances were sent by a variety of means, including banks such as the Emigrant Savings Bank, mercantile houses, shipping firms, exchange agencies, private letters and returning emigrants, and also by the new postal money order system which was started in 1871 between the United States and the United

Kingdom (Ó Gráda 1998; Casey 2006, 305–9). It seems that emigrants from the poorest families were the most faithful in sending money home. So we find, for example, Elizabeth Hagan on 12 February 1877 in Windermere, near Ballarat, Australia, dictating a letter (because she was unable to write) to her cousin Mary Hagan in Irish Street, Dungannon, and reporting that she has sent £5 to her sister in New Zealand following the mental breakdown there of her husband and that she hoped that her brother John in Dungannon would also send some money 'as maney [sic] pound she sent home when she could spare it' (CMS IED 9706244).

Over-persistent requests from home, however, might have the effect of alienating the immigrant, as Patrick MacGill reported in his *Autobiography of a Navvy*: '"Send home some more money, you have another brother," ran the letters, and a sense of unfairness crept over me. ... I rebelled against the imposition and did not answer the letter' (1914, 110). As long as the immigrant remained single with parents alive, the money tended to be sent regularly, especially for Christmas, St Patrick's Day (17 March) and Easter. As responsibilities in the new world increased and obligations in Ireland decreased, smaller sums were sent. Immigrants were aware that the 'American' money was being used to pay the rent, pay shopkeepers' bills, replace the thatch with slate, repair floors, walls or doors, replace a cow or horse, pay for an apprenticeship in trade or for the education of a younger member of the family, or to cover the costs of a funeral wake. Less commonly, it might be used to add to the family savings or buy land. This was what Schrier calls the first branch of the 'golden stream' being sent back to Ireland (1958, 122).

The second branch of that stream, in the later nineteenth and early twentieth centuries, was targeted at the support of religious, social or political institutions. Money might be sent for building a new parish church or local hospital, or support of a political campaign, such as Fenianism or the Land League, in response to a personal letter, or even a visit, from the parish priest or political leader, such as that by James Stephens in 1864 (Neidhardt 1975, 14–15). John Francis Maguire, after an extensive tour among the Irish in America, reflected on whether 'the ocean of sentiment for Ireland and hatred for England' that he had found there was likely to evaporate, and concluded that it 'may subside – so may the sea; but, like the sea, the first breath will set it in motion, while a storm would lash it into fury' (Maguire 1868, 610). It has been strongly argued that while most immigrants retained an interest to a greater or lesser degree in the affairs of the 'old country', only among the Irish was this interest 'so emotionally rooted that it was transmitted to the second, third, and even fourth generations' (Schreier 1958, 123; cf Bade 2003, 49, 90). In this sense the process of 'arriving' took a long time to be completed. Many first-generation immigrants continued throughout their lives to alternate between seeing their new world as the 'land of plenty and sweet liberty' and the 'land of the stranger'. For the Presbyterian Thomas Mellon, whose own family were 'waked' on their departure for Derry and Pennsylvania, the mental picture of his home-place remained as clear as a photograph, so much so that he felt compelled in old age to return to the family home, Camphill Cottage in the townland of Castletown, near Omagh, Tyrone (now part of the Ulster American Folk Park) to see for himself if all was really as he remembered it (Lambkin 2002, 47–9; 2008).

The stories of individual migrants and the story of the group as a whole can therefore be structured according to these three stages. For example, the chapters of Margaret Brenan's story (Dunnigan 2007) are 'Life at Home' and 'The Leaving' (leaving); 'The Journey' (crossing); and 'Life in America' and 'Return Migration' (arriving). The Irish as a group might be said to have finally arrived in their new worlds when the emigrant stream from Ireland dried up or was reduced to a trickle, as in South Africa and Australia by the 1920s, and the Irish ceased to play a distinctive role in politics, or as in the United States when the election of J. F. Kennedy as president signalled the 'arrival' of the Catholic Irish. For many this was the highly emotional completion of the 'long journey home' of their group, which has been seen as a move 'from ghetto to suburb' (McCaffrey 1992, 10–46). However, as long as emigrant streams continue to feed new worlds, the situation of the first- and second-generation immigrant remains ambivalent, as in the case of one English-born son who remembered how his Irish-born father at their home in England in the 1950s received 'regular letters from his sister, who still lived at "Home", telling him about her children, his brother and the latest on friends and neighbours and keeping him up to date with news about his sister in Brooklyn. She'd send huge bunches of shamrock over each year for St Patrick's day and a turkey at Christmas' (Ward 2002, vii). Arriving at Euston Station in 1952, Edna O'Brien found it 'a jungle, grim and impersonal ... This was to be home. It had nothing to recommend it ... But I had got away. That was my victory' (1976, 126–7; for comparison with Brian Moore's arrival in Liverpool, see Dawe 2007, 99–100; Delaney 2007, 10–11). For how many has the experience of arriving in 'Celtic Tiger' Ireland at the end of the twentieth and in the early twenty-first century been similar?

3
A Three-Way Process: Immigration, Internal Migration and Emigration

The overview of migration in Irish history as a three-stage process given in the previous chapter featured emigration more than immigration because over these 400 years it has been the dominant direction of flow. However, it is important to realise that the leavings, crossings and arrivals of Ireland's emigrants, from Hugh O'Neill to Edna O'Brien, have been paralleled by those of its immigrants. Migration is not simply a one-directional process of movement between a sending society and a receiving society, but rather a two-directional process: few if any sending societies receive no return migrants or new immigrants – even in the worst year of the Great Famine, as we shall see in chapter 10, Ireland received some; and few receiving societies, such as France, send no emigrants. Additionally, in both predominantly sending societies and predominantly receiving societies, there is internal migration. While it is true that migrating within a country generally involves fewer practical difficulties and much less physical hardship and emotional intensity, internal migration differs from international migration in degree rather than in kind. Not only does it have the same three-stage structure and involve similar practical, physical and emotional challenges, internal migration also affects and is affected by both immigration and emigration. Therefore, if we are trying to view migration comprehensively, we need to see it not as a two-directional process but as a three-directional or three-way process of immigration, internal migration and emigration.

As we noted in chapter 1, migration studies is concerned with exploring five basic questions: Why does migration occur? Who migrates? What are the patterns of 'old worlds' and 'new worlds' and of the flows between them? What are the effects of migration on the 'old world'? What are the effects of migration on the 'new world'. Here we are also concerned with a sixth question: What effects do the three main directions of migration (immigration, internal migration and emigration) have on each other? Seeing not only the three directions of migration as separate flows but also as interactive aspects of one 'three-way' process is a challenge, and to that we now turn.

Migration force-field

Each of the three directions of migration flow can be accounted for at any given time by the interaction of push and pull factors, which may be common to all three directions or specific to two or only one of them. Often these push and pull factors are imagined as being like magnets. One historian, for example, offers a rule of thumb in this way for the pull factor of towns in rural–urban migration: 'the range of the attractive force was largely related to the size of the city and the dynamics of its growth' (Bade 2003, 44). So in trying to visualise the causes of migration we can imagine the attractive and repulsive forces of multiple sets of magnets of varying strengths, situated in various old and new worlds, and in the intervening spaces between them, which combine to generate the highly complex and turbulent 'magnetic' field in which migration takes place. The idea of 'sets' of magnets is crucial because, as Leslie Page Moch points out, 'migration to the city is better understood as a pulsing two-way current between town and country rather than as attraction to a magnet', and this observation (as in the case of the Wall Street Crash of 1929) applies equally to the push and pull forces that operate between countries and affect immigration and emigration (2003, 103). The point is not always well understood that, as well as exerting pull forces, 'new worlds' can also exert push forces. For example, the Wall Street Crash weakened the pulling power of the United States on potential emigrants in Ireland and at the same time increased its pushing power on Irish immigrants in the United States, resulting in a reduction in emigration and increase in return migration. Similarly, 'old worlds' can exert pull forces as well as push forces. Indeed, it is the pulling force of the 'old world' which is 'home' that accounts largely for the 'immobility' or 'non-migration' within national borders of the majority of the world's population (see Appendix I). The pulling power of 'home' is as it were the 'gravitational' force that has to be overcome by a combination of other forces in order for migration to take place. Repelling and attracting in varying degree, all these sets of pulsating magnets in and between old and new worlds interact to constitute a fluctuating balance of forces. It is within their force-field that migrant decisions are shaped and taken and migrant moves made.

Migrant decisions

Migrant moves are influenced but not wholly determined by the current state of the force-field in and between old and new worlds. A further critical force is the power of individuals to decide whether or not to 'go with the flow'. As Jackson has remarked, there is a strong analogy between the decision to marry and the decision to migrate, with the former indeed often entailing the latter:

> This, usually voluntary, decision is rather like the decision to marry. It becomes possible to isolate in a particular environment a variety of predisposing causal factors which lead to the net result. One is left, nevertheless, with a fascinating range of questions regarding the actual factors of selection in the decision-making process which lead some to migrate or marry and particular others to remain as they were.
>
> (1969, 5)

While many may opt for whatever course at any given time appears to offer them 'the line of least resistance' (staying put or migrating in a particular direction), others may demonstrate highly independent decision-making. In responding to the 'Goldilocks question' (what course is 'just right' for me in this situation) some may choose to stay put or migrate 'against the flow'. In other words, it is a mistake in thinking about the migration force-field to see migrants, any more than those who stay, as 'mere passive bits of flotsam on some alleged historical tide' (Akenson 1993, 11, 37).

Individual migrant moves aggregate to form the three main migration flows. Each flow develops a momentum of its own so that it exerts push and pull forces on the others. This interaction of migration flows is evident, for example, in Ireland in the seventeenth century when a marked increase in the strength of the immigration flow (the Plantation of Ulster) affected both internal migration (movement of the dispossessed from fertile to marginal land) and the emigration flow (movement out of Ireland to Europe in the wake of the Departure/Flight of the Earls). A more recent example, observed over the course of his lifetime by Garret Fitzgerald (b. 1926), is the remarkable sequence in some family migration stories of emigration and return:

> a number of those who have recently returned to work in Ireland after having had to emigrate in the late 1980s had as children been brought back to Ireland by parents who returned here in the 1970s after themselves having had to emigrate in the 1950s or early 1960s.
>
> (2003, 106)

All these push and pull forces – in tension with each other at the micro-, meso- and macro-levels – constitute what we call the overall 'migration field'. Since the strength of each of these forces is rarely constant for extended periods, the balance of forces in the migration field fluctuates over time, resulting in migration flows of changing character, strength and direction. Our concern in Part II will be to examine in detail continuity and change over four centuries in the three main directions of migration and in the interaction between them. For the moment we are concerned with getting an overview of the three-way process, and here an analogy may be helpful with the world of sub-atomic physics and the search for a 'unified field theory', which will unify all the fundamental forces of nature and the interactions between them into a single theoretical framework. If we think of a theoretical framework for migration in this way, we can imagine individual migrants as being like particles in a sub-atomic universe, where the individual trajectory of each particle is accounted for by the interaction of its particular charge with all the push and pull forces of its universe. The World Systems theory of Wallerstein (1975; Hopkins and Wallerstein 1982) and structuration theory of Giddens (1984; Robertson 1992, 138–45) provide alternative, highly developed frameworks for considering the interaction of the agency of individuals and prevailing socio-economic structures and climates. Garner sums it up neatly in saying that 'around the bodies of migrants emerges a force field of anxieties and tensions engaging both the "national" and the "migrant"' (2004, 197).

'Uncertainty principle'

A further aspect of the sub-atomic world that might be useful in this regard is the 'uncertainty principle', which states that increasing the accuracy of measurement of one force increases the uncertainty of the simultaneous measurement of another force. This seems to apply to the human brain and to the writing of history, at least in the sense that the more detailed the research of an historian into one aspect of a phenomenon (such as immigration, internal migration or emigration in the case of migration) the more difficult it becomes to know in equivalent detail about its other aspects, let alone about how they all interrelate (Lowenthal 1985, 238). Foregrounding and highlighting one aspect comes at the price of backgrounding and hiding the others. So far as migration in Irish history is concerned, we find that historians have tended to treat immigration and emigration as separate phenomena rather than as different aspects of the same phenomenon. We also find that by comparison with emigration, immigration and internal migration have been little studied, especially the latter. Cormac Ó Gráda, for example, refers to 'the unimportance of immigration in modern Irish history' (2006, 1–2; Dooley 2004, 134–6). Without denying its lack of importance between the early eighteenth and late twentieth centuries, our aim here is to promote the idea that, notwithstanding the relative smallness of some migration flows at some times, it is important at all times to try to see the different directions of migration as parts of a whole.

The 'sub-atomic' image of the complexity of fluctuating forces operating on myriad particles may help us appreciate the complexity of migration, especially at the micro-level. There political, economic, social and religious forces interact on particular individuals, holding some (usually the majority) in the 'worlds' where they are settled, but causing others to migrate. However, having zoomed in to the finest-grained microscopic level, we need also to make sense of overall patterns by zooming out to the telescopic level, and here we may find useful the thought-experiment proposed by Robert Scally:

> If one could have scanned the earth from an orbiting satellite for the move-ment of peoples, its surface would have appeared fitfully dormant until the sudden buzzing and swarming which followed the Napoleonic wars. Liverpool would immediately attract the eye as a center of the boiling activity.
>
> (1984, 16)

Our aim in Part II is to scan the earth from the angle of what we might call 'Scally's satellite', ranging across the last 400 years to get as clear a picture as possible of the 'field' of Irish migration. This means zooming in and out between the global, national, regional and local levels in order to examine the changing tension between immigration, internal migration and emigration. In his *Primer*, Akenson uses an alternative image, that of the spotlight that can be moved to focus on different parts of the stage (1993, 12–13). For now we may get an overview, or at least a rough impression, of how the view from the satellite or the spotlight changed by considering, century by century, the attempts of four individuals – Sir William Petty, Arthur Young, Thomas Colby and Father John O'Brien – to obtain 'satellite' views of Ireland and the migra-tion of its population.

Sir William Petty

In the seventeenth century, Sir William Petty (1623–1687) produced *Hiberniae Delineatio*, the first county atlas of Ireland (1685), based on his 'Down Survey'. Petty has been described as 'the greatest figure in Anglo-Irish cartography' for his attempt to integrate topographical mapping with the registration of the quantity, value and ownership of property (Andrews 1975, 18). Seeing the population of Britain and Ireland as a whole, he thought Ireland 'much under-peopled' or 'thin-peopled', contrasting it with 'thick-peopled' England. Far from seeing things in his day as being 'just right', Petty was concerned in par-ticular with what he saw as the dangerous imbalance in the distribution of Catholics and Protestants in the two islands, and so he proposed a radical rebalancing scheme in *The Political Anatomy of Ireland* (1691, 120, 100). As finally submitted to the Catholic King James II, his proposal would have involved 'transplanting' large numbers of Catholics (one million of his esti-mated total of 1.3 million) to England and 'transplanting' an equivalent number of Protestants from England to Ireland (Lansdowne 1967, I, 48).

Arthur Young

In the eighteenth century, Arthur Young (1741–1820) made observations and comments on 51 localities throughout the four provinces in his *Tour in Ireland* (1780), which Maria Edgeworth considered to be 'the first faithful portrait of its inhabitants' (Young 1970, I, xii). Young, like Petty, tried to see the big picture as well as local detail:

> As to the number of people in Ireland, I do not pretend to compute them, because there are no satisfactory data whereon to found any computation ... the number was computed by Sir W. Petty in the year 1657 to 850,000; in 1688 at 1,200,000 ... I cannot conclude this subject, without earnestly recommending to the Legislature of Ireland to order an actual enumeration of the whole people ... Such a measure would ... place the great importance of Ireland to the British Empire, in that truly conspicuous light in which it ought ever to be viewed ... the common idea is, that there are something under three millions in Ireland.
>
> (Young 1970, II, 121–2)

Unlike Petty, who did not see it as significant in his day, Young was particularly interested in emigration and reported that 'upon going over to Ireland I determined to omit no opportunities of discovering the cause and extent of this emigration'. His radical conclusion, against the prevailing view, was that 'emigration should not, therefore, be condemned in states so ill-governed as to possess many people willing to work, but without employment' (1970 vol. II, 56, 58).

Thomas Colby

In the nineteenth century, in the spirit of Young's recommendation that there should be an 'actual enumeration of the whole people', Thomas Colby (1784–1852) directed the British Ordnance Survey in making the first detailed map survey of Ireland. Colby saw his task as 'at once a work of science and scholarship, an aid to commerce and industry, and an instrument of government that could take its users far beyond the needs of local taxation'. His map survey (1833–46) resulted in complete coverage of the island by almost 2,000 6-inch (1:10,500) sheets – an achievement that 'challenges comparison with William Petty's "Down Survey" of mid-seventeenth-century Ireland' (Andrews 1975, 88, 87). As one of Colby's colleagues noted, 'many of the instructions of Dr Petty and Colonel Colby might be printed in parallel columns, so remarkably have the same circumstances produced the same results, from minds very similar in some respects to each other' (Larcom 1851, 324). Needless to say, the Ireland represented by Colby's Ordnance Survey, and the 'Great Census' of 1841 that complemented it, was very different from that of Petty's Atlas of 1685. The total population in 1841 was calculated to be 8,178,000, and in that year 71,392 were recorded as having emigrated overseas. Along with the making of the first edition of Ordnance Survey maps, Colby had ordered the compilation of Parish Memoirs which would detail social and economic aspects of life at the local level. One of the 'heads of inquiry' was emigration, and so we know, for example, that in 1834 emigration from the parish of Tamlaght Finlagan, Londonderry, to Quebec and St Johns, New Brunswick, was on the increase (Andrews 1975, 147; Day and MacWilliams 1994, 92–3).

Father John O'Brien

In the middle of the twentieth century, Father John O'Brien, an Irish-American priest, was the first commentator to discuss the Irish world-wide coherently in terms of both 'homeland' and 'diaspora'. Whereas Colby had been observing the population of Ireland in the 1840s at over eight million, O'Brien saw it in the 1950s at just over four million. Emigration was approaching what turned out to be the peak year of 1957 (60,000 emigrants) when O'Brien published *The Vanishing Irish: The Enigma of the Modern World* (1954). Introducing this volume of essays by 15 contributors, he gave the stern reminder that 'for more than a century emigration has been like a huge open sore on the bosom of Ireland, robbing her of her lifeblood', and warned that 'all economists and sociologists are agreed that, if this ominous trend continues, in another century the Irish race will have vanished, much like the Mayans, leaving only their monuments behind them' (1954, 26, 7). Like Petty, having diagnosed the problem – in this case that of being 'the country with the fewest and the latest marriages in the civilized world' – O'Brien offered a prescription:

> To help break the log-jam of excessive bachelors it would be well for the Government to import about 5,000 men – Italians, Lithuanians, Bohemians, Germans and Poles – who would marry young Irish girls and set an example for the marriage-shy bachelors of Eire. Their example, reflecting the custom of every other Christian country, would do more than a ton of abstract preachments.
>
> (1954, 228)

By 2007, numbering about six million with 10 per cent foreign-born – including many Italians, Lithuanians, Bohemians, Germans and Poles – the inhabitants of the island seem far from vanishing. However, the current state of Ireland's migration balance seems not much closer to 'just right' than it seemed to either Petty or O'Brien, as indicated by the radical proposal of one recent commentator:

> Too much Cosmopolitanism dilutes the very Hibernianism that makes us Irish. Finding that particular sweet spot, where we get the best economic

performance point without undermining our culture, is almost impossible ... Now that Ireland has become an immigrant nation ... we should consider what type of immigrants we want ... the Diaspora ... the exiled Irish will be the saviours of a successful Ireland ... Let us ... call ... them home.

(McWilliams 2007, 263, 274)

But another commentator, Donald Keough, former president of the Coca-Cola Corporation, warns that such a proposal may already be too late because 'Irish-Americans view Ireland as more mentally distant with every passing generation' (*Irish Times*, 3 November, 2007; Hayward and Howard 2007, 57). While the people of Ireland are certainly not vanishing in Ireland, they may still, as O'Brien feared, be vanishing in the diaspora.

Looking back at Europe over these four centuries from the perspective of Scally's satellite, we can see how Ireland constitutes a special case. The island's population grew from about two million in 1700 to 4.4 million in 1790 and to 8.5 million in 1845, in the latter period at the phenomenal rate of 1.3 per cent per annum, compared with 1 per cent in England, 0.8 per cent in Scotland and 0.4 per cent in France. However, over the nineteenth century as a whole, during which the rest of Europe experienced population growth, Ireland's was the only population to decline – from 8.5 million in 1845 to 4.4 million in 1914. This was due mainly to emigration, as for example in the 1860s when the rate of natural increase in the population was at 8 per 1,000 and net emigration was at 12 per 1,000 (Kennedy and Clarkson 1993, 158–84).

Across the countries of Europe the balance between immigration and emigration flows varied. Between 1870 and 1900 immigration in France, for example, was dominant, while immigration and emigration were more or less in balance in Britain, and immigration replaced emigration as the dominant flow in Germany. Over the 400-year span, the balance between immigration and emigration in Ireland varied greatly: immigration was dominant in the first half of the seventeenth century; immigration and emigration were almost in balance in the second half of the seventeenth century; emigration was dominant from the eighteenth through to the late twentieth century, when immigration became dominant again. Migration within Ireland was limited by the absence of any extensive deposits of iron or coal and consequently by the comparatively slow rate of industrialisation and urbanisation. Only two major conurbations developed, both on the eastern side of the island, attracting internal migrants from a generally poorer western zone. Between 1800 and 1900 the capital, Dublin, grew from 182,000 to 290,000, while Belfast, in the north-eastern region where textiles and shipbuilding were important, grew from 25,000 to 350,000, making it the fastest-growing centre in the United Kingdom. Nevertheless, it is only since the 1960s that more than 50 per cent of the population of the 26 counties have been living in towns and cities (as compared with the six counties of Northern Ireland, where the tipping point was reached in the 1920s).

Such has been the long dominance of emigration in Ireland's three-directional process of migration that, before proceeding to the detailed examination of Part II, we need to look at three features (other than the American Wake, discussed in chapter 2) that mark it out as distinctive in Europe. These are the early origin and persistence of emigration over four centuries, the low rate of return migration and the high rate of female emigration. Given such an emigration flow, Ireland's immigration and internal migration flows were minor by comparison.

Persistence

No other modern European tradition of emigration has been marked by starting so early and persisting so long. We have an icon of its origin in Thomas Ryan's painting *Departure of the Earls,* and we have one of its persistence through to the end of the twentieth century in Petra Fox's painting *Small Island,* inspired by Brian Lenihan's famous interview comment that 'After all, we can't all live on a small island' (*Newsweek*, 10 October 1987; see front cover of Ó Gráda 1995). The origin of the Norwegian tradition of emigration, for example, can be traced to the iconic sailing of the ship *Restauration* from Stavanger in 1825, remaining at a high level to the 1950s. Emigration from Italy was persistently high only in the period 1880–1920. This is not to imply that the rate of Irish emigration was uniformly high. Like other migration flows it went through peaks and troughs in response to fluctuating economic and political conditions, but, even in 'trough' years, apart from major wars, the rate was still relatively high. As we shall see in Part II, from 1825 there was a shift to 'mass' migration from all parts of the island.

Emigration 'culture'

Persistent emigration over four centuries is best explained in terms of the development of a self-sustaining culture. We have seen in chapter 2 how the development of mechanisms such as the American Wake, emigrant letters and religious and political organisations facilitated the continuous reproduction of the main phases of the migration process (leaving, crossing, arriving), with the result that migration, and the 'emigrant trade' in particular, became embedded in Ireland and its diaspora as part of the way of life. Miller discusses this 'self-perpetuating dynamic', showing how, after the Famine in particular, the processes of commercialisation of agriculture and emigration were 'circular and interdependent: commercialisation produced social and cultural changes [such as the switch to impartible inheritance] which mandated and encouraged an emigration which facilitated more commercialization and changes which in turn promoted more emigration, *et cetera*' (1985, 424–6). As well as sending remittance money as part of the strategy of sustaining the family home in Ireland, relatives also sent the 'American parcel', a staple in the west of Ireland until the 1960s, including newspapers and later glossy magazines and mail order catalogues, which had a destabilising effect in showing how different life could be overseas. Letters sent home to Irish-speaking areas encouraged parents to want their children to learn English. Successful returned emigrants, embodying this difference, were particularly effective agents of social change, which included a new, unsettling attitude of 'independence' among tenants and employees, and further emigration. The 'mental map' of the girl from Co. Galway, who explained to Horace Plunkett that rather than migrate internally to join relatives on a farm only 30 miles away she preferred to emigrate to New York City 'because it is nearer', illustrates how many might think they knew more about Boston or New York than about Dublin, Cork or even parts of their own counties (Miller 1985, 25).

Regional spread

The persistence of emigration had a cumulative effect. Although the poorest regions contributed disproportionately to the emigration flow over the long term, they were not the first to be penetrated. These tended to be in the immediate hinterland of ports and 'a notch or two up the economic scale' (Miller 1985, 140; O'Day 1996, 191). Their example gradually spread to poorer regions, in part by internal migration, as the canal and railway networks were spreading to connect coast and interior more closely. Recent research has shown how important planned group migration schemes have been in both overcoming initial inertia and sustaining momentum, by getting new migration streams established and encouraging individual migrants (Duffy 2004). These include schemes as diverse and widely separated over time as the seventeenth-century Cromwellian internal migration to Connacht and the emigration of Sarsfield's army to France as a condition of the Treaty of Limerick, and in the twentieth century the Irish Free State's internal migration of farming families from Connacht to Leinster and wartime agreements with the United Kingdom for labour migration. Such schemes were based on the assumption that they would lead to 'chain' migration. Thus the presence of Gaelic chiefs in Continental courts acted as a 'magnet' for subsequent migration by their followers and extended kin groups. Convicts transported to Australia were entitled, and indeed encouraged, to arrange for their families to join them on their release. In the 1830s Lord Palmerston estimated that assisting 2,000 to emigrate from his estate in Co. Sligo in the 1830s led to a further 4,000 leaving in the following 18 months. Ninety girls sent from Co. Clare to the United States by Vere Foster in the 1880s paid, within four years, for the passages of 94 others (Duffy 2004, 12). Such schemes accounted for only a small proportion of total emigration: 3.2 per cent between 1815 and 1845 when over one million emigrated, and about 1 per cent between 1846 and

1852. However, their 'priming' effect was often highly successful, especially when substantial participation by women was achieved (Fitzpatrick 2000, 261). Unlike men, the women tended to continue sending remittances to their relatives in Ireland even after they were married, helping to ensure that chains with their own as well as their husbands' families were established and sustained. It has been argued that the even gender balance of Irish emigration has much to do with female literacy (O'Dowd 2005, 269), and women's role in establishing 'female chains' of endorsement or networking that 'unfettered a woman's migrating decision' (Casway 1991, 130; see also Nolan 1989).

'Chain' migration and migration 'fever'

The operation of the system of chain migration was observed by the Ordnance Survey Memoir writers in the 1830s:

> it is a usual system in this, as in other parishes, to send out the younger members of a family to act as pioneers for the others. A constant correspondence is kept up and each emigrant is generally furnished with his outfit by another who has gone before him.
>
> (Day and McWilliams 1996a, 31)

The 'pioneering' stage is illustrated by John Dennison (of Pennsylvania) writing to his brother (in Co. Down) in 1789:

> I have given you a small account of the country to you and if you thought it answered you to come I would be fond to see you here ... if you ware heare and settled nigh to me I would not see you want until you would have time [to] fix yourself.
>
> (Parkhill 2004, 67; PRONI, T/2294/1)

The next stage in the development of a family chain is illustrated by Joseph Anderson (of Pennsylvania) writing home to Co. Londonderry in 1840:

> I am arrived here safe with my relations ... I rested two weeks with John and David. I then set out to work about thirty miles distant from John's Brother. Robert and I works for the one man. A young man can do better here than in Ireland ... no rents and every man here is Lord of his soil.
>
> (Parkhill 2004, 68; PRONI, D/1859/3)

Such letters were held to 'spread the contagion of emigration' (Day and McWilliams 1996b, 15). As emigration penetrated districts for the first time it was usually described in terms of disease. Thus we find references in Ireland (and Scotland) to emigration 'fever' earlier than elsewhere in Europe (Jackson and Page Moch 1994; Harper 2003, 23–4). By the later nineteenth century, when there was scarcely any district in Ireland that emigration had not penetrated, the 'disease', though now less 'fevered' in character, was endemic.

Patterns

Whether or not it was conceived in such feverish terms, emigration was spread by the development of new migration streams. As noted in chapter 1, some patterns of chain migration at work in the late nineteenth century had originated in the seventeenth and eighteenth centuries, with the United States receiving emigrants mainly from the west of Ireland, and Upper Canada mainly from Ulster; Scotland receiving them mainly from the north-east, and England mainly from eastern and southern coastal regions. New patterns developed in the nineteenth century, with Australia receiving many emigrants from the south-west and north midlands, New Zealand from Ulster and Argentina from Wexford, Westmeath and Longford. As migration streams developed, so did various support systems, including, from the late seventeenth century, indentured servant schemes (enabling mainly single men otherwise unable to raise the fare to make the crossing); credit schemes (enabling 'redemptioners' to have their passage paid for by friends or relations on arrival); and bounty schemes (enabling those introducing immigrants of a suitable age and occupation to be rewarded by grateful colonial governments). Eventually the system developed, first in Philadelphia, to enable Irish immigrants to buy a passage from a local shipping agent, who then notified his associate in Ireland, who in turn notified the beneficiaries that their ticket had been paid (Parkhill 2004, 70). Newspapers, by carrying advertisements for such schemes and publishing letters by passengers who had successfully made the crossing, contributed to the 'information feedback fuelling the exodus' (Duffy 2004, 96). Getting emigrant streams started usually needed group leadership and organisation, as in the case of Presbyterian ministers with their own congregations in the early eighteenth century, and landlords and land agents with their tenants in the nineteenth century (Murnane and Murnane 1999, 174–96). Apart from sending criminals and vagrants to the colonies, governments in the eighteenth century generally disapproved of emigration.

Assisted migration

In the nineteenth century governments shifted to official tolerance and even approval of schemes to assist emigration, convinced in part by the evidence that it was cheaper to pay for the overseas passage of the impoverished than to support them at home in the workhouse. Provided they were not too impoverished, colonial governments might be glad to receive them and so emigration assistance was often extended from the writing-off of rent arrears and payment of the passage to support with clothing, luggage, transit accommodation, landing money and entry into the new labour market. Without government assistance, emigration to Australia and New Zealand would have been slow to develop, the obstacles of distance and lack of information being particularly acute for landlords, land speculators and individual emigrants alike. That said, passages paid for by earlier individual emigrants 'dwarfed all other sources of finance' (Guinnane 1997, 110). Whatever way Irish communities abroad were established, the migrant stream to them tended to continue, as the writer John Sheridan put it, 'as a sort of human osmosis' (O'Brien 1954, 182).

Ambivalence

The 'culture' of emigration which was well established as part of the way of life in Ireland before the Great Famine was sustained by ambivalence afterwards, as evidenced by Nationalist newspapers which, while opposing in their editorials further assisted emigration as leading to 'extermination', continued carrying advertisements for shipping lines operating to the United States and publishing articles of advice to intending emigrants (Duffy 2004, 94). The persistence of emigration in the twentieth century, which dismayed and embarrassed Nationalists whose rhetoric predicted that independence would halt emigration, was matched by continuing ambivalence, especially after the switch of main destination in the 1920s from the United States to England, and even beyond public recognition of the problem by the Commission on Emigration and Other Population Problems, 1948–54.

Countering emigration

One of the few proactive steps against emigration taken by the Irish state in the twentieth century was the repatriation scheme of the 1930s for Irish unmarried mothers in Britain (Earner-Byrne 2004). Another was the series of internal migration schemes, from the 1930s to the 1950s, for resettling farmers from Connacht to Leinster, which included Éamon de Valera's dream of establishing a community of native Irish speakers at *Ráth Chairn* (Rathcarne, Rathcarran), Meath, in the heart of the Pale, a little over 20 miles from the capital. It is striking how the terms 'colony', 'settlement' and 'pioneers', used to describe such schemes, 'reverberated down the centuries of Irish history', pointing to fundamental continuities in the migration process that transcend particularities of time and place:

> When the time of departure arrived, there was great sadness and the urge to go seemed to have died in some. Many were lonely at leaving their homeland. Every dyke, fence, rock and mountain held a meaning and a memory for them ... On the Friday preceding the move, fifteen of the school pupils bade goodbye to the teachers and went to their homes in the tiny villages of Srahwee, Woodfield, Althore and Derryheigh. On the following Sunday morning they went with their parents and grandparents to Mass in Killeen

Church and afterwards prayed by the graves of their kindred in the nearby cemetery. ... On Wednesday ... the final meeting place for departure was the school. They took a long last look at the familiar scenes and haunts of childhood and youth, bade farewell to Killeen church where they were baptised and wed, and for some of them, farewell to the resting place of their parents. The convoy of migrants crept slowly up the road. Neighbours gathered round and all were weeping bitterly.

(Whelan et al. 2004, 180, 182)

This was a group of ten families leaving Cregganbaun in south-west Mayo in 1955, not 1855 or 1755, and crossing not to America but to Kiltoom, Westmeath. 'Arriving' on the fertile plains of the east midlands, as with migration overseas, took time:

a division between migrants and local populations often persisted for years in many regions. There was limited social interaction between both communities who were separated in the chapel, in the graveyard, and in terms of intermarriage for the first generation.

One son of a Mayo migrant, born in Kildare, provides evidence of continuing connection with the 'homeland': now in his forties, he speaks with a distinctive Mayo accent and refers to the people of the west as 'his people'. Another son of a Mayo migrant recalls his father telling him about disputes in the early 1950s on the streets of Kilcock, Kildare, between migrants from Mayo and Connemara on the one hand, and the local, settled population on the other (Whelan et al. 2004, 180, 187, 182, 195; P. Mac Éinrí pers. comm.).

In the 1990s, with the dramatic reversal of migration flow from net emigration to net immigration, the persistence of high-level emigration was over (Fanning 2007, 2). If Ryan's *Departure of the Earls* serves as an icon of its modern origin, and Fox's *Small Island* of its persistence, the photograph of the 2007 election poster (Plate 24) may serve as an icon of its demise. However, a major component of net immigration has been return migration from the diaspora, as in 1999 when there were 47,500 immigrants to the Republic of Ireland, of whom just over half were returners. To the extent that it has been based on the promise of return, and to a very limited extent on actual return, the Irish migration tradition is circular rather than linear. In this sense, given the open-ended relationship between diaspora and homeland, it still persists.

Return

In the three-way migration process a linkage is made between emigration and immigration by those emigrants who return, because they join in the immigration flow. While emigration may have been a 'pleasing idea' to some, most emigrants, as noted in chapter 2, promised to return and many desired 'to lay their bones in their own country'. Emigrants who did return we consider as forming part of the immigration flow, although they form such a distinctive group that they are often treated separately. In the case of Ireland, relatively few returned. Compared with the returning 'golden stream' of remittances, the 'trickle' of returning emigrants was minute (Schrier 1958, 103; Fitzgerald 2007). Over 50 million Europeans emigrated between 1815 and 1914, primarily from Britain and Ireland in the first half of the century, from parts of Scandinavia and several German states in the mid-century, and from southern and eastern Europe in the decades before the First World War. What is still not widely appreciated is that, overall, as many as between a quarter and a third returned to their countries of origin. In the case of Ireland, only about a tenth did (Baines 1985, 28, 126). However, by the end of the twentieth century, the Irish experience of return migration was no longer exceptional in Europe. The American Wake was a thing of the past. In the 1980s, during the renewed phase of net emigration, before the flow reversal of Celtic Tiger Ireland, the so-called 'new wave' emigrants were being thought of as 'climbing social ladders' in the 'benign tax fields' of western Europe and the United States (Corcoran 1999). As we have noted, many of these mainly middle-class migrants were ambivalent about describing themselves as emigrants in the traditional sense, seeing themselves as 'sojourners' rather than 'settlers', engaged as much on a quest for self-fulfilment as escape from poverty, with a likely prospect of return.

Types of returners

As well as the difficulty of distinguishing between 'first-time emigrants' and 're-emigrants' in the emigration flow, not to mention distinguishing between long-term 'emigrants' and short-term 'sojourners', we have the difficulty of distinguishing and quantifying a wide variety of types of returners in the immigration flow. Many of them, because they resist easy classification, form part of what analysts call the 'statistical awkward squad' and constitute the 'dark figure' in international migration, which accounts for much of the difference between gross and net migration (Richards 2005, 88). More fundamentally, categorising migrants is problematic because of the 'myth of return' (Anwar 1979) to which most, if not all, are subject: no matter how well 'settled', immigrants generally keep their minds open to the possibility that one day they will return, if only as a safety net. What is clear is that rates of return relate to perceived conditions in both receiving and sending countries. For example, tenant emigrants leaving for freehold land (like the Mellon family) are less likely to return than skilled craftsmen leaving for cities; those without marriage ties in the new country are more likely to return than those with; and although only around 25,000 Irish, mainly male, emigrants went to South Africa in the nineteenth century, that was the country from which they were most likely to return: in 1904 it had a first-generation Irish population of only 18,000 (Bielenberg 2000, 222). Also, rates of return were conditioned by personal factors, which could be highly complex in that most immigrants belonged to 'three different worlds': that of the immigrants; that of the receiving country; and that of the old country (Emmer and Mörner 1992, 288–9; Wyman 1993).

'Returned Yanks'

The improvement in communications that came in the 1860s with the transition from the age of sail to the age of steam meant that, having compared conditions such as wage rates in all three 'worlds' and made the decision to emigrate, it was possible for the first time to know that one could relatively quickly and easily return should changes in the labour market so dictate. Thus a Norwegian farmer, smitten by 'America fever' in the 1860s, might have more easily reversed an ill-considered decision to leave than a similarly circumstanced Scottish Highlander in the 1770s (Harper 2005, 4; see also Devine 1999, 475–6). In the 1880s, about the same time as the 'stage Irishman' was becoming a familiar feature in the United States, the 'Returned Yank' was still a relatively rare figure in the Irish landscape (MacGowan 1962, 145; Smyth 1992, 72). However, they were sufficiently familiar to be given a central role in Irish fiction, such as that of George Moore, Daniel Corkery, Frank O'Connor, Seán O'Faolain and Máirtín Ó Cadhain (Hart 1982; Doyle 1998). Typically, Returned Yanks could be recognised by their propensity to dress expensively and colourfully, to be ostentatiously generous when buying drinks in public houses, and to sprinkle their conversation liberally with distinctively accented North American expressions such as 'I reckon', I calculate' and 'I guess', leading them to be referred to in some places by locals as 'the I-guessers' (Shrier 1958, 29–30). One such was Margaret Brennan of Carrownamaddy, south Roscommon, who first emigrated to Boston in 1902 aged 18, made her first return visit in the spring of 1911, when it was suggested that she should marry 36-year-old Patrick Dowling who owned 30 acres nearby, and returned again in 1913 to marry him and stay (Dunnigan 2007, 54–66). The figure of the 'Returned Yank' proved an enduring one, and some of the same distinguishing characteristics and motivating factors found in accounts of the late nineteenth century can be found in accounts of the twentieth century, including films such as *The Quiet Man* (1952) and *The Field* (1990). The establishment in 1931 of the Ford motor works at Dagenham, 12 miles east of Charing Cross, London, attracted an exodus of Cork migrants who became known as the 'Dagenham Yanks':

Take the 'Dagenham Yanks', for example. Men with winklepickers and blue suits and more money than sense home for the holidays from Ford's giant Essex complex, regaling the clientele in hostelries from Shandon to Barrack

Street in Cockney tones as polished as their brown shoes, the jingle louder in the first week home than the second. By which time nature would out and the accent had re-tuned itself to the mellifluous local sing-song, 'Jeez boy, that's a great pint of Murphy's, all the same ahh!'

(Mac Éinrí 2005, 419)

The transition to the age of air travel in the 1960s, and especially greater afford-ability of air fares from the 1990s, has greatly facilitated the possibility of frequent return to the 'homeland' for both emigrants and their descendants.

Return migration and migration studies

As an emerging academic discipline, the trajectory of migration studies has tended to follow that of migration itself in that the phase of 'return' has been the last to receive full scholarly attention (Harper 2005). Not surprisingly perhaps, concern tended to be focused first on emigration (mainly from Europe) and its impact on receiving societies (mainly in North America), being extended subsequently to concern with its impact on sending societies, and eventually, once its massive scale was appreciated, further extended to include return migration. A strong argument had held sway that return migration was of negligible importance. For example, Fender asserted that most emigrants to the United States had 'burned their boats'. Not only had they made a final break from their neighbours and extended families, they had also 'cut the apron strings of imperial hierarchy and the purse strings of Government preferment'. This was 'the emotional and conceptual break with the past so crucial to the adaptation to new circumstances' (1992, 355).

However, this view of emigration as an irreversible rite of passage has been challenged, for example, by Gerber, who shows that in the age of sail, as well as in the age of steam, there were significant numbers of emigrants from Europe to the United States who continued to 'live ... and think in multina-tional and transnational patterns that are neither here nor there, neither in homelands nor hostlands, but in both simultaneously' (2000, 35). Bruce Elliott (2005) has shown how, even in the Irish case, it is misleading to claim that emigrants generally 'burned their boats'. Climbing the social ladder to 'respectability' and achieving full adult status through 'domesticity' – marry-ing and setting up an independent home – remained primary migration goals in all eras and locations. 'Settling down' might be achieved as well back in the old country as in the new, depending on individual circumstances.

Local tradition in Ireland frequently recalls the movement of single women who emigrated to America to work for a few years in order to save for a dowry that they would bring back to Ireland in anticipation of marriage to a farmer's son (Neville 1992). Relatively little is known about this phenomenon, one example of which is beautifully described by Richard White in *Remembering*

Ahanagran (1998; see also Neville 1992; Murphy 1997; Clear 2007, 66). Similarly, little is known of those obliged to return to look after elderly parents; or of young children who were sent home to Ireland to be reared by grandparents (Fitzpatrick 1989, 567). This latter group, whose most famous member was de Valera, may well have been, as Smyth suggests, more common than is generally recognised (1992, 72). Once again we are returned to the importance of unravelling the complexity of migration at the local and individual level by making use of records such as those of the National Archives of Ireland (Maher 2004).

Research themes

Themes of current research on return migration include 'the motives of returners, the mechanisms by which they maintained links with the various places where they had alighted, or put down roots, or the economic, social, cultural impact they made on the adopted countries they left and the homelands to which they returned' (Harper 2005, 2). The negative side of Ireland's relatively high emigration rate has long been recognised. What has not been so well appreciated has been the equally negative aspect of its low rate of return migration. The investment overseas in Ireland's human capital was largely realised abroad, rather than eventually back at home. The migration mechanism that worked positively as a 'safety-valve' also depleted the store of progressive and innovative energy. Further research is needed to assess the implications of low return for Irish society. Return migration was not just a feature of the nineteenth century, of course, and five main reasons, which hold good for all eras and locations, have been identified to explain why some, sooner or later, made emigration into a round trip: success in the receiving country; failure; homesickness; a call to return to take over the family farm or other property; rejection of life overseas' (Wyman 2005, 21).

Homesickness

The nature of 'homesickness' in particular offers a key to better understanding of not only return migration but also new immigration. Recent research, based on analysis of emigrant letters and oral history interviews, has shown how homesickness is not just a passing phase which sufferers get over or grow out of. Nor is it a constant emotion which festers and deepens over time. Rather, it comes and goes with the phases and events of the individual's life course. Approaching retirement, for example, men and women may experience a resurgence of homesickness and a growing desire to live out the rest of their lives in their 'home' country. It turns out that homesickness is as much about problems with life in the new world as about missing the old world. Gender analysis has offered useful insight into why women migrants in particular, for example around the birth of the first child, in the absence of the support network of family and friends they would have had 'back home', might suffer acutely. It has also revealed a covert form of male homesickness, felt most by those who fail to establish themselves in the role of breadwinner, with a resulting collapse of masculine identity. Conversely, for those on course to achieving their migration goals, momentary pangs of longing for 'the absent' might be offset by engagement with the challenges of the present and the prospect of eventual success. What this research emphasises is 'how the causes of return were often deeply rooted in pre-migration experiences, and how the prospect of return changes – sometimes in unexpected ways – throughout the life course of the 'settled' migrant' (Thomson 2005, 128). Miller's thesis, that most Irish emigration was conceptualised in terms of 'exile', would suggest that Irish emigrants were predisposed more than most to homesickness – something borne out, for example, by the woman who admitted to an Irish Folklore Commission collector in the 1930s that she had never been happy in America: 'I never got up a morning in it but I thought how nice it would have been to be rising in Ballighan and seeing the sun on top of the Cruach' (quoted in Wyman 2005, 22). Most emigrants may not have thought of home every morning, but few could avoid it around Christmas or St Patrick's Day, when letters, like the actual sequence that inspired the song *Kilkelly, Ireland* by Peter Jones (*c.*1970), would exhort return. Until that might be a practical possibility, tokens, such as portrait likenesses or photographs, might be sent in reply, along with remittances, as a surrogate for the emigrant (see Plate 14).

Fitting back in

For those who did return, especially those coming back permanently, fitting back in to a place that was no longer the same as that which had been left could prove as much of a challenge as the initial immigration (Corcoran 2003; Jones 2003; Ní Laoire 2007a, b, c; Trew 2005, 2007). More research is needed into the extent to which return was to the home community or to elsewhere in Ireland, and how reintegration was achieved, including the returned 'exiles' of various 'Troubles' across the four centuries and, most recently, elderly Irish repatriation schemes such as 'Aisling' (http://www.aisling.org.uk) and 'Safe Home' (http://www.safe-home-ireland.com). The return strategy for a number of returners in the late nineteenth and early twentieth centuries, for example, seems to have been to become a publican with a sideline as an official emigration agent, representing one or more of the shipping lines (Molloy 2002). While some returners acted formally as agents, most did so informally, providing information and encouragement, and thereby helping to sustain the emigration flow (Harper 2005, 4).

Homecoming

An increasingly strong feature of return migration in the late twentieth and early twenty-first centuries is that of 'homecoming' by emigrants and descendants of emigrants – an effect in part of what has been called the 'postcolonial unsettling of settler society' (Basu 2005, 134). The recovery of family history, now aided greatly by the Internet, is associated in particular with the increasingly multicultural nature of new world societies and the sense of one's ethnic identity gradually being absorbed into the 'melting pot' (Glazer and Moynihan 1970). In particular, it is associated with the 'new white ethnic movement: the desire of white suburban, middle-class, assimilated citizens to effectively dissimilate themselves and recover a more distinct, particular ethnic identity' (Waters 1990). It is also associated with a more general 'culture of victimisation' – a preference for identifying with the oppressed rather than with the oppressors – which has been described generally as 'Holocaust envy' (Novick 1999, 190), and, in the Irish case, as the 'MOPE' ('Most Oppressed People Ever') syndrome (Kennedy 1996, 221). This goes a long way to explaining how the term 'diaspora', with its primary connotation of the Jewish experience and meanings of exile, loss, dislocation, powerlessness, pain and longing for an ancestral homeland, especially after Alex Haley's influential television series *Roots* (1977), comes to have been appropriated by others, including Irish and Ulster Scots, as a useful and desirable term, and why so many 'roots tourists' make the 'return' to what they see as their homeland, even though they may never have been there before. An example of such a quest is that of the Tasmanian-born Christopher Koch who 'returned' to Ireland in search of Margaret O'Meara, his Tipperary-born great-great-grandmother (2002).

Forced migration and repatriation

There is a growing literature on forced migration and repatriation to homelands where violent conflict was the cause of the migration (Manning 2005, 133–8; Eltis 2002; Long and Oxfeld 2004; Crawley 2006). The distinction between free and forced migration, which hinges on who makes the decision to leave (the migrant or some other individual) is evident from comparing the eighteenth-century experience of indentured servants, such as those from Ireland and Germany described by Marianne Wokeck (2002), and slaves and convicts. The former were not usually 'forced on board ship, chained and kept behind temporary barricades so that they could not see their homeland before setting sail'; nor were they 'subjected to special measures to restrain suicide during the actual sea voyage', whereas the latter could expect 'all or most or these things' (Eltis 2002, 6).

In the case of Ireland, migration due to violent conflict and natural disaster has been a persistent theme of the history of the last 400 years, including the displacements induced by Plantation after 1607, the Cromwellian policy of transplantation in the 1650s, the 'ethnic sorting-out' of the 1790s (Miller 1985, 68–9), the 'genocide' or 'holocaust' of the Great Famine (Foster 1988, 318–44; Morash 1995, 68, 186), and further 'sorting-out' in the 1920s (Parkinson 2004) and the

1970s (Conroy et al. 2005). However, Akenson has argued provocatively that there has been 'very little forced emigration' and that Irish historians have been mistaken in seeing Irish emigrants as 'passive flotsam on the fast-running tide of modern history' (1993, 36–7). Similarly, Patrick O'Farrell adopted a more positive interpretation of convict transportation in Irish migration to Australia (1986, 22–53). Such a view has been countered, for example, by O'Callaghan (2000) in *To Hell or Barbados: The Ethnic Cleansing of Ireland*. In global perspective, the scale of forced migration in Irish history may have been relatively small, but this detracts neither from the intensity of the suffering of those involved nor from the force of the perception that it has been great. Irish Travellers, for example, trace the origins of their migratory lifestyle to the displacements of the 1650s or the late 1840s (Gmelch 1975, 16; Hayes 2006).

In the twentieth century various programmes of return have been organised for forced migrants and their descendants, such as those run recently by the government of New Zealand for the Maori people, or by the United Nations in Bosnia, Rwanda and Kosovo. These usually provide financial aid for travel, restitution of land and houses, resettlement in a different region of the home country, or sometimes social aid for reintegration. Criticism of such pro-grammes has noted that a lack of infrastructure – especially employment opportunities – often does not allow for 'sustainable return' and leads to sub-sequent re-emigration or, in some cases, a transnational lifestyle where travel between multiple 'homeplaces' becomes the norm (Black and Gent 2006). As we shall see in chapter 12, the effort in the 1930s by the Fianna Fáil govern-ment to establish new Irish-speaking colonies within easy reach of Dublin by promoting internal migration from the Connemara *Gaeltacht* was a kind of 'transplantation to Connacht' in reverse. More recently, migrants returning to a pre- or not quite post-conflict Northern Ireland have received little support (Trew 2005, 110; 2007, 2008).

Linear and circular migration

Both 'exiles' and 'sojourners' see migration as a cyclical rather than linear process in that it is completed by return. Paradoxically, this may also be true for 'pilgrims' or 'adventurers', who tend to see emigration as a straight line into permanent settlement in the receiving country: many of them may regard the phase of 'arriving' in the 'new world' as incomplete until they have made a return visit to their original home, as was normally promised in the Irish case at the American Wake (Miller 1985, 565). The communal aspiration, expressed by the famous Percy French song 'Come Back, Paddy Reilly, to Ballyjamesduff', was fulfilled by few (Fitzgerald 2005). One such was Thomas Mellon, who made one return visit in 1882, at the age of 69, to the original family home in Castletown, Tyrone. For Mellon, who never had any intention of returning to settle permanently, the single day he spent there was immensely satisfying:

> Before coming I had supposed that I should want to stay or return here for several days; but I am satisfied: what more could I see or know if I returned again? So farewell to the home of my childhood. Adieu to the reality of its beautiful presence, but its sweet memory will remain to the last!
>
> (Mellon 1885, 306; Lambkin 2002, 46)

This sense of satisfaction has to do with the completion of unfinished business. In this case the emigrant was concerned to see for himself whether or not the 'photographic' memory of his childhood home, which was vivid for him all his life, was just as he remembered it. There is also a strong sense that he was revisiting the family home for the sake of his parents and uncles – something that they had not been able to do for themselves (Lambkin 2008a). Descendants of emigrants as 'roots tourists' report a similar sense of acting on behalf of ancestors who, despite the promise to return they had more than likely made on departure and renewed repeatedly in reply to letters from 'home', for whatever reason, never did return. The emotion involved, evoked so well by George Moore in his masterpiece short story *Home Sickness* (1931), can be so strong that in some cases the descendants of emigrants feel impelled to 'return' and settle. The return of the second- and third-generation cohorts is a recent reality of the expanding economy of Celtic Tiger Ireland which was probably never envisaged by the first generation of migrants (O'Connor 2006).

Gender

The persistence of emigration in Irish history has long been understood as stretching back to 1607 and the flight of the Earls, who were the archetypal 'Wild Geese'. However, as Patrick O'Sullivan reminds us, it turns out that 'for all these centuries, we have been talking about "Wild Geese" when really we were only talking about wild ganders' (1995, 11).

Geese and ganders

In reassessing the gender balance in the emigration flow, scholars have recently shown how the Irish in foreign military service in continental Europe were not exclusively men, and how the 'astronomical percentage' who left Ireland in the early modern period, starting with the 10,000 who left Ireland for Europe between 1585 and 1625, 'involved men, women and children from all levels of society' (Henry 1995, 23). It has been argued, perhaps unfairly, that Seán Keating's iconic painting *Economic Pressure* (1936), by presenting a 'typical' emigrant scene', reinforces the myth of the emigrant male and the stay-at-home female (see Plate 23) (Travers 1995, 146). It is clear now that, by the middle of the nineteenth century, about half of the Irish diaspora was female, and that from 1871 to 1971 a greater rate of female than male emigration was the norm, to such an extent that we can speak of a 'de-feminisation' of the Irish country-side and, by extension, a 'feminisation' of the Irish diaspora (O'Sullivan 1995, 1). While the European norm was for a much greater number of men to emigrate (the ratio was about 2:1), this broadly even gender balance is another charac-teristic which marks the Irish experience of emigration as distinctive (Lee 1989, 376).

Male and female 'geographies'

The Irish case seems less surprising when it is remembered that one of Ravenstein's 'laws of migration' is that 'females are more migratory than males within their country of birth', and that emigration is fundamentally an extension of internal migration (see Appendix II). In the move from country-side to town, a more or less even gender balance was evident across Europe (Bade 2003, 43–4). Given that women have largely shared a common range of pressures and motivations, various arguments are made nevertheless as to how they have experienced migration differently from men (Bauer and Thompson 2004; Kofman 2004; Silvey 2004). For a start, the 'geographies' of men and women could be very different – at home, on the street, in the labour market, in church and in society in general – making it important to study men and women both separately and together. In mid-Victorian Liverpool, for example, 'many women were less clearly socially and economically segregated than their menfolk' (Letford and Pooley 1995, 109). McSorley's pub in New York, which was established in 1854 and barred women until the 1970s, stands as an icon of these different geographies (Griffin 1998, 151). One formulation of gender difference is that 'while men move through the family networks to find work, women move through job networks to find a family' (Bertaux-Wiame 1982, 192). What many women seemed to have hoped for in the nine-teenth century, according to one analysis of emigrant letters, was 'economic achievement sufficient to secure "respectable" marriages and the status and authority of homemakers' (Miller et al. 1995, 60). As one historian puts it, 'the entire human drama of the transition from a traditional Irish rural economy to a metropolitan industrial and technical economy is one of the astonishing historic departures of modern times' (Clark 1995, 127). In order to interpret what this has meant for the women who took part, we need to trace their changing 'employment worlds' in pre-industrial, industrial and post-industrial settings. By tracing at the individual level, studies such as that of Marilyn Cohen (1995; 1997) are revealing the chain migration, residence strategies, employment patterns and indicators of vertical social mobility of women who otherwise have left little historical documentation.

Gender perspective

The absence of this gender perspective in Irish history was striking as recently as 1990 when the publication of *Migrations: the Irish at Home and Abroad*, a collection of essays by male authors only, provoked anger at the 'indirect censorship implicit in the book' (Kearney 1990; O'Carroll 1995, 192–3). The traditional, patriarchal view which sees womanhood as having a particular essence with specific characteristics, such as caring, gentleness, emotion and intuition, was based on the idea that these derived from the inevitable biological differences between female and male. In rejecting this, feminism has insisted on distinguishing socialisation (into gendered roles) from biological difference, seeing gender as an identity, like ethnicity and class, which may be de-emphasised or manipulated to suit different needs and situations (Kells 1995). Thus, in considering the migration of Irish women over 400 years, we need to bear in mind the complex ways in which the changing categories 'Irish' and 'women' have been combined, as, for example, in the case of the female Irish Traveller, born in England and reared in Ireland, who told a researcher: 'I don't even call myself Irish. I call myself a Traveller that's all. We have no really set place anyway. We haven't really got a set country' (Gray 2004, 5, 75). Following in the wake of pioneering studies such as those by Diner (1983), Nolan (1989), Walter (2001) and Lambert (2001), the gendered approach, which highlights female experience and questions the role and image of women in relation to that of men, has altered migration studies considerably. As we have already seen, gender analysis has yielded useful insights into the nature of homesickness, including how both men and women might suffer acutely at certain life stages (Murphy 1997; Walter 2001; Ryan 2003).

The changing balance

The changing proportion of women to men who emigrated before about 1800 is difficult to gauge without accurate records. For example, the system of indentured servitude favoured males, just as that of domestic service later favoured females. In 1745–8, the only period for which such data are available before the peaks of Irish emigration to North America in the early 1770s and early 1780s, only 13.5 per cent of 546 indentures recorded for Irish immigrants were for women or girls (Wokeck 1999, 201; Doyle 2006b, 178). However, it is clear that substantial numbers of women who married Irish-born men emigrated and played a crucial role in establishing overseas communities, first in Catholic Europe and then more widely, just as British-born women had done in Ireland in the seventeenth century. In the eighteenth and early nineteenth centuries, Irish emigration was distinctive for the high numbers of single females emigrating when the European norm was for women to leave in family groups (Baines 1991, 47). Many women moved internally from the countryside to the towns. Some stayed, taking the places of town women who emigrated. Others, demonstrating the linkage between internal migration and emigration, stayed for a while and then emigrated. In the nineteenth century, Poor Law Guardians invested particularly in emigration schemes for females, recognising that initial investment would eventually pay dividends, as much in the interest of the receiving as the sending society, by 'setting in motion a whole series of chain migrations' (McLoughlin 1995, 85). The greater rate of female emigration from the middle of the nineteenth century was in contrast, for example, to the dominance of males in the emigration stream from Sweden (Bade 2003, 255–6). The only recent Census decades in which more men than women emigrated from Ireland were those of major British wars, when many Irish men joined the British armed forces (1891–1901, 1911–1926, 1936–46), and 1951–61 and 1981–91, which were years of exceptionally high unemployment (Walter 2003, 1147).

Trajectories of domestic servants

On average Irish female emigrants were younger than males, with a surprisingly large proportion between the ages of 15 and 19 going into domestic service (Travers 1995, 147). The term 'outsiders inside' has been used by Bronwen Walter to describe the ambiguous position of Irish women, especially those going into the domestic service of the middle classes in Britain and the United States (2001, 9). Many such women succeeded in achieving 'respectability', particularly through the education of their children, as indicated, for example, by the upward mobility of the large numbers who went on to become schoolteachers and nurses (Nolan 2004, 76–7; Ryan 2007a, b). One assessment of the contribution of succeeding first generations of female immigrants in North America is that 'the diffusion of female-supported families from a rural Irish base into metropolitan societies with their developing urban patterns has constituted a notable source of social stability amid tides of economic disruption and spiritual dislocation' (Clark 1995, 127). However, many women must also have wondered whether they had sacrificed too much in pursuing the dream of 'love and liberty' and achieving domesticity, as in the case of Ellen Finn, the wife of a day-labourer in Barrytown, New York who, through her work as a laundress, 'purchased a house and lot that cost her fourteen hundred dollars', but was left 'very thin and old looking' (Miller et al. 1995, 61). The substantial minority of households headed by women are seen as 'persistent symbols of the poverty often faced by women living without men' (Cohen 1995, 143). Similarly, the many men who failed to achieve domesticity through migration must have wondered if they had not sacrificed too much in pursuit of the dream of 'settling down' (Elliott 2005, 154–5).

Breaking the silence

An important stage in breaking the silence about women's migration was the Irish Government Commission on Emigration and Other Issues (1948–54). Its final report recognised the lack of opportunities in rural Ireland to keep women there, without, however, recommending changes to the inflexible family inheritance system that was largely responsible for making emigration 'an enforced requirement rather than a free choice' (McCullagh 1991, 206). Following the Great Famine, the norm was for farms on the death of the father to be inherited by the eldest son, rather than divided among the children. One daughter might stay by marrying a neighbour's eldest son but others could not be supported as single adults, especially after men took over dairying and poultry-keeping, which traditionally had been women's farm work (Bourke 1993). By way of compensation, and to improve their prospects as providers of remittances from abroad, girls generally achieved higher levels of education than boys (Nolan 2004). A North/South difference emerged in 1923 with the introduction of the marriage bar in the Irish Free State, preventing women once they married from remaining in civil service occupations or teaching. The bar remained in force until accession to the European Economic Community in 1973. In Northern Ireland, where there was no such restriction on women's participation in the workforce, emigration rates for women were about the same as for men, not significantly higher.

South/North differences

As well as lack of employment opportunities at home, socially restrictive attitudes to women, based on the teaching of the Catholic and Protestant Churches alike, encouraged the seeking of greater freedom outside Ireland. This was especially the case with those finding it difficult to conform to a narrow definition of womanhood, including single women, lesbians and those who became pregnant outside marriage (Earner-Byrne 2004, 155; Ryan 2004). In the 1980s new anti-abortion legislation and the initial rejection of legislation permitting divorce in the South reinforced a social climate felt by many to be stifling. A study of emigrants in London in the early 1970s found that 'a larger proportion of women than men indicated that they did not intend to return to Ireland', leading to the conclusion that 'emigrant women would be less likely to embrace the "Erin's children in exile" interpretation of emigration so beloved of Irish politicians, at home and abroad' (Travers 1995, 164). Migration, especially to England, would appear to have operated both as a resource in concealing pregnancy (and hence preserving 'respectability') and as a means of expanding sexual possibilities for many Irish women in the twentieth century. In the 1970s, following the outbreak of civil conflict, the conditions of migration from Northern Ireland and public perceptions of it became markedly different from those in the South (Gray 2004, 27, 5; Trew 2007).

In the South the character of female migration changed in the 1980s, when those leaving were predominantly middle class and migration in Northern

Ireland continued to be conditioned particularly by the Troubles. In the 1990s more men than women were leaving. With Ireland being refigured as a 'global nation', intellectual skills replacing physical strength as a labour market requirement, and fewer women leaving, the new emphasis was on individual choice in pursuit of self-fulfilment and career advancement (Gray 2004, 8). Research into this recent migration has been making especially effective use of life-course oral narrative methodology, highlighting in particular the experience of older women emigrating in search of employment, women who are left behind and women who emigrate to escape domestic violence (Kelly and Nic Giolla Choille 1995, 191; Trew 2006, 2007). As one commentator concludes, 'sometimes a woman needs a room of her own and 500 dollars a month ... to reassemble the lifeimages/lifewords of her own herstory [*sic*]. Sometimes this room can only be found 3,000 miles away from what Adrienne Rich calls "that most dangerous place, the family home"' (O'Carroll 1995, 198). 'Irishness' in Ireland, for women as for men, is not found to be the same as 'Irishness' in London. Interestingly, one study noted 'the repeated *slippage* in the women's accounts ... from "Irish women" to "Irish people"' (Gray 2004, 19; emphasis added).

'Uneven assimilation'

In migration studies generally, the concept of 'uneven assimilation' has been found helpful in understanding the variety of choices made by migrants about living in the new world among the ethnic group, or socialising or seeking a partner within it, or simply keeping one's accent. Emerging from work on the Irish abroad is a wide range of voices with different perspectives, including one, for example, which objected vehemently to the new stereotype that 'the bright and the brilliant and the beautiful and the adventurous take off, you know ... and all the boring daisies and common, ugly ones like ourselves stay here and keep the home fires burning' (Gray 2004, 85). It remains a moot point whether the relatively unrestricted freedom to move in a rapidly globalising world, which has brought with it the freedom to choose to 'belong' in both Ireland and, say, London, has rendered migration any less of an 'uprooting' experience for men or women. Gray contrasts a past when emigrants were 'gone' and 'settled down' with a present where they 'come and go' and concludes that the present is possibly even more 'unsettling', both for those who go and for those who stay (2004, 162). This raises the question of how those of mixed backgrounds of various kinds may sustain multiple belonging by frequent modulation between different cultures and communities.

Something of this ambivalence is captured by Keating in his painting *Economic Pressure* (Plate 23). So far as gender is concerned, part of the painting's appeal is that it requires a close look to decide whether it is the woman or the man who is leaving.

The view from 'Scally's satellite'

Viewing the three-way process of Irish migration over the four centuries from 'Scally's satellite', we are struck not only by the 'fitfully dormant' movement of people on the earth's surface before the Napoleonic Wars and the 'sudden buzzing and swarming' that followed. The contribution of Ireland to the overall migration picture is marked by these three particular features: the persistence of its emigration flow from the seventeenth century through to the late twentieth century; the small proportion of return migrants in the immigration flow; and the high proportion of women in the emigration flow. In Part II, where we shall observe continuity and change in more detail over shorter periods, we may expect to find evidence of the distinctive features of Ireland's three-way migration process. Zooming in more frequently to the local level, we may also expect to encounter the bewildering diversity of individual migration stories that constituted the characteristic patterns of Ireland's three-way migration process. Before that, however, we need to consider in more detail the possible outcomes of the process.

4

A Three-Outcome Process: Segregation, Integration and Modulation

We know now that major outcomes of Irish migration over the last four centuries have been: the conflicting projects of 'Making Ireland British' and 'Making British Ireland Irish'; the urbanisation of a predominantly rural population; the formation of a global Irish diaspora; and the formation of parts of the diasporas of other countries in Ireland. New ways of thinking about Ireland's diaspora of about 70 million people world-wide, Catholic, Protestant and other, who are descended from the ten million who left the island between 1607 and 2007, have helped bring about a resolution of the British–Irish conflict in Northern Ireland and a peaceful accommodation of large numbers of immigrants across the whole island.

However, these outcomes seemed far from inevitable as the story unfolded. In the first place, to speak of 'the Irish diaspora' before the 1990s is anachronistic (as we discuss in chapter 15). Given the general European trend of rural–urban migration, the eventual urbanisation of Ireland did increasingly seem likely, but it was a long time in coming, with the rural–urban balance that had tipped in the six counties of Northern Ireland in the 1920s not tipping in the 26 counties until the 1960s. The persistent conflict stemming from British immigration in the seventeenth century appeared intractable in Northern Ireland even beyond the Belfast/Good Friday Agreement of 1998. The lasting reversal to net immigration in the late 1990s was experienced by many as a shock. Because these outcomes of the migration process did not become obvious until near the end of our four centuries, further discussion is deferred to Part III. Nevertheless, before proceeding to the more detailed survey of Part II, we need to look more closely at the possible outcomes of the migration process and the attitudes of each migrant generation to them.

As noted in chapter 2, the third stage of arrival (whether migration is inward, within or outward) generally results in segregation or integration (Mac Éinrí 2007, 216). In practice, however, at least as far as individual migrants are concerned, the outcome rarely seems clear-cut: many continue throughout their lives to modulate between seeing their new world as the 'the land of the stranger' and the 'land of plenty and sweet liberty' (Sheridan 2007, 141). In 1876 Peter Coyle for example, wrote from the silver mines of Nevada to his mother in the townland of Altanagh, Tyrone, saying, 'I am lonely to hear from you', and that 'the women are very scarce in this country. I have not seen a white woman this seventeen months, only one and she was not a very good one neither'. Two years later he wrote, 'Dear mother, I am sorry that the times are so bad in that country with you but it is a poor country when it is at its best. It would be better to be in prison in this country than to live there' (Shields 1984, 78). At the same time, those already settled in the receiving society may modulate between acceptance and rejection of their immigrants. Such a fluid and dynamic, two-way modulating process of continual readjustment and renegotiation takes place in the kind of 'third space' described by Homi Bhabha (1994) and Ed Soja (1996), between the extremes of integration and segregation, and may result in a continuing state of 'migrancy', as described by Iain Chambers (1994). In the next chapter we shall encounter another example of modulation (in the sense of negotiating a sinuous path between opposites) in the debate among historians about whether early modern Ireland is more appropriately considered as a kingdom or a colony, or as 'somewhere between the colonial model of North America and the experiences of the kingdoms of mainland Europe'. Therefore, as well as seeing migration as a three-stage, three-way process, we also need to see it as a three-outcome process of segregation, integration and modulation between the opposites.

Within/beyond the Pale; inside/outside the melting pot

The basic choice to be negotiated by both international and internal migrants and their receiving societies or communities in the process of arriving is between segregation, or apartheid, and integration. In the sixteenth and seventeenth centuries in Ireland, the old policy of immigrants from Britain and their descendants segregating themselves from the natives by excluding them 'beyond the Pale', or in 'Irish streets' or 'Irishtowns' within it, was extended by further 'plantation'. A strict policy of segregation might be difficult to enforce, as witnessed, for example, by the repeated ordinances that were deemed necessary in Dublin against native Irish people becoming freemen of the city, against their being taken on as apprentices in the trades and against even their dwelling within the franchises of the city (Lennon 1989, 35).

In contrast, the policy in the United States of the 'melting pot' (see Plate 10), and in Canada of the 'mosaic', was one of integration. The earliest reference to America as a melting pot describes it as a place where 'individuals of all nations are *melted* into a new race of men' (de Crevecoueur 1782). Well grounded in the biblical image of the 'refiner's fire' (Malachi 3:2), this new industrial-scale sense of a 'crucible' in which various 'metals', their 'impurities' having been removed, are 'amalgamated' to form a new 'super' identity, was popularised by Israel Zangwill's play *The Melting Pot*, first produced in Washington, DC in 1908. The hero announces that 'America is God's Crucible, the great Melting-Pot where all the races of Europe are melting and re-forming! ... Germans and Frenchmen, Irishmen and Englishmen, Jews and Russians – into the Crucible with you all! God is making the American.'

However, in practice admission to the crucible was often resisted by the receiving society, especially on the grounds of 'race'. When barriers to integration were put up by the receiving society, immigrant groups responded with the survival strategy of self-segregation and ethnic solidarity. When integration was permitted, it often took the form of 'assimilation' to the established dominant culture (white, English-speaking and Protestant in North America), leaving no detectable contribution by other immigrant groups to the character of the homogeneous whole (Myrdal 1944; Takaki 1979; Ignatiev 1996; Roediger 1999; Black and MacRaild 2000, 155–7). This approach was satirised in the cartoon 'The Mortar of Assimilation', which appeared in *Puck Magazine* (26 June 1889): it pictures the mortar of 'Citizenship' packed with figures in different national costumes, including a recalcitrant Irishman, being pounded with the pestle of 'Equal Rights' by 'Miss America' (recalling the figure of Liberty in Plate 6), whose costume is the Stars and Stripes.

Stews and salads

Another way of thinking about the process of arriving has been in the looser sense of a cooking pot in which a 'stew' is cooked. The basic idea that the community is like a cooking pot or cauldron is an old one, attested in the early Irish law tracts where the 'true ruler' (*flaithemain fír*) is described as 'a cauldron that cooks together every raw thing: *coire con-berba cach n-uile n-om*' (*Corpus Iuris Hibernici* 2215.40-2261.2; Kelly 1988, 18, 236, 240). In the modern version, immigrant identities are seen more appreciatively than in the melting pot – like different kinds of meat in a Hungarian goulash, which retain their solid structure while being 'blended' with the whole. In the 1960s, as a way of moving beyond what was seen as the excessive blending of the cooking or melting pot, the 'salad bowl' metaphor became popular in thinking about how quite separate identities might be retained while still being in harmonious relationship with each other. In the 1970s Canada in particular pioneered this multicultural approach, based on the work of the Ukrainian-Canadian Paul Yuzyk (1967), in addressing the needs of the First Nations Canadians, English-speakers and French-speakers, and the new immigrant minorities. This was in contrast to the idea of homogeneous nationality, as favoured for example by France. The outcome in the Canadian case was described as a 'cultural mosaic' (Gibbon 1938; Porter 1965).

In the ghetto

Those not permitted or unwilling to integrate, whether as ingredients of the melting pot, stew pot or salad bowl, or as tesserae of the mosaic, found themselves segregated in 'ghettos' of various kinds, a metaphor popularised again by Zangwill in *Children of the Ghetto* (1892), published the year before Frederick Jackson Turner first outlined his thesis about American identity-formation and the role of the closing 'frontier' (Turner 1920; Billington 1971). A first experience of segregation in the new world might well have been in a quarantine station, such as Castle Garden or, from 1892, its successor, Ellis Island in New York, Grosse Isle in Canada or Hobart Town in Australia (O'Gallagher 1984). Immigrants who were able to afford first- or second-class tickets were normally exempt from such places (Schepin and Yermakov 1991; Figorito 2006). The experience of the quarantine station was followed in many cases by segregation in urban working-class districts with distinctive ethnic identities, where, as we have seen, the 'ghetto' provided essential shelter when no other survival strategy was available. There is an extensive literature on the process of ghettoisation (Cutler et al. 2007), which has been studied, for example, in relation to the residential experience of the Irish in mid-Victorian Britain (Pooley 1989) and an Irish neighbourhood in Buffalo, New York, in the nineteenth and twentieth centuries (Jenkins 2003).

Modulating

In the postmodernity of the late twentieth and early twenty-first centuries, there has been much discussion of different models of integration and of how modern migrants, situated in 'diasporic space' between 'new world' and 'old world' are negotiating the possibilities of being integrated in both, as if modulating, as in music, between different 'keys' of belonging (Mac Éinrí and Lambkin 2002, 138; Mac Éinrí 2007a, 233). The idea of modulating between different ways of seeing one's situation in the world is useful for suggesting both the 'seamlessness' of human experience in general and the coherence of the experience of the migrant who fits neither the exile (yearning to return) nor the emigrant (determined to stay) type. Seasonal, internal migrants, for example, were used to 'balancing between agricultural and urban work' (Page Moch 2003, 129). This balancing between worlds might even be achieved by overseas migrants. Although we have emphasised emigration in the Irish case as an irreversible rite of passage, some in the age of sail as well as in the age of steam managed to return more or less frequently and continued to 'live ... and think in multinational and transnational patterns that are neither here nor there, neither in homelands nor hostlands, but in both simultaneously' (Gerber 2000, 35).

Of course, for some in the in-between situation of crossing between old and new worlds, the switch of mood might be far from smooth, as in the case of the migrant we encountered in chapter 2 'vacillating between hope and fear'. Even committed, permanent emigrant settlers could experience deep ambivalence about their new world, like the Swedish emigrant Peter Cassel, who in 1845 founded the settlement of New Sweden, Iowa and wrote home to say, 'this country can be *at the same time* both a Canaan and a Siberia' (Barton 1994, 14–15; our emphasis). For most migrants it was never a simple choice between old world and new world because they effectively belonged to 'three different worlds': that of the immigrants, that of the receiving country and that of the old country (Emmer and Mörner 1992, 288–9). This means that the outcomes of migration at the level of individual migrants are highly diverse, varying over time according to changing circumstances and attitudes in all 'three worlds'. The sending society might vary between encouragement to go and encouragement to return'; the migration policy of the receiving society might vary between segregation and integration; and the migrants and their descendants might vary in their commitment to 'joining in' or 'keeping apart', or in finding a way to do both. The limits of what may be possible in 'becoming' someone else are explored by Eva Hoffman in *Lost in Translation: A Life in a New Language* (1989). Enda Delaney for example, writing of the Irish in post-war Britain, draws attention to the ambivalences of their 'inner histories':

> Most retained a deep loyalty to home in the abstract sense of place rather than the Irish nation-state, yet recognized the material benefits of living in this 'strange' land. Others readily acknowledged the damaging consequences of Catholic hegemony of social and cultural life in independent Ireland, but still viewed Catholicism as an important component of individual identities. Some went as far as expressing anger at Britain's historical role in Irish history yet just as instinctively identified 'tolerance' and 'fair play' as core English values.

> (2007, 8)

Therefore, in trying to comprehend the complexity of migration, we should see it not just as a two-outcome process of segregation and integration but as a three-outcome process, which includes varying degrees of modulation between segregation and integration, seen, for example, in the 'retuning' of the accents of the 'Dagenham Yanks' referred to in the previous chapter, or in the migration story of one Cork boy and his father and older sister:

> I was in my early teens when World War Two began. My father had served in the Royal Leinster Fusiliers in world War One and had been

wounded in action in that conflict. So at about fifteen years having left the Primary School I persuaded my parents that England was my future and in company with my older sister joined my father in wartime Wiltshire.

On Saint Patrick's Day I wear my shamrock with pride but come November 11th, I am equally proud to wear my 'poppy' and remember those who made the supreme sacrifice for the well being of both countries.

(Mac Éinrí 2005, 419)

Finally, before turning to survey Irish migration more closely over these four centuries, we should note that scientific investigators like Sir William Petty, Arthur Young, Thomas Colby, Father John O'Brien and Dr Garret Fitzgerald have not been the only ones to view it imaginatively, as if from a satellite. When Sister Agnes of the Convent of Mercy, Charleville, Cork, composed the hymn 'Hail, Glorious Saint Patrick' in 1853, she was developing the global perspective of the prayer 'Hail, Holy Queen' (*Salve Regina*), cited as an epigraph to this book. As well as envisaging the Blessed Virgin Mary looking down on 'the 'banished children of Eve' in 'this valley of tears', Sister Agnes boldly imagined St Patrick alongside her 'high in thy mansions above' and 'looking down' not only on 'Erin's green valleys', but also on 'thy people, now exiles on many a shore'. The subsequent popularity of the hymn, sung especially on St Patrick's Day, was a marker of the strength of the family relationship between homeland – 'our native home' and 'the land of our birth' – and diaspora – 'wheresover we roam' (Litvak 1996, 80; Cronin and Adair 2002, xviii).

The spread of 'Hail, Glorious Saint Patrick' throughout the homeland and the peoples of Ireland world-wide – at least their Catholic parts – is a reminder that artefacts and ideas as well as people migrate. Another striking example of the relationship between the homeland and its migrants scattered world-wide is the Irish-language song *Seachrán Chairn tSiadhail* (The Shaughraun or Wanderer of Carnteel) which originated in the late eighteenth century in the village of Carnteel, near Aughnacloy, Tyrone. Its popularity, as well as the familiarity of such figures in Irish and European life generally, may well have been a factor in the phenomenal success of *The Shaughraun*, the melodrama by Dion Boucicault, which was first performed in New York in 1874 (O'Sullivan 1994, 9). The song was later tracked by the Dublin-born and Protestant Gaelic League activist Seosamh Laoide (Joseph Lloyd) in the four provinces of Ireland and also in the United States, from where Mr J. J. Lyons of Philadelphia had sent back to Ireland a version which was published in the *Tuam News*:

The following song is very popular among the natives of Ulster in America. I often heard it sung at weddings, christenings and other social gatherings, in the city of Philadelphia. It is written from the dictation of Mr. Conn MacNeilis, a native of the parish of Iniskeel, Co. Donegal.

So here we have an illustration of the creative tension between the different directions of migration: the immigrant background of the student of the song (implied by Loide's originally Welsh family name, Lloyd); the internal migration of the song itself within Ireland; its emigration to the United States (attached to a named individual migrant); and its eventual return to Ireland – its *seachránaidhe* (wandering) paralleling that of the eponymous *Seachrán* (Laoide 1904, 45–6, 34–5).

The changing tension in the three-stage (leaving, crossing, arriving), three-way (immigration, internal migration, emigration), three-outcome (segregation, integration, modulation) process of migration – creative and otherwise – is the theme of Part II and its more detailed survey of four centuries of the 'fitfully dormant', 'swarming', 'buzzing', 'boiling' activity of migration in Irish history.

Plate 1 *The Departure of O'Neill out of Ireland* (1958), Thomas Ryan, courtesy of the artist

The backward look of the departing Hugh O'Neill is framed by the blessing hand of the friar, representing the Faith, and the flag, representing Fatherland, Ireland. In the far distance is the western shore of Lough Swilly, where O'Neill will shortly meet up with O'Donnell and take ship for Europe. Some of the migrants' 'sea-stores' are being carried by the two figures in front of the friar and the bare-foot boy beside the flag-carrier has his bundle in his hands. There are ritual aspects to the leave-taking of the two couples to the left of the friar: the woman with child in arms faces her husband as he clasps her hand; the other woman is weeping. Probably weeping also is the child beside O'Neill being held by his mother. The boy in the right hand corner holds out one hand to the dog while the other clasps a set of rosary beads. The steadying hand on O'Neill's elbow indicates the ambiguity of the moment. Would the emigrants return, or would this be a last look back? Completed shortly after the 350th anniversary, the painting now hangs in the State Apartments in Dublin Castle (Fitzgerald 2007).

Plate 2   Map of Ulster (1591), Francis Jobson, TCD MS 1209/17, Trinity College Dublin

Nine ships (five single-masted, four double-masted, and three with faces showing) are crossing between Britain and O'Neill's Ulster, before the outbreak of the Nine Years War (1593–1603). The proximity of Britain is indicated at the top by the southern tips of Islay and the Mull of Kintyre. Marked vividly on the north-east tip of Ireland (Torr Head) is the site of 'ye Scottes warnenige fyer' [the Scots warning fire], which, according to the 1835 Ordnance Survey Memoir for the local parish of Culfeightrin, was 'celebrated as having been the place on the summit of which the Scots who had migrated or invaded this country used to light beacons for the purpose of alarming and calling to their assistance their countrymen in Argyllshire' (Horning 2004, 208).

Moving around the coast from west to east, the ships indicate the estuaries, ports and river valleys that were used by the settlers in penetrating inland: 'L. Yearne' (Lough Erne); 'Donnegall' (Donegal); 'L. Silley' (Swilly); 'L. Fooll' (Foyle) and 'Derre' (Derry); 'The Bande' (Bann) and 'Colrane' (Coleraine); 'The bay of Carigforgus' (Carrickfergus) and 'Carigforgus' and 'Bellfaste' (Belfast); 'Strangforde' (Strangford); 'Dundrum'; 'Carlingforde' (Carlingford) and 'The Newrye' (Newry); 'The Baye of Dondaulke' (Dundalk) and 'Dundaulke'.

In 'Logh Eaugh' (Lough Neagh), what is today called Coney Island is marked as 'Island Sydney', named after the Lord Deputy, Sir Henry Sidney (1529–86) who was responsible for the defeat of Shane O'Neill and the Compositions of Connacht and Munster. To the west of Lough Neagh is marked O'Neill's capital of 'Dungannon' and above it 'the stone whereon they make ye onels' (the O'Neill inauguration site at Tullaghogue, demolished by Mountjoy in 1602). Also marked is the pilgrimage site of 'S. Patricke his Purgatorie' (St Patrick's Purgatory, Lough Derg). To the south of 'Strabane' and 'Newtown' (Newtownstewart) is marked the hill of 'Sleue Trime' (*Sliabh Troim*), later called Bessy Bell, beneath whose eastern slope today is the Ulster-American Folk Park. Ulster is bounded by 'Parte of the Province of Connoughe (Connacht)' and 'parte of the Province of Leomster (Leinster)'. The density of detail in the mapping indicates the frontier between the more familiar east and the largely unexplored west. For more on the cartographer Francis Jobson and his pioneering fieldwork, see Andrews (1997, 104–9).

Plate 3 *Belfast 1613*, **Sketch for Mural in Belfast City Hall (1951), John Luke, Collection Ulster Museum, Belfast**

The central figure is Sir Arthur Chichester, enemy of Hugh O'Neill and Lord Deputy (1605–15). He reads the Town Charter of Belfast awarded in 1613. The bell on which he stands and the nearby anchor are the punning symbols of Bel-fast. He is framed by signs, some of them anachronistic, of the town's linen and shipbuilding industries: to the left, bundles of flax, a woman at a spinning wheel, a handloom weaver, lengths of linen on a bleach green, the market house and court house, and a bolt of finished linen being inspected; to the right, blacksmiths, rope-makers and shipwrights; and to the rear, the arched bridge across the Lagan, with the forest of ship masts behind, the glass-works chimney, and the two church towers, the larger Anglican and the other Presbyterian. The hourglass on the loom suggests the stereotypical Protestant attitude to time and work ethic. Beyond the town in the middle distance is a road winding through the ordered countryside, past whitewashed cottages to the limestone quarry. Beyond it again is the forbidding, wooded height of the Cave Hill (translated from the Irish *Binn Uamha* 'peak/cliff of the cave', also known as *Beann Mhadagáin*: 'peak of Madagán', McKay 2007, 39), suggestive of the natives still living in the uplands. On its summit in June 1795, Wolfe Tone, Henry Joy McCracken, Thomas Russell, Samuel Neilsen and other United Irishmen pledged themselves to rebellion.

Grouped around Chichester is a family of three generations: the father, holding the hand of the younger son who is turned to face the viewer; the older son with stick and dog; the wife with child in arms; the marriageable sister or daughter; and the white-bearded grand-father leaning on his stick. The sticks of the boy and the old man echo the pikes of the guards flanking Chichester. This immigrant group contrasts with the family groups around O'Neill in Plate 1, especially with that of the departing husband taking leave of his wife with a child in arms. The strong presence of children, including the young girl seated happily on the bleach green with cat and kitten, also indicates that these immigrants are anchored fast and determined to remain as permanent settlers.

John Luke (1906–75) had worked both in Belfast's shipyards and in its York Street Flax-spinning Company before moving to London to study at the Slade School of Art. He worked on the Northern Ireland government's pavilion at the Glasgow Empire Exhibition in 1938 and was commissioned to paint the large mural in the dome of the City Hall, Belfast, for the Festival of Britain (Newman 1993, 140–1). His representation of industry, godliness and prosperity possibly tells us more about 1951 than 1613 and Unionist efforts to stress the apartness of British Ireland from Irish Ireland, imagined here to lie beyond the Cave Hill.

Plate 4 *The North Gate Bridge and Jail, Cork City* (*c.* 1770), **Nathaniel Grogan, Crawford Municipal Art Gallery, Cork**

The bridge marks the point of transition between urban and rural worlds. The boat being rowed under the bridge over the River Lee is approaching the masts of ships that indicate the proximity of the sea. Leaving the city is a lady of quality being driven in a carriage that is about to overtake a woman carrying a basket on her head and a man carrying a sack on his back. Arriving in the city is a man on horseback who doffs his hat. All who arrive and leave by this route pass through the decorated gateway arch of the four-storey jail. The French traveller Chevalier de Latocnaye, writing in about 1798, described how 'it would seem as if it were wished to hinder the wind from drying the filth, for the two ends of the street are terminated by prisons, which close the way entirely and prevent the air from circulating' (quoted in Crowley et al. 2005, 67, see also 161, 69).

Four figures are leaning on the parapet of the bridge while another, in the bottom right-hand corner, is resting on the outside city wall with a creel or basket of turf. Between them three men, one wheeling a barrow of stones, are engaged in repairing the breach in the wall. Close by stand three ladies of quality in conversation, with a beggar squatting behind them. Even in the later eighteenth century Irish town governors saw themselves as upholders of English urban civility. The position of the beggar outside the city gate and its jail may be taken as symbolic of the desire to prevent the entry of undesirable immigrants from the countryside. As Avril Thomas puts it, 'the visible boundary of the curtain wall may have had psychological implications in terms of urban pride, exclusiveness and restrictiveness, at which we can only guess now' (1992, 132). It was the north and south gates that were closed against starving in-migrants in 1847 (see chapter 10).

The Cork-born Nathaniel Grogan (1740–1807) was a returned migrant, having served in the British army in America and the West Indies (Strickland 1989, I, 413–15).

Plate 5 *Street scene at St Patrick's Cathedral, Dublin* (c. 1810), **Private collection; formerly with John Nixon, Agnew & Sons, London**

The view is looking south down Patrick Street. Behind the viewer is the River Liffey, Wood Quay and Christchurch Cathedral. Ahead on the left, on the oldest Christian site in Dublin, is the tower of St Patrick's Cathedral, with the largest ringing peal in Ireland, and where the first public clock in Dublin was placed. The Huguenots worshipped in the Cathedral from 1666 to 1861. Ahead on the right lie the Liberties, described by the Rev James Whitelaw in 1798:

> The streets are generally narrow; the houses crowded together; the rears or back yards of very small extent, and some without accommodation of any kind. Of these streets a few are the residence of the upper class of shopkeepers or others engaged in trade; but a far greater proportion of them, with their numerous lanes and alleys, occupied by working manufacturers, petty shopkeepers, the labouring poor and beggars, crowded together to a degree distressing to humanity.
>
> (Bennett 2005, 152)

In the centre foreground the street fiddler has an overturned wheelbarrow at his feet. To the left is a wigmaker's shop, and to the right, under the sign of the 'Bunch of Grapes', is the establishment of 'Denis O'Dogherty', offering 'choice cordials', including 'Whiskey and Rum'. An altercation is in progress between two men brandishing a stick and pitch fork, while another man at a first floor window uses a stick to tumble a flower pot onto the head of his neighbour. Nixon's Hogarthian vision of early nineteenth-century Dublin reveals a street scene of tumult and disorder in a city which had experienced generations of immigration from the countryside. The scene encountered by William Carleton when he arrived in the city in 1818 (see chapter 9) cannot have been much different.

Plate 6 *Liberty Welcoming the Arrival of the Immigrants* (1800), John James Barralet, Winterthur Museum, Delaware, USA

This picture is remarkable as a representation of the three stages of migration (leaving, crossing, arriving). Three handmaidens escort two newly arrived immigrant children to the person of Liberty, at the entrance to her temple, seated beside the shield of the Republic and its cornucopia. Arrival in the new world, with its Greek and Roman inheritance of democracy, is contrasted with departure from the barbarism of the old world, represented in the far distance by the castle and prehistoric stone circle. The three-masted ship at anchor represents the transatlantic crossing. Significantly, the children are given priority over their immigrant parents: two men and two women follow; one man carries two bolts of linen and the other a box, possibly containing tools, while the two women unload a spinning wheel. The implication is that while the parents bring with them welcome skills, it is their children who will become American citizens most fully under the tutelage of Liberty.

The political context of the picture is intriguing. Barralet, born in Dublin of French Huguenot parents, had arrived in Philadelphia only a few years previously (Strickland 1989, I, 25–8). Notwithstanding his own Irish background and the probability that the immigrants represented are Irish (or German), he has framed the picture with symbols of Wales: the three feathers of the Prince of Wales (the future George IV, who was Prince Regent during the madness of his father, George III , 1811–20), crossed leeks, harp and goat. Barralet's composition appears to have been influenced by the 1782 print 'America Triumphant and Britannia in Distress', in which America is depicted as the Greek goddess Minerva (http://www.loc.gov/exhibits/us.capitol/thirtn.jpg).

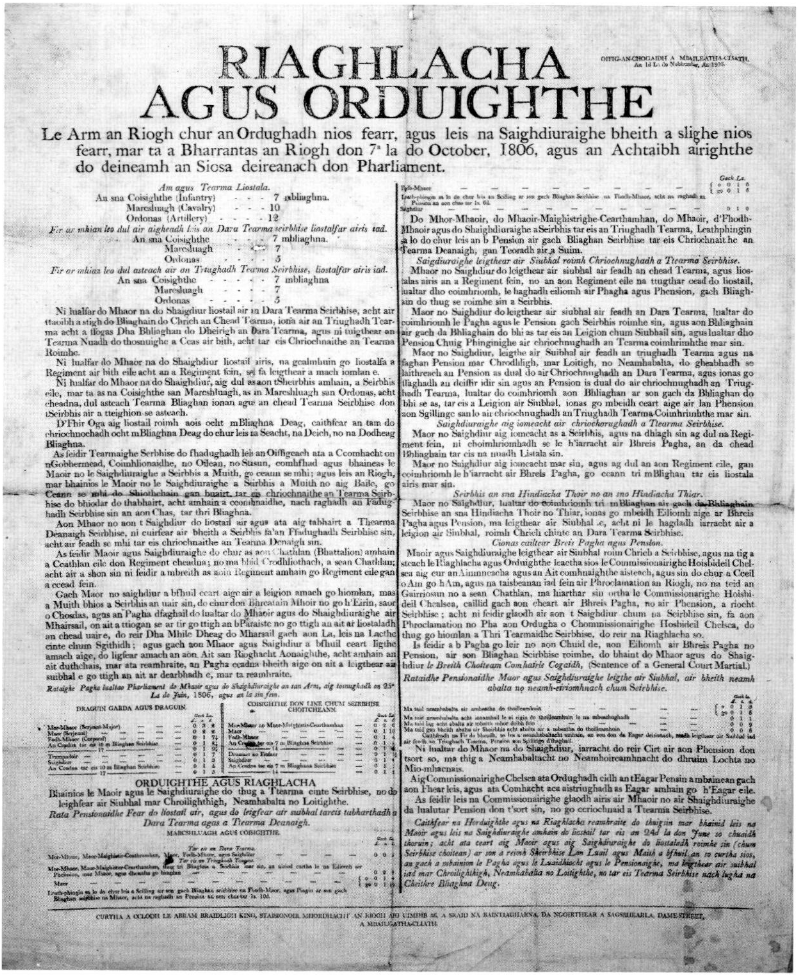

RIAGHLACHA
AGUS ORDUIGHTHE

Le Arm an Riogh chur an Orughadh nios fearr, agus leis na Saighdiuraighe bheith a slighe nios fearr, mar ta a Bharrantas an Riogh don 7ᵃ la do October, 1806, agus an Achtaibh airighthe do deineamh an Siosa deireanach don Pharliament.

Plate 7 ***Riaghlacha agus Orduighthe*** **(Rules and Regulations): A Proclamation issued by the War Office, a branch of the Chief Secretary's Office in Dublin Castle (1 November 1806), National Library of Ireland**

About 5,000 copies were made of this Irish-language version of the recently revised 'Rules and Regulations for the Better Ordering of His Majesty's Army'. Although there were about 3.5 million Irish speakers in a population of about five million, few could read. The posters were therefore probably more important for their sign value in signalling the changed attitude of the British government, now desperate to recruit as widely as possible in the war against Napoleon. Between 1793 and 1815 an estimated 150,000 Irishmen served in the British Army, mostly abroad as military migrants (Kissane 1994, 44–5).

The Stationer of His Majesty the King (*Staisionoir Mhordhacht an Riogh*) is identified at the bottom of the proclamation as 'Abram Braidligh King' of 36 Dame Street, Dublin, just around the corner from the Castle, and not far from Patrick Street (see Plate 5). Abraham Bradley King (1773–1838) had his country seat at Marfield, Stillorgan, Dublin, and was sometime deputy grand master of the Orange Order, alderman 1805, lord mayor 1812–13 and 1820–1, and was knighted in 1821 (Hill 1997, 319).

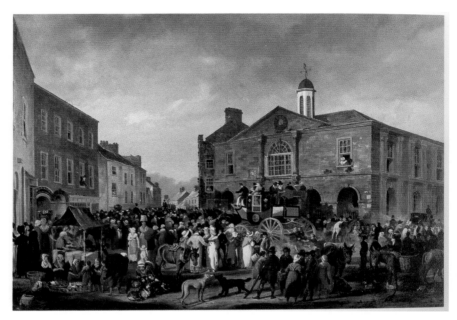

Plate 8   *The Market Square, Ennis* (*c.* 1820), William Turner De Land, Frost & Reed Gallery, London (sold at auction, Christies, May 1997)

Unlike Cork, Ennis was not a walled town. However, the two-storey market house and courthouse (like Belfast's, shown in Plate 2) represents the regulation of relations between the town and countryside, including migration in and out. In the centre, a group of four men and three women of quality stand in conversation. In the bottom left corner, two ladies of quality inspect fabrics, while four other women squat beside the temporary fabric stall, minding baskets of poultry and eggs and a pile of cabbages, as well as four children. In the bottom right corner stands a donkey loaded with two creels of turf (Ó Dálaigh 1995, 12–13). The figure closest to a beggar is the man in the centre with the crutch and ragged left trouser leg. Altogether the scene is more orderly than Dublin as shown in Plate 5.

The Bianconi car (see chapter 9) indicates the town's position in the transport network. Having arrived from Cork, it is leaving along the Gort road north to Galway, fully laden with goods and passengers, possibly emigrants.

Plate 9 *Emigrants at Cork* (*c.* 1840), Anonymous pupil of Nathaniel Grogan, UCD Delargy Centre for Irish Folklore and the *National Folklore Collection*

A family group of four men (with possibly a fifth making his way down the steps to the two-masted ship), four women and two children are preparing to take their leave. Their mood seems mixed, reflecting perhaps both the optimism of the emigrant and the sadness of the exile: the woman standing in the centre smiles, while the seated woman, whose face is completely hidden by her hood, may be weeping, or possibly breast-feeding. A greater proportion of those who made their way across the Atlantic before the outbreak of famine in late 1845, were in moderately prosperous family groups, headed by what contemporaries called 'snug farmers'. One such family was the Mellons of Castletown, Tyrone, who sailed from Derry to St John New Brunswick in 1818.

The family in this picture is framed on the left by the seated beggar and on the right by two women and an exotic-looking man. They may be hoping to make a sale from the makeshift stall of shiny tin cans and kettles. Such items might be added to whatever supplies and equipment are already in the two trunks. Emigrants at this stage were still largely responsible for their own cooking on board.

The north gate and the centre of Cork city lies to the left of the picture, which is looking north from Merchants Quay across the River Lee to St Patrick's Quay and the high ground of Montenotte, named after the Battle of Montenotte, near Genoa, 1796 (Mac Éinrí 2005, 419). As a single-masted ship arrives, the two-masted, single-funnelled paddle-steamer is leaving, probably for Bristol, but possibly for New York. In 1838, the Cork-based, Quaker-inspired St George's Steam Packet Company had produced the *Sirius*, the first steam-powered vessel to voyage to America (Crowley et al. 2005, 174–5, 180).

Plate 10 *Five Points, Sixth Ward, Manhattan, New York City* (*c.* 1850), Geoffrey Clements, Bettmann Picture Archive, New York

The upturned table legs and other furniture on the carts crashing in the foreground indicate people moving home. Some leave as others arrive. Five Points was the archetypal 'melting pot', a confluence of African, Irish, Anglo and later Jewish and Italian cultures in contact. The top-hatted figure in the left corner looks on, suggesting Charles Dickens, who described his visit to the neighbourhood in *American Notes* (1842):

> There are many by-streets, almost as neutral in clean colours, and positive in dirty ones, as by-streets in London; and there is one quarter, commonly called the Five Points, which, in respect of filth and wretchedness, may be safely backed against Seven Dials, or any other part of famed St. Giles's.

Compared with Ireland, it seems more similar to Dublin (Plate 5) than Ennis (Plate 8). As well as filth and wretchedness, Five Points was notorious for violence and vice, described by Herbert Asbury in *The Gangs of New York* (1928). The sign 'Young Ladies Seminary' at the top right may have been misleading. Having been poorly drained in the 1820s this part of Manhattan was left by the rich to the influx of poor immigrants, first emancipated African Americans and then Irish during the years of the Great Famine (1845–50). What was Five Points is today covered by the city and state administration buildings of Foley Square (named after prominent Tammany Hall district leader, Thomas F. 'Big Tom' Foley, 1852–1925). It was sufficiently close to be within walking distance of the docks on the southern tip of Manhattan island, but sufficiently far away for the comfort of Wall Street (Anbinder 2002).

Plate 11 *The Irish Emigrant Homeward Bound* (1850), Erskine Nicol, National Library of Ireland

Making a contrasting pair with *Outward Bound* (see Donnelly 2001, 196–7), Nicol's *Homeward Bound* presents the now prosperous migrant on the quayside in New York. Unlikely to have been living in Five Points, he weighs up the opportunity to return to Dublin, apparently preferring the 'fast-sailing Barque *Washington*' to a steamship. He has probably been influenced by the contents of the letter that lies discarded beside the whiskey jug. Unlike him, the large majority of post-Famine Irish emigrants to America did not become 'Returned Yanks' (see chapter 2).

Several features seem to indicate how Paddy had prospered on the road to respectability and 'becoming white' (Ignatiev 1996; Kenny 2000). His straw hat and tail coat suggest a connection with the cotton plantations of the south, as does the black figure beyond and the bale of cotton numbered '22'.

The Edinburgh-born Erskine Nicol (1825–1904) arrived in Dublin in 1845 to teach art. In his work he was repeatedly drawn to the theme of Irish emigration.

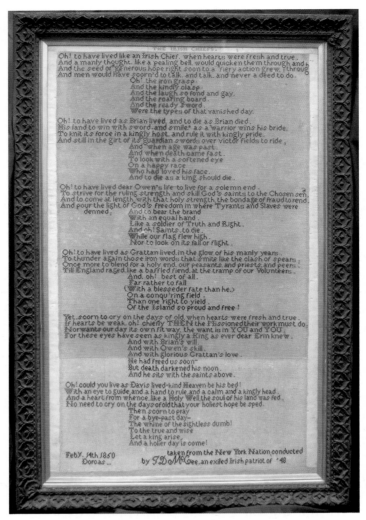

Plate 12 *The Irish Chiefs*, **needlework sampler (1850), Dorcas McGee, courtesy of the owner, John Sutton, Ocean Grove, Australia; photo Brendan Meegan, Belfast**

This migrant object was made in Ireland in 1850 and brought to Australia in 1853. Its trajectory illustrates the complexity of relations between homeland and diaspora (see chapter 12). The 'Dorcas' named at the bottom was the sister of 'TD [Thomas D'Arcy] McGee, an exiled Irish patriot of '48', who had escaped to New York after the failure of the 1848 Young Ireland Rebellion. In New York he had 'conducted' [founded and edited] the *New York Nation*, in protest against the closure of the *Nation* newspaper in Dublin and the imprisonment in Kilmainham Jail of its editor, Charles Gavan Duffy. The poem 'The Irish Chiefs', first published in the Dublin *Nation* in 1846, was by Duffy. One of the chiefs referred to, Owen Roe O'Neill, was a returned emigrant (see chapter 5).

Dorcas already had experience of emigration, having sailed with her brother from Wexford to Quebec in 1840, aged 14, arriving eventually with their Aunt Bella in Providence, Rhode Island. She displayed the sampler in her new homes in Castlemaine and Melbourne, as did three successive generations of her family in Australia, proudly proclaiming their Irish connection.

Part II

In-Within-Out-Migration, 1607–2007

Introduction

We embark on our more detailed, chronological survey of migration in Irish history with the Departure, or Flight, of the Earls in 1607. That iconic moment is a gateway in the dual sense that it not only opened the way for the outflow that resulted, eventually, in what we call now the modern Irish diaspora; it also opened the way for the inflow of the Plantation of Ulster which resulted, again eventually, in a separate Northern Ireland. We end in the 400th anniversary year of 2007. As the year in which devolved government was restored in Northern Ireland, this may or may not prove to be a landmark date in the unfolding story. Whatever the case, it is the vantage point from which our survey was conducted, limited in its own way as were those, in their days, of Sir William Petty, Arthur Young, Thomas Colby and Father John O'Brien.

Our approach to these four centuries is based on the idea that migration is a useful prism through which to view societies as a whole since the migrants who are moving home and resettling are in relationship with the majority, in both their old and new worlds, who remain settled. Eight chapters deal with about 50 years each, with one chapter focused exceptionally on the decade of the Great Famine (1845–55). Each chapter is divided in the same way into three sections: on immigration, internal migration and emigration. This should make it easier to cross-refer between chapters, or to read about a particular aspect of migration continuously from chapter to chapter. The presentation of immigration, internal migration and emigration in the same sequence in each chapter is also a constant invitation to see them interacting as 'in-within-out-migration', with each as a three-stage (leaving, crossing, arriving), three-outcome (segregating, integrating, modulating) strand of the three-in-one process of migration.

Surveying the migration landscape from 1607 to 2007, as if from 'Scally's satellite', we already know the outline of what to expect: immigration dominant in the first half of the seventeenth century; immigration and emigration almost in balance in the second half of the seventeenth century; emigration dominant from the eighteenth century through to the late twentieth century; and immigration dominant once again in the late twentieth and early twenty-first centuries (this time with significant return migration), and internal migration relatively modest by European standards but steady throughout. Also, we may expect that the landmark dates of migration history will not necessarily correspond with those of our more familiar political chronology (on the broader question of periodisation in migration history, see Moch 1999). Figure 5 shows ten of the most prominent intervening dates in popular Irish history (the 1641 Rising; the battle of the Boyne; the 1798 rebellion; the Act of Union; the 1848 Rebellion; the battle of the Somme and the Easter Rising, both 1916; Partition 1920; the outbreak of the Troubles 1969; the Belfast/Good Friday Agreement 1998. Below are shown ten of the most important intervening dates in Irish migration history (the famine in Scotland of 'Black '97'; the iconic start of mass emigration from Ulster to North America 1718; the famine in Ireland of 1741; a step-change in emigration to North America 1756; 'Black '47'; a point of maximum emigration 1907; closing of the 'golden door' to the US 1929; another point of maximum emigration 1957; and the sustained switch to net immigration 1994.

A comparison of the two sets of dates gives some indication of the distinctive features that we may expect to emerge from looking century by century at the action of migration in Irish history.

5
Irish Migration, 1607–1650

The thoughts that occupied the minds of the Earls of Tyrone and Tyrconnell as they prepared to depart from Rathmullan on 14 September 1607 remain a mystery, caught as they were between the forces holding them in Ireland and those drawing them to Europe. Until his death in Rome in 1616, Hugh O'Neill, Earl of Tyrone, like many other 'exiles', lived with the ebb and flow of circumstances that altered the likelihood of his return. The power vacuum created by the Flight was eventually filled by the Plantation of Ulster, which acted like a magnet in offering a huge landed resource to new immigrants, especially those whose potential for upward social mobility and material success in their homelands was restricted. In Ireland they would be drawn to the most favourable niches for settlement.

Over the course of the century the attractive force of Ireland waxed and waned. In the later 1620s a grave subsistence crisis checked the inflow of British migrants and at the same time propelled migrants from Ireland eastward to Britain and beyond to continental Europe. Political crisis also checked the inflow. The Rising which broke out on 22 October 1641 sent shockwaves across the three kingdoms and the inflow of settlers into reverse as many returned 'home' to Britain. The relationship between the arrival of newcomers and the departure of natives requires nuanced analysis. For some natives the arrival of the new settlers meant direct displacement, perhaps downward social mobility to tenant status or movement onto poorer marginal land, perhaps relocation to a different Irish county or emigration overseas. Study at the local level, where the historical record permits, reveals a diversity of experience among those who arrived, those who stayed and those who left. As the new immigrants came to terms with colonising Ireland, emigrants, departing mainly for continental Europe, saw themselves variously not only as exiles, like the Earls, but also as adventurers, even colonialists, in the growing empires of France and Spain.

Immigration

A 'razed table'

When Lord Mountjoy was appointed Lord Deputy in Ireland in January 1600 he declared his intention to make Ireland a 'razed table' upon which, as one historian puts it, 'the Elizabethan state could transcribe a neat pattern' (Foster 1988, 35). Although such ambitious and confident statements had been issued before, and would be issued again, by 1650, despite the destructive warfare of the 1640s, a new outline pattern remained discernible. This British imprint was neither neat nor all-embracing, but during the course of the two preceding generations profound changes had been fashioned by the new settlers. The project of 'Making Ireland British', as it has been called, had made real progress, motivating Oliver Cromwell to attempt to fulfil the aspirations of his Elizabethan predecessors (Canny 2001, vii–xi, 55–8).

Volume and origins

How many migrants came to Ireland during the course of these five decades? A generally accepted estimate is about 100,000 – roughly three-quarters from England and Wales and one quarter from Scotland (Canny 1988, 96; 1994, 62). Recognising that many immigrants were never officially documented, our best guess is that immigrants of English, Welsh, Scots and indeed Manx descent increased from around 5 per cent of the population in 1600 to close to 20 per cent by 1641 (Smyth 2006, 100, 430; Gillespie 2007, 58). Not all British settlers who moved to early seventeenth-century Ireland settled permanently. Some returned to Britain after varying lengths of stay, some moved back and forth between Ireland and Britain and others migrated onward within both the old and new worlds. We know, for example, that traders journeyed from south-west Scotland to markets and fairs in north Down and back again in the same day (Stevenson 1920, 48–9; Canny 2001, 395). In many ways the narrow north channel continued to function as a corridor as much as a border between the Irish and Scottish worlds (McLeod 2004, 4–4, 78–9, 89–94). Although migrants from Britain made up the vast majority of those coming to early Stuart Ireland, there was also a small trickle of immigrants from continental Europe, particularly into the larger port towns – some arriving directly, others via Britain and London especially, which already had a sizeable population of continental aliens by 1600 (Whyte 2000, 98–9; Luu 2005). One successful planter, Matthew De Renzy, a German native, came to Ireland in 1606 when his London textile business folded (Mac Cuarta 1993, 1; Connolly 2007, 349, 399–400). A few Dutch settlers were also to be found among those taking up land in Munster while other Dutch and a few French migrants were active in the commercial life of early seventeenth-century Dublin (Canny 2001, 360, 369–70). One of those supplying the expanding city with glass from the works he established in Birr, Offaly, was Abraham Bigoe (originally Bigault), a Protestant migrant from Lorraine, in eastern France, who arrived in Ireland in 1623 (Austin et al. 1993, 31). There was even the exotic curiosity of a native American Indian who, having taken the English name John Fortune, came under attack by insurgents in the Rising of 1641 (Canny 1998, 161).

Migration and mixing

Data on the ages of migrants on arrival in Ireland are limited. They were likely to be disproportionately young adults (16–25), not unlike those who moved within Britain or left for new world destinations (Clark and Souden 1987; Horn 1998a, 171; Whyte 2000, 90). The demographic dynamism of planter society in the decades before 1641 may also reflect a somewhat earlier age at marriage than was the case in England at the time (Gillespie 1985, 53). Furthermore, males had a good chance of marrying a partner who was also a settler. Writing of this period, Canny notes that 'the migration was also distinctive in the high percentage of women it included', compared to migration from Spain to New Spain and, it might be added, from England to the Chesapeake (Canny 2001, 211–12). Some migrants travelling from England to Munster did so as family groups, while most settlers who married in Ireland did so within their own ethnic group. Intermarriage between natives and newcomers, Catholics and Protestants, would appear to have been more common in Munster than in Ulster. One historian dealing with issues of ethnic identity in the late 1640s has referred to intermarriage as 'extensive' by this stage (Wheeler 2002, 156; see also Connolly 2007, 400). In Ulster also, English settlement was more regularly interspersed with Scots settlement, and intermarriage between these settlers appears also to have remained the exception, although by no means unknown, particularly as the century wore on. We do know that by 1639 provision for the children of mixed marriages was being discussed by Catholic clerics (Jackson 1970; Foster 1988, 70–1; Elliott 2000, 130). The depositions relating to the 1641 Rising provide ample evidence of the experience of significant numbers of settler women, including those who were single, married or widowed (O'Dowd M. 1991b, 95–9; Canny 2001, 348). Although most natives were Catholic, not all were, and not all settlers were Protestant: some natives converted to Protestantism and at least a few English settlers coming to Munster were Catholic recusants escaping persecution. Similarly, in Ulster by no means all Scots planters, such as the Hamiltons of Abercorn, were lowland Protestants (MacCarthy-Morrogh 1986, 191–7; Hill 1993, 24–43). Of course, we should also draw attention to one other group of Catholics who were coming into Ireland in this period, those who were return migrants, largely from the continent. Limited scholarly attention has so far been directed towards this group and it is impossible to suggest an estimate of scale, but clearly mercantile, military and educational migrants did return to Ireland after time spent abroad. Catholic clergy receiving religious training abroad were anticipated to return to their native land in support of the Counter-Reformation effort. Undoubtedly, the return of Owen Roe O'Neill to Sheephaven Bay, Donegal, in July 1642 was powerfully symbolic, as the departure of his uncle Hugh had been 35 years before. With him came some 200–300 veterans, many of whom had been away for decades and many of whom, like O'Neill himself, would end up buried in Irish soil (Casway 1984; Henry 1993, 59–60).

Origins and skills

Prominent in discussion of the skills, social background and economic potential of migrants from Britain to Ireland has been a debate about the relative extent of progress made by planters in Munster and Ulster. This was sparked by Canny's claim that 'the retarded social condition of Ulster as compared to the settled parts of Munster in 1641' was an effect of those drawn towards the southern province being predominantly from the more economically advanced regions of south Wales and south-west England (Canny 1985, 27–9; 1986, 96–100). The validity of this thesis, particularly the suitability of the sources used to support it, has been challenged (Gillespie 1986, 90–5; Perceval-Maxwell 1987, 59–61). However, the origins of migration flows into Munster and Ulster were clearly concentrated in different regions of Britain, which inevitably influenced the skills, technology and knowledge that migrants brought with them. Also the mainly pastoral agricultural tradition of Ulster made it more like Scotland, while a tradition of more arable farming made much of Munster seem more like lowland England, reflecting similarities of topography and soil quality on both sides of the Irish Sea. Despite different rates of development, urbanisation and commercialisation across the island, we can detect a great deal of continuity with the economy of the sixteenth century. As Gillespie concludes, 'the settlers expanded what already existed rather than transforming it radically' (1991, 32). Even in terms of the built environment they often preferred to take over existing settlement sites, just as earlier Anglo-Norman settlers had done.

Seizing opportunities

Above all else, Ireland after 1607 was somewhere an individual could get rich rapidly, as did Richard Boyle, first Earl of Cork, who in 1588, at the age of 22 and of modest means, arrived in Munster from Canterbury, Kent. By the 1620s, through service to the crown and his own enterprise, he had amassed an enormous landholding and was one of the wealthiest men in the three kingdoms (Canny 1982). Similarly, the career of Sir Arthur Chichester from Raleigh, Devon, who became Lord Deputy in Ireland in 1605, demonstrates the rapid rise of a determined soldier-adventurer (McCavitt 1998). At the heart of such spectacular transitions was the acquisition of land. Not surprisingly, the opportunities to participate in colonisation in Ireland appealed more to those eager to check or reverse downward social mobility than those stable or already rising at home. Although inheritance patterns and strategies among the propertied of seventeenth-century England may have been more flexible than was once thought, younger sons, still a potential problem for their families at home, found Ireland consistently alluring (Wrightson 2002, 61–4; Gillespie 1993, 134). Men 'in a hurry' could find ready assets to strip. The Irish woodlands in particular were denuded as many newcomers exploited the opportunities to profit from the timber or iron trades, generally with little thought of conservation or renewing assets. Security considerations could either augment or cloak financial interests. In 1642 the Protestant Dublin lawyer Robert Bysse informed his brother that the wood at Artaine (now Artane, *Ard Aidhin*, a northside suburb of Dublin) should be felled in order to provide fuel and remove a hiding place for woodkern (outlaws) (McCracken 1971, 57–111; Neeson 1991, 57–78; Nicholls 2001, 181–206; Ní Mhurchadha 2005, 47; Smyth, 2006, 94-9). One such newcomer was Toby Caulfield, born in 1565 in Great Milton, Oxfordshire. He came to Ireland first with the Earl of Essex in 1599 and stayed on to be rewarded with handsome land grants, following the Flight of the Earls, as collector of the Earl of Tyrone's rents. Energetically clearing the woods in what had been the heartland of Tyrone's territory, he simultaneously reduced cover for woodkern and wolf, provided materials for his splendid new home, Castlecaulfied, and made a massive profit from the timber to boot. He was a model Elizabethan prospector, settling on the frontier, the achievement of church and state objectives coinciding, more or less, with his own (Bardon 1992, 128: Craig 1948, 3-8; John Lynch, pers. comm.). A recent trend is to consider such settlers in Ireland in the context of the wider contemporary British diaspora in both the old and new worlds: so we find them judged to have been 'more skilled and to have fared better than those who migrated to New England' (Whyte 2000, 110, 140), and in terms of prosperity they 'probably outstripped … most migrants to North America and the West Indies' (Canny 1994, 64–75; Ohlmeyer 1998, 135–47; Barber 2005, 280–99). In the early twenty-first century historians, reflecting contemporary concerns, have focused to a greater extent on the manner in which migrants to the new world and Ireland impacted on the environment and came to change the relationship between the land and those settled on it (Taylor 2001, 46 9; Aalen, Whelan and Smout 1996, 67–106, 122–34).

Old and new worlds

The contexts from which migrants were drawn, as well as those in which they settled, were crucial. What we know about the geography of recruitment for Irish and other overseas colonial projects tends to support the conclusion that migrations across the Irish Sea and across the Atlantic were more often complementary than competitive. The greatest geographical overlap, in terms of recruitment of settlers, occurred in the south-west of England. From there, those migrating beyond England's shores moved in significant numbers to the Chesapeake, the Caribbean and to Munster. New England, however, drew most strongly upon the south-eastern counties of England, particularly East Anglia, which was less significant in relation to migration to Ireland. Migrants to Ulster tended to be drawn particularly from south-west Scotland and north-west England, regions as yet little engaged in the transatlantic movement. From what we know about newcomers to Leinster and the Irish midlands, it was western England and Wales which largely supplied the flow (Fischer 1989, 35–6; Gillespie 1993, 135–6; McFarlane 1994, 164; Horn 1998a, 177; Canny 2001, 362–84). Even where there was regional overlap, the timing of migration could be different. Migration to Ireland was heavier in the opening two decades of the century, whereas migration across the Atlantic gathered pace after 1630 (Whyte 2000, 119–20; Canny 2001, 212). It may be the case that future local studies in Britain, focused more on the issue of migration decisions and patterns, will cast more light on the interrelationship between movements to a variety of destinations.

Although significantly more migrants crossed the Irish Sea than the Atlantic during this half-century, there was a more concerted effort through print and spoken word to promote new world destinations. Most promotion, however, was by word of mouth and therefore not now retrievable by historians (Games 2002, 40). Generally, the closer and more familiar a destination and the fewer the intervening obstacles, the more attractive it is likely to be. For potential migrants from anywhere in Britain, Ireland, visible on a clear day from many western vantage points, was much more a known quantity than transatlantic colonies, months away by sail. For migrants contemplating the latter option the stakes were even higher and the inducements therefore had to be strong. Thus, the Virginia Company's propaganda portrayed the colony as a veritable *El Dorado* ('The Golden'), the fabled city of gold in South America sought by many, including Sir Walter Raleigh, who had led an expedition in 1595 up the Orinoco through what is now Venezuela. Little did prospective migrants realise that their transatlantic futures were more likely to entail relentless toil in tobacco plantations than the mining of precious metals. Bad as the reputation of Ireland was following the Nine Years War (1594–1603), few of those making their way as servants to the Chesapeake could have known of the risks to their health imposed by the punitive climate and environment on the James river (Wright 1973, 134; Canny 1998, 164). We should not read too much into the absence of such a direct promotional effort by the crown in relation to Irish colonisation. Its geographical proximity and strategic sensitivity meant securing successful settlement in Ireland was for Elizabethan and Stuart governments not just desirable but essential. From the outbreak of the

Desmond rebellion in Munster in the 1580s, 'plantation' became 'an instrument of royal policy and private enterprise ... put to work for the purpose of the state' (Ohlmeyer 2004, 38).

Private enterprise and government planning

'Private enterprise', within the framework of government planning, was the main engine in this half-century driving the peopling of Ireland with British Protestants, like Toby Caulfield, who would simultaneously serve their own interests and those of the crown. Some argued that government should eschew the risks of reliance on private investment in colonisation for the security of a planned and direct controlling influence. An example of what is more familiar today as a 'public–private partnership' scheme was advocated by the Somerset parson Richard Eburne in his 1624 treatise *A Plain Pathway to Plantations*. Before 1641, however, the crown remained all too conscious of its limited resources and the necessity of harnessing self-interest in pursuit of the state's strategic goals (Wright 1973, 139). Needless to say, the very definition of self-interest in the context of early modern governance was markedly different from that which applies today. In understanding the centrality of the king himself in planning the official Ulster Plantation of 1609 we should recall James's experience with plantation as a policy option in Scotland, especially in the islands of Lewis and Harris, and his keen interest in seeing developments in Ireland as a part of his desire for real union of the English and Scottish crowns (Kishlansky 1996, 77–8; Ohlmeyer 1998, 124–47).

British settlement in Ulster by 1640 had been most effective in the counties of Antrim and Down, which had been subject to informal colonisation sponsored by private enterprise. Settlers there took advantage of both the debts of native landowners, like Conn O'Neill, to acquire estates and control of the long-established Anglo-Norman infrastructure. Hugh Montgomery and James Hamilton, two large landholders from south-west Scotland, did most to sponsor migration and settlement on the lands in north Down which they acquired in 1605 (http://www.hamiltonmontgomery1606.com). In the second decade of the century Scots flooded into this area. Some saw in Ulster the opportunity to prevent or recover from downward social mobility, others a place to escape the law. Some came, saw and returned; others stayed. Despite being considered a 'private enterprise' plantation, however, the state was far from uninvolved. Settlers had to seek 'denization' from the government to confirm legal status and inheritance rights. At the same time, the Scottish Privy Council sought to regulate migration in accordance with its own interests. In September 1630, when both Ireland and Scotland were experiencing bad harvests, the government in Edinburgh, with an eye on the domestic food supply, ordered that emigrants returning to Scotland should be turned back. Yet, only five years later, the same body, fearing a drain on the supply of suitable tenants, ordered that migrants leaving Scotland for Ireland required their landlord's permission (Gillespie 1985, 28–31, 50–2). Although these informal private enterprise plantations had much to commend them, we should remain cautious about over-emphasising the contrast with what had gone before and what would follow. Self-interest also shaped the construction of the historical narratives crafted later in the century.

Capital and commitment

The Virginia Company can be viewed as a model for those planning the Official Plantation of Ulster in 1609. The Honourable the Irish Society, established by the Common Council of the City of London to manage the lands it was allotted, had many close connections with the Virginia Company. However, the contrasts were as telling as the similarities. While the capital employed in both enterprises was joint stock, the former was pursued by private interests in pursuit of profit with encouragement from the crown, and it was the crown that took the lead in the latter and turned to the London Companies as the body best able to capitalise the project. Even though the London Companies were less than enthusiastic to engage in the project, they could not resist the pressure imposed by the crown (Moody 1939, 96–8; Curl 1986, 34). Over the course of the following decades, the London Companies poured significant sums into the project, but regularly fell short of government requirements. Not least among the challenges facing The Irish Society was the attraction of settlers. A full five years after the various 'proportions' were allotted, the Haberdashers Company doubted its ability to attract tenants of 'any sufficiency' in London, 'men being so loathe to remove from hence that have any good means to live here' (quoted in Canny 2001, 222). The solution to the problem was arrived at by leasing to single individuals who could fulfil the contractual obligations. Thus, the Haberdashers' proportion was acquired at an annual rent of £350 by a Scot, Sir Robert McClelland, who set about peopling the land with tenants from his own home place at Bomby, near Kirkcudbright in Galloway, many of whom brought subtenants with them. Also attracting Scots tenants from elsewhere in Ulster, McClelland oversaw on the lands of a London company the evolution of what has been described as 'a Scottish world in miniature' (Canny 2001, 222–3). A similar pattern was observable with respect to the Fishmongers' proportion. In this challenging new environment of ethnic and cultural mixing, a poorish, rural British tenantry set about bettering themselves by being more innovative (Hunter 1999, 234). Immigrants faced with the challenge of establishing effective settlements could make little headway without coopting the assistance of the native population. Archaeological evidence from the excavation in Co. Londonderry of dwelling houses at the Mercers' Company plantation settlement by the River Bann at Movanagher, near Kilrea, points to a process of 'economic levelling' and a world in which 'the necessities of everyday life likely increased both interaction and material accommodation' (Horning 2001, 396). So by 1650 the old pattern that underlay the new plantation pattern inscribed on Lord Mountjoy's 'razed table' was being hidden unevenly.

Internal migration

'A mobile and fluctuating population'

Migration in about 1600 has been described as 'a striking aspect of the population geography of Ireland' (Butlin 1977, 148). During this half-century, particularly at its opening and close, political, military and economic forces were generating high levels of internal population mobility (Smyth 2006, 384). British colonisation certainly accounted for some of this, but it is clear that Irish society, well before the Nine Years War, was far from static or sedentary. 'Traditionally', observes Duffy, 'Gaelic Ireland has been perceived as containing a highly mobile and fluctuating population' (2001, 122). Reports of contemporary colonial officials and observers, though prone to exaggeration and misinterpretation derived from cultural difference and subjective agendas, tended to suggest that mobility was common within native Irish society (Harrington 1991, 27–111). In Ulster especially they were struck by the predominantly pastoral economy and the mobility of often huge herds of cattle and those who tended them. Gaelic lords moved their herds around as they collected tribute or engaged in warfare. Cattle-raiding or 'creaghting' (Ir. *creacht*, 'cattle raid') combined with the practice of transhumance or 'booleying' (*buaile*, 'summer pasture') added to the impression – especially in summer – of a rural society 'on the move' (Nicholls 1972, 117; O'Dowd 1986, 130; Duffy, Edwards and Fitzpatrick 2001; Smyth 2006, 74). Ongoing, low-level conflict between Gaelic lords, which had been virtually endemic in the decades before 1600, meant military personnel, including mercenary soldiers, notably the Scots gallowglass (*gall-óglach*, 'foreign warrior'), were mobilised across the country (Hayes-McCoy 1937; Brady 1996, 136–59). In addition were all those who followed these private armies in the field. Cattle raids, 'stealths' and dynastic feuds also created new migrants as victims of violence became civilian refugees (see the illustration 'An Attack by Kern on a Homestead' by John Derricke 1581, Quinn 1985, Plate II). As well as this forced migration, there was some voluntary movement by those at the base of the social pyramid from one lord to another. In the context of low population density (a total of less than one million on the whole island) even those with very limited rights could and did in this respect 'vote with their feet' (Lennon 1994, 46). Later sixteenth-century evidence confirms the migration of tenants shifting between lordships and the concerted efforts of the Gaelic elite to control it, as town councils similarly tried to control internal migration (Canny 1970, 27–35; O'Dowd 1986,

129). Many native Irish tenants continued, of course, to pursue the same strategy during the opening decades of the seventeenth century, seeking out the best working conditions and contractual terms. Indeed, the colonists in Ulster complained of their inability to compete for leases with Irish tenants willing to pay higher rents to sustain a foothold on what they no doubt considered the 'home' place (Elliott 2000, 93–4).

Making way

Although settlers might lament native competition, the establishment of Planter society in Ulster meant for many displacement of the old order, and here the interconnection between inward and internal migration is clear. For the many who were able, one way or another, to remain on the land they formerly occupied, there was an acute sense of eroded status as they were forced to adjust to becoming mere tenants at will rather than proprietors. The slow slide into debt in an increasingly commercial world only sharpened the sense of loss. For others less able to compete, the Plantation generally meant displacement from the more fertile lowlands to the less fertile uplands or poorly drained bog land. Viewed from today's perspective, this was a long drawn-out process over the course of the seventeenth and eighteenth centuries, which reflected economic forces more than any deliberate or concerted policy of expulsion (Moody 1938, 63). Although the nature and motivation of such displacement are not entirely clear, we can see that its pace and scale were variable. Armagh, particularly the fertile baronies of Oneilland East and West around Lurgan and Portadown, allotted to the English as part of the Plantation scheme, proved as popular with settlers as it had been with O'Neill's tenants, who were now displaced and resettled on the boggy land of the southern shore of Lough Neagh. It is hard to escape the conclusion that the violence evident in this area during the Rising in the autumn of 1641 was the result of the sharp erosion of social status and displacement in the preceding generation (MacCuarta 1993, 3; Simms 1993, 135; Elliott 2000, 93; McCavitt 2001, 245–63). Some of those displaced by plantation in Ulster migrated outside the province entirely, seeking refuge to the south-west in Leitrim and to the south-east on the Cooley peninsula, areas which may still have been considered to be parts of the northern province (Smyth 2006, 462).

Colonial spread and a shifting frontier

Research over the last generation has adjusted our perspective on the peopling process, of which government plantation schemes were only part. It is now clear that many remained migrants long after their arrival, willing to move on in search of a better settlement niche within Ireland. Even though they may have had a particular initial destination in mind, settlement on the 'frontier' might not necessarily mean permanent settlement (Smyth 2000, 158–86;

Canny 2001, 213, 316; Smyth 2006, 421–50). Just as there was chain migration from Ireland to Britain and continental Europe, and later to the new world, so now there was chain migration to Ireland from Britain as successful pioneers signalled to others back home to follow (Duffy 2006, 23).With the growth and spread of a market economy, tenants themselves became consumers in a land market, seeking the best available deal. Landholders, both settlers and natives, could show their eagerness to attract new tenants.

In the particular context of the Ulster Plantation, Philip Robinson, drawing on the work of Swedish colonial theorists, introduced the idea of 'colonial spread' to chart British settlement, which was consolidated in the coastal lands adjacent to the ports of entry in the north and east, while the rich, fertile river valleys served as migrant corridors for substantial and permanent penetration of the provincial interior (1984, 116–19). Environmental factors conditioned movement and settlement across Ireland too, and Nicholas Canny has subsequently described similar examples of 'colonial spread' in contemporary Munster and Connacht. There is good evidence to suggest that the emerging landlord class appreciated early on the need to acquire the best and most easily accessible land in order to gain an edge in the competitive market for tenants, without whom the land would remain unprofitable and incomes wither. This informal 'colonial spread' indicates the limitations of government control on British migrants, who were far from being mere pawns. Canny makes this clear in his landmark work *Making Ireland British*, by considering in turn the British presence in all four provinces during Sir Thomas Wentworth's tenure as Lord Deputy, 1632–41 (Canny 2001, 152, 385, 336–89).

The grass is greener

The fragmentary nature of the evidence makes the tracing of migrant decisions difficult, but we can see, for example, the widespread 'breaking of boundaries' in relation to migration out of Antrim and Down into the six escheated counties, and out of the province of Ulster as a whole into Connacht and north Leinster. We can see the process by which the counties of Leitrim and Sligo, and the port town of Sligo in particular, became increasingly populated with British (mainly Scots) settlers. Mary O'Dowd, in studying early modern Sligo, elucidates such 'overspill' migration from the official Plantation counties by attempting to reconstruct the perspective of a contemporary migrant. She suggests that Scottish families on arriving in remote parts of Donegal and Fermanagh must have reviewed their options after 'looking around them with despair and fear at the isolation and barrenness of their new homes'. Whilst some committed to the erection of sturdy bawns, others decided to move on, westwards towards the sea, or southwards, where Sligo as an established port offered a better prospect of security and contact with home and the wider world (O'Dowd 1991b, 147; Fitzgerald 2005b, 43–8).

A Dublin Plantation?

The importance of the British settlement of Ulster in this period seems obvious to those familiar with the twentieth-century history of Partition, the Troubles in Northern Ireland and the continuing importance to contemporary politics of both the numerical balance and distribution of Protestants and Catholics. Not so obvious is the central role of Dublin, rather than Carrickfergus or embryonic Belfast, in the whole framework of seventeenth-century colonial settlement. Already by the opening decade of the seventeenth century, Dublin showed several signs of becoming a 'contested space' in the age of Reformation, as 'New English' Protestants began to pose a threat to the 'Old English' Catholic, urban and largely mercantile elite and their municipal power (Lennon 1989, 215–18; Simms 2001, 65). As well as the city of Dublin, the county was also being transformed during these decades as New English settlers acquired land (Smyth, 2006, 225–73). Canny, in demonstrating the extent of British settlement in the province of Leinster, also points to the growing number of British inhabitants in the city from the 1580s. The British in Dublin were socially diverse, and included landed gentry, merchants and more humble artisans. By 1641, as depositions following the Rising illustrate, there were well-developed links through land, trade and credit between the city and both the immediate 'Pale' hinterland and the entire island, including Ulster. As the legal and administrative centre, Dublin drew in the wider settler population on a regular basis. Consider, for example, the testimony given in the deposition of James Hoole, a merchant of Dublin City, originally from Thornton, Lancashire, about 4 miles north of Blackpool. Hoole claimed that as a consequence of the Rising he had lost timber worth £35, which he had bought in order to build a ship. His losses, however, were incurred at Kilrea, on the once well-wooded banks of the River Bann, near Movanagher, in Co. Londonderry. In this sense we see Dublin developing as the hub port for British settlement throughout the country, as did Philadelphia in the American colonies a century later (Bailyn 1987, 25–6, 345–6; Smith 1990, 44–5, 154–5). At the same time, Old English merchants in Dublin were similarly networked into a wider commercial, Irish community (Canny 2001, 362–70).

'... in the town but not of it'

Dublin's population was accelerating fairly rapidly throughout most of this period. In 1600 it was a city of about 10,000 inhabitants, but by 1660 their number had quadrupled to about 40,000 (Cullen 1992, 251; compared with 962 in Carrickfergus and 589 in Belfast, Bardon 1992, 146). It almost certainly had more extramural housing than is shown in John Speed's splendid map of 1610 (Simms 2001, 41), which leaves out most of the simple mud-walled, thatched cottages erected by the marginal poor and portrays a much neater boundary than was the case between the relatively densely populated countryside and the city. Throughout the later medieval period, Dublin's city assembly issued numerous bye-laws and ordinances which were aimed at excluding Gaelic Irish migrants from establishing settlement within the city limits or immediate hinterland (Lennon 1989, 35, 120). As the New English power base established itself in the city, the desire to keep such settlement at bay was sustained. While this process had a particular religious and ethnic dynamic in Dublin, it was in many ways mirrored across contemporary Europe, where rural-to-urban subsistence migrants, unable to afford the purchase of their freedom, were driving the development of poorer suburbs (Cowan 1998, 132; Friedrichs 1995, 218). As has been observed of such migrants in contemporary English towns, 'they were in the town, but not of it, and segregated in particular areas they created formidable problems of social control' (Clark and Slack 1976, 94). Increasing numbers became part of a makeshift economy and lived lives marked by unsettledness (Fumerton 2006, 12). Inevitably such migration accelerated during subsistence crises or famines when the rural poor made for the port towns. In Ireland, the years between 1627 and 1631 witnessed such a crisis and added impetus to the growth of suburban poverty in Dublin (Gillespie 1984, 5–18; Fitzgerald 1997, 101–23) In 1635, Sir William Brereton, former MP for Cheshire, passing through Dublin, noted how 'this city is extending its bounds and limits very far'. More explicit evidence emerges from a petition of the previous year drawn up by the Common Council of the city assembly. Here complaint was made about the 'many beggars and other vagabonds' who 'meet and presumptuously build cottages upon the commons and highways of the suburbs of the city' (Gilbert, iii, 1889, 298-9, 303–4). In this way poor migrants were able to exploit long-standing boundary disputes between the city assembly and the Liberties (the area outside the city walls) to establish makeshift dwellings.

For betterment or subsistence

By no means all of those moving to Dublin from elsewhere in Ireland fitted into this category and the developing city, as an expanding port and service centre, offered new employment which, although fairly tightly regulated, attracted young migrants from rural Ireland and provincial towns. Indeed, internal migration between the more developed port towns may have been more significant than later as the interior of the country in the early seventeenth century remained largely underdeveloped and sparsely populated (Connolly 2007, 282–3). Crises, however, brought contagious disease and death that were not restricted to the urban poor and so created spaces for new in-migrants who aspired to join the ranks of the free in Dublin (Clark and Slack 1976, 92–3; Gillespie 1989, 89). Following Clark and Slack's distinction between *betterment* and *subsistence* migrants, Gillespie suggests that in periods of less severe crisis, like the early 1620s, rather than the deeper crisis of the late 1620s, pressures may have been sufficient to encourage Dublin's young males and first-generation immigrants to look elsewhere, including overseas, in search of improvement (1989, 89).

Emigration

An iconic beginning

Few events in Irish history possess the iconic and enigmatic power of what has come to be known as The 'Departure' (*Imeacht*) or 'Flight' of the Earls (*Teitheadh na nIarlaí*). The leaving of Ireland by the Earls of Tyrone and Tyrconnell and their company of followers, from Lough Swilly, Donegal, on the feast of the Exaltation of the Cross, on 4 or 14 September 1607 (Old and New Style Calendar), has long been taken as marking the end of the old Gaelic order and the beginning of the largest and most ambitious British Plantation in Ireland (Akenson 2005, 171–2; Connolly 2007, 274). As well as this, it can serve to mark the beginning of what we now understand as the modern Irish diaspora (McCavitt 2002, 7). As A. M. Sullivan put it in *The Story of Ireland*, 'if [1607] witnessed the disappearance of Milesian Ireland, it witnessed the first appearance in history of that other Ireland, which from that day to the present has been in so great a degree the hope and glory of the parent nation – *Ireland in exile!*' (1867, 343). It is of course true that there was already a long tradition of Irish migration to continental Europe, but the departure of those who had come close to establishing Gaelic hegemony across the island only a few years earlier proved a powerful precedent for those who followed them in leaving Ireland. Ryan's *Departure of the Earls* (Plate 1), painted at the time of 350th anniversary, conveys a strongly Nationalist, 'faith and fatherland' inter-pretation of the event which parallels other depictions of departure, such as that of 1851 in the *Illustrated London News* of a priest blessing departing emigrants at their cottage door (Griffin 1981, 40; Coogan 2000, 234–5). Yet many of those who saw Ryan's painting at its first viewing in 1958 will no doubt have sensed the ironic contrast with the constant stream of contemporary emigrants leaving from the pier of Dún Laoghaire harbour for Britain. While the migrants of 1607 were arguably as much chain migrants as pioneers, and as much aspiring military returnees as tragic exiles, the shadow they cast on Irish emigration has proved long and profound. The scale and direction of the outward flows of the seventeenth century is illustrated in Figure 1.

Idle swordsmen become wild geese

If the Flight of 1607 established a noble precedent in the popular imagination for the emigration of the following four centuries, behind it was the defeat at the battle of Kinsale in 1601, which established patterns that would persist throughout the seventeenth century. After Kinsale 'idle swordsmen' became 'wild geese', transferring what was often their only skill – martial expertise and physical hardiness – to the forces of the continental Catholic monarchs. Thousands went to the Spanish army in the Low Countries to join up with Irishmen there since 1586 (Henry 1992; Edwards 2004 292–3). Rather than necessarily seeing these migrants as the progenitors of a distinctive Irish tradition of political/military exile, Connolly points to similarities with other poorer and peripheral European states such as Scotland and Switzerland, which also provided prolific recruiting grounds for the major European powers (2007, 380). Alongside those who went voluntarily were those compelled to remove themselves from Ireland. The government, desperate to reduce the costs of the garrison in Ireland, was ever eager to reduce the internal threat by transporting overseas all who might again take up arms against the crown. Sir Arthur Chichester as Lord Deputy of Ireland claimed to have transported after 1605 some 6,000 native soldiers to serve in the armies of the Protestant powers of Sweden and Denmark (McCavitt 1998, 147–8; Edwards 2004, 293–4). The scattering or diaspora created in the wake of the battle of Kinsale was neither exclusively military nor male. We find an Irish military 'community' in Spanish Flanders in the early seventeenth century, well integrated through marriage and wider links with the local population of Walloons and Flemings, which has been contrasted by one historian with later Irish communities less well integrated in England and America (Henry 1992, 78–9, 88–9). Significant numbers of others went directly to Portugal and Spain (O'Scea 2004, 17–37). Those departing in the years which followed the defeat at Kinsale also included migrants more accurately categorised as civilian refugees. These early years of the century were marked by serious harvest crises and outbreaks of plague, which exacerbated the scorched earth campaigns to subdue Gaelic resistance and stimulated a significant flight abroad. The flight of the poor in these years to both England and France, and the actions of authorities in London and Paris to expel them, together reflect the range of the ripple effect from the defeat at Kinsale and subsequent disruptions. (Fitzgerald 1992, 13–35; Lyons 2000, 363–82).

Economic pressures and social status

The peak in emigration from Ireland to the continent after 1601 and 1607 would be followed by similar exoduses in the early 1650s and early 1690s, as we shall see in the next chapter. For now we should note that later Romanticism, associated with the flight of the Wild Geese after such defeats, can have a distorting effect on our picture of both military and overall migration patterns to seventeenth-century Europe. Éamon Ó Ciosáin, analysing migration from Ireland to France in the century after 1590, demonstrates how patterns reflected economic and social conditions in Ireland as well as diplomatic relations. Between 1634 and 1660 an estimated 30,000 Irishmen entered French service and, while there were predictable peaks and troughs in the recruitment of mercenaries, strong demand in France as in Spain helped sustain the flow to Irish communities on the continent. Both powers were keen to recruit in Ireland, seeking licence as and when diplomatic relations allowed, and to take advantage of push factors there to sustain military campaigns in Europe. While rank-and-file soldiers who had little alternative employment in Ireland made up the bulk of migrants, the officer class had long seen Catholic Europe as a destination where their noble status would be both recognised and rewarded (McGurk 1992, 36–62; Stradling 1994; Ohlmeyer 1995, 101–2, 107, Murtagh 1996, 294–314; Ó Ciosáin 2001, 98–102). Accordingly, they made sure, if they could, to leave Ireland equipped with evidence of their family history, or failing that acquired it later, particularly in the form of pedigrees authenticated by genealogists, such as the Chevalier Thomas O'Gorman (de Fréine 1956; Stradling 1994, 158).

Mercantile migrants

Military migration constituted the single largest element of Irish movement to Europe throughout the century, but it was only one of several strands (Silke 1976, 608–11; Cullen 1994, 121–2, 139). Already evident by 1607 was a well-developed mercantile network linking Irish ports with western Europe. The import and export trade led to the exchange of people as well as goods, and merchant clusters, developing sometimes into larger colonies, were established in several continental ports from the later sixteenth century. In turn, expatriate Irish merchants often acted as magnets to other migrants. The efforts of a new wave of scholars, both Irish and European, working in archives across the continent, have provided many fresh insights into Irish migration to early modern Europe. In ports such as La Coruña in Galicia we can observe the progress of a man like Robert Comerford of an Old English, Waterford merchant family. Settled in the port from the late 1580s, he established himself as a major supplier to the Spanish navy and as 'consul to foreign nations'. By the time of his death in 1623 he was one of the leading merchants in La Coruña and offered a good example of how Old English Catholic merchants from Ireland could take full advantage of the rapidly developing Spanish Atlantic empire (O'Scea 2001, 40). Closer to Ireland, Brittany similarly provided rich opportunities for Irish merchants, exporting hides, fish and agricultural produce and importing wine. The origins of a Irish mercantile presence in the Breton port of St Malo may be traced to the early sixteenth century and by the 1660s there may have been over 1,000 Irish merchants and traders resident in Brittany as a whole (Lyons 2001, 107–26).

Sustaining the faith

As well as by military service, trade and commerce, migration from Ireland to the continent was driven by a desire for a Catholic education. In the later sixteenth century as the Counter-Reformation effort intensified, a network of

Catholic religious houses, secular and regular, including convents and colleges or seminaries (modelled – ironically – on Calvin's seminary at Geneva) were established across Catholic Europe (Casway 1991, 117). By 1600, the Old English in particular were opting to send their sons to Louvain, Salamanca or Paris rather than follow the traditional path across the Irish Sea to Oxford, Cambridge or the Inns of Court in London. Nonetheless, in pointing to changing patterns we should remain conscious of continuity and acknowledge that the process was one of gradual alteration rather than dramatic shift (Cregan 1970, 95–114; McGrath 2004, 217–36). As an example of continuity, consider the case of William Dongan who in 1609 was examined by the authorities at Chester as he made his way from Lincoln's Inn, in London, to Dublin. Accused of attempting to import 'papistical' texts and superstitious relics, his trunks were also found to contain items of high English-style fashion (Ní Mhurchadha 2005, 56–7).

Students abroad faced pressure between the competing interests of self and church, not altogether dissimilar from pressure between self and state interests affecting migrants to Ireland. The Counter-Reformation missionary effort required trained priests to sustain the faith in the hostile environment of a reformed Ireland, but young clerics witnessed the possibilities of advance and a more congenial living within the Church in Catholic Europe, or even within overseas empires. Exploration of the evolving continental network of Irish colleges has not only cast light on Irish migration and settlement in Europe but also served to provide a mirror to tensions and divisions at home. Clearly evident in the admissions policies and internal politics of the colleges are divisions between Old English and Native Irish constituencies, as well as the manifestation of distinct and competing regional identities. The Alcalá college, for example, favoured students from Ulster (Henry 1993, 52–6; O'Connell 2001, 61). The evidence drawn from the continent can tell us much about the overall reaction of native to newcomer and the stresses between the former at home and abroad (Canny 2001, 403–32; Kearney 2007, 283–7).

The early modern Irish diaspora in Europe

Emerging in particular from the publications of the 'Irish in Europe' project, based at the National University of Ireland, Maynooth, is a significantly clearer picture of Irish migration to early modern Europe, which has generated new questions and possibilities for further research (O'Connor 2001; O'Connor and Lyons 2003; 2006). Thanks to this work we can now compare Irish migrants and the way they integrated in different places, but we still await detailed comparative study of the Irish and other ethnicities settling in a single place. Thomas O'Connor has referred to the extent to which Ireland, Spain and France in the early modern period were 'not discrete "nations", in the modern sense, but collections of regions with differing levels of economic, social and cultural relations with other British and European regions' (2001, 21). This new research, in the archives in Ireland, Britain and Europe, reveals a tangle of interconnection and interdependence, and a clear sense emerges of migrants moving within a network that we can meaningfully describe as the Irish diaspora (O'Connor 2001, 12). Just as our interpretation of Ulster Presbyterian emigration to the new world in the eighteenth century has shifted to a greater emphasis on economic rather than religious factors, so too the emphasis on the effect of 'political turmoil' on earlier migration to Europe by Irish Catholics has been adjusted to take greater account of the 'economic' (O Connor 2001, 12). We may anticipate further research to explore all of these overlapping diasporas and cultures in contact across old and new worlds. The National Library of Ireland in 2007 launched a major exhibition, *Strangers to Citizens: the Irish in Europe, 1600–1800*, paying special attention to the issues of integration and assimilation processes of Irish migrants (*Irish Times* 5 January 2008).

Knockfergus on Thames

Migration in response to economic crisis is evident in the years around 1605 when we find Irish migrants passing through England on their way to and from the continent. Some were military men with their families, but there was clearly a larger refugee phenomenon which manifested itself across both the Irish Sea and the English Channel. In June 1605 the Privy Council in London warned the Lord Warden of the Cinque Ports on England's south coast about the entry of 'base people from Ireland', who as beggars had been deported from France and made their way to London. Later the same year we learn from a letter sent by the Lieutenant of the Tower of London to Lord Salisbury of the development of a form of Irish shanty settlement, probably not very different from those that would emerge around Dublin. Similar reports of Irish settlement in London are to be found almost two and a half centuries later. The report to Salisbury described a 'cluster of base tenements' rapidly constructed in the city's east end and known to its impoverished Irish inhabitants as 'Knockfergus' (alias Carrickfergus or 'Carigforgus'; see Plate 2). Associated with this Irish settlement, in the eyes of the Lieutenant were the issues of social control, which would become increasingly familiar in urban Britain and Europe in the centuries ahead, illegitimate children, unruly youth, multiple lodging, overcrowding, begging and petty crime (Lees 1979, 63–87; Fitzgerald 1992, 24–5; Turton 1999, 122–56). Thus, by 1605 we can observe Irish migrants settling in Britain as a distinctive part of the larger group of mobile or vagrant poor (Beier 1985, 62–5; Slack 1988, 98; Treadwell 1998, 321 n.55).

Trafficking the mobile poor

By the later sixteenth century the Irish were to be encountered as vagrants particularly across Wales and western and southern England, with London acting as the most powerful magnet (Beier 1985). An ongoing regular traffic, which may already have included some element of seasonal agricultural labour, accelerated substantially with the dislocation caused by warfare and subsistence crises. The series of failed harvests between 1627 and 1631 resulted in a sizeable flow of subsistence migrants from Ireland; this appears to have peaked between 1629 and 1630. Given the sums of money raised specifically to address this problem by the authorities in the ports around the Severn estuary, with Bristol Corporation chartering seven ships for repatriation to Ireland in 1629 alone, we can appreciate the volume of the movement. The survival of one particular examination by Somerset justices from May 1630 provides a closer view of the flow when the master of the barque *Peter* of Dungarvan, Waterford, and his servant and a number of poor passengers were examined following the interception of the vessel as it sought to drop some 40–80 passengers at a quiet cove near Portishead Point, known locally as Battery Point, 10 miles west of Bristol. One of the passengers, described as a poor tailor from Co. Clare, declared that he and his wife and two children had travelled south-east to Youghal, Cork, with a view to obtaining a passage to England but, enjoying no success, had moved on to Dungarvan, Waterford. Here they were advised that Maurice Keysons (alias Curry) ran a regular trade in 'trafficking' poor people into England and they agreed terms with him. Despite Keysons' claim to have been acting patriotically, there is little to suggest that he had much genuine interest in the welfare of his passengers, who were encouraged to sell all to pay him, obliged to leave what few provisions they had on board, then to be disembarked into shoulder-high water. No doubt there were many such episodes during these years (Fitzgerald 1994, 199–200).

A backwash from crisis

Political and military crises also drove ripples of migration east across the Irish Sea. Following the outbreak of the Rising in October 1641 there was an exodus similar to that after the end of Tyrone's rebellion (1594–1603). Large numbers of British settlers across the island sought refuge in the Irish port towns and the majority of those who perished in the late autumn and winter of 1641 probably did so as, hungry and cold, they undertook the journey. Of those thousands of settlers who reached a port, many eventually managed to obtain a passage across the Irish Sea to Britain's west coast (Lindley 1972, 143–76; Young 2007, 219–41). From Derry, in the north, many made their way to the west of Scotland and sought assistance from the government in Edinburgh. From Dublin, others descended on Chester. Among them was Alice Stonier, a widow whose husband had been pressed as a soldier and died at Drogheda, who found herself in early 1642 with five children to support in an increasingly crowded Dublin. With the encouragement of overstretched city governors she was persuaded to return to England and seek relief in the parish of her birth or last settlement. So she returned to Leek, Staffordshire, on the edge of the Peak District near Newcastle-under-Lyme, where she was given relief and assistance in placing her daughters in service (O'Dowd M. 1991a, 99–100). Generally, however, those returning from the British diaspora in Ireland could not be sure whether they would be welcomed as returned British colonists or shunned as Irish beggars (Fitzgerald 1994, 156–230). It is also worth noting that in early 1644, following the arrival of troops from Ireland to support the Royalist cause in the West Country, terms such as 'English-Irish' and 'Irish-English' were in circulation, reflecting the diverse backgrounds of the new arrivals (O'Hara 2006, 94). Overtly religious issues could also play into such migration, as when Ulster's Scottish Presbyterians, already under pressure from poor harvests and troops quartered on them, reacted in 1639 to the imposition of Wentworth's 'Black Oath' by fleeing across the north channel (Gillespie 1985, 81–3).

In perspective: east and west

Knowing how the history of the next four centuries turned out, we tend to project back and assume that the Elizabethans and Jacobeans thought of North America as we do – as more important than Ireland. However, for the Privy Council in London in 1607, the implications of the Departure of the Earls loomed very much larger on their political and diplomatic agenda than the establishment of Jamestown, Virginia on the other side of the Atlantic: somewhere in the region of 50,000 Irish migrants went east to England and Europe; only 10,000 went west to the Americas (Cullen 1994, 139; Mark Kishlansky, pers. comm.). Similarly, we may need to adjust our view of just how important Ulster was as a part of Scotland's diaspora since, in the first half of the seventeenth century, eastern Europe was far more important than Ulster as a destination of Scottish emigration (Smout, Landsman and Devine 1994, 85; Murdoch 2000).

Transatlantic connections

The need to revise preconceived notions has also been to the fore in the debate among historians over the last generation as to whether early modern Ireland is more appropriately considered as a kingdom or a colony, or as 'somewhere between the colonial model of North America and the experiences of the kingdoms of mainland Europe' (Bottigheimer 1978, 45–66; Ellis 1985; Canny 1988, 1991; Brady 1995, 64–86; Howe 2000, 21–7; Gillespie 2006, 6; Smyth 2006, 421–50; Connolly 2007). More central to our purpose here, however, are the close connections which were forged in this period between settlers and adventurers in Ireland and across the Atlantic. The very title of the most recent study of Cork and south Munster, *Old World Colony*, highlights the centrality of the developing relationship, which through trade as well as migration linked Ireland's southern shore in particular with English colonial enterprises in the New World (Dickson 2005, xiii). From the later Elizabethan period we can observe an overlap in personnel which shaped a relationship between colonial settlement in both destinations. Adventurers, such as Sir Walter Raleigh, Humphrey Gilbert, Richard Grenville and Ralph Lane, engaged in colonisation projects in both Ireland and the new world (Quinn 1991, 16–28). Although these remained the sporadic initiatives of individuals, they nonetheless forged links and established transatlantic networks that supported more significant developments later in the century. The importance of these initial pioneers is highlighted by the effect of failure, as in the case of the abortive transatlantic crossing from Ulster of the *Eagle Wing* in 1636, which dampened Presbyterian enthusiasm for emigration for several generations, the leaders of the pioneering venture having returned not to Ulster but to Scotland (Dickson 1966, 19; Doan 2000, 1–18).

Trade and migration in the emerging Atlantic world

From the second decade of the seventeenth century the flow of trade and people between Munster and the new world accelerated. Prominent individuals, notably Captain William Newce, Lieutenant John Shipward and Daniel Gookin, came to appreciate the potential Munster offered as a supply base for the emerging colony in Virginia. In addition to provisions and livestock, these men supplied settlers. For example, when Gookin left his estate at Carrigaline, Cork, for Virginia in 1621 he carried some 80 passengers. An active pirate community in west Cork also served to link the province with the wider Atlantic world, while English ships which called into ports such as Youghal or Kinsale recruited others, with varying degrees of compulsion, to travel with them to mainland America or the West Indies (Smith 1947, 62–6; Appleby 1989–90, 76–104; Quinn 1991, 21–5; Canny 2001, 313–16). Here we have a clear sight of the early emergence of a strong relationship between mercantile trade and migration: to the colonising adventurer the human cargo of potential settlers was as valuable as provisions, livestock, tobacco or timber. Although we should not exaggerate the scale of Atlantic migration in these decades, the geographical range of settlement remains impressive. By 1650 Irish migrants had registered their presence on the far side of the Atlantic from Canada, through New England, New York, Virginia, the West Indies, to the Amazon basin in South America (Miller 1985, 137–51; Lorimer 1989; Beckles 1990, 503–22; Quinn 1991, 28–33; Cullen 1994, 126–7; Hershkowitz 1996, 12; Canny 1998, 148–69).

While the vast majority of Irish emigrants to the new world in this period, and indeed later, followed channels pioneered by English colonisers, we should not overlook the small number who did not. These included Michael Donquan, an Irish labourer in St Malo, who accompanied Jacques Cartier to Atlantic Canada in 1535. Going initially to Europe and then on to engage in the transatlantic colonial initiatives of France and Spain, they also pioneered Irish settlement in destinations that would become important in the future (Lyons 2001, 110). Further research into such points of contact between a plurality of cultures and over-lapping empires, especially in the Caribbean and Atlantic Canada, may prove revealing.

Conclusion

Politically, the beginning of Ireland's seventeenth century is taken as being marked either by the Battle of Kinsale, 1601, or the accession of James VI and I and the Treaty of Mellifont, 1603. Viewed in terms of migration, the Departure or Flight of the Earls in 1607 is a more powerful marker, both of the beginning of the modern Irish diaspora and of the renewed project of 'Making Ireland British' through immigration. Plantation proceeded relatively smoothly and the British diaspora in Ireland, as we might call it, expanded considerably. The colonial frontier was extended and new settlement was consolidated within an urban, market framework where new settlers and natives who migrated from the surrounding countryside, settled alongside each other in the kind of pattern indicated by the English, Scotch and Irish Street names of Ulster towns like Downpatrick and Armagh (Buchanan and Wilson 1977 ,7).

The orientation of Irish Catholic migration towards Europe since the later sixteenth century was symbolically confirmed by the Flight of the Earls; there-after the attractions of settlement in Spain and France in particular sustained movement by migrants seeking economic advantage as well as those seeking asylum (Swords 2007). Nonetheless, the peaks of outward movement correspond closely with the transfer of large numbers of military personnel and their follow-ers after the crushing defeats of 1601 and 1649. Viewing Europe as a whole, we can see the Irish, like the Scots and others on the periphery, being drawn to the armies of the powers contesting the Thirty Years War. In looking at Scotland and the Plantation by James VI of the islands of Harris and Lewis in particular, we may see both parallel and precedent for the government's scheme for its frontier through Plantation (Ohlmeyer 1998, 124). Although we have focused on the numbers of Scots beginning to move south and west towards Ireland, we should not ignore the much larger numbers migrating east, often to take advan-tage of trading opportunities in the Baltic states. Nor should we ignore signs of a developing westward orientation in Irish migration towards the Atlantic world.

The first generation of settlers in Ireland could still think of home as being in Scotland, England or Wales and return there if forced by changing circum-stances. In this sense the decade of warfare which followed the Rising of 1641 represented the most significant disruption to the project of 'Making Ireland British'. After 1649, however, immigration would take off again as Cromwell determined to make a fresh start on Plantation and to inscribe indelibly on Mountjoy's 'table' a new settlement pattern.

6
Irish Migration, 1650–1700

The flows of immigration and emigration over our four centuries came closest to equilibrium during this half-century. Ireland's draw on the population of its neighbouring island remained strong and immigration in these five decades was actually greater than in the previous half-century. Inflows and outflows were particularly strong in the wake of the Cromwellian and Williamite military victories of 1649 and 1690 respectively. As in the first decade of the century, the 1650s saw emigration by large numbers of Irish Confederate forces to the Catholic continental powers, which added to the attraction of Ireland to the point that new settlers arrived and former settlers were sufficiently encouraged to return. The final decade of the 1690s proved decisive in consolidating British settlement in Ulster as newcomers were both pushed from Scotland by devastating famine and pulled into a buyer's land market. Although the Cromwellian transplantation to Connacht is still remembered as a brutal example of deliberate migration policy, it demonstrates how limited early modern governments were in their power to engineer the societies they desired. Warfare, the land market, the economic cycle and urban growth did more to shape patterns of internal migration than government policy. Strong ties with Europe persisted, but emigration to the new world, particularly the West Indies, increased significantly. To potential Irish migrants, the Americas in 1700 seemed somewhat closer and the Atlantic less broad than in 1607.

Immigration

The volume, origins and rhythm of migration

About 190,000 migrants arrived in Ireland from Britain during these decades. As before, approximately two-thirds (110,000) were from England and Wales, and the other third (80,000) from Scotland (Canny 1994, 64; Smout, Landsman and Devine 1994, 87–8). This migration, again as before, was characterised by distinct peaks and troughs rather than a steady, regular, annual flow, with marked peaks at the opening and close of the half-century. A peak in the 1650s saw an average of 8,000 immigrants a year entering the island (Smyth 2006, 100). Estimating the flow from Britain in this decade, however, is particularly difficult. Our only contemporary guide to social statistics is Sir William Petty (1623–87), a physician-turned-political economist. Calculations based on his figures suggest an inward movement of some 100,000 English and Welsh migrants during the Cromwellian period, 1649–60 (Petty 1672, 17–18; Canny 1994, 62; Smyth 2006, 100). Taking into account the somewhat inflated estimates offered by Petty and the fact that he did not include the pre-1641 settlers who returned to Ireland after leaving during the wars of the 1640s, this figure of 100,000 immigrants does not appear wildly inaccurate. Scottish immigration, into Ulster in particular, was also heavy during this decade, with something like 20,000–30,000 migrants crossing the north channel in the years immediately before 1660 (Houston 1992, 62).

The later 1670s saw a further peak in immigration from Britain (Smyth 2006, 100, 385). The final peak in the 1690s was almost exclusively composed of Scots taking up favourable opportunities to acquire and rent land in Ulster as an escape from devastating famine. It is likely that somewhere in the region of 50,000 migrants were involved in this crucial 'topping up' of British settlers in Ireland, in particular of Scots settlers in Ulster (Fitzgerald 2004, 79). Although the rate of immigration, year on year, was generally more sluggish in the three decades between 1660 and 1690, cumulatively the volume of movement was still substantial. Religious conflict in Scotland and economic opportunities in Ireland served to sustain the migration flow from Scotland to Ulster, with somewhere in the region of 10,000–20,000 Scots arriving. New settlers also came from England and Wales and were more evenly distributed across the island: about 10,000 between 1670 and 1700. Allowing for an additional 5,000 during the steady movement of the 1660s, we have about 15,000 English and Welsh immigrants arriving between 1660 and 1700 (Gillespie 1988, xvii–xviii; Canny 1994, 63). This scale of immigration across the island was spectacular in contemporary European terms: by 1700 almost 30 per cent of the entire population was of recent British origin (Smyth 2006, 100). As had been the case before 1650, some immigrants returned to Britain, temporarily or permanently. For example, between 1688 and 1690 significant numbers of the Scots settled in Ulster returned to Scotland, recoiling from the increasingly strident Jacobite regime under the Earl of Tyrconnell (Simms 1969, 40–59; Young 2004, 11–32). Overall, the key point to stress is that the largest numbers of British settlers migrating to Ireland did so after the era which is traditionally framed as Plantation Ireland (1556–1641).

Continental migrants

While most immigrants came from Britain, some came from further afield. Undoubtedly, the most significant group were Calvinists from France, the

Huguenots (Old French from Swiss German *Eidgenosse*, 'confederates'), some of whom were step-migrants who had spent some time in England. These refugees arrived in three main phases: 1662–69; 1681–7; 1692–1705. Precisely estimating the scale of this migration is again difficult. By the end of the second phase there were probably something like 500 Huguenots settled in Ireland, and by 1700 about 2,000. Though relatively modest in scale, this immigration of highly skilled linen weavers and craftsmen had a dispropor-tionate impact on the host society (Caldicott, Gough and Pittion 1987, 211–21). Other immigrants from Europe are also found among the growing number of specialist artisans documented in town and countryside. Recent research suggests those from the French, German and Dutch territories may have constituted as much as 20 per cent of this segment of settler society (Smyth 2006, 385). As well as Huguenots, there were small numbers of other continental immigrants, including not more than a few hundred continental Jewish and Dutch immigrants, most of whom were concentrated in Dublin and involved one way or another in trade.

The shaping of British Ireland

The impact of immigration across the island after 1650, as before, was uneven. In broad terms, British settlement consolidated pre-1641 patterns with the strongest migration flows directed towards the established provincial planta-tions of Ulster and Munster, and also towards the growing economic, adminis-trative and social hub of Dublin. Nonetheless, the large volume of British settlers arriving, particularly in the later 1650s, came to settle predominantly on the land, and the Cromwellian land settlement served to expand the distribution of the British presence in Ireland to a marked degree, if not necessarily quite as intended by the government. The gap between theory and practice, already evident in the Plantation schemes of Tudor and early Stuart Ireland, is clearly detectable once more in the 1650s (McKenny 1995, 181–200; Canny 2001, 552–78; Smyth 2006, 198–224). Generalisations about the actual patterns of British settlement as they worked out on the ground are hazardous and the process of studying the patchwork implementation of the land settlement at a local level is still only developing (Byrne 1997). Trends already evident by the 1660s tended to consolidate those already in place during the preceding decades. In Ulster, for example, the second half of the seventeenth century witnessed an important augmentation of British settlement. By the opening years of the eighteenth century, British Protestants, and Scots Presbyterians in particular, were much more thickly settled throughout much of west Ulster than had been the case before the 1641 Rising. This migration and settlement pattern was strongly compounded by the very sizeable influx of the 1690s (Gailey 1975, 2–22; Macafee and Morgan 1981, 58–62). English settlers, predom-inantly from the north-west of England, were also continuing to arrive in

Ulster, particularly in the east and south. This movement was stronger during the 1660s and 1670s than subsequently (Morgan 1976, 9–12; Gillespie 1988, xvii–xvii). Those adventurers who came to Ireland in the wake of Cromwellian confiscations to take up their landholdings were primarily drawn from southern England, particularly London and the West Country (Foster 1988, 112). English and Welsh migrants were also settling in not insignificant numbers across Leinster and Munster during the 1660s and 1670s (King 1997, 22–32; Dickson 2005, 176–81).

Islands of civility

Thomas Dineley, an English antiquary who toured Ireland in 1680, offers some insight into this process in his description of one south Leinster village in Co. Carlow, Staplestown (formerly Ballinacarrig, *Baile na Carraige*). With its church, rectory and mill on the River Burren, surrounded by the residences of largely English and Protestant artisans and craftsmen, Staplestown came close to the kind of model urban settlement envisaged by the planners of the Cromwellian era (Maxwell 1954, 103). Across Ireland at this time, the impact of sustained, high-level immigration was increasingly evident in the landscape as the new settlers led the way in felling timber, draining and enclosing land, establishing nucleated settlements like Staplestown, and sponsoring industrial and commercial enterprises (Smyth 2006, 100).

It is likely that many of those settled in Co. Carlow had arrived in Ireland through the port of Dublin and, while many undertook onward migration, others went no further than the capital. Still too often neglected in accounts of British settlement in seventeenth-century Ireland, Dublin can be viewed as an alternative 'overseas' urban destination for the numerous contemporary rural–urban migrants in Wales and western England (Canny 1994, 62–3; Barnard 2003, 280–1). By mid-century, Dublin was well on its way to becoming the second city to London. The population, estimated at 40,000 in 1660, had grown to around 60,000 by 1700, making Dublin the metropolitan centre of an 'Irish Sea province' (Smyth 2000, 168; Sheridan 2001, 68).

Growing capital of an Irish Sea province

One such migrant was George Bewley, who came to Dublin in 1698. A Quaker born in Cumberland, Bewley crossed the Irish Sea as a young man in order to take up an apprenticeship with the aptly named Edward Webb, a Dublin linen draper. In common with many others who left the English countryside for the growing towns and cities during the later seventeenth century, Bewley recorded his apprehension at making the 'crossing' from a rural to urban environment. That his apprenticeship in Dublin had been arranged by Quaker friends who travelled regularly on business between the north-west of England and Dublin hints at the important networks that criss-crossed the Irish Sea and connected Dublin with a wider British hinterland (Gillespie 2001, 234). Other migrants to Dublin and Leinster were drawn from across England and Wales. We know, for example, that John Bufton left Coggeshall, near Colchester, Essex, during the 1680s for Dublin and eventually moved north to Drogheda, at the mouth of the River Boyne, where he became a port official. Whilst in Ireland he kept up a fairly regular correspondence with his brother, a woolcomber, who remained in Coggeshall. These migrant letters are, unfortunately, rare survivals from the period (Clark 1987, 272). Had a greater quantity of such material survived it could have provided a basis for potentially revealing comparative analysis with surveys of contemporary transatlantic correspondence (Cressey 1987).

Migration channels

Although rural–urban migration within Ireland played a part in the demographic expansion of Dublin between 1650 and 1700, it is clear that the main engine behind this population growth was immigration from Britain, making it 'an island of Protestantism surrounded by a sea of Catholicism'. By 1700 approximately two-thirds of Dublin's recorded inhabitants were Protestants (Fagan 1998, 9–52). Migrants were drawn from across England, Scotland, Wales and their offshore islands to settle throughout Ireland. A sprinkling of individual settlers of Scottish origin certainly made it to the southern province of Munster, while those from southern English counties such as Devon and Kent, as well as East Anglia, were to be found in Ulster. Nonetheless, geographical proximity, as usual, was critical in shaping the main migratory patterns. This is clearly evident in relation to migration from Scotland, where the model of a settlement frontier is particularly applicable. The process of colonial spread, discussed in the previous chapter, had continued in the decades after 1650. Disregarding the official boundaries of the Ulster Plantation of 1609, the concentration of Scots settlement by 1700 could be observed decreasing southwards along an imaginary line running from Fair Head in north-east Ulster to Mizzen Head in south-west Munster. Accessibility as a determining factor was evidenced by strong Scots settlement around northern ports of entry such as Londonderry, Coleraine and Donaghadee, and along the river valleys of their hinterlands, such as the Foyle, Finn, Bann and Sixmilewater (Macafee and Morgan 1981, 58–9; Robinson 1984, 109–24; Gillespie 1985, 113–94). The process of southern and western expansion from an Ulster core may be conceptualised as an expanding frontier and comparisons with Virginia and the American colonies have been pursued by historical geographers. Important in both frontier contexts was the migration of family units capable of sustaining the family farm through at least the first two generations (Smyth, 2006, 428–30). As in the decades before 1641, perhaps the single heaviest regional concentration of British migrants bound for Ireland after 1650 came from the south-west of Scotland. The origins of migrants during the large-scale migration of the 1690s still requires detailed study, but it may be the case that the geographical range from which migrants were drawn was more extensive than had been the case during the early seventeenth century. This seems likely because the serious famine which drove migration from Scotland between 1695 and 1699 was truly national in scope, but particularly severe in northern and eastern Scotland, which had previously been less well represented in the migration to Ireland (Flinn 1977, 164–86; Tyson 1986, 32–52; Cullen, Whately and Young 2006, 250–76; Macinnes 2007, 217–19). Undoubtedly an area for future research will be to understand the specific contexts which conditioned British migrants to leave home and seek to establish settlement in Ireland during the seventeenth century.

Ethnic networks

Other regional migration patterns, like that which linked south-west Scotland and north Ulster, can be identified. In the two decades after 1660, migrants from the north of England were particularly important in settling a belt of land stretching from Belfast Lough, down the Lagan valley, across north Armagh and west down the Clogher valley into Co. Fermanagh. Confirmation of this pattern can be found in records of the Quaker meeting at Lurgan, in north Armagh. Of some 30 families recorded as settling there during the later seventeenth century, a third were from Yorkshire, a fifth from Cumberland and the remainder from Lancashire, Northumberland and Westmoreland (Gillespie 1988, xviii). Geographical proximity was also a key determinant of British settlement patterns across Leinster. Here the main ports of arrival, Drogheda and Dublin, provided access to Cos Meath, Louth, Kildare and Wicklow and the Irish midlands more generally. The majority of these British settlers were drawn from north-west England and north Wales. Many went no further than the port towns. The population of Dublin, as we have seen, was roughly two-thirds Protestant by the close of the century, and Drogheda was even more Protestant (75 per cent) as early as 1670 (Connolly 1992, 147). For later seventeenth-century Dublin there is clear evidence of the regional origins of British settlers in the city. In 1671 the Welsh gathered for a feast and to hear a sermon preached by a Welsh minister, and in the same year inhabitants with roots in Cheshire, including Dublin's mayor, John Totty, gathered in St. Werburgh's church for a sermon by a Cheshire cleric. By 1700 Dubliners celebrating their Welsh ethnicity were congregating on St David's Day (Gillespie 2001, 235). In Munster, the regional origins of settlers reflected both geographical proximity and the long-established trading relationship with south Wales and the south-west of England. In Youghal, Cork, for example, we find in the 1670s a leading trader, Samuel Hayman, modulating between Ireland and England. Originally from Minehead, Somerset, he retained a house there and close contact with his brother (Barnard 1993, 345).

Taking ship

Reinforcing the influence of geographical proximity in shaping migration patterns was the establishment of chain migration as pioneer migrants encouraged and assisted others to follow them from their region of origin. British landholders, who had taken up lands in Ireland under the various plantation schemes, particulary the Scots in Ulster, sought to draw tenants from their lands in Britain to settle their new Irish estates. The consequences of this strategy, initiated in the first half of the century, were increasingly evident after 1650 (Barnard 2003, 221). Another important but often neglected consideration is the issue of how migrants actually crossed the Irish Sea (see Plate 2). Here the pattern of mercantile relationships between ports in Ireland and Britain was hugely influential. The vast majority of migrants who came as the occupiers of land or as artisans and craftsmen, rather than as landholders, made use of the numerous small trading craft which traversed the Irish Sea. Most vessels entering the Munster ports of Waterford, Youghal and Kinsale were from the ports of the Severn estuary, while those using the Ulster ports used the route from south-west Scotland and from coal-exporting Whitehaven in Cumberland. Throughout this period a growing proportion of Irish merchant shipping was operating from the port of Dublin, and trade with ports such as Chester and Whitehaven was significant in providing a means for migrants to make the crossing (Cullen 1968, 32, 82).

Snapshots of migrant motivation

Understanding the motivation of migrants coming to Ireland in this period presents a real challenge to historians confronted with source material which very rarely addresses the question explicitly. Only a tiny proportion of the documents which can shed light on migration were consciously fashioned for that purpose. We have very little by way of migrant correspondence or personal journals that would allow us to reconstruct full migration stories. We get partial and fleeting glimpses of migrants and their individual circumstances – snapshots rather than extended footage. Nevertheless, some generalisations about motivation are possible. As in the opening decades of the seventeenth century, the attraction of Ireland to voluntary immigrants was primarily economic. The continuing availability of relatively cheap land and the greater opportunity for rapid upward social mobility drew many who may have considered themselves materially circumscribed and their social standing under pressure in Britain. The opportunities in the Irish land market were handsomely augmented following the wars of the 1640s and early 1650s, and again in the 1690s. The Cromwellian, Restoration and Williamite land settlements created openings for acquisitive British settlers, but more often than not served simply to shuffle landholdings among those who already held estates in Ireland. Landholders in the wake of war wanted to re-people their estates and rejuvenate their rent rolls rapidly. Thus, rents set at modest levels and on favourable leasing terms could offer a new tenant an attractive opening. At the same time, immigrants from Britain increasingly settled in an urban context, either in the port towns and cities or within the growing network of smaller provincial, country towns and villages. By 1700 there was a sizeable labouring Protestant population that was most conspicuous in urban Ireland (Barnard 2003, 280–1).

Ireland and British local/regional diasporas

There is even less evidence of the direct promotion of Ireland or active recruitment of migrants in Britain after 1650 than before, which indicates that other, more informal influences were at work in stimulating movement across the Irish Sea. We have already observed the region-specific nature of migration from Britain to Ireland, and it is interesting to note that the north and west regions of England, which were important sources for migration to Ireland, were relatively less important at this stage in feeding transatlantic migration. Similarly, the extent of movement from Scotland to colonial America or the West Indies before 1700 was relatively limited, certainly in comparison with the flow to Ulster (Whyte 2000, 103–37). The extent to which Ireland and the new world were now in competition with each other as destinations for potential British emigrants still remains unclear. Local or regional studies which consider more fully the interrelationship of migrant flows and their interplay and impact on the sending society should in future add to our understanding.

An open frontier

In the decades after 1650, in spite of a slowing down and then reversal in the rate of demographic expansion in England and Wales, access to land there was problematic for many, as was the securing of economic independence, particularly in northern England and the Scottish lowlands. Aspiring small tenant farmers could still look to Ireland as an 'open frontier' with affordable access to land which was suited to their mainly pastoral mode of farming (Sharpe 1987, 35–42; Houston 1992, 28–34; Whyte 2000, 113). We should caution against any assumption that early modern migrant behaviour was less complex than that of modern migrants. As we know only too well from attempting to understand the individual motivation of later Irish emigrants, generalisations, based on partial evidence or inferred from macro socio-economic trends, may be at best simplistic, at worst misleading. British migrants arriving in Ireland in the seventeenth century were likely to have been influenced by the same mix of personal, family and local circumstances that affected Irish migrants heading in the opposite direction in the nineteenth and twentieth centuries.

Relief from religious persecution

Although the main causes of immigration appear to have been primarily economic, the role of religion and religious persecution in influencing migrants should not be neglected. For three groups in particular religious belief played a significant part in influencing their decision to emigrate and the manner in which they settled. First, there were the more radical, covenanting Presbyterians from south-west Scotland who continued to cross to Ulster, both during the 1650s and after the re-establishment of the Episcopalian church in 1660. Friction between them and the state was correlated closely with the rhythm of migration to Ireland between 1660 and 1690. Second, nonconformists from England – Presbyterians, Quakers and Baptists in particular – also moved to Ireland in the hope that state persecution would be less rigorous there. Following a sizeable influx in the 1650s, Quakers from the north-west of England continued to migrate to south Ulster and Leinster in the following decades, as they did in smaller numbers from the south-west of England to Munster. Third, religious persecution also accounted for the immigration of those from beyond the British Isles, such as the Huguenots (French Calvinists) already mentioned. Again, the volume and timing of their arrival correlated closely with the persecuting zeal of the French crown (Caldicott et. al. 1987; Kilroy 1994; Gillespie 1995; Harrison 1995; Herlihy 1996; Greaves 1997). It was also in the decades after 1660 that we find the origins of a small Jewish community in Ireland. In about 1660 a number of Sephardi (from Portugal and Spain) Jews, mainly from prosperous mercantile families, made their way to Dublin from Amsterdam via London. These immigrants were then followed by Ashkenazi (from Germany) Jewish immigrants, following the same migration path, but generally poorer than the Sephardi pioneers. In subsequent decades, relations between these two branches of the Jewish faith in Dublin remained more harmonious than in many other parts of Europe, prompting their presentation as something of a model for later Jewish settlements on the transatlantic frontier (Weiner 2001, 276–82).

Internal migration

Patterns in shade

Study of internal migration in Ireland in the half-century after 1650 remains relatively neglected, as for the earlier seventeenth century. In comparison to what has been published on this subject in relation to contemporary England and Scotland, the outlines in Ireland remain particularly hazy. A major difficulty again is the relative paucity of source material which could be exploited to measure internal migration in any systematic way. The kind of municipal, legal and church records which have been used to uncover internal migration patterns in England and Wales were kept or survive to a much lesser extent in

Ireland. We should not underestimate either the English-language bias of the surviving documentary records or the gulf of incomprehension that existed between two language communities in the seventeenth century. While more extensive and imaginative use has been made of Irish-language sources by scholars, migration patterns within native Irish society remain, if not hidden, firmly in the shade (Palmer 2001, 40–74; Smyth 2006, 454).

Non-mobile migrations

Before considering internal migration caused mainly by government policy, both deliberately and incidentally through Plantation and transplantation, we should also recognise the extent of 'non-mobile' migration (see Appendix I), caused by the completion of the 'shiring' process, which had begun in the late twelfth century under the Anglo-Normans. The final shiring after the Flight of the Earls made the new 'county' of Tyrone a very different place from the old 'lordship' of Tyrone. Similarly, the new Castlecaulfield (named after Sir Toby Caulfield) was very different from the old *Baile Uí Dhonnaíle* ('territory of O'Donnelly', Toner 1996, xix; McKay 1999, 37; marked as 'Dunnalley' on Jobson's map of 1592, see Plate 2). As a result, the 'non-mobile' migrants – those who 'stayed put' – found themselves willy-nilly moved into a 'new world'.

Cromwellian crisis

There can be little doubt that Ireland about 1650 was in flux and suffering a profound demographic crisis. The direct impact of warfare, famine and plague between 1649 and 1653 brought an estimated minimum reduction in the population of between 15 and 20 per cent (from about 1.5 million to 1.3 million) – a major demographic crisis by any reckoning (Lenihan 1997, 19–20). When Henry Ireton, the New Model Army commander, travelled across Munster in the summer of 1650 he reported a desolate and depopulated landscape. Mid-Ulster in particular had experienced an exodus of refugees, many of whom made their way out of the province altogether. Undoubtedly the impact of displacement was variable, occasionally showing up in the surviving sources as a marked decrease, increase or no significant change in the population of different areas, as has been noted in several county Dublin townlands during these years (Smyth 2006, 158, 271). Worth noting is the tradition among modern Irish Traveller families that attaches the origin of their migratory lifestyle to these years (Gmelch 1975, 16).

Native mobility and settler suspicion

Specific data about movement within the Irish countryside remain elusive. Protestants in Ireland, often from something of a distance, continued to make observations about what they considered to be the excessively mobile, even nomadic existence of the native Catholic tenantry. Their 'strange' tradition of accompanying livestock from winter to summer pastures and back caused alarm or disparagement, initially at least (see John Derricke's illustration *An Irish Lord Feasting in the Open Air*,1581, Quinn 1985, Plate III). Mobility among the native Irish was a concern, especially to those haunted by the memory of 1641 and alive to the threat posed by the figure that contemporaries referred to as the 'tory' or 'raparee'. These rural brigands continued to operate, particularly in remoter upland areas of the country, into the early eighteenth century (Ó Ciardha 1997, 141–63). A frustrated agent on one Donegal estate in 1665 contrasted the permanently settled Protestant population with the Catholic tenantry who 'snail-like, carry their houses on their heads, and will easily so abscond themselves as never more to be seen by us' (Barnard 2003, 289).

Transplantation: stretching capacity

The most prominent feature of internal migration in this period was the forced transplantation to Connacht, undertaken by the government in the wake of the Cromwellian conquest, 1649–52. The most ambitious plans for wholesale removal of Catholics to the Connacht counties of Galway, Roscommon, Mayo and Clare, promoted by army radicals, were not carried through. However, the eventual land settlement made provision for the forfeiture of the estates of those who had not remained consistently loyal to the parliamentary forces during the preceding decade and Connacht landholders themselves were also obliged to relocate within the province. As things were, the logistical task of overseeing the migration of those deemed guilty proved overwhelming and, in the context of much official disorganisation, significant numbers of greater and lesser landholders remained in place (Dickson 1991, 227–31; Smyth 2006, 182–7). The government itself eventually recognised that it was stretching its own capacity beyond breaking point and, if the evidence relating to Co. Limerick is more widely indicative, it is likely that the relocation of only about half of those due to be transplanted across the Shannon was ever completed (O'Mahony 2000, 29–52). Nonetheless, the memory of the horrific migrant choice, 'Hell or Connacht', was sufficiently bitter to be sustained by subsequent generations of Irish Catholics (Simington 1970).

Expanding the frontier

Of course, settler society was itself far from static. Recent immigrants and second- and third-generation settlers continued to engage in 'colonial spread' as farmers and tenants moved on in search of better land, a more favourable leasing arrangement or simply an alternative settlement opportunity. The growing numbers of migrants, particularly Scots, coming to Ulster after 1650 and most spectacularly after 1690, reinforced British settlement on the southern and western boundaries of the 1609 Plantation scheme and beyond. New settlers and the sons and daughters of earlier settlers moved south into Leinster counties such as Longford and west towards Leitrim, Sligo and Mayo in north Connacht (Kennedy, Miller and Graham 1991, 35–7; O'Dowd M. 1991b, 140, 163). Evidence from the fragmentary remnants of the parish registers of Blaris, near Lisburn in the Lagan valley, and from north Armagh estate records covering these years point to fairly high rates of population turnover. Just as predominantly Scots migrants spread out from the settlement 'cores' of the Foyle and Bann basins, so migrants, drawn to a greater extent from the north and west of England before 1680, looked south and west, beyond the Lagan valley, towards the Clogher valley in south Tyrone and the better farming lands of east and north Fermanagh (Morgan 1976, 9–15; Gillespie 1988, xvi–xxv). This restored continuity with earlier internal migration patterns, after the disruption of 1641.

Consolidating the citadel, confronting the marginal poor

Looking at movement within the countryside, we are on firmer ground with rural–urban migration. Irish towns in general were expanding during this period but, as in Scotland and England, a growing proportion of the population was concentrating in towns at the top of the urban hierarchy, particularly the capital cities, Edinburgh, London and Dublin. Dublin's share of the Irish population increased from an estimated 0.5 per cent in 1600 to approximately 4 per cent in 1700 (Butlin 1977, 93; Whyte 1995, 18). As noted above, roughly two-thirds of Dublin's estimated 60,000 inhabitants in 1700 were Protestant. In 1660 Dublin was both the largest and the most British settlement on the island (see Map 2). While it should not be assumed that Protestants were absent from those defined as the city's poor, there can be little doubt that the vast majority of those identified as the 'problem poor' or the 'sturdy, foreign poor' were at least nominally Catholic. Many of these indigent inhabitants may not even have owned one identifiable hearth and so escaped the notice of official enumerators. Many continued to be rural migrants who erected shanty-style cabins in the poorer western suburbs or the poorer districts beyond the city walls at the mouth of the Liffey. Here they eked out an existence as best they could, relying on a range of subsistence strategies, within and without the law. In this regard Dublin was little different from most pre-industial European cities (Butlin 1965, 92–7; Friedricks 1995, 218). The city fathers continued to try to exercise social control and to exclude those deemed ineligible for citizenship or unworthy of officially sanctioned alms.

Subsistence and opportunity

Civic activity predictably peaked at times of economic hardship or subsistence crisis, when the flow of rural migrants was likely to be heaviest, as in the difficult year of 1674. It was reported from the Waring estate in east Ulster that as a consequence of the want of bread and shortage of seed, landholdings, even entire townlands, had been deserted as the tenant families had 'gone off' to beg a living. In the early 1680s, when harvests failed again, Dublin corporation renewed its campaign to have the city beadles exclude those poor found begging without the badge issued to the 'deserving, resident poor' in an attempt to regulate casual alms-giving. There is also evidence that prostitution, often the resort of impoverished young women from the countryside, was a particular concern in Dublin at this time. Although problems with the migration of the rural poor into urban centres were most pronounced in Dublin, they were evident in most Irish towns. Where soldiers and mariners congregated, local governors seemed most exercised by the issue and in this respect there was continuity with the previous half-century (Fitzgerald 1994, 353–403; O'Dowd 2005, 88, 98). Of course, not all of those migrating towards the port towns were poor. Although Belfast was still only a modest town compared to what it would become, we find there an expansion in trade accompanied by an inflow of men from the surrounding countryside, seeking new mercantile opportunities. Between the late 1670s and the early 1690s these included second- and third-generation Ulster-Scots such as David Butle, Edward Brice and James Stewart from Co. Antrim, William Sloane from Co. Down and Robert Lennox from Co. Londonderry, who moved into the port and set up as merchants (Agnew 1996, 12; Gillespie 2007).

Military migration

It is hard to exaggerate the extent to which throughout the seventeenth century Ireland was a highly militarised society and how much this influenced migration patterns. Warfare as well as economic crisis swelled the numbers compelled to take to the road, as during the Cromwellian campaign of the early 1650s when there was significant population turnover in port towns like Waterford and Galway, particularly an exodus of Catholic merchants (Barnard 1975 50–5; Smyth 2006, 358). Military migrants were as central to immigration and internal migration as they were to emigration. Just as the servitors (military crown servants) of the early seventeenth century had been critical to the peopling and defence of Plantation Ireland, so were soldier adventurers as settlers and speculators in the 1650s. Soldiers featured as internal migrants during warfare and after as the demobilised negotiated re-entry into civilian life. Across early modern Europe, in states and communities less war-torn and militarised than Ireland, the spectre of the 'idle swordsman' loomed large as a threat to settled society (Beier 1985, 93–5; Jütte 1994, 26–7; Bartlett 2002). Colonial society in Ireland, from the first plantation schemes of the mid-sixteenth century, was slow to shed anything of the character of the garrison. Although less disruptive than the warfare of the 1650s, the Williamite campaign (1689–91) and the settlement that followed the Treaty of Limerick (3 October 1691) had the same kind of impact, particularly on migration overseas.

Emigration

Defeat and exodus

Our only estimate of emigration in the five decades after 1650 of just over 70,000 is offered by Cullen (1994, 139). Corresponding to immigration, there were peaks in the 1650s and again in the 1690s, reflecting the large numbers of military personnel and their followers who departed in the wake of military defeat. In excess of 35,000 men left for Spain and France in the wake of Cromwellian victories in the early 1650s. Later, about 18,000 troops went to France during 1690–91 (Cullen 1994, 124, 139). As in the early seventeenth century, these migration flows were not made up exclusively of male soldiers. Wives, partners, daughters and female camp followers also left Ireland for the continent. The failure of many women to obtain a passage for France from Cork following the surrender at Limerick in 1691 etched another powerful image of tragic parting on Irish Catholic minds. Many of them, however, may eventually have found their way to France, following the precedent set by Irish women in preceding generations. It is estimated that for every ten rank-and-file soldiers, four dependants followed (Casway 1991, 120–1; Cullen 1994, 139; O'Dowd 2005, 98). Military conflict across Europe stimulated significant migration, and in recalling the highly militarised nature of seventeenth-century Ireland we should see it as part of a wider continental pattern.

Chains of connection: Catholic Ireland and the continent

What can be defined broadly as military migration made up the dominant emigrant stream to Europe, but there continued to be movement which was not directly related to military recruitment or military conflict in Ireland. Trade, as well as the continuing demand for Catholic lay and religious education which was no longer permitted in Ireland, continued to pull and push emigrants from Ireland to Europe. Not all such migration, of course, was on a permanent basis, but it is likely that at least 5,000 migrants fell into this category (Cullen 1994, 139). Movement to Europe continued to draw very heavily, if not exclusively, on Catholic Ireland. Emigration from Ulster after the 1650s appears to have declined somewhat from its already modest level (Henry 1993, 37–60). The south-eastern counties of Ireland continued to be over-represented in the stream and the southern port towns accounted for significant numbers of mercantile and religious migrants. Regional migration patterns, as with British emigration to Ireland, were strongly influenced by geographical proximity to destinations. The influence of family and local networks in chain migration was already strongly evident in the later seventeenth century. For example, Luke Quirke, an Irish mariner recently arrived in St Malo, Brittany, wrote to his cousin, John Kearney, also in France at the time, asking, as often seen in the transatlantic correspondence of later centuries, 'how all our poor friends in Clonmel do?' (Lyons 2001, 121; O'Connor 2001, 21). France represented the primary destination for continent-bound migrants during these decades, reflecting the hunger for men of Louis XIV's expanding armed forces and the establishment of major Irish colleges at Nantes and Paris (Ó Ciosáin 2001, 93–106). Spain too continued after 1650 to offer settlement opportunities for Irish military personnel, merchants and scholars, but the relative importance of Spain within the Irish diaspora was undoubtedly on the wane (Stradling 1994, 155; O'Connell 2001, 63; Downey and MacLennan 2006). Further east smaller numbers of Irish military migrants, particularly of the officer class, were occupying positions in the Austrian and Polish service (Silke 1976, 609–10; Downey 2002). Already by 1700, we can detect the fibres of connection between migration to old world Europe and to the new world as Irish migrants and their descendants fed into expanding European empires, in the Caribbean, French North America and Spanish Central and South America.

The draw of London

Migration from Ireland to Britain in the 50 years from 1650 has received limited attention. Each year on average 150 migrants were arriving in England on a permanent or semi-permanent basis: 7,500 in total (Cullen 1994, 139). Although they came from a wide range of social backgrounds, the strong association with poverty and vagrancy persisted. Indeed, as the effect of the Settlement Act 1662, which strengthened the armoury of the state against what it deemed the illegitimate migration of the poor, combined with the slowing rate of population growth, the proportion of the poor of Irish origin who were tramping the roads of Restoration England may even have increased (Beier 1985, 172; Slack 1988, 194). At the same time, the level of elite concern about the issue relaxed somewhat as there were fewer, less sustained food crises in Ireland after the early 1650s. London, regardless, continued to draw migrants from across the British Isles. On the basis of a sample of over 4,000 deponents who came before the London church courts between 1665 and 1725 it has been calculated that 12.1 per cent of males and 9.1 per cent of females had origins outside England and Wales. This reflected an increase in the number of London's non-English in-migrants, including significant numbers of Irish (Earle 1994, 47–8). The more satisfactory integration of Britain and particularly London into our emerging picture of the early modern Irish diaspora remains high up the future research agenda (Ohlmeyer 2007, 499–512).

Commerce, provisions and the Caribbean

By 1700, Irish emigrants were significantly more likely than those of a century before to consider the prospect of crossing the Atlantic. This reflected the steady growth in Ireland's transatlantic trade, particularly during the second half of the century. Cork city and the other Munster ports became increasingly involved in the export of provisions, mainly barrelled butter, salted beef and pork to the Caribbean (Truxes 1988, 147–69; Dickson 2005, 135–48). This trade, generally carried on by English vessels, provided the means for increasing numbers of indentured servants to make their way to the West Indies, particularly but not exclusively those islands in British posession. This migrant flow, stretching back to the 1630s, was significantly augmented by another forced migration scheme of transportation during the Cromwellian period. Estimates of the scale of transportation in the 1650s range from less than 12,000 to 50,000 (Gwynn 1932, 139–286; Blake 1942–3, 267–81; Foster 1988, 107; O'Callaghan 2000, 85–6). Notwithstanding the lasting impression this forced migration made on family memories on both sides of the Atlantic, evidence for the logistics of contemporary shipping and population size in both Ireland and the West Indies supports acceptance of a figure towards the lower end of this range. As well as this forced migration, there was significant voluntary migration to the same destination so that by the 1690s the planters of Barbados, nervous about the possibility of Irish Catholic field hands and slave labour jointly fomenting violent revolt, petitioned against further Irish Catholic immigration (Beckles 1990, 503–22). The Caribbean island with the greatest Irish presence, made up of both Catholic servants and landowners, was Montserrat, where close to two-thirds of the population was of Irish ethnicity in 1678. On the basis of his special study of the island and the role of its Irish colonists, Akenson asks in his title what would have happened *If the Irish Ran the World* and finds small difference (Akenson 1997a, 109, 171–87).

The Origins of Irish-America

Irish migration to the Caribbean was already connected with settlement on mainland colonial America. From the mid-seventeenth century, indentured servants and the sons of farmers, planters and merchants were moving from Barbados to South Carolina and the Irish made up a proportion of these. There was also migration directly from Ireland. One estimate claims that as many as 100,000 emigrants had left Ireland for the American colonies before 1700, but such a high figure seems doubtful (Smyth 1992, 51). Two promotional pamphlets published by the South Carolina proprietors were printed in Dublin in the 1680s and such literature may have played a part in influencing individuals such as John Barnwell to cross the Atlantic. Despite having what appeared to be reasonable prospects at home, Barnwell left Dublin for Carolina in 1700 for no other reason, claimed a contemporary observer, than 'a humour to go to travel' (Weir 1983, 392). Colonies further to the north, such as Maryland and Virginia, offered opportunities for indentured servants, not least in the developing tobacco plantations. Not all Irish Catholic immigrants of this era were confined to the ranks of bonded manual labour. On 1 October 1688 Charles Carroll, from a landed family in Co. Tipperary, arrived in Maryland, via London. Carroll thrived in his new position as attorney general to Lord Baltimore, even though he admitted finding acclimatisation to the humid environment difficult (Hoffman 2000, 36–60). Scattered evidence of an Irish presence in New York and New England has also been presented (see Glazier 1999 under individual colony entries). Moving further up the Atlantic coast we encounter a corner of the Irish diaspora which even at this early stage had its own distinctive character. From at least the 1620s Irish seafarers were joining vessels from the south-west of England, particularly in Waterford, to travel to the rich fishing grounds on the banks of Newfoundland, returning home in the autumn. A small proportion would appear to have settled more permanently from the 1670s, establishing a basis for later, more substantial Irish settlement (Quinn 1991, 28–33; Mannion 2001 257–93; Pope 2004, 232 6; Trew 2005, 45). As this case shows, Irish transatlantic migration, like British migration to Ireland, could be circular.

In search of a new frontier

The last quarter of the seventeenth century, rather than 1717–18, is now generally taken as the starting point for the emigration of Ulster Presbyterians to colonial America (Kirkham 1997, 76–80). It is clear that the difficult years 1683–4 saw Scots settlers in west Ulster nervous about religious persecution and payment of the next instalment of rent, and using the threat of emigration as a bargaining tool with landlords. We know that a number of Presbyterian ministers from east Donegal, such as Francis Makemie of Ramelton (1658–1708), who went on to become the 'father' of American Presbyterianism, made their way to the Chesapeake in the early 1680s, memories of the abortive *Eagle Wing* expedition of 1636 having faded somewhat. Reports from Maryland and New Jersey during this and the subsequent decade suggest that there was a larger-scale movement, totalling about 1,000 by 1700 (Kirkham 1997, 77–8). Thus, at the same time as tens of thousands of Scots were entering Ulster, taking advantage of favourable land leasing terms or fleeing from devastating famine, others were already exchanging old world frontiers for new. Also among those Protestant dissenters pioneering the transatlantic migration path were the Quakers. The inducement to join other Friends enjoying religious liberty in William Penn's colony of Pennsylania, founded in 1682, was strong. In the years after 1682 and during the early decades of the eighteenth century Quakers from Ireland shaped trans-oceanic networks that expressed and strengthened both their spiritual and commercial identities (Myers 1902, 1969).

Conclusion

Looking back we see a half-century starting and ending with decades of heavy population turnover. The forces generated in the wake of warfare in the 1650s and 1690s resulted in an increase in the numbers on the move into, within and out of the island. The frontier of British settlement was mainly driven west as the volume of immigration from the neighbouring island increased. Transplantation to Connacht, though never as thorough in execution as in conception, displaced internal migrants, but undoubtedly fewer than did economic forces. Dublin virtually doubled in size through immigration from Britain and a continuing stream of rural and provincial migrants. As well as physical internal migration, 'non-mobile' migration continued as many found themselves, without going anywhere, in a new British world – part of what we may now call 'the British diaspora' (Horn 1998a). The evolving and overlapping parish and congregational frameworks of official and unofficial churches reminds us of the complex mental mapping and local identity construction that was in progress in early modern Ireland.

Immigration into Ireland during the seventeenth-century continues to be viewed from the perspective of the destination and in terms of what we might crudely classify as pull factors. The most recent general survey text of seventeenth-century Ireland, while acknowledging the significant Scots influx of the 1690s, makes no reference to the devastating famine then prevailing in Scotland (Lenehan 2008, 200).

The sight of large numbers of defeated soldiers departing as 'Wild Geese' after the signing of the Treaty of Limerick (1691) is a reminder of how important the motif of the military exile was to be to political nationalism in the nineteenth century. However, we should not neglect the diversity represented by the myriad individual accounts, stories of success and the seizure of opportunities overseas as well as those of bitter hardship for the vanquished. Catholic Ireland was also developing a diaspora with new opportunities: colonised at home but colonising abroad, retaining or even improving their status in Europe, and reaching out, in a variety of enterprises, across the North Atlantic. At the same time, in the 1690s we see the consolidation of Scots settlers in the north, which proved critical in laying down settlement patterns that persist to the present and, like those departing for the continent, they were both pushed and pulled. In the event, many chose to leave a frontier that was closing for the one that was opening in North America.

7
Irish Migration, 1700–1750

Those whose lifetimes spanned this half-century must have noticed a stark change underway: in 1700 Ireland was a country of net immigration; in 1750 it was a country of net emigration, which would continue for nearly 300 years, until the short-term reversal of the early 1970s. Following the surge in the later 1690s, large-scale immigration from Britain declined fairly sharply. The correspondingly high emigration to Europe stayed at a high level and from the second decade of the eighteenth century was supplemented by an increasing flow across the Atlantic. The shift was most evident in the north as the paths of arriving immigrant Scots crossed those of departing Ulster-Scots pioneers as they left for America. Immigration dried up, first from Britain and then from continental Europe, as push factors in Britain and Europe weakened and pull factors in colonial America strengthened.

Simply getting enough to eat was difficult for many in Ireland and the underlying weakness of the agricultural economy was exposed by brutal famines in 1728–9 and 1740–1 which, along with a shift from tillage to grazing and proto-industrialisation, especially in linen manufacture, drove much internal migration and emigration. Continental Europe continued to offer rank-and-file 'Wild Geese' the chance to put bread on the table and those of the officer class the possibility of preserving their military rank and social status. The 'Ascendancy' in Ireland, although enjoying greater security and stability within an expanding British empire, still sensed a double threat: from dissenting Scots immigrants at home and disaffected Catholic emigrants abroad. The flows of emigrants, east and west, during the half-century were more or less evenly balanced. However, this would not turn out to be an enduring feature of the emerging modern Irish diaspora and nothing approaching a similar balance would be witnessed again until the twentieth century.

Immigration

The migrant stream dries up

Estimating the volume of British immigration in this half-century is made more difficult by the steady decline that set in after 1700. However, it is clear that the inflows from Britain started to reduce from about 1700 – first into Munster and last into Ulster. By 1715 the inflow of continental Protestants had also dried up and it was clear that the era of large-scale immigration was over. Some migrants would still head west across the Irish Sea in search of opportunities, but these were now increasingly directed towards Ireland's relatively modest urban network. One exception was John Walker, a distant ancestor of the television entertainer Graham Norton (Walker). Born in 1691, he left the Wentworth estate in Stainsborough, near Barnsley in south Yorkshire, to cross to Ireland in 1713, arriving to take up a lease on the Fitzwilliam estate, founded in Co. Wicklow in the 1630s by Thomas Wentworth (www.bbcwhodoyouthinkyouare.com/stories).

The new pattern of landownership in Ireland was consolidated after the Williamite settlement, with the Catholic share of landed property reduced from 22 per cent in 1688 to 14 per cent in 1703. This meant fewer enticing bargains in the Irish land market after 1700, reducing the power of an important pull factor for both substantial landholders and more modest tenant farmers (Cullen 1981 39–60; Dickson 2000, 117–30). In 1702 Sir Robert Southwell advised Sir John Perceval that 'English tenants are best and safest for you, even at ten in the hundred [ten per cent] cheaper than the Irish'. The problem for Perceval, however, in pursuing the advice of his elder was that such tenants were thin on the ground as Munster, unlike Ulster, received no Williamite reinforcement of British settlers (Dickson 2005, 177). The Scots, who had come to Ireland in such large numbers in the 1690s to acquire land and take up attractive leases, were now more likely to look further west to the American colonies. Furthermore, the severe famine of that decade in Scotland and the heavy excess mortality and emigration that resulted did much to 'take the steam out of Scottish population growth' (Whyte 1995, 124). Similarly, in England and Wales the steady reduction of population growth which had set in about 1650 persisted until around 1730, when population began to grow more strongly again. Nonetheless, the first half of the eighteenth century was the period of most modest emigration from England and Wales, not only to Ireland but across the globe (Wrigley and Schofield 1981, 531–4; Horn 1998b, 30–5). Offering any estimate of British migration to Ireland for this period is precarious but it seems clear that migration per decade was now measurable in thousands rather than tens of thousands, and that a greater proportion was on a temporary rather than permanent basis: Canny, for example, estimates that between 1700 and 1775 roughly 10,000 English migrants arrived in Ireland

(1994, 64). If one includes Welsh and Scottish migrants and those migrating on a temporary rather than permanent basis, this should be taken as a quite conservative estimate.

A tide of dissent

Scottish immigration continued to cause particular tensions in Ulster in the decade 1695–1705. Members of the Established Church, already outnumbered at the end the Williamite war in many areas by Presbyterians, were now faced with the virtual doubling of Presbyterian ministers and congregations (Connolly 1992, 167). The 'pamphlet war' within Protestantism around the turn of the century betokened Anglican fears and growing Presbyterian confidence. One pamphlet of 1697 by Thomas Pullein, Bishop of Dromore, captured the fevered mood well: complaining of the many thousand families of zealous Scots covenanters recently arrived, he suggested that their preachers, like those coming from a country infected with plague, should be compelled to 'perform their quarantine' (Hayton 1976; Fitzgerald 2004, 80). Ulster's natives were no less disturbed by the fresh influx. As late as 1715, Bishop McMahon of Clogher noted that 'Calvinists [Scots Presbyterians] are coming over here daily in large groups of families, occupying the towns and villages, seizing the farms in the richer parts of the country and expelling the natives' (Dunlop 1995, 21). This suggests that somewhat delayed internal 'colonial spread' was underway on the settlement frontier after the strongest pulses of direct immigration from Britain. The sectarian 'sorting out' of south Ulster, begun a century before, was still being played out in competition for farms between natives and newcomers.

'Magpies on the eastern margin of the Irish Sea'

We have only fleeting glimpses of this lower level of British immigration during the first half of the eighteenth century. In his forensic analysis of Irish Protestant society, Toby Barnard illustrates how the state and landed society in Ireland continued to offer positions and patronage disproportionately to those described colourfully as 'magpies on the eastern margin of the Irish Sea' (2003, 146). John Evelyn, son of the famous diarist, along with the English MPs Francis Robartes and Thomas Meddlycott, arrived successively in Dublin during these decades to take up the lucrative position of Revenue Commissioner. Land agents like Richard Musgrave were attracted from the north-west of England to the fertile Blackwater valley in Co. Cork. Another agent known to us only by his surname, Hume, arrived from Yorkshire to work on the Malton estate on the Wicklow/Wexford border in the early 1730s. Education and the professions attracted others. In the opening decade of the century, Daniel Burgess, a former cleric from England, took up the position of head teacher at the Earl of Orrery's endowed school at Charleville, Cork. In 1738 another English minister, Rev. William Preston, was inducted into a handsome living, estimated at an annual £200, in Co. Carlow.

Going west and passing through

Marriage also could lead to migration. A woman from Wales who married into a Co. Roscommon family in the 1730s complained of the backwardness of her new environment and her sense of social isolation – an indication that even by the second quarter of the eighteenth century rural Connacht could still feel, to a recent arrival at least, like the frontier. Perhaps, it was in Connacht that Protestant society felt most isolated and Protestants still clustered geographically in knots of settlement in a predominantly Catholic environment. In 1749 a census of the diocese of Elphin (stretching from Sligo to Athlone) revealed that just under a tenth (9.7 per cent) of the population was Protestant, mostly Anglican but with some Presbyterians and a small body of Quakers (Legg 2004, xiv).

Opportunities for apprenticeship and training also attracted immigrants. In 1719, Walter Burton, an officer in Chancery in Dublin, agreed to take on a youth from Wales; and a decade earlier James Reynolds, a Dublin butcher, had contracted to take on a butcher's son from Merionethshire. Such apprenticeships were probably most common in trades that involved the processing and use of agricultural produce, such as those of the butcher and shoemaker. Military migration also continued. We know that some officers with roots in England, like Samuel Bagshawe and Adolphus Oughton, settled more or less permanently after their period of service in Ireland. Many more, however, stayed for a few months or years only, adding little as they sojourned, and taking little as they departed, passing 'like shooting stars across the Irish sky, only to embed themselves in British soil' (Barnard 2003, 75, 86, 106, 119, 163–4, 192, 222, 231–2, 308, 309).

Imported skills for a building boom

The growing desire of those within Irish landed society to display their wealth and cosmopolitan tastes created new employment and patronage opportunities for specialist craftsmen and artists from beyond Ireland's shores. The engravers Giles King and Andrew Miller and painters Peter Lens, John Simpson, Benjamin Wilson and James Worsdale crossed the Irish Sea in this period attracted by the promise of work, mainly in Dublin. Others came from further afield. James Mannin, a French-born landscape painter, was working in Dublin by the 1740s; Johann Van der Hagen, an artist born in the Hague, was in Dublin by 1720; Isaac Vogelsang, a landscape and livestock painter, born in 1688 in Amsterdam, also spent a period working in Ireland before his death in London in 1763 (Strickland 1989, I, 580; II, 17, 100, 109, 354, 473, 491, 544, 563). Outside Dublin, the fashion, sometimes passion, for establishing Irish country estate houses also offered opportunities for skilled craftsmen and artists from abroad.

Looking to Protestant Europe

While the opening decades of the new century saw a marked decline in the volume of immigration from Britain, immigration from continental Europe remained significant until about 1715. The later seventeenth century, as we have seen, saw a deliberate effort by the government to promote settlement by French Protestant Huguenot refugees (Caldicott, Gough and Pittion 1987). Even during the final decade of the seventeenth century there had been a growing awareness in Ireland of the significance of continuing Protestant immigration in the face of declining migration from England and the unimpressive progress of the Irish Reformation. An official memorandum of 1694 had concluded that 'it is only by such that the kingdom can be made secure and profitable to England, by balancing the numbers of the Irish, for England can't spare many to plant in Ireland'. London's governing elite was becoming increasingly aware of the potential of Britain's new world empire and its call on Britannia's children (PRONI T3222/1/10; Connolly 1992, 302; Richards 2004, 67–90). In the government's eyes, especially those of Whig administrations, foreign Protestants had gone from being a supplement to the immigration of British Protestants to being a virtual replacement. Such immigrants were also perceived as a positive influence within the host society, especially as entrepreneurs and developers of new technology. Thus, government encouragement and royal patronage helped with the step-migration of Louis Crommelin, a Huguenot refugee engaged in the linen business, first in his native Picardy and later in Holland. He was finally enticed to set up business near Lisburn, Antrim. By 1701, with a workforce of some 70 Huguenots, Crommelin had established the first large-scale bleaching establishment in Ireland at Hilden, and four years later offered wider encouragement to the fledgling industry by publishing *An Essay Towards the Improving of the Hempen and Linen Manufactures in the Kingdom of Ireland* (Collins 1994, 11–13; Best 1997, 21–5; Mackey 2003, 99–122).

Immigrants and entrepreneurs

At the same time, other Huguenot refugees were being attracted to developing estate villages where textile production was taking place, the foremost example being Portarlington in Queen's county (Laois), where the chief patron was Henri de Ruvigny, Earl of Galway, himself a French Protestant immigrant. He encouraged refugees to settle in a village where many of the veterans of the Huguenot regiments during the Williamite war had established themselves as pioneer migrants (Powell 1994, 43–9; Hylton 1999, 415–35). The largest Huguenot community in Ireland, and the centre to which most new immigrants were attracted, was Dublin itself. By 1710 Huguenots made up as much as 5 per cent of the city's population and expressed their distinctive identity through their churches and charities (Dickson 2000, 48; Barnard 2001, 205). While some conformed to Anglicanism, most preferred to remain committed to the more Calvinistic doctrines and practices they had adhered to in France. The need to attract and retain such immigrants was felt so strongly that those who persisted with their nonconformity were permitted a greater degree of licence by the church and state than other Protestant dissenters, though this did little to promote harmony within the Huguenot community in Dublin, which,like that of Ulster's Presbyterians, showed a propensity for disputation and schism (Forrest 1995, 96–110).

Rhineland to Rathkeale

The most prominent example of direct government intervention in the peopling process came with the appointment in 1709 of a commission to oversee the settlement in Ireland of Protestant refugees escaping persecution, hunger and warfare in the south Rhineland region of the Palatinate (Kurpfalz, later Bayern-Pfalz). In the same year some 800 families arrived and were intended to be settled on the estates of 43 Irish landlords. The scheme, however, ran into difficulties and by 1713 only 260 families remained in the country, the majority having made their way back to England. Those who did remain were mainly poor peasants, concentrated in Cos Limerick and Kerry, who conformed to the Church of Ireland but retained for generations a separate linguistic and cultural identity, and were not universally accepted by their neighbours. Aware that other refugees from the German Palatinate had emigrated to North America, some of those in Ireland reacted to increasing rents, particularly in the late 1750s, by following them across the Atlantic. A further phase of Palatine emigration from Ireland during the 1820s and 1830s reflected the limited opportunities for betterment in rural Ireland and an atmosphere of competition and tension with the local community. By the mid-nineteenth century most vestiges of distinctive Palatinate settlements in Ireland had disappeared as a consequence of both onward migration and assimilation, although their heritage is still cherished by the Palatine Museum in Rathkeale, Limerick. The Palatines, not unlike the Scots migrants of the 1690s, exchanged, within a couple of generations, the role of immigrants to Ireland for that of transatlantic emigrants from it. Not unlike the Jewish minority in Ireland in the twentieth century, as we shall see later, the Palatines were able to reconnect within their own diaspora and enjoy the benefits of more consolidated settlement elsewhere (Hempton 1988, 155–8, 166–7; O'Connor 1989).

Internal migration

A developing urban network

Between 1700 and 1750 the proportion of Ireland's population living in towns of over 10,000 inhabitants continued growing steadily, from about 5 to 7 per cent (Whyte 1995, 16). Much of the growth was in Dublin, which doubled in size from 60,000 to 120,000 (Sheridan 2001, 68). Similarly, Cork doubled from under 20,000 to 41,000 (O'Flanagan et al. 2005, 160). The lesser but still substantial growth of market towns and estate villages during this period also indicates rural–urban migration. Given the reduction in immigration from Britain, this migration into the towns must have come mainly from the surrounding countryside (Cullen 1986a, 181–4; Crawford 2002, 97–120; Hood 2003, 139–58).

The capital and its hinterland

Dublin mirrored the position of London in Britain, without dominating the urban hierarchy to the same extent. While Dublin attracted migrants from all over the island, the fact that population growth and house construction was least rapid in rural Leinster suggests that Dublin drew particularly heavily on the 'Pale', at this stage the area within about a 30-mile radius of the city (Dickson 1983, 188). As Dublin's commercial, political, administrative and cultural dominance increased after 1700, the city offered a widening range of opportunities for both urban and rural migrants from the provinces. Much of the linen manufactured in Ulster made its way south to Dublin to be sold or exported, strengthening the routes of communication that migrants might follow (Dickson 1983, 183). Servicing the growing demands of the capital's population and particularly its elite created employment opportunities, but Dublin was also evolving as a location for manufacturing. By mid-century thousands gained an often precarious livelihood in the production of textiles, weaving silk, wool and linen. The Smithfield St. Paul's area of the city, north of the Liffey, although designed to meet the demand from higher-status citizens to be housed in extramural suburbs, developed in a different direction as the better-off opted for rival developments like that on St. Stephen's Green. The backyards of Smithfield's properties came to house industrial enterprises, while the warehouses and alehouses lent the district an air very different from the original intention of the designers (Twomey 2005, 14, 24). So a particularly strong link developed between Dublin and its rural hinterland, and the growing familiarity with the capital that came with the increased frequency of coming and going served to ease the path of migrants.

The road to Dublin and beyond

Records relating to later emigrants can sometimes serve to throw light on previous movements within Ireland. Jane McDaniel, aged about 30 in 1700, gave testimony before the Consistory Court of the Bishop of London that she had been born at New Towne (Newtownards) in Co. Down. When she was about 22 years of age she had gone to Dublin, where she had gained employment as a servant with an upholsterer in Capel Street, then worked at a public house called the 'Indian Queen' on Essex Bridge (later Grattan Bridge, between Parliament

Street and Capel Street), before gaining a position with Mr Dugan, a tailor in Michael's Lane in the city (Bennett 2005, 33, 25). On marriage to a tailor called Arthur, she and her husband left for London (Earle 1994, 192). McDaniel's step-migration, from Newtownards to London via Dublin, is probably representative of thousands of those who came to Dublin from elsewhere in Ireland. In 1695 about 17 per cent of the city's population were servants: 7 per cent male and 10 per cent female, foreshadowing a gender imbalance that would be just as evident in the nineteenth century. We know that in contemporary Britain servants were highly mobile and that during the later seventeenth and early eighteenth centuries the majority were female (Fagan 1998, 22; Whyte 2000, 75, 80; O'Dowd 2005, 133–43). As well as this, McDaniel's migration story is representative in the sense that initial migration from country or smaller town to capital city was often a step to migration overseas. Dublin, like other growing cities, was acting as a revolving door, tempting migrants in and sending others out simultaneously.

The hungry tramp to the ports

As far as we can tell, McDaniel's migration story – taking her to a place where there were greater chances of employment and marriage – is one of 'betterment'. Others, as ever, arrived as subsistence migrants, especially in years of failed harvests, concerned only with survival. The deep-rooted structural weakness of the Irish economy was reflected in the frequency with which serious food shortages occurred and threatened life on a very substantial scale. In this half-century there were two major famines – in 1727–30 and 1739–41 – which set off subsistence migration right across Ireland. Even in Ulster, where the linen trade was beginning to strengthen the regional economy, failed harvests took their toll. Primate Boulter, who travelled on visitation through Ulster in 1727, reported that thousands of families had deserted their homes in search of food and many streamed south towards Dublin, already thronged with hungry residents and migrants (Kelly 1992a, 78–9, 92). In mid-June 1740, at the other end of the island, it was reported that the streets of Cork city 'were so covered with beggars that there is no passing for them' (Bardon 1992, 175; Dickson 1997, 26). Following the famine of 1728–9, Arthur Dobbs, in his essay on *The Trade of Ireland* (1731), expressed alarm at what he saw as the abnormally high level of subsistence migration. Cullen has suggested that short-term fluctuations in the hearth money taxation returns – for example, a drop in the early 1740s of almost a third in Kerry and Sligo – reflect population mobility more than excess mortality (Cullen 1981, 90–1). Bearing in mind that a consequence of the 1740–1 famine was a fall in population of between 10 and 15 per cent (as drastic as the decline of the 1640s), the impact on migration, both internal and external, must have been considerable, comparable with both Scotland in the 1690s and Ireland in the late 1840s (Smyth 2006, 384).

The continuing absence of any statutory, national system of poor relief exacerbated the tendency for those at the margin of subsistence to respond rapidly to crisis by migrating. Newly arrived in Dublin, they tended to congregate round the port where ships importing foodstuffs were most likely to dock and discharge their cargoes. They also added to the number of makeshift dwellings erected along the arterial routes on the outskirts of the city. By the 1670s, more inhabitants were living beyond than within the city walls, and the extent of the suburban ribbon development spreading out from the city centre is shown clearly in Brooking's map of 1728, and even more extensively in Rocque's map of 1756 (Sheridan 2001, 66–158; Cullen 1992, 252–77). At the same time as subsistence migrants were being pushed by hunger to the city, betterment migrants, pushed more by ambition, were being pulled to it by the numerous positions left vacant at all social levels by excess mortality during the famine of 1740–1: this is clear from the stark fact that there was no significant decline or growth in Dublin's population (Dickson 1983, 178).

The changing face of urban Ireland

An effect of the overall growth of Dublin's population from internal migration was a change in its religious profile. In 1700 it was about two-thirds Protestant. As the influx of immigrants from Britain, almost exclusively Protestants, dried up, the continuing flow into the city from the rest of Ireland, which was predominantly Catholic, tipped the balance, so that by 1750 numbers of Protestants and Catholics were roughly equal. As the Catholic component of the population grew steadily during these decades, it was increasingly the case that 'communities of people of the same religion, social status and employment' began to 'congregate in distinct areas of the city' (Kelly 2005, 14). In Munster, where the flow of fresh immigration had already dried up by 1700, a similar trend was underway in Limerick, Cork and Waterford, which had their Irish-speaking populations replenished regularly with new arrivals from their rural hinterlands (Smyth, 2006, 414).

Chains of connection with the countryside

Up to the 1740s in Dublin, suburban development was mainly in the west and north and we have some evidence that in-migrants tended to cluster, according to their province and even county of origin, along the arterial route that led into the city from 'home' in the north, west or south. Barnard has identified a particularly strong presence of gentlemen and clergy from Ulster in the north-side parish of St Michan's. It is likely that settlement lower down the social scale followed the same kind of pattern and that, for example, the clientele of some alehouses reflected a common rural origin. This pattern of what might be called a regional diaspora presence in the city, sustained by chain migration internally, has been observed in relation to such premises in eighteenth-century English cities (Clark 1983; Barnard 2003, 241).

Seasonal agricultural labourers

Seasonal migration by agricultural labourers is also evident in this period, although similarly difficult to quantify. Such movement within Ireland almost certainly existed before 1700 (Quinn 1966; O'Dowd A. 1991, 1–8). Most likely to occur where a zone of poorer land and excess labour was close to a relatively rich agricultural zone, we have early evidence in Gaelic poetry of seasonal migration from the uplands of south Armagh and north Monaghan to the fertile lowlands of Co. Meath (Ó Fiaich 1971, 80–129). During the 1720s and 1730s this type of migration seems to have expanded fairly rapidly and by the 1740s a larger-scale movement from Connacht to Leinster was detectable (Cullen 1986a, 169–70).

Southern Ulster colonies

Just as the government and Irish landowners were keen to encourage the settlement of Protestants from abroad who were deemed to be industrious and progressive, individual landowners were occasionally inclined to sponsor internal migration of tenants whom they perceived to possess similar qualities. In 1736, for example, Sir Maurice Crosby developed plans to 'establish a colony of northerners' in Co. Kerry; and elsewhere in Munster similar projects were attempted to bring proto-industrial Protestants south from their Ulster stronghold. In the following decade, agents on the Temple estate in Co. Sligo and on the Smythe estate in Westmeath were making efforts to entice skilled Ulster Protestants south with the promise of looms, spinning wheels and even livestock. Ultimately, the numbers involved in this type of sponsored migration did not prove great, but the attempt itself demonstrates the high reputation which Protestant tenants continued to enjoy among landowners across the island well into the eighteenth century (Barnard 2003, 247; Dickson, 2005, 177, 204–5).

Emigration

Old and new world migrations

The claim has often been made, especially by historians working in North America, that the era of emigration from Ireland effectively began with the surge in emigration by Ulster Presbyterians in the years around 1718 (Jones 1960, 22–3; Daniels 1991, 77–8). However, as we have seen, emigration to continental Europe throughout the previous century had been very substantial, and after 1650 there had also been significant emigration to the Caribbean. Overall, the rate of emigration in relation to population remained as low during this half-century as it had been during the seventeenth century (see Figures 1 and 2).

How many crossed the Atlantic?

What happened was that while the flow eastward to Britain and Europe was sustained, migration west across the Atlantic accelerated significantly, with a gradual shift away from the islands of the Caribbean towards the mainland American colonies. The scale of this emigration has been a point of contention for some time. As for earlier periods, which have not attracted such controversy, the absence of passenger lists and the partial survival of port records mean that the actual total of emigrants is irrecoverable, but there has been extended debate about estimating the total – an indication of the perceived importance of the issue. Not surprisingly, estimates of the number of emigrants from Ireland to North America between 1700 and the outbreak of the American Revolutionary War in 1775 spread over a broad range. The most specialised work on the subject up to the 1960s was by R. J. Dickson, who put emigration from Ulster alone at 120,000 (1966, 19–81). Later, Kerby Miller put total emigration from Ireland in the period at between 250,000 and 400,000 (1985, 137). This was broadly in line with previous estimates of emigration from Ulster alone as presented in the American literature (Hansen 1940, 41; Leyburn 1962, 179–83). It was also in line with the assumptions about volume made by those who had undertaken research in Ireland as well as in America (Lockhart 1975; Doyle 1981, 52). Then Graeme Kirkham, pushing back in time, demonstrated that emigration from Ulster between 1680 and 1720 had been significantly greater than previously acknowledged and further suggested that Dickson's estimate (120,000) was low (Kirkham 1988, xv–xvi; 1997, 76–118). However, at about the same time, Marianne Wokeck was working on a detailed analysis of the port records of colonial Philadelphia and the other Delaware ports, where most Irish and German immigrants entered the American colonies. Having found that no more than 52,695 emigrants from Ireland passed through these ports between 1729 and 1774, she proposed a downward revision of Dickson's estimate (Wokeck 1989, 141; 1999, 167–219).

While Miller's estimate (250,000–400,000) represents the maximum of the range, Cullen's represents the minimum: 65,000 (1994, 140). The argument for revising Dickson's estimate downward was based on a major criticism of his method: that while using the information provided in contemporary shipping advertisements to calculate the ratio of passengers to registered tonnage of vessels carrying emigrants, he had failed to take into account that such advertisements routinely exaggerated the tonnage of vessels. However, the most recent contribution to the debate concludes that 'Dickson's high-end figures are far too low and that Ulster emigration before 1776 may have ranged up to 250,000 or more' (Miller and Kennedy 2003, 656–9). As in earlier periods, with little prospect of the available evidence yielding greater precision, we may at least proceed confidently with this indicative range for the total numbers emigrating from Ireland to North America between 1700 and 1775: 100,000–250,000.

Emigration from four provinces

There is also debate about the relative importance of emigration from Ulster compared with the rest of the island. One estimate, at the lower end of the range, is that between 1700 and 1775 emigration from Ulster was 66,100 and from the rest of the island 42,500; and furthermore that between 1700 and 1750 emigration from Ulster was 17,500, significantly smaller in gross terms than the 22,000 from the rest of Ireland (Fogelman 1992, 698; adapted by Horn 1998b, 32). Another estimate, however, suggests that emigration from Ulster in the same period was marginally greater than from the rest of Ireland (Wokeck 1999, 167–219). Whatever is the case about emigration between 1700 and 1750, there is consensus about what was happening between 1750 and the outbreak of the Revolutionary War in 1775. These were particularly busy years when the flow from Ulster was significantly greater than that from the rest of the island. Totalling between 40,000 and 80,000, the outflow from Ulster in these 25 years accounted for between a quarter and a third of the total number of transatlantic migrants between 1700 and 1775 (Wokeck 1999, 167–219).

Continuity with migration to the east

The development of this major migration stream across the Atlantic did not result in a corresponding reduction of migration from Ireland east to Britain and continental Europe. Indeed, this was the half-century when the emigration flows east and west came closest to equilibrium, which in itself suggests that new pools of potential outward migrants were emerging. Smyth describes the establishment of 'a commercialising pastoral monoculture' by which broad swathes of the island's interior witnessed the impoverishment and marginalisation of former rural dwellers who were forced to make way for sheep and cattle. The cleared woodlands made way for the grazier economy and not unlike the post-Famine decades of the nineteenth century, the 'hewers of wood and drawers of water' were left to go under or go abroad (Smyth 2006, 455). Military migration to service in the armies of continental European powers, which had been the central dynamic behind Irish emigration in the previous century, continued to exercise significant influence during the first half of the eighteenth century. Cullen suggests that it remained numerically the most significant stream and that it was actually greater than it had been during the seventeenth century. During these five decades something like 35,000 Irish soldiers entered the service of European armies and navies, and this recruitment relates only to rank-and-file personnel: many thousands more went to the continent to seek positions as officers. Furthermore, migration for other reasons – professional, educational and commercial – all continued to be important in drawing hundreds of migrants, almost exclusively from Catholic Ireland, to Europe every year (Cullen 1994, 140).

War and peace

The significance of the diasporic Irish Catholic community in Europe in influencing contemporary politics in Ireland and sustaining Irish Jacobitism in particular has been illustrated by Ó Ciardha, who reminds us of the intricate recruiting networks which linked the continental powers with Ireland. Along with trading and privateering networks, these gave substance to the idea of a community abroad linking exiles in ports such as Calais, St Malo, Bilbao, Genoa and Leghorn (Ó Ciardha 2002, 35–6, 376). Ironically, it was during periods of demobilisation that the linkages of the exiled Irish were most clearly revealed. Following the Treaty of Ryswick in 1697, the French were obliged to reduce their armed forces significantly and for the large numbers of Irish they employed, especially given the unwelcoming condition of Ireland after the Williamite war, this spelt disaster. Redundant soldiers and their dependants fell into poverty, swelling the numbers of vagrants and criminals in rural France. Some of those who found themselves in this position turned to piracy; others used their network of contacts to gain employment in the Spanish military or even took the option of crossing the Atlantic (Bracken 2001, 127–42).

In spite of defeat, there was a persistent sense of expectation by Jacobite sympathisers that the Protestant interest in Ireland could yet be overturned by a turn in the military fortunes of Britain's rivals. Much of the Gaelic poetry of the period reflects this sense of yearning in exile for return (Ó Buachalla 1996). As Smyth reminds us, 'Catholic Irish exiles played a key role in the new national awareness' which 'synthesized Tridentine Catholicism, loyalty to Gaelic and gaelicized cultural norms and a consciousness of the territorial integrity of the island' (2006, 452). For their part, Protestants gave regular expression to their fear of the threat posed to their ascendancy by Irishmen serving in foreign armies. The London-born and Oxford-educated Hugh Boulter, Archbishop of Armagh (1724–42), claimed in May 1726 that numbers of lusty young fellows were quitting the country on the pretence that they were going to England for work (Ó Ciardha 2002, 33).

To Europe through Britain

The choice for migrants was not simply between going to Britain or to the continent. As in the previous century, there was step-migration through Britain and on to continental destinations. Continuing cross-Channel links have been demonstrated by Linebaugh in his analysis of those hanged at Tyburn in London. During the eighteenth century, 171 Irish men and women were executed there, of whom 8 per cent had been soldiers. Many ended up in London after service on the continent and, with their experience of firearms, many appear to have become highwaymen or robbers in or about the capital – London versions of the tories and rapparees of Ireland. Particularly prominent in the opening decades of the century, they were still making their presence felt about

1750. In November of that year, Thomas Reynolds, Irish-born and with a record of service in Flanders, was arrested in London while recruiting men for the Irish brigade in the French army – indicating a substantial Irish presence in Britain, particularly in the capital (Linebaugh 1991, 297–300). New online access to records of Old Bailey proceedings between 1674 and 1834, based on ethnicity, provides an additional and rich resource for reconstructing the migration stories of many of those who followed this path (www.oldbaileyonline.org).

Training abroad

Between 1700 and 1750 something like 12,500 Irish migrants moved to Britain, including some 5,000 from the professions; 5,000 skilled, semi-skilled workers and seasonal labourers who failed to return; and 2,500 recruits for the British and imperial service (Cullen 1994, 140). Ethnic patronage networks were already connecting those Irish migrants in the legal and mercantile world of London with the emerging overseas empire (Bailey 2007). Britain offered Protestants alternative opportunities for education and professional training that proved popular: for example, in the early eighteenth century nearly one in ten of entrants to the Inns of Court in London came from Ireland. Ulster Presbyterians, for whom there was still no alternative in Ireland, continued heading mainly for the universities of Glasgow and Edinburgh. Catholics, for whom also there was no alternative in Ireland, headed mainly for the Irish colleges on the continent. Catholics and Protestants were to be found together receiving medical training in the Dutch university of Leiden (Barnard 2003, 121, 129).

Nascent imperial opportunities

For Irish Protestants in particular, the growth of the first British empire and what has been referred to as the 'fiscal-military state' opened up new avenues for advancement (Brewer 1989; Bartlett 2004, 61–90) The rise of Arthur Dobbs, a major landowner in south Antrim, to become Governor of North Carolina in the early 1750s was one such individual, but we should remember that there were already significant opportunities in the distant east as well as in the west (Clarke 1957). By the later 1730s Ulster Protestants were already influential in the East India Company, with three wealthy nabobs able to trace their roots back to Derry. This migrant pathway was one which would also expand in the century ahead (Barnard 2003, 202–3; Hewson 2004). From lower down the social scale there was substantial recruitment in Ireland into regiments of the British army garrisoned there. Stationed throughout Britain and its empire, these regiments took many Irish men and women with them.

Dublin, Cork and London

A change in the pattern of subsistence migration to Britain is detectable in this half-century. In earlier crises, such as those of the late 1620s and early

1650s, the dominant flow had been from the Munster ports to those of the Severn estuary and then onwards to London. By 1750 there had been a shift and the dominant flow was now between Dublin and the north-west of England, so that greater numbers of Irish were now tramping their way south-east, through the English midlands, towards London. With Holyhead a very minor port at this time, Parkgate, replacing silted-up Chester, served as the main port of arrival from Dublin. From the 1690s, the port records of travellers passing through, and also those of the Cheshire county Quarter Sessions, note the problems caused by impoverished Irish arrivals, many of whom were intent on gaining seasonal agricultural work. The increase in vagrant 'passes' issued to such migrants in Cheshire and Buckinghamshire illustrate this northward shift and the growing importance of the Dublin/Parkgate/London axis (Place 1994, 172–91; Fitzgerald 1997, 101–22). Temporary seasonal migration was clearly a key component of this flow, but as with all such migration there were those who did not, for a variety of reasons, return to Ireland. As well as these unexpected non-returnees, there were others who went with the aim of obtaining other kinds of employment and of settling permanently. We see this indicated in 1724 by the order of the Tin Plate Workers Company in London that its members should stop taking on unskilled Irishmen (Ebbenwhite 1896, 26). A decade later in 1736, low-wage Irish labourers in the city caused more violent reaction: there were serious riots when local workers expressed their frustration at the presence of Irish building workers, perceived to be undercutting agreed wage rates. The subsequent inquiry found also that master weavers in the Spitalfields and Shoreditch districts had been taking on increasing numbers of Irish workers (Rudé 1959, 53–62). The mobility of such Irish labour was impressive. In May 1741 in London, Andrew MacManus explained to the chaplain of Newgate gaol how he had been driven by curiosity to leave Dublin for England. As a journeyman thread-dyer he had walked (probably from Parkgate) to Manchester, where he gained work for about six months, before walking on to Staffordshire and ultimately to London (Earle 1994, 52). Internal migrants kept flowing into Dublin and it is likely that many of them, having become seasoned to urban life in the second largest city in the British Isles, felt a particular draw towards the largest, London. It seems clear that across the social spectrum connecting chains between the two were being developed (Clark and Gillespie 2001).

Seditious ideas in motion

While McManus's move to London shortly before 1741 may well have been motivated by curiosity, it is quite possible his decision to leave – like that of many others – was influenced by the serious famine that set in after 1739. At the same time the threat of a Jacobite rising was increasing and observers in England were becoming more sensitive to the Irish presence. In October 1745, for example, Charles Cavendish reported to a friend his concern about the numbers of Irish who had been coming to London recently, especially those he had encountered on the road from Hertfordshire on his way in to the north of the city. Rumours of a Jacobite conspiracy were rife and among those with surnames of Irish origin questioned by the authorities was a shoemaker, Patrick Rice (Rogers 1975, 5–27). Only four years before, at the height of the famine in Ireland, there had been a similar threat to imperial order on the other side of the Atlantic. At Hughson's tavern on the New York waterfront, conspirators from many backgrounds had gathered to plot the destruction of the Fort George garrison on St Patrick's Day 1741. Between 30 and 35 Irish persons were involved, including Daniel Fagan, Jerry Corker, John Coffin, William Kane and Edward Murphy (Linebaugh and Rediker 2000, 174–88). So we glimpse the outworking of emigration, forced and otherwise: disaffection abroad and fear at home.

Conclusion

Until relatively recently historians have tended to consider the first half of the eighteenth century in Ireland as a comparatively quiet period – a lull between the political violence of the seventeenth century and that of the later eighteenth century, which climaxed in the 1798 Rebellion. Similarly, traditional tellers of Ireland's story, preoccupied with political conflict, have found no 'memorable dates' between 1700 and 1750. However, recent research, focused on the prevailing and countervailing currents of economy and society, has revealed a period of contrasts: domestic peace and growth in certain areas, but also fragility and tension coming to a head in the Jacobite Risings of 1715 and 1745, and in actual famines in 1728–9 and 1740–1. Looking back from the vantage point of 1750, we see 1728–9 and 1740–1 as 'memorable dates' when migrants were driven by want towards the towns, across the Irish Sea and further overseas. Unlike Britain, but not unlike many other parts of Europe, Ireland had yet to break free of crisis-driven excess mortality and the imperative to move in order to survive. However, recovery from the famine of 1740–1 was fairly rapid. By 1750 early signs were apparent of the great expansion in trade, rural commercialisation, population and emigration that was to come.

8
Irish Migration, 1750–1800

Ireland's dramatic population growth took off in these decades, but migration was not the main factor driving it. Paradoxically, the increase took place in spite of net emigration. The immigration flows from Britain and Europe were so reduced that the Protestant community was scarcely able to sustain itself, with southern landowners in search of new Protestant tenants instead looking north to Ulster. The main internal migration flow from the countryside to Ireland's towns and cities was less strong than elsewhere in north-west Europe and less crisis-driven in character than it had been before 1750. However, the population was far from static, especially in the turbulent 1790s. Fundamental changes in the emigration flow got underway in the aftermath of the Seven Years War (1756–63) and *before* the American War of Independence (1775–82), arguably making the former rather than the latter the major division of the century. After 1763, the importance of Britain and North America as emigrant destinations increased as that of Europe declined. The 'modern' practice of prior payment for transatlantic passage started to replace the 'early modern' practice of indentured servitude, especially in Ulster, and increasingly emigrants responded to the strengthening force of opportunities in the new world rather than to problems in the old. Transition to a pattern of emigration which was essentially 'modern' was underway, although it would be a further generation until the phenomenon could be properly described as mass emigration.

Immigration

Demographic dynamism

Ireland's demographic regime in the later eighteenth century sets it apart from the rest of Europe. It took well over 100 years – between 1700 and 1835 – for the population of Europe as a whole to double; whereas it took only 50 years (1750–1800) for that of Ireland to double, from about 2.3 to 4.6 million (Livi Bacci 1999, 11). What drove such a dramatic increase has been the subject of debate, similar in vigour to that about the scale of emigration to North America in the first half of the century. However, one factor emphatically rejected as a significant contributor is immigration (Clarkson 1993, 172–8; Macafee 2005, 69–88). So we have the paradox (most evident in Ulster) of a country of net emigration (though still on a relatively modest scale) sustaining simultaneously a highly dynamic annual population growth rate of 1.5 per cent or more, which is almost without parallel across the regions of Europe. The flow of immigration from Britain – reduced so dramatically by 1715 – remained a trickle. There was less incentive to emigrate from Britain where, even though the pace of population growth was quickening, the industrialising towns and expanding military needed most of the rural–urban migrants they could get; and for those in Britain who did consider emigration, North America and the developing overseas colonies were now much more attractive than Ireland. The frontiers of settlement and opportunity had moved from across the Irish Sea to beyond the oceans (Whyte 2000, 119–23; Richards 2004, 67–90).

Protestant interest and the British diaspora in Ireland

Although less than 10,000 immigrants are thought to have arrived in Ireland from England between 1700 and 1775, this did not mean, as noted in the previous chapter, that Ireland's British 'colony' was isolated from its homeland. The Protestant Ascendancy, as it was increasingly referred to, had accommodated in one way or another the large majority of those who had migrated from Britain. Barnard's dissection of the mid-century Irish Protestant population of about 400,000 (about 17 per cent of the total) offers some insight into the opportunities open to them in the colonial infrastructure, although the fragmentary nature of the evidence means that about 90 per cent of them remain hidden from us (Barnard 2003, 326). Those who came to Ireland to occupy a niche in the church or state, like the London-born Archbishop of Armagh Hugh Boulter mentioned in the previous chapter, had little guarantee of a warm reception as already settled Irish Protestants, equally hungry for preferment, were prone to see them as interlopers and rivals. In practice, the generally meagre livings of the Church of Ireland (as Dean Swift had found them earlier in the century) attracted few external candidates, but anger could be directed at outsiders who were frequently appointed, on substantial incomes, to the bench of bishops: in 1800 nine of the 22 were of English or Scottish origin (Barnard, 2003, 98–9; McDowell 1979, 164). Similarly, Scottish-born Presbyterian ministers saw employment opportunities in Ireland, in Ulster in particular, which occasionally meant competition with Irish-born ministers, educated like them at the universities of Glasgow and Edinburgh.

'… shuffling the pack of soldiers'

The military establishment in Ireland undoubtedly accounted for much more migration than the established and dissenting churches. A network of barracks was extended across the island from the 1690s and the economic spin-off for garrison towns and their traders was significant. Between the military and the locals there was a good deal of social interaction, including partnerships and marriages which might result in the settlement of some of British origin in Ireland. Militating against this, however, was what has been called 'the frequent shuffling of the pack of soldiers' as officers and men shifted back and forth across the Irish Sea (Barnard 2003, 206). In some cases a tour of duty in Ireland might lead to a more extended residence. Samuel Bagshawe, from Derbyshire, arrived in Ireland in the 1740s in the train of the new Lord Lieutenant, the Duke of Devonshire. As a colonel – on what he no doubt considered an insufficient salary of £230 – he moved between the worlds of Dublin Castle and the barracks of provincial towns such as Bandon and Limerick, eventually marrying the daughter of a substantial Fermanagh landowner, settling down and getting himself elected in 1761 to the Irish House of Commons. That Bagshawe's trajectory was rare is reinforced by the suggestion that he had 'stayed in Ireland longer than he had expected or wanted'. Now that the lure of land and timber was gone, we find few parallels to the servitors who emerged from the Nine Years War, like Sir Toby Caulfield, to underpin the establishment of Plantation society. The vast majority of Bagshawe's fellow officers 'passed like shooting stars across the Irish sky only to embed themselves in British soil' (Barnard 2003, 186–7, 192).

Servicing the Ascendancy

There were other niches in Irish colonial society open to British migrants. A range of offices in the administrative network centred on Dublin Castle needed staffing, as well as the professions, so there was 'an impressive stream of immigration from Britain into business in the Irish cities, especially Dublin' (Cullen 1981, 127). Trinity College continued to draw in a small number of students from 'across the water', mainly from the Irish Sea fringe. Landlords, both resident and absentee, required agents and often preferred to recruit from Britain, as is the case of Lord Kingsborough, who in 1777 appointed Arthur Young as agent on his massive Mitchelstown estate in Co. Cork (Young 1970, I, 458). The issue of absentee landowners, which became increasingly contentious in the later eighteenth century, itself illustrates the migration of some at least within landed society: as larger landowners moved between their residences on either side of the Irish Sea, so might their domestic servants move with them (Malcolmson 1974, 15–35; Barnard 2003, 211–16; Dickson 2005, 98–103). Irish landowners as patrons of the arts also provided openings, as Strickland's classic reference work on Irish artists shows: British-born artists working in Ireland in this period include William Ashford (Birmingham), who arrived in Dublin in 1764 and was buried in Donnybrook churchyard 60 years later; Samuel Collins (Bristol) worked as a miniaturist in Bath before financial difficulties forced him to cross to Dublin in 1762; Horace Hone (London) lived and worked in Dublin 1782–1802; Faithful Pack (Norwich), the son of a Quaker, worked as portrait and landscape painter in Dublin 1787–1821, before retiring to London; Thomas Snagg (London) was attracted to Dublin by the theatre in 1770 and continued to paint there as an amateur until his death in 1812; James Tassie (Glasgow), a stonemason, modeller and sculptor, arrived in Dublin in 1763, stayed several years and then moved on to London; and Francis Wheatley (London), one of the greatest artists of later eighteenth-century Irish life, alternated between Dublin and London until his death in 1801 (Strickland 1989, vol. I, 7, 190, 509; vol. II, 209–13, 393–7, 422–7, 519–27). This indicates how Dublin in particular, as the second city of the empire, attracted those in search of a career opening or relaunch, but there is little doubt that the flow of ambitious migrants was greater out than in.

Scots investors

The Scots in the later eighteenth century, even more than in the seventeenth, were drawn to Ireland by commerce and opportunities in the skilled labour market. Although concentrated in the north, they were not restricted to Ulster. Around mid-century, for example, John Damer, busy overseeing the construction of Damer Court at Shronell near Tipperary town, imported up to 60 skilled and specialist workmen directly from Scotland. Many moved on when the project was completed, a few taking a local bride with them, but some remained in Tipperary on the estate (Butler 2006, 169). Damer was by no means alone in seeking skilled labour beyond Ireland for such building that was underway throughout the Irish countryside. Those completing the Grand Tour sometimes brought back more than just aesthetic inspiration. In addition, what has been described as 'a stream of Scottish traders' began operating out of Cork city from the 1760s, highlighting a more general movement of Scots into the Irish wholesale trade and industry during the later eighteenth century (Dickson 2005, 161; Cullen 1981, 127).

We are fortunate to have at least one detailed account of the career of a Scots mercantile migrant to Ireland during this half-century. John Anderson was born about 1747 in Galloway, about 12 miles south-west of Dumfries in the small coastal village of Portling. His surviving narrative of step-migration stresses familiar themes, detailing the crucial role of education in his rise from humble origins to business success, first in Glasgow, where he settled, traded and married in the early 1770s. In 1780, at the height of the American War of Independence, he crossed to Cork city and took full advantage of the opportunities in the buoyant provisioning trade, setting himself up as an export merchant. A decade later, with the profits of trade and loans, he acquired an estate near the garrison town of Fermoy, 22 miles north-east of Cork city. Over the course of the next generation, until his bankruptcy and death in 1820, Anderson epitomised the spirit of the improving entrepreneur, eager to realise the full economic potential of his new country and to leave a lasting impression on the landscape of his adopted home (Brunicardi 1987).

Cosmopolitan Dublin

As well as the relatively small number of immigrants from Britain, there were others from further afield. The popularity of the Grand Tour with the landed class encouraged a fashion for European crafts and artistic styles, while the ongoing investment in 'big houses' required continental as well as British craftsmen and artists. As Arthur Young noted, 'the badness of the houses is remedying every hour throughout the whole kingdom, for the number of new ones just built is prodigiously great' (1970, I, 151). Dublin and the port cities, not surprisingly, were home to the majority of Ireland's small ethnic minorities. Dublin's role as a cultural centre, enhanced by the establishment of annual sessions of the Irish Parliament in 1785, offered opportunities for artists, musicians, actors, performers and teachers which attracted some from continental Europe. One, Gaetano (better known as Chevalier) Manini, born in Milan, moved from London to Dublin in the 1790s in order to carry on his work as a painter specialising in historical and mythological subjects (Strickland 1989, II, 99). It is clear that Irish merchants profited as a consequence of the slave trade and that there was a presence, albeit a small one, of negro servants in Ireland's port cities. Previously hidden connections between Ireland and Africa in this period are only now being fully revealed (Shyllon 1977; Rodgers 2000; 2004; McGrath 2007). The exceptional character of a black face in later eighteenth-century Dublin is evidenced by the fact that the presence of Lord Edward Fitzgerald in the city's streets was heralded by the appearance of his black servant, Tony Small. The noble lord had brought the freed slave, who had saved his life in the American War of Independence, back across the Atlantic in 1782 (Tillyard 1998, 38–9, 61–2, 239–40).

Moving on, catching up

At the same time, the long-established minority communities of Jews, Huguenots and Palatines were not being replenished: the small Jewish community in Dublin, according to one estimate, declined significantly (Darby 1988, 171). That Jews and others were regarded as suspect, at least by Ireland's legislators, is suggested by the Irish Naturalisation Act of 1783 (in force until 1846) which specifically excluded Jews (Weiner 2001, 280). Similarly, the experience of those Palatine settlers who had come to Ireland in Queen Anne's reign (1702–14) was now one of depletion: the majority moved on to the new world around 1760 when their originally favourable leases expired. Here we can see diasporic reconnections being forged as old world refugees and their descendants moved on to 'catch up' with those from the Palatinate who had crossed the Atlantic half a century before (O'Connor 1989, 68–71). Although there were still some continental traders and merchants residing permanently or temporarily in Ireland's ports, their numbers were also declining because of the disruptions of international warfare: the long-term trend was away from trade with Europe and towards trade with Britain and the Atlantic world.

Internal migration

Rural population growth outstrips urban

Despite its dramatic population expansion during this half-century, Ireland lagged behind most of Britain and the rest of north-west Europe in terms of rural–urban migration. The proportion of people living in towns of more than 10,000 in 1750 was 5 per cent; by 1800 it had grown to only 7 per cent, compared with 18 per cent in Britain and Europe (Cowan 1998, 132–3). Comparing Irish and Scottish rates of urbanisation, Whyte observes that 'during the eighteenth century more rapid population growth in Ireland reduced the relative demographic importance of Irish towns compared with Scotland where population growth was slower and urban expansion more rapid'. While Scotland was rapidly approaching the point when it would be as urbanised as England, the rate of urbanisation in Ireland, compared with the century before 1750, was slowing down. (Whyte 1995, 28, 15–17).

The emergence of Catholic Dublin

Although it is true that its rate of expansion was somewhat slower in the second half of the century than in the first, Dublin was certainly growing faster than other Irish towns, particularly in the 1750s and 1760s. The capital was still pulling away from the 'chasing pack' of provincial centres and Cullen describes its growth as 'astonishing'. Between 1750 and 1800 Dublin kept adding around 1,000 new inhabitants to its ranks every year (1992, 251). In about 1750 the religious balance tipped, giving a Catholic majority for the first time since the sixteenth century. Higher Catholic fertility may have been one factor in the gradual change, but the declining stream of immigration from Britain, evident since the 1690s, was more significant (Fagan 1998, 45). Most important of all, although we have little evidence for reconstructing patterns, was ongoing migration of Catholics into Dublin from the countryside and provincial towns. An increasing range of services, an expanding port and the development of manufacturing, combined with expansion of the city's metropolitan role, can only have increased the magnetism of Dublin, pulling wider and deeper on its hinterland (Dickson 1983, 177–92). Based on backward projection from the 1841 Census, David Dickson suggests that it was Leinster and the counties bordering Co. Dublin in particular which supplied the greatest proportion of new arrivals in this half-century. The pull of Dublin had also been strong on south Ulster from the 1720s: apart from the brisk trade in live cattle, a significant proportion of the 3,000 linen weavers working in Dublin probably had roots in the north (Dickson 1983, 183, 188; Cullen 1992, 252). From our post-Partition perspective (i.e. after 1920) it is rather easy to forget that Dublin was the capital of the whole island and to overlook its strong connections with the northern province. Prior to the establishment of the White Linen Hall in Belfast in 1783, Dublin as the national market attracted south those engaged in manufacture and trade. Dublin's Linen Hall, erected in 1728 off North King Street, close to the main arterial route north to Ulster, was surrounded by evidence of internal migration: Coleraine Street, Derry Street, Lisburn Street and Lurgan Street (Bennet 2005, 153).

By the 1760s, the movement into Dublin of craftsmen and apprentices from the provinces was probably starting to be restricted by the early organisation of labour into combinations. In 1782 a leading worsted manufacturer, looking back to a golden age of deregulation, asserted that 'about 1750 ... the people of every part of Ireland could ... get work freely in Dublin' (quoted in Dickson 1983, 188). The efforts by combinations to protect wage rates and working conditions by restricting recruitment eventually encouraged government and manufacturers towards what today might be called decentralisation – in effect rural 'putting-out' in the textile industries and the relocation of some other industries from the city.

Ribbon development and rural-urban links

After 1750, migrants coming in to Dublin were settling along 'a very marked social gradient from west to east', evident, for example, in the guide to the city published in 1780 by Robert Pool and John Cash (Sheridan 2001b, 136). Broadly speaking, the east side of the city with its elegant streets was home to the gentry, and the west side to the merchants and mechanics. Although Pool and Cash made little reference to the poor, almost every other visitor to the city lamented their abundance and miserable appearance. They were concentrated in the western parishes where industrial activity and overcrowded, rundown housing were most evident. The east–west contrast in the 1790s caught the eye of one French exile, Chevalier de Latocnaye, who praised the wealthy streetscapes of the east but not the 'dirt and misery of the quarters where the lower classes vegetate' (1796–7, 18–19, quoted in Sheridan-Quantz 2001, 280). As poorer migrants crowded into the west of the city, as they had done for well over a century, settlement stretched out further along the main arterial routes. In 1775, another continental visitor, Richard Twiss, noted the scenes of suburban roadside poverty: 'the outskirts of Dublin consist chiefly of huts, which are termed cabins; they are made of mud dried, and in these miserable dwellings, far the greater part of the inhabitants of Ireland linger out a wretched existence'. Cultivating tiny patches of potatoes and consuming whiskey prodigiously, 'these beings', as Twiss described them, seemed 'to form a distinct race from the rest of mankind' (1776, 29–30, quoted in Sheridan 2001b, 146). It is possible that the rapid ribbon development of such dwellings had the effect of exaggerating the extent of poverty in the eyes of such travellers (Cullen 1986b, 133).

Particular patterns of in-migration have also been identified by Cullen as established Protestant weavers and artisans gradually gave way to Catholic in-migrants from the Leinster hinterland: those from Kildare settled particularly in the Liberties, south-west of the Castle, and this localised migration stream persisted down to the Great Famine (1845–50) and beyond. The Earl of Kildare in proclaiming 'they will follow me wherever I go' had also drawn migrants from his patrimony towards the south side of the city (Hegarty 2007, 206). Those from Meath to the north, on the other hand, settled particularly around Smithfield, north of the Liffey. As probably had been the case in the first half of the century, these patterns were reflected in political allegiances and in the development of pubs or alehouses with particular regional or county connections (Cullen 1992, 252; Nolan 2006, 572).

A mobile servant class

Of course, internal migration also took place within Dublin. The east–west social gradient notwithstanding, rich and poor were never rigidly segregated. As the census of Dublin conducted by Rev. James Whitelaw in 1798 confirms, no parish in the city was without both rich and poor residents. De Latocnaye noticed that Dublin's numerous beggars were concentrated, at least by day, among the homes and shops of the better-off east end, from which, with its busy docks at the mouth of the Liffey, the demand for labour would not allow the poor to be excluded. The parish of St Mark's in the docks area south of the Liffey, according to Whitelaw's estimate, was as much as three-quarters 'lower class'. Rich and poor were also integrated by domestic service: by 1800, approximately one in ten Dublin inhabitants were employed as 'living in' domestic servants (Maxwell 1936, 122; Sheridan 2001b, 141–6). The lower echelons of household staff were likely to have been recruited from beyond the city. The Bishop of Elphin, for example, brought from his Roscommon diocese the niece of his housekeeper as a maid for his daughter. The turnover and circulation of domestic servants between estates and city households further stimulated rural–urban migration (O'Dowd 2005, 134).

Prostitution was another aspect of the metropolitan economy in which the lives of rich and poor intersected. At one end of the spectrum was Margaret Leeson, born in Killough, near Delvin, Westmeath, who became one of the best-known and well-heeled brothel owners in this period. Leeson and the more genteel among her workers could boast customers from the international as well as the local elite. At the other end, in one-room brothels in notorious red light districts such as Smock Alley (now West Essex Street), young women who had, for a variety of reasons, left home, plied a trade which perhaps only in its early stages brought them contact with those of the middling sort or above. The records of the first Magdalen Asylum, founded in 1767 in Leeson Street by Lady Arabella Denny, born in Lixnaw, Kerry, for the reform of those who had 'fallen into' prostitution, hint at the rural origins of many of the 388 women who entered the institution in the following three decades: those who described themselves as skilled in 'country business' probably had a background in farming or household service on a country estate (O'Dowd 2005, 130-1; Raughter 1992; Lyons 1995; O'Dowd 2005, 130–1; Boyd 2006, 140–50).

Turnover in the towns

The rest of the urban network, from the major port cities and provincial centres to the modest villages barely distinguishable from the surrounding country-side, also drew in rural migrants, albeit on a much smaller scale. Recently, there has been a flush of fresh research into Irish towns in this period, but without uncovering much about the process of in-migration. What does seem clear is that a complex array of factors resulted in fairly wide variation nation-ally, with some settlements expanding on the back of steady inward migration and others stagnating, unable to attract new residents (Simms and Andrews 1994; 1995; Borsay and Proudfoot 2002; Holton, Clare and Ó Dálaigh 2004). Given the absence of detailed studies of internal migration as it related to urban development, we should guard against any temptation to assume that eighteenth-century Irish towns were places where the same resident families persisted generation after generation with little change. In the city of Armagh, which was really more accurately described as a country town, there was sig-nificant population turnover: of the 92 surnames recorded in the hearth money rolls of 1664, no more than 29 could be found in the city a century later. The remarkable fact that Armagh virtually doubled its population in the single gen-eration after 1770 indicates a steady stream of newcomers from an ever more populous rural hinterland settling in the city (Clarkson and Crawford 1985, 22; Crawford 2005, 55). Similarly, an analysis of later eighteenth century Derry city, comparing it with the townlands of its immediate hinterland, suggests an accel-eration of turnover in property occupancy in the city after 1750, and the local newspaper, the *Londonderry Journal*, gives further information on who was moving where within the town (Thomas 1999, 372).

Changing denominational complexion

If the scale of inward migration of provincial towns never rivalled that of Dublin, there was a similar shift in their denominational balance. Increasingly, Catholics established themselves as traders, professionals, craftsmen and humbler residents within settlements which had been founded or expanded through immigra-tion from Britain in the seventeenth century, to the point that they formed majorities. This trend, which would accelerate in the next half-century, was evident in Ulster and to an even greater extent in Munster in the later decades of the century. By the 1770s, the arterial routes into Tallow (Waterford), and even the Protestant stronghold of Bandon (Cork), were showing a significant build-up of poor ribbon development. As on the outskirts of Dublin, primitive cabins with a tiny plot of land were occupied almost exclusively by Catholics who, having neither quite left the countryside nor arrived in the town, eked out a precarious existence in this liminal zone (O'Flanagan, 1988, 124–48; Crawford, 2002, 107). That such ribbon development was common to towns across the island is suggested by the English traveller John Bush, who in 1764 noted 'the generality of dirty entrances to them, and the long strings of despicable huts or cabins that most of them are prefaced with' (O'Brien 1918, 370).

Subdivision and seasonal spalpeens

Most migration into the towns (recalling Ravenstein's first 'law of migration', see Appendix II) is likely to have been short distance – within the province at least, if not within the county. However, there were also substantial numbers of temporary or seasonal migrants who might go further afield. Paintings by artists and accounts by travel writers, such as John Bush and Arthur Young, give the impression of a society marked as much by movement as settlement (Haddington 1991; Hadfield and McVeagh 1994; see Bishop 1999, 57 for Nixon's depiction of Dublin shortly after the Union; see also Plate 5). A much more rapid increase in population was underway in the countryside than in the towns, resulting in an increase in tillage, which was further encouraged by the wars in North America (1775–82) and in Europe after 1793. Not surprisingly, the number of seasonal agricultural migrants, the spalpeens (*spailpíní*; from *spailp* 'spell', as in *spailp oibre* 'spell of work'), increased, travelling, as before, from predominantly poorer, upland, grazing districts, often in the west, to those regions of most developed arable production, mostly in the east midland grain belt, particularly during the harvest season. Robert Bell, an Ulsterman who travelled through the island in the 1780s, noted the work of the spalpeens in prime arable counties such as Dublin, Meath and Kildare (O'Dowd 1991, 13). Rapid expansion in the rural population also resulted in more poverty and an increase in vagrancy and begging. The signs were there that the scale of the problem would become almost overwhelming for the government, as it did in the early decades of the nineteenth century (Geary 1999, 121–36).

The mobile poor

With so little evidence surviving, we can know little of the migratory patterns of those at the lowest social levels in Ireland, but what we do know generally of the mobile poor in pre-industrial societies suggests that long-distance movements or island-wide circuits may not have been exceptional (Moch 2003,

119–22). Analysis of the admissions journal of the Limerick House of Industry from the 1790s suggests that many of those taken from the streets of the city and incarcerated were from well beyond the immediate mid-west region (Limerick City and County Archives, GB/NNAFO101698). Periodically, the problem of vagrancy was exacerbated by demobilisation. A substantial increase in Irish recruitment to the British military in itself stimulated migration within Ireland and beyond, and if large numbers were demobbed at a time of high unemployment, which occurred in 1782–3, social problems became particularly acute (Kelly, 1992b 38-62; 1992/3 61–88; Hay and Rogers 1997, 158–61).

Attracting northern artisans

Religious balance was also altering in the countryside. As noted in the previous chapter, following the rapid reduction of immigration from Britain in the early years of the eighteenth century, landowners keen to maintain their estates with Protestant tenants were increasingly forced to look north to Ulster. In the counties bordering Ulster such migration might be interpreted as little more than a continuation of the process of colonial spread identified in the seventeenth century. No doubt this was welcomed, for example, by landlords in Sligo, where, in the eastern parishes especially, the Protestant population continued to expand from 1750 until about 1830 (Cullen 1981, 194). Elsewhere, estate owners concerned as much with the loyalty of their tenants as with their industriousness, still preferred where possible to take on Protestant tenants. More enterprising landowners and agents, particularly in the northern half of the island, did what they could to tempt Protestant tenants to move south or west, particularly those skilled in spinning and weaving. There were some concerted schemes, similar to those undertaken before 1750, to import Protestant proto-industrialising colonies into largely Catholic areas. The most substantial initiative of this kind was the Earl of Arran's project in the 1790s to establish a linen-producing estate village at Mullifaragh, a few miles north of Ballina, Co. Mayo, which attracted a substantial number of Presbyterian weavers from Ulster. The contemporary estimate that the colony numbered as many as 1,000 workers may have been exaggerated, but the alacrity with which it was attacked in 1798, following the arrival of the French at Killala under General Humbert, indicated the risks involved in such schemes of internal colonisation in the fraught political climate of the 1790s (Stock 1800; Freyer 1982 edn , 66; Jordan 1994, 61, 82–4).

1790s refugees

Mayo witnessed another inward migration of Ulster weavers in the 1790s, but in this case the migrants were Ulster Catholics fleeing from the violent aftermath of the Protestant victory on 21 September 1795 in the sectarian affray near Loughgall, Co. Armagh, known as the Battle of the Diamond. The subsequent campaign of intimidation, stretching across north Armagh west into Tyrone and east into Down, drove out thousands of Catholic refugees, many of them linen weavers, towards predominantly Catholic areas. Some moved elsewhere within Ulster, some left Ireland altogether for Scotland and America, but most went west to Fermanagh and Connacht, especially the area around Westport, on the Mayo coast. Indeed, the particular violence of the attack in 1798 on Arran's colony at Mullifaragh was probably not unconnected with this migration by Ulster Catholics (Cullen 1981, 252). The ripple effect of the sectarian violence centred in north Armagh reached at least as far south as Tipperary, where even as late as the twentieth century a distinctive 'Ulster Irish' was evident among those referred to locally as the 'Oultachs' (*Ultachaigh*), remembered in local tradition as the descendants of the Ulster men and women who had moved there in the 1790s (Ó Fiaich 1990, 7–19; Elliott 2000, 226). A balanced perspective of how the 'sectarian disease' operated in this period at the level of the parish is given in Kyla Madden's study of Forkhill, south Armagh (2005, 3–9).

Curfew and control

Such internal migrants, like immigrants, were generally viewed by the authorities with suspicion, especially in the years preceding the Rebellion of 1798. Dublin Castle was alert to the spread of seditious ideas by those who were, or pretended to be, itinerant craftsmen and traders, such as journeymen weavers, chapmen and pedlars. Once recruited into the United Irishmen, James (Jemmy) Hope, a former journeyman weaver from south Antrim, travelled throughout the country, spreading the republican message and organising. Following the outbreak of violence in 1798 it was little surprise that the army should seek to restrict movement by imposing a strict curfew in hotbeds of radicalism like Belfast, where Henry Joy McCracken was arrested attempting to escape to America via Larne (Madden 1846, 1998 edn, 9; Stewart 1995, 239–40).

Emigration

Reblocking the story

Historians generally take the American War of Independence (1775–82) as marking the main division of the eighteenth century, and historians dealing with migration between Ireland or Ulster and North America in particular have tended to use it in dividing the 'long' eighteenth century into three periods: 1689–1715; 1715–75; and 1775–1815. However, recent research supports the case, as far as migration is concerned, for taking the Seven Years War (1756–63) as marking the main division of the century. Of course, there were significant changes in migration after the Revolutionary War: there was an acceleration in the decline of indentured servitude – long-established as the main mechanism by which migrants with limited means could gain a foothold in the new world (Morgan 2000, 123–4; Fogleman 1998, 44); and the creation of the new United States at the expense of the British Empire had great implications for emigrants from Ireland, Britain and continental Europe. Nonetheless, there was considerable continuity to the extent that the disruption of the Revolutionary War can be seen as a trough between the two most significant peaks in emigration between Ireland and North America, in the early 1770s and early 1780s.

A mid-century transition to 'modern' migration

The character of emigration in the 1760s, especially after the Seven Years War, bore greater similarity to that of the 1780s than that of the 1740s, as has been argued most forcefully by Cullen. Characterising eighteenth-century emigration decisions on the whole as being 'more conscious and less involuntary' than previously suggested, he asserts that, from at least 1760, emigrants appear to have been behaving more individualistically as compared with the more collective behaviour of the previous decades. In addition, he detects the departure of greater numbers of skilled migrants with more enterprising attitudes, foreshadowing the 'modern' mass migration of the nineteenth century more than reflecting the patterns of the early modern period. Taking the long and broad view, Cullen's striking contention is that 'the 1760s constitutes the greatest single watershed in the history of migration overall'. In other words, it was during the two decades of the 1760s and 1770s that 'the modern world was born' (Cullen 1994, 144–9).

The 'transformation thesis' of Cullen, centred on the inter-war years 1763–75, is supported by the innovative work of Wokeck in comparing the flows of German and Irish immigrants into the Delaware ports between 1730 and 1775. She found that after 1763, and particularly during the peak years of the early 1770s, Irish immigrants were much more likely to have paid for their passage as modern migrants, rather than to have exchanged their freedom for their crossing as indentured servants in the early modern way. As noted in the previous chapter, it was during these years that the proportion of emigrants leaving the northern ports was greatest and that the contrast in the character between the northern and southern outflows was greatest: while emigrants from southern ports were still predominantly young, single, indentured servants, those from northern ports were predominantly members of family groups who had paid for their passage (Wokeck, 1999, 167–219).

Reading partition into the eighteenth century

Once again we should be wary of the danger of projecting the present back on the past and seeing two entirely separate transatlantic flows that correspond somehow with contemporary Nationalist and Unionist divisions. This propensity is evident in a good deal of the earlier literature, especially before the emergence of professional Irish history writing in the 1930s (Hanna 1902; Glasgow 1936; Marshall 1943). It has proved hard, even for professional historians in the later twentieth century, to avoid a 'separate and different' approach to emigration in the eighteenth century, coloured by post-Partition hindsight. For example, R. J. Dickson's *Ulster Emigration to Colonial America, 1718–1775*, published in 1966 and still a fine work of scholarship, only fleetingly mentions the probability of emigrants from Ulster taking ship in ports outside Ulster; and all but rules out the possibility of Ulster Presbyterians having done so (Dickson 1966, 4). However, as Wokeck points out, 'several ships from Ulster stopped in these southern ports ... and probably gained passengers whilst there' (1999, 195), confirming the observation of Lockhart 20 years previously (Lockhart 1976). Rather than focusing separately on Scotch-Irish or Ulster-Scots migrants and southern Irish migrants, we should seek to understand the whole geography of Irish migration patterns as more nuanced and interconnected, following Doyle's injunction to bear in mind that 'where an emigrant came from, and at what date, tells most about the outlook and skills he brought, not the mere fact of his being Scots Irish' (2006, 160).

Ethnic identities

Another perspective is provided by Tom Devine, who argues in a different direction against a segregated analysis by suggesting that 'Ulster Scots emigrants to America deserve to be considered as one distinctive element in the more general Scottish diaspora of the eighteenth century' (2003, 148). Bearing in mind that the peak volume of Scottish migration to Ulster occurred as recently as the 1690s, it would not be surprising to find a strong sense of Scottish identity sustained among the many Presbyterians who left Ulster for America during the opening decades of the eighteenth century. (Fitzgerald 2004, 71–85). However, we should not overlook evidence that suggests that in the new world such migrants showed little sign of objecting to being described as Irish. In short, the issue of ethnic identity and labelling seems to have been much more fluid than would later be the case (Miller et al. 2003, 8, 442–51; Doyle 2006, 151–4).

A variegated picture

Already we can detect specific districts which might be described as 'emigration hotspots' and sense just how varied the pattern of emigration was across the island. As we discuss in chapter 15, the Irish diaspora of 1800 is best analysed as an aggregate of local diasporas constituted by the networks of relationships between the peoples of particular townlands, parishes, towns and counties and their emigrants (O'Connor 2006, 153–63). In order to see the variegated pattern of emigration we need more studies at the local level; for as one leading historical and cultural geographer of this period warns, 'given the enduring local bases of eighteenth century Irish life, the historiography is still haunted by these regional ghosts, which rise up to mock premature generalizations' (Whelan 1990, 165).

Emigration as a positive sign

In what Whelan calls the northern zone of proto-industrialisation, we find heavy emigration, precociously modern in character, and so we may ask what features of this zone help explain its early migration modernisation. Travellers were quick to detect increased prosperity on entering the 'linen country' of south Ulster. As early as the 1750s both John Wesley, the peripatetic Methodist leader, and Edward Willes, a circuit judge, described the outward signs of wealth and comfort derived from the widespread cottage-based production of linen cloth (Crawford 1994, 27–8). The core area of weaving was in the 'linen triangle' between Lisburn, Dungannon and Newry (Crawford 2005, 106). This was surrounded by an outer zone, stretching south and west, where flax spinning was more important in supplementing household incomes (Crawford 1994, 18–37; Dickson 2000, 140). It was in the 'linen triangle' that entrepreneurial middlemen came to dominate the finishing stage of bleaching, reaping the rewards of early investment in mechanisation. Fundamental to understanding the connection between linen, prosperity and emigration is the point made by Cullen, who cautions against the tendency to read backwards from the following century the pervasive view that emigration was a sign of economic weakness: the appropriate perspective on emigration in the later eighteenth century is seeing it, says Cullen, as 'one of the very bases of the strength of the society' (1994, 144–9). To this extent we might see emigration in this region of the country at this time as having certain parallels with later emigration from urbanising, industrialising southern Scotland (Devine 1992, 1–15). John Dunlap, who left Strabane, Tyrone, aged ten in 1757, flourished in America to be remembered as the printer of the Declaration of Independence. Having prospered from the War of Independence (1775–82), Dunlap secured his place among the Philadelphia elite of the early Republic and enthusiastically recommended the United States to eager readers and listeners at home. In the spring of 1785, writing to his brother Robert, in Strabane, no doubt expecting his news to be read aloud and circulated, he offered a ringing endorsement of the merits of his newly independent country: 'the young men of Ireland who wish to be free and happy should leave it and come here as quick as possible, there is no place in the world where a man meets so rich a reward for good conduct and industry as in America'. Thus, a widening pool of potential migrants in Ireland learned of new opportunities across the ocean (McCaughey 1992, 99-109; PRONI T 1336/1/20, CMS IED 8910144).

Modernisation, commercialisation and migration culture

How, then, did emigrants, wishing to avoid forfeiting their freedom as indentured servants, raise the capital required to purchase a passage across the
Atlantic and fund successful settlement in America? Men weaving cloth or
women spinning flax could hope to save, but departing tenants in Ulster
could also hope to realise liquidity through what was popularly known as the
'Ulster Custom': the departing tenant's right to dispose of his saleable interest
in his tenancy to the highest bidder, subject to the landlord's approval,
including the value of any improvements he had carried out and also the difference between the competitive market rent and the 'fair' rent he actually
paid (Crawford 1975, 5–22; Dowling 1999, 3–7; Connolly 1998, 538–9).
Substantial resources were needed to move an entire family group across the
ocean, as in this half-century significant numbers did. For younger sons of relatively prosperous farming families, strategies to avoid downward social
mobility were required and already by the later eighteenth century, America
was seen as the answer by inheritance-conscious parents and children.
Primogeniture and transatlantic kinship networks were already playing an
important part in shaping emigration from Ulster. Furthermore, passage
money to America was evident as an inheritance to kin in Ulster from earlier
emigrant relatives (Gilmore 2005, 2–3). Most emigration from Ulster after 1750
drew from those areas in which the market economy was most developed
and it was not simply a coincidence that these were often the areas where
immigrants from Britain settled a century before. Again we glimpse the fibres
connecting immigration and emigration, so that we may speak of a 'culture
of migration' developing across generations in certain specific localities.
In places like Ardstraw in the Foyle valley and Aghadowey in the Bann
valley, fresh Scots immigration around 1700 had been intensive and these districts were equally active at an early stage in the American emigration of the
eighteenth century (Dickson 1966, 27–8; McCourt 1999, 303–20). The mobility evident in settler society in seventeenth-century Ulster along the key
migration corridors was sustained into the eighteenth century, although the
main direction of flow was now reversed (Gillespie 1988, xvi–xxv; Dowling
1999, 127).

Dissent, literacy and the new world

Bearing in mind that at this stage about two-thirds of emigrants were Ulster
Presbyterians, we need to ask why this group especially opted for emigration
to America. A strong communal memory of religious persecution in Scotland
had much to do with it, combined with both a negative experience of further
religious discrimination and even persecution in Ulster, and their extremely
positive self-image as pioneer settlers on an expanding British frontier, first in
Ireland and then America (McBride 1997, 23–6, 31–3, 62–3; Griffin 2001,

12–15, 157–8). As emigrants they had the advantage of relatively high levels of literacy – a benefit derived from a church government that placed so much emphasis on the importance of individual Bible reading, combined with the influence of the Scottish enlightenment and the high value that it placed on education (Kirkham 1990, 74; Lunny 1994, 56–70). Therefore news of America, especially shipping news, circulated more readily in Ulster. Most importantly, those contemplating emigration had access to first-hand accounts of the new world that were increasingly sent back home in letters by the pioneer emigrants. Just as in the seventeenth century, reports of abundant rich land and timber flowing back from Ireland were all the more persuasive when they came from a familiar and reliable source. Also arising from vigorous theological engagement, many internal divisions and splits developed within Presbyterianism in Ulster and these spurred some to seek fuller freedom of religious expression across the Atlantic. There, like rich land and timber, it was not always easily obtained and both during the American Revolution and after many found themselves engaged in an immigrant struggle against an Anglican hegemony not dissimilar to that which they had left in Ireland (Griffin 2001, 16–17). The distinctiveness of Presbyterians in relation to Anglicans and particularly Catholics in this period would decline with time, as would their over-representation in the emigration flow.

Trading a human cargo

As well as all this, linen production and the export of finished cloth were central to the emigration flow from Ulster. The emigration trade, as Truxes has argued, is really best considered as a part of Ireland's trading relationship with the American colonies. The great increase after 1763 in transatlantic trade, especially in flaxseed, meant an increase in the number of transatlantic ships and their availability to emigrants. As the volume of imported flaxseed rose, so did the importance of the ports: not only Dublin and Belfast which took the largest proportions, but also the smaller ports of Derry and later Newry. The owners and masters of vessels bringing flaxseed east across the Atlantic did not want to make the return trip with an empty hold. While other cargoes, such as finished linen cloth and flour, could be loaded for export to the American colonies, ships arriving in a port like Derry or Newry in the autumn or early spring and ready to return to the middle colonies could seek instead a human cargo. The notorious delays emigrants experienced prior to embarkation in this era stemmed in part from the time needed for the alterations necessary to make a vessel ready for passengers (Truxes 1988, 132, 206–9; Hood 2003; MacMaster 2005). Whatever other factors encouraged overseas emigration early in Ulster, without the network in place to provide passage across the ocean it would not have got underway.

A sentence to sail

Not all ships, of course, were taking the increasing number of voluntary emigrants, who were the agents of Cullen's 'transformation' thesis. Some carried large numbers of forced emigrants: those convicted by the courts in Ireland to serve a term, usually seven years, sometimes 14, as 'transportees' in the American colonies. From the enabling legislation of 1703 to the start of transportation to Australia in 1791, there were between 9,000 and 18,500 – a not insignificant proportion of the emigrant flow, even at the minimum of the estimated range. Whether these individuals considered themselves as exiles more than emigrants is impossible to know, but some were able to make the return journey to Ireland or Britain, sometimes to re-offend (Ekirch 1987, 24–5, 46–7, 114–16; Garnham 1996, 162–3, 259–60; Fitzgerald 2001, 114–32; Kelly 2003, 112–35).

Increasing migration to Britain

Although the volume of the emigrant stream to North America overtook that to Britain and Europe in this period, emigration to Britain nevertheless continued to increase, particularly after 1780. The numbers of seasonal agricultural labourers and the itinerant poor, not always easy to differentiate, accounted for a good deal of temporary migration, but early industrial development, particularly in northern England and southern Scotland, attracted more permanent settlement, which caused some official anxiety during the turbulent 1790s (Elliott 1982, 133–50, 178–89, 282–90; O'Dowd 1991, 5; Place 1994, 172–92; McRaild 1999, 44–9; 2006, 8–9). Although groups of Irish migrants roaming the British countryside might appear less exotic and threatening than they had in the early seventeenth century, they were still feared as carriers of contagious diseases; and a correlation has been documented between surges in subsistence migration and outbreaks of disease, particularly typhus (Schellekens 1996, 29–42). The scale of the problem of the itinerant Irish poor, reflecting strong population growth in rural Ireland, may well have been on the increase again. A survey of adult street beggars conducted in London in the 1790s revealed that just over a third (33.95 per cent) originated in Ireland, and evidence relating the passage of Irish vagrants through Wiltshire suggests a significant acceleration in the traffic during that decade (Corfield 1982, 103; Church 2000; Cole 2000).

Old and new worlds connected

By the final decade of the century, with a growing Irish presence in the southern hemisphere, we can see the outlines of a fully global and already diverse diaspora. The strong Irish presence in Australia from the 1790s among the transported convicts was to prove a mixed blessing to the voluntary Irish immigrants who arrived in the following century (O'Farrell 1986, 22–53;

Carroll-Burke 2000, 54–5; Reece 2001, 231–54). In 1801, on the other side of the world in Chile, the funeral of Ambrose O'Higgins, governor and captain-general, marked an influential Irish presence in the Spanish colony. Making good use of his aristocratic Irish pedigree, O'Higgins had enjoyed success as a central figure in the Spanish empire. Others, like the merchant and genea-logist Thomas O'Gorman, whose family was from Clare, developed important trade links between Spain and South America during the later eighteenth century (Kirby 1992, 94, 97–8). Here we see a continuity developing between early modern and modern patterns of Irish emigration: those who in the fol-lowing century would make use of British imperial trade links to establish Irish settlements in Argentina would capitalise also on the older links with South America established through the earlier Irish presence in imperial Spain (McKenna 2003, 43).

In the wake of '98

The failed rebellion of 1798 resulted in a strong emigrant flow and there is a similarity between this and the earlier flow of 1728: a significant proportion of those departing were responding to a crisis, being pushed by a repressive gov-ernment in 1798 and by famine in 1728. However, it is the difference between the two exoduses that is most striking: whether they were Presbyterians from Antrim and Down or Catholics from Wexford and Kildare, the emigrants of the 1790s were distinctively 'modern'. Some revolutionaries made it to Britain or Europe, others were transported to Australia, but the majority, cer-tainly many thousands, ended up on the far side of the Atlantic (Elliott 1982, 241–365; Weber 1997, 141–66; O'Donnell 1998). Here they contributed to the strong current of Anglophobia which characterised the early Republic and laid the foundations of nineteenth-century Irish-American nationalism (Wilson 1998; Parkhill 2003).

Conclusion

Focusing on migration alters our perception of the importance of the American War of Independence (1775–82), which historians normally take as marking the main division of the eighteenth century. The peaks of emigration occurred in the years immediately before and after the war, indicating that this rather than the Seven Years War, regarded by some as the first 'world war', that opened the way to 'modern' emigration. The increasing population generated increasingly complex migration patterns. As regional and local studies show, there was wide variation in the extent to which these played a part in the development of the Irish economy, but looking back from the vantage point of Arthur Young in 1780 it had generally been positive. The government's interest in the migration of the masses was less developed than it would become before the Great Famine, but the final decade of the eighteenth century demonstrated the concern of those in power to control suspicious movement and hence regulate the migration of ideas it considered seditious. Had the events of 1798, 'The Year of the French', taken another turn, migration patterns would have been very different in the century ahead. In fact, by 1800 the outlines were in place of the pattern of nineteenth-century mass emigration within the English-speaking world. The predominance of the trans-Atlantic route was already clear, as was the future importance of British North America (later Canada) as a destination of arrival and settlement.

9

Irish Migration, 1800–1845

This was the half-century in which Ireland became truly a country of 'mass' emigration. After the Act of Union in 1800, the country was little more attractive as a destination for immigrants than before. Those who did come were mainly from Britain looking for a place of opportunity, but too few to promote much closer integration of the two islands. The population continued to grow dramatically and this, combined with slow economic growth, had the effect of entrenching structural poverty, indicated by the growing number of vagrants and beggars. Despite a surge of reforming energy, government had not come to grips with the problem before 1845 and the catastrophic years of famine. Increasing numbers of temporary seasonal labourers joined departing emigrants on the new steam-propelled vessels plying between Dublin and other east coast ports and Liverpool. Many families from the snug farming class took passages via Liverpool across the Atlantic. Though many now arrived in the ports of British North America (Canada), their ultimate destination lay south of the 49th parallel in the United States. The British government sought through assisted emigration schemes to keep migration restricted within the empire, but its early experiments proved discouraging.

Immigration

A distant groom

Although the Act of Union was thought of by many as a 'marriage', there was little affection in Britain for its Hibernian bride (Bartlett 2001, 243–58; Dougherty 2001, 205–15). Impressions of the Irish in Britain tended to be coloured by first-hand experience and second-hand reports of the increasing number of immigrants travelling through or settling in the emerging industrial heartlands and the capital, London. In 1845 as the Great Famine began, despite the 175 Commissions and Special Committees appointed since the Union to enquire into Irish affairs, it seemed to well-wishers that the English actually knew less about Ireland than they knew about West Africa (Woodham-Smith 1962, 32, 122). This becomes evident when we consider the main types of immigrants arriving in Ireland from Britain: civil servants, soldiers, land agents, churchmen and tourists.

An ' Irish Raj'

British civil servants in Ireland found themselves in a very different situation from, say, those in India, who faced little or no competition from locals. The now long-settled Protestant community felt itself to have a much stronger claim than newcomers on the posts of an Irish administration which employed a total of almost 5,000 (McDowell 1964, 4). Even though the number of vacancies was increasing as government extended its reach more than it did in Britain, particularly in education and Poor Law reform, these posts tended to offer only short-term career advancement for new arrivals. Relatively few found satisfyingly permanent niches in the 'Irish Raj' (MacDonagh 1961, 320–50). Some, like Thomas Colby of the Ordnance Survey, were drawn or sent to Ireland by the new spirit of government improvement and intervention. Another such was Alexander Nimmo, born in 1783 in Kirkcaldy, Scotland and educated at the universities of Edinburgh and St Andrews, who arrived in 1810, aged 27. He had been recommended by the leading civil engineer Thomas Telford as one of nine engineers attached to the recently formed Commission to inquire into the nature and extent of Irish bogs. Resident in Connemara, Nimmo worked hard to develop the infrastructure of the west and alleviate poverty until his death in Dublin in 1832 (Villiers-Tuthill, 2006). The career of the Scottish surveyor William Bald followed a similar path: arriving in Ireland in 1809 from Burntisland, Fife, his work took him to Co. Mayo in 1815 and later to Antrim for the building of the spectacular coast road that would take travellers from Larne to Ballycastle (Andrews 1985, 287).

A growing garrison

The growing military garrison accounted for a much larger migration flow. In the late eighteenth century it had been between 10,000 and 12,000; in the nineteenth century it peaked at 30,000, and for most of the first half of the nineteenth century its size was double the garrison of contemporary Britain. From the Union in 1800 to the Boer War of 1899–1902, it remained official policy to garrison Ireland with troops from Britain, although, as we shall see, the Irish presence in the army in Ireland increased as recruitment there accelerated (Spiers 1996, 335–57; Cookson 1997, 257–8). Recent research shows that though billeted in a well-developed network of barracks, officers and men were part of local society, sometimes taking up residence outside the barracks, marrying local women, fathering children, frequenting local alehouses and shops, attending local events and bolstering the often thin congregations in the local Protestant churches on Sundays (Harvey and White 1997; Butler 2006, 227). Some chose to leave the army and settle locally, many of them finding employment in the police force. The first inspector general of the Royal Irish Constabulary, James Shaw Kennedy, whose 1837 book of rules and regulations did much to shape the character of the force, was a Scot originally from Dalton, Kirkcudbrightshire, who had served previously in the light infantry (Malcolm 2006, 70). Overall, the effect of this military inflow was ambiguous: on the one hand, growing numbers of Irish Catholic recruits in the British forces and British soldiers and seamen marrying Irish Catholic women could be seen as promoting Ireland's integration within the United Kingdom; on the other hand, the very retention of such a large military garrison marked Ireland as a special case where government was anxious about its ability to maintain control.

Staffing the estate

Like the civil service and the military, domestic service was expanding as a sector of employment and in the 'big house' the higher positions – the public face of below stairs – were often filled by British-born and trained migrants (Luddy 2000, 53). If the extent and style of the house expressed its owner's status, so too did the manners of the butler or lady's maid. As in England, a mark of aristocratic status was the presence of a French cook. The estate office, domain of the land agent, was also often staffed – as in the previous century – by recruits from Britain, especially Scotland. Many landowners, particularly in the north and west of Ireland, looked to Scotland for models of agricultural improvement and estate rationalisation. Although modern scholarship questions whether there was any substantial difference between the Irish and Scottish agricultural economies in this period, there is no doubt that the latter enjoyed a better reputation at the time (Solar 1983, 70–88). Lord Palmerston, following this trend, sought to improve his estate in Co. Sligo in 1828 by recruiting a new 'agriculturalist' from Scotland, John Lynch, whose family name suggests an origin in Ireland (Power 2004, 113). William Blacker who had oversight of the Gosford estate in Co. Armagh was busy a few years later bringing in other agriculturalists from Scotland and allotting each a subdistrict of the estate to improve. These trouble-shooters or 'peasant chasers', as they were sometimes called by contemporaries, were in strong demand. By 1836 Blacker had recruited up to 60 such men, but many had subsequently moved on to estates across the country, responding to requests from landlords or their agents eager to engage their services (Greig 1976, 34–5; W. H. Crawford pers. comm.).

Missionary migrants and the Second Reformation

The various Protestant churches also continued to recruit in Britain, especially with the renewal of evangelical missionary effort in the 1820s, often referred to as the Second Reformation, which was expressed in the establishment of a wide range of new missionary bodies, such as the Scripture Readers' Society, the Hibernian Bible Society and the Home Mission of the Irish Presbyterian Church (Bowen 1970, 110). All varieties of Irish Protestantism, as one historian observes, 'saw themselves as operating within a denominational environment that spanned the Irish Sea'. Furthermore, they tended to see themselves as working in collaboration where 'what mattered was not one's secular but one's spiritual citizenship' (Holmes 2005, 210–11). The main thrust of the Second Reformation was in the west of Ireland, especially through the medium of the Irish language, and its most influential evangelical migrant was the Anglican Rev. Alexander Dallas from Colchester, Essex. Although he first arrived in Ireland in 1840, he had been preaching about Ireland and in touch with Irish Evangelicals since the early 1820s. In 1843 he founded the Society for Irish Church Missions, going on to take advantage of what he saw as 'the God-given opportunity of the Great Famine to spread Protestantism throughout Connacht' (Bowen 1978, 208–12; Lalor 2003, 267). Another prominent evangelical immigrant was Asenath Nicholson from Vermont, USA, who first arrived in 1844 to spend a year travelling extensively throughout the island, mostly on foot and alone. When the Great Famine struck, she returned to Ireland to work among the poor, buying and distributing food and Bibles, returning finally to the United States in 1852 (Murphy 2002; Lalor 2003, 782–3).

Tourists and *terrazzo* workers

Otherwise, few immigrants from beyond Britain were attracted to Ireland in the early nineteenth century, little encouraged by the manner in which it was reported to the outside world: its rural poverty was notorious, even before the Famine. However, there was a regular, seasonal trickle of curious observers from overseas, some attracted by the spectacular scenery which by 1800 had already made Killarney an 'international success story' as a tourist destination (Hooper 2001, 8–75; Dickson 2005, 423). Neither was there much more than a trickle to replenish the older-established religious minority communities. It was reported – though probably an exaggeration – that only three Jewish families were resident in Dublin in 1805, and, as with all minority communities below a viable threshold, 'marrying out' steadily diminished numbers. In 1820 a synagogue was established in Stafford Street and moved 15 years later to a somewhat larger building at St Mary's Abbey (Hyman 1972, 92; Keogh 1998, 6). The Catholic Emancipation Relief Act of 1829 provided something of a fillip to immigration from continental Europe, particularly from the Italian peninsula, as the huge programme of new church building across the island created a demand for foreign stonemasons, *terrazzo* workers and skilled church decorators. As before, Dublin's many places of public entertainment continued to offer niches for foreign musicians, artists and performers, who might supplement their incomes by offering tuition to the sons and daughters of the better-off. As well as these first-time arrivals in Ireland, there was also a small flow of returned emigrants, re-migrating particularly from the United States in years of economic downturn, such as 1819, 1837 and 1842 (Fitzgerald 2005, 32–54).

'Bryan Cooney' between worlds

The best-known European immigrant of this era, Carlo (Charles) Bianconi (1786–1875), arrived in Dublin from Italy in 1802 as an apprentice to a resident print dealer, Andrea Faroni. The young Bianconi progressed from selling his master's wares on Dublin pavements to peddling them on foot across much of Leinster and east Munster, gradually learning English and eventually going into business very skilfully on his own account, first in Carrick-on-Suir, Waterford, and later in Clonmel, Tipperary, where the locals, translating to the vernacular, referred to Bianconi as 'Bryan Cooney', or 'Bryan of the Corner' (a reference to his premises on the corner of Johnson Street). In the local humour we sense just how exotic such immigrants were in pre-Famine small town Ireland. The rest of Bianconi's migration story is instructive. He strove to integrate into his adopted country and county, Tipperary. Despite the demands of running an island-wide business, he became actively involved in Irish politics, occupying at various times during his long life the offices of mayor, magistrate, grand juror and deputy lieutenant of the county, and enjoying a lasting personal friendship with Daniel O'Connell. We can see the immigrant entrepreneur establishing a kind of equilibrium in modulating between his Irish 'new world' and his Italian 'old world'. Occasionally he was to be found in Waterford, riding along the quays of the busy port, looking out for a vessel from Italy and an opportunity for conversation in his native language. In 1833 on the death of his father, Pietro, he made the return journey to his native village of Tregolo in the municipality of Costa Masnaga, about 22 miles north-east of Milan. Having reconnected with his family, to whom he made generous gifts, he returned to Ireland in melancholy mood, stopping in mountain woods and on the shore of Lake Como to recall scenes of his youth. Back in Ireland, the objects on display in the round entrance hall to his 'big house' at Longfield, Tipperary, expressed his sense of double-belonging: busts of Catalini, the Italian singer, and Seneca, Nero's tutor, along-side those of O'Connell and Father Mathew. Also in the hall was a bust of the Duke of Wellington and balancing it – but at a discreet distance in his private study– a portrait of the Emperor Napoleon, presented by Bonaparte himself to his grandmother Bianconi (Maxwell 1954, 238–49; Bianconi and Watson 1962; Nowlan 1973, 82–95).

However representative and unusual Bianconi's migration story may have been in its different aspects, his major contribution in the decades before the coming of the railway was to facilitate movement within Ireland. From 1815 he pioneered the development of a horse-drawn passenger car network which greatly improved communication between Irish provincial towns, particularly in the west (see Plate 8). As a result it became easier for the increasing number of internal migrants and emigrants to move, baggage and all, to the towns and ports.

Internal migration

William Carleton and the road to Dublin

One of the internal migrants too poor to take advantage of the kind of travel offered by Bianconi was William Carleton. In 1818, aged 24, he arrived in Dublin on foot from his native Clogher valley, Tyrone, via Newcastle, Co. Dublin, where he had been working as a hedge-school master, and Maynooth, Co. Kildare. As he recalled almost 50 years later, he walked in through Dublin's ever-expanding suburbs, along what he called 'the great southern road', which eventually became James's Street where the city's workhouse (soon to become a foundling hospital) had been strategically located more than a century before, at St James's Gate (compare the location of Cork Jail in Plate 4). With only 2s 9d in his pocket, Carleton thought it better to stop in the suburbs rather than proceed to the heart of the city (see Plate 5). Turning left off James's Street, he arrived in the ominously named Dirty Lane, near Usher's Quay (later Bridgefoot Street), and acquired a bed for the night in modest but comfortable lodgings at number 48 (Bennett 2005, 26, 264). His funds having soon run out, the landlord gave him 3d and escorted him across the road to the door of a cellar, which, upon being firmly kicked, opened to reveal something worse, so Carleton thought, than the entrance to Dante's Inferno: in the cellar surrounding a blazing fire were the bodies of men and women, some lying in 'shakedowns' (straw covered with a sheet rag) others still up, but clearly suffering the effects of 'liquors of every description'. Here were the vagrants and beggars who by day swarmed the streets of the city's east side (Carleton and O'Donoghue 1896; 1996, 160–6). One commentator has interpreted Carleton's sense of repulsion as an affront to his 'bred-in-the-bone rural respectability', pointing out that he would have encountered wandering beggars many times previously but in rural settings where they seemed to have 'a certain dignity and mystical significance', whereas in the Dirty Lane cellar 'the green country lad felt for the first time the creeping touch of a leprous obscenity' (Kiely 1947, 60–2; Carleton and O'Donoghue 1896; 1996, 6–7). The irony is that many of the ghastly inhabitants of Carleton's cellar were probably, like him, migrants from 'respectable' rural Ireland. As we have already noted, this suburban underworld was far from new. The location of the workhouse on James's Street as early as 1704 points to the persistence of inward migration from the south and west, and the failure of many new and unskilled arrivals to secure employment in the capital.

'Mobile over medium distances'

This is the only pre-Famine period, to our knowledge, in which Irish internal migration has been the subject of specific research. In the 1960s, an historical geographer investigated internal migration as part of a wider study of the regional variability of emigration patterns. With the exceptions of Dublin and Belfast and their surrounding counties, he found that movement in and out of most counties was generally in equilibrium: most moves were short distance, and internal mobility overall was not sufficient to seriously distort analysis of emigration patterns (Cousens 1965). Subsequently, Nicholas and Shergold, two Australian researchers, analysed data collected from the legal 'indents' drawn up for almost 4,000 Irish men and women transported to the penal colony of New South Wales between 1817 and 1839. Challenging Cousens, they suggested that 'the Irish were not only mobile before the Famine, but were mobile over medium distances'. Those most likely to move were the young and skilled and those working or seeking work outside the agricultural sector. As one might expect, female migration was found to be heavily influenced by marriage options. Overall, at least a third of the sample group had changed their county of residence at least once and the strong pull of Dublin and Belfast on their rural hinterlands was confirmed, with Dublin attracting almost a fifth of all migrants (Nicholas and Shergold 1990, 22–43).

Dublin underworld

Dublin's population at this time was expanding more rapidly than at any point since the early seventeenth century, but not its economy (Sheridan 2001, 68). As noted above, the new spirit of enquiry in government resulted in a stream of reports concerned with the condition of the lower classes. Surveys of pre-Famine Dublin society reflect a kind of migration between two spaces separated by status rather than physical distance. As one historian observes, investigators such as Whitelaw (1805), Cheyne (1818), Wilde (1841) and Willis (1845) 'introduced the reader to the topic as if writing about a foreign land ... a voyage to "another world", where the "natives" were depicted as "denizens" and "poor creatures"' (Prunty 1998, 18). The persistent failure to grapple effectively with the problems of poverty well before 1800 and after 1845 – not just in Ireland – was a result of opinion formers and policy makers continuing to view those who daily negotiated dire poverty through a variety of subsistence strategies as inhabitants of a different 'world'.

Institutional deterrent

Just as the location of the workhouse in James's Street hints at the inflow of poor rural migrants to the city from the south and west, so the erection in 1773 of the House of Industry on the north side of the Liffey in Channel Row (later North Brunswick Street) indicates a similar effort to 'deal' with poor migrants flowing in from the north and west. Of course, such institutions, including those established in the cities of Cork, Waterford and Limerick, were hopelessly inadequate to the huge scale of the national problem. Their forbidding architecture was intended to deter all but the most desperate, as they did before the New Poor Law of 1838 and after. John Foster, an elderly itinerant beggar from Connacht, gave eloquent voice to the mental distance between rich and poor when he told the Poor Law Inquiry in 1836 that he would rather have 'the free range outside' where he could keep supple his joints 'by a walk through the country' (quoted in Geary 1999, 121). The failure of the 1838 Poor Law to tackle the problem of vagrancy and begging effectively meant that previous attitudes prevailed: ratepayers in a number of Poor Law Unions in the early 1840s demanded a return to the old custom of casual alms-giving as they came to see toleration of local beggars on their streets as both cheaper and more effective in deterring an influx of beggars from elsewhere (Geary 1999, 121–36).

A municipal answer to a national question

Dublin's north-side House of Industry was effectively a national institution, dealing with large numbers of poor not native to the city. As reported in 1818, of the 10,000 who passed through it three years previously, it was observed that a 'great measure' were 'adventurers from the kingdom at large', and no doubt some of them were demobilised troops returned after the victory at Waterloo (quoted in Prunty 1998, 203). The fear of the urban elite that they faced a problem raging out of control, compounded by the associated fear of contagious disease, resulted in the establishment in 1817 of The Association for the Suppression of Mendicity in Dublin. Its members raised and invested the sizeable sum of £9,507 in putting to work about half of the 6,000 begging on the streets and encouraging the rest to leave the city limits. That most of these beggars were female should not surprise us since across Europe they elicited a more generous response from alms-givers than men, and it was a common strategy for the travelling wives of seasonal migrant labourers to beg during the summer months of absence from home (Prunty 1998, 201–18; Geary 1999, 123–4). Outside Dublin the picture was similar, as for example in Drogheda where between the cotton slump of 1826 and the outbreak of the Famine there was a marked increase in urban poverty (McHugh 1998). Nor was begging confined to the towns: in the countryside, especially in the 'hungry months' when the old crop had run out and the new crop was not yet in, beggars were on the move, often seeking potatoes rather than cash.

A tide rising in the west

Rapid population growth, particularly strong before 1830, was accelerating the subdivision of landholdings, particularly in the west, and forcing agricultural labourers to supplement meagre incomes through seasonal migration to harvest work in richer areas, both in Ireland and across the Irish Sea. As transport networks improved, internal seasonal migration seems to have peaked before the Famine, while migration to Britain continued increasing after it. We glimpse this seasonal migration in various reports commissioned by the Westminster parliament: during the difficult late 1810s, as many as 3,000 people from Co. Roscommon were estimated to be looking for harvest work in the Kilcock district of Co. Kildare alone. Similarly, large numbers were found moving from west Cork to the vicinity of Cork city; from the remoter parts of Kerry to the vicinity of Limerick city; from the midlands east towards Kildare; and from north Monaghan to Meath and Dublin; with the largest flow of all coming from Connacht to the richer eastern counties (O'Dowd 1991, 14–15, 39, 58, 65). We also get glimpses of northern movements in the 1830s in the Parish Memoirs produced by Colby's Ordnance Survey – another expression of the government's new spirit of enquiry which penetrated to the local level. For example, in one Co. Londonderry parish it was estimated that:

> from 80 to 100 persons have emigrated to harvest in England and Scotland from the parish of Lower Cumber within the current year. Those persons are chiefly the youths of both sexes and of the cottier class. There are many instances of man and wife, newly married and of the above class, going together to harvest. … There are very few instances of persons going to harvest to the southern or western parts of Ireland … though artisans and labourers and persons in various occupations go to Dublin, Cork, Galway, Belfast, Drogheda and many other seaports and inland towns to procure employment from the above parish.
>
> (Day and McWilliams 1995, 50)

Migrant labourers, as ever, were particularly vulnerable to fraud and abuse, and their working conditions were often extremely harsh. One group from Clare, working in Kilkenny and Tipperary, gave evidence in 1835 that they were treated worse than 'the slaves in India' – a choice of comparison reflecting perhaps the increasing flow of Irishmen into the ranks of British regiments serving in India. In some cases, disputes (often about recovery of wages) might lead to a farmer appearing before a magistrate at the petty sessions, but few migrant workers, far from home, had the time or inclination to wait for the law to take its course. Oral evidence, collected in the twentieth century, illustrates the wide variety of pejorative names applied to migrant workers, many of which, such as 'culchie', are likely to have originated before the Famine. It seems also that the most numerous group from Connacht enjoyed the poorest reputation and were most likely to be given a hostile reception (O'Dowd 1991, 46–56, 130, 203–5, 229).

Stepping up the professional ladder

As well as at the lowest level, there was also internal migration higher up the social scale. The expansion of government at every level created new openings for the sons of small farmers and an emerging urban middle class which often required a move or a series of moves. For example, even before the Famine a job in the police service, whether in the Royal Irish Constabulary (RIC) or one of the metropolitan forces, was thought by many of the small farming class a better option than emigration. Thus, William Waters, a Wicklow-born Protestant, served between 1810 and 1820 in Dublin as one of many rural recruits before joining the RIC. By 1840, when he retired with a pension, he had had successive postings in Galway, Mayo and Down. His son, Abraham, born in Dublin in 1816, joined the force in 1835 and over his career served in all four provinces. Similarly, Robert Dunlop, from a Protestant small farming family in Clough, Co. Antrim, joined the RIC in 1843, aged 17. With three other young Ulster recruits he travelled from Belfast to Dublin by steamship to be trained at the newly built barracks in Phoenix Park. His personal diary reflects the perspective of a greenhorn recruit: his role in preventing O'Connell's monster meeting at Clontarf; agreeable times spent in Dublin; and his circuits around rural Leinster. Training complete, the young constable was able to rely on the influence of his friend, the head constable, to secure him a posting back in Ulster; but at the last minute the commandant switched him from Fermanagh to Longford in the province of Leinster, leaving him crestfallen: 'I certainly did not know where the county Longford was, or by what way I should get to it.' It seems probable that the commandant suspected a breach of the RIC rules that sought to prevent corruption in getting favourable postings or postings to which a constable was already connected: possibly Dunlop had family connections in Fermanagh (Malcolm 2006, 63, 79–80). To some extent, such careers provided alternatives to emigration and had the effect of integrating rural and urban worlds. But internal migration could also prove a stepping stone to emigration, as it did for the many Irish policemen who transferred to colonial forces overseas – increasingly so after the Famine (Malcolm 2006, 70–1, 132–3).

Emigration

Pre-Famine Ireland?

Those below the level of the propertied class at the beginning of this half-century were more likely to have been concerned with the dangers of famine than with the proposed Act of Union. The harvests between 1799 and 1801 were bad and the government, stretched by war against Napoleon abroad and fearing social breakdown at home, tried hard to intervene, helping to ensure that excess mortality was measured in tens rather than hundreds of thousands (Dickson 1989, 107; Wells 1996, 163–94). It is a measure of the scale of the disaster that was still to come in the 1840s that this famine, and the ones that followed it in 1817–19, 1822 and 1831, took place in a period that we persist nevertheless in referring to as 'pre-Famine' (Mokyr 2006, 47).

Continuity and change

The extent to which emigration also helped to contain the rate of mortality is debateable. With Britain also badly affected by the subsistence crisis, increasing numbers of emigrants took the more expensive option and headed for North America. The pattern of the previous period persisted: departures were still disproportionately from the Ulster ports and Ulster Presbyterians still made up a majority of those going to the new world (Jones 1969, 46–68). As later during the Great Famine of the 1840s, many who left were the better-off or 'snug' farming families, driven to commit their resources to relocation more by despair at their future prospects in Ireland than present poverty and hunger. The Lord Lieutenant, Cornwallis, alarmed by the loss of such valuable economic and political support, attempted to curtail it, eventually by bringing in the Passenger Act of 1803. However, we should be wary of assuming that few emigrants were starving, in contrast to the emigration of the Great Famine, when so many were. Although it was true generally that the poorer an individual, the more limited was the geographical range of their migration, we should not underestimate the ingenuity of poor and hungry migrants. Certainly by the 1830s a strong presence of those from the labouring bottom third of Irish society was evident in the transatlantic flow. Migrants in the decades before 1845 were increasingly conscious that expanding America could find places for those with little more to offer than a strong back, impressive stamina and sheer determination.

Steering human capital

A new tension emerged in the first decade of the nineteenth century between the interests of the government and those of individual emigrants, particularly Catholics preferring emigration to the United States, as evidenced by Cornwallis's Passenger Act 1803. As well as trying to assist transatlantic migrants on humanitarian grounds, the government was also seeking to redirect migration by adjusting the permitted ratio of passengers to tonnage in favour of British and Irish-owned vessels, making the cost of passage in foreign, especially American, vessels more expensive and therefore less attractive (Adams 1932; 1980, 85–6; McDonagh 1961, 61–4). Rather than permitting unchecked emigration that would promote the growth of the United States as an economic competitor and assist the emergence there of an Irish-American community, the idea was to experiment in assisted emigration schemes that would invest 'human capital' in British North America (Canada), South Africa and Australia, to the mutual benefit of colonies and homeland (Akenson 1993, 141–53; Bielenberg 2000, 215–35; Kenny, 2004, 90–122). Any measure that might result in the closer integration of Ireland, just like Scotland, into the wider British imperial world was welcome in principle (McDonagh 1961, 22–53). Well before the Great Famine, however, it was evident that the government was fighting a losing battle in its efforts to tempt the growing number of Irish Catholic emigrants away from the 'honey pot' destinations of a rapidly urbanising and expanding United States. Emigrant ships might be encouraged or forced to sail to ports in British North America, but once arrived there was no guarantee that immigrants would take up residence in the broad expanses of Upper Canada and not drift south, as did the Mellon family who, having arrived in St John, New Brunswick from Derry, immediately took another ship south to Baltimore, Maryland, in order to join their relatives in Pennsylvania (Houston and Smyth, 1990; Mellon 1994, 15–16; Elliott 2002).

A call to arms

A neglected figure in the relationship that developed between Ireland and Britain after the Union is that of the Irish military migrant, now more likely to be wearing a British uniform than any other (Bartlett 1990, 173–82). Warfare with France from 1793 had massively increased demand for manpower, and the drum beat of the recruiting party was increasingly heard across rural Ireland, as in Wales and in the west and highlands of Scotland (see Plates 7 and 18). A striking piece of evidence of the pressure is held by the National Library of Ireland: a proclamation of terms and conditions of service in the British army which was really a recruiting poster – one of 5,000 printed in October 1806 for the War Office in Dublin Castle when Napoleon was in the ascendant. What makes it remarkable is that its language is Irish, without translation (Kissane 1994, 44–5). Such recruitment campaigns were clearly successful: it is estimated that by the end of the war in 1815 with the final defeat of Napoleon at Waterloo, about 150,000 Irishmen had served in the British military; even greater than the number of the civilian emigrants who crossed the Atlantic during those 22 years (Spiers 1996, 335)

If the Seven Years War can be thought of as the first 'world war', then the Napoleonic Wars constituted the second, with the result that most Irish recruits to the British forces were moved overseas. Even those who served no further afield than continental Europe might end up within the overseas empire, as did the many veterans of Waterloo who were rewarded with land grants in British North America. Many such Irish soldiers and sailors encouraged further emigration, as did significant numbers of demobilised troops, returning to hard times in rural Ireland after service in the war with America (1812–15) and circulating stories of the bounty that they had witnessed in the new world (Miller 1985, 203). After 1815, the Irish – Catholics in particular – continued to make up a significantly disproportionate element of the British army: in 1830 there were more than 40,000 Irish non-commissioned officers and other ranks – 42 per cent of the army as a whole; and although this proportion declined gradually, it remained at around 30 per cent for the rest of the nineteenth century. This included increasing numbers of Irish recruited in Britain itself (Spiers 1996, 337).

Dispirit strands

The experience of one individual illustrates the complex, intertwined strands of migration patterns during the first half of the century. Maurice Shea, a labourer, born in 1794 at Prior near Tralee in Kerry, joined the Kerry Militia when he was 18 and a year later enlisted in the 73rd Foot (see Plate 19). Three years later he fought at Waterloo, surviving to be discharged with the rank of corporal in 1822, on a pension of 6d per day, suffering according to his record from a general debility as a consequence of fever and wounds received on service in Ceylon (Sri Lanka). On his return to Kerry in 1823, he married 14-year-old Mary O'Connor from Cahirciveen, joined the British Auxiliary Legion at Cork, and as a lieutenant saw further active service in the Spanish Civil War (1833–39). When the Legion was disbanded in 1838, he returned once more to Ireland and in 1847, at the height of the Great Famine, with his wife and six children he emigrated to Canada – four of the children dying soon after disembarkation. Despite contracting fever himself, Shea recovered and went on with the remainder of his family to settle in Montreal where he gained employment, first in the constabulary and then in Montreal jail. When he eventually died in 1892, aged 98, he had the distinction of being the last survivor of the entire British army at Waterloo (Lagden and Sly 1998, 205–11). Thanks to Shea's remarkable longevity, the details of his migration story were preserved, giving an idea of those of his countless unrecorded fellow migrants.

The shift to mass migration

The decades between the Union and the outbreak of the Great Famine witnessed two major developments, which not only affected emigrants like the Shea family but were critical in the longer term in shaping the broad patterns of the century ahead: the scale of migration increased dramatically

to become 'mass' migration; and Liverpool became the dominant migration port (see Plate 17 and Figure 3). Although precise data, as before, are
not available, we do have better evidence in this period, thanks to the passion for statistical enquiry among those like Colby, which was spreading
in governments generally. One result was much improved record-keeping,
especially in the form of the passenger lists that captains of ships were
required to present to the authorities on arrival in North American ports
(MacDonagh 1961, 58–9). Ironically perhaps, the Act of Union did not result
in improved record-keeping of migration between Ireland and Britain since
this was now officially deemed internal migration within a single United
Kingdom. Nevertheless, we can be confident that just over a million emigrants
left Ireland for North America and about half a million for Britain. Compared
with the scale of emigration in the later eighteenth century, not just in terms
of absolute numbers but also as a proportion of the total population, it is
clear that the 'mass' migration, although still generally thought of as beginning with the Great Famine of the 1840s, was already underway from 1825
(Coleman 1999, 107). While almost half of transatlantic emigrants were
arriving in ports in British North America, mainly Quebec and St John,
New Brunswick, as many as half of these moved on to settle south of the
49th parallel – an indication of the extent to which Canada was a country
of emigration as well as immigration (MacRaild 1999, 10; Kenny 2000,
45–6). The second main destination for migrants from Ireland in this period
was Britain. Our best method of estimating seasonal migration and step-
migration through Britain is to compare change between National Censuses,
held every ten years from 1821, and it is on that basis that we can say that
between 1800 and 1845 about half a million Irish migrants settled there,
permanently or semi-permanently (MacRaild 1999, 10).

Postponement and redirection

Thus we see the tradition of 'mass' migration to North America and Britain
established well before the Great Famine. The 'gear shift' or 'transformation'
in the aftermath of the Napoleonic Wars was recognised by historians as
early as the 1930s (Adams 1932, 68–70). As well as this, there was a steadier
outflow than had been evident in the preceding century. Financial panic
in the United States in 1819, and even more so in 1837, cut back departures
sharply, but recovery was more rapid than previously, suggesting improved
communications between potential chain emigrants in Ireland and their
transatlantic contacts (Miller 1985, 195). Furthermore, in such times of
crisis in America a greater proportion of emigrants had the option of redirect-
ing to Britain; 'stepping' across the Irish Sea, settling for a while to build
up more capital, and then pressing on to the ultimate goal across the
Atlantic.

Gateway to the new world

The second major development in this period was the emergence of Liverpool as the single most important port of embarkation for Irish transatlantic migrants. By 1825 Liverpool's pre-eminence was secured and while ports in Ireland, including Dublin, Belfast and Derry, Sligo and Cork, continued to offer direct passages across the ocean, none could hope to compete with Merseyside. Still in the age of sail, Liverpool was the main transatlantic emigrant port of choice, not only for emigrants across the whole of Britain and Ireland, but also for emigrants across northern and eastern Europe: the huge scale of its operation gave it a clear commercial edge, making the prices it offered for a passage the most competitive.

The vast majority of Irish migrants were in transit to North America, but many who arrived on Merseyside moved no further. By mid-century Liverpool was the most distinctively Irish city in Britain, ahead of Glasgow and Manchester, with almost a quarter of its inhabitants Irish-born, earning it the nickname 'the capital of Ireland'. As early as the 1790s, observers were noting an influx of Irish and Welsh migrants – a strong indication of the transition that was underway. The port that in the eighteenth century had been a key player in the trans-shipment of millions of slaves across the Atlantic was now gearing up for fare-paying passengers (Scally 1984, 7; Aughton 2003, 97; Belchem and MacRaild 2006, 305–8; Belchem 2007). Transition from the age of sail to steam started in 1819 when the first steamship sailings between Liverpool and Dublin were made; five years later the City of Dublin Steam Packet Company launched its Dublin–Liverpool service. By the following decade a great range of ports in Ireland were directly connected by steamship service to Liverpool (Pearsall 1989, 111–20; McRonald 2005, 17–37). The network now was in place that would facilitate mass emigration during and after the Great Famine.

Conclusion

If not well 'married', Ireland and Britain after the Act of Union of 1800 became more closely integrated, not least through what was now technically internal migration, mainly from west to east. Looking back from Thomas Colby's vantage point in 1845, the British diaspora in Ireland had received few new migrants, while the much greater numbers that crossed from Ireland to Britain either did so temporarily or as part of a 'stepwise' strategy intended ultimately to achieve the crossing to the United States. The mid-point in this half-century, 1825, marked not only the emergence of Liverpool as the main hub of the Irish diaspora, but also the point at which Catholics displaced Protestants as the majority component of the emigrant flow. Although the subsistence crisis which followed the end of the Napoleonic Wars may have reminded some of earlier migrations driven by hunger, few contemporaries could have predicted the tragedy that was to come. The working of the 1803 Passenger Act indicated the limits of the government's effectiveness in regulating migration – limits that were to become so painfully apparent in the decades ahead.

10
Irish Migration, 1845–1855

So cataclysmic was the impact of the Great Famine on Ireland that in a survey like this the decade between 1845 and 1855 requires its own chapter. With the appearance of the potato blight in the autumn of 1845 the strength of the forces driving internal migration and emigration was dramatically increased. Although traumatic in the extreme, this did not mark a complete break with the past because while new migration flows were started in some areas, well-established flows were reinforced in others. The task of assessing change and continuity is made all the more difficult because few historians deal with the 'pre-Famine', 'Famine' and 'post-Famine' periods in a unitary way, and because so few have set out to identify continuities we are less conscious of them (Lee 2005, 211). Insofar as they can be reconstructed, the individual migration stories of the Famine generation exhibit a broad diversity, but all were affected by the general atmosphere of panic and the urge to escape. In popular imagination, the legacy of the Famine looms large over the entire Irish migration tradition, distorting the way many see both the century before and the century after: replica ships of this period, such as the *Jeanie Johnston*, are assumed erroneously to be 'coffin ships'; emigrant ancestors, who in fact left earlier or later, are assumed to be Famine victims; and the Irish diaspora is assumed to have been generated entirely by the Great Famine. For many Irish Americans, this compression of memory into the Great Famine experience has made it 'the basis of their origin myth', so that 'the coffin ship is to them as the *Mayflower* and Columbus's caravels have been to others' (Comerford 2003, 84). However understandable such over-simplification or lumping may be as a response by descendants to the trauma of ancestors, taking the long view of Irish migration we can see that much more than this awful scattering explains the Irish presence world-wide (Kennedy 1996, xv).

Immigration

Everyday life went on

Famine immigration sounds like an oxymoron, and indeed a survey of the huge outcrop of new research on the Great Famine around its 150th anniversary in 1995 confirms the impression that migration during this decade was exclusively outward (Donnelly 2001 23–5; Daly 2006, 92–110). However, more recent research has highlighted how much variation there was across the country as a consequence of the potato failure, emphasising the extent to which everyday life went on. It turns out that immigration, admittedly on a very modest scale, did continue.

Absentees return

Immigration from Britain – by civil servants, soldiers, land agents, churchmen and even tourists – seems to have stayed at about the same level as in the previous half-century. In addition, the crisis itself was the main reason for some making the move to Ireland. For example, the philanthropist Vere Foster, having been engaged since 1846 in sending relief from England to the distressed poor in Dundalk, decided in the spring of 1849, very much against the flow, to take up residence permanently on his family's estate in Co. Louth, eventually moving to Belfast where he died in 1900 (McNeill 1971, 43–7; Hartley 2006, 130–1). Similarly, Frederick Blackwood, first Marquis of Dufferin and Ava, was so moved by the horrific scenes he witnessed on his visit to Skibbereen in 1847 that he moved from England to settle on his family's estate in Co. Down (Dufferin and Ava and Boyle 1847; Hickey 2002, 198, 344). Elizabeth Grant of Rothiemurchus in the Scottish Highlands arrived in the summer of 1851 on her Irish husband's Wicklow estate, three miles south of Blessington, and kept a personal diary of the next five years of her life between their Baltiboys country seat and the Dublin season (Pelly and Tod 2005).

Munster needs you

Whilst some returned to estates in Ireland and others married into them, migrants from Britain in the closing stages of the Famine came in search of opportunities to gain land bargains and establish a new estate. One such was Lieutenant-Colonel Henry Horatio Kitchener. In the autumn of 1849, in ill health on half-pay and in search of a future role, he visited his younger brother Phillip, recently appointed land agent to the Earl of Dunraven, in Adare, Limerick. There he came upon the modest but bankrupt estate of Ballygoghlan, straddling the Limerick/Kerry border. By April of the following year he had acquired the property on favourable terms and crossed the Irish Sea again to settle there. With him he brought his wife and son, two young

Englishmen to help make the estate more agriculturally profitable, and later a nephew who acted as tutor to a second son, Herbert, born in June 1850. Clearly Henry Kitchener approached the challenge with enthusiasm, writing a letter to *The Times* in the year of his arrival in which he urged others to follow him in what he may have conceived as something of a second Munster Plantation. Herbert, who eventually became the recruiting icon of the British army in the Great War, gave little indication in later life that he thought of himself as Irish or even Anglo-Irish. His family left Ireland for Switzerland in 1862 when he was twelve. However, he did return occasionally to Dublin and the Curragh of Kildare, and he recalled working as a boy in the fields of his father's estate, alongside the local labourers (Pollock 2002, 7–15).

One man's distress ...

Another who moved to Ireland specifically because of the Famine was the renowned French chef Alexis Soyer, who was tasked with devising the most nutritious yet economical recipe for use in the soup kitchens of Merrion Square, Dublin (Kinealy 1994, 121). Also arriving in 1845 from Scotland to teach art in Dublin was the painter Erskine Nicol (see Plates 11 and 15). Others moved to Ireland or returned, as before, to further their careers. One such was Robert Burke, the future explorer of Australia, who had been born in Galway in 1820, left Ireland for education in Flanders, and gone on to join the Austrian army, rising eventually to the rank of captain. Notwithstanding the awful prevailing conditions, he returned to Ireland in 1848 to take up a post in the Royal Irish Constabulary. He re-emigrated five years later, this time to Australia (Henry 1997). Evidence of immigration from beyond Britain during this decade is sparse but it does appear that the small Jewish community in Dublin, numbering by now a few hundred, continued to expand slowly, due in part at least to fresh immigration from continental Europe (Hyman 1972, 155).

Famine, folklore and Victorian planters

Contemporary perceptions of immigration could be very different from the reality. A widespread belief of government, farmers and tenants alike appears to have been that thousands of English and Scottish farmers were ready and willing to move in and take over vast tracts of Irish land. This spectre of 'Victorian planters' figures prominently in the folklore of the Famine: for example, Thomas Magner, a Tipperary blacksmith born in 1860, informed the Irish Folklore Commission in the 1930s that the lands left vacant by those who died during the crisis, and by those who were assisted to emigrate to Australia, were 'taken by Scotch people who were imported at the time' (Póirtéir 1995, 249–50). But however welcome to Irish landowners such tenants might have been, few in practice had any notion of exchanging Renfrewshire or Tyneside for Roscommon or Tipperary: the 1851 Census recorded only 579 English and Scots farmers resident in Ireland as a whole, and by 1861 this had increased to just 886 – on average about ten new settlers per county (Vaughan 1994, 39). Notwithstanding the evidence of continuing immigration, it is hard nevertheless to think of a period in which Ireland offered less attraction to prospective immigrants.

Internal migration

Succour in the towns

How much internal migration was there during this famine decade? As noted in the previous chapter, there has been little research. Cousens concluded that 'the tendency to rush for succour to the towns was on the whole short-lived and insignificant' and that 'migration within Ireland during the Famine was remarkably restricted' (1960, 120). Challenging this view, Ó Gráda has made the general assertion that 'all famines induce people to move in search of food and in order to escape disease; there is much movement from rural areas into the towns' (1997, 148). As usual in such cases, the truth probably lies somewhere between, but the extreme nature of the crisis and the fragmentary surviving historical record means that precision in measuring the scale of internal migration is even more difficult than measuring excess mortality and emigration. In relative terms we can be confident that internal movement exceeded immigration but was significantly less than emigration. As the authors of *Mapping the Great Irish Famine* put it, 'the rivulets of internal migration were as nothing compared to the flood of people out of the country' (Kennedy et al. 1999, 40).

The 'long meadow'

Internal migrants, moving mainly from the countryside to the towns, as before fell into three main categories: those who stayed on permanently; those who stayed temporarily and returned home; and those who went on to emigrate. Here we are reminded of how internal migration and emigration are connected: by no means were all of those who crossed in the holds of emigrant vessels clearly decided on that course when they left home, many going simply to the port towns in search of subsistence but ending up bound for Britain or North America. Just as many of those who sought a transatlantic passage from Liverpool ended up going no further, so many others remained 'trapped' in the Irish port towns (Neal 1988, 80–104; Gallman 2000, 2–3). Even for those whose minds were set on emigration from the outset, a myriad of circumstances could complicate and delay their departure. The widespread extent of contagious disease, the want of ready money and the fact that demand for shipping consistently exceeded supply meant that many of those who hoped to spend only hours in a port might end up spending weeks, months or even longer. There was little that was neat and orderly about the emigrant experience of the Famine years, even in cases where the state or individual landlords provided assistance. In the case of the assisted emigration of the tenants of Ballykilcline townland, near Strokestown, Roscommon, in the winter of 1847, not all made it as far as Liverpool:

> it is all but certain that some who failed to board ship in Liverpool either slipped out of the march near home or perished from some cause on the road, ending their journey at some point to join thousands of other aimless or hopeless spectres lining the 'long meadow'.

> (Scally 1995, 176)

The gradual return to something like normality during the early 1850s was noted by the Poor Law Commissioners in 1856, when they reported 'an almost total disappearance of deaths by the roadside through want of the necessities of life' (quoted in Clear 2007, 127).

Family break-up

Many of those who ended their days on the roadside in this way were indeed refugees from famine for whom migration was primarily an act of desperation. Count Strelecki, representing the British Association in Ireland, reported to a parliamentary committee in 1849 that roadside deaths were so frequent that they went virtually unnoticed (Robins 1995, 126). As in 1629, 1729, 1741, 1801, 1817–19, 1822 and 1831, a main consequence of food crisis was a rise in the already sizeable vagrant population. Any survey of local newspapers and municipal administrative records during these years is likely to reveal evidence of such migration. Throughout Ireland, but particularly in the west where famine hit hardest, market towns acted as magnets to those in their impoverished rural hinterlands. In the early summer of 1848, the efforts of the Poor Law Guardians of Ennis, Co. Clare, to jail the multitudes of idle persons and beggars who had arrived in the town following a spate of evictions in the surrounding district, were only thwarted by the disease-ridden and already overcrowded state of the county prison (Ó Murchadha 1998, 178; see Plate 4). The conditions prevailing in Ireland during the later 1840s must also have increased the numbers of child migrants circulating within Ireland and moving beyond her shores as the crisis served to fragment families and orphan many. The vast majority of these remain anonymous to us, but we know something of the experience of young Owen Peter Mangan, from near Cootehill, Cavan. Just before the potato blight took hold his father died and he and his four elder brothers were dispersed after their mother remarried. While he sought desperately to find his mother again, following her and her new husband around the north of Ireland, his brothers ended up in Rome, Durham, Philadelphia and New Orleans. Mangan, eventually able to contribute to the family income, was set up with a job in a Drogheda cotton mill in 1853, and then with three young friends took the two shilling crossing to Liverpool (Fitzpatrick 1984, 23–4; Harris 1995, 143–5; Gerry Fitzgerald pers. comm).

The threat of strangers

The pulling power of the larger port towns on desperate rural migrants was even stronger. As well as the same kind of casual or official relief, there was the hope of closer access to food imports and possibly a chance to escape to Britain or America. The response of urban governors or Guardians, already struggling to deal with the plight of the resident poor, was, as usual at such times, both fearful and hostile. The principal cause of death in the late 1840s was contagious disease rather than starvation and the role of the itinerant poor in the spread of infection was well established in the minds of towns-people, who watched as mortality rates soared (Crawford 1997, 137–50; Geary 2004, 181–209). Their response could seem draconian, as in Cork in the spring of 1847 when the Lord Mayor ordered officers to man the city gates to prevent the arrival of any more rural paupers. The sense of threat and fear was mani-fest in the newspaper reports which painted a picture of poor wretches from the country, lurking in the suburbs, and then under cover of darkness slipping into the city to transmit their pestilential infections. A month after this measure was put in place, it was estimated that there were no fewer than 20,000 'strangers' in the city, whose population was normally about 80,000. In October of that year one Poor Law Guardian likened the state of the city – under threat from the starving hordes in the countryside – to that of Rome facing the Goths and Vandals (Kinealy 1994, 172; O'Mahony 1997, 169). In the newspapers, those seeking entry into the city workhouse were described as 'walking masses of filth, vermin and sickness' (Robins 1995, 120). In Belfast, for long inaccurately believed to have largely escaped the impact of the potato crop failure, a local newspaper reported that at Christmas 1846 there were 'starving wretches hourly swarming into the streets from the country' (Bardon 1982, 97; Kinealy and MacAtasney 2000, 143).

The broken people

Like Belfast, it was believed subsequently that Dublin had been lightly affected during the Famine, but recent research has demonstrated that it was far from escaping – confirmation of the lone view of an eminent architectural historian who had likened the city to 'a gigantic refugee camp' (Craig 1969, 309; Ó Gráda 1999, 167). The *Dublin Medical Press* noted as late as the spring of 1850 how 'strangers from different parts of the country, especially Mayo, Galway, and other western counties all presented the same listless, stupid, care-worn aspect, and the same miserable squalid appearance' (Ó Gráda 1999, 173). Institutional provision for the poor when famine hit – only seven years after the passing of the Poor Law of 1838 – was still underdeveloped across the country, especially in the rural west where it was most needed (Crossman 2006, 19–37). Furthermore, the Poor Law of 1838 did not really alter the fact that unlike the community-based outdoor relief system in Britain, Ireland's first statutory social services were based on the indoor relief of the national system of workhouses. If determined to stay outside the workhouse, as many were, there was little incentive to remain in one's place of birth or residence (Burke 1987, 300). As late as 1918, a report described Dublin as

> the rest house or alms house to which people broken in health, character or fortune come from all over Ireland, to shelter or hide themselves or to take advantage of its numerous hospitals and almost innumerable over-lapping charities.
>
> (Cowan 1918, 14)

So it is not surprising to find that in the spring of 1850 about a third of the patients in the Cork Street Fever Hospital, at the south end of the Liberties, had been resident in Dublin for less than 20 weeks (Ó Gráda 1999, 173). Similarly, Belfast institutions were reported to be crowded with inmates and patients who were drawn to the city, sometimes from further afield than Ulster (Kinealy and MacAtasney 2000, 109–38).

Death by destitution

It is unlikely we will ever know how many died on country roads and urban streets during the Great Famine. Their deaths were even less likely to be recorded officially or commemorated than the deaths of those residing in their local parish or subject to some form of indoor relief or care. However, the verdicts of coroners' juries carried in the newspapers allow some insight into their plight. In February 1847 the *Freeman's Journal* noted the deaths of John Mullherin and his wife Ellen, who some months previously had made their way from Co. Leitrim to Dublin: existing in squalid conditions in the yard of a house in Hendrick Street, on the north side of the Liffey, the couple were deemed to have died of destitution (Ó Gráda 1999, 168–9). While starvation stemming from destitution could and did kill many, it was the diseases associated with malnutrition, especially relapsing fever and typhus, that accounted for most of the estimated one million Famine dead. Internal migration, which resulted in the congregation of crowds in towns, spread disease; something not lost on contemporaries, who referred to it generally as 'road fever'. Needless to say, the 'unseen lethal baggage' that migrants carried was at its most deadly in the 'black' year of 1847, when atrocious winter weather added to the lethal mix (Geary 1995, 82–3; Crawford 1997, 145–6; 1999, 121–37).

Dublin and Belfast populations increase

Another category of internal migrants we can identify, with the benefit of hindsight, are those who made a permanent change of residence. Once again we are largely dealing with rural–urban migrants. They are revealed by comparing the Census of 1851 with that of 1841. For example, we find that in Dublin and Belfast, where cholera caused substantial excess mortality, their populations nevertheless increased by about 6 and 30 per cent respectively, through in-migration (MacArthur 1956, 306–7; Vaughan and Fitzpatrick 1978, 28, 37; Froggatt 1989, 134–56). Similar increases in the populations of other Irish cities and towns registered by the 1851 Census were in large part due to an increase in the numbers resident in workhouses, hospitals and various charitable institutions (Butlin 1977, 132). A less obvious feature of internal migration was short-distance migration within towns. In Dublin this resulted in the development of slum tenements through 'the steady out migration of the better off to the new suburbs, leaving the medieval core to decay, and the burden of its poor to be carried by those who remained'. Tensions surfaced in April 1847 when the Board of Guardians of the North Dublin Union complained that the South Dublin Union, despite having a greater proportion of highly valued property to draw on, was not doing its fair share to shoulder the burden imposed by the streams of migrant poor coming to the city (Prunty 1998, 23, 286; Brady 2001, 265). Similar developments took place elsewhere, as in Londonderry where thousands of paupers arrived to settle beneath the city walls in the Bogside (Hume 2002, 27–32). These were among those who survived. The number of dead as a result of the Famine – those departed to the 'next world' rather than to some 'new world' in Ireland or beyond – is estimated at one million (Ó Gráda 1999, 85).

Emigration

The long shadow of Black '47

The sheer scale of emigration during the Great Famine decade is staggering: 2.1 million adults and children left Ireland (Donnelly 2001, 178). The vast scale of the exodus becomes even more apparent when we realise that 'more people left Ireland in just eleven years than during the preceding two and one-half centuries' (Miller 1985, 291). However, worse was to come. Looking forward, the huge Famine emigration takes on a slightly different perspective: in the 65 years between 1856 and 1921, between 4.1 and 4.5 million adults and children left Ireland (Miller 1985, 346). Bearing this in mind is particularly important because of the way the extreme crisis of the Famine years, with the spectre of 'Black '47' and the 'coffin ships', still distorts the popular imagination. It is little wonder that it should, considering the circumstances in which the phrase 'coffin ships' was picked up from the 'sailing coffins' remark made by Thomas D'Arcy McGee in a speech to the Irish Confederation on St Patrick's Day 1848:

> The towns have become one universal poorhouse and fever shed, the country one great grave-yard. The survivors of the famine and pestilence have fled to the sea-coast and embarked for America, with disease festering in their blood. They have lost sight of Ireland, and the ships that bore them have become sailing coffins, and carried them to a new world, indeed; not to America, but to eternity!

McGee's reference to 'sailing coffins' created a sensation and before long the vessels that had carried Famine migrants across the Atlantic were all referred to as coffin ships (Wilson 2008, 191–2). However, we should be wary of the assumption that all Irish emigrants, before and after this decade, were similarly famine-driven and accommodated in coffin ships (Ó Gráda 1999, 104–14). Indeed, we might also caution against the assumption that all who left during the course of this decade might be so depicted. We should bear in mind that even if Ireland entirely escaped the potato blight, it is very likely that hundreds of thousands of migrants would in any case have left Ireland's shores in the five years after 1845.

Hoping to step through Britain to the new world

While the wide spread of contagious disease included the middle and upper classes, there can be little doubt that the Famine dead came predominantly from the poorest third of the population and that it was among the surviving poor that the pressure to emigrate was keenest. Those taking the cheaper option of crossing to Britain were generally poorer than those who took the Atlantic crossing. Again, we find that estimating the scale of migration across the Irish Sea is difficult because no official records or shipping lists were kept in relation to those who, especially since the Union, were regarded as internal migrants. About 300,000 Irish migrants settled permanently in Britain during this decade, particularly in ports such as Liverpool, but given the central role of Liverpool in transatlantic migration, much larger numbers must have spent some time there, following the well-established strategy of 'stepwise migration', which used Britain as a platform for onward trans-oceanic migration (MacRaild 1999, 33; Belchem and MacRaild 2006, 328–30; Pooley 2006, 180–95). However, the times in Britain were not propitious for accumulating the savings necessary for an emigrant voyage that cost between £3 and £5 for the ticket alone. For Irish paupers disembarking from a cattle ship in Liverpool in 1847, the prospects of escaping the poverty trap in one of Britain's growing cities were generally slim, but better in some places than in others. Just as recent research in Ireland has revealed wide geographical variation in the impact of famine, so there was variation in how Irish immigrants were received in different regional and local contexts across Britain (Lees 1979; Devine 1991; Akenson 1993, 191; McRaild 1998; Neal 1998; Swift and Gilley 1999; O'Leary 2000; Belcham 2007).

Fear of refugees from famine

In Leeds a Poor Law official described the Irish applying for relief in 1847 as 'a peculiar tramping people', but the extent to which this was something novel and a fair characterisation of the Irish in Britain as a whole has been challenged (Fitzpatrick 1989, 636; Lee 2005, 188–90). Striking, however, is the sense of continuity with earlier centuries found in records of the late 1840s. Echoing our earlier example of the interception of illegal Irish immigrants on board the *Peter* near Bristol in 1629, we find in 1847 the master of the *Lady Ann of Kinsale* being fined by a court in Cardiff after he was observed landing some 40 Irish paupers on the south Wales coast. In the same year, an Irishman attempting to struggle ashore near Penarth was reported drowned after becoming trapped in a mud flat (Neal 1998, 71; O'Leary 2000, 81). Again, as in 1629, the scale of repatriation was considerable, with numbers peaking in 1847 when over 15,000 were ordered to be removed from Liverpool. According to the law, those who claimed poor relief in a parish in England or Wales and were deemed not to have been 'settled' within that parish could be refused relief and ordered to be removed to their original parish of settlement or birth. Despite the many practical difficulties, the threat of removal served some purpose for Poor Law officers under pressure. While some went voluntarily and others exploited the provisions in order to get a 'free' passage back to Ireland, those forcibly removed were often caught in disputes about responsibility between officials on either side of the Irish Sea which showed them little respect and left bitter memories (Rose 1976, 25–45; Neal 1998, 217–38). 'Irish fever' was the term generally given in Britain to the range of contagious diseases associated with famine, adding to anti-Irish sentiment already circulating in port cities such as Liverpool and Glasgow. The popular press often wrote in terms of the Irish 'swarming' or 'herding', as did the *Liverpool Mercury* when it made an explicit link between the removal of Irish migrants and the reduction of mortality rates in the city. Again we see continuity: it has been demonstrated that the correlation in the public mind of migration and disease, so evident in the 1840s, stretched back into the eighteenth century (Schellekens 1996; Neal 1998, 138). The behaviour of officials in Scotland was no better, especially in Glasgow which received the heaviest influx: Irish paupers were still being removed from Scotland as late as 1910, when the enabling legislation was eventually repealed (Collins 1993, 392).

'Coffin ships' in context

The majority who left famine-stricken Ireland in this decade made their way across the Atlantic, mainly to the United States, which received about 1.5 million;

a further 340,000 settling permanently in Canada. The attractions of the less well-regulated and cheaper emigrant shipping route from Liverpool to the Canadian ports, particularly in 1847, meant that, like Britain, Canada received Famine migrants in transit to the United States (Kenny 2000, 97, 102–3). After 1847, the direct emigrant flow to American ports, New York City in particular, became dominant. The higher levels of mortality experienced on board these vessels (up to 30 per cent), and subsequently at the quarantine station of Grosse Île on the St. Lawrence River, were shocking, but should not obscure the basic point that the large majority of transatlantic emigrants in the Famine decade survived the crossing (O'Gallagher 1995; Kenny 2000, 102). In comparative perspective, mortality rates on ships leaving Irish and British ports in 1847–8 were significantly lower than on German ships bound for New York – a point that should serve to warn us against easy assumptions about migration during this period (Ó Gráda 1999, 106–7).

Following well-worn routes

A small proportion of Famine emigrants arrived in Australia: about 23,000 or less than 2 per cent of the total outflow (O'Farrell 1986, 63). Between 1850 and 1855, when famine conditions were gradually abating, major gold strikes in Australia drew tens of thousands of Irish migrants, from California as well as from Ireland; less famine-driven and more attracted by the prospect of striking it rich in the outback (Akenson 1993, 96). Before 1855 only a few thousand Irish had arrived in New Zealand, of whom the majority were military personnel and young, male step-migrants who had moved on from Australia in search of gold or land (Hearn 2000, 56–8). Numbers similar to those in New Zealand were arriving in Argentina where, despite the introduction in 1848 of an assisted migration scheme, there was no Famine-related surge (Murray 1919, 163; McKenna 2000, 202). In emigration to South Africa, there was a peak between 1848 and 1850 with about 9,000 arriving in the Cape and Natal (McCracken 2000, 255). Given that much larger numbers were undertaking passages across the south Atlantic and the Indian Ocean, it may seem curious that more Irish did not opt for the shorter journey to the Cape. In presenting South Africa as 'the land the Famine Irish forgot', McCracken suggests that their reluctance is explained mainly by the negative experiences of previous migrants; the determined resistance of both the colonial authorities and the settled population of the Cape to further Irish immigration; and the fact that America, Britain and even Australia were simply more familiar as possible destinations and offered the prospect of greater mutual ethnic support (McCracken 1997, 41–7). We have here an indication of the influence of a long-established culture or tradition of mass migration on potential emigrants, who generally prefer to leave as chain migrants rather than pioneers, and follow the well-worn routes.

Acceleration and innovation

We can say something too about where in Ireland emigrants tended to come from, although hard evidence is limited. In many counties of the west and south where destitution and mortality was most severe, emigration was a restricted option for most survivors, who were too impoverished or weak to get out (Cousens 1960, 119–34; Ó Gráda and O'Rourke 2006, 132). However, in some of the worst affected counties in north Connacht, such as Sligo and Leitrim, where in some districts there was already a strong, pre-Famine tradition of emigration, heavy rates of emigration continued (Donnelly 2001, 184). Similar continuity was evident in other regions of strong pre-Famine emigration, such as south Ulster, and the midland counties. That said, there was still a large increase in counties without comparably strong pre-Famine traditions of emigration, such as Mayo, Galway, Kerry and Clare. In broad terms, we can say that emigration during the Famine was heavier in the western half of the country than in the east, and that after 1845 the southern province of Munster was more fully represented in the emigrant flow than before (Ó Gráda 1999, 113–14). We should also note that at parish level there was considerable local variation in emigration rates, which may be revealed progressively by local studies of the country's 62,205 townlands (Crawford and Foy 1998, 16, 18, 21; O'Dalaigh et al. 1998).

The panic to escape

The potato blight, for which no effective remedy was found until the 1890s, was first reported in July 1845 but its impact was not fully felt until September, when the emigration season for that year was almost over. Nevertheless, 1845 was the busiest year recorded in terms of departures, with an estimated 75,000 leaving the country. In this sense the Famine exodus that followed was building on a well-established base. The fact that the previous generation had regularly experienced partial, localised crop failures, and that the worst effects of the blight were not evident until the late summer, help to explain the modest rise in emigration during the first half of 1846. However, when the full extent of crop failure became clear in the late summer and early autumn of 1846 there was a surge in departures: by the end of the year 100,000 had left. The following year was the most horrific: 'Black Forty-seven' (Sullivan 1867, 556). Although the precise origin of the term is obscure, it may be taken as a reflection of both the depth of the crisis and the bitterness of the subsequent memory. Widespread and unprecedented panic was reported among those determined simply to get out of Ireland (MacDonagh 1956, 320). The stampede to the ports was driven not only by fear of hunger, disease and death and included not only the poor but large numbers of the farming class, who had already been feeling the financial pressure of the new poor rate and feared greater burdens to come. In the spring of 1847 in Munster the *Southern*

Reporter described 'panic amongst the better class of farmers', who fearing the recalling of loans and increasing rates, had 'thrown up their farms to the landlords, drawn out what money they had been saving for years from the bank and left a country in which they saw nothing but famine staring them in the face' (CMS IED 9310531).

The extreme crisis tends to mask the fact, but for many, as we can see from the evidence of emigrant letters, 'everyday life' went on. Especially in the 'old zones' with long-established traditions of emigration, many who could not be classed as refugees – just as before and later – chose more or less freely to realise capital and leave Ireland to start again elsewhere (Fitzpatrick 1997, 161; Owens 2005, 30; Doyle 2006b, 215, 219). However, even if we suppose that in this decade as many as 800,000 emigrants would have left a 'famine-free' Ireland as voluntary 'emigrants' rather than as involuntary 'exiles', we cannot neglect the fact that *all* those who left, whether they liked it or not, were classed as 'Famine emigrants' (Lee 2005, 213–14). In this sense 'Black '47' was black for everyone.

Risking winter storms

In the hysteria to escape many took risks they would never normally have contemplated, especially in crossing the Atlantic in the winter of 1846–7. In the first place, much greater numbers than usual were prepared to risk leaving as 'pioneer' rather than chain migrants, without any family member or friend waiting to help them on their arrival. As noted previously, the transatlantic emigrant trade since the eighteenth century had usually been confined to the 'emigration season': it was not unusual for vessels departing in the summer months to advertise their departure as a final opportunity to cross the Atlantic before winter set in. The phenomenal demand for an emigrant passage overcame the established reluctance of shippers and passengers to run the risk of encountering the fury of North Atlantic storms from November through to March. Referring to Christmas 1847, the *Sligo Champion* reported how emigrants 'destitute of clothes' were 'leaving the country in the very depth of winter, on the eve, too, of a festival most sacred and holy in the estimation of the pious Irish peasantry'. It concluded that 'the dread of starvation forced those poor people to brave the perils of the deep, at a time when emigrants never before attempted to cross the Atlantic' (CMS IED 9502029). Winter departures increased the risk of encountering storms and shipwreck. As luck would have it, the winter of 1846–7 was exceptionally cold and stormy. Given the numbers of older vessels of dubious seaworthiness that were drafted into service to meet the exceptional demand such as the *Exmouth of Newcastle* (mentioned in chapter 2) these fears were real enough, particularly for those sailing from the smaller Irish ports. Even more perilous for the bulk of emigrants, however, was the increased impact of stormy seas on the usual emigrant hazards of dampness, which could accelerate the course of dysentery and other diseases; and seasickness, which could lead to dehydration and fatally weaken the already frail. In the overcrowded and insanitary conditions between decks the passenger's life was made all the more unpleasant (Coleman 1972, 128–54; Scally 1984, 5–30).

Arrival during the winter months brought additional problems. The *Quebec Mercury* in late October 1847 reminded its readers that 'winter seals up almost every channel of industry' and predicted that there would be little alternative to begging for the new arrivals from Ireland (CMS IED 9601283). In the United States, the unseasonal influx sharpened the usual 'nativist' response to immigrants, as reflected in November 1847 by the warning of Jacob Harvey, President of the New York Emigration Society, that 'no emigrant should brave a winter's passage; this should be discouraged on all hands; they bring misery on themselves and a heavy tax upon our cities'. He concluded, 'it is not right to crowd our streets at a season when we cannot attempt to send them into the country' (CMS IED 9311550).

A variety of experience

The intensive research of the last 20 years has revised the overwhelmingly negative view held previously, especially by historians of Irish-America, of how Famine immigrants adjusted on arrival in the new world. We now know that the majority were not from the deeply impoverished poor of the monoglot Irish-speaking, rural west. We also appreciate better that – in contrast to the winter weather of 1846–7 and the 'cold' economic climate in Britain – the Famine Irish were arriving in America at a relatively propitious time. Sustained economic growth was expanding the labour market with a rapid growth of domestic service jobs in middle-class American homes, for which the large numbers of young, female Irish immigrants were well able to compete. Research based on the records of the New York Emigrant Savings Bank has revealed the highly impressive performance by newly arrived Irish savers, subverting strongly held, preconceived notions about the Famine Irish immigrant in New York city (Fitzpatrick 1997b, 68; Lee 2005, 212; Casey 2006, 302-31; Doyle 2006, 218–19). However, this revised, much more positive view needs to be balanced by awareness that the poorer migrants who left for Britain were arriving in a country already in the depths of a recession and political crisis, where there was now an added urgency to the debate about the 'Irish burden' being imposed on those paying the poor rate (MacRaild 1999, 63–4; Neal 1998, 239–76).

A delayed peak in departures

The anxiety and urgency of the flight of 'Black '47' declined somewhat in the following years, but the peak in terms of the volume of emigration was not reached for a further five years. The Emigration Commissioners estimated that the total number of emigrants in 1852 was a staggering 368,764 (Kinealy 1994, 298). By 1854 the total had declined to 150,209. The next year, 1855, the annual number of departures fell below 100,000 for the first time since 1845 (78,854). Although famine conditions continued in some western counties such as Clare into the early 1850s, the good harvest of 1849 saw a significant improvement in conditions nationally (Kinealy 1994, 298–300). However, it should be noted that the total volume of emigration was some 30 per cent higher in the four years after 1849 than it was during the four years before it. Such a delay in the peak of emigration during a subsistence crisis was not unusual, but the exodus of the early 1850s is best seen both as an epilogue to the flight from Famine and as a prologue to the persistently high emigration of the post-Famine decades.

One in twenty assisted

If poverty, particularly in the rural west, prevented many from emigrating; how did others cover the costs of their journey? Some were provided with financial assistance, however, the government's role in sponsoring emigration was very limited, despite the circulation of various outline colonisation schemes in government circles. Relatively modest numbers of mainly women and children were given assistance under the Poor Law to leave the work-houses for Australia and Canada, but such schemes made a minimal impact, not least because it was rarely from the poorest Poor Law Unions that such emigrants were sent. Assisted emigrants, leaving the workhouse for distant shores, were content to go and passages were as popular with inmates as they were with those paying the local poor rate (Gray 1999, 299–315; Parkhill 2001, 41–54; Crossman 2006, 29–32). Some emigrants were assisted by their landowners, who in the drive to improve and rationalise their estates often drew on funds or credit from outside Ireland to ship out 'surplus tenantry'. Although such schemes could make a bitter and lasting impact, not only on the emigrants themselves but also on their descendants and those left behind in Ireland, in fact no more than one in 20 emigrants left in this way (Kinealy 1994, 304).

Resourceful strategies

So the vast majority of emigrants had to defray costs from their own resources. In the evidence collected by the Irish Folklore Commission in the 1930s we find stories of how emigrants raised money by selling land, livestock and household goods, or by soliciting aid from friends. Two resourceful Donegal emigrants, James Morrow and William McIlhinney, worked their passage to America as members of the crew on board a ship from Derry (Póirtéir 1995, 244–60). Others pawned clothes and household goods for cash, but this strategy appears not to have been as common as one might assume (Fitzpatrick 2001, 79–89). Some, particularly in areas where emigration had been well underway before the Famine, received remittances from family members or friends abroad, which helped to cover the costs of the passage, serving to remind us again of the continuities as well as contrasts with pre-1845 emigration. This in itself inclined Famine emigrants to consolidate the patterns of settlement overseas already established by 1845. Those not already linked to a chain might try the pioneer strategy by which one member of a family, often the father, would depart in the hope of establishing a foothold overseas from which to assist the remainder of the family to join them later. Family fragmentation was a regular occurrence during the late 1840s, as evidenced by the significant increase in advertisements placed in the 'Missing Friends' section of the *Boston Pilot* newspaper and also the large number of children named on the passenger lists of these years who appear to have been crossing alone (Harris and Jacobs 1989; see CMS IED under SHP – Shipping (Passenger) Lists). The emotional strain and personal trauma imposed by hard decision-taking can only be imagined. In May 1847 the *Freeman's Journal* reported the story of Ann Nowlan of Roscommon. Her husband had died, leaving her unable manage the 10-acre farm, so she gave up the place for a mere £15, sold a mare and a cow for £9 and got a little more for a few agricultural implements and household goods. However, she still fell short of the £27 she needed to take herself and all her children to America (Ó Gráda 1999, 148). Stepwise migration provided another option by which an initial journey across the Irish Sea, on board a cattle ship, could be completed for 2–3d and the £2–5 necessary for a passage across the Atlantic subsequently gathered there. Such sums were a huge hurdle for many. For a labourer with a family to feed whose weekly wage might average 6 shillings, achieving the cost of an emigrant passage would take months of disciplined saving (Ó Gráda 1999, 64).

A bitter legacy

Although it accounted for no more than a tiny proportion of the overall exodus, we should not forget that there was also a violent political response to the Great Famine in 1848 by the Young Irelanders, which resulted, as in 1798, in forced emigration: some of the movement's leaders, including John Mitchel, William Smith O'Brien and Thomas Francis Meagher, were transported to Van Diemen's Land (Tasmania); others, like Thomas D'Arcy McGee, escaped into exile in the United States (Sloan 2000; Wilson 2008; see also Plate 12). Although the later careers of these individuals took divergent trajectories, the memory of the Famine as mediated by the writings of Mitchel and the memories of Famine migrants in America fed into the significant development of the violent Irish Republican tradition in the diaspora in the next generation (English 2006, 162–71).

Conclusion

Looking back from the vantage point of 1855, the worst was over in terms of excess mortality by 1848. Also over was the peak emigrant year of 1852 when 368,764 left (the greatest number in all four centuries). The country having been stripped of about three million people, the task of the survivors and their descendants was reconstruction, which sadly depended on continuing emigration well into the second half of the twentieth century.

11
Irish Migration, 1855–1900

The impact of the Great Famine was felt throughout the rest of the nineteenth century and into the twentieth. Emigration persisted at a level higher than in any other country in Europe and thought of as a chronic haemorrhage, it resulted in steady population decline. The force-field of Irish migration had experienced a massive distortion. As well as the expulsive force of the Famine, the huge numbers of its emigrants now abroad exerted a relentless pull on those back at home. As well as its scarring psychological effect on the survivors, recent research has pointed to the Famine's long-term physical damage, in terms of both those who were prevented from being born and those who were born seriously damaged by malnutrition or starvation (Clarkson and Crawford 2001, 163).

The spaces vacated by those who emigrated were never close to being filled by immigrants. Most who arrived in Ireland in the later nineteenth century were driven by oppressive force or severe poverty in eastern Europe or southern Italy rather than attracted by the prospect of economic opportunity or an Irish welcome. As a result, the streets of Irish towns and cities remained remarkably homogeneous. While movement into them from the countryside continued, especially into Belfast, most Irish migrants who made the transition from rural to urban living in this period did so through emigration. In different ways the bicycle and the train transformed mobility and widened horizons. Contrary to what is still widely assumed, Protestants from Ireland continued to emigrate throughout the nineteenth century and into the twentieth. Although a minority of the emigrant flow since about 1825, their numbers, compared to the eighteenth and early nineteenth centuries, were much greater. Viewed as part of the huge nineteenth-century European diaspora of more than 50 million people, the Irish diaspora, both Catholic and Protestant, stood out from those of other countries because about half its emigrants were female, they all were so much less likely to return and so many of them ritualised their leaving as if it were a death. Even though we devote more pages in this chapter to emigration than to immigration and internal migration combined, they cannot adequately reflect the complexity and diversity of such an exodus.

Immigration

A minor resurgence

In the Famine's aftermath, immigration, as before, was minute compared to emigration, but by comparison with previous immigration, the 1880s and 1890s saw the most significant inflow since the seventeenth century. The single largest migrant stream into Ireland, as before, was technically internal migration from Britain, within the United Kingdom. The only estimate of the scale of this flow is offered by Fitzpatrick, who suggests that in the mid-Victorian period it represented about a twelfth of the flow in the opposite direction. Although this serves to emphasise its relatively small scale, it was still sufficiently large to overshadow in-migration from beyond Britain (Fitzpatrick 1996; MacRaild 2006, 8). As the vast majority of those crossing the Irish Sea left Ireland for industrialising Britain, we can detect at least one significant counter-stream: skilled labour from Britain coming to Belfast, particularly in the generation after 1880. As Lynch has demonstrated, the proportion of the rapidly growing city's population born in England or Scotland increased by almost half (4.9 per cent to 7.2 per cent) between 1881 and 1911. Employment in the shipyards and linen factories of Belfast offered couples and families real opportunities to migrate to double-income status (2001, 21-7). Jewish immigration from continental Europe, evident to a limited extent before 1855, expanded significantly towards the end of the century. Since there was very limited legislation to control the entry of aliens in place before 1905, it is difficult to be precise about numbers, but the Census returns for these decades reveal a significant surge in the 1880s and 1890s: in 1881 in Ireland as a whole there were fewer than 500 Jews, but by 1901 there were 3,898 mostly settled in the cities, with 2,048 in Dublin, 708 in Belfast, 359 in Cork and 171 in Limerick (Keogh 1998, 6–12). These recent arrivals were mainly forced migrants, seeking asylum from the persecution and pogroms that swept Russia and eastern Europe in the last quarter of the nineteenth century. Compared with other countries, Ireland was a very small part of the wider Russian Jewish diaspora of over two million people who left homes in continental Europe between 1880 and the start of the First World War (Klier and Lambrosca 2004). The large majority settled ultimately in North America, but in 1901 there were about 250,000 Russian, Russo-Polish and Romanian aliens resident in England and Wales. Relatively little industrial development and limited employment and business opportunities, combined with the small size of the long-established Jewish community, made Ireland a relatively unattractive destination.

New streams of Jewish immigration

Nevertheless, setting aside migration from Britain, Jewish immigration in this period was 'the largest influx into Ireland since that of the French Huguenots two centuries earlier' (Ó Gráda 2006, 10). In the stories of those who arrived in Ireland we see chain migration at work, with those arriving in Dublin and Cork having come mainly from the province of Kovno in Lithuania, and from the settlement of Akmijan in particular (Keogh 1998, 7–11).

Louis Goldberg left Russia in 1882 for the United States but was set ashore at Queenstown (Cobh), where he had the good fortune to meet another Lithuanian Jew, Isaac Marcus, who often went to the docks in order to offer assistance to newly arrived co-religionists. Having rested a few days with a Jewish family in Cork city, Goldberg proceeded to walk the 158 miles to Dublin. Arriving there from the south, like Carleton in 1818, he purchased a pedlar's licence with money borrowed from a fellow Jew and returned to Cork, selling Catholic holy pictures along the way, in the manner of the young Bianconi. By the mid-1880s he had done well enough to rent a house in Limerick and bring his mother over from Russia to join him (Ryan 1997, 167–70; Ó Gráda 2006, 17). In Belfast, where according to the 1861 Census there were about 60 Jewish residents, their connection was mainly through trading links with Germany in the linen industry. The community was formally constituted in 1871 and the first synagogue opened in Great Victoria Street. As in Dublin, this economically comfortable elite group was joined by several hundred refugees from Russia and eastern Europe, whose diversity of place of origin, religious practice and class resulted in tension between 'old' and 'new' immigrants, indicated by their use of separate places of worship until 1904 (Warm 1998, 224–5). Differences were even evident in their burial ground in Belfast city cemetery, where the 'poorer class of Jews' were prohibited by the Corporation between 1884 and 1929 from erecting headstones or monuments on graves (Hartley 2006, 108). Similar tensions between 'old and 'new' immigrants were paralleled in other diasporas, including the Irish.

Chains from Casalattico

Immigration from Italy accelerated in the quarter-century following the death of Bianconi in 1875. There was very heavy emigration from southern Europe and from southern Italy in particular but, unlike Ireland, as many as 40 per cent of emigrants from Italy remained within Europe. Of these only a tiny proportion settled in Ireland, but their presence has left lasting traces. As earlier in the nineteenth century, Italian stonemasons, church decorators and *terrazzo* workers found employment in cities like Belfast, benefiting from the expansion of Catholic church-building and the increasingly fine interiors required for the passenger liners being built in the shipyards. The Victorian splendour of the Crown Liquor Saloon on Belfast's Great Victoria Street (1885) owes much to the late-night work of skilled Italian craftsmen, and customers leaving such licensed premises at closing time might well have encountered Italian immigrants in the streets selling roast chestnuts or later chips from a coal-fired cooker and cart. Some of these street traders eventually became café owners, such as Guiseppe Cervi who in 1886, having been joined by his wife, Palma, opened a fish and chip shop in Dublin's Great Brunswick Street (later Pearse Street). He also invested in a lodging house in Little Ship Street, at the rear of Dublin Castle, in an area that soon came to be known as Little Italy. In Belfast, a small Italian community, many of them musicians, developed in the area of Little Patrick Street and York Street. Establishing migration chains, Italian immigrants in Ireland were predominantly part of the diaspora of the Lazio region, south of Rome, coming in particular from the province of Frosinone and the village of Casalattico. The intimate links established between villages in the *Mezzogiorno* and Dublin or Belfast mirrored those between villages in Ireland and particular new world towns and cities, like the link between the Blasket Islands off the coast of Kerry and Springfield, Massachusetts (Power 1988; Fitzgerald 2008). As well as these immigrants from beyond Britain, of course, the flow from Britain continued, including James Pearse, father of Patrick, arriving in Dublin from Birmingham during the church-building boom of the 1860s to work as a stonemason. He settled, as did the café owner Cervi, in Great Brunswick Street (Le Roux 1932, 2; Dudley Edwards 1977, 1). Just as Patrick Pearse, the Republican icon, was descended from an English immigrant, so too the great Unionist icon, Edward Carson, was the grandson of a Scottish immigrant to Dublin in the mid-ninteenth century (Lewis 2005, 1).

Immigrants could also become internal migrants. In Cork during the 1870s, among those locked up for begging were two Italian men in their thirties and a 27-year-old 'Mahometan' (Clear 2007, 133).

Internal migration

Some towns grow but most stagnate

In this half-century we find the population of the major port of Queenstown (Cobh), Cork, almost doubling, from 5,142 in 1841 to 9,082 in 1891 (Vaughan and Fitzpatrick 1978, 34–5). Evidence of that growth is to be seen today in St Colman's Roman Catholic cathedral, which still dominates the town: it was begun in 1868 to replace a much smaller parish church that was no longer fit to accommodate the increasing numbers of internal migrants attracted from the surrounding countryside by the new opportunities on offer (Dennehy 1923, 32, 53; Broderick 1994, 112–15). In stark contrast, the vast majority of Irish towns were shrinking as Ireland's urban network became overall a net loser of population (Vaughan and Fitzpatrick 1978, 28–41). It was a bitter irony that Queenstown's growth depended on attracting hundreds of internal migrants to service the needs of the hundreds of thousands who were passing through what was becoming Ireland's main emigrant port. The overall reduction in its urban population made Ireland stand out in Europe: in few other places were so many making the transition from rural to urban life by leaving their native country (Bade 2003, 41–5; Moch 2003, 126–31). Most provincial towns failed to grow, or actually lost residents, because those who would normally have been expected to arrive in them as internal migrants from the surrounding countryside instead became emigrants. They did so because, between 1850 and 1921, as one commentator starkly puts it, 'Ireland as a whole neither urbanised nor industrialised' (Royle 1993, 260). There was, however, a more striking exception than Queenstown to the non-urbanisation rule: Belfast. Indeed, Belfast's rate of population growth in the later nineteenth century was unrivalled in Britain. Linen, shipbuilding and engineering mainly drove the expansion of what had been a town of about 30,000 in 1815 to a city of 386,974 in 1901 (Budge and O'Leary 1973, 28; Maguire 1993, 69–70; Lynch 1998, 7). Suburban infilling between small settlements to the east, like Holywood, along the south shore of Belfast Lough, and the expansion of the shipyards and city docks in the second half of the century gave Belfast its modern character (see Plate 16). Such was the atmosphere there at the close of the century that one historian has well compared it with that of the contemporary Gold Rush towns of the American West (Gray 2006).

Industrial opportunities

Internal migrants were attracted into satellite towns around Belfast such as Lisburn, whose population almost doubled in the half-century after 1841, from about 6,000 to 12,000 (Vaughan and Fitzpatrick 1978, 36–7). Patterns of internal migration and settlement were determined largely by the location of new industries and facilitated by an expanding transport network. From the early 1850s, powerloom weaving factories were being erected in towns such as Portadown, 30 miles south-west of Belfast. It was, however, the routes of the newly opened railway lines that did most to boost this town's appeal to prospective migrants. In 1852 the new line from Dublin linked up with the Ulster Railway at Portadown, fixing its importance as a major junction. Had the route through Armagh been taken, as originally proposed by the Railway Commissioners, the pattern of internal migration would have been quite different (Butlin 1977, 133–4; Crawford 2001, 874–6). As it was, Portadown's population grew: in 1851 it was 3,091; in 1901 it was 10,092. By contrast, Armagh's population in the same period shrank from 10,245 to 7,588 (Vaughan and Fitzpatrick 1978, 36–7). So, as industrialisation proceeded and the reservoirs of rural labour emptied, mainly overseas, there were some winners in the hierarchy of provincial towns but more losers.

Mostly passing through Dublin

Although Dublin's population continued to grow slowly, it was in a sense the biggest loser, providing a sharp contrast with Belfast. Between 1851 and 1911 the proportion of the Dublin workforce engaged in manufacturing declined from 35 per cent to 22 per cent (Daly 1981, 224). Unlike Belfast and many British and continental European cities, Dublin was not creating the industrial manufacturing jobs which sustained consistently high levels of new employment, demographic growth and strong inward migration. One historian concludes that 'migration into the city was extremely low', suggesting that the number of internal migrants arriving between 1881 and 1891 was only 6,500, a quarter of the total that emigrated from Co. Dublin to Britain and the United States. The number was almost certainly lower in the 1880s, when emigration rates were particularly high, than during the 1890s, when the recession in the American economy had a braking effect on emigration. Nevertheless, there is no disputing the fact that the flow of internal migrants into Dublin was very weak compared with emigrant outflow (Daly 1981, 222–3). The 1881 Census shows that 38 per cent of the inhabitants of Dublin (city and county) had recorded birthplaces outside the county. While every county in Ireland was represented in this group, it is clear that most had arrived in Dublin from the immediately surrounding counties, particularly those to the south. It was also clear that most were female, many of whom, no doubt, sought employment in domestic service.

Continuing poverty

Even though trans-oceanic migration was becoming less physically challenging, it remained by and large a young person's enterprise and, as earlier in the century, the sick, elderly and poor were well represented in the inflow to Dublin, ending up in public institutions or begging on the streets (Prunty 1998, 197–9). Throughout the second half of the nineteenth century, prosecutions for vagrancy remained proportionately highest in the cities, particularly in Dublin, with a predictable falling off in numbers after the Famine, but evidence suggests an increase in homelessness after 1875. Increasingly, arrests for vagrancy suggested the predominance of men among the wandering poor or perhaps they were simply more likely to be taken by the police. More vagrants in this later period were 'strangers' in the place of arrest, more likely to have travelled some distance, but less likely than one might anticipate to have originated in the poorest western province of Connacht. At the turn of the century, increasing numbers of tramps entered the workhouses as 'night-lodgers', often returning to the roads by day. Whilst the stark horrors encountered in the late 1840s may have passed, the migrant life of the poor rarely exhibited much of the romance of freedom attached to it by more comfortable observers. As Clear concludes, 'most destitute people on the move went round and round a shrinking circle of deprivation as monotonous as it was debilitating' (2007, 127–35).

Derry: growing together

Another contrast to Dublin was Derry, which had developed like Belfast, albeit to a lesser extent, doubling its population: in 1851 it was just under 20,000; in 1901 it was just under 40,000. Like Queenstown in the south-west, Derry in the north-west combined the functions of railway terminus and emigrant port, with emigrants from the 1870s onwards being tendered down Lough Foyle to the larger steamers from Liverpool, Glasgow and Belfast waiting in the deep-water anchorage at Moville. Although the modern city is today effectively divided by the River Foyle, the pattern of internal migration was not simply one of migrants from the predominantly Protestant eastern hinterland settling on the east bank in the 'Waterside' and those from the predominantly Catholic western hinterland settling on the west bank in the suburbs of the 'Cityside', including the Bogside: the degree of religious integration in the later nineteenth century was significantly greater than in the later twentieth century (Poole 1999, 557–71).

One of those moving into Derry in the 1850s was the step-migrant Thomas Gallaher, who arrived in Sackville Street as one of nine children from his family's farm at Templemoyle, between Coleraine and Derry, to set up his own tobacco business. Leaving Derry six years later in 1863, he arrived in Belfast to set up in the same business, first in Hercules Street and later in York Street, becoming eventually one of the city's captains of industry. Unusually sensitive to the situation of his employees, many of whom like him were rural–urban migrants, he reduced working hours and introduced paid holidays (Hartley 2006, 178–9).

Females on the Foyle

An unusual feature of Derry was its gender balance: the 1891 Census showed a slightly higher proportion of females in the city and its liberties than for Ulster as a whole (52.6 per cent compared with 51.7 per cent). However, the Censuses also show that in the 1870s and 1880s the proportion of females emigrating from the city and county was only 43 per cent compared with 47 per cent for Ireland as a whole (Census of Ireland 1892, 689, 759; Vaughan and Fitzpatrick 1978, 16, 262). The apparent anomaly is largely accounted for by the fact that Derry offered more employment opportunities for women than for men, especially in shirt manufacture where outwork could be undertaken in the home, often in the surrounding countryside as well as in the town, and increasingly in the city's factories. In 1902 the workforce in the shirt industry was 80 per cent female. The attraction of female labour in particular into the city had the concomitant effect of embedding higher levels of male unemployment and hence emigration (Ollerenshaw 1985, 85–6; Daly 1997, 27–8). Here again we see the threads connecting internal migration and emigration. We might also note that Derry's significant employment opportunities for women served to reduce the scale of prosecutions for prostitution in the city. Dublin, however, even by the end of the period, when arrests for the offence nationally were well down from the 1850s and 1860s, was noted as the prostitution capital of Europe. Young women from the country and provincial towns could still end up plying their trade in the capital, just as they had done in the preceding centuries (Clear 2007, 135–8).

Reaping a harvest

Although internal migration, like immigration, was marginal compared with the massive flow of emigration, and largely concentrated as rural–urban migration in Ulster, there were other cases elsewhere worth noting. In the previous chapter we observed how for some the emigrant journey might get 'stuck' and this continued to be the case in ports of emigration such as Dublin, Belfast and Cork, where many inhabitants fitted the bill of 'disappointed emigrant', with a few of them being more or less bitter returnees. As well as this, there was still some internal migration that was not rural–urban. Although the peak of internal seasonal agricultural labour migration had been reached before the Famine and the bulk of such labour was now directed towards Britain, some continued to the end of the century. This was especially evident in Munster where seasonal migration from the western county of Kerry remained important well into the twentieth century: 400 such workers were recorded as being resident there in 1905, of whom 90 per cent remained within Ireland. Such internal migration has been described as 'quite clearly defined' and consisting mainly of 'short distance moves into more fertile parts of the same county or to neighbouring counties'. Even by the last decade of the century 'temporary harvesters and potato diggers were still employed in large numbers on an annual basis' and were making a 'tidy living' (O'Dowd 1991, 69, 78–80). Harvesters of another kind were the clergy, whose careers could involve considerable internal migration, as in the case of the Rev. Richard Rutledge Kane who was born in 1841 in Omagh, Tyrone, and moved as a boy with his family to Belturbet, Cavan. Having become first a minister in the Primitive Methodist Church, Kane migrated to ministry in the Church of Ireland, arriving successively in Dundonald (Down), Dorset (England), Tullylish (Down) and finally Belfast, having become along the way not only Grand Master of the Orange Order, member of Masonic Lodge 314 and Vice-President of the Ulster Loyalist Union and Belfast Conservative Association, but also an Irish-speaker and patron of the Gaelic League – a reminder of how complex an individual migrant's trajectory might be (Hartley 2006, 58–9).

Joining up, joining together

There was also some internal migration in the countryside as mostly 'strong' or middling farmers – moving up or down the social ladder – purchased and rented farms. For the most part, however, farming families remained settled in the 'home' place, with some members staying and the others migrating – mostly emigrating. Some managed to stay in Ireland, such as those that joined the police, but even managers in the police found the retention of staff difficult against the relentless tide of emigration and the lure of better opportunities elsewhere. As ever, marriage often resulted in internal migration, with women generally more likely to move away than men, and middle-class men more likely to go further afield for a partner than lower-class men, as in the case of police officers whose wider social contacts made them more likely than constables to marry a partner from outside their county of residence (Herlihy 2005; Malcolm 2006, 64–5, 70). Here we may also note the impact of the bicycle, especially in the countryside, as increasing ownership extended horizons beyond the bounds of the parish (Griffin 2006).

Emigration

Their destiny is America

Although annual rates declined from the peak of 1852, the staggering scale of emigration in the Great Famine decade persisted for the rest of the century and beyond: between 1855 and 1900 more than three million adults and children left Ireland; and in no single year did fewer than 30,000 leave. The broader European context helps us to see this in perspective: between 1840 and 1900 about 26 million left Europe for the new world. In all the countries of Europe in the later nineteenth century, with the single exception of France, emigration was a major aspect of life (Baines 1991, 7–12; Moch 1992, 147). Of course, each country's experience was distinctive and the Irish experience, as discussed in chapter 3, stood out in at least three respects: persistence, high rate of female emigration and low rate of return. By the end of the nineteenth century, emigration was as deeply engrained in social life as it could be for, as one contemporary observer put it, 'children learn from their childhood that their destiny is America; and as they grow up, the thought is set before them as a thing to hope for' (O'Riordan 1905, 292; quoted in Fitzpatrick 1996, 637). Also fundamental to sustaining the mass migration, as noted in chapter 8, was the expansion of the rail network, which brought a station within 30 miles of most people, and the transition from sail to steam, made largely during the course of the American Civil War (1861–65), which resulted in shorter, safer crossings and the extension of the normally restricted 'emigrant season' between March and October.

Many young men and women of 20

Whereas males generally predominated in the emigration flows from other European countries, the balance in the Irish flow between males and females remained more or less even. Between 1852 and 1900, the proportion of females emigrating (from the 26 counties later to become the Republic of Ireland) was 49.2 per cent (Akenson 1993, 166). By contrast, the proportion of females emigrating in the same period from Europe to the single most important destination, the United States, was 39.4 per cent (Gabaccia 1996, 91). Only in the flow of Jews from eastern Europe in the last two decades of the century was there a gender balance similar to that of the Irish (Moch 2003, 153).

The even gender balance is not accounted for by the emigration of family groups, which declined relatively after the Great Famine. The largest component of the emigrant flow was now made up of young single women, who may well have already entered the labour market but were still unmarried. Female emigration was most pronounced in Connacht and the rural west and least in the greater Belfast region and the more urbanised east (Fitzpatrick 1984, 7–8; 1999, 257). Employment opportunities for women in rural Ireland in relative terms were even more limited than they had been before the Famine, with the collapse in domestic spinning being particularly significant in the north. By the final decade of the century there was also a marked decline in the number of women employed in agriculture (Daly 1997 18–19; Bourke 1993, 37–8). There was a growing discontent with life in rural Ireland, sharpened by an awareness of the advantages on offer in America, as regularly described in that most trustworthy source of information, the emigrant letter (Miller, Doyle and Kelleher 1995, 43).

Migrating to marry

As well as a general growth in discontent in post-Famine rural society, there was also 'the very large increase in the proportion who never married'. Some of those who had rejected marriage entered religious orders, and while some migrated and became nuns, others became nuns and migrated as missionaries (Clear 1987; Guinnane 1997, 96; Walsh 2002, 141–4). Larger numbers of young women, often working for a relative on a small farm, were aware of the huge numbers of marriageable Irish men now overseas and those who sought marriage increasingly saw the chances of a suitable match as being a good deal higher in an American city than in their local parish. The recollection of one young immigrant who left Co. Clare in 1879 may not have been untypical: 'every Sunday night a crowd of us had a party at a friend's house, maybe a dance .... It was at one of these dances ... that I met my husband. I was then eighteen and a year later we were married' (Nolan 1989, 76). Once arrived in America, Irish women were found to be 'nearly always more likely to marry than the men' – an indication of their greater readiness to 'marry out' and move up the 'social ladder' (Foley and Guinnane 1999, 33). Marriage to a man with at least the same national if not regional or local origin as themselves was a desired outcome for many young women emigrants, but the attractions of economic, social, personal and sexual independence away from home should not be underestimated. Few young women could look forward with any enthusiasm to life within the patriarchal, small farm environment in rural Ireland. The expression on the face of the intending emigrant in *Letter from America* by Brenan may be interpreted as one of quiet anticipation, as we see concern and perhaps a little envy in that of her inheriting older brother (see Plate 13; Mary Sullivan pers. comm.). In the marriage market of the new world, the fact that the vast majority of women were English-speaking and literate gave them a marked advantage over immigrants from continental Europe. Of course, this advantage applied also to Irish men, but in relative terms Irish women were more advantaged in the labour market, especially in domestic service. In 1900 it was still the case in the United States that over 70 per cent of employed Irish-born women were engaged in domestic and personal service (Miller, Doyle and Kelleher 1995, 54). Despite the not always favourable representations of them in the popular press and theatre, there remained in middle-class American households a strong demand for 'Bridgets' or 'Biddys'.

Domestic service beckons

While the ready supply of such unskilled labour kept wages down and made domestic servants affordable for an increasing proportion of American families, this employment had several advantages for Irish immigrant women. Free lodging within the household and the provision of a uniform helped offset modest wages and still allowed remittances to be posted back to the family farm in Ireland. As one historian concludes:

> Domestic service provided the core of Irish female employment. It supplied the destinations to which millions of young Irish women went, choosing by themselves, and along female chains of family and friends, to leave Ireland and come to America.
>
> (Diner 1983, 93)

Although the work was long and hard, life in a better-off American household exposed the immigrant to polite American values and manners, helping the process of 'arrival' in the host society (Hotten-Somers 2003, 227–42). The effect of Irish immigration on the United States during this period was profoundly evident. As one historian has dramatically expressed it, 'None would suggest that an Irishless United States in 1900 would have been a Hamlet without the prince. But few would dispute that it would have been a very different and a poorer play' (MacDonagh 1956, 387).

Emigration for keeps

The relatively low rate of return or re-migration to Ireland (part of the immigration flow) is a second distinctive feature of Irish emigration to North America. As Schrier puts it, 'the outstanding fact about this American return tide was its minuteness' (1958, 130). Whereas the average rate of return for immigrant groups in the United States is estimated to have been about 30 per cent, the Irish rate is estimated to have been about 10 per cent; and some have even suggested as low as 6 per cent (Gould 1980; 't Hart 1982; 1985; Fitzpatrick 1984, 6–7; Miller 1985, 426; Wyman 1993, 10–11). However, more recent work by David Fitzpatrick has led to the conclusion that between 1871 and 1921 'return movement to Ireland, once rare and spasmodic, became commonplace', and that by the 1890s 'the "Returned Yank" as well as the Irish-born tourist had become a familiar figure in rural Ireland'. The British Parliamentary Papers relating to emigration reveal that for every 100 Irish passengers who left for extra-European destinations between 1895 and 1913 about 44 returned (Fitzpatrick 1996, 633–7). Whatever the actual balance between temporary and permanent returnees, the Irish experience of return migration appears to have been somewhat less exceptional than was once thought.

The difficulties of return

By European standards, the rate of Irish return migration between 1855 and 1900 was low, but it seems there was substantial variation according to time and place. There were surges in re-migration in the 1860s, as the transition from the age of sail to the age of steam was completed, and in 1874 when fares from the United States to Ireland were halved. While the Irish may never have come back home to the same extent as emigrants from Russia, the Balkans or Italy, return rates to Scotland and Wales were not very different (Wyman 1993, 11). Major downturns in the US economy also stimulated increases in the rate of return, most clearly in the deep recession of the mid-1890s, when A. B. McMillan, writing in April 1894 from Pittsburgh to her sister Eliza in Newtownards, Down, apologised for not being able to assist her financially and lamented her decision to leave: 'times is very dull in this Country, I sometimes think that if I had the money I would go Back Home again'; and the next letter the following spring found her 'all alone with very little to do' (PRONI D1195/3/39; 1195/3/41; CMS IED 9310349; 9310733).

Often sensed in emigrant correspondence is the vulnerability of the emigrant in the harsh environment of industrial America when times were hard or sickness threatened. Charles Mullen, recently arrived in Brooklyn from Sligo, wrote home a few days after Christmas in 1883 to his uncle and aunt, reporting that he was unemployed and ill; that 'this country is not what I thought it was'; that he was 'sorry now I ever came' and that his mother and father were 'disgusted with the place' and intended to return to Sligo as soon as possible, like 'the Hundreds here who would be glad to get Back to Ireland if they could' (PRONI T1866/9; CMS IED 8809051).

Actual return did not guarantee successful reintegration however, as in the case of the 41-year-old New Yorker admitted in 1884 to Castlebar prison, Mayo, as a vagrant (Clear 2007, 131). Return migration also seems to have been more common in the north-west and in northern Leinster, where a more open market in land may have provided the means to purchase a farm (Fitzpatrick 1989, 567). Those who came back with a little capital and little desire to farm could invest in a pub or spirit grocery, which many appear to have done. Often the licensee would 'double up' as an agent for one of the shipping companies and a returnee was clearly well qualified by experience for this work (see Plate 22; Molloy 2002, 99, 110, 132, 182, 210, 243). For the great majority of trans-oceanic Irish emigrants during this era, however, thoughts of an ultimate return do not appear to have been to the fore at the time of departure and the difficulties of reintegration for both those who succeeded and those who failed in the new world were equally well understood.

A rational strategy

A further distinctive aspect of emigration from Ireland particularly evident in this period was the 'American Wake', discussed in chapter 1. As with return, there seems to have been considerable variation in the practice of this custom in time and place and Fitzpatrick has pointed out that the much shorter transatlantic crossing in the age of steam and the increased possibility of return 'encouraged emigrants to leave Ireland with less fuss than before' (1996, 637). Whatever the emotional intensity of the last farewell, many families waiting patiently for those Christmas letters from Boston, Bolton or Brisbane, relied heavily on their contents (Ó Gráda 1994, 228–9). Emigration was if nothing else a rational strategy to deal with pressures on individuals and families. As Catriona Clear suggests, 'people emigrated to better themselves and, sometimes, the families they left behind them' (2007, 63)

Educated to emigrate

It is in this half-century that we see in emigrant correspondence the widespread impact on literacy of the system of national schools in Ireland which had been established in 1831, well ahead of most other European countries. By 1850 there were about 4,500 national schools educating 250,000 children. By 1900 there had been a five-fold increase: 8,700 schools with 1,250,000 children (Hyland, in Lalor 2003, 342). The role national education played in promoting literacy and accelerating the transition from the Irish language to English was central to the preparation for emigration, as teachers pointed out the special significance for many of their pupils of the maps and pictures of the world on the walls and in textbooks (Nolan 2004, 27–8). As one migrant native Irish-speaker recalled:

> *Bhíodh seandaoine an cheantair anon is anall go hAlbain blianta roimhe seo agus bhíodh siad i gcónaí ag casoid go rabh drochbhail á tabhairt orthu ó tharla nach rabh beagán léinn agus Béarla acu. Cuireadh chun na scoile mé féin. ... ar scor ar bith d'fhoghlaim mé féin scríobadach bheag léinn agus cha rabh mé ábalta cuntas a chur chun an bhaile cá rabh mé agus caidé bhí mé a dhéanamh.*

[Older people had been going to and from Scotland for years and they were always complaining that they were looked down on because they had neither education nor English. So I was sent to school. ... anyhow, I got together a little bit of learning and there was no place I went to for the rest of my life that I wasn't able to send an account home of where I was and what I was doing.]

(Mac Gabhann 1959; 1996, 27, 29; MacGowan 1962, 10, 12)

To a land down under

Through the national schools generations were prepared for migration to the English-speaking world, and for the further-flung destinations of the Antipodes state funding could help defray the costs of a passage. Although Australia had acted as destination for convict transports, workhouse paupers and orphans, it would be misleading to think of this destination mainly as a dumping ground for Ireland's social problems. The authorities in Australia knew the kind of emigrants they wanted and agents shaped the pattern of recruitment significantly. The desire to attract Ulster Protestants and what MacDonagh describes as the 'petit bourgeoisie' met with a good deal of success (1986, 161; Haines 1997, 233). Set in a comparative frame with migration to the United States, Campbell demonstrates the predominantly rural nature of their settlement patterns and the diversity of Irish-Australian experiences (Campbell 2008).

'A reading people' for the English-speaking world

In South America, we find the exception that proves the rule in terms of Irish emigration between 1855 and 1900: apart from Argentina which by 1900 had received from Ireland no more than 30,000 people, the vast majority of Irish emigrants left for destinations in the English-speaking world (McKenna 1992; Lalor 2003, 43–4). Knowing that it would be particularly helpful in the kind of employment open to them, girls especially were keen to acquire literacy before leaving school – something suggested by the young girl reading in Brenan's painting *The Letter from America* (see Plate 13). According to Fitzpatrick, 'the proportion of emigrants able to read and write seems to have risen from three-fifths in the 1870s to well over nine-tenths by the Edwardian decade' (1996, 615). As the Earl of Carnarvon remarked in 1884 on how information about life in the British colonies made its way back to every village and parish, 'the rising generation are learning to read and write, and the next generation will be a much more reading people than the last' (Hansard's Parliamentary Debates, March 28, 1884, Vol. 286, Third Series, Colonies, 987–1001; CMS IED 9907097).

As well as sending back bank notes or money orders, letter writers communicated information about comparative wage rates and the state of labour markets, concluding with advice to prospective emigrant, coded according to current circumstances, like traffic lights showing red or green: a 'red light' usually meant only postponement and when the 'green light' was given the letter often contained a pre-paid ticket (Fitzpatrick 1994, 6–36; Hatton and Williamson 1994). Thus Annie Moore, now immortalised in bronze in both places, made the crossing from Queenstown (Cobh) to Ellis Island (New York) in 1892, with her two younger brothers, to join their parents.

Peaks and troughs

There were peaks in the 1860s and 1880s and troughs in the mid-1870s and mid-1890s. Within the broad trend we also find regional variation, as in the mid-1870s when the Irish agricultural economy was at its most buoyant: more young men and women in rural Ireland decided to remain at home, but the flow from Ulster remained strong, suggesting perhaps some parallel with the more ambitious outlook of contemporary emigrants from urbanising and industrialising southern Scotland.

A patchwork of local diasporas

By 1900 there were few local communities in rural Ireland that did not have a particular association with some district, town, suburb or village in the United States, Britain, Canada or Australasia, so that, as we discuss further in chapter 15, we may see the Irish diaspora as a patchwork of local diasporas. Although such connections were mainly with the United States, especially since in this half-century it was overwhelmingly the main emigrant destination, we should not neglect other destinations: not only Britain – the second most important destination – but also the others, including South America, with which the counties of Westmeath, Wexford and Longford were particularly connected, sending between them three-quarters of the emigrant flow to Argentina (McKenna 1992, 80).

Growing diversity across Britain

The Irish remained 'by far the most important migrant group in Britain during the nineteenth century' – proportionally more significant in Scotland than in England or Wales – and recent research has done much to challenge the stereotype of an impoverished people, settled in ghettos in the poorest quarters of the big cities, by bringing to light the richer and more varied experiences of immigrants elsewhere (Aspinwall 1991; MacRaild 1999, 185, 43; Swift and Gilley 1999). Opportunities in mid- and late Victorian London opened for certain kinds of Irish migrants in a variety of fields, including the arts, theatre, journalism, politics, the law and medicine, and these achievements deserve fuller recognition (Cullen and Foster 2005, 10–11, 25). As its rate of replenishment slowed and its average age increased (more in England than Scotland), so the Irish community in Britain lost some of its vitality (Davis 1991; Collins 1993; Fitzpatrick 1996a, 655). Just as in 1700 the paths of many Scottish immigrants arriving in Ulster had crossed those of 'Ulster-Scots' leaving for North America, so now in 1900, as Devine has pointed out, the paths of many Ulster immigrants arriving on Clydeside crossed those of 'Scottish' emigrants leaving for North America, who were first- and second-generation immigrants in Scotland from Ireland. The long-established tradition of seasonal migration to Britain, particularly between the north of Ireland and Scotland, continued, resulting in ongoing cultural exchange in language, music, song, dance and sport in both directions, but by 1900 it was starting to decline, mainly because of farm mechanisation, and to diversify especially into construction and factory work (O'Dowd 1991, 24; McIlvanney and Ryan 2005). To some extent Ulster might be thought of as being somewhat more akin than other Irish provinces to Scottish emigration patterns in this period in that large numbers were leaving and transferring their skills to a global employment market, not from a rural but from an urban, industrial context (Devine 1992, 1–15).

Empire, migration and mining

Emigration to Australia took off in the early 1850s, driven mainly by the attraction of precious metals, especially prospecting in the goldfields of Victoria. Among those making the long voyage was Dorcas, sister of Thomas D'Arcy McGee, who eventually settled in the new gold-mining town of Castlemaine, Victoria (see Plate 12). The reputation of Australia in Ireland changed 'from that of prison to El Dorado' as the number of Irish-born in Australia reached its peak of 222,696 in 1891 (O'Farrell 2001, 90, 328). Following the lead given by Akenson (1990), an impressive concentration of research, mainly by scholars in New Zealand, has revealed the distinctiveness of the Irish experience of 'arrival' there, where much of the flow resulted from mining-related step migration from California and Australia (Fraser et al. 2000; Patterson 2002; 2006; McCarthy 2005). In the overseas environment that was probably most like 'home', the Irish pattern of settlement across the archipelago, which was more scattered than in Australia, resulted in a relatively muted expression of ethnic identity (O' Farrell 2000 34; Hearn 2000, 74). Although the empire and access to the opportunities it offered never reconciled the Hibernian 'bride' to the Union of 1800, we should not underestimate the evidence pointing towards a degree of successful integration occurring in later nineteenth-century Canada, Australia and New Zealand (Gray 2004, 13).

Seeking assistance

Government, Poor Law Unions, landlords and philanthropists all played a part in assisting the emigration of individuals and families overseas. Much depended on the attitude of the receiving society to assisted migrants. In Australia and New Zealand, for example, governments between 1830 and 1880 assisted migrants with the long crossing and set up a network of agents in Ireland, making clear that their ideal settler was a young Protestant woman from an Ulster farming family, preferably with connections already established 'down under', but in practice colonial governors found it difficult to be quite as selective (O'Farrell 1989, 670–1; Akenson, 1990, 14–15). Many of those who were assisted, or 'shovelled out', in the end considered themselves fortunate, not necessarily lamenting the spadework of those who sought to gain by their absence. For Poor Law Guardians and landlords in the bleak 1840s and again in the difficult 1880s, providing assistance was seen as aiding rationalisation of the congested countryside, initiating chain migration that would perpetuate the process (Moran 2004, 219–23).

A variegated picture in rural Ireland

Viewed at the national level, it seemed that the earlier prediction made about Ireland in London by the exile Karl Marx had come to pass: 'her depopulation must go yet further, that thus she may fulfil her true destiny, that of an English sheep walk and cattle-pasture' (1867; 1906, VII, XXV, 153). However, there was marked regional variation in the rate of change in post-Famine Ireland. Agricultural labourers were quicker to disappear and strong grazier farmers to emerge in the midlands than in the west, where change in family structure and emigration patterns might be delayed beyond the 1880s. These were the districts defined in 1891 as 'congested', where the conservative practice of land subdivision was slowest to change (Breathnach 2005, 117–18).

Few spaces at home

This regional variation is a reminder of the diversity of migration experience discussed further in chapter 15. Like fingerprints, no two trajectories matched exactly and we can see this expressed in the new type of evidence that becomes increasingly available from the 1860s – photographs. Whether of an individual, family or other group, each 'snapshot in time' begs questions about the story of each person: how did they come to be there, and what happened to them next? Examining photographs of farming families, the insistent migration question is where all the children would go when only one, normally the eldest son, inherited the land. By the 1870s and 1880s, families tended to be smaller and embarked on later than in the previous generation. Especially in the grazier farming belt of the Irish midlands, commitment to primogeniture and consolidation of the family farm left 'many young men of twenty', in the phrase of John B. Keane, forced to search for a livelihood elsewhere. As well as in the photographs, we can see the threads connecting the stayers and the emigrants in the paintings of Jack B. Yeats (a migrant himself from rural Co. Sligo): set alongside each other, his depictions of the departing labourer – leaving the land with his trunk on the back of the cart, or waiting on the station platform in his Sunday best – make a stark contrast with the settled snug farmer, the publican and the priest (Booth 1992, 62; Pyle 1993).

The Irish in the empire and against the empire

Much has been written in the last decade or so about Ireland's nineteenth-century engagement with the British empire, but it remains hard to sum up, with the picture complicated recently by much new work on the Irish in India (Foley and O'Connor 2006). Akenson's emphasis on the collaborative role of the Irish has provoked strong reaction from Nationalist and post-colonialist perspectives and the debate seems set to continue – evidence in itself of the continuing legacy of Irish migration (McDonagh 2005). Connected with the issue of collaboration is that of the role of emigrants and their descendants – as in previous centuries – in the nationalist politics of the homeland.

In the previous chapter we referred to the forced migration of Young Irelanders after the failed Rebellion of 1848, and their contrasting later careers illustrate the complexity of diasporic politics. Escaping in 1852 from Tasmania to the United States, Thomas Francis Meagher became a journalist in New York, commanded the pro-Union Irish Brigade during the American Civil War and was appointed temporary governor of Montana. John Mitchel, who escaped from Tasmania to the United States the following year, published his hugely influential *Jail Journal*, tried his hand at farming in Tennessee, became a leading supporter of slavery and the southern cause in the American Civil War, acted as financial agent in Paris of the Fenian Brotherhood and shortly before his death in 1875 returned to Ireland to become MP for Co. Tipperary. Having been pardoned in 1854, William Smith O'Brien returned from Tasmania to Ireland and took no further part in politics, except to denounce Fenianism. Having escaped in 1848 directly from Ireland to the United States, Thomas D'Arcy McGee moved to Montreal where he became prominent in the movement for Canadian confederation, returned to Ireland briefly in 1868 where he denounced Fenianism, and shortly after his return to Canada was assassinated by a Fenian. Another Young Ireland leader, Charles Gavan Duffy, author of the poem 'The Irish Chiefs' (see Plate 12), who had been arrested but not transported in 1848, emigrated in 1854 to Victoria, Australia, where he eventually became premier and speaker of the assembly, and was awarded a knighthood by Queen Victoria (Connolly 1998).

The Fenian Brotherhood was founded simultaneously in Ireland and the United States in 1858 by James Stephens and John O'Mahony as an expression of its aim to embrace both homeland and 'the Irish abroad'. Capitalising especially on the patriotic fervour of many Irish soldiers demobbed after the American Civil War, it mounted unsuccessful attempts to invade Canada in 1866, 1870 and 1871. In 1867, it attempted a further rebellion in Ireland, which also failed. However, this was not to be the last example of diasporic involvement in the project of remaking Ireland Irish (Senior 1991; Comerford 1998).

Conclusion

In this half-century, the population balance between Protestants and Catholics had shifted in favour of the former (almost 4 per cent more of the population in 1901 than 1861 were non-Catholic). This was more to do with the preponderance of Irish Catholics within the post-Famine exodus than any revival in immigration from Britain. However, the decline of the 'Big House', already evident by 1900, more than anything else perhaps was indicative of the state of British Ireland. Immigration to Ireland's cities, particularly by Jewish and Italian immigrants in the final decade of the century, brought a notable ethnic minority presence to urban Ireland, but as part of the Jewish and Italian global diasporas the presence was tiny. Analysis of rural–urban migration patterns in this period reveals the growing contrasts in the performance of towns, cities and regions, though most towns and cities remained net losers through migration. The limited extent of significant industrial development in Dublin sapped the capital's capacity to generate wealth and employment and its reduced capacity to compete with overseas urban centres in the English-speaking world was clear to see. Belfast by contrast accelerated its growth through industrialisation. Not unlike nearby Glasgow, it did so in the context of continuing and substantial emigration.

Focusing more on the experience of the individual migrant than the social phenomenon of emigration in the post-Famine decades, it could be argued that the transport revolution of the 1860s was more crucial than any other process or event. Again we are reminded of important differences between political and migration chronologies. The year 1863 marked the tipping point between the age of sail and the age of steam: thereafter the majority of those crossing the Atlantic were powered by steam. The annual emigration rate between 1855 and 1900 never dropped below 30,000. At its lowest level in 1876, an estimated 37,000 left (Bew 2007, 296). Had this buoyancy of the Irish agricultural economy been sustained, emigration might well have fallen to the more modest levels of the early twentieth century more rapidly. 1892 is also significant as the year when Ellis Island was opened in New York, with Annie Moore from Ireland leading the immigrant stream ashore on its first day. Yet, in many ways this marked the passing of an era of Irish emigration, the growing maturity of Irish-America reflected, for example, in the foundation of the Scotch-Irish Society of the United States of America in 1889 and that of the American-Irish Historical Society in 1897. By 1900 Belfast, having created the industrial jobs to sustain strong in-migration from rural Ulster, could boast a population greater than the capital, Dublin.

12
Irish Migration, 1900–1950

As migration within and between most parts of the world accelerated in the twentieth century, there was a gradual decline in the importance of Europe (Hoerder 2002, 443–583; Castles and Miller 2003; Bayly 2004). Global economic and political forces, already significant in shaping Irish migration patterns in the century before 1900, became all the more powerful in the century ahead (MacLaughlin 1997, 7–10; O'Toole 1997; Kuhling and Keohane 2007, 55–62; Inglis 2008, 106–14). We might think of Irish emigration as a component of one phase of globalisation eventually giving way to immigration to Ireland as a component of a second phase (O'Sullivan 2006, 118).

The high point of European emigration to North America came in 1907 (Baines 1991, 7). There was a reorientation of the main direction of Irish emigration in the 1930s, not unlike that of the 1760s, away from Europe and towards North America, only this time the shift was from America and towards Britain (see Figure 4). The Wall St Crash of 1929 and the Depression that followed largely dashed the American dream in Ireland and the great majority of emigrants now made the shorter but less promising crossing of the Irish Sea. Although the Partition into two separate jurisdictions in 1920 altered the context within which migration decisions were made, its impact on the volume of emigration flows, north and south, was marginal. The irony of Britain becoming the main emigrant destination so soon after the establishment of the Irish Free State (1922) was not lost on governments in Dublin, London or Belfast. Even during the economic war with Britain (1932–8), Dublin proved powerless to intervene. As the demand for labour in Britain increased during the Second World War, so did the immigrant flow from Ireland. Few immigrants were attracted to Ireland. The development after Partition of two clearly distinct and divergent economies and also two separate systems for the collection of statistics made seeing the island's migration patterns as a whole more difficult. Rural–urban migration, north and south of the border, continued, mainly into the greater Dublin and Belfast areas, although its scale was still modest by contemporary western European standards. For both, for the time being, the era of rapid expansion was over.

Immigration

West Britons and Irish Irelanders

As before, immigration from Britain continued at a low level, even less noticed now because of its long persistence. The Union had been in place for a century and the idea of Ireland as 'West Britain', like Scotland as 'North Britain', was well established since O'Connell had first mooted it in Westminster in 1832:

> The people of Ireland are ready to become a portion of the Empire provided they be made so in reality and not in name alone; they are ready to become a kind of West Briton if made so in benefits and justice; but if not, we are Irishmen again.

D. P. Moran, who coined the term 'Irish Ireland' and who founded *The Leader* in 1900, having worked in London from 1888 to 1899, had absolutely no time for such modulation. For him, 'West Britons' were those who did not measure up to his definition of 'Irish Irelanders', such as those who welcomed 'the Famine Queen' Victoria, when she arrived for the fourth time in 1900 and mourned her death in 1901. The eventual outcome of the competing projects of 'Making Ireland British' and 'Remaking Ireland Irish' was still far from clear. Belfast recorded its highest proportion of residents born in Britain (7.2 per cent) a decade before Partition in 1911. This reflected the employment opportunities for skilled and semi-skilled workers in the industrial city linked into the industrialising south of Scotland and north of England. From this point on, however, the proportion of British-born residing in the city continued to decline until a slight revival brought the figure up to 3.4 per cent in 2001 (Boal 2006, 79).

A declining minority

The Jewish community, which had become the largest immigrant group from beyond Britain in the second half of the nineteenth century, started to experience a slowdown in its rate of replenishment from continental Europe. Situated on the periphery, with a stagnant economy and a growing reputation for anti-Semitism, Ireland in this half-century was little more attractive as a migration destination than previously. In Limerick city there was outright opposition to Jewish settlement on 11 January 1904 when a sermon preached by the Redemptorist Father John Creagh had an incendiary effect: many of those who heard it joined in an attack on the nearby Jewish quarter centred on Collooney Street. Disturbances in the city lasted more than a fortnight and there was a boycott of Jewish businesses, lasting until the autumn, by which time the majority of Limerick Jews had left, some leaving Ireland altogether. However, the Limerick 'pogrom' of 1904 was an isolated case and the majority of Jewish immigrants arriving in the early twentieth century did not receive a hostile reception, as indicated by the absence of any mass popular movement promoting anti-Semitism, although this may have had less to do with tolerance than with the small size of the Jewish community, which never exceeded much more than 5,000 (Keogh 1998, 26–53; Rivlin 2003, 34, 91; Keogh and McCarthy 2005, 1–5; Ó Gráda 2006, 11).

Those to attract, those to repel

A change in the general attitude to immigration in Ireland and Britain, also in 1904, was indicated by the Bill introduced by Arthur Balfour's Conservative government to implement recommendations of the Royal Commission on Alien Immigration, set up in 1903. This was a response in part to the lobbying of organised labour concerned at the impact of increasing numbers of Jewish pauper immigrants on the domestic labour force, especially in the East End of London. Having failed at the first attempt, the Alien Immigration Act became law in 1905. It was based on the notion of discriminating between 'good' and 'bad' immigrants. The latter – the ones to be refused entry – were defined as those unable to prove that they were seeking asylum from persecution. In practice the new system discriminated against the poor, as in the case of Isaac Black, who arrived in England from Poland in 1905 and was refused entry on the grounds that he did not possess the minimum of £5 now required by law. Returned to Hamburg, Germany, he was able to obtain the necessary money there from a philanthropic society and this time made a successful crossing. By the 1930s Black had established a prosperous house furnishing business in Belfast and had been able to bring his brother Alexander to join him in what by this time had become Northern Ireland. In spite of increasingly lax enforcement and a generous appeals procedure, Jewish immigration to Ireland declined, most preferring to join the much larger Jewish communities in London, Paris, New York and, after 1948, in the new state of Israel (Klier and Lambroza 1992; Keogh 1998, 54; Rivlin 2003, 31; Winder 2004, 199–200).

Two states with little appeal

Following Partition, neither part of the island became more attractive to immigrants. The continuing perception of Ireland as a contested space or conflict zone, offering few economic opportunities, meant there was little revival in the modest migration flow from Europe that there had been in the generation before the First World War. The economy of the Irish Free State, over-dependent on the agricultural sector, remained weak and there was no significant expansion in the labour market. Northern Ireland benefited from the continuing flow of revenue from the British Treasury in London (about 80 per cent of total government revenue) but the major domestic industries suffered severely in the inter-war depression (Johnson and Kennedy 2003, 452–86). Needless to say, immigration was never in danger of becoming a priority social policy issue for ministers in Dublin or Belfast. Notwithstanding assertions by the Dublin government of independence, especially in the issuing of passports from 1924, there was close practical co-operation with Belfast in the regulation of cross-border traffic (Fitzpatrick 1998, 137–43). Before the opening of Dublin airport in 1941 and the onset of large-scale air passenger traffic in the post-war years, the Irish Free State effectively relied on British immigration controls, especially at the English Channel ports (Weldon 2002, 121–9; Engerman 2002).

Aliens and refugees

Implementing protectionist economic policies and conservative social policies, the official attitude to the very small numbers who did request rights of residence and citizenship was less than welcoming (Keogh 1998, 115–21). The issue of citizenship in the Irish Free State was eventually dealt with by the Irish Nationality and Citizenship Act 1935: those entitled to Irish citizenship included anyone born within the Irish Free State on or after 6 December 1922 and anyone whose father was an Irish citizen at the time of his or her birth. Provision was also made for a naturalisation procedure and the automatic denaturalisation of anyone who became a citizen of another country on or after reaching 21 years. A new Aliens Act, also in 1935, determined the regulation of migrants entering the territory of the Irish Free State from destinations other than the United Kingdom (which retained its special status). The workload of the Department of Justice, which was responsible for implementation of the Aliens Act, increased with applications from many seeking asylum from political and religious persecution, especially in Germany. Officials, pleading the weakness of the state's industrial base and pressure on its land resources, admitted that their interpretation of the Act was 'not liberal'; as a result – in line with many other small European states – few refugees from Nazism arrived in Ireland (Ferriter 2004, 387).

As war approached, the state began to monitor its alien population more closely. The files of the Department of Justice and Irish military intelligence reveal that in 1939 there were 2,354 resident aliens, with 864 (37 per cent) in the greater Dublin area. Most were American (1,143), with only five other nationalities registering more than 100 citizens – German (194), Italian (188), Belgian (142), Russian (133) and French (133) – and a sprinkling of others including Polish (39), Spanish (10) and Chinese (1).

Most immigrants 'returned Yanks'

It is indicative of attitudes to immigration that no separate record was made of those who had arrived from the United Kingdom or Commonwealth countries.

It is probable that a substantial number of Canadians were resident in 1939 and a smaller number from the Indian subcontinent, including refugees escaping communal conflict in northern India. Some of this group met Jawaharlal Nehru when he visited Dublin in 1949, the year India gained independence and Ireland left the Commonwealth. (Fraser 1996, 77–93; Kapur 1997, 37–8; Keogh 1998, 115–21). Though incomplete, the list prepared in 1939 strongly confirms the view of Ireland as peculiarly mono-ethnic or homogeneous in western Europe. The 1946 Census not surprisingly revealed that as many as 96.7 per cent of the population of the 26 counties had been born within the territory and that only 1 in every 200 residents was born beyond Ireland and Britain (Redmond 2000, 20). Outside Greater Dublin, even in 1950, one's best chance of encountering someone exotically 'foreign' was in meeting a 'Returned Yank'.

The impact of warfare

As in each of our previous half-centuries, international warfare disrupted migration. In this half-century almost ten of the 50 were years of war. The states involved, as Bade reminds us, 'faced internal fronts in which labour migrants and immigrants from enemy countries were transformed into enemy aliens and threats to internal security' (2003, 175). On the outbreak of war in 1914 some 30,000 Germans of military age resident in Britain and Ireland were rounded up and interned. Those arrested in Ireland were sent mainly to camps on the Isle of Man, where most spent the rest of the war. It is hard to know how many chose to return to Ireland. On the outbreak of war again in 1939, the Irish Free State's policy of neutrality made for a very different situation. As one of the governments involved in the hostilities, Stormont compiled a list of enemy aliens, identifying 200 Germans, 155 Italians, 32 Austrians and 24 Czechs. Although most had arrived in Northern Ireland in the 1930s as refugees, they were almost all arrested in the spring of 1940 and moved to the internment camp at Huyton in Lancashire (Barton 1995, 30).

Under suspicion

As usual, war tested the identities and loyalties of immigrants from countries now hostile. Victor Fiorentini and his wife, for example, had arrived in Derry from Italy after the First World War and opened a thriving restaurant business on the Strand Road, specialising in fish and chips and homemade ice-cream. Having helped to establish the Derry branch of the Fascist party after Mussolini's rise to power in 1922, Fiorentini was a concern for the local police in 1939 and he was given a friendly warning that should Italy enter the war in support of Hitler, as happened on 10 June 1940, he would be interned. Just in time, he escaped by car the short distance over the border to Muff in Co. Donegal, where he endured 'three-years' exile', living with his father-in-law, who also was of concern to the authorities because he was employed by the Londonderry Harbour Board as a pilot on Lough Foyle. Despite fears that the movements of Allied shipping might be reported by him to Rome or Berlin, Fiorentini was eventually able, using cross-border diplomatic channels, to convince the Northern Ireland authorities that he had no interest in espionage and he was permitted to return to his wife and business in Derry (Fisk 1983, 460–1).

The American influx

During the war there was short-term but large-scale immigration to Northern Ireland in the shape of over 300,000 military personnel, mainly after 1943 from the United States. Its impact on many places was great, as in Derry where the population almost doubled with the influx of over 40,000. Virtually a new town was constructed around the Langford Lodge airfield on the Antrim shore of Lough Neagh near Crumlin. Described at the time as 'the fastest growing suburb of L.A.', it was suggested that nothing like it had been seen 'since the Pilgrim Fathers went the other way'. In response to the 'Protestant Sunday' enforced throughout Northern Ireland, some US military migrants would 'escape' temporarily to Donegal or even Dublin. As many as 1,800 'inter-allied marriages' took place, resulting mostly in the emigration of local brides to the United States (Bardon 1992, 575; Kelly 1994, Barton 1995, 94–5, 101, 107).

Migration heritage and political propaganda

The new US presence presented an opportunity to the Northern Ireland government to match Dublin in efforts to turn the Irish-American heritage to its advantage. Increasingly popular literature in the north would reflect the desire of Unionists to highlight the contribution of the Scotch-Irish or Ulster-Scots to the story of the making of modern America. As Irish Protestants had been passed over in the narrative of Irish-America, so now were Catholics in the telling of the story of Ulster-America. Thus, in the bicentennial year, the Rev. Ian Paisley set out to explain *America's Debt to Ulster* (1976) and to refute 'a fallacy given great credence both in the United States of America and in parts of Ireland that the United States is under an infinite debt to the Southern Irish for their foundation as a nation'. Paisley sought to prove that 'American independence was in fact pioneered by men of Ulster stock', citing the words of W. F. Marshall that 'Southern Ireland made no mark on the United States till the 19th century' (Paisley 1976, xii, 73; see also Cromie 1976; Allen 1982). Marshall had published *Ulster Sails West: The Story of the Great Emigration from Ulster to North America in the 18th Century, Together with an Outline of the Part Played by Ulstermen in Building up The United States* in 1943, just as the Americans started arriving in large numbers.

Internal migration

From west to east

The 'new town' of Langford Lodge was one of the few examples of urban development in this period. As the process of urbanisation across Europe continued drawing internal migrants into the towns from the countryside, Ireland as a whole continued to lag behind: migration for most continued to mean emigration. Despite the border created in 1920 between north and south, the direction of internal migration was still predominantly from west to east. The 1911 Census reveals that in eight of the nine counties on the western seaboard, the proportion of those born in another Irish county was less than 10 per cent, whereas four of the five counties with the highest proportion – over 20 per cent – were on the eastern seaboard. All five of these surrounded the two major cities of Dublin and Belfast, reflecting their continuing, though in Belfast's case waning, power of attraction on their extensive hinterlands (Guinnane 1997, 123). Looking at patterns in the South between the Censuses of 1926 and 1951, we see that of the nine newly established planning regions, the only one that showed growth (7 per cent) was the eastern region, which was more or less coterminous with the old 'Pale' around Dublin. The decline in the other regions was sharpest in four of the five western regions, indicating internal migration to the greater Dublin area. Similarly, the greater Belfast area after 1900 continued attracting rural migrants, mainly from the rest of Ulster, but at an increasingly slower rate than in the later nineteenth century. Indeed, in the opening decade of the twentieth century, just as its splendid new City Hall was being completed on the site of the old Linen Hall (1898–1906), Belfast was making the transition to being a net loser through migration. At the same time Greater Metropolitan Belfast continued to expand steadily demographically as rural migrants moved into and inner city migrants moved out to the suburbs (Boal 2006, 57–83; Gillespie and Royle 2007). At about the same time as Partition, the population balance in Northern Ireland tipped from the rural to the urban. The tipping point in the South would not be reached until the 1960s (see Figure 6).

Comparing this half-century with the previous one we see that the rate of inward migration to Dublin was accelerating while that to Belfast was slowing down. Despite the slowdown, the Planning Advisory Board in Northern Ireland in the late 1940s was seeking to encourage industry to locate, or relocate and develop in inland provincial towns, such as Lurgan and Portadown, rather than in the disproportionately large port city of Belfast (Boal 1967, 172–3).

Planning a Leinster *Gaeltacht*

In the South, the new government sought to address the structural problems of agriculture in part by assisting internal migration from west to east. Before independence, the Congested Districts Board (established 1891) had tried to promote the rationalisation of landholding in the west through local, short-distance resettlement schemes (Dooley 2004, 132–6; Breathnach 2005, 137–42). After the election victory of de Valera's Fianna Fáil party in 1932, the vision of the new government included agricultural self-sufficiency, to be brought about through a reverse of the shift from grazing to tillage which had been so evident in the late nineteenth century. It was believed that reducing congestion in the rural west and stemming the flood of emigration could now be cleverly combined with the extension of the *Gaeltacht* through the creation of new Irish-speaking colonies within easy reach of Dublin. These aims resulted in new schemes, implemented by the Land Commission (which took over the functions of the Congested Districts Board in 1923), to promote internal migration from relatively poor, rural Connemara in the west to relatively rich, rural east Leinster, particularly Co. Meath. As commented on further below, this was a kind of 'transplantation to Connacht' in reverse, marking the wider effort to reverse the 'Making Ireland British' project in favour of 'Remaking Ireland Irish'. Little by way of national solidarity, however, was displayed by many of those in Meath, where slogans appeared reading: 'No more migrants allowed here' and 'This land is not for Connemara people. It is for Meath men'. Although no more than a few hundred families had made this internal migration, by the start in 1939 of the 'Emergency' as it was called, the importance of the policy to the government is indicated by the fact that land redistribution and assisted migration schemes accounted for 10 per cent of total public expenditure. By the late 1930s the Department of Finance was doing all that it could to curtail plans for further colonisation schemes by the Department of Lands. Furthermore, the continuing strong sense of psychological exile manifested by those whose physical journey barely exceeded 100 miles serves to remind us that the traumatic sense of breaking ties with the 'home place' could affect internal migrants quite as strongly as those who crossed oceans (Dooley 2004, 132–55; Whelan, Nolan and Duffy 2004, 175–96).

Leaving the islands

At the same time, there was continuing unplanned migration from Irish-speaking areas, such as the Blasket Islands off the Kerry coast. In 1916 the population was at its highest (176) but steady emigration, mainly to the United States, and Springfield, Massachusetts in particular, resulted in the official evacuation of those who remained in 1953 (Moreton 2000, 202–3; Royle 2003, 97; Ferriter 2004, 379). One of the famous Blasket Island storytellers and writers, Peig Sayers (1873–1958), had wished to emigrate but could not raise the cost of the passage to America (Coughlan 2003, 963–4; 1999). Another, Muiris Ó Súileabháin (1904–50), in his autobiography *Fiche Blian ag Fás* [Twenty

Years A-Growing], describes his sister's *tórramh Meiriceánach* (American Wake) and his own migration story: his leaving of the island on Tuesday, 15 March 1927; his crossing by boat to the mainland of Ireland; his *amharc déanach* (last look back); his onward journey by train; his arrival in Dublin where he joined the Garda Síochána; his posting to Connemara; and his return to the island two years later on holiday (Ó Súileabháin 1933; 1976, 174–6, 192 194; O'Sullivan 1933; 1953, 216–19, 241, 242).

'New Dubliners'

Despite limited industrial development, and against the overall trend of population decline, the population of Dublin almost doubled between 1901 and 1951: from 291,000 to 576,000. Between 1926 and 1951 the proportion of the population of the state living in Greater Dublin increased from under 15 to over 20 per cent (Sexton 2003, 816). Unlike Belfast, Dublin's expansion in the first half of the twentieth century was significantly greater than in the second half of the nineteenth. However, for many arriving from the west settlement in the inner city, especially in the slums of the north-side tenements, or even in the new inter-war suburban housing estates, might mean, as before, little improvement in their standard of living. One of the very few studies of these 'New Dubliners', published in the 1960s, draws on fieldwork interviews conducted in the late 1940s. It found strong threads of continuity between their urban 'new world' and the rural 'old world' from which they had come, which had been so thoroughly described by Arensberg and Kimball (1940, 98–122). Although the study detected greater intimacy and maturity in inter-generational relations among the 'New Dubliners', overall it concluded that migration had made little difference to them in relation to class status, the role of women and religious observance (Humphreys 1966, 2–3, 230–51; Ferriter 2004, 500–1).

'Going to Dublin was like going to Australia'

One 'New Dubliner' arriving in the inner city in 1935 was 16-year-old Tom Lynam, who had only come from as far west as Marlinstown, near Mullingar, Westmeath, to take up his first job as a shop assistant. Despite growing up within a 2–3-hour bus journey of Dublin, this was only the second time he had been in the capital. Writing his memoirs in the early years of the twenty-first century, he recalled that 'going to Dublin was like going to Australia' and that accordingly his mother had fretted greatly about him. Considering himself a mere *gábín* (awkward and simple person) he joined many other young men standing at the tables provided at the back of the General Post Office in O'Connell Street to compose his weekly letter home to his mother, different only from those being sent from London, New York or Sydney to mothers all over rural Ireland in that his letter had no enclosure: throughout those early years he remained dependent on the 'pocket money' his mother sent him;

and when she died in 1943, he regretted not having been able to afford to bring her on a visit to Dublin. From his account we can see how much this young internal migrant had in common with those who emigrated, including chain migration: it was his sister Josie, already working in Dublin, who had set up his first job interview, and he also had welcoming cousins, Lilly and Molly Cunningham, living in Glasnevin in the north of the city. Yet we also see that Dublin was not quite Australia: he could take the bus home for holidays, or cycle there in the summer – and here we may note that some of the family did visit Dublin on special occasions, such as the Fairyhouse races or All Ireland finals at Croke Park. However, his case also reveals the threads connecting internal migration and emigration: the family farm in Marlinstown had been purchased by his grandfather in about 1862 on his return from the United States (Lynam 2004, 2, 55–7, 62–3, 95–7).

The gateway to Britain

As in previous centuries, arrival in Dublin from the countryside turned out to be for some a preparation or seasoning for emigration, when the 'taste for city life' was acquired, along with the qualifications needed to pursue it elsewhere, especially in England. The 14-year-old Maura Murphy, whose memoir was a bestseller in 2005, arrived in 1942 in Dublin from Clonmore, Offaly. She was employed as a domestic servant, eventually married a soldier stationed in Portobello Barracks and left with him for Birmingham, where he had got work as a labourer in motorway construction (Murphy 2004). From the 1920s this pattern of step-migration to Britain increased (Delaney 2000, 49–50).

Belfast attracts east Ulster Protestants

In Belfast, which had briefly overtaken Dublin as Ireland's largest city in the 1890s, the rate of rural–urban migration slowed from the turn of the century and a religious imbalance in the inflow became more evident (Hepburn 1996, 113–15; Clarkson 1997; Boal 2006, 58–83). Inward migration was heavier from predominantly Protestant north Down and south Antrim than it was from the more Catholic Glens of Antrim or the shores of Lough Neagh. In both Northern and Southern Ireland, the 'county' market towns, in contrast to the late nineteenth century, generally saw modest population expansion, with less expansion in the west where emigration rates remained heaviest. In the western, predominantly rural county of Tyrone, we can see the change in the proportion of those living in towns of 2,000 or more: in 1926 it was 13 per cent; in 1951 it was 18 per cent (MacAfee 2000, 450).

Professional migration and all Ireland mixing

As well as rural–urban migration, migration between towns and within towns continued. In both states there was continuing 'career migration' by those such as civil servants, bank managers or clergy who could expect to be posted away from home or transferred on a regular basis. In the decade which followed the foundation of the Garda Síochána in 1922, members, especially those with families, often complained about the frequency with which they were required to move (McNiffe 1999, 91). Before 1922, officers in the Royal Irish Constabulary had been among the key agents of inter-provincial migration on the island so that large numbers of those who grew up in the early twentieth century with grandparents in more than one province owed their mixed heritage to the RIC (Herlihy 2005). Within the towns, migration was mainly by the better-off, retreating from the centre to semi-rural suburbs. From the 1930s, when a new approach emerged to deal with the decayed housing stock of the urban core, there was also working-class migration out to new housing estates, especially in Dublin (Prunty 1998; Brady and Simms 2001; McManus 2002; Ó Maitiú 2003).

Non-mobile migration and partition

As well as all this 'mobile' migration, Partition had enforced 'non-mobile' migration on all the inhabitants of the island – not by moving them physically from an 'old world' to a 'new', but by redesignating their 'old world' as 'new' (Bade 2003, x; see Appendix I). Thus all were 'moved', whether they liked it or not, from the 'old world' of British Ireland to the 'new worlds' of the Irish Free State and Northern Ireland. Those who anticipated that they would end up on their preferred side of the border after the deliberations of the Boundary Commission (1924–5), but did not found this 'non-mobile migration' most traumatic (Rankin 2001, 980; Hand 1969). Interestingly, the Irish precedent of non-mobile migration was 'not lost on the supporters of Pakistan or the Indian National Congress whose leaders were still fighting for a united India and fearful of creating "Ulsters" on the sub-continent' (Fraser 1996, 91).

Cross-border migration

Some of those who did not like their new position responded by migrating and so, notwithstanding the predominant west to east direction of internal migration, there were also south–north and north–south cross-border flows. The flow from south to north appears to have been very small, as is evident particularly in the greater Belfast area: from Partition, the proportion of Belfast residents born in the 26 southern counties declined fairly steadily, in 1991 the figure was less than a third of what it had been in 1926 (1.8 compared to 5.5 per cent). There was nothing new in such a small flow from the south to the island's only industrial 'success story' in the north, which could be traced back to the 1841 Census (Budge and O'Leary 1973, 30; Boal 2006, 79). As Britain became the main destination of emigration from the 1920s on, the general impression from the North was that 'the South of Ireland is turned eastward rather than northward' (Heslinga 1979, 101). Nevertheless, the government of Prime Minister Basil Brooke (1943–63) continued to monitor southern Irish labour coming north to work. Brooke himself regarded 'immigration' as a 'burning question'. When it seemed that Westminster might not sanction the Stormont government continuing to issue residence permits after the war, some ministers favoured having the Government of Ireland Act 1920 amended to give Stormont the necessary powers, but it proved impossible to formulate a practicable scheme that would discriminate in favour of 'loyal' southerners, and so the attempt was abandoned (Barton 1996, 83).

Leaving 'cold houses'

Eastward orientation was also evident in the more or less forced migration that took place in the wake of the 1916 Easter Rising and the Anglo-Irish War (1919–21). Most retreating members of the southern Protestant and Unionist minority went east across the Irish Sea. However, some retreated north: the Censuses show that between 1911 and 1926 about 24,000 of those born in the 26 counties had taken up residence in the six counties. Reference was made in debates in the newly established Northern Ireland parliament – then sitting in central Belfast until its move to the new Stormont building in the suburbs of East Belfast in 1932 – to 'hundreds of families' fleeing into Northern Ireland from as far south as county Kerry (/stormontpapers.ahds.ac.uk). In fact, the great majority of southern Unionists migrating north were arriving in Northern Ireland from the Ulster 'border counties' of Donegal, Cavan and Monaghan, which had been 'moved' into the Irish Free State. Most settled just over the border, especially in towns like Enniskillen. As a result, the Protestant population of Co. Monaghan declined between 1911 and 1926 by about 2,000 – almost 25 per cent (McDowell 1997, 130; Dooley 2000, 47).

A bitter tide of refugees

By comparison, there was a greater flow from north to south in response to sectarian tension and violence. 'The Troubles' between 1920 and 1922 in Belfast and other northern towns, including Derry, Lisburn and Banbridge, resulted in retreat by substantial numbers of the Catholic and Nationalist minority: about 23,000 people were forced from their homes in Belfast – 25 per cent of the Catholic population of the city (Gallagher 2004; Parkinson 2004, 13). As after the Battle of the Diamond in 1795, some sought refuge in the surrounding countryside, some in Scotland on Clydeside, and others in the South. In the summer of 1922, over 200 northern refugees were being accommodated in a Dublin workhouse and others in Marlborough Hall, while the new Irish Free State government made a particular point by requisitioning for the same purpose the headquarters of the Orange Order in Kildare Street. Some moved as far south as Cork city, but were met there with a less than charitable welcome (Parkinson

2004, 64–6). Needless to say, the legacy of both these forced migration flows – south to north and north to south – was bitter and long-lasting, exacerbated in 1935 by further trouble in Belfast, which resulted in more forced migration (Bardon 1992, 488–95; Fitzpatrick 1998, 118–19, 142, 164; Elliott 2000, 374–5).

Emigration

Two emigrant nurseries

The Government of Ireland Act 1920 and Partition, confirmed by the opening of the Northern Ireland parliament and the signing of the Anglo-Irish Treaty in June and December 1921, resulted in the emergence of two new reservoirs of emigration – both mainly to Britain – where previously there had been one. While the rate of net population loss through migration from the North was only about two-thirds of that from the South, it nevertheless remained substantial by European standards (Delaney 2002, 3–19; Sexton 2003, 799–800). The rate of emigration for Northern Catholics was more than double that for Protestants, but we should not assume this meant easy mixing with other Irish abroad. Only in the early twenty-first century are we beginning to appreciate some of the complex identity issues involved for both Northern Catholics and Protestants (Trew 2007, 22–48).

Britain takes over as the primary destination

As already noted, it was in this period that Britain overtook the United States as the main destination of emigrants. The introduction of immigration quotas in 1924, aimed mainly at restricting 'new' migrants from southern and eastern Europe and Asia, also affected the Irish, but only marginally, since the flow from Ireland had been declining significantly from the turn of the century. The decisive factor in reorienting the main flow of Irish emigration was the fall-out from the 'Crash' of the Wall Street Stock Exchange on 24 October 1929. The switch in direction was signalled dramatically by the stream of 'Returned Yanks', as reported by the *Donegal Democrat*:

> Patriots foretold that a time would come when the exiles would come back to the motherland; they were only waiting for the dawn of freedom; then they would return. That day has arrived, but how very different from the one the prophets foretold. The wild geese are returning, but their footsteps are slow and their faces are haggard. They are here because they can no longer get bread or work in the land of their adoption.
>
> (7 November 1931, quoted in O'Brien 2003, 86)

Also because of the Crash, the number of emigrants leaving independent Ireland for destinations other than Britain had plummeted: in 1930 about

16,000 left, mainly for the United States; in 1931 the number was only 1,500. Concentrated like so many other European ethnic groups in municipal and public sector employment, 'Irish America' was highly vulnerable to the budget-cutting of the Depression. The sting of unemployment and poverty in America was soon felt in Ireland, particularly in the west where the American letter had been so important to sustaining both the small farm economy and the continuing emigrant flow. Compared to the United States, the British economy was less severely hit by the Depression, but severely enough to decrease substantially the migration flow to it from Northern Ireland. However, in the flow from the South, where the conditions of unemployment relief were even less favourable, there was no significant decrease (Delaney 2000, 88). From the mid-1930s, Irish migrant labour was proving flexible and adept at exploiting niches in the new 'sunrise' industries of England in the midlands and south-east – pioneering pathways and establishing networks that would prove crucial for the following generation (O'Brien 2003, 78–97).

The 'cheap hotel'

Despite the eventual economic recovery of the United States, Britain would remain the main destination of emigration through the 1940s and beyond. Previously, the response in Ireland to downturns in the US economy had tended to be postponement of emigration rather than redirection. The rapid redirection now of flow to Britain proved traumatic for many, and not just for those who left: against all Nationalist expectation, emigration to the mainland of the recently deposed colonial power, with whom an economic war was still being conducted, not only continued, but increased. Traditionally regarded as second-best to the United States as a migration destination and 'more like a cheap hotel than a home', Britain was now the best (Mac Raild 2000, 64).

Continuity in the rural west

Nevertheless, there was much continuity in emigration between the later nineteenth and early twentieth centuries. The after-effects of the Great Famine were still evident in the disappearance of the cottier class, although not evenly. Between 1900 and 1914 emigrants were leaving mainly from the rural west, with about four in every five crossing the Atlantic to the United States. Most were from Connacht. In the midlands and central Munster, the shift from tillage to grazing reduced the demand for agricultural labour and as the cattle herds grew, so the human population shrank (Fitzpatrick 1984, 11–13; see Plate 15).

A *Titanic* snapshot

In the more industrialised north-east, economic depression helped to entrench the gradual decline of the traditional heavy industries, shipbuilding included, and emigration increased (Travers 1988, 7). For the years before 1914, a snapshot of transatlantic migration is provided by the ill-fated maiden voyage of the Belfast-built *Titanic*. Among those embarking at Queenstown for the crossing to New York in third-class was 17-year-old Ellen Corr, fourth of ten children from a small farming family in Corglass, about ten miles north of Longford town. Her sisters Honor (20) and Mary (19) were already living in New York and the latter was married. Fortunate to survive the tragedy, Ellen eventually joined her sisters. Finding employment in New York at the Royal Hotel, John Street, she eventually became head waitress and was married in St Patrick's Cathedral to Patrick Sweeney, another Irish immigrant.

Not so fortunate was a fellow passenger, Andy Keane, a talented 23-year-old hurler from Derrydonnell, about five miles south-west of Athenry, Galway. Despite considerable success on the sports field he had chosen to emigrate, having in the United States two sisters and a brother, who had sent home the money for his passage. Although the family farm was a sizeable 120 acres, it had recently been inherited entirely by the eldest son, Patrick. Having purchased his ticket in Athenry from Mahon's shop for £7 15s, Andy arrived in Queenstown with a bag containing his hurling medals, a dozen hurley sticks and his melodeon. He never arrived at the house of his brother John in Auburndale, about ten miles west of Boston. His two sisters returned to Derrydonnell permanently.

Less typical but also in third class was 31-year-old Thomas Morrow from Drumlough, about a mile south of Rathfriland, Down, crossing to join his brother Waddell, who was not in New York but working as a ranch hand on the prairie in Alberta, Canada. A strict Presbyterian and master of his local Orange Lodge, Morrow was described subsequently by a fellow passenger, Lawrence Beesley, as a well-groomed, melancholic individual, standing apart during the crossing as his fellow passengers danced to traditional music, his gloom perhaps in part a reflection of the passage earlier that same month of the Third Home Rule Bill (Beesley 1912; Moloney 2000, 53, 96–7, 153–4).

Changing context of reception

The first decade of the twentieth century had been the highpoint of European emigration to the United States with about eleven million arriving, mainly through the immigration station of Ellis Island, New York. However, the Irish component of that flow in gross terms had been declining since the 1880s. The Irish and the Germans were no longer the dominant ethnic groups they had been in 1855 when Castle Garden, the predecessor to Ellis Island, had opened. With immigrants from southern and eastern Europe now in the majority, the circumstances in which the Irish arrived were greatly changed. By 1910 American cities had become so multicultural that those immigrants from Ireland who were determined to live as far as possible within Catholic,

Irish-American enclaves found it increasingly difficult to avoid what was regularly presented to them, not least by their own Catholic clergy, as 'the Italian problem' (Brown 1991, 110). At the same time, many had made it into mainstream American society, advancing the status of the Irish as an immigrant group ahead of more recent arrivals. For example, by 1910 Irish-American women made up the largest single ethnic group among public elementary school teachers in many American cities, paradoxically achieving higher social status by becoming servants of the poor rather than servants of the rich (Nolan 2004).

Against the flow – migration within the empire

As to the United States, emigration between 1900 and 1950 to all other overseas destinations (except Britain) declined. Up to 1914, the colonial governments of the British empire fought an uphill battle, through the advertising of their emigrant agents in Ireland and selective subsidies, to compete with the lure of the United States, and with the relatively quick and cheap crossings to New York being offered by the major shipping lines (Harper 2004, 41; Breathnach 2008, 32–45). One such emigration agent was James Smyth, who in 1891 arrived in Canada aged 18 from Castledamph, a mile east of Plumbridge in the Glenelly valley, Tyrone, to be employed subsequently as an agent of the Canadian government to return frequently to Ireland until 1914 and tour the northern half, calling on part-time emigration agents and giving public lectures about the attractions of Canada (see CMS IED 0606010; 0410228; also Plate 22).

After Partition, a modest emigrant flow continued to Canada, South Africa, Australia and New Zealand, and in the flows from both southern and northern Ireland a disproportionate number were Protestants, many of them taking advantage of well-established family chains and networks. The Empire Settlement Act 1922 resulted in government assistance for Northern Ireland emigrants going to Australia or Canada, even though the Stormont government had little interest in promoting a depletion of the majority Unionist community. Relatively large numbers of Protestants left Northern Ireland in the uncertain years of the 1920s for Canada, with smaller numbers leaving for South Africa, Australia and New Zealand. Decline generally set in during the 1930s, and between 1939 and 1945 the flow was halted by war, as it had been between 1914 and 1918 (Akenson 1993; Kenny 2004).

Migration and the Great War

Recent research has drawn attention to the huge impact of the First World War on life in Ireland, not least in terms of recruitment to the British armed services in which over 200,000 Irishmen served (Fitzpatrick 1996, 388). As in previous centuries, the majority of those recruited in Ireland saw service abroad. Estimating the numbers is difficult, partly because Irishmen were recruited throughout the diaspora as well as the homeland – in Britain, the United States and throughout the empire. What we do know is that somewhere between 25,000 and 49,000 died, the majority in Flanders on the Western Front (Jeffery 2000, 35).

Sapping the struggle

While most who survived returned to Ireland, war as usual resulted in the long-term emigration of some, especially those who, having become familiar with Britain as 'Blighty' during periods of training, leave or recuperation, decided to settle there on being demobbed. These included Charles Fitzgerald and Douglas Lambkin, from Portmore, Antrim and Dublin city respectively: having served with the Royal Medical Corps and the Royal Dublin Fusiliers in France, they settled in Salford, Lancashire and Golders Green, London.

The impact of the war on women in Ireland was more limited than in contemporary Britain, not least because of the absence of conscription in Ireland (Lambkin, R. 1992; Lynch 1998, 156–7; Jeffery 2000, 29–30). Nonetheless, some women were drawn into the wartime economy, particularly those in the industrial north-east, and some thousands crossed the Irish Sea for employment in Britain, especially in nursing (Hill 2003, 67–8).

The lack of official record-keeping makes it difficult to estimate the scale of civilian migration from Ireland to Britain between 1914 and 1918, but there can be little doubt that the flow increased as crossing to North America became increasingly dangerous and virtually impossible after 1915. There can also be little doubt that the 'turning off' of what the British authorities regarded as the 'safety-valve' of transatlantic emigration was a factor in the dramatic change in the political climate that took place in the wake of the Easter Rising. At the General Election in 1918, Sinn Féin was most successful in the rural west where the voting population contained greater numbers than usual of restless young men and women, 'kicking their heels' as they waited for a crossing to New York. Throughout the Anglo-Irish War (1919–21), Sinn Féin fretted about the danger of renewed emigration sapping the lifeblood of their armed struggle against the British forces. Similarly, Unionists in the newly established Northern Ireland from time to time expressed concern about the depletion of Orange lodges through emigration – persuasive evidence, if evidence were needed, of 'the social and political importance of emigration' (Fitzpatrick 1996, 633).

Sorting out and taking stock

While the population of the 26 counties of the Irish Republic declined continuously from the middle of the nineteenth century to 1961, political violence resulted in a particularly sharp dip between 1911 and 1926. The Protestant community shrank by 32.5 per cent in this period (Sexton and O'Leary 1996).

Subsequently, the fate of southern Protestants was presented as an awful warning to northern Protestants in the rhetoric of extreme Unionists such as Ian Paisley. This asserted that decline was the cumulative effect of successive crises – Home Rule, 1916, the War of Independence, Partition, the Civil War – which, combined with the attitude of the Nationalist and Catholic majority in independent Ireland, more or less 'forced' large numbers of Protestants to emigrate. The lesson to be learned was that if ever northern Protestants allowed themselves to fall into the same position under 'Rome Rule', their fate would be the same. Despite being ill-grounded in historical evidence, this view has proved remarkably persistent.

Reacting to the 'great betrayal'

The decline of the Protestant community in southern Ireland is not simply explained by the ending of the Union with Britain in 1921, the uncertainty surrounding the establishment of the Irish Free State and the consequent withdrawal of the British army and other public servants, many of whom were Protestants. It is certainly the case that 'at the very least over 60,000 Protestants who were not directly connected with the British adminis- tration left southern Ireland between 1911 and 1926' (Bowen 1983; Delaney 2000, 71, 72). We may conclude that many of these southern Unionists were reacting to Partition as the 'great betrayal' (Inglis 1962, 12). It is also the case that the Protestant minority in the South was uncertain about its future. In April 1922 the Church of Ireland Archbishop of Dublin, J. A. F. Gregg, called on the new government in the South

> to take the necessary steps to protect a grievously-wounded minority, and to defend the Protestants of west Cork from any repetitions of these atro- cities, and to save the Protestants there and in other parts of the South from threatened violence and expulsion from their homes.
>
> (Seaver 1963, 24; Hart 1998)

In May, Gregg led a deputation from the General Synod to the provisional government to enquire 'if they were permitted to live in Ireland or if it was desired that they should leave the country' (Bowen 1983, 24; Delaney 2000, 69). This was all part of the sectarian 'sorting out' consequent on Partition. At the same time, Catholics were coming under pressure in Northern Ireland. Between July 1920 and July 1922 Catholic relief organisations estimated that in Belfast between 8,700 and 11,000 Catholics had been driven out of their jobs and 23,000 Catholics had been forced out of their homes (Bardon 1992, 494). Some northern Nationalists, like southern Unionists, also seeing the 'great betrayal', reacted similarly by emigrating (O Connor 1993, 336; Elliott 2000, 377–8).

'The long retreat'

It is still not widely appreciated that the emigration of Protestants from the newly created Irish Free State needs to be seen in the context of a longer-term decline. What has been called the 'long retreat' of Protestantism in Ireland, studied in relation to Co. Longford by Kennedy and Miller (1991), had begun in the early eighteenth century with the slowing of the immigration flow from Britain (see chapter 7). However, it remains true that Partition, as well as accelerating the decline, brought it into sharper focus and largely determined the negative way in which the South was perceived by Unionists in the North. Looking on, they witnessed the struggle of minority religious communities, particularly the Church of Ireland, to assert the integrity of their distinctive identities, as in the case of Gregg's plea against 'absorbtion':

> It is not necessary to be Gaelic in order to be Irish. On the other hand, the Gaelicisation which is recommended to us, added to other factors of our environment, would involve our absorption, the incorporation of the minority into the majority, with the inevitable loss of the religion we prize (which is an integral part of our identity).
>
> (*Church of Ireland Gazette*, 12 May 1939)

A stifling environment

The policy of 'Gaelicisation', with an emphasis on Nationalism in the teaching of history and the requirement of proficiency in the Irish language for entry to the civil service, resulted in some Protestant parents opting to educate their children in Britain or Northern Ireland (Delaney 2000, 78). Although Akenson judges that, so far as the state was concerned, 'the Protestants were tolerated and well treated as a religious minority but were penalised and ill-treated as a cultural minority', for many Protestants the distinction between cultural and religious ill-treatment was hard to see – especially in the light of the Catholic Church's attitude to mixed marriages, which constituted roughly 15 per cent of marriages by Protestant males (Akenson 1988, 109–15). The effect of pressure from the Catholic Church on Protestants marrying Catholics to ensure that any children were brought up as Catholics, which applied equally in the North, was particularly evident in the South (Morgan et al. 1996; Wigfall-Williams and Robinson 2001). In the 1930s, when Samuel Beckett has one of his fictional characters exclaim that 'it is always pleasant to leave this country' he was no doubt expressing the sentiments of many who found the dominant cultural environment stifling (*Murphy*, written in London 1936, quoted in English 2006, 324). The possibility that the small Protestant community remaining might disappear altogether fuelled the fear of northern Protestants for their own future and helps to account for the gerrymandering of local government electoral boundaries and the local allocation of housing in favour of the Unionist interest (Lalor 2003, 437; Hennessey 2005, 72–3). This in turn affected internal migration by accentuating the tendency of Protestants and Catholics to 'self-segregate' when choosing where to live (Boal 2000).

The Second World War and migration

When war broke out in 1939, the political situation in Ireland was very different from that in 1914. Nevertheless, about 120,000 men and women were recruited to the British armed forces: 50,000 from Northern Ireland and 70,000 from the neutral South (Docherty 2000, 92–3; Roberts 2004, 274). Even greater in number was the flow of Irish workers arriving in Britain for employment in the expanding wartime economy. Whereas since Partition there had been unregulated freedom of movement between the Irish Free State and the United Kingdom, even during the economic war, now both governments were forced to introduce regulation as a result of an IRA bombing campaign in Britain in 1939 which resulted in over 200 explosions, starting in January and culminating in August with an explosion in Coventry which killed five people and injured 70. The Westminster government had responded in July by introducing the Prevention of Violence Act, which required Irish citizens to register with the police. In effect this 'cast a veil of suspicion over the Irish in Britain', regardless of the fact that most of the IRA members involved, including the 16-year-old Brendan Behan arrested in Liverpool within ten hours of his arrival, had travelled from Ireland specifically for the campaign, and there was no evidence that the long-settled Irish immigrant population was involved (Holmes 1989; Delaney 2000, 94–5). We may also note here the difficulty of many Irish immigrants in Britain in getting due recognition of their distinctive identity as Unionists or UK citizens in the host community, where they tended to be lumped together with Catholic Irish immigrants as 'Paddies' (Pooley 2000, 191).

Labour migration

In turn, the Dublin government responded to the requirement of the British authorities that all persons travelling to Britain should carry official identification by issuing identity cards that could be applied for at local police stations. This had the effect of strictly curtailing travel across the Irish Sea, including travel from Northern Ireland: permission to enter Britain was given for 'business of national importance' only, and those who returned to Ireland were not permitted to re-enter Britain (Delaney 2000, 117). The new form of record-keeping indicates the scale of the flow: between 1941 and 1945 the number of permits issued in Dublin for travel to Northern Ireland and Britain was 170,000 (Connolly 2000, 122–3; Delaney 2002, 34).

Uncomfortable realities

For the first time, the pressure of wartime circumstances had forced the for-mulation of concrete policies on migration between Ireland and Britain, much to the embarrassment of the government in Dublin (Delaney 2000, 151). The large numbers still leaving neutral Ireland voluntarily for civilian and military work in Britain were painfully at odds with de Valera's vision of the nation as 'home', as expressed in his *Radio Éireann* broadcast on St Patrick's Day 1943:

> Before the present war began I was accustomed on St Patrick's Day to speak to *our kinsfolk in foreign lands, particularly those in the United States*, and to tell them year by year of the progress being made towards building up *the Ireland of their dreams and ours* – the Ireland that we believe is destined to play, by its example and its inspiration, a great part as a nation among the nations.
>
> Acutely conscious though we all are of the misery and desolation in which the greater part of the world is plunged, let us turn aside for a moment to that ideal Ireland that we would have. The Ireland that we dreamed of would be the *home* of a people who valued material wealth only as a basis of right living; of a people who, satisfied with frugal comfort, devoted their leisure to the things of the spirit – a land whose countryside would be bright with *cosy homesteads*, whose *fields* and *villages* would be joyous with the sounds of industry, with the romping of sturdy children, the contests of athletic youths and the laughter of happy maidens, whose *firesides* would be forums for the wisdom of serene old age. The *home*, in short, of a people living the life that God desires that men should live.
>
> (www.rte.ie/laweb/ll/ll_t09b.html; our emphasis)

The fear of returnees

Irish ministers had been nervous in 1939 about the impact on their fragile economy of the possible forced return of large numbers of Irish migrants from Britain and they had justified not preventing further emigration on the prin-ciple that it was the prerogative of the individual to decide how best they could 'sell' their labour, and that in practice it would be difficult to police the land border with Northern Ireland. As Allied victory approached in 1944, the same fear resurfaced and they tried to persuade the London government to stagger the return of migrant labour to Ireland as the British economy inevitably started to scale back to peacetime levels (Delaney 2002, 40). This fear of return migration highlighted the real impotence of the government regarding emi-gration, and little would change in the 1950s to shorten the queues on the pier at Dún Laoghaire, waiting for the Holyhead boat to Britain. After 1947, restrictions on Irish migrants to Britain were lifted as they continued to be regarded as a valuable source of labour. Although there had been some unpleasant incidents in the inter-war years concerning the churches in Scotland and some local figures in Liverpool, the reception of the Irish in Britain was generally good compared with how New Commonwealth migrants were received in the 1950s (Delaney 2000, 297).

Conclusion

Looking back from the vantage point of 1950, we see the familiar landmark dates of the two world wars; the Government of Ireland Act 1920; The Easter Rising 1916; and the Third Home Rule Bill in 1912. Regarding migration, we see an even more decisive event in the Wall Street Crash in 1929, when the idea of America as the land of opportunity, pervasive in Ireland since the eighteenth century, was shattered. Ironically as the Atlantic became ever quicker to cross, the main direction of emigration flow switched to Britain. The immigration flow, tiny by comparison, indicated the island's relative isolation, economic weakness and conservative social climate, in both the North and South. Neither new state seemed secure as the rural–urban transition continued. In Northern Ireland the Unionist majority depended in part on greater numbers of Catholics than Protestants continuing to emigrate, and in the South emigration acted simultaneously as a safety-valve for social stability and as a threat to the long-term viability of the state. As what turned out to be the extremely severe winter of 1947 approached, the economic and social malaise that was driving emigration seemed ominously symbolised by the newsreel footage of Dubliners being bussed into the surrounding countryside to help in the urgent task of saving the storm-damaged harvest (RTÉ *Seven Ages*, programme 3). A century on from the Great Famine and 'Black '47', the task of reconstruction seemed far from complete.

13
Irish Migration, 1950–2007

There was a dramatic transformation in the second half of the twentieth century when net emigration – dominant since the beginning of the eighteenth century – was reversed to net immigration. In the 1950s the prospect of such a transformation was almost unthinkable: as was reported at the time, if a little over-dramatically, 'all economists and sociologists are agreed that, if this ominous trend continues, in another century the Irish race will have vanished, much like the Mayans, leaving only their monuments behind them' (O'Brien 1954, 7; Delaney 2000, 203). With the tradition of emigration as strong as ever, there seemed no end to it: 'the common talk amongst parents in the towns, as in rural Ireland, is of their children having to emigrate as soon as their education is completed in order to be sure of a reasonable livelihood' (Government of Ireland 1958, 5). In Northern Ireland, emigration was smaller in scale but the prospects at home seemed little better. Neither the Republic of Ireland nor Northern Ireland had much experience of inward migration arising from British decolonisation. However, their emigrants in Britain and their descendants did. Having been the largest immigrant group by far since the eighteenth century, the situation of the Irish in metropolitan Britain, as in the United States at the end of the nineteenth century, changed greatly in the 1960s with the impact of New Commonwealth immigration (Walter et al. 2002).

Eventually, improved economic performance helped to slow the flow in the 1960s to the extent that briefly in the early 1970s the Republic of Ireland became a country of net immigration, but not Northern Ireland where 'the Troubles' were underway. With the downturn in the economy that followed, net emigration resumed in the 1980s, persisting until the emergence of the 'Celtic Tiger' economy in the 1990s, when the dramatic shift was made to net immigration, which has been sustained to the present and looks likely to continue.

Immigration

An unpromising start

In the 1950s, when the level of immigration to both the Republic of Ireland and Northern Ireland was minimal, there were few signs of the dramatic trans-formation that was to come. One group of refugees of the kind that would become familiar in the 1990s did arrive. In November 1956, the Republic of Ireland, acting in concert with other western European countries as a signa-tory to the 1951 Geneva Convention, offered asylum to refugees from the uprising in Hungary (http://foreignaffairs.gov.ie/policy/hr/hrunstr.asp; for reflections on the 50th anniversary see *Irish Times*, 14 October 2006). More used to coping with emigration than immigration, and lacking administrative systems and an appropriate legal framework, the state appeared ill-equipped for the challenge of receiving 541 Hungarians. As early as December the gov-ernment was requesting Canada to take the 500 who had expressed a prefer-ence for settling there. By the spring of 1957 about 20 had returned to Hungary and 100 were settled in Ireland – 70 with temporary employment. The remaining group – about 350, including 100 children – were housed in a disused army camp at Knockalisheen on the north side of Limerick city. Frustrated by the delay in any agreement between Dublin and Ottawa, the majority went on hunger strike. By mid-August only 175 Hungarians remained and in mid-September a party of 117 sailed from Ireland to Quebec, marking an unpromising start to Ireland's post-war role as a receiving society (Ward 1996, 131–41; Galvin 2000, 200–1; Ward 2000; Fanning 2001).

Asian arrivals

As before, most immigrants arrived individually rather than as part of a government-assisted scheme. One such was Johnnie Chada, who arrived by bicycle in Sligo town in 1953 on a January evening, having made the crossing from the Punjab, where he had qualified as a mathematics teacher, married and taken part in the struggle for independence. He sold clothes, travelling by bike rather than on foot, as had Bianconi and Goldberg, and was successful enough to be able to secure a house in the town and bring over his wife and daughter. By 1969 he was employed teaching mathematics in the local college and he considered himself and his four children 'fully integrated into the Sligo community', which voted him 'Sligo Man of the Year, 1987' (Kapur 1997, 90). Also from the Punjab, from the small village of Sanghol about 20 miles west of Chandigarh, Diljit Rana arrived in Northern Ireland in 1966 and opened a small restaurant in Belfast; going on to establish a major property development and hospitality company, he was appointed to the House of Lords in 2004 and chosen in his homeland as 'Non-Resident Indian of the Year, 2005' (Northern Ireland Museums Council 2005, 18).

The arrivals of Chada and Rana were separated by the Commonwealth Immigrants Act 1962 which, applied in practice to the Republic of Ireland as well as to Britain and Northern Ireland, as part of the Common Travel Area. The Act made entry rather more difficult for immigrants, but in Northern Ireland separate legislation which introduced a more attractive employment voucher scheme resulted in increased migration by professionals from India and Pakistan. Also beginning to arrive in Ireland in the 1960s were Chinese immigrants, mainly from the New Territories of Hong Kong, with the first Chinese restaurant opening in Belfast in 1962 (Northern Ireland Museums Council 2005, 18, 20).

A return to net immigration

The Dublin government's publication of *Economic Development* and its *Programme for Economic Expansion* in 1958 marked the start of two decades that have been described as a 'golden age' (Ó Gráda 1997, 29). Economic improvement flowed from increased foreign investment and job creation, which reduced emigration rates fairly swiftly and increased, albeit much more slowly, immigration. As Ireland, along with the United Kingdom, joined the European Economic Community (EEC) in 1973, the tipping point was reached with net immigration being recorded for the first time since the foundation of the state, and indeed since about 1700. Most of those arriving were returned emigrants, many of them with families, choosing now to come back with skills and expertise acquired abroad to take advantage of new opportunities opening up (Mac Éinrí 2001, 47). Economic conditions north of the border in the 1960s were also favourable, resulting in modest net immigration, although most were officially internal migrants from elsewhere in the UK, coming as students or to take up positions in the public sector (Lee 1989, 515, 539; Compton 1995; Ó Gráda 1997, 212; Sexton 2003, 817). After the outbreak of the Troubles in 1969, there was little to attract return migrants to Northern Ireland and so it is not surprising that there was no increase in immigration in the early 1970s to parallel that in the South. Indeed, patterns of migration north and south increasingly diverged as membership of the EEC boosted the southern economy, especially in the agricultural and public sectors (Hitchens et al. 1993, 53; Sexton 2003, 814). For the first time an economic case was being heard for reunification (Fitzgerald 1973, 63–85; O'Donnell and Teague 1993, 240–1). However, the 'feel better' atmosphere of the early 1970s changed sharply in the wake of the massive increase in the price of oil in 1973 and the economic depression of 1979–80 and the main direction of migration again reversed. Notwithstanding the deep political and religious divisions, both parts of the island, in comparison with the ethnic and cultural diversity of the rest of western Europe, remained until the early 1990s remarkably homogeneous and a consequence of negligible immigration was 'less exposure to alternative attitudes to fertility, religion and authority' (Coleman 1999, 108).

Irish idyll

A small flow of immigrants with an influence disproportionate to their numbers had been arriving from continental Europe since the 1950s, seeking escape from land-locked Europe and attracted particularly by the natural beauty and slower pace of life on the west coast of Ireland, as described by Heinrich Böll in his *Irisches Tagebuch* ('Irish Diary', 1957). In Conor MacPherson's play *The Weir* (1997), the publican refers to these immigrants generically as 'the Germans', regardless of the fact that many were from Scandinavia and elsewhere, an echo of the way that even emigrants going to Australia were given an American Wake. Also arriving in the 1980s from Britain, during the Thatcher government (1979–90), were some who considered themselves as political dissidents. Letters in the pages of Irish newspapers during the decade, sometimes without apparent irony, decried those 'swarming' from England into areas like west Cork as 'New Age travellers', later to be described as 'welfare migrants'. The flow of return migration from Britain continued, reflecting even deeper recession in the UK economy and some improvement in opportunities in Ireland, which resulted in a surge in the early 1990s (Corcoran 2003, 303–4).

Northern invisibility

The very small immigrant flow into Northern Ireland was indicated by an absence of any reference to it in the guidebook published by the government in the 1950s, which simply stated that 'roughly two-thirds of the population belong to various Protestant denominations and one-third are Roman Catholics' (Shearman 1955, 35). By the 1980s there were about 1,000 people from the Indian subcontinent living in Northern Ireland and 600 in the Republic, working mainly in the retail drapery trade and in catering. Questions of ethnic diversity and multiculturalism did not begin to be seriously researched or debated until the 1990s (McCann, O'Siochain and Ruane 1994; Irwin and Dunn 1997). The titles of two studies indicate the position of ethnic minorities metaphorically: *Out of the Shadows* (Mann-Kler 1997) and *Divided Society* (Hainsworth 1998).

The Celtic Tiger magnet

The main direction of migration flow in the South reversed once more to net immigration in the mid-1990s. This time the change was lasting, reflecting the boom of the Celtic Tiger economy. Between 1993 and 1999 the annual growth rate exceeded 8 per cent and the overall increase in employment was 25 per cent (Clinch et al. 2002, 24–52). In the year to April 2006 a record 87,000 immigrants entered the Republic, while only 17,000 left – a net inward flow of 70,000. Even

allowing for the underestimation of inward migration this presents a remarkable transformation from the position in the later 1980s (Fahey 2007, 27–8).
The population boom of the 1970s, now feeding through, helped to ensure
that the market's new appetite for labour was met by young Irish people.
However, this was a relatively short-term gain because, in the long term, traditionally high fertility rates were in decline and today the overall fertility rate
is 1.98, less than half compared with 4.0 in the 1960s (MacÉinrí 2006, 108).

In search of asylum

From the mid-1990s a number of key trends were apparent. First, the Republic
of Ireland's inward migration flow was high by comparison with other EU countries, in large part due to the high proportion of return migrants in the flow:
between 1995 and 2000 about 250,000 arrived, representing about 7 per cent
of the 1996 population of 3.6 million. The Census demonstrated that by 2002
16 per cent of the total population of the state had lived outside Ireland and
that of these more than half (9 per cent of the total population) were returned
migrants (Ní Laoire 2007a, 2). As in the 1970s, the majority of these – albeit a
declining majority – were returning Irish emigrants, and the rest mainly citizens of the United States and other EU countries. However, in contrast with
the 1970s, about 29,400 of those arriving (12 per cent) were from countries
beyond the EU and the US. Also arriving in steadily increasing numbers were
asylum seekers: in 1992 there were 39 applications and in 2000 there were
10,938. Despite the fact that by 2000 Ireland had received the smallest number
of asylum seekers in the EU (2.4 per cent of the total) and they constituted less
than 10 per cent of all immigrants to Ireland, the issue of asylum and the
granting of refugee status dominated media coverage. This did little to clarify
the distinction between refugees seeking sanctuary from life-threatening circumstances, and economic migrants exercising the right to freedom of movement of labour (Cullen 2000; Mac Éinrí 2001, 56).

Struggling to come to terms

Relative to population, Ireland ranks fifth among EU states in terms of applications received and it has been argued that the procedures established by the
Irish government 'embody aspects of institutional racism' insofar as the dual-
track system for determining refugee status was based prejudicially on race.
The weaknesses of the interview system, the government's increasingly
narrow interpretation of asylum, the increasingly rapid rejection of applications since 1999 and the highly restrictive regime imposed on applicants in
Ireland have led asylum seekers to be seen as the 'most disempowered group
in Irish society' and their presence as marking 'the nadir of the putative values
of the Celtic Tiger' (Fanning 2002, 102–8, 180–1; Loyal 2003, 79; Lentin and
McVeigh 2006). However, this remains a fluid area of government policy. As

recently as January 2007, the 'Celtic and Christian people' speech by Enda Kenny, the leader of Fine Gael, sparked further debate about what the appropriate response to the challenge of net immigration should be, prompting one letter writer to comment that mature and open debate is greatly needed because 'four hundred years on, we haven't quite come to terms with the last period of mass immigration in this country' (*Irish Times*, 25 January 2007; 2 February 2007).

The North – no longer isolated

By comparison, changes in the pattern of immigration in Northern Ireland in the 1990s were slower and on a smaller scale. Nonetheless, by 1997 about 20,000 were from minority ethnic groups – 1.5 per cent of the population (Hainsworth 1998; McVeigh 1998). Given greater political and economic stability and the younger age profile of immigrant groups generally, this proportion has increased as expected (Hainsworth 1998, 18; Watt and McCaughey 2006, 42). The prominence of immigration-related issues in the media, including racism, attacks on members of ethnic minorities, people trafficking, migrant workers employed in the low-wage 'black economy' and the detention of asylum seekers in prison while awaiting determinations on their applications, indicates the extent to which Northern Ireland is no longer so isolated from the main currents of European migration (Harvey and Ward 2001; Tennant 2003; Bell, Jarman and Lefebvre 2004; Jarman and Monaghan 2004; Shuttleworth and Green 2004, 118; Shuttleworth and Osborne 2004, 188; Betts and Hamilton 2005). One noteworthy point concerning the particularity of the integration process for recent immigrants to Northern Ireland relates to the fact that the vast majority of migrants have, in fact, as a consequence of their religious backgrounds, sought integration disproportionately with the Catholic community. Northern Ireland, unlike the Republic, has not experienced immigration by African Pentecostals (Ugba 2007, 168–84; Johanne Trew, pers. comm.).

Essential skills

Keeping the issue of asylum seekers and refugees in proportion, we see the continuing importance to the Republic government's National Development Plan of return migrants, who have until recently constituted about half of the recent immigration flow, and other labour migrants (Mac Éinrí and Walley 2003, 17). Prosperity and well-being are seen to depend on immigrant labour to meet skills gaps, such as in the health service. A shortage of trained nurses in Ireland – unimaginable to an earlier generation – encouraged the Irish government, as well as relying on intermediate agencies, to recruit in the Philippines, making provisions to expedite the issue of visas and permits as necessary. By 2002 there were about 2,500 Filipino nurses working in Ireland, but many of those coming to the end of their two-year contracts were migrating to

Britain, Australia or other developed countries, where better terms and conditions could be found. When it became clear that essential skilled labour was being lost, the government responded by offering better conditions of service, including altering visa restrictions to allow nurses to be joined in Ireland by family members (*Irish Examiner*, 20 December 2002; Mac Éinrí and Walley 2003, 27–44). Viewed from Manila rather than Dublin, we can clearly see the demand-driven character of such high-skill migration and appreciate the competitive western marketplace in which the Irish Health Service now has to compete. In contrast, it has been observed that the largely male, middle-class influx of sporting labour to Ireland, north and south, has been received more positively (Carter 2005, 204).

Seeking to meet the challenges

More broadly, the government has been criticised for the inadequacy of its response since 1993 to the challenges of making the transformation from sending to receiving society. In Europe, Germany, for example, has faced similar challenges (Bade and Weiner 1997, 3–12). A report by the Immigrant Council of Ireland in 2003 warned that domestic and global conditions were likely to sustain high levels of immigration and that consequently a much broader, coordinated approach than a narrowly economic one was needed to ensure appropriate policies for dealing with issues of social inclusion, not least regarding the education of both new arrivals and their hosts (Ward 1998; Curry 2000, 137–52; MacÉinrí and Walley 2003). So between 1991 and 2002 the share of foreign-born persons living in Ireland rose from 6 per cent to over 10 per cent, including about 1.3 per cent born in Northern Ireland (Ruhs 2004). In the United Kingdom as a whole, the share of foreign-born persons increased between 1951 and 2001 from about 4 per cent to 8 per cent, whereas in Northern Ireland the highest estimate of the foreign-born share of the population in 2006 was 2.5 per cent (Watt and McCaughey 2006, 42).

Accession state migrants

In 2004 the Republic of Ireland, like the UK and Sweden, chose not to impose transitional restrictions on admission to its labour market and accordingly the numbers arriving from the new EU accession states, especially Poland, Latvia, Lithuania and Estonia, were substantial. Between 1 May 2004 and 30 September 2005 more than 94,000 accession workers obtained a Personal Public Service (PPS) number in Ireland; this is about 70 per cent of the number arriving in the United Kingdom, which has a population about 15 times greater. The number of applicants declined sharply to 4,305 in 2005 in line with a world-wide fall and partly in reaction to the narrowing of entitlement to citizenship by the Irish Nationality and Citizenship Act 2004 (which replaced the 1956 Act, which previously had replaced the 1935 Act) and the adoption of a fast-track processing system for applications. Government policy is still evolving in response to the greater ethnic and cultural diversity of the population, as indicated by the 167 languages spoken – a reflection in large part of the 27,000 who arrived as asylum seekers and are now legally settled. A new Equality Act came into force in 2004, bringing Ireland into line with protective legislation across the EU, and further legislation is planned concerning economic migration and integration into Irish society (Doyle, Hughes and Wadensjö 2006; MacÉinrí 2006, 106–15). It has been estimated that by the 2020s it is likely that migrants and their descendants will constitute a fifth of the population of the Republic, so the need for concrete policy formation in the area of integration management cannot be delayed (MacÉinrí 2007b, 248).

Local initiatives

Although not nearly as marked, there has been a continuing increase in immigration to Northern Ireland. According to the Census of 2001, the number of residents born outside the United Kingdom was 26,659, which may underestimate the 'non-indigenous' in the population by as much as a half. Compared to the scale of immigration flows in the past, the increase has been particularly marked after the accession in May 2004 of a further ten states to the EU, whose combined population is over 70 million. Similar challenges in terms of appropriate provision by central and local government now face Northern Ireland, particularly measures to combat racially motivated crime. Initiatives, such as those of the South Tyrone Empowerment Programme (STEP), directed by Bernadette McAliskey, and those in Cavan of the County Development Board, Community and Voluntary Forum and Multi-cultural Network, are concerned with integration as a 'two-way' process as distinct from 'one-way' assimilation (Moroney 2006). Another factor set to help sustain immigration is the increasing the proportion of the population of pensionable age (Hamilton 2006, 38–45).

North–South perspectives

Looking forward, as well as seeing similarities in the challenges being posed by immigration, we still see a strong contrast between south and north. This is how the *Irish Times* summed up the situation in the south in 2005:

> We have already become a substantially multicultural society, largely because nearly a quarter of a million people have immigrated here since the mid-1990s, drawn by the availability of work in a rapidly growing economy. An estimated 6 per cent of the population are classified as "non-nationals", with UK and EU nationals numbering 3.4 per cent, and Asians, Africans, and non-EU Europeans making up 0.5 per cent apiece, as do Muslims. At least 166 different nationalities are recorded here. The 24,000 Travellers represent 0.6 per

cent of the population. The flow of people to Ireland has been one of the strongest in the EU and has been significantly extended since 10 new states joined in May last year.

(28 January 2005)

Reacting to the publication in 2007 of an international attitudes survey that described Northern Ireland as a 'world capital of bigotry', this is how the *Belfast Telegraph* summed up the situation in the North:

Even allowing for Northern Ireland's insular nature, isolated from the Republic, Britain and mainland Europe, there is something radically wrong that should not be ignored. ... Could the reason be that, almost from birth, the two communities divided by religion and politics learn to be suspicious not only of each other, but of those who do not share their values? Many are hostile to outsiders, particularly of another religion.

(8 February 2007)

Internal migration

Taking the strain

As before, the main direction of internal migration continued to be from the rural west to the urban east. The continuing close relationship between countryside and town is neatly captured in a photograph taken not far from Dublin's city centre as late as 1958: a herd of cattle is being driven casually along the road in Phibsborough, followed by a double-decker bus, many bicycles and a few cars (MacCarthy Morrogh 1998, 154; Piaras Mac Éinrí, pers. comm.). Almost half a century later, although the speed of the traffic is little changed, cattle are no longer seen and the ratio of bicycles to cars is reversed. The contrast in the quality of life between then and now was starkly evident when Dublin came to a standstill on Wednesday, 22 November 2006: a burst water pipe resulted in seven-hour traffic jams on the M50 orbital route and on the N11 entering the city from the south-east, marking perhaps, as one journalist suggested, the day that 'the concept of Dublin as a functioning metropolis finally imploded' (*Sunday Times*, 26 November 2006).

Into the city

Between the 1951 and 2002 Censuses the increase in the proportion of the population living in Dublin City and County was spectacular – from about 23.5 per cent to 28.5 per cent – and the proportion living in Leinster increased from 45 per cent to 54 per cent. The population share of the three other provinces – Munster, Connacht and the three Ulster counties – declined accordingly. However, Dublin was not the only city to experience strong growth:

between 1946 and 1996 Cork and Galway almost doubled and trebled their populations. It was in the course of these decades that the Republic of Ireland made the transition to being a predominantly urban country: in 1946 the proportion of the population living in the countryside or small towns and villages was over 60 per cent; by 1996 it was down to 42 per cent (CSO 2000, 14–16). Figure.6 shows the 'tipping point' having been reached by 1971. In Northern Ireland this same point of transition had been reached about the same time as the foundation of the state.

Travellers too

The impact of the rural to urban transition is seen starkly in the lives of Irish Travellers, who switched from the horse-drawn to the modern caravan. Currently numbering about 25,000 in the Republic and 1,500 in Northern Ireland, with substantial communities in Britain and North America, they now 'cluster in towns, often in appalling conditions giving rise to health problems and tension with non-Traveller neighbours'. During the 1950s and 1960s significant numbers of Travellers began to make the migration from countryside to town and city as their traditional economic base collapsed (Helleiner 1993; Kirk and Ó Baóill 2002; Ní Shuinéar 2003, 1071–2, 1074; Crowley 2005; Hayes 2006, 233). A report by the Irish Traveller Movement in late 2006 pointed to the widespread failure of local authorities to provide transient halting sites which would allow Travellers to engage in nomadism, which they consider to be an integral part of their collective identity (*Irish Times* 12 December 2006).

Rural–urban revelations

The process of moving from countryside to town altered perceptions generally, as for example in the case of Polly Devlin, who grew up in the 1940s and 1950s in a 'remote, almost medieval area' of Co. Tyrone, in the townland of Muinterevlin in the parish of Ardboe on the south-west shore of Lough Neagh:

> it was only when I went to Belfast, and saw in the poor traditionally Protestant areas, children playing who had the same narrow limbs and white faces which I associated with the children of my own faith, that I realized these were the physical marks and characteristics of the poor and not of caste.
>
> (1983; 2003, 156)

Urbanisation and the commuter belt

Compared with other countries, in 1970 the rate of internal migration in the Republic was still low. Inter-county migration was just 12 per 1,000 population – less than a fifth of the rate in the United States (68 per 1,000) and

France (64 per 1,000), and only a third of the rate in Northern Ireland (36 per 1,000). Nevertheless, starting from a relatively low base of urbanisation as one of the most sparsely populated countries of the EEC, with a population density of 50 per sq. km compared with Northern Ireland's 100 per sq. km, the change appeared dramatic. The county of Dublin was the origin of about a fifth and the destination of about a third of all inter-county migrants. It formed the heart of the region designated for planning purposes as the east, along with Kildare, Meath and Wicklow, which saw fairly rapid growth in industrial and service employment in the early 1960s. By 1970 the inflow to Dublin was predominantly in the age groups 15–19 and 20–24, with women outnumbering men by three to one. Also by 1970 there was increasing 'counter-urbanisation' in the eastern region as significant numbers of Dublin-born moved out to neighbouring counties but continued to work in Dublin, extending their commuting distance considerably (Hughes and Walsh 1980, 15, 53; Meredith 2006).

A spatial strategy

These trends accelerated rapidly during the later 1990s when job creation, particularly by multinational companies, was clustered in the Greater Dublin region. As house prices soared in the city, many more of those who worked in Dublin sought to buy houses in satellite towns and in outer Dublin or commuter belt housing developments, many of which were poorly serviced by health, education, shopping and leisure facilities. Boundaries between clearly defined urban and rural worlds evaporated as Ireland edged towards a state which has been described as 'ex-urbanisation' (Corcoran, Keaveney and Duffy 2007, 252). A major negative effect was congestion on a road infrastructure unable to cope with the rate of economic development. Although Dublin's relative growth has been less spectacular than many larger cities, such as those in the United States, current demographic projections forecast that over the next three decades Greater Dublin will account for a growing proportion of the national population. In the Census year of 2002 the government responded with a National Spatial Strategy, aimed at achieving a better balance of social, economic and physical development across Ireland, supported by more effective planning. However, the preliminary report of the 2006 Census illustrates the continuing need for a more even spread of population growth across the country. Whereas parts of the Dublin commuter belt around Fingal and parts of Co. Meath showed population expansion in the preceding four years of over 20 per cent, other centres, such as Sligo in the north-west, grew by only 3 per cent (Department of the Environment and Local Government 2002; www.irishspatialstrategy.ie; www.cso.ie/census/2006preliminaryreport; *Irish Times*, 25 July 2006). Given the limited success of government in decentralising economic activity, the challenges ahead appear formidable (Clinch, Convery and Walsh 2002, 96–9). Greater Dublin in 2007 was coming close to occupying the same area as Los Angeles and likened to an 'oozing oil slick' that would soon 'gobble up Athlone, Kilkenny and Wexford' (*Sunday Times*, 18 February 2007, 19). Similar trends are evident in Northern Ireland, as indicated by its Regional Development Strategy. So, for example, the commuting relationship between Dungannon, at the end of the M1 motorway, and Belfast is developing in a way similar to that between towns like Naas and Dublin (Department for Regional Development 2001).

The 'lost city of Craigavon'

The Northern Ireland government attempted to influence internal migration in the 1960s with its decisions to site a new town and a new university in predominantly Unionist locations. Rather than relieve pressure on Belfast and spread urban development by expanding the second city of Londonderry/ Derry, which was largely Nationalist, the decision was taken in 1966 to follow the recommendation of the Mathew Report (1963) and build the new town of Craigavon east of the Bann, between the predominantly Unionist town of Portadown and the more evenly balanced Lurgan, with a target population by 1981 of 100,000. The project was directed in its initial stages by Geoffrey Copcutt, another Scots migrant improver, the architect of Cumbernauld New Town near Glasgow. As in the earlier plantations of north Armagh, natives were displaced. Stormont vested some 6,000 acres at £250 per acre, and farming families, many there for generations, had to give up their land and move out. As it turned out, the levels of inward investment and job creation proved insufficient to attract the projected number of migrants to move from the Greater Belfast area and from western urban and rural areas. From the mid-1970s special financial packages were offered as an inducement to move, but not all who came to claim this prize remained for the long term. During the 1970s, with widespread intimidation on both sides, housing estates became almost wholly Protestant or Catholic. When Goodyear, the main employer, closed in 1983, Craigavon council was accused by the Fair Employment Agency of anti-Catholic bias and surplus public housing was used to accommodate people displaced by political violence in Belfast, which heightened existing tensions in the area. In 2001 the population of the Craigavon urban area was about 58,000 and in 2007 media commentators were going in search of 'the lost city of Craigavon' (O'Dowd 1993; Flackes and Elliott 1994, 131; Adair et al. 2000; McKittrick and McVea 2000, 39; Lalor 2003, 252, 780; Hennessy 2005, 40-1; Newton Emerson, BBC 1 NI 10.35 pm, 3 December 2007).

Deep wounds

Following the report of the Lockwood Committee on Higher Education (1965), a similarly controversial decision was made to locate the New University of Ulster on the east bank of the Bann in the predominantly Unionist town of

Coleraine rather than develop Magee University College in the largely Nationalist Londonderry/Derry. Magee College had been founded in 1865, becoming a
college of the Royal University of Ireland in 1880 and associated with Dublin
University (TCD) from 1908. Whatever the merits of the case, Eddie McAteer,
leader of the Nationalist Party, regarded the decision as a 'deep wound inflicted
on the North-West as a whole', and it, along with the Craigavon decision, came
to be included in the list of grievances identified by the Civil Rights movement in 1968 (Osborne 1982; Lee 1989, 417; Purdie 1990; Hennessy 2005,
39). The New University of Ulster in Coleraine (1968) failed to attract the
expected number of students and was merged in 1984 with the more successful Ulster Polytechnic, established in 1971 at Jordanstown, between Belfast and
Carrickfergus.

Conflict and migration management

During the violent decades of the 1970s and 1980s, internal migration, some
of it forced, increased substantially the Protestant share of the population in
core Unionist-dominated districts in the eastern half of Northern Ireland and
also the Catholic share of the population in the district council areas near the
border (Boal and Douglas 1982; Compton and Power 1986; Kennedy 1986).
Unlike other areas where governments have sought to prevent, control or resolve
conflict by managed migration policies, such as in Malaya and South Africa in
the 1950s, France in the 1960s, Singapore and Sri Lanka in the 1980s and the
Torres Strait Islands (part of Queensland, Australia) in the 1990s, no large-scale
resettlement schemes were attempted in Northern Ireland (Yiftachel 1992;
Christopher 1995; Quine 1996). One of the possible political solutions to
the conflict that was considered at various stages was repartition. A con-
fidential memorandum on redrawing the border and population transfer
in July 1972 set out a contingency plan which envisaged that areas where
there were Catholic majorities would be ceded to the Republic and also
considered the possibility of forced movement of approximately one-third
of the population across the new border (PRONI: PREM 15.1010). The difficulties with any kind of repartition were later set out by Liam Kennedy
(1986; Loughlin 2003).

As Enda Delaney has observed, 'the question of the relationship between
sectarian violence (and threats of violence) and patterns of migration is a sensitive subject which is often neglected in standard accounts of Irish history'
(2000, 70; Miller 1985, 378). The difficulty in disentangling migration influenced
by political conflict from migration that would have taken place anyway is
compounded by both inadvertent and deliberate misinterpretation of Census
data. Although current trends, such as the growth of the Catholic share of the
population and increased residential segregation, appear indisputable and may
seem a cause for Nationalist optimism and Unionist pessimism, it has been

argued that 'their precise scale and character remain unknown' and therefore media reports of the extent of residential segregation may be exaggerated (Anderson and Shuttleworth 1994, 80, 93; 1998; Ó Gráda 1997a, 209).

Sectarian 'sorting out'

Nevertheless, it is clear that a major sectarian 'sorting out', like that after the Battle of the Diamond in north Armagh in 1795, took place between 1969 and 1972, when an estimated 60,000 people, mainly in the working-class areas of north, west and inner east Belfast, moved home (Brett 1986, 65–70). Before the 1980s and war in the Balkans, this was one of the largest movements of civilian population in post-war Europe. Its scale may be appreciated by recalling that during the Belfast Blitz in May 1941 some 220,000 left the city, seeking alternative accommodation in surrounding farmhouses and rural towns. Internment – effectively a form of 'internal exile' – was reintroduced on Monday, 9 August 1971 and continued until Friday, 5 December 1975. During this period a total of 1,981 people were detained, of whom 1,874 were Catholic/Republican, while 107 were Protestant/Loyalist (Brady et al. 1975; Burton 1978; Spjut 1986; Bardon 1992, 572). Geoffrey Beattie, who grew up in the 1950s in Legmore Street in the old mill village of Ligoniel, north Belfast, in an area later known locally as 'Murder Triangle', recalled how his neighbours, the Rocks family, had to leave their house during the Troubles:

> One night somebody took a shot at a man down at the turn-of-the-road and then, it was said, this gunman had escaped by running into the Rocks' house and over their yard wall. So the following night somebody fired into the Rocks' house. Nobody was injured but the Rocks moved to the top end of Ligoniel, "to be with their own kind" as my mother put it. She meant other Catholics.

Beattie also recalled his surprise at discovering in the course of his research at the Public Record Office (PRONI) that the Rocks family originally moved into the nextdoor house in Ligoniel as long ago as during the First World War (2004, 3, 153–4).

A river runs through

Internal migration related to political violence has also been evident in Northern Ireland's second city. As noted in chapter 11, Londonderry/Derry has been divided by the River Foyle between the mainly Catholic Cityside (on the west bank and to the north) and the mainly Protestant Waterside (on the east bank and to the south). From 1971 to 1991 the Catholic population increased by 36 per cent (from 40,188 to 54,658), compared with a Protestant decrease of 31 per cent (from 15,907 to 10,924). This change took place in the context of an increase of 8 per cent in the city as a whole (from 65,214 to 70,503). The Waterside population increased in this period by 12 per cent (from 18,812 to 21,389). This was largely accounted for by an increase in the Protestant population of 27 per cent (from 7,849 to 9,935), but even in this traditionally Protestant area the Catholic population increased by 4 per cent (from 7,708 to 8,032). In contrast, the Catholic population on the Cityside increased by 42 per cent (from 33,951 to 48,233) while the Protestant population declined by 83 per cent (from 8,459 to 1,407). Poole and Doherty (1996b) found that of the 39 towns they investigated, Londonderry/Derry was the fourth most segregated. A measure of the degree of segregation is their finding that in order to achieve spatial integration of Protestants and Catholics in the city it would be necessary for 71 per cent of the population to move. A study in 1995 by Templegrove Action Research found evidence in some areas that the Protestant population was 'residualising', that is, the younger, more able and employed were moving out and leaving an elderly, benefit-dependent, unemployed core. Another indication of the eastward trend of internal migration by Protestants was the decision taken in 2006 that the only remaining non-Catholic secondary school on the Cityside, Foyle and Londonderry College, should be relocated to the Waterside. In the opening years of the twenty-first century there was little indication of change in these trends (Shirlow et al. 2005, 16). Indeed, a front-page headline on New Year's Day 2008 read 'Derry's Protestant exodus shock': editorialising on the news that fewer than 500 Protestants now remain on the west bank of Derry, less than 3 per cent of the 18,000 housed there in 1969, the *Belfast Telegraph* urged that 'the latest figures from Derry should make every thinking person in Northern Ireland reflect on the nature of the society we are building'.

Living apart

Further 'sorting out' in the first phase of the Troubles, 1969–73, resulted in greater community segregation in Northern Ireland as a whole (Darby 1986, 25; Poole and Doherty 1996a). In 1969, 32 per cent of the population lived in 'mixed' streets (defined as less than 91 per cent of one community or the other, Protestant or Catholic). By 1972 the proportion had dropped to 23 per cent. Conversely the proportion living in 'unmixed' streets (defined as 91 per cent or more of one community) increased. In 1969 the majority of Protestants (69 per cent) and Catholics (56 per cent) were living in 'unmixed' streets. By 1972 these majorities had increased to 78 per cent and 70 per cent respectively (Poole 1982). Considered in terms of the Census enumeration districts of about 500 persons each, between 35 and 40 per cent of the Northern Ireland population was living in 'segregated' areas in 1981 (Compton and Power 1986, 34). It is important to note the marked unreliability of the 1981 Census, but mapping of the 1991 Census data confirmed that 90 per cent of wards in the Belfast Urban Area were either mainly Protestant or mainly Catholic (Boyle and Hadden 1994, 35; Boal 1995, 26–9).

Ethnic patchwork

The 13 'peace lines' of Belfast are the result of a further attempt to manage conflict through 'non-mobile' migration. Constructed to separate Catholic and Protestant neighbourhoods into distinct 'worlds' and to allow movement between them to be regulated, they form an 'ethnic patchwork' that reflects the consequences of 'an incomplete ethnic sorting' (Murtagh 2002, 45, 47). At the same time, there has been a drive to improve the quality of housing and this may have contributed significantly to the notable fall in violence in the region in the 1980s by comparison with the 1970s, with paramilitary strongholds tending to be 'in the remaining rundown and congested enclaves and in the more soulless estates put up in the 1960s and early 1970s' (Bardon 1992, 793). Within Northern Ireland, there has been a process of 'repopulation' of the countryside or 'counter-urbanisation' in selective areas, mostly in traditionally Catholic areas in the south and west close to the border with the Republic, especially Newry and Mourne, the west of Fermanagh and the south-west of the Londonderry District Council Area. This trend has accentuated religious lines of division in rural areas and threatens the long-term survival of distinctive local Protestant communities. For example, in his study of 'Glenanne', Brendan Murtagh found that selective 'exiting' of the younger, more able members threatened the 'critical mass' any community needs if it is to be 'institutionally complete' (2002, 42, 119; Stockdale 1992; 1993). Related to the concept of 'critical mass' is that of the 'tipping point', when critical mass is lost and the community collapses through rapid 'exiting' or migration (Gladwell 2000; Murtagh 2002, 35). Some, including Boal (who makes use of Hirschman's 'exit-voice' polarity theory, see Appendix II), have been dismissive of 'the Holy Grail of tipping point', pointing out that much change in choice of residence is characterised by gradual progression rather than by a dramatic, isolated shift. Nevertheless, it is clear that during periods of violence, ethnic sorting is accelerated and results in greater spatial polarisation (Boal 1987, 126, 118). As political effort in recent years has been put increasingly into mitigating the economic and social effects of Partition by promoting cross-border cooperation, a great deal of research effort has been concentrated on understanding the effect on communities of the international border and also the 'peace lines' which function as 'borders within borders' (Whyte 1983; Smyth 1995; Anderson and Bort 1999; Doherty and Poole 2000; Jarman and O'Halloran 2000; Hughes and Donnelly 2001; Bairner and Shirlow 2003; Shirlow 2003; Coakley 2004; Jarman 2004; Poole 2004; Coakley and O'Dowd 2005; Conway and Byrne 2005 – an excellent on-line annotated bibliography; Harvey et al. 2005; Jarman 2005; Shirlow and Murtagh 2006).

The conflict and housing

As well as the reintroduction of internment, it has been argued that government attempted from the 1970s to manage the violent conflict through internal migration by 'systematically and deliberately creating ghettos in which dissident populations may be easily contained' (Hillyard 1983, 47; 1997). Reviewing the literature, Murtagh identified three main allegations of manipulation of population movement by the security forces:

> The first was that, through the planning and housing system, the Northern Ireland Office (NIO) engineered population movements in a way that led to a more homogeneous and manageable ethnic map. Second, that the security forces were involved in the detailed design and layout of housing developments in order to police and secure them more effectively. Third, that key planning decisions such as the construction of Poleglass in West Belfast or the demolition of Unity Flats in the North of the city were dictated by broader political concerns.
>
> (2002, 163–4; see also Brett 1986, 79)

Notwithstanding his difficulty in getting access to all parts and levels of the decision-making process, Murtagh found little evidence to support these allegations and concluded that after the fall of Stormont in 1972 the planning service in Northern Ireland was not used 'to manage conflict, guarantee dominance or reproduce spatial advantage as it was in South Africa and Israel' (2002, 168–9, 171, 177). Nevertheless, he did find 'absence of a clear and explicit policy on the connection between housing, planning and the spatial dimension to the conflict'. He further concluded that the resulting uncertainty 'has given space to conspiratorial theories in a society where anecdote can quickly become accepted as fact'. Attempts by the newly established Housing Executive to pioneer 'mixed' housing developments sparked violent reaction, such as in Manor Street, Belfast, where 17 new dwellings had to be demolished. In the light of this experience, the Housing Executive opted to go with the flow, concluding that this 'demonstrated the need to plan housing developments responsibly and in a way that did not threaten lives and property' (Brett 1986, 70–2; NIHE 1987). The scale of the problem is indicated by the fact that in 1976, 25,000 houses were damaged by violence and in 1986 the Housing Executive dealt with 1,118 cases of intimidation (Flackes and Elliott 1994, 12, 36; Neill 2004).

Demographic realignment

With regard to internal migration in the private sector, one study found 'religion' to be the key variable in house search behaviour. Another study found two almost 'self-contained' housing markets in Craigavon, operated by separate estate agents, developers and landowners. As with housing, so it was with the transfer of land, which has been analysed in terms of 'dual land markets' with limited 'seepage' between them (Kirk 1993; Paris et al. 1997; McPeake 1998; Adair et al. 2000). In response to the ongoing threat of political violence, real and imagined, there has been continual 'demographic realignment' in local communities, mainly through internal migration rather than emigration. Alongside the 'normal' technological change and economic restructuring of post-industrialisation common throughout the island, this ranks as an additional major social change, and its result has been a deepening of the cleavages between the two communities (Boal 2000; Murtagh 2002, 33–4).

Ethnic cleansing?

Paramilitary organisations, as well as influencing urban migration, also influenced rural migration by so-called 'ethnic cleansing', especially in border areas. Since its formation in 1970, the Ulster Defence Regiment had by the end of 1990 suffered on average the loss of one member every 39 days – 188 killed in all – and another seriously injured every 19 days. Particularly in rural areas, a very high proportion of adult male Protestants had joined the UDR and because most served part-time and lived in the community they were 'dreadfully vulnerable'. Ken Maginnis, who reached the rank of major in the UDR before being elected a Unionist MP, argued that because so many eldest sons and wage-earners had been targeted with the aim of driving Protestants from their farms and jobs west of the Bann, it was clear that Provisional IRA attacks on the UDR were not only sectarian but 'genocidal'. Protestants in west Cork in the 1920s had similarly believed that the IRA campaign there had been 'sectarian' (Bardon 1992, 807; Hart 1998, 291–2; Dawson 2007, 217–20). In Northern Ireland in 2007 there was serious concern about a spate of arson attacks on Orange Halls (*Belfast Telegraph* 21 December 2007).

Segregation or integration

The progressive polarisation of the two communities in segregated areas, through both forced and voluntary migration, is embodied by the 'peace lines' which 'concentrate violence, cut through housing markets, blight land and project negative images to visitors and investors'; and at the same time also 'protect, build solidarity and enhance cultural identity' (Murtgagh 2002, 63–4). An example is the single, shrinking Protestant enclave of the Fountain on the Cityside in Derry, outside the city walls to the south of St Columb's Church of Ireland cathedral, where a study found that 29 per cent of the community thought that segregation had brought some degree of community protection; 52 per cent thought that it helped to enhance their identity; and 57 per cent thought it had given freedom for cultural expression (Templegrove Action Research, 1995). Given that the traditional coping strategy of moving to areas of greater segregation has made sense to most people and 'works', and also that there is an inverse relationship between the degree of assimilation between two ethnic groups and the degree of residential segregation that exists between them, the prospect for a shared future seems bleak (Boal 1969; 1987, 112; see Poole and Doherty 1996a, b for a review of the research literature pursuing this insight). The two main choices available for conflict management or resolution being between segregation (separation) and integration (sharing), the choice preferred by the Belfast Agreement was integration and 'the promotion of a culture of tolerance at every level of society, including initiatives to facilitate and encourage integrated education and mixed housing' (Boyle and Hadden 1994; NIO 1998, 18). In practice planners have tended to favour segregation, occasionally being accused of 'discrimination', as with the development of the large Poleglass housing estate in west Belfast (now part of the city of Lisburn) and the cessation of housing programmes in Protestant areas, which was claimed by some (with echoes of the policy of 'de-Arabisation' in Israel) to be 'de-Protestantising' the city (Murtagh 2002, 176–7). More recently, the Housing Executive has again taken up the challenge of moving beyond a policy of 'benign acceptance' of segregation, and powerlessness in the face of the very 'wickedness' of the problem, to develop policies designed at overcoming the tendency to segregation and promoting 'sharing'. Government policy likewise has become clearly committed to 'A Shared Future' (Murtagh 2002, 37; Community Relations Unit 2005). In October 2006 20 families moved into Carran Crescent outside Enniskillen, Fermanagh, the first mixed-community social housing scheme in Northern Ireland in a generation (*Belfast Telegraph* 30 October 2006).

Cross-border issues

With regard to internal migration on the island post-Partition, we should note cross-border migration in both directions. The upheaval of political violence between 1969 and 1972 resulted in the movement of northern Catholics across the border reminiscent of that during the early 1920s. By mid-August 1971, in excess of 5,000 northern refugees, many escaping sectarian rioting in Belfast, moved south of the border, with many being accommodated by the Dublin government at Gormanstown army camp, Meath, between Drogheda and Dublin. In the years of the Troubles others followed this path, while it was not unknown for southern Protestants to be forced out of the southern border counties of Donegal, Cavan and Monaghan. The continuing issue of displaced persons from Northern Ireland remained relatively forgotten until research recently revealed its scale (Conroy, McKearney and Oliver 2005, 23–51). Another issue was that of cross-border workers, highlighted by the Irish European Cross Border Workers Association in a submission to the Minister for Finance's Committee on the Taxation of Cross Border Workers (March 1995). It argued that cross-border workers living in the Republic were being discriminated against because, while gross pay levels in Northern Ireland were much lower, taxation rates in the Republic were higher, and therefore 'the effect of allowing this situation to continue will be to create a sort of uni-directional economic partition of Ireland where it will become financially impossible for anyone who works in Northern Ireland to live in the Republic of Ireland'. Such matters became the concern of the various cross-border bodies established after the Belfast/Good Friday Agreement 1998.

Emigration

Leaving the 'sinking ship'

As late as 1994, it was possible for a leading Irish writer, Joseph O' Connor (b. 1963), to testify to the continuing centrality of emigration in Irish life: 'emigration is an utterly ingrained part of the Irish psyche. Growing up in Dublin, you expect emigration to happen to you, like puberty' (1994, 17). This serves as a reminder that social attitudes are slow to reflect structural change in the economy and that even when it is more buoyant, many people, particularly the young, still leave from the ports and airports in search of work. Similarly the former Irish rugby international Hugo MacNeill recalled returning to Dublin from Oxford in the mid-1980s, where he was researching a thesis on the Irish unemployment problem, to play a friendly match between the 'stayers' and the 'rats', the latter being made up of those, like him, who were thought to have 'left the sinking ship' (*Sunday Times* 16 May 2004; Ferriter 2004, 674). As it turned out, many of those who had left returned in the 1990s, demonstrating once again change in migration patterns in response to boom and bust in the economic cycle, and prompting the former Taoiseach Garret Fitzgerald to point out that:

> a number of those who have recently returned to work in Ireland after having had to emigrate in the late 1980s had as children been brought back to Ireland by parents who returned here in the 1970s after themselves having had to emigrate in the 1950s or early 1960s!
>
> (2003, 106)

The 'black fifties'

In recent years there has been much discussion of how dark the so-called 'black fifties' actually were, with some recalling a time of unremitting gloom and others insisting that there had also been progress and optimism in spite of the undoubted economic setbacks (Fallon 1998; Doherty and Keogh 2003; Keogh, O'Shea and Quinlan 2003; Savage 2003). However the austerity of the 1950s is remembered, from the vantage point of 'Celtic Tiger' affluence in the early twenty-first century it is difficult to see the emigration statistics as an indicator of satisfaction with the homeland. The forecast at the time was dire, summed up by the title of O'Brien's *The Vanishing Irish* (1954). The tens of thousands of Irish citizens taking the boat train to Britain have been referred to by one commentator as marking the 'psychological implosion' of the country (interview with John Bradley, RTÉ *Seven Ages*, programme 4). Net emigration from the Republic was at an annual average of 14.1 per 1,000 (Kennedy 1994, 23). The peak year of the decade was 1957 when almost 60,000 left, and roughly three out of every five children growing up in the 1950s were destined to leave at some stage (Delaney 2002, 164–5; 2007, 12–13). Emigration from Northern Ireland, though much higher than in the 1930s and 1940s, was still much lower by comparison, at an annual average of 6.6 per 1,000 (Kennedy 1994, 23). Britain was still the main destination, now as dominant as the United States had been a century before, receiving about 80 per cent of emigrants from North and South (Walsh 1974, 107).

The safety-valve

Deep-seated prejudice against emigration to Britain persisted in Ireland long after Britain replaced the US as the main destination, with England in particular tending to be regarded by the middle classes as 'a kind of vast Irish slum where none of the better people went, not even on holidays' – although some were prepared to concede that if it were not for England they would have had very little (Ryan 1990, 46, 50). Particular concern was expressed at the time for the moral well-being of female emigrants, who it was feared might succumb to material temptations and abandon their faith in accommodating to a hostile lifestyle. Nevertheless, politicians consistently refused to attempt any restriction on the free movement of labour and also to allocate public funds to centres which assisted Irish migrants in Britain. Emigration acted for a time as a 'safety-valve' and it was recognised that 'if emigration were to be stopped tomorrow conditions favourable to social revolution might easily arise'. However, by the late 1950s there was also widespread recognition that emigration was jeopardising the survival of the independent Irish state (Delaney 2005, 64–5; Ferriter 2006, 239–52).

Men and women

Although the literature still tends to present the emigration of the 1950s as predominantly male, the gender balance was still remarkably even (Ryan, 1990, 54; Daly 2006b, 83, 85). Popular literature on the theme probably compounded the impression that the emigrants were predominantly male: after all, the musical evocation by John B. Keane (1928–2002) of leaving his native Listowel, Kerry, for England was entitled 'Many Young Men of Twenty' (1961). In spite of the severe increase in male unemployment in Ireland, between 1951 and 1961 the gender ratio of the emigration flow was 876 females to 1,000 males (Travers 1995, 147–8; Ó Gráda 1997, 95). The significance of females in the flow was acknowledged in the final report of the Commission on Emigration (1948–54), but it stressed the importance of social rather than economic factors in shaping their decision to leave (Travers 2003, 351). This was to ignore the obvious point that more higher-status jobs, such as in nursing, teaching and the civil service, were available to Irish women in Britain than at home (Delaney 2000, 184–5). The expectations and priorities of women in rural Ireland were changing, but there was as yet limited evidence that the insensitivity or even downright hostility of the state was relenting (Travers 1995, 163; Daly 1997 49–51; Hill 2003, 243; Cullen Owens 2005, 237–47). There is little doubt that the public profile of male migrants from Ireland remained higher in the 1950s, especially as represented by the large number of 'unskilled workers' still filling the traditional niche of 'navvy' in the host labour market on construction sites, building roads, motorways, dams or power stations, such as London's Bankside Power Station (now Tate Modern), to which, for example, the Dublin-born Douglas Francis Lambkin moved in 1960 from other civil engineering work near Newcastle upon Tyne, with his Northern Ireland-born wife and four children (Delaney 2000, 135–8; Cowley 2001, 166–9). Although continuing to leave for lower-status employment, women from Ireland were increasingly represented across the spectrum of higher-status jobs opening to women in post-war Britain. Their presence as nurses was particularly apparent in the embryonic National Health Service, even if, as recalled by one nurse interviewed for the *Irish Empire* television series, it was often taken for granted (1999, programme 3, Littlebird Productions).

The government perspective

Attempting to address the apparently relentless exodus, the inter-party government in 1948 had established the Commission on Emigration and Other Population Problems. To the extent that the strategy was intended to sideline an embarrassing issue, it backfired, generating instead a debate that was vigorous by comparison with the neglect evident in the 1920s and 1930s (Delaney 2000, 190–1; Daly 2006b, 139). The Commission's final report in 1954 contained a massive amount of data on the national picture, but was light on policy recommendations, which included 'decentralisation' and the supply of running water and internal sanitation. This reflected a governing elite that was still doggedly anti-urban and anti-industrial in outlook. The obvious conclusion was that the surest route to stemming the haemorrhage of Irish people was through policies that would deliver economic growth and job creation, particularly through industrialisation and urbanisation, and that would offer an alternative locally to rural migrants leaving for urban life in Britain or beyond; in short, the replacement of emigration by internal migration (Daly 2006b, 18, 42–3). The breakthrough came with the publication in 1958 of the

White Paper *Programme for Economic Expansion*, under the name of the Secretary of the Department of Finance, T. K. Whitaker (Ó Gráda 1997, 213).

The 'crowded cohort'

After the peak of 1957, the rate of net emigration fell steeply over the next five years. A slight resurgence in the later 1960s was followed by the sudden switch to net immigration in the early 1970s, which persisted until the onset of world-wide economic recession in the early 1980s, when industries such as steel-making, shipbuilding and car assembly, which had enjoyed a transitional period of protection after joining the EEC in 1973, started to be dismantled. In early 1983 severe deflationary measures by the government accelerated the increase in unemployment: in 1979 this had been at 7.8 per cent, and by 1985 it was at 18.2 per cent. Compounding the problem was the arrival in the employment market of the children of the 1960s 'baby boom', and so for many of this 'crowded cohort' there seemed no choice but to emigrate (Walsh 1989, 19; Kennedy, 1994, 12–13; Ó Gráda, 1997, 31; Tansey 1998, 69–71; Gray 2004, 4–5). For those still in Ireland who remembered the 1950s, there was a strong sense of *déjà vu* with the return to mass emigration. Some, however, sensed a discontinuity with the past and talked more optimistically of better educated, 'new wave' emigrants, going overseas with good prospects of return. One of those who did remember the 1950s was the Minister for Foreign Affairs, Brian Lenihan. Asked in an interview by *Newsweek* about the issue his reply included the oft-repeated 'small island' sound-bite:

> I don't look on the type of emigration we have today as being in the same category as the terrible emigration of the last century. What we have now is a very literate emigrant who thinks nothing of coming to the United States and going back to Ireland and maybe on to Germany and back to Ireland again. The younger people in Ireland today are very much in that mode ... It [emigration] is not a defeat because the more Irish emigrants hone their skills and talents in another environment, the more they develop a work ethic in a country like Germany of the U.S., the better it can be applied in Ireland when they return. After all, we can't all live on a small island.
> ('The New Emigrants', 10 October 1987; Whelan 1987; Gray 2004, 30–1).

Small Island

In the following year, 1988/9, an astounding gross total of 70,600 people (about 2 per cent of the population) left the country (Mac Éinrí 2001, 47–8). The painting *Small Island* by Petra Fox, inspired by Lenihan's comment, repays close attention for the message it conveys, far more nuanced than the misleading interpretation made by the media of Lenihan's 'small island' comment (see front cover of Ó Gráda 1995).

The 1980s leavers

As before, the majority of those leaving were the young: in 1988 emigrants aged 15–24 made up 68.8 per cent of the total. Those leaving were also predominantly female – 75 per cent of the total. In contrast to the unskilled manual labourers of the 1950s, many had completed secondary and tertiary education and acquired professional qualifications as a result of the expansion of the education sector from the 1960s (Shuttleworth, 1997, 304–22; Redmond 2000, 45–51). During the 1980s the proportion of unemployed graduates rose from 20 per cent to 40 per cent – hence their description as 'new wave' emigrants. However, in practice, especially for those leaving the rural west, the contrast with the past could be more apparent than real, for, as Jim MacLaughlin observed, 'while a minority of Irish male emigrants are climbing social ladders abroad, many more are simply climbing ladders' (1997, 144–5, 153).

The 'illegals'

Of course, however well educated young emigrants may have been, their qualifications did not necessarily guarantee ease of entry to labour markets overseas. Britain was still the main destination, especially London and the south-east, accounting for about 60 per cent of those leaving the Republic. When emigration was at its peak, between 1987 and 1990, it is probable that around 15 per cent left for the United States, a large proportion of them 'undocumented', with a further 15 per cent leaving for other destinations worldwide. The remaining 10 per cent left for other EU countries and, taking the long view, we may see this growing trend as a kind of 'reconnection' with Europe after the very small flow in the nineteenth and earlier twentieth centuries (Courtney 2000, 306). The major English-speaking global metropolitan centres of London, New York, Boston and Sydney offered this 'new wave' the best opportunities. A study of the 'New Irish' in New York city found many of them to be working clandestinely, tied into a bar scene which encouraged them to associate with other Irish 'illegals', rather than with the 'Old Irish', who by this stage had largely 'arrived'. On being interviewed, it became clear that these 'new' migrants were exploring a different kind of modulation or 'double-belonging', both enjoying the relative social and financial freedom of the US, but resisting the notion that they would make it their permanent home (Almeida 1992, 196–221; Corcoran 1993).

The tension between the 'old' and 'new' Irish in New York was especially evident in 1991 when the Irish Lesbian and Gay Organisation mounted a vocal protest against the decision by the Ancient Order of Hibernians to deny them a place in the traditional St Patrick's Day Parade, which was criticised as 'a solemn, quasi-militaristic display of staunch Roman Catholicism, self-righteousness, and Irish republicanism'. Similar inter-generational tension was evident in Britain where attempts were also being made to promote a more diverse and inclusive definition of Irishness, including that of the so-called 'Plastic Paddy' in Britain (Arrowsmith 2000, 35; Dezell 2000, 17; Kenny 2000, 237-8; Almeida 2001, 80–1, 122; Cronin and Adair 2002, 223–5). As concern about immigration in Ireland continued in 2007, so did the debate about the status of Irish illegals in the US, not least between Niall O'Dowd and Trina Vargo (*Irish Times* 20 November 2007).

The northern 'brain drain'

Meanwhile, in Northern Ireland more inclusive definitions of Irishness and Britishness were a long way off. With political violence at its height between 1971 and 1976, emigration, always much higher than for any other part of the UK, increased, and as the violence continued into the 1980s, between 10,000 and 15,000 left each year (Eversley 1991, 81; Delaney 2002, 6). In the 1980s population increase resumed, but there was still significant net out-migration (Kennedy 1994, 4, see Figure 1.1 and Table 1.1; Trew 2007). In the media there was less talk of 'new wave' emigration and more of a 'brain drain', with particular concern for the disproportionate number of Protestant students leaving for higher education in Britain and the effect that their low rate of return was having on the religious and political balance. From 1921 to 1969, Catholics were significantly over-represented in the outflow from Northern Ireland, but during the 1970s and 1980s the position was reversed as more Protestants left – a transformation that enhanced the growing confidence of Nationalists, but did nothing for the ebbing confidence of Unionists (Eversley 1991, 91–2; Osborne et al. 1991, 112–15; Ó Gráda and Walsh, 1995, 259–79; Delaney 2002, 17). A consequence of the 'continuing haemorrhage' in the 1980s and 1990s of young Protestants to universities and colleges in Britain with few returning to live in Northern Ireland has been a rising representation of Catholics in the highly qualified sector of the workforce (Shuttleworth and Osborne 2004, 80, 16, 61, 84, 186, 188; Osborne, Smith and Hayes 2006).

Nevertheless, the rate of out-migration compared with the Republic was low and this continued to be taken by many in the late 1970s and 1980s as a continuing indicator of Northern Ireland's higher 'British' standard of living. Although not experiencing the radical transition to net immigration in the 1990s, net emigration from Northern Ireland in that decade was marginal, averaging only about 500 each year (Shuttleworth and Osborne 2004, x–xi). However, the still declining Protestant share of the population in the Republic and the still increasing Catholic share of the population in Northern Ireland were taken as indicators of the insecurity of the Protestant majority in Northern Ireland, and the 'brain drain' of young Protestants from Northern Ireland continued to be of grave concern (see Kennedy 1994, 9, Table 1.2; Osborne, Smith and Hayes 2006, 1–7; Trew 2007, 22–48).

Coming home

One young Protestant, Lucy Caldwell, who was happy as an 18-year-old to have left 'boring, introverted and self-obsessed' Belfast for Britain in 1999, had vowed never to return, but when she did in 2006 she was pleasantly surprised to find a much changed city:

> when the various paramilitary organisations announced their respective ceasefires in the latter half of 1994, we were 13 and just starting third form, contemplating what GCSEs we'd begin studying for the following year – some girls declared that their parents swore that if ever there was a united Ireland, they'd be on the next ferry to Scotland.

Now, both Caldwell and her best friend who also emigrated 'haven't ruled out the possibility that one day we might – just might – end up coming home, after all', concluding that 'in the end, after everything, 'home' is still Belfast' (*Belfast Telegraph* 4 January 2007).

They did go away you know

As noted above, and as is evident in the individual case of Lucy Caldwell, disentangling migration caused by political violence from that caused by 'normal' economic pressures is fraught with difficulties, but it has been claimed that 'even during the unrest accompanying the H-block hunger strikes [1981], the main cause of emigration throughout the 1980s and into the 1990s was lack of work' (Bardon 1992, 795). However, there was emigration very directly related to the conflict, albeit on a much smaller scale than what has been presented as economically-driven emigration, resulting from both governments and paramilitary organisations 'forcing' individuals out. In 1974 the Prevention of Terrorism Act was rushed through parliament in the wake of the Birmingham pub bombings, echoing the Prevention of Violence Act 1939, referred to in the previous chapter. As well as giving the government the power to arrest and detain suspected terrorists, it gave the power to exclude from Great Britain, Northern Ireland or the United Kingdom as a whole persons alleged to be involved in terrorism associated with Northern Ireland. Accordingly, the Secretary of State excluded 31 people from Northern Ireland between November 1974 and December 1987: eleven of these orders were made in 1981, the year of the hunger strike; there were no exclusions in 1985 and 1986; and only one in 1987 (Hillyard 1993; Flackes and Elliott 1994, 453, 457). Paramilitary organisations on both sides also operated a policy of excluding or 'exiling' from Northern Ireland and the issue of 'on the runs' or 'political refugees' (from both the state and from paramilitary organisations) was still a live issue in 2007. In the lead-up to elections in March, it was feared that it might 'break the peace process', and the Northern Ireland Office sought to assure Unionists 'that no amnesty is planned for IRA fugitives, the so-called on the runs or OTRs [about 20 in total]', a very small segment of the estimated 11,000 northern migrants living as displaced persons in the Republic (Byrne 2004; Conroy, McKearney and Oliver 2005, 23–51; *Belfast Telegraph* and *Irish Times*, 13 February 2007).

Sharing the fruits

Viewed from the vantage point of 2007, the record of governments north and south in assisting the emigrants they felt largely powerless to retain has been judged harshly. Even in better times, efforts to share the Celtic Tiger cake with the 'forgotten generation' have seemed less than generous. One of the most recent analysts of the population haemorrhage which afflicted Ireland in the half-century since Independence judges the official relationship with the twentieth-century diaspora as decidedly one-way: 'successive Irish governments failed to provide assistance and support for Irish emigrants, although they were more than happy to use these networks to promote tourism or advance causes such as the antipartition campaign' (Daly 2006b, 20). However valid the judgement made with hindsight, predicting the future of migration flows and determining policy accordingly is a precarious business, as illustrated by J. J. Lee's commentary, from the vantage point of 1992, on Brian Lenihan's 1987 'small island' speech:

> It is probable that he [Lenihan] was expressing a fairly widespread, if largely silent, assumption among the population. As long as this belief continues, so will emigration. It will be occasionally interrupted when the international economy slumps and the jobs temporarily vanish abroad. But it will resume as soon as the British, American and European economies revive. It seems likely to be as active in the last decade of the 20th century as in the first decade, and to continue into the twenty-first century unless we find a way of creating jobs that has eluded us for most of this century.
>
> (1992, 20)

Coming to terms

That it seemed unlikely to Lee and many others that the elusive way of creating jobs would be found serves to underline how inexact the science of migration forecasting is. The 'silent assumption' about emigration and the effects it has had on the 'archaeology of the modern Irish mind' has begun to be explored by oral narrative projects such as 'Breaking the Silence' (2002) and 'Narratives of Migration and Return' (2003–6) and Northern Ireland Emigrant Narratives (2006–8) (Lee 1989, 375; Gray 2002; Trew 2005; 2007; Ní Laoire 2006, 2007a, b; discussed further in chapter 15). The 'small island' legacy of net emigration, which had hampered the response to the Hungarian refugees of 1956, was still undermining efforts to come to terms with the challenge of net immigration, which in 2007 looked like being sustained indefinitely.

Conclusion

The Commission on Emigration and Other Population Problems which reported in 1954 revealed the many aspects of a huge social problem but provided few answers because the Commissioners were still bound by the traditional view of emigration. It was the Whitaker Report of 1958 which set in place a strategy for tackling Irish economic underdevelopment and thus emigration. The contrast between North and South was most apparent at the major turning point of 1973, when both the UK and the Republic joined the EEC. As political violence in Northern Ireland drove emigration higher, net immigration was recorded for the first time since Independence, and indeed since the beginning of the eighteenth century. In 1995, the fruits of spectacular economic growth in the Republic resulted in a return to net immigration, which would be sustained in the following decade. Imbalances in the distribution of a now more prosperous population threatened many rural communities with continuing decline, while the towns and cities, particularly Dublin, suffered congestion, which severely reduced the quality of life for many. There were few signs in 2007 that Irish migration patterns were likely to alter fundamentally in the decades ahead. In the South more than 400,000 people – 10 per cent – were foreign-born and it seemed evident that an increasing minority of this minority would become permanent residents. With a similar trend underway in Northern Ireland, this amounted to the biggest shake-up in the composition of the island's population since the seventeenth century.

Plate 13 *Letter from America* (1875), **James Brenan, Crawford Municipal Art Gallery, Cork**

Brenan's painting suggests a representative narrative. We may imagine the family of linen workers (Plate 6), the 'snug' farming family (Plate 9) and the homeward-bound Paddy (Plate 11) as having left such a cottage in Ireland. The envelope of the letter from America, possibly from an older son or daughter, uncle or aunt (like Dorcas McGee's Aunt Bella, Plate 12) lies on the corner of the table. The father sits, holding in his left hand the pre-paid ticket that has arrived, possibly from Five Points (see Plate 10). He cups his right hand to his ear, listening intently as his younger, bare-foot daughter reads. Presumably, she has had the benefit of a National School education, unlike her older sister who is the next to emigrate. The family group is framed between the pot of potatoes on the left (a reminder of the Great Famine) and the open door, leading to the railway station and port. Their faces express a mixed mood, between the resignation of the mother and the quiet anticipation of the older daughter. The eldest son, due to remain and inherit the farm from his infirm father, also sits, contemplating how its future depends on the success of his sister in her new world. Perhaps he is also a little envious. Shortly, she will be given an 'American Wake' (see chapter 2). The likeness on the windowsill (perhaps of Daniel O'Connell or Father Matthew) may become a migrant object, like Dorcas McGee's sampler (Plate 12), given to the departing emigrant as a keepsake.

James Brenan (1837–1907) was an internal migrant from Cork, where he was head of the Cork School of Art, to Dublin, where he was head of the Dublin Metropolitan School of Art.

Plate 14 *Gold Diggers Receiving a Letter from Home* (*c.* 1860), **attributed to William Strutt, Art Gallery of New South Wales, Sydney, Australia**

One of the gold diggers holds a letter that starts 'My dear Tom'; the rest is indecipherable. On the barrel beside him that serves as a table is a bundle of letters. It includes an envelope addressed to Mr T. Godfrey, Ballarat, Australia, with a circular postmark from London and also a photograph, perhaps a likeness of his wife. The letter would have taken three months to arrive. It may contain bad news as there is a hint of a tear in his eye (Macdonald 2005, 114). The steadying hand of a fellow migrant on his shoulder recalls that on the elbow of Hugh O'Neill (Plate 1). Whether English, Scottish, Welsh or Irish in origin, gold diggers welcomed such letters as one of their few pleasures. Many of them had previously tried their luck in California, and many would later move on from Australia to the gold fields of the South Island of New Zealand.

One gold digger, Michael Normile of Caheraderry, Clare, emigrated from Liverpool to Australia with his sister Bridget in 1854 (the year after Dorcas McGee, see Plate 12). He wrote home from Lochinvar, a few miles inland from Maitland, New South Wales, to his father on 1 April 1855, saying 'I received you [*sic*] welcome letter on the 25th March dated January 1st 55 which gave me and my Sister an ocean of consolation ...' (Fitzpatrick 1994, 70, see also chapters 3 and 15).

The Devon-born William Strutt (1825–1915) emigrated to Australia in 1850. He returned to England in 1862, having for 18 months tried his hand at gold-digging in Ballarat, Victoria, about 65 miles north-west of Melbourne.

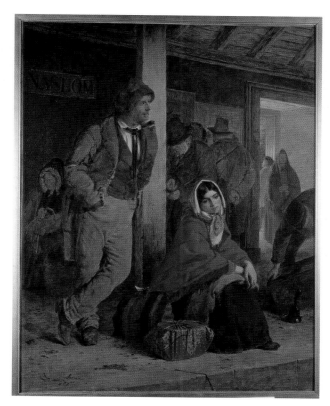

Plate 15 *Irish Emigrants Waiting for a Train* (1864), Erskine Nicol, Sheffield Galleries and Museums Trust, UK/The Bridgeman Art Library

The male emigrant in Plate 11 and the female emigrant in Plate 13 we may imagine as having waited for a train in similar fashion. The sign on the platform confusingly shows '...NASLOM'. It is clear from the other copy of this painting in the collection of Tate Britain (NO1538) that '...NASLOE' was intended (Arnold 1977, 126). This must be Ballinasloe (*Béal Átha na Slua*, 'mouth of the ford of the hosts') in east Galway, site of one of the oldest and largest horse fairs in Europe. It was the terminus of the Grand Canal which, like the more northerly Royal Canal, connected Dublin in the east with the River Shannon in the west. The railway station had opened on 1 August 1851 on the Dublin–Galway line.

Beside the hat box tied up with a scarf is a dual-purpose carpet bag. It is folded and latched up on the sides as a travelling bag, but it could also be opened out as a rug for keeping warm in drafty, unheated railway carriages, or on board ship. In 1864 the Civil War economy of the Union was cranking up. The emigrants are probably travelling the 34 miles west to Galway, rather than east to Dublin. In Galway they could have headed north to Derry, or south to Cork, or to the Galway Line/Royal Atlantic Steam Navigation Company, formed in 1858, for a crossing to Boston via Newfoundland.

One advertisement on the back wall is for '...ndlater Wine'. The firm of Findlater had been founded in Dublin in 1827 by the Scottish-born Alexander Findlater (1797–1873), who had emigrated from Greenock to Newfoundland before arriving in Dublin. The other advertisement is for 'Thorley's Food ... ..ttle' [i.e. for Cattle], an ironic reminder of the post-Famine switch from arable to grazing that resulted in an increase in the cattle population and decline in the human population.

Plate 16 *View of Belfast, Sydenham, Belmont and Glenmachan* (*c.* 1861),
J. H. Connop, Belfast Harbour Commissioners

Looking across Belfast Lough from the Co. Antrim side to Co. Down, the recently constructed villas indicate the growth of Belfast's suburbs. Belfast (out of the picture 2 miles to the right) then had a population of 120,000, compared with 20,000 in 1800. As the wealthier merchants moved out of the town centre, Sydenham, with its fine views of lough and mountain, was one of the areas that attracted those seeking a country mansion. At the outbreak of the American Civil War the transition from the age of sail to steam is nearing completion as the, two-funnelled, two-masted paddle-steamer heads out of the Lough towards Bangor and Clydeside or Merseyside. Arrivals and departures are regulated by the East Twin Island (now gone) with its beacon and two-storey house for harbour officials. The steam train of the Belfast and Co Down Railway heads along the coast from Bangor towards Belfast. It has just passed Tillysburn station and is approaching Sydenham station (both smaller than Ballinasloe station in Plate 15). In the middle distance is Stormont Castle and beyond it Scrabo Tower and Strangford Lough. The reclaimed land in the bottom right is today Victoria Park and beside it, on more reclaimed land, is George Best Belfast City Airport (Black 1983, 15).

Plate 17   Aerial view of Liverpool (1859), John Isaac, Liverpool Record Office, Liverpool Libraries

This view comes close to that imagined by Robert Scally (see chapter 3):

> If one could have scanned the earth from an orbiting satellite for the movement of peoples, its surface would have appeared fitfully dormant until the sudden buzzing and swarming which followed the Napoleonic wars. Liverpool would immediately attract the eye as a center of the boiling activity.

(1984, 16)

For a generation before and after the Great Famine (1845–50) this was the way out for millions of Irish and other west and north east Europeans. The many Irish who passed through, such as those evicted from Ballykilcline, Roscommon (see chapter 10), and the many who stayed, made a lasting impression on the city. Recalling Five Points in New York (Plate 10), the Irish tended to congregate around 'core streets' in the 'instant slum' of the North End with its purpose-built court housing, and in the failed middle-class suburb of the South End. The most famous 'Irish' pub was strategically positioned opposite Clarence Dock, the disembarkation point for Irish passenger traffic, immediately recognisable by the effigy of St Patrick, shamrock in hand, high on its walls (Belchem and MacRaild 2006, 330, 334).

Liverpool, previously a major port of the African slave trade, is now a major hub for European emigration.

Plate 18 *Listed for the Connaught Rangers* (*c.* 1880), Elizabeth, Lady Butler, Bury Art Gallery, Museum and Archives, Lancashire

From the middle of the eighteenth century large numbers of Irish Catholic recruits joined the ranks of the British military, now serving the Empire rather than Britain's European rivals. Many never returned, dying or settling in the colonies. The characters in Derry-born George Farquhar's play *The Recruiting Officer* (1706), which were drawn from his life in England, illustrate the recruiting process:

> If any gentlemen soldiers, or others, have a mind to serve Her Majesty, and pull down the French king; if any prentices have severe masters, any children have unnatural parents; if any servants have too little wages, or any husband too much wife; let them repair to the noble Sergeant Kite, at the Sign of the Raven, in this good town of Shrewsbury, and they shall receive present relief and entertainment.

Here we see a latter-day Sergeant Kite, his corporal and two drummer boys escorting two young men away from their coastal village in county Kerry, probably to the railway station in Killarney or Tralee. Unlike the 'convoy' that was part of the 'American Wake', no neighbours are in evidence. Again the mood is mixed. While one looks resolutely forward, the backward look of the other is directed to the wallsteads of a cottage – a reminder of the deaths and emigration of the Great Famine, and the evictions of the Land War (1879–82). However, having taken the 'king's shilling', both wear round their hats the temporary uniform of red and blue ribbons, as does the sergeant.

This picture can be seen as answering the well-known song 'Arthur McBride', first collected about 1840 in Limerick, in which the eponymous Arthur and his cousin do not go along willingly with Sergeant Harper, Corporal Cramp and the 'wee drummer'. The Connaught Rangers had served in the Peninsular War (1808–14), the Crimean War (1854–56) and in India from 1857 (the year of the Indian Mutiny) until 1870. They would go on to serve in the Sudan (under Lord Kitchener – see chapter 10), in South Africa during the Boer War (1899–1902), and in France during the First World War.

The Swiss-born Lady Butler (1846–1933) arrived in Kerry in 1877 on her marriage to Tipperary-born Sir William Butler, an Irish Catholic soldier with strong Nationalist sympathies (Usherwood and Spencer-Smith 1987, 70; Spiers 1996, 338).

Plate 19   Maurice Shea (1794–1892): last known survivor of Wellington's army at Waterloo, Alan Lagden, Brightlingsea, Essex

This photograph was taken in Canada about 1875, towards the end of this man's impressive migration story, which included not only survival at the battle of Waterloo, but also in Ceylon and Spain, as well as transatlantic emigration to Canada with his family in the worst year of the Great Famine (see chapter 9). He may well have seen a copy of the British Army proclamation (Plate 7) posted in Tralee in his native Kerry. It was printed when he was 12 years old, about the same age as the drummer boys in Plate 18. The Proclamation announced the recent extension of the age limit on recruitment to the Infantry (from 25 to 30) and the reduction in the minimum height requirement (from 5' 6" to 5' 5") for 'growing Lads from Seventeen to Nineteen Years of Age'.

Plate 20 *St. Patrick's Day in America* (1872), anonymous (possibly by John Reid), American Antiquarian Society, Worcester, Massachusetts

A mother in mourning, probably the widow of a deceased Irish-American Union soldier, pins a sprig of shamrock to her son's lapel as her daughter watches the passing St. Patrick's Day parade. The son with drum appears prepared to make the same sacrifice as his father through service in the military, the route to acceptance and respectability for many Irish-American families. Their 'double-belonging' is represented by the hanging of the military portrait between the flags of Ireland and the United States.

The picture can be seen as answering the negative ghetto image of the Irish in Five Points (Plate 10) and the hostile stereotyping by the German-American Thomas Nast in cartoons such as 'The Day We Celebrate: St Patrick's Day, 1867' (Jones 1976, 88–9). The family Bible beside the statue of Virgin and Child is a reassuring signal of the Christianity shared by Protestant Americans and Irish-American Catholics. The picture of St Patrick indicates continuing connection with the homeland, as does the slogan on the banner being waved by the daughter, 'God Save Ireland'. The song of that name was written by T. D. Sullivan in 1867. We may imagine it being sung on this occasion. Like 'Hail Glorious Saint Patrick', composed in 1853 (see chapter 15), it pictures the close relationship between homeland and its diaspora:

> Girt around with cruel foes, still their courage proudly rose,
> For they thought of hearts that loved them far and near;
> Of the millions true and brave o'er the ocean's swelling wave,
> And the friends in holy Ireland ever dear.
>
> 'God save Ireland!' said the heroes;
> 'God save Ireland!' said they all …

Plate 21 *Breaking Home Ties* (1890), Thomas Hovenden, Philadelphia Museum of Art

For many families, migration did not stop on the far side of the ocean as the next generation moved on. Here the son takes leave of his mother, perhaps heading from their town west to where the American frontier is closing, or from their farm into the town (http://www.philamuseum.org/collections/permanent/47809.html).The prosperous interior contrasts with that of Brenan's *Letter from America* (Plate 13), but the mood is similar. The father carries a carpet bag, like the one on the platform of Ballinasloe station (Plate 15). At the door stands a man with a buggy whip, waiting to drive to the station.

Thomas Hovenden (1840–95) was born in Dunmanway, Cork. Orphaned during the Great Famine at the age of six, he studied art in Cork city, leaving for further study in London, New York, Paris and Brittany. He returned to the United States in 1880 and died in Plymouth Meeting, Pennsylvania. One of his ancestors, Henry Hovenden, was in the company of Hugh O'Neill on his departure from Ireland in 1607. The family, originally from Hoveden (now Howden), 20 miles from the city of York on the road from Beverley to Doncaster, had been granted land in the new Queen's County (Laois) in 1555 during the reign of Mary Tudor, along with the families of Cosby, Barrington, Hartpole, Bowen, Ruish and Hetherington (Ó Muraíle 2007, 413).

Plate 22   *The Publican* (1913), Jack B. Yeats, A. P. Watt Ltd (on behalf of Anne Yeats and Michael B. Yeats)

The publican is a spirit grocer, as indicated by the stack of paper cones on the counter, probably for selling tea. The poster behind advertising 'America', possibly the 'American Line' shipping company, indicates that he is also an emigration agent. Perhaps he himself is a 'Returned Yank' (see chapter 3). The hand in his pocket, like that of the prospective 'Returned Yank' in Plate 11, suggests prosperity if not greed. He turns an additional penny or two by facilitating the Atlantic crossings of the local landless labourers and aspirant housemaids, allowing them, once the fare was paid, some credit 'on the slate', in expectation of the family getting its Christmas letter from America, with a remittance enclosed. One emigrant who purchased his ticket on the *Titanic* for £7 15s in such a shop was the hurler Andy Keane of Derrydonnell, Galway (see chapter 12).

The London-born Jack Butler Yeats (1871-1957) was a friend of the playwright John Millington Synge who described the kind of figure depicted here as:

> the groggy-patriot-publican-general-shop-man who is married to the priest's half-sister and is second cousin once-removed of the dispensary doctor, that are horrid and awful. This is the type that is running the present United Irish League anti-grazier campaign, while they're swindling the people themselves in a dozen ways and then buying out their holdings and packing off whole families to America.

(Booth 1992, 62)

Plate 23 *Economic Pressure* (1936), Sean Keating, Crawford Municipal Art Gallery, Cork

It is not immediately clear whether it is the man who is taking leave of the woman or vice versa (see chapter 3). Women were as likely as men to have purchased tickets from agents such as the publican in Plate 22. Now, after the Wall Street Crash of 1929, the emigrant's destination is almost certainly Britain and not America. There are strong elements of continuity in the scene: the embrace of the couple and the woman's tears (see Plate 1), the one-masted boat (see Plate 2) and the dress of the man standing in the shelter of the rock (see Plate 18). Child clings to parent, or spouse to spouse like the blasted tree clings to the rock. Not all the inhabitants of such islands were able to cling on. The Great Blasket, for example, was finally evacuated in 1953 (see Chapter 12).

The Limerick-born Seán Keating (1889–1997) left for Dublin aged 20, moved on to the Aran Islands and London, and returned to Ireland in 1916. He was the model for the man seated cross-legged beside the weeping woman in Thomas Ryan's *The Departure of O'Neill out of Ireland* (Plate 1).

Plate 24   Election poster, Ravenhill Road, Belfast, 2007; photo Brian Lambkin

This photograph was taken on the morning of 7 March, when 108 new members were elected to the restored Northern Ireland Assembly. The Democratic Unionist Party, led by Ian Paisley, and Sinn Féin, led by Gerry Adams, emerged as clear winners. Anna Lo of the Alliance Party was the first person of Chinese origin to be elected to a parliamentary institution in Europe. Born in Hong Kong, she arrived in Northern Ireland in 1974 (see chapter 16).

Martyrs' Memorial Church in the background is the headquarters of the Free Presbyterian Church of Ulster, also led by Paisley. Built in 1969, its dedication to the Protestant martyrs of the sixteenth century is a reminder of the religious background to the Departure/Flight of the Earls in 1607 and the Plantation of Ulster that followed. The biblical injunction to remember that 'Time is Short' (I Corinthians 7: 29–31) recalls the symbolism of the hourglass placed on the loom in Luke's picture of Belfast in 1613 (Plate 3).

Figures

Maps

Explanatory note

For reasons explained in the Preface, Figures 1–4 can only be indicative rather than definitive. They are intended to show, century by century, the changing size of the population of the whole island, the main directions and scale of outward migration, and an estimated emigration rate. All estimates are gross figures. The emigration rate is calculated on the basis of the estimated mid-century population and the total number of emigrants for that century.

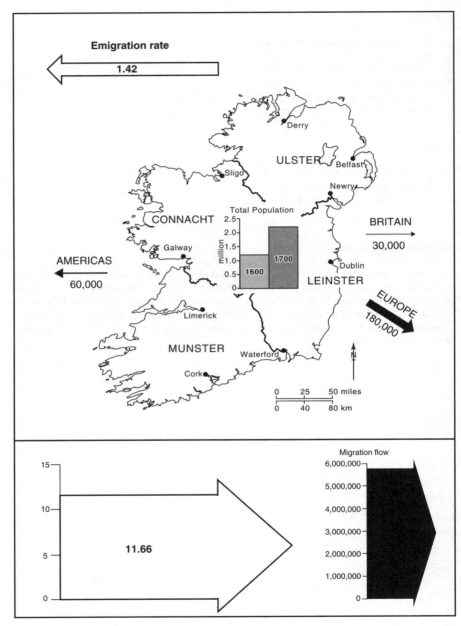

Figure 1. Irish emigration flows, 1600–1700

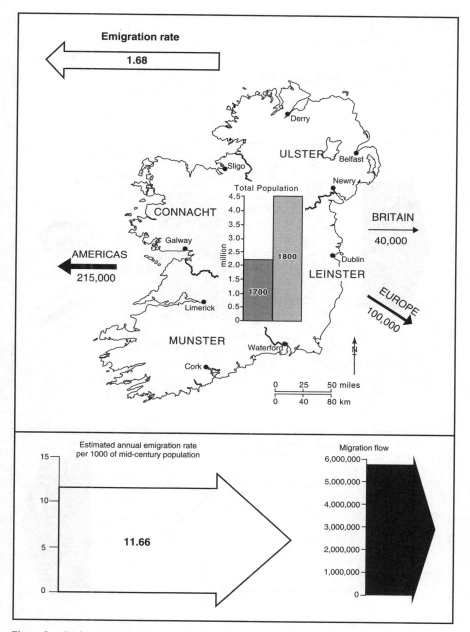

Figure 2. Irish emigration flows, 1700–1800

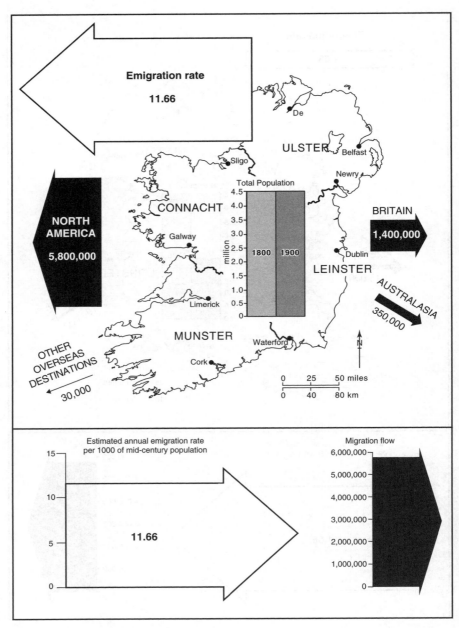

Figure 3. Irish emigration flows, 1800–1900

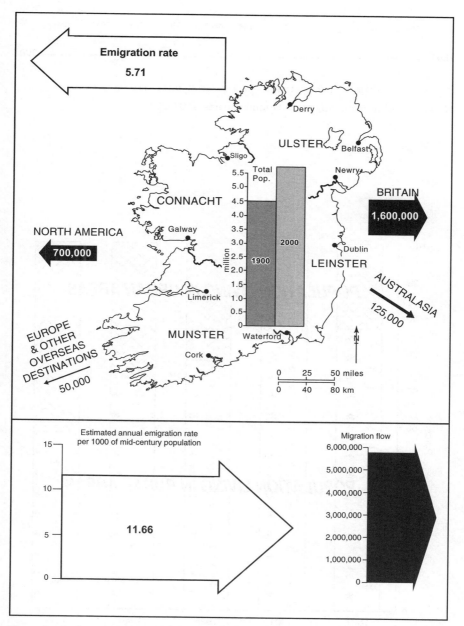

Figure 4. Irish emigration flows, 1900–2000

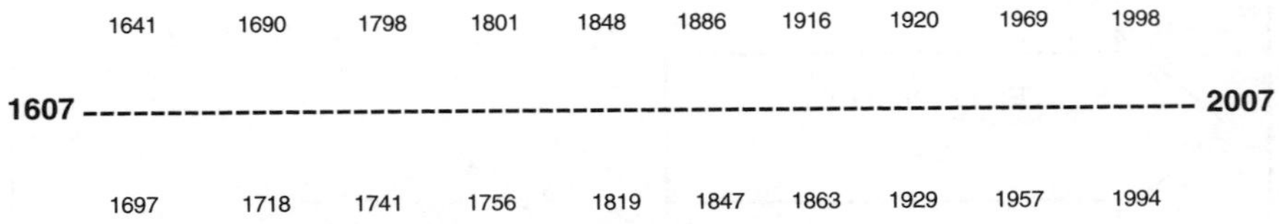

1641
1690
1798
1801
1848
1886
1916
1920
1969
1998
1607
2007
1697
1718
1741
1756
1819
1847
1863
1929
1957
1994

Figure 5. Political and migration landmark dates, 1607–2007

100
90
80
70
60
50
40
30
20
10
0
Percent
POPULATION LIVING IN URBAN AREAS
POPULATION LIVING IN RURAL AREAS
1881
1901
1926
1946
1971

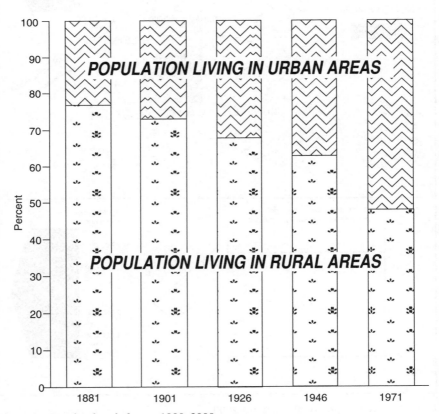

Figure 6. Rural–urban balance, 1900–2000

Map 1. Provinces and counties of Ireland

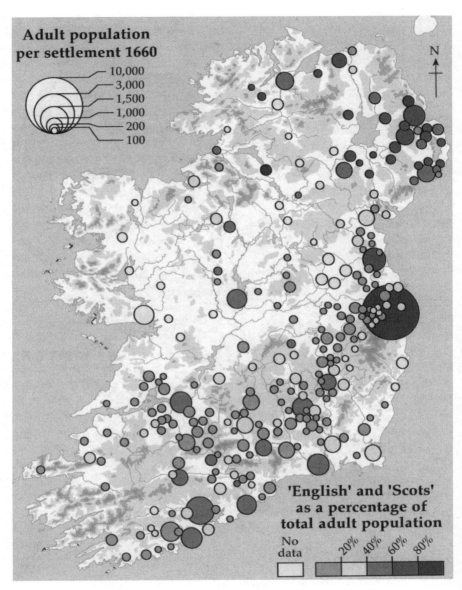

Adult population
per settlement 1660

— 10,000
— 3,000
— 1,500
— 1,000
— 200
— 100

'English' and 'Scots'
as a percentage of
total adult population

No
data   20% 40% 60% 80%

Map 2. Ireland's urban network *c.*1660

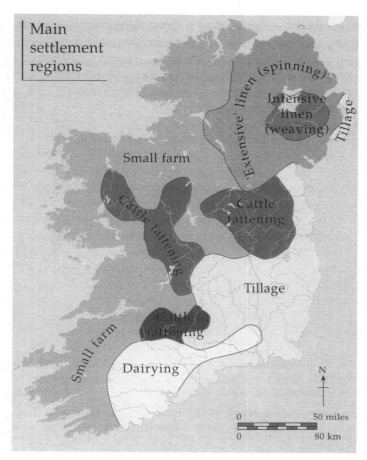

Map 3. Main settlement regions, 1700–1800

Part III

The World in Ireland – Ireland in the World

Introduction

Taking the long backward look, as it were from 'Scally's satellite', beyond1607 to the end of the last Ice Age (about 10,000 years ago) when the land we now call Ireland was uninhabited, we can see the migration process getting under-way as the first immigrants established the pattern of successive 'arrivals' that has persisted through the last 400 years to the present (Manning 2005, 86–90). The concern of this final part is with what we can observe today as the cumu-lative outcome of migration in Irish history, which can be summed up by the term 'through-otherness'.

There was renewed interest in the idea of 'through-otherness' when the Northern Ireland Assembly was restored in 2007 (Paul Gillespie, *Irish Times* 12 May 2007). It had been popularised by Seamus Heaney in a lecture given at the University of Aberdeen in 2001, entitled 'Through-Other Places, Through-Other Times: The Irish Poet and Britain'. He had drawn the term from the poem 'Armagh' by W. R. Rodgers, which begins:

> There is a through-otherness about Armagh
> Of tower and steeple,
> Up on the hill are the arguing graves of the kings
> And below are the people.

Heaney pointed to Rodgers' migration heritage (his father was of indigenous Irish stock and his mother of Scottish Planter ancestry) and suggested that in his life 'there is something analogous to the triple heritage of Irish, Scottish and English traditions that compound and complicate the cultural and polit-ical life of contemporary Ulster', but for Rodgers 'it wasn't a question of the otherness of any part of his inheritance, more a recognition of the through-otherness of all of them'.

Interestingly, the English or Ulster Scots word 'through-other' or *'throo-ither'*, meaning 'in a mess' or 'things mixed up among themselves,' is a sign of itself, being a word for word translation of the Irish *trí chéile* (Macafee 1996, 356; Heaney 2002, 366, 381; Hillan 2005, 90). We are reminded of the 'through-otherness' of the 'world' of sub-atomic particles, discussed in chapter 3 in relation to the 'force-field' or matrix of migration. The idea of the through-otherness of Ireland is illustrated well by Patrick O'Connor in *All Ireland is in and about Rathkeale* (1996).

However selective or comprehensive we choose to be in our view, the three-stage, three-direction, three-outcome process of migration has resulted in the 'through-otherness' of Ireland and the world: the rest of the world – or parts of it at least – being made manifest *in* Ireland through immigration (including return migration); the countryside being made manifest *within* the town and the town *within* the countryside through internal migration; and Ireland being made manifest *out* in the rest of the world through emigration.

In chapter 14 we consider the presence in Ireland of what we might call the British diaspora and the diasporas of other countries, including those of Israel, Italy, Poland and Nigeria. In chapter 15 we consider the presence, mainly in the large urban centres of Ireland, of what we might call regional, local and family diasporas, and the presence throughout the world of the family, local and regional diasporas that together constitute the global Irish diaspora. In the final chapter we consider current trends in the three directions of Irish migration and the importance, for a harmonious outcome in future, of a better public understanding of migration in Irish history.

14
In: the British and Other Diasporas

Until recently, what has been referred to by Irish nationalists as 'the British presence in Ireland' has rarely been thought of as part of the 'British diaspora' (Horn 1998; Bridge and Fedorowich 2003). This is because the collective scattering of British migrants world-wide has normally been thought of in the distinctive terms of empire, or 'settler colonies' (Manning 2005, 149). Unlike the exiles and emigrants of other non-imperial countries, so the argument goes, British migrants as 'colonists' were effectively internal migrants within the empire: for them it was not emigration but 'home flitting to another part of the same land' (Richards 2004, 227; Brendon 2007). However, this special pleading neglects the fact that not all British emigration was to imperial destinations; many went, for example, to the United States, and as in other countries British emigration could act as a 'safety-valve', whether to imperial destinations or not (Moch 2003, 148). Also, British migration was fundamentally no different from that of other groups as a three-stage, three-way, three-outcome process, and therefore the outcome of British emigration can reasonably be described as the formation of a British diaspora, albeit of a distinctive type. The process of decolonisation after the Second World War highlighted the importance of the British homeland in relation to its diaspora: many of both its colonists and their descendants and its colonised and their descendants chose to exercise their right of 'return'.

Diaspora

Diaspora was not a familiar term in relation to European migration before the 1990s. Previously, diaspora (from the Greek *diaspeirein* meaning 'to sow or scatter seeds') had been associated, almost exclusively, with the forced dispersion of the Jewish people, as in the Greek translation of the Old Testament 'thou shalt be a *diaspora* in all kingdoms of the earth' (Deut. 28, 25). Originally, however, it did not mean forced dispersion exclusively: it was used in antiquity, for example, by Thucydides to describe the voluntary 'dispersal' of Greeks throughout the Mediterranean (*History of the Peloponnesian War*, II, 27). It is in this broad, neutral sense of 'scattering', including both forced and free dimensions, that 'diaspora' has recently come to be applied in migration studies, although not without controversy (Waters 1990; Lloyd 1994; Akenson 1997; 2000). Having first been extended by analogy with the migration experience of the Jewish people to that of Black Africans, diaspora, meaning simply the emigrants of any country and their descendants, has spread to become a 'universally popular', albeit 'slippery', concept (Hickman 2002, 8; Lee 2005, 183, 186). It has become what Raymond Williams (1985) called a 'keyword' in our culture, like 'community' (Black and MacRaild 2000, 151–3). A very recent example shows how widespread and versatile it now is: 'the Northern Irish classical musician diaspora i.e. the best undergraduate, postgraduate and young professional Northern Irish musicians based around Britain, Ireland and abroad' (*Irish News* 15 December 2007). A report in the *Belfast News Letter* on the Foyle Ulster-Scots Festival was headlined 'The Cultural Diaspora in Londonderry' (17 December 2007).

Diasporas and diasporans

A diaspora can be defined more precisely as:

> a social-political formation, created as a result of either voluntary or forced migration, whose members regard themselves as of the same ethno-national origin and who permanently reside as minorities in one or several host countries. Members of such entities maintain regular or occasional contacts with what they regard as their homelands and with individuals and groups of the same background residing in other host countries. Based on aggregate decisions to settle permanently in host countries, but to maintain a common identity, diasporans identify as such, showing solidarity with their group and their entire nation, and they organize and are active in the cultural, social, economic and political spheres. Among their various activities, members of such diasporas establish trans-state networks that reflect complex relationships among the diasporas, their host countries, their homelands, and international actors.
>
> (Sheffer 2003, 31; 9–10)

The advantage of using this newly developed migration terminology based on 'diaspora' is that it offers 'a de-centred approach in which migration, migrants and their multi-generational societies are seen as phenomena in themselves and not simply in relation to their countries of origin and reception' (Stradling 1994, 158; Mac Éinrí 2000, 1). It is estimated that there are currently about

300 million people living 'in diaspora', about 3 per cent of the world's population, but it is extremely difficult to estimate what proportion of them behave or would describe themselves as 'diasporans'. What distinguishes 'diasporans' from the 'settled' people in both their sending and receiving societies is that they are 'people who try to be at home abroad', or who are 'in but not of the host society'. The term 'diaspora space' was coined by Avtar Brah (1996) as a way of comprehending 'the relationship between the host nationals and the migrants within a polity dominated by the former' (Garner 2004, 158). Diaspora, therefore, is a collective term that refers to both people and place: it includes all the emigrants of a particular homeland and their descendants, and all the spaces in all the receiving societies in which they live.

Visualising such a formation is difficult, but in the first 'anatomy' of the Irish diaspora Donald Akenson offers a vivid metaphor that can be applied more generally:

> Now in many ways, the Irish diaspora is similar to a Fabergé egg. It is a marvellously complex phenomenon. Details, though fascinating in themselves, are subordinated to the larger picture, since they all interrelate and are all subject to the whole. And, like the Fabergé egg, the diaspora has to be viewed as a three-dimensional object if it is to be appreciated. One has to look at the phenomenon from all sides and to rotate it 360 degrees in every plane to grasp its full character. In fact, the same is true of several other major cultural constellations – for example, the remnants of the world-encircling Spanish empire, the French-derived cultures world-wide, and the dispersions of the several Oriental cultures. Yet, we almost never look at these marvellous ethno-cultural patterns as a whole. Instead, we slice them up. … Like constellations of enamelled pearls on a gilded egg, they [Irish immigrants in America] cannot be interpreted on their own. The story of the Irish in America makes sense only within the context of a world-encircling history.
>
> (1993, 4–5)

Although Akenson stops short of describing 'the remnants of the world-encircling Spanish empire' and the 'French-derived cultures world-wide' as diasporas, the idea that there is such a thing as the Spanish diaspora and the French diaspora no longer seems strange. The current discourse of diaspora was initiated and developed in the late twentieth century, not without opposition, by a small group of intellectuals and political leaders in relation to European and other migrations (Tölöyan 1991). In the case of Ireland, the idea of an Irish diaspora (discussed in chapter 15) was associated in the 1990s in particular with the presidency of Mary Robinson. Recently, it has been applied to the British Isles by Eric Richards in *Britannia's Children: Emigration from England, Scotland, Wales and Ireland since 1600* (2004, 7–9).

Thinking about the world-wide spread of the peoples of Europe and their legacies, we come back to the question of when migrants and their descendants finally 'arrive'. The Plantation project of the British immigrants to Ireland in the seventeenth century and the homeland from which they came has been described as 'Making Ireland British' (Canny 2001). Similarly, the project of Irish Nationalists (at home and abroad), at least since the Act of Union 1801, can be described as 'Making British Ireland Irish' or 'Remaking Ireland Irish' and it is important to realise that migration in various forms (including the immigration of colonists, the forced emigration of natives, the return migration of natives from exile, and the forced emigration of colonists) was central to both projects, in theory and practice. The violence against settlers in 1641, for example, was a result of native Irish resentment at their families' land losses a generation earlier and the wish to reverse the Plantation by expelling the settlers, on the grounds, as contemporaries expressed it, 'that the land was theirs and lost by their fathers'. As Brian Mac Cuarta also points out, 'underlying this attitude lay the belief that Protestantism was heresy, and its adherents were heretics' (2007, 154, 162). The two projects in contention necessarily entailed an 'either/or' outcome – either British or Irish – summed up in the slogans 'Not an Inch' and 'Brits Out'. New thinking about the relationship between homeland and diaspora, influencing the Belfast/Good Friday Agreement of 1998, has opened up the possibility of a 'both/and' outcome – both Irish and British.

A major contribution of migration studies has been to demonstrate the inadequacy of the old Chicago School model of inevitable assimilation in the 'melting pot' (Park, Burgess and McKenzie 1967). Migrant identity is now much better understood as depending on the unpredictable outcome of interaction between three sets of choices, made by sending society, receiving society and migrants themselves (Cohen 1985; Brettell and Hollifield 2000, 77–96). Thus, even though migrants and their descendants might both acquire legal belonging as citizens in their 'new world' and retain their 'old world' citizenship, it is hard for them to feel they that have 'arrived' in the former and still 'belong' in the latter if, in practice, both treat them as 'foreigners'. In this context, the issue of migrant identity is seen to be much more complex than the so-called 'Tebbit test', named after the suggestion made by the British Conservative minister Norman (now Lord) Tebbit in 1990 which makes it simply one of immigrants choosing to support either the national sports teams of their receiving society or those of their sending society. Given the spread of new methods of communication (internet, email, satellite television) and travel back and forth (cheap and frequent transport connections), maintaining multiple identities within the one 'global village' – being 'at home' in both new and old worlds – seems a more viable option than ever before, in what has been called 'third space' (Bhabha 1994, 38–9).

Maguire, dealing with Vietnamese migrants who came to Ireland a generation ago, refers to those who 'belong, but differently so'. They maintained relationships with two 'homes', while feeling like strangers in both. Others interviewing Pakistanis and other Asians in Northern Ireland record descriptions which speak of 'living in between two worlds' (Maguire 2004, 97–8, 160; Wilson and Donnan 2006, 150). The Polish footballer Lukaz Adamczyk, now playing for the Northern Ireland club Glentoran, when asked in November 2007 whether he would be supporting Northern Ireland or Poland, which were in the same qualifying group for the 2010 World Cup, replied: 'I will support both teams because my life is here now'. The viability of the option in itself, however, is no guarantee that equality of respect and parity of esteem will be the outcome. As Steve Garner observes, 'recent patterns of racist attitudes ... appear to overlay the longer-standing ones of anti-Semitism and anti-Traveller racism' (2004, 68, 168–97).

The case of British immigrants in Ireland and their descendants is complicated first by the idea of Britain as a set of separate homelands (England, Wales and Scotland), and later by that of Ireland as an additional homeland within the United Kingdom (1801–1921). In effect, therefore, Ireland has been simultaneously a part of the British diaspora (even though it was not called such in the past) and part of the British homeland. The whole island remains part of the British diaspora in the sense that immigrants from Britain and their descendants still live there, and Northern Ireland remains part of the British homeland. More particularly, Ireland is part of the diasporas of England, Wales and Scotland. Each homeland is in fact part of the diasporas of the others, making England, for example, part of the diasporas of Scotland, Wales and Ireland (Richards 2004, 9–10). In this regard, Ireland as a homeland stands out mainly because of the extraordinary circumstances and size of the immigration flow that it received from England, Wales and Scotland in the seventeenth century.

Of course, as well as being part of the British (English, Welsh and Scottish) diasporas, Ireland, as a receiving society, is also part of others. During the long centuries of net emigration, it was a relatively minor part of only a few, including the Huguenot, Jewish and Italian diasporas, but with the return to net immigration in the late twentieth and early twenty-first centuries and the foreign-born population at over 10 per cent, it is now part of far more. Although it is difficult to know precisely, it seems likely that, since the immigrant flow reduced to a trickle in the early eighteenth century, only a small minority of immigrants arriving in Ireland have done so with the intention either to renounce any connection with their homeland or refuse, as far as possible, any accommodation with their receiving society. It seems to be the case that the majority and their descendants have endeavoured to negotiate a middle course, like Carlo (Charles) Bianconi (chapter 9), and Joyce's Leopold Bloom:

when 'the citizen', suspicious of Bloom's Jewishness and acting like a 'gate-keeper', asked, 'What is your nation?', Bloom answered 'Ireland … I was born here' (1975, 330). In this sense Ireland is what André Levy describes as 'a community that is both a center and a diaspora' (2005, 90–1, 109).

Most immigrants and their descendants in Ireland, as elsewhere, have been, in varying degrees, 'diasporans' – people trying to live 'at home abroad' and 'in but not quite of the host society'. Even the New English of the 1630s, whose ostensible aim was to transform the whole of their receiving society into as complete an extension as possible of their homeland, exhibited the 'in-between' characteristics of the diasporan, for they 'would have found it necessary to establish relationships with the indigenous population, as servants, labourers, tenants or traders'. In such a through-other society, 'there was also a degree of intermarriage' (Connolly 2007, 400).

This seems to have happened in the case of the poet W. R. Rodgers (1909–69), although the paternal and maternal family names of his father, Robert Skelly Rodgers of the townland of Artana, Dromara, Down, and his mother, Jane Ferris McCarey of Dundonald, Down, all seem to have been 'thoroughly Scots Presbyterian in origin'; the McCareys having been in Ireland longer than the Rodgers, 'probably since Cromwell's day' (O'Brien 1970, 17–18). Nevertheless, Rodgers, known as the 'Catholic Presbyterian', was fascinated as much by the native as by the Planter element in his lineage, including the location of the Rodgers family in one of the last Irish-speaking areas of Co. Down and the likelihood that their name was originally McCrory (*Mac Ruaidhrí*; Nini Rodgers, pers. comm.). Rodgers described himself as having had 'a tongue in both my parents cheeks' so that he could 'take the word out of two different mouths'. It was from this dual perspective that he had seen Armagh as 'through-other in its history of Celt and Dane, Norman and Saxon', with its 'arguing graves of the kings' whose descendants (as Heaney also pointed out) 'continued to hold sway until the Flight of the Earls in 1607' (2002, 364).

The through-otherness of Rodgers' individual migration story is of itself instructive. Born and brought up in Mountpottinger, east Belfast, he migrated internally to the predominantly Ulster-English area of Loughgall, Armagh, where he served as minister of Cloveneden Presbyterian Church, and then externally, first to London where he worked in the BBC, thanks to a fellow migrant Louis McNeice, and later to California, where he regarded himself as 'an Irish missionary to America – his church neither Presbyterian nor Roman but Irish'; and when he died there his ashes were returned to Ireland for burial in Cloveneden (O'Brien 1970, 93, 100).

To the extent that Ireland's immigrants and their descendants have remained 'in diaspora', connected with their homelands, they have brought the world into Ireland, and likewise emigrants have brought Ireland into the world.

15
Within-Out: the Irish Diaspora

As well as immigration having made Ireland at the national level part of the British and other diasporas, many more diasporas have been formed within Ireland, at the multiple levels of province, county, parish, townland and family, by internal migration, mainly from the countryside to the towns. In Part II, for example, we encountered eighteenth- and twentieth-century migrants, from Ulster and Connacht respectively, settling in Munster and Leinster and retaining an identification with their original provincial 'home' (chapters 8 and 12). Bearing in mind Akenson's warning about losing sight of the whole when 'slicing' it down into its component parts, we look in this chapter at the outcomes of internal migration and emigration together, examining more closely how diasporas are constructed at multiple levels, not only outside Ireland but also within.

Slicing the whole of the Irish diaspora and its homeland into sub-sections reveals another aspect of through-otherness: it is made up of interconnected sets of ever-smaller 'home' communities and diasporas, nested like Russian dolls. In the case of Ireland, for example, we can move down from the national level of the whole island and its world-wide diaspora, through provinces, counties, baronies, parishes and townlands, to the smallest unit of all – the family household. Thus, the dispersed members of these multiple 'homes', scattered elsewhere in Ireland and beyond, can be thought of as constituting regional (provincial, county, barony), local (parish, townland) and family household diasporas (Smyth 1997, 28, 32, 40). Before looking at these multiple 'homes' and their diasporas at regional, local and family household levels, and then at the global Irish diaspora, we focus on the smallest component part of any home or diaspora: the individual.

Individual migrants

It is a principle of migration or diaspora studies, as in the social sciences generally, that in order to understand migration in all its complexity, as well as counting and classifying the migrants we need to reconstruct the stories of as many individual migrants as possible. This is especially true of the first 250 years of our four centuries when the fragmentary nature of the historical evidence makes quantitative analysis based on reliable statistics extremely difficult, if not impossible. For this reason, historians, not only those working in the early modern period, have been pioneering new analytical methods, such as 'isonymy' and 'prosopography'.

Isonymy

Isonymy is the analysis of surname distribution in order to measure the relationships between different populations. A pioneering project by Smith, MacRaild and Hepburn, based at the universities of Durham, Ulster and Sunderland, has been successful in mapping (using GIS technology) relationships between populations in Ireland and England and so shedding light on migration streams. For example Consett, the County Durham iron and steel town, with a known history of Irish migration from Tyrone and Monaghan, showed this history to be reflected in its patterning of Irish surnames. Similarly, the sectarian residential segregation of Belfast is well-known and the pattern can be easily mapped using the 1901 census. The project used isonymy to see whether names were associated with sectarian identity. If this could be demonstrated in Belfast, where the sectarian segregation of the population is well attested, then the method could be used to identify the 'isonymic footprint' of segregated populations elsewhere, even in the absence of primary evidence of religious affiliation (as is the case with the English census data). A not surprising perhaps but nevertheless very important finding of the project was that analysis by isonymy of electoral divisions within Belfast at the 1901 census did indeed show a profound correlation not only of surnames but also of forenames with religious denomination. The potential of isonymy is now well established as a complement to traditional historical or geographical methods.

Prosopography

The method of prosopography is the collective biography of groups, such as politicians, merchants or domestic servants, based on individual biographies. The aim of the prosopographic method is to understand the history of various groups, in political, economic, social, religious and cultural terms, by using a range of disciplines, including genealogy and family history, onomastics (personal and place name studies), demography (population studies) and migration studies, to isolate various series of persons having political or social characteristics in common, and then analysing each series in order to distinguish between details that are specific to individuals, and constants and variables that are common to the whole group. Much of the 'hidden' history of individuals turns out to be related to their occupations and their status within the family, and so by taking this systematic approach to reconstructing individual biographies we advance our understanding of the history of institutions of all kinds, not least that of the family (Werner 1997).

The leading example of this approach in early modern Irish migration studies is the *Irish in Europe Project*, which has resulted in a series of fine studies (O'Connor 2001; O'Connor and Lyons 2003; 2006). Leading examples in the modern period are the monumental *Oceans of Consolation: Personal Accounts of Irish Migration to Australia* by David Fitzpatrick (1994) and *Irish Immigrants in the Land of Canaan: Letters and Memoirs from Colonial and Revolutionary America, 1675–1815*, by Kerby Miller and his team (Miller et al. 2003; see also Gerber 2006: 19–23, 271–4). Donald Akenson's two-volume *An Irish History of Civilization* (2005a, b) has brilliantly extended the method of reconstructing individual biographies and presenting them intricately connected on the grand scale. These 'inner histories', as Enda Delaney explains, 'can only be probed by looking beyond the traditional documentary sources of historical enquiry (2007, 8).

Since the reconstruction of individual stories, including their contextualisation, is at the heart of migration studies, it may be useful at this point for the reader to revise (in the sense of look over again) the few named individuals mentioned by way of illustration in this book. To that end they are set out chronologically, under the headings of immigration, internal migration and emigration, in Appendix III.

Revision

Revising these individuals quickly highlights gaps in the attempt to make coverage of Irish migration as comprehensive as possible. Immediately apparent is how few of our named individual migrants are female, children or elderly. We have noted how young single adults predominated in the emigrant stream and how 'unlike other immigrant groups in the New World, the Irish rarely travelled with or sent for their parents' (Clear 2007, 60). Further work may uncover more of the 'hidden' history not just of the 'wild ganders' but also the 'wild geese', as Patrick O'Sullivan has demonstrated in the case of Marie Louise O'Morphi (Murphy): a second-generation Irishwoman born in France, she arrived in Paris from Rouen to become mistress to Louis XV, having been born the daughter of a shoemaker, Daniel Murphy, who probably arrived in France after the Treaty of Limerick in 1691 (O'Sullivan 1995, 11; see also Knox 2007). Apart from Michael Davitt (aged 4), Thomas Mellon (5), and Herbert Kitchener (12), none of our named migrants are children. Although the names of many are known, especially from ship passenger lists, little research has been done on the migration experience of children, although the potential is good. For example, one database of Census records compiled by

John Perkins, yields intriguing details of the four children of Daniel Flynn (40) and his wife Eliza (27), who in 1817 were living in the military barracks in Whitehaven, where Daniel was a pensioner and sergeant in the Royal Cumberland militia. The record does not state where the youngest child Ellen (1) was born, but Maria (2) had been born in Walmer Barracks, near Dover; John (4) had been born at sea, 'off Cape Horn Lat. 52'47S Long. 35'14W'; and the eldest, Mary K (5), had been born in Melbourne, Australia.

Exploring biographical records

We have been conscious particularly of our difficulty in providing examples of internal migration – a reflection of both the relatively scant attention that has been paid to this aspect by scholars and the elusive nature of the surviving evidence. It will be noted too that we have referred to more individuals in the early modern period than in the modern. This reflects mainly the need to offset the greater lack in the early modern period of quantitative evidence and also the greater inaccessibility of qualitative evidence that gives biographical information. We have directed the reader for further exploration to the abundance and diversity of biographical materials for Australia and North America especially in the later eighteenth and nineteenth centuries as presented by Fitzpatrick in *Oceans of Consolation* (1994) and by Miller, et al. in *Irish Immigrants in the Land of Canaan* (2003). There is also, for example, a wealth of written and oral history material to be explored relating to the migration stories of Irish singers and musicians, not least those collected by Captain Francis O'Neill (1848–1936), whose own migration story from Tralibane near Bantry, Cork, to Chicago is itself of great interest, as is that of his collaborator, James O'Neill from Co. Down (Carolan 1997; Vallely 1999, 285–6; Trew 2000, 307; Moloney 2002). Critical attention is also being brought by Liam Harte (2003; 2004; 2007) to the considerable body of autobiographical writing by Irish migrants of the nineteenth and twentieth centuries, such as that by Lynam (2004) and Murphy (2005) referred to in chapter 11. This is evidence of what might be called the 'democratisation' of memoir writing. Such material for the earlier centuries is comparatively rare, but we do have the eye-witness account of the Departure/Flight of the Earls by Tadhg Ó Cianáin (Walsh 1916; Ó Muraíle 2007), so just as the message of the previous chapter was of the need for more local studies, so here it is for more reconstruction of migration stories at the level of the individual (Halfacree and Boyle 1993).

Representative individual migration stories

A further question about the migrants that we have named here is the extent to which they are representative of their group, and without a series of similar cases it is difficult to be confident. So, for example, we found that while the ship on which the Mellon family sailed may have been typical of the early nineteenth century, the length of their voyage (12 weeks) was unusually long, the average being 5–6 weeks. Likewise with migrant correspondence, we need a series of similar letters before we can get a sense of how typical, for example, was the case of Patrick McAuliffe. In 1884 he was living in Port Augusta, near Adelaide, Australia, when he received a letter from his father in Croughcroneen, near Lixnaw, Kerry, with a reminder of his promise to return home:

> After many years we are bewailing your absence ... We have as much welcome for your empty letter as if it was loaded with gold and you had no right to leave your Mother so long in trouble. Her hart [sic] is broke from thinking of ye all and it is many a silent tear she had shed for the last seven years ... Dear Patrick your home is still in Crough, waiting for you. I hope you wont fail in coming.
>
> (Richards 2005, 93)

We may wonder how often emigrants came under such emotional pressure to return, and in passing we may also note how such correspondence gives voice to the dialect and accent of 'home' (Baldassar 2001; Montgomery 2006). It seems likely that a great deal of such correspondence remains in private hands, as indicated recently when an unusually large, two-way collection of 900 letters, written between 1891 and 1926 by James Smyth in Ontario, Canada and his family in Castledamph near Plumbridge, Tyrone, was added to the Centre for Migration Studies Irish Emigration Database (CMS IED 309001).

Migrant objects

As well as correspondence, other migrant objects can illuminate individual stories. Generally, migrants bring some material possessions with them from their 'old world' to the 'new world', including objects that have been deliberately selected more for their sentimental than practical value, as expressions of 'old world' identity, and such objects may assist in opening up the migration stories of their owners. For example, in about 1910 Mrs Brenda Carroll of Randwick, near Sydney, recalled her grandmother, who had arrived in Australia in 1866, standing in front of an enormous portrait of Robert Emmet and wailing 'Oh, my poor country' (O'Farrell 1986, 206). Migrant objects of this kind function as 'icons' of connection with the original 'homeland', but relatively few are to be found in museum collections in Ireland and Europe generally (Proudfoot 2003, 174; Lambkin 2006, 23, 32). One example is the walking stick or cane now in the collection of the Ulster-American Folk Park, Omagh, which belonged to Thomas Mellon. As he explained in his autobiography, it had originally belonged to his earliest known ancestor, who had arrived in Ireland from Scotland in about 1660, and, having been passed down the generations in Ulster, it was brought by the family with them to America (1994, 410–11). Another migrant object that has recently come to light in Australia is a needlework sampler (Plate 12), which has stimulated the reconstruction of the migration story of its maker, Dorcas, an emigrant to Australia who turns out to have been a sister of the Young Irelander Thomas D'Arcy McGee, who emigrated first to the United States and then to Canada. The sampler's trajectory illustrates the phenomenon of what has been called 'ethnic fade' in the 'fabric' of the Irish diaspora – the gradual loss of value that results in such objects being relegated from display and eventually disposed of, and it also shows how the process of reconstructing the migration stories of emigrant ancestors may result in the process of 'ethnic fade' being arrested (Lambkin and Meegan 2005; Lambkin 2005a, b).There may be many more such objects still unattended to in museum collections or in private hands whose migration stories could likewise be reconstructed.

Oral history

In such a case the evidence of oral history is vital in reconstructing both the provenance of the object and the migration stories of its owners. The technique of oral history is being applied more widely in migration studies, as in the work of Louise Ryan on Irish nurses in Britain (2003; 2004; 2007a; 2007b). One example, recorded by another researcher illustrates internal migration leading to emigration. Maureen H. told him how she had:

> left a small Midlands farm in 1934 and took a job in a draper's shop in Dublin in preference to entering domestic service locally. Three years later she emigrated to New York without telling her parents. Here she found herself in domestic service where she remained until she married six years later. Asked why she was willing to enter service in America but not in Ireland, she insisted that it was different.
>
> (Travers 1995, 164)

Another female emigrant told the same researcher how she had:

> left a small holding in Achill in the late 1940s. Faced with the choice of an arranged marriage or emigration, she chose the boat-train to Britain. Forty

years later, she described her feelings: 'I didn't think much of it at the time. I'd worked with my sister in Scotland from when I was fourteen [as a seasonal worker]. Still I missed home and cried every night for a year … But I never dreamed of going back. There was nothing for me there.

(Travers 1995, 164, 165)

Three more recent oral history projects about Irish migration, following a biographical life-narrative approach, have sought to recover a wide range of individual voices and make them accessible in audio archives. The first of these, 'Breaking the Silence: Staying at Home in an Emigrant Society' (2000–2) collected interviews with 78 non-emigrants aged 60–65, focusing on their lives in Ireland in the 1950s, when emigration reached almost 500,000 (http://migration.ucc.ie/oralarchive/testing/breaking/index.htm; Gray 2002; Trew 2005, 109; Ní Laoire 2007c). The subsequent 'Narratives of Migration and Return' project (2003–6) collected a total of 92 interviews, in both the North and South, which explored the experiences of some of the first large wave of emigrants who began returning in the late twentieth century (http://migration.ucc.ie/nmr/index.html). The 'Northern Ireland Emigrant Narratives' project (2006–8) collected interviews with 48 Northern Ireland emigrants, one of whom left in the mid-1980s as an adult to settle on Merseyside. She said she believed that Northern Ireland people had been 'completely abandoned … Nobody noticed us going, nobody's ever tried to look at us, why we might have gone, you know, both Protestants and Catholics. I left because … the pain was too much.' Her story contrasts with another who left at the age of eight in the 1950s:

the fact that I left the wee six counties – the grand wee province, 'Norn' Ireland, the truncated fascist Orange statelet, whatever – I think broadened my perspective, and I think hearing my father's perspective being broadened when he was with the fleet air arm, you know, and met Catholics and saw a new world.

(NIENJDT-18; Trew 2008)

Detailing the big picture

If each new migrant narrative collected is considered as a further 'pixel' to be added prosopographically to the 'big picture' of Irish migration, then we may appreciate how the more narratives are collected the more fine-grained the picture obtained. Ronald Wells (2004) has argued for a moral imperative to the task of recovering as many individual migrant stories as possible, not only those of people now living and those who achieved fame in their day. He is particularly concerned with the stories of the forgotten, who died in transit, citing the injunction in the book of *Ecclesiaticus* to 'sing the praises of famous men, our ancestors in their generations', and not to forget them because:

> some of them left behind a name, so that others declare their praise. But of others there is no memory. They have perished as though they never existed. They have become as though they had never been born, they and their children after them.
>
> (44: 1; 8–9)

The task of recovering even the names of individual migrants, let alone their migration stories, on such a scale is beyond the scope of any conceivable team of professional researchers and would require the sustained collaboration of as many as possible of those who are engaged in local and family studies (McCarthy 2007, 7–8). Yet the collection of more stories of itself would not add to our understanding. As structuration theory explains (Appendix II), social life is not simply the sum of all activity at the local level. By the same token, however, social activity cannot be completely explained from the global level, so we need the approach of prosopography, working up from individual migrant to the global level of the national homeland and its diaspora, through the multiple levels of family, local and regional 'homes', and their diasporas.

Family, local and regional homes and diasporas

One of the most exciting developments recently in the writing of Irish history is that local studies are increasingly being done at the level of Ireland's smallest spatial network: the townland. Pioneering publications include *Townlands in Ulster* (Crawford and Foy 1998) and *Irish Townlands* (Ó Dálaigh et al. 1998; see also Lambkin 1998). A further shining example is Peter Carr's monumental study of *Portavo*, a single townland on the north Down coast, between Bangor and Donaghadee (2003, 2005). Just as the whole of Ireland can be seen as an aggregation of about 60,000 townlands, so the whole of the Irish diaspora can be seen, from this bottom-up perspective, as an aggregation of 'townland diasporas', each with its own story, which is in turn made up of the stories of its families (Muhr 1996, 360–4; 1999, 5). Although awareness of the townland as the basic social unit that constitutes the parish has been largely lost in urban communities, it survives strongly in dispersed rural communities, reinvigorated by the campaign of opposition in Northern Ireland to the introduction in the 1970s of postcode addresses and rural road names that bore little relation to the townlands they passed through. This combined with a revival of interest in urban townlands, as evidenced by the poster maps produced in the early 1990s by the Ultach Trust/Iontaobhach Ultach of the townlands of Belfast, Omagh and Moyle (Ballycastle), makes the townland network, which covers the entire island, a valuable framework not only for the study of rural communities, but also of urban and suburban 'neighbourhoods'.

Townland diasporas

On this basis, a strong case can be made for extending townland studies to include the 'townland diaspora' (Crawford and Foy 1998, 3; Prunty 1998; 2004; Fitzgerald and Lambkin 2004). Most townland studies, urban, suburban and rural, engage to some extent with immigration, internal migration and emigration. How could they not? But, so far as emigration is concerned, beyond quantifying the numbers who left, and perhaps referring to the destinations to which some went, it is rare, so far, for local historians to demonstrate an interest in the continuing diasporic relationship between the emigrants and their 'home' townland, as illustrated particularly by letters, remittances and return visits. An example of a townland study that takes a closer interest than most in its emigrants is that of Gallon, near Newtownstewart in west Tyrone (Bradley 2000). This shows McLaughlins leaving Gallon for the United States, Canada, England (Huddersfield), Scotland (St Johnstone), Wales and Australia (Sydney); Brogans leaving for Philadelphia; and McGarveys leaving for San Francisco. One of the McAnena family emigrated to Scotland to find work with a farmer in Ayrshire and later on a hydro-electric scheme in the Highlands. Members of the Morris family went as priests and nuns to the United States and England. Included in the study is a photograph of one of the Quinn family, taken the day before she emigrated to Philadelphia. Collectively, these individuals, with their families and their descendants, have constituted the world-wide 'Gallon diaspora'. Their continuing relationship with their 'home townland' is illustrated well by return migration: one of the McConnell family who had emigrated to the United States in the 1950s came back to buy a farm in Gallon, as did one of the Bradleys, who had emigrated to Australia. Similarly, a study of the townlands of Inishatieve and Altanagh in the parish of Termonmaguirk, Tyrone, highlights their connection with Philadelphia as revealed by surviving letters (Shields 1984).

For completeness, the same approach to the townland's emigrants should be applied to its immigrants, who make it part of the local, regional and national diasporas of other countries. One study, of what we might call 'the English diaspora' in Ireland, traces the seventeenth-century story of immigration in Kerry and Fermanagh by members of the Blennerhassett family back to their migration origin in the village of Blenerhassett near Norwich, Norfolk. Another examines *The Planters of Luggacurran, County Laois: A Protestant community, 1879–1927* (Cunningham 2006, 92; Coffey 2006). Similarly, the Morelli family in Derry and elsewhere in Ireland are part of the diaspora of Casalattico, a *commune* (municipality) in the province of Frosinone, in the region of Latium, Italy (Fitzgerald 2008). However, David Fitzpatrick's *Oceans of Consolation: Personal Accounts of Irish Migration to Australia* (1994), even though it does not use the term diaspora, remains the best model for studies seeking to situate individual migrants in relation to their home townland. The recently published study of the emigration and return of Margaret Brennan of Carrownamaddy, south Roscommon, illustrates the rich potential of the local historian focusing on the relationship between the townland and its diaspora (Dunnigan 2007). Another powerful example is the *Gaeltacht i gCéin* project in the *Ceantar na n-Oileán* area of Connemara, about 12 miles west of Galway. This involved no less than mapping all of the living persons born in the local area of *Leitir Mór* (Lettermore) and *Leitir Mealláin* (Lettermullan) area who subsequently migrated, as well as all those still living there.

Multi-levelled relationship with 'home'

It is not only rural townlands like Gallon and Carrownamaddy that can be studied in this way but also urban townlands, such as Ballymagee in Bangor, Down (Millsop 1998). Research at the townland level reveals, in the most local community context of all, the operation of the diaspora's smallest component parts in the form of the migration stories of the individual family members, who constitute the family's diaspora. At this point, family history, local history and migration studies merge as the local–global connection is made. The multi-levelled relationship with 'home' is expressed poignantly in graveyards around the world, on headstones where individuals are identified by their country of origin. Often identification is made not just by country of origin but also by county, town or even townland, as was the practice in Ireland (see http://www.historyfromheadstones.com). One such example is the gravestone in Fairview, near Boise, Idaho, which identifies Thomas Kittle as 'Native of Cavan Co. Ireland died April 22 1877 Aged 34 years'. Another is that in Arrowtown, South Island, New Zealand, which identifies John McKibbin, died 1894, as 'native of Marshallstown, Downpatrick, Co. Down, Ireland' (Muhr 1999, 4; Sullivan 2005). Attachment to local place-names in the homeland was also evident in songs of Irish emigration, which are 'often powerfully evocative of home places and counties of origin' and also represent the 'whole gamut of emotions' experienced by emigrants (O'Connor 2006, 159–61; see also Moulden 1994; 2001; Moloney 2002, 3–4).

Just as individual and family stories can be reconstructed from gravestone inscriptions and death, marriage and birth records, so we can reconstruct the formation and operation of family diasporas from migration records, such as ship passenger lists and emigrant letters, accessible, for example, on the CMS Irish Emigration database. Miller's *Emigrants and Exiles* (1985), which makes extensive use of selective quotation from emigrant letters, received some criticism for paying insufficient attention to their context. This turns out to have been a *felix culpa* for it has stimulated highly detailed and contextualised reconstructions of family migration stories on a monumental scale. These include Cecil Houston and William J. Smyth's *Irish Emigration and Canadian Settlement: Patterns, Links and Letters* (1990); David Fitzpatrick's *Oceans of Consolation* (1994), based on letters between Ireland and Australia; Kerby Miller's own (with Doyle, Boling and Schrier) *Irish Immigrants in the Land of Canaan* (2003); and Angela McCarthy's *Irish Migrants in New Zealand, 1840–1937: 'the Desired Haven'* (2005). A further added value of studying the diaspora at the level of the family is that it is possible to observe more clearly the operation of intra-diaspora connections, as well as diaspora–homeland connections. For example, in 1851 we find John Williamson in Cohoes, New York State, writing to his brother Benjamin in Leeds, England, with news about their brothers, James in Illinois, and William gold-digging in California, as well as news about their parents 'back home' in Richhill, Co. Armagh (PRONI T2680/2/5; CMS IED 9007146). Family diasporas can also be reconstructed from oral history interviews, such as those collected in the archives of the *Breaking the Silence* and *Narratives of Migration and Return* projects (Gray 2002; Trew 2005; 2007; Ní Laoire 2007c).

Growing migration complexity

The idea of the 'Irish diaspora' gradually took hold in the 1990s because of persuasive new thinking about Irish migration that required a new term to help comprehend its complexity. Previously, Irish emigrants and their descendants as a group had been thought of more simply, by themselves and by those in Ireland, as 'the Wild Geese', 'the Irish Overseas', 'the Irish Abroad', or just 'the Emigrants', and also as 'Ireland in exile' (Sullivan 1867, 343). However, as the work of Ruth-Ann Harris on the 'Missing Friends' columns in the *Boston Pilot* newspaper illustrates, the sense of connection between emigrants and homeland developed gradually through multiple levels of attachment:

> We ... see good evidence of patterns of chain migration and the clustering of migrant streams – that is, there would be a spill of persons from one parish while in an adjacent parish there would be no 'Missing Friends' sought. .. Bound first by attachment to townland, then to parish and in some cases to barony, they saw themselves as emigrants from Kenmare or Carrickmacross or Omagh. It would take the experience of being in America to create a national Irish identity.
>
> (2000, 172)

The development of 'county' enclaves in the new world, such as 'Kerry' and 'Cork' in the Fourth and Seventh Wards of New York, could also result in the formation of 'county societies'. As Gillmor observes, 'attachment to county extends across the oceans and in some respects it may even be intensified amongst Irish emigrants' (2003, 46; O'Connor 2006, 153). In contrast, the Ancient Order of Hibernians was organised by parish, neighbourhood or sometimes occupation, but never by county origin (Ridge 1996, 276–8; Delaney 2005). The Orange Order as a 'transnational' organisation similarly sustained diasporic identities in a 'global Orange network' of 'fraternal greetings: travelling warrants and universal handshakes' (Bryan 2003; Hume 2005, 73–81; MacRaild 2005b, 311; 2006, 56).

Networks of networks

The same basic structure of 'home' and dispersed 'family' network is evident whichever way we slice a 'home', from the macro-level of the national homeland, down through the meso-level of its regions, to the micro-level of the local communities and family homes of the individual migrants. And the same is true however we slice their diasporas (Delaney and MacRaild 2007, ix–xii). For example, the largest slices that Akenson (1993) deals with in his 'anatomy' of the Irish diaspora are (in order): New Zealand, Australia, South Africa, the rest of the British Empire, Britain (dividing into England, Scotland and Wales) and North America (dividing into the United States and Canada). These are what we might call intermediate or 'meso-diasporas'. Similarly, the slices dealt with in O'Sullivan's *The Irish World-Wide* series are: England, Europe and Argentina (1992a), and the United States, Britain and Australia (1992b). These 'meso-diasporas' may in turn be sliced. For example, the North American slice, which is also referred to as *Irish America* (Byron 1999; Meagher 2001) and *The Irish in North America* (Glazier 1999), can be split in two: *The Irish-Catholic Diaspora in America* (McCaffrey 1997) and a separate non-Catholic, Scotch-Irish, Ulster Scots or Irish-Protestant Diaspora (see http://www.ulsterscotsagency.com/instituteofusstudies.asp). As a vital corrective to this slicing, we are reminded by Akenson in his *Primer* of

> the fundamental fact that neither in the history of the Irish homeland nor in any nation of the Irish diaspora, can one segregate from each other the three main components of post-Reformation Irish history, the Ulster-Scots, the Anglo-Irish, and the Irish Catholics.
>
> (1993, 256)

At this intermediate level, 'meso-diasporas' are named as parts of the global Irish 'macro-diaspora'; it is understood that the 'homeland' to which they relate is still the whole of Ireland. Below this level, sets of 'micro-diasporas' are named, conversely, as parts of the 'homeland', ranging from the province down to the county, barony, parish, townland and family. This idea has been pioneered by Donna Gabaccia in *Italy's Many Diasporas* (2000). As examples of some of Ireland's many diasporas, we can single out the diasporas of Connacht (province), Roscommon (county), Kilglass (parish), Ballykilcline (townland) and McDermott (family). The diaspora or 'dispersed family' of each of these 'home' units is potentially scattered across the world (Scally 1995; see http://www.ballykilcline.com). The very naming of the national diaspora's components not only according to parts of the rest of the world but also to parts of Ireland is indicative of a complex, two-way dynamic or dialectic between diaspora and homeland (Skinner 1982).

Features of diaspora

Some generalisations seem valid for the whole of the Irish diaspora, such as Meagher's proposal that the key influences on the development of any ethnic community 'in diaspora' are

> the vitality of local economies and the breadth of opportunities they afforded; the rules of politics; the ethnic origins, power, and endurance of local elites; and the time of arrival, cultural predilections, and numbers of other immigrant or racial groups.
>
> (2001, 14–15)

It may also be valid, in part at least, with regard to internal migration within the homeland. However, as J.J. Lee reminds us, 'only open-minded research, based on respect for the evidence, can determine in any specific case the place of the diasporic dimension in the total life experience of emigrants themselves and of their descendants' (2005, 187). That warning points to the need for more 'local' studies to test the evidence for sub-diasporas at different levels in different time periods. An indication of the ever-extending reach of local studies is that the *Encyclopedia of the Irish in America* (Glazier 1999) was able to include separate entries for each state of the United States.

Local Irish diaspora studies

Good examples of local studies, covering longer or shorter periods at the intermediate level, where sub-diasporas are still identified by migration destination, include: Liverpool (Neal 1997; Belchem 2007), Dundee (Collins 1997), Cumbria (MacRaild 1998), Tyneside (Neal 2000), Wales (O'Leary 2000) and Huddersfield (Gilzean and McAuley 2002); St Malo (Lyons 2001) and Cadiz (Fannin 2003); San Francisco (Walsh 1979), Butte, Montana (Emmons 1989), and 'the South' (Gleeson 2001); eastern Canada (Mannion 1974, 2001), Ontario (Akenson 1984; 1993, 310–13), Toronto (McGowan 1999), New Brunswick (Toner et al. 1988), Sydney, Australia (Grimes 1992); and Montserrat (Akenson 1997a). Useful here as an analytical tool is the idea of O'Sullivan that earlier work in migration studies tends to fall into three broad categories: oppression history (highlighting the victim status of migrants); compensation history (high-lighting the achievements of exceptional migrants); and contribution history (highlighting the immigrant role in nation building; for example, the role of the Catholic Irish in Australia or the Scotch-Irish in the American War of Independence). Of the three, contribution history is the largest (O'Sullivan 1992, xviii–xix). As O'Sullivan points out, these approaches 'tend to fragment the Irish migration experience – they do not allow us to look at the inter-connectedness, over space and time, the world-wide-ness of the Irish migra-tions' (1992, xvii–xix; xx). Incidentally, this is the closest that O'Sullivan came in *The Irish World Wide* series to describing the 'diaspora' without actually using the term, before going on to adopt it in 1997 in founding the on-line Irish Diaspora Studies scholarly network (http://www.irishdiaspora.net). Also requiring further investigation are relations between Irish and other migrants in diaspora.

Comparative studies

The full value of such local studies is only realised when they are set in com-parative perspective, which may be trans-local as well as transnational, and also when an attempt is made to integrate them into our understanding of the whole. Good examples are the work of John Mannion (1974), comparing three provinces of Canada; David Doyle (1989; 1994), comparing Australia and Britain with the United States; Marilyn Cohen (1995), comparing Gilford, Co. Down (place of migration origin) with Greenwich, New York (destina-tion); Donald MacRaild (2000), comparing Britain and the United States; Bronwen Walter, comparing Irish women in Britain and the United States (2001); and William Jenkins (2007a; 2007b), comparing Irish Catholics in Buffalo and Toronto. A particularly controversial example of comparative study is that by Malcolm Campbell (2000; see also 2008) which aimed 'to evaluate the validity of American explanations for the failure of Irish emigrants to settle on the land' by comparing the Irish in Minnesota and south-west New South Wales. Campbell argues that 'the Irish in Minnesota and south-west New South Wales in the mid-nineteenth century were not worlds apart' and concludes by calling for 'the abandonment of stereotypical assertions about what the Irish did not do (or could not do) on the land' (2000, 188–9).

Micro-diaspora studies

So far there have been fewer studies at the level of the 'micro-diaspora', which is identified by place of migration origin in Ireland, but the prospect for more work of this kind is good. Local studies in Ireland continue to proliferate at the county and parish levels and increasingly these pay attention to the dimension of migration, especially in the *History and Society* county series, which devotes separate chapters to emigration from Derry (McCourt 1999); Fermanagh (Fitz-gerald 2004); Galway (Moran 1996); Kilkenny (Mannion and Maddock 1990); Tyrone (Fitzgerald 2000) and Wexford (Elliott 2001). The Co. Cavan diaspora has been explored by Mary Sullivan (2006). Similarly, the Maynooth series of town-land studies initiated by *Irish Townlands* (Ó Dálaigh et al. 1998) has continued to do so, including Dunnigan (2007). Local studies, whether at the meso or micro level, can range from being based broadly on all available sources of evidence to being based narrowly on particular sets of records, such as those of the work-houses in Ulster or the Emigrant Savings Bank in New York (Parkhill 1997; Ó Gráda 1998; Casey 2002). Another important possible unit of study, with which emigrants strongly identified for good or ill, is that of the landed estate, such as that of the Palmerstons in Sligo (Power 2004), the Shirleys in Monaghan (Duffy 1997) or the Clotworthy estate in Antrim, which was developed as 'a small island of English settlers in a sea of Scots' (Rees 2000; Duffy 2004, 7).

Having considered the relationship between the Irish homeland and what we now call the Irish diaspora in terms of its component parts of family, local and regional homes and diasporas, we now turn to consider the emergence of the term Irish diaspora in the 1990s and its significance as an outcome of emigration from Ireland over four centuries.

From Irish abroad to Irish diaspora

There was of course awareness of the Irish diaspora *avant la lettre* when the emi-grants and their descendants were referred to collectively as 'the Irish abroad', 'the Irish overseas' or the 'Wild Geese', as for example by A. M. Sullivan in *The Story of Ireland* (1867). As we noted in chapter 5, recent research on the Irish in Europe in the seventeenth century has revealed a tangle of inter-connection and interdependence and a clear sense of migrants moving within a network that we can meaningfully describe as the Irish diaspora (O'Connor 2001, 12). Following the nineteenth-century coinage of Thomas D'Arcy McGee (1825–68), the emigrants (at least the Catholic ones) were also referred to as the 'world-divided Gaels' or the 'sea-divided Gaels' (Wilson 2008, 271); and as summed up by Joyce, in connection with 'the black 47' and 'coffin ships', as 'our greater Ireland beyond the sea' (1922; 1975, 328). We have also noted how they were described by Sister Agnes, in the famous hymn she composed in 1853, as members of St Patrick's 'people' who are 'now exiles on many a shore'. A strong sense of collective identity, transcending local and regional affilia-tions, was evident in the departing emigrant's promise as expressed in the final verse of one of the most popular emigration songs:

> So now to conclude and to finish my ditty,
> If ever friendless Irishman chances my way,

> With the best in the house, I will greet him in welcome,
> At home on the Green Fields of America[y].
>
> (Moloney 2002, 9)

Those at home in Erin's Green Valleys and those going into diaspora on the Green Fields of America and elsewhere were predisposed to maintain old connections with home and with each other, and to make new ones. Over time, however, and notwithstanding de Valera's St Patrick's Day radio broadcasts which included reference to 'our kinsfolk in foreign lands', the homeland showed little evidence of cherishing its diaspora.

Presidents Robinson and McAleese

'Cherishing the Irish Diaspora' was the title of an influential speech made by President Mary Robinson (1990–97) in 1995 to the joint Houses of the Oireachtas in Dublin. In it she quoted Eavan Boland's poem 'The Emigrant Irish', criticising the dominant attitude of the homeland to them ('Like oil lamps we put them out the back / Of our houses, of our minds') and proposing the possibility of a new 'cherishing' approach of equality of respect and parity of esteem. This was to be achieved between homeland and diaspora through constructive dialogue. Robinson and her successor, Mary McAleese (1997–), are largely responsible for popularising the idea of an Irish 'diaspora' with the status of a 'fifth province'. This grew out of creative thinking about the development of a 'non-territorial and post-nationalist Ireland', including the Irish overseas, which had been advanced in the 1980s by Richard Kearney (1988; 1990) and others. An outworking of this, as part of the Northern Ireland Peace Process, was the Amendment to Article 2 of the Irish Constitution, following the Belfast/Good Friday Agreement 1998, which, without using the term, effectively recognised the special position of the Irish diaspora by declaring that 'the Irish nation cherishes its special affinity with people of Irish ancestry living abroad, who share its cultural identity and heritage'. This effectively gave to the Irish diaspora the 'special position' which previously had been given to the Catholic Church by Article 44.1 of the 1937 Constitution. This had been removed in response to the outbreak of conflict in Northern Ireland by referendum in 1972, which was also the year of the referendum on accession to the EEC (Drudy and McAleese 1984, 38–40, 59–60; Böss 2002, 139).

The subtlety of this move has been to re-imagine those of Irish identity in Northern Ireland as being 'in diaspora', rather than in part of the national territory. Although not expressed formally in the Belfast Agreement as a reciprocal commitment, it is strongly implied that Northern Ireland, as part of the United Kingdom, should likewise cherish its special affinity with people of Northern Irish or British identity living abroad (including those in the

Republic of Ireland) who share its cultural identity and heritage (Mac Éinrí and Lambkin 2002, 135–6). Underpinning this bold political development is the notion of a diasporic 'third space' in which multiple identities can be sustained (Bhabha 1994, 38–9).

Tensions

In the Irish case there have been tensions between homeland and diaspora, and also within each, when equality of respect and parity of esteem have not been so evident, as for example in hostile responses to the best-selling song *Fairy Tale of New York* by the 'London-Irish' Shane McGowan (1988), the best-selling memoir *Angela's Ashes* by Frank McCourt (1996), the reinterpretation of Irish dancing in *Riverdance* (1994) by the Irish-Americans Michael Flatley and Jean Butler, and the stance taken by the Ancient Order of Hibernians in the 1990s to exclude the Irish Gay and Lesbian Organisation from participation in the New York St. Patrick's Day Parade (Almeida 2001; Ó Cinnéide 2002, 46–57; Mac Éinrí 2002, 143–3; Foster 2007, 148, 151, 159).

Testing relationship

A major test of the nature and strength of any relationship is the behaviour of the partners when one of them is in crisis; and in the case of the Irish homeland and the Irish diaspora the crises have been mainly in the former, with emigrant remittances as evidence of continuing commitment from the diaspora. Although the reaction of emigrants from Ireland and their descendants, Catholic and Protestant, in different parts of the diaspora to the Northern Ireland crisis has yet to be assessed comprehensively, various studies, such as those of the United States (Clark 1977; Cronin 1987; Wilson 1995, 2005; O'Clery 1996), Britain (Hickman 1995; Halpin 2000); Canada (Trew 2005; 2007), and the comprehensive survey of Irish communities abroad (Walter et al 2002), indicate how complex it has been in terms of place, time, range and scale; some choosing to hide their connection with the homeland, others to highlight it through support for the 'armed struggle' or the 'peace process'. It seems clear at least that both the protracted conflict of the Troubles and the eventual Belfast/Good Friday Agreement would not have been possible without mobilisation of the diaspora, including major investment in the economy, North and South (Dumbrell 2000; Thompson 2001; Lynch 2004; Aughey 2005, 83–7; Tonge 2005, 175–87).

Conversely, the homeland–diaspora relationship can be tested by the response of the homeland to the difficulties of its emigrants and their descendants abroad. In the 1980s, for example, the Irish government supported the campaign to regularise the position of Irish 'illegals' in the United States (Corcoran 1993). Similar support was given to the campaign by the Irish Lobby for Immigration Reform that got under way in January 2006, led by

Niall O'Dowd, editor of the New York-based *Irish Voice*, on behalf of the illegal Irish workers in the US, estimated controversially to number between 25,000 and 50,000. The government also published in 2002 the *Report of the Task Force Regarding Policy on Emigrants* with a commitment to implement its recommendations, although subsequent progress has been minimal. Consideration of the homeland–diaspora relationship shows how variable it may be according to circumstances on both sides: sometimes it suits to emphasise the 'emigrant' aspect of belonging in the 'new world'; at other times to emphasise the 'exile' aspect of belonging in the 'old world'. This was evident, for example, in the presidential careers of Andrew Jackson and J. F. Kennedy. Jackson (1829–37), although born in America and a member of the Protestant elite, found the Irish background of his parents, who had emigrated in 1767 from Boneybefore, near Carrickfergus, Antrim, and also his membership of the Ancient Order of Hibernians, increasingly useful in attracting Catholic votes (Glazier 1999, 480–1; Doyle 1981). Kennedy (1961–3) had Irish Catholic roots back to his paternal great-grandfather Patrick, who had emigrated in 1848 from Dunganstown, Wexford, that were well known; he had therefore to work hard at demonstrating his American pedigree in attracting Protestant votes, as in his famous make-or-break speech in September 1960 to the Protestant ministers of Houston, Texas, and in his telling a congressional hearing, 'There is an old saying in Boston that we get our religion from Rome and our politics from home' (Carty 2004, 5, 71). In this case there was no question of migrant modulation: by home he did not mean Ireland.

Adopting diaspora

The gradual adoption of the term 'diaspora' by students of Irish migration can be traced from its earliest use by Father John O'Brien, who referred to the relationship between 'we of the Diaspora' and 'Eire' (1954, 8), through Cullen (1994), to Enda Delaney's article in the *Encyclopedia of Ireland* (Lalor 2003, 294–6). Tellingly, this entry takes up three columns, compared with the complementary entries on 'The Irish Abroad' (2 cols) and 'Emigration Patterns' (2 cols). That the term is absent not only from Miller's *Emigrants and Exiles* (1985) but also from O'Sullivan's *The Irish World Wide* series (1992–7) indicates its relatively swift rate of adoption since the 1990s (Delaney, Kenny and MacRaild 2006). Similarly, a development can be traced from the stark distinction between 'emigrants' and 'exiles', elaborated by Miller (1985) and critiqued by Akenson (1993, 34), towards a more nuanced understanding of the complex motivations of individual migrants who might both see themselves and be seen, in varying degrees at different stages of their trajectories, as both 'emigrants' and 'exiles'. The idea of diaspora was taken up in an increasingly rancorous debate between so-called 'revisionist' and 'anti-revisionist' historians and others in the 1980s and 1990s, with revisionists challenging the restricted, traditional view that Irish migrants were the victims, not the builders of empire; that they were Catholics, but not Protestants; that they went to the United States, but not Canada, Australia or Britain; and that they settled in urban, but not rural, areas (Kearney 1990; Brady 1994; O'Day 1996).

Catholics *and* Protestants

A major challenge to the argument that the Irish tradition of emigration was 'exceptional', by virtue of having been generated by uniquely oppressive conditions, was mounted by Akenson, who, for example, drew attention to 'the almost universally ignored fact that *the bulk of the Irish ethnic group in the United States is at present, and probably always has been, Protestant*' (1993, 219; emphasis in the original). Akenson's 'anatomy' of the Irish diaspora (1993) and O'Sullivan's pioneering *Irish World Wide* series (1992–7) have been followed by other studies, including Crawford (1997), Blethen and Wood (1997), Bielenberg (2000) and Fitzgerald and Ickringill (2001). There has also been a more popular account by Coogan (2000) and the large-scale television series by BBC Northern Ireland, RTÉ and SBS Independent, Australia, *The Irish Empire*, complete with a book of the series (Bishop 1999). The independent initiatives that resulted in the founding of the Irish Centre for Migration Studies at University College Cork (1997) and the Centre for Migration Studies at the Ulster-American Folk Park, Omagh (1998) were further responses to needs generated by new ways of thinking about the Irish migration tradition. Something which is still lacking in the Irish case is a comprehensive 'atlas' of the Irish diaspora, highlighted by its simplistic treatment in the *Penguin Atlas of Diasporas* (Chaliand and Rageau 1995), which maps emigration from Ireland to North America and Britain at the time of the Great Famine, neglecting to include previous and subsequent emigration to these and other destinations (Mac Éinrí and Lambkin 2002, 139–40; Fitzgerald 2006). Nevertheless, the effect cumulatively has been to develop public understanding of Irish migration in terms of the relationship between diaspora and homeland and the entanglement or 'throughother' nature of 'emigrant' and 'exile' elements in the emigration flow.

This 'diasporic' perspective offers a way of transcending fixation on the nation-state as the primary unit of historical analysis. It offers a further benefit when seen as part of both a 'world systems' approach (Mac Laughlin 1994) and the process of 'globalisation' – 'the compression of the entire world and the development of consciousness of the whole world as a single space' (Robertson 1992) . Kenny, basing his argument on the case of the Irish diaspora, has gone so far as to claim that combining diasporic, comparative, transnational and cross-national approaches makes possible 'a unitary approach to global migration' (2003a, 140; 2003b, 226). In this new, globalised framework, where each nation-state, as well as being a homeland, is seen as part of another homeland's diaspora, there is an urgency about mutual respect and parity of esteem. So, for example, we may compare the present Irish diaspora of about 70 million, generated by about 10 million emigrants over 400 years, with the Italian diaspora of about 60 million generated largely by 26 million emigrants since 1878, and see how both they and their homelands are interrelated by migration (Gabaccia 2000). In this comparative frame, the inconsistency of speaking, for example, of Irish 'illegals' in the United States in a neutral or even sympathetic way, while treating new (legal) migrants in Ireland in a hostile way, becomes even more apparent. There is a danger, following the reversal of the net migration flow in the 1990s, that the long tradition of Irish emigration will be forgotten, in which case lessons from it will not be learned, or it will be remembered in a partial, wholly negative way that fails to empathise with new migrants. A worrying, unspoken question detected by some researchers is, 'why should we welcome strangers when our own had to leave?' (Mac Éinrí and Lambkin 2002, 147).

Several key questions relating to the 'operational validity' of the concept of diaspora remain, including the issue of who or what determines when membership of a 'diaspora' ends (Lee 2005, 183–7). Was a Protestant emigrant of the nineteenth century, the descendant of a seventeenth-century immigrant from Britain, part of the Irish diaspora, part of the British diaspora, or both? Dealing with the eighteenth century, Devine considers that 'Ulster Scots emigrants to America deserve to be considered as one distinctive element in the more general Scottish Diaspora of the eighteenth century' (2003, 142, 148). However, one of the authorities that he cites in support described these same migrants as 'Irish' but 'with a difference' and as 'the Irish of the North' (Leyburn 1962, 142–3; 327–8). As individuals and groups may vary their self-descriptions according to changing circumstances, this issue remains elusive.

There is still much of the Fabergé egg network to be mapped, for as Akenson reminds us:

> spanning as it has done the globe, the diaspora is therefore not comfortably within any single ambit. There is no possibility of any one person, or even a team of scholars, capturing it all. It can only be approached with humility, as an extremely complex, often unfathomable, frequently awe-inspiring, collective human creation.
>
> (1993, 14; see also MacRaild 2000, 46; Fitzgerald 2004, 41)

So, to deepen our understanding of how this whole world-encircling 'constellation' or 'ethno-cultural pattern' is constituted, we need to keep slicing it down to its smallest component parts, at the microcosmic level of local and family diasporas, and the atomic level of the individual migrant – disaggregating in order to re-aggregate.

Delimiting diasporas

What has been called the 'feel-good' rhetoric of the 'fabled 70 million' of the 'global Irish family', especially as used by politicians, has prompted challenging questions. How are the limits of the Irish diaspora to be determined? If Irish-born emigrants, their children and grand-children are included, what of their descendants, especially when, over generations, they 'marry out' of the ethnic group? How will we know when the diaspora is at an end? (Lee 2005, 186). Perhaps fhe main criticism is expressed by Breda Gray when she says that to speak of 'the strength of a global family, which has turned the tragedy of emigration into a huge success story' (as President Mary McAleese did in Omagh 2001) effectively 'subsumes the gender, class and racial hierarchies that structure the diaspora to the assumed unity of interests of the global Irish family'. In short, such rhetoric is 'less about social justice or social inclusion than capitalising on the human potential of the diaspora in the interests of the nation', a tendency we shall discuss further in the final chapter (Gray 2004, 151, 154). Such rhetoric may also function as a way of talking about the relationship between the living and the dead that is acceptable in secular as well as religious terms: 'diaspora' is closely related to the ecclesiastical idea of 'communion', as in the case of the Roman Catholic communion for whom 'home' on earth is Rome, while Anglicans and Presbyterians have a somewhat similar regard for Jerusalem, and also for Lambeth and Geneva.

Family of families

The idea of the nation and its diaspora being, like the church, a 'family of families' has unrivalled explanatory power for the understanding of Irish migration, especially when it is remembered how fluid families are. As President McAleese also pointed out, they 'come in all sizes, from *The Little House on the Prairie* to *Angela's Ashes*'. Families are dynamic, continually combining (as on marriage, adoption and fostering), splitting (as when children leave the old 'home' of their parents and make new homes) and recombining (as when members who have been 'cut off' reconnect). Potentially, the Irish diaspora may have an unlimited future, in the sense that, like the extended family and the nation, it is an 'imagined community' of the living and the dead; 'imagined' in a similar way to the nation which, as Benedict Anderson explains, 'is imagined because the members of even the smallest nation will never know most of their fellow-members, meet them, or even hear of them, yet in the minds of each lives the image of their communion' (1983, 6).

Like all communities, the Irish diaspora is constantly changing, not least in number, extent and character, so that to speak of it in the singular may be misleading, as if to imply an essential continuity over the preceding four centuries. Nevertheless, it is a reasonable convention to speak about a single Irish diaspora in the sense that lines of continuity can be traced, comprehending all those connected with the island of Ireland through migration. Although connections may be broken suddenly, or fade gradually over many generations, the possibility remains open, at the level of the family at least, for reconnections to be made, for 'fade' to be brightened, and thus for the relationship between diaspora and home to persist, even when actual emigration flows have been reduced to a trickle or dried up entirely. Alternatively, we may think of diasporas 'waxing and waning' (Van Amersfoort 2004). An example of this came in 2006 with the reawakening of interest in the 'Scottish diaspora' in Ireland at the commemoration of the 400th anniversary of the settlement of the Hamilton and Montgomery families in Co. Down (see http://www.hamiltonmontgomery1606.com). So the concept of diaspora, in its two main aspects, seems set to frame the unfolding story of Irish migration. Looked at one way, Ireland is seen as a part of the global, multi-levelled diasporas of most countries of the rest of the world. Looked at the other way, Ireland is seen as a global aggregate of its own multi-levelled, local and regional diasporas. These are the two main aspects of Ireland's 'within-out' through-otherness: the world in Ireland-Ireland in the world.

16
Conclusion: Migration in Irish History

In chapter 1 we noted that, whether we view it from a religious or secular standpoint, much of our thinking about the future is coloured by our own experience of migration, our understanding of historic migration, and the prospect of becoming homeless. One example that we encountered in our survey (chapter 10) was Thomas D'Arcy McGee's description of the Famine emigrants' ships as 'sailing coffins' that 'carried them to a new world, indeed; not to America, but to eternity!' The bitterness of his irony depends on an understanding of the long tradition of Christian thinking about trans-migration to the next world, illustrated by the three 'pilgrim' and 'exile' extracts quoted as epigraphs to this book (from the seventh-century poem about St Columba, *Do-ell Érinn*; the eleventh-century prayer *Salve Regina*; and the seventeenth-century *The Pilgrim's Progress from This World to That Which Is To Come*). It also depends on an understanding of migration in Irish history.

As we have seen, communities and migrants alike try to manage or cope with migration as a way of getting themselves closer to the conditions that they deem 'just right', whether that means moving in the direction of a more open or more closed society. As we have also seen, there is a fundamental choice to be made in the organisation of social groups at all levels: between integration (doing everything together), segregation (doing everything apart) and modulating (alternating more or less skilfully) between the two (Boyle and Hadden 1994; Mac Éinrí 2007). As Steve Garner concludes: 'the question-ing process is crucial to re-assessing who and what constitutes the Irish "we" at the beginning of the twenty-first century'. The same applies to the British 'we' (2004, 253). In this final chapter we consider briefly the outlook for Irish migration as it appeared in 2007, attempt to summarise the story that has emerged from this survey of the last 400 years, and ask again how the challenges of the present may be met more effectively by having a better understanding of migration in Irish history.

Counting uncertainties

Considering how things looked in 2007, it is ironic to return to the caveat that we entered in the Preface about the difficulty of offering anything other than approximations of numbers of people migrating before the middle of the nineteenth century and the era of scientific census-taking. A major concern expressed in both jurisdictions was uncertainty about exactly how many immigrants there were on the island. In the Republic of Ireland the national household survey for the third quarter of 2007 put the number of non-Irish nationals aged 15 and over at 341,600, just under 10 per cent of the population, but in December the Central Statistics Office admitted that the number of foreign nationals living in Ireland may have been underestimated by more than 85,000 (*Sunday Tribune* 2 December 2007). This paralleled ongoing uncertainty about the accuracy of British government's immigration statistics, while confidence about the accuracy of internal migration and emigration statistics remained relatively high.

Outlook 2007

Three books published in 2007 give some indication of how migration was then viewed: Bryan Fanning (ed.)'s *Immigration and Social Change in the Republic of Ireland*, Roy Foster's *Luck & the Irish: A Brief History of Change 1970–2000* and David McWilliams' *The Generation Game*.

Immigration and Social Change

In his introduction to the 14 articles that make up *Immigration and Social Change in the Republic of Ireland*, Fanning wrote of 'a profound disconnection between official Ireland and an increasingly diverse real one' (2007, 2). On the one hand, legislation and administrative rules were found to prohibit discrimination on the basis of race, and, on the other, to sanction discrimination against non-citizens. Attention was drawn to the removal of the citizenship birthright from Irish-born children of immigrants in 2004. The evidence was found to suggest a desire to control immigration and social change resulting from immigration – for example, in the campaign by the state to encourage the return migration of former emigrants. However, a free market ideology appeared to be prevalent within Irish immigration policy, with less of a welcome for return migrants with low skills – a case of 'cherry-picking' rather than 'cherishing' the diaspora (Hayward and Howard 2007).

On the whole, immigrants were found proportionally more likely to be educated to degree level than Irish citizens, to be employed in the professional and technical sectors, and not significantly more likely to be engaged in out-of-hours employment or shift work. However, immigrants were found not to be employed to the level suggested by their educational qualifications and were far less likely to be members of a trade union. The state policy of isolating asylum seekers from the mainstream of society was often described as 'a state akin to limbo, a place where lives are on hold'. It was argued that lessons for integration could be drawn from case studies of the relatively long-established Vietnamese and Bosnian immigrant communities, and of the more recently arrived African Pentecostal communities, by examining issues of family reunification, education, the different perspectives of older and younger generations within immigrant communities, and the challenges facing both immigrant-led organisations and Irish political parties (2007, 4).

On the question of social cohesion, Fanning pointed to 'a family resemblance between social inclusion goals and integration goals', but warned of the need for more debate:

> there has been relatively little explicit discussion of how immigrants should be integrated into Irish society ... The multi-cultural model championed by liberal thinkers such as Bhikhu Parekh has come under criticism in Britain, while in the Netherlands the murders of Pym Fortuyn and Theo Van Gogh have led to some questioning the Dutch approach to diversity. In France the debate on the wearing of the hijab and other 'ostentatious' forms of religious expression has concluded, after well over a decade, with a law, passed by a majority on the left and on the right, which bans such practices outright.
>
> (2007, 5)

However, it is curious that Fanning's book was confined strictly to the Republic of Ireland. Although the immigration policy of the Republic remains closely tied to that of the United Kingdom (in order to avoid having to introduce new border passport controls), it made scarcely any reference to Northern Ireland, let alone the idea that immigration is a common issue and that each jurisdiction might have something to learn from the other in their approach to integration (Little 2003; Marranci 2003; Bell, Jarman and Lefebvre 2004; Chan 2006; Watt and McCaughey 2006; Gallagher 2007; Loyal 2007).

A Brief History of Change, 1970–2000

Immigration featured in Foster's analysis of the last 30 years, but not to the extent of being given a chapter to itself. He registered how in the late 1990s immigrants 'poured into the country', constituting 'a rapid and obvious phenomenon', forming 'a pattern undreamt of twenty years before' and presenting the 'challenge of immigration' (2007, 9, 34, 188). On the negative side, observing a 'mushrooming' of racist incidents, Foster noted that 'those cosily termed the "New Irish" have not always received a hundred thousand welcomes' and that 'the influx of immigrants from less privileged parts of the world were creating a new underclass – but not one that was yet making any indentation upon established political party lines' (2007, 9, 34, 97; see also Flanagan 2007, 200–41). On the positive side, for Ireland at least, he noted that the large majority of incomers were destined for unskilled work or the health service, that 'Protestantism within the Republic has also received a numerical boost from certain sectors of recent immigration' and that immigration contributed to a modest revival of the Irish language in the 1990s in 'eroding the old pietistic attitude to the "first national language"', with the added bonus of evidence that 'learning Irish socializes immigrant children by putting them on a level with their equally ignorant native-born peers'. Finally, he noted the positive effect on popular culture of large-scale immigration, not just from eastern Europe and the Philippines but also from Africa, with the establishment of 'communities of young Irish people who were *actually* black, and who were beginning to develop a musical and cultural style using a mixture of traditions'. This, he concluded, was 'an illustration of how immigration may prove to be one of the defining characteristics of Irishness in the twenty-first century, just as emigration did in the twentieth' (2007, 34, 60, 97, 175, 174, 150).

So far as internal migration was concerned, Foster refered to plans for the decentralisation of government services and attempts to establish Limerick, Cork or Waterford as alternative metropolitan centres which were 'abandoned or came to grief in clientelist politicking, as the population figures for Dublin headed towards 40 per cent of the state as a whole'. Foster also criticised the continuing 'abuse of the coastal environment ... with ribbon development of single dwellings' (2007, 161).

Although Foster recognised that by 2001 Ireland had arrived at the top of the list of the most intensively 'globalised' countries, he had little to say about the relationship between the homeland and the Irish diaspora. He referred to 'the intense interest in Ireland sustained by the Irish diaspora, projecting back images of the island to itself' (indeed, acknowledging that 'this book may itself be part of that process'), but he did not refer to any reciprocal interest being sustained by the homeland in the diaspora (2007, 6). In so far as he took cognisance of the diaspora, he was highly critical of the 'movement of roots-discovery among people of Irish stock, born and living abroad, where the recent vogue for identity politics sometimes goes with a curious brand of late-nineteenth-century racial essentialism, as well as unreconstructed Anglophobia' – a view that now seems dated and not to ring true with our experience of visitors to the Ulster-American Folk Park (2007, 177–8). He did discuss 'the glamour of the American connection' in relation to the Northern Ireland peace process, including, for example, the importance of the St Patrick's Day 1977 statement by Tip O'Neill, Daniel Moynihan, Hugh Carey and Ted

Kennedy, which condemned support of the IRA by Irish-Americans (2007, 138–9). He did discuss Presidents Robinson and McAleese, but not their work in developing relations with the diaspora. As Foster saw it, the question of what Ireland was doing for its diaspora did not arise.

Re-imagining Ireland

The view of migration taken by McWilliams in *The Generation Game* could scarcely have been more different from Foster's. Not content with confining himself, like Foster, to analysing the social change of the last 30 years and presenting 'a map of the landscape receding so bewilderingly behind us', McWilliams proposed a bold project for 're-imagining Ireland', based on developing the relationship between homeland and diaspora. In contrast to Foster's rather upbeat assessment of 'lucky', albeit 'crooked', Celtic Tiger Ireland, McWilliams diagnosed not just crookedness but 'degeneration', including imminent collapse of the property market and immigration as a major threat. He did not share Foster's benign view of the 'New Irish', including the 'communities of young Irish people who were *actually* black'. Referring to those attending the Lithuanian Saturday school in Inchicore, McWilliams, a Dublin-born returned emigrant, wrote, 'these people are as much New Irish as I was New English when I lived in London' (2007, 152).

To avoid degeneration and achieve 'renaissance', he proposed a 'post-nationalist, national project', focused on the Irish diaspora as the nation's most important asset, involving the creation of a 'Greater Ireland'. Referring repeatedly to the emigrants and their descendants as 'the exiles', he pictured making Ireland 'the mother ship of a global tribe so that people can come home, recharge their Irishness and go back out into the world again, satisfied that they know where they come from and who they are' – contrary to the spirit of Robinson's idea of 'cherishing', according to which expressions of Irishness in Ireland and in the diaspora are treated as being of equal value (2007, 243, 259, 274), Significantly, he made no reference to the work of Presidents Robinson and McAleese and others in developing the concept of diaspora and never referred to the homeland and diaspora as the global Irish 'family', as popularised by McAleese, preferring instead the more manly 'tribe', presumably because his project was not only about 'soft' culture but also about 'hard' business, designed to result in global economic advantage for Ireland.

The overheated rhetoric, including the implication that all 'the exiles' (Ulster Scots included) are in some sense maladjusted, was unfortunate. However, McWilliams did succeed in raising the question of what the peace process amendment of 1998 to Article 2 of the Irish Constitution should mean in practice. Thinking about how the nation should 'cherish its special affinity with people of Irish ancestry living abroad who share its cultural identity and heritage', McWilliams made concrete proposals, including offering, as in the case of

Israel, passports and the 'right of return' to all descendants of emigrants; offering their teenage children the opportunity to visit Ireland and participate in specially designed summer *Gaeltacht* schemes; providing a world-class on-line genealogy service that would stimulate and support the reconnection of homeland and diaspora; and creating a new Department of the Diaspora. Not all of this was well thought through and it contained as one reviewer pointed out, backward-looking elements that would have pleased Myles na Gopaleen (*Irish Times*, 13 October 2007). Disturbingly, the insistence on an Irish-speaking *Gaeltacht* experience indicated an exclusive view of Irishness as Catholic and Gaelic. Even though McWilliams did emphasise that 'our exiles include the Ulster Scots exiles in Canada and the southern states of the US as much as the Catholic Irish Diaspora all over the world', his neglect of the Protestant, Catholic and other British in Ireland (English, Scots and Welsh) and the Ulster Scots (not to mention the Ulster English) outside Ireland in Britain, Australia, New Zealand and elsewhere, indicated a blind-spot about how the Republic of Ireland and Northern Ireland might work together in reaching out to people of Irish ancestry living abroad who share their cultural identity and heritage, both Irish and British (2007, 264, 265, 267, 270).

Capitalising on the diaspora

The big idea of capitalising on the diaspora as an asset and advocating a 'Greater Ireland' beyond the sea was not new and McWilliams' project can be seen as a postmodern variant on a Romantic nineteenth-century theme as expressed, for example, by the Irish Race Convention of 1896 (http://www.archive.org/details/proceedingsofiri00irisuoft; Carroll 1978, 51–3, 127–31; Fleming and O'Day 2005, 767) or by the Rev Augustus Thébaud SJ (1808–85). Born in Brittany, Thébaud was the first president of St John's College, New York (later Fordham) after it was handed over to the Jesuits by Archbishop John Joseph Hughes, and Thébaud wanted to see the property market in Ireland freed up and then the diaspora used to restore a Catholic gentry to Ireland:

> Is there no room for a plan whereby Irishmen, who have grown rich in foreign countries, may become purchasers of the land thus offered for sale [through the Encumbered Estates Courts]? ... could not the fathers spare one son at least, whom they might devote to the noble purpose of becoming Irish again, and settling on an Irish estate, and marrying there? This would seem an easy and simple manner of recreating a Catholic gentry in the island.
>
> (1879, 484)

Nevertheless, McWilliams' proposal of 'creating a network of global citizens, who may have two identities, two addresses, two allegiances, but one homeland'

(2007, 264), seemed likely to stimulate the debate called for by Fanning et al. about integration; about how in future we will choose between integrating and segregating, or modulating between the two – the desideratum, as McWilliams put it, of becoming 'more Hibernian [or Britannic] yet more cosmopolitan at the same time' (2007, 258). A further sign of the times in 2007 that this debate was likely to gather momentum was the announcement in November, at the inaugural US-Ireland Forum in New York, that University College Dublin was to establish the John Hume Institute for Global Irish Studies. As the university's President Hugh Brady said, 'We have to ask ourselves, in the future, will the global Irish family be seen as an agent for change or as an historical curiosity'.

'Just right' migration balance

The differences of view between Fanning et al., Foster and McWilliams that were evident in 2007 about current migration and the 'New Irish' in particular return us to the question of the seventeenth-century immigration from Britain and the arrival of the 'New English' (Connolly 2007, 397–403). The 'unfinished business' of their migration only now looks like coming close to a lasting, peaceful resolution. One sign of this is the Ulster-Scots Agency (*Tha Boord o Ulstèr-Scotch*), which together with *Foras na Gaeilge*, the agency set up to promote the Irish language, constitutes the North/South Language Body, established as a result of the Belfast/Good Friday Agreement of 1998. The remit of the Ulster-Scots Agency is 'the promotion of greater awareness and the use of Ullans and of Ulster-Scots issues, both within Northern Ireland and throughout the island'. Significantly, the Agency has supported the translation into Ullans (Ulster-Scots) of *The Pilgrim's Progress* (*Alang tha Pilgrim's Pad*), which begins: '*Yinst A wus wannèrin amaing tha reuch grunn* [English 'rough ground', translating 'wilderness'] *o this here warl ...*', on the grounds that 'it has been the most popular religious book in Ulster next to the Bible'. If we are aware of the painfully protracted outworking of Ireland's seventeenth-century immigration, and anxious to manage our migration process in future to get it as close as possible to 'just right' in its stages, directions and outcomes, then what can we learn from having mapped the migration history that continues to recede so bewilderingly behind us?

Looking back over the last 400 years from the vantage point of 'Scally's satellite' in 2007, studying the fluctuating forces that constituted Ireland's migration 'field' and the interaction of its migration flows, it is hard to see any time, the present included, when contemporaries thought they were close to enjoying the 'Goldilocks' condition of an equilibrium that was 'just right'. Any claim is likely to fail the migration test, as did that made for the Ireland of the 1930s by Arensberg and Kimball in their famous *Family and Community in Ireland* (1940):

> Their brilliantly articulated model of West Clare society in the 1930s portrays a community in equilibrium, having apparently acquired the secret of eternal stability. It would be difficult to glean from this account of the Irish countryman that 165,000 emigrants left Clare between 1851 and 1920, or that the population of the county had fallen from 212,000 in 1851 to 95,000 in 1926. Emigration scarcely intruded into this classic portrait of a serene society, at peace with itself and the world, functioning like a beautifully balanced clockwork mechanism, a perfect *gemeischaft*.
>
> (Lee 1989, 651; see also Akenson 2005, II, 582–3)

In the seventeenth century, when Sir William Petty was surveying Ireland, there was immigration of about 260,000 settlers from the island of Britain and emigration of about 130,000. These numbers may seem relatively small, the total of emigration for the whole century being less than that of single years of the Great Famine (1845–51). However, given that the population of Ireland in the mid-seventeenth century was about two million (as compared with over eight million at the time of the Famine), the emigration of 130,000 represented about 6 per cent of the population. Most of these Irish emigrants (about 90,000) moved to continental Europe. Mostly they were military migrants, leaving in particularly large numbers after the military reverses of 1601, the early 1650s and 1691. In the second half of the century the British Caribbean became a significant destination for about 30,000 emigrants. Over the whole century about 10,000 people (some of them returning settlers) continued the long established tradition of movement from Ireland to Britain.

In the eighteenth century, when Arthur Young visited Ireland, there was less immigration and much more emigration. The island's population had grown slowly to about 2.4 million by 1750, but there was emigration of about 265,000, so the emigration rate had increased to about 11 per cent. The main emigration destination was now North America. About 110,000 emigrants crossed the Atlantic from Ireland in the decades before the American Revolution (1775–81) with about a further 40,000 crossing between 1782 and 1800, making a total of about 150,000 emigrants for the whole century. About 60 per cent of these were from the northern province of Ulster and at least two-thirds of these were Presbyterians with Scottish ancestors (who had been part of the immigrant stream to Ireland in the previous century). Migration to Europe remained strong, especially in the first half of the century and particularly by Irish Catholics from the south-eastern counties. About 60,000 in total left for the continental mainland, attracted by opportunities for military service, education and trade. About 50,000 moved to Britain. And with the start of convict transportation in the 1790s, about 5,000 Irish people were moved to Australia.

In the nineteenth century, when Thomas Colby conducted the Ordnance Survey, the greatest number of people by far emigrated from Ireland. Over the whole century the total number of emigrants was almost seven million, and the emigration rate was almost eight times greater than in either of the preceding two centuries (see Figures 1–3). North America remained the dominant destination with a staggering five million emigrants crossing the Atlantic between 1800 and 1900. The great majority settled in the United States. In the first half of the century about 400,000 of these settled in British North America (later Canada). The second most important destination was Britain, which probably received about 1.5 million emigrants. As continental Europe had declined as a destination for emigrants from Ireland, Britain's colonies had become increasingly important. During the century about 350,000 moved to Australia, about 80,000 to New Zealand and about 15,000 to South Africa. The only non-English-speaking country to receive large numbers of emigrants from Ireland was Argentina, which had close trading links with Britain. About 30,000 went there.

Over the whole of the twentieth century, in which Father O'Brien worried about 'The Vanishing Irish', the total number of people emigrating from the island of Ireland, north and south, was about 2.5 million. Given the much smaller total population in 1951 of 4,331,514, the emigration rate was about 56 per cent (compared with 6 per cent, 11 per cent and 85 per cent in the preceding three centuries). Britain overtook North America as the dominant destination in around 1929 when about 1.2 million emigrated to Britain with about 1.1 million emigrating to North America, with more than two-thirds of these departing before 1930. About 150,000 went to other overseas destinations. Following the accession of the Republic of Ireland to the EEC in 1973, there has been a re-emergence of emigration to continental Europe. By the end of the twentieth century Ireland had become again, for the first time since the seventeenth century, a country of net immigration.

Thus we arrive at a total figure of about ten million emigrating from the island of Ireland over the last four centuries. In the broader European context we can appreciate just how significant this was. Between 1821 and 1914 about 44 million people emigrated from Europe world-wide, of whom about six million were emigrants from Ireland (Baines 1986, 9; 1991, 10). In 1890 two out of every five Irish-born people were living outside Ireland (most of them in the United States – about five million emigrating there between 1820 and 1920). As has been argued, we need to see Irish migration, like that of any other country, within a comparative framework (Kenny 2003). When we look at Europe we find that no other country has been so affected by emigration (Baines 1986; 1991). As well as its long duration and large scale, three features of Irish emigration tend to set it apart from most European countries. First, the numbers of males and females in the emigrant stream from Ireland were more or less balanced, whereas from most European countries there were more males than females. Second, only about 10 per cent of emigrants from Ireland ever returned, whereas from most European countries about 30 per cent did. Third, a special ritual of leave-taking was developed in Ireland, known as the 'American Wake' or 'Living Wake', which was modelled on the traditional community neighbourhood ritual of death and practised by both Catholics and Protestants of the lower and middle classes. The emigrant 'wake', attested well before the Great Famine and persisting into the twentieth century, seems to have been unparalleled elsewhere in Europe (Miller 1985, 556). That so few returned and so many married within their ethnic group largely accounts for the diaspora of about 70 million people scattered around the world today who claim some connection with Ireland, either directly through emigration or indirectly through descent from emigrants.

If we look for an icon of the origin of the emigration flow that resulted in the formation of this modern Irish diaspora, and of the counter-flow of immigration that resulted in the formation of Northern Ireland, we may find it in Ryan's *The Departure of the Earls* in 1607 (Plate 1). If we look for an icon of the persistence of that emigration flow, we may find it in Fox's *Small Island* (see front cover of Ó Gráda 1995). And if we look for an icon of the current state of the competing projects of 'Making Ireland British' and 'Remaking Ireland Irish', we may see it in the May 2007 election poster on Belfast's Ravenhill Road, outside the Martyrs Memorial Free Presbyterian Church of the Rev Ian Paisley (Plate 24). This shows the face of Hong Kong-born Anna Lo, Chief Executive of the Chinese Welfare Association and the first candidate from an ethnic minority immigrant background to contest a winnable seat in the Northern Ireland Assembly, which was restored in 2007. Chinese media reports described her as the first Chinese person to be elected as a lawmaker anywhere in Europe. Lo's election was paralleled in the Republic of Ireland in June when Rotimi Adebari, a 43-year-old Nigerian who had arrived seven years previously as an asylum seeker, was elected in Portlaoise, Laois, to become the island's first black mayor.

In making its future, our society, however defined, is bound to continue wrestling with how to make things 'just right' – not too closed and not too open. Migrating hopefully from the relative 'wilderness' of the present to the 'gold-paved city' of the future, this means making decisions about what, if anything, we should write over our 'gates'; about what laws and regulations we should have as binding on ourselves, including our emigrants; about what restrictions we should place on access to our resources; and about what kind of commitments, if any, we should require of and make to immigrants who arrive seeking sanctuary and citizenship. As much as that of other countries, the story of migration in Irish history points to the long-term costs that are incurred when stayers and migrants erect, or fail to remove, barriers that inhibit full participation in society.

We began our survey in 1607 with the departure of the Earls, O'Neill and O'Donnell, and we close in 2007 with the departure of the ministers, Paisley and McGuinness. The Earls left in September, without the official permission of James I and VI, King of England, Scotland and Ireland, and arrived eventually in Rome, seeking the protection of Pope Paul V, and hoping to return. In September 2007 there was much talk of the increasingly likely prospect of the Queen of Great Britain and Northern Ireland, Elizabeth II, arriving in Dublin and of Pope Benedict XVI arriving in Belfast on state visits. Then in December the First Minister Ian Paisley and Deputy First Minister Martin McGuinness left for the United States, not only with official permission but with almost universal approval; they arrived in Washington seeking the support of President Bush, and returned safely. It seemed that a peaceful way had been woven between the contesting projects of Making Ireland British and Remaking Ireland Irish. If it was not exactly a 'sewing together' (*comúaim*) that was 'just right', then at least it was 'through-other' in the way advocated by Heaney. In part, this peaceful outcome has been thanks to action based on new thinking about the significance of the 'fitfully dormant', 'swarming', 'buzzing' and 'boiling' activity of migration in Irish history, and of its outcomes: the British and other diasporas in Ireland and the Irish diaspora world-wide.

In *Migration in World History*, Patrick Manning's project was to 'illustrate the recurring patterns of human migration' and to 'show how they underlie the pattern of endless reformulation, innovation and exploration that characterizes our species' (2005, 14). Concluding *Migration in Western Europe since 1650*, Leslie Page Moch saw in those patterns hope for the future:

> Currently, global migrations indisputably bring the world together, enriching the choices of cuisine, music, and public culture in a way that seems to be more obvious now than in the past. Yet migrations also offer a great and singular challenge to the quality of public life, human and civil rights legislation, and to the policies of inclusion and exclusion of western Europe. One must hope that this challenge will not result in a resurgence of ethnic persecution and ideologies of dominance.
>
> (2003, 200)

In closing *Migration in Irish History, 1607–2007*, we share this hope for the through-otherness of the world in Ireland and Ireland in the world.

Appendix I
Types of Migration

As well as in stages, migration can be analysed according to different types and several typologies of migration have been developed (Cohen 1997; Manning 2005). At the most basic level we distinguish simply between 'external' and 'internal'. External migration takes place 'from inside to outside', or *between* two 'worlds'; whereas internal migration takes place 'inside' or *within* a 'world' – usually defined as a state or nation. Making a further distinction, we interpret external migration as either emigration (out-migration) or immigration (in-migration), according to whether our focus is mainly on the leaving or the arriving of the migrants. Since one person's emigration is another's immigration, it is well to realise that they are two aspects of the same process – migration – rather than two separate processes. Although the 'worlds' from which migrants emigrate and into which they immigrate are usually defined as states or nations, we should also note that writers about migration sometimes define 'old worlds' and 'new worlds' as units smaller than that of the state or nation. In the Irish case these 'worlds' might be provinces, counties, towns, parishes or townlands, and someone writing about what is technically 'internal' migration between, say, Cork and Dublin, or Belfast and London, might refer to it as movement between the 'the world of Cork' and 'the world of Dublin', or 'the world of Belfast' and 'the world of London', as if it were 'external migration'. Thus, even though it takes place *within* the 'world' of the nation or state, internal migration may be treated as if it were external migration in cases where it is thought of as taking place *between* two of the many different 'worlds' from which that of the nation or state is constructed. This close relationship between internal and external migration is particularly evident in the case of migration between Ireland and Britain before Partition in 1920, and after between Northern Ireland and Britain: whereas a Unionist might think of moving to Britain as internal migration within the United Kingdom, a Nationalist might think of it as emigration. Unless qualified otherwise, we have used 'internal migration' in this book to mean migration within the island of Ireland.

Having clarified the distinction between internal and external, we can distinguish further types of migration according to the motivation of the migrants and the duration of their migrant 'stream' (Peterson 1958). According to motivation, migration may be either 'voluntary' or 'forced'. In broad terms, people migrate when their economic situation is relatively poor or when their personal security is in danger, as from natural disasters or political conflict (Bauder 2006). This may seem straightforward, but in practice it is often difficult to distinguish between those who left 'voluntarily' and those who were 'forced out' – as in the case of the 44 million who emigrated from Europe between

1815 and 1914 (Baines 1986, 9). Not so, however, in the case of the 12 million West Africans who, over more than three centuries of legalised slavery (1502–1865), were taken to the new world (Braziel and Mannur 2003, 2).

To the present day a main concern of migration policy is to discriminate between voluntary 'economic' migrants and 'asylum seekers', who seek to be granted the status of 'refugee'. Although casually used to mean any displaced person forced to leave their home, as in the case of a natural disaster, 'refugee' in the technical, legal sense under the 1951 United Nations *Convention Relating to the Status of Refugees* is defined as:

> one who owing to a well-founded fear of being persecuted for reasons of race, religion, nationality, membership of a particular social group, or political opinion, is outside the country of his nationality, and is unable to or, owing to such fear, is unwilling to avail himself of the protection of that country.

So identifying the motivation of migrants also involves consideration of others, especially those causing forced migration. Here we should also note a form of forced migration which is not so obvious: 'non-mobile' migration. Although no physical displacement is involved, we can still see at work the core migration process of disassociation, transition and re-association. It is illustrated most clearly perhaps by the redrawing of national boundaries in Europe after the First and Second World Wars when, without physically moving home, millions found themselves moved, for better or worse, out of their 'old country' and into a 'new country' (Davies 1997, 926–7; Meinhof 2002). Again the obvious Irish case is that of Partition in 1920 when Ireland, then all part of the United Kingdom, was divided into the two new 'worlds' of the Irish Free State and Northern Ireland (Coakley and O'Dowd 2005; 2007).

According to the duration of the 'stream', migration may be classified according to the following types: pioneer, chain, seasonal, step and return. Pioneer migrants (whether internal or external) are the first from their families or communities to out-migrate or emigrate to a particular destination. Especially in the case of emigration to a 'new world', they may establish a 'bridgehead' and subsequently both encourage and assist relations and friends to join them, thereby establishing a 'chain' between old world and new which may extend to successive generations. Thus, in chain migration migrants 'follow in the footsteps' of the pioneers, as for example in the case of the 'chain' established in the late nineteenth century between the Allihies copper mining area of west Cork and the copper mines of Butte, Montana (Emmons 1992, 83; see also Mulligan 2001a; 2001b; 2004). We also see the power of chain migration expressed in the song 'The Green Fields of America': the singer remembers 'the time when old Ireland was flourishing / When most of our tradesmen did work for good pay' and contrasts it with the present when 'the lint-dams are gone and the looms are now idle' and the tradesmen are gone, including 'winders of baskets and creels', 'journeymen', 'ploughboys' and 'fiddlers'; concluding that 'since our manufactures have crossed the Atlantic / It's now we must follow to America' (Moloney 2002, 9).

'Seasonal migration', which may be internal or external, takes place between 'home' and a semi-permanent place of work elsewhere (as formerly with Irish 'harvest-workers' in Britain, and now with Irish construction workers world-wide). Step migration takes place in stages between places, either within a country (internal) or between countries (external), as in the case of those who emigrated from Ireland in pursuit of gold and went first to North America, then on to Australia, and finally to New Zealand (Hearn 2000, 84–5; Fraser 2007). Return migration is out-migration or emigration in reverse: from the new residence back to the old.

As well as distinguishing these different aspects or types of migration (internal, external, forced, voluntary, pioneer, chain, seasonal, step, return, non-mobile), we need also to apply the standard method of the social sciences and distinguish more specifically between groups of migrants in terms of their ethnicity, gender, politics (nationality, party or military affiliation), economics (class, occupation), social service (law and order, health, education), religion (creed or denomination) and culture (arts and sciences). Thus, for example, different types of 'career' migration, such that of soldiers, police, clergy, teachers, bank officials, domestic servants or musicians, may be singled out for investigation. High-skilled transnational migration of the kind promoted by multinational corporations tends to result in 'expatriate' or 'sojourner' patterns of migration. An important special aspect of chain migration is family reunification. In Europe between 1974 and the mid-1990s (as labour immigration was suspended in the wake of the 1974 oil crisis) family reunification exceeded in volume both labour migration and forced migration (P. Mac Éinrí, pers. comm.).

Types of migration in global perspective

The process of human migration accounts for how groups and individuals have come to be scattered and concentrated around the world in the way that they are today. Taking the long view into the deep past, back to the emergence of *Homo sapiens* about 200,000 years ago, migration is the process that accounts for the peopling of the earth 'out of Africa', from our east African 'homeland' (Manning 2005, 16–17). We now understand migration as a global process that has shaped the evolution of virtually all societies in the modern world, albeit to varying degrees (Cohen 1995; Lucassen and Lucassen 1997; Hoerder 2002). In contrast to the relatively small scale and slow rate of migration over the millennia, the scale of migration since the sixteenth century has increased enormously, and over the last 30 years in particular (Castles and Miller 1998). Today about 200 million people in the world live outside the country of their birth compared with 1970 when the number was less than half that (Mac Éinrí 2003; International Organisation for Migration 2003). The increase has given rise to the notion of an 'international migration crisis', according to which the developed countries of the North are seen as being about to be swamped by floods of migrants driven by poverty, violence and chaos in the South. This has been exacerbated first by the end of the Cold War and more recently by the events of 11 September 2001, which moved migration – especially refugee migration – to the top of the security agenda (Reimers 1998; Zolberg and Benda 2001). Nonetheless, according to the Global Commission on International Migration (2005), the overwhelming majority of people in the world (6.5 billion) are still settled in their country of birth and the proportion of migrants 'remains rather modest at around 3 per cent' (191 million). In the European Union, for example, migrants from outside and internal migrants represent about 3.5 and 1.5 per cent respectively of its population of 487 million. This indicates a strong propensity to remain 'at home'. Most migrants aspire either to settle permanently in their 'new world' or return eventually to their 'old world'. Some move frequently as seasonal migrants or as members of transnational families which span countries of origin and destination. Only a tiny minority of migrants are truly 'nomadic' in the sense of being either 'homeless' or continually on the move between multiple 'homes'. These few include some of the world's very poorest and richest for whom 'transit is a permanent lifestyle' (Melucci 1989; Sigona 2003; Ní Shuinéar 2006, 81).

Useful for setting Irish migration in global perspective is the typology of Manning (2005, 13–14). He sees migration in terms of the boundaries of human communities, four basic types of migration, the processes of cross-community migration, the role of migration in social development, and the long-term impact of migration. His four basic types of migration are: within and across community boundaries; home-community migration; colonisation; whole-community migration; and cross-community migration. He classifies migrants as colonists; settlers; sojourners, itinerants, invaders, and as whole communities. He focuses on the interplay of what he calls 'institutions of migration': families within and across communities; migratory networks; and the migrants themselves.

Appendix II
Migration Theory and Irish Migration Studies

The roots of the discipline we now call migration studies go back to the 1880s and the work of E. G. Ravenstein (1834–1913), who postulated a set of 'laws of migration' that are still regarded as having fundamental validity (Ravenstein 1885; 1888; Jackson 1969, 6; Lee 1969, 282–3; Grigg 1977; Daniels 1990, 16; Brettell and Hollifield 2000, 27–9, 35–6; Delaney 2000, 9; Guinness 2002, 11–12). They can be grouped in summary form as follows:

Internal migration

- The majority of migrants go only a short distance.
- The natives of towns are less migratory than those of rural areas.
- Large towns grow more by migration than by natural increase.
- Migration increases in volume as industries and commerce develop and transport improves.
- The major direction of migration is from the agricultural areas to the centre of industry and commerce.
- The major causes of migration are economic.

Out-migration (internal and external)

- Migrants going long distances generally move by preference to one of the great centres of commerce or industry.
- Most migrants are adults: families rarely migrate out of their country of birth.
- Females are more migratory than males within the country of their birth, but males more frequently venture beyond.

Step migration

- Migration proceeds step by step.

Stream and counter-stream

- Each current of migration produces a compensating counter-current

Ravenstein's 'laws' were subsequently refined by Everett Lee (1966).

As noted in chapter 1, some migration scholars have found Lee's broad definition unwieldy, even though it excludes 'the continual movements of nomads and migratory workers, for whom there is no long-term residence, and temporary moves like those to the mountains for the summer' (Lee 1969, 285). They have preferred to restrict their view of migration to changes of residence that require the individual to 'readjust' completely in terms of job, friends and neighbours (Bogue 1969; Whyte 2000, 1). However, some organisational theorists, following the insight of Jackson about the deep structure or core process of migration (1969, 5) and also work by Hirschman (1970), have analysed movement between the domestic home and the workplace or school as a type of migration, arguing that these destinations are best understood as 'second homes' (Lambkin 2001). Whatever the merits of narrower or broader definitions of migration, the application of Lee's simple criterion of 'moving residence' has proved valuable for understanding the nature of mobility in a population by distinguishing 'migrants' from other 'movers'. We usually think of migration as being linear between points A and B, where A is the 'old home' and B is the 'new home' (Jones 1990). Migration is therefore different from 'circulation', which is movement around a fixed residential base and includes short-range journeys, such as those made daily from home to work, school or the shops and back, and also long-range journeys, such as those made in the course of employment, education or leisure which may last days, weeks or even months. Although there is no universally agreed definition, journeys lasting more than a year are often counted as migration. But since migration often results in 'return migration' – increasingly so with the advent of cheaper air-fares – the distinction between migration and circulation is far from clear-cut.

The basic way of explaining migration is still to say that it results from the tension between 'push' and 'pull' forces, which are mainly economic: the attraction of another location only has meaning when compared with conditions at home (Baines 1991, 21). 'Push' forces include lack of employment opportunities, low wages and population pressure in the 'old world' that is 'home'. 'Pull' forces include better employment opportunities, higher wages and a higher standard of living in the 'new world'. The basic popular explanation of the push and pull factors involved in Irish emigration is expressed in the song 'The Green Fields of America': the singer imagines that 'the green fields' are 'calling' him daily and it is on them that he will put 'an end to my misery and strife', because there he will get 'ten dollars a week', which is 'not very bad pay', and there will be 'no taxes or tithes to devour up your wages' (Moloney 2002, 9).

The basic assumption is that migration can be explained by reference to changes or fluctuations in the labour market of the sending and receiving societies. A further assumption is that there is some mechanism for feeding back information about economic and social conditions from the receiving society to the sending society. In the nineteenth and early twentieth centuries this information was fed back through newspaper advertisements, a new literary genre of 'Advice to Emigrants' and the network of agents that made up the 'migration industry', but still most effectively by the traditional method of emigrants writing letters home or returning in person (Baines 1991, 44–5; Castles and Miller 1993, 97–8).

According to Marxist and neo-Marxist analysis, push and pull forces are seen as operating within a core–periphery framework: the 'underdeveloped' global periphery acts as a reservoir of cheap labour (and raw materials) for the manufacturing industries in the 'developed' global core (Delaney 2000, 17). This model is used to explain both international migration from 'developing' countries to 'developed' countries and also internal migration from the 'developing' countryside of the state to its 'developed' urban centres.

However, a difficulty with the push–pull model is that of assessing the relative importance of forces at work in any given case. Recently, there have been fruitful developments in migration theory, contributed by various disciplines. From economics has come a switch in focus from the migration 'decision' of individual migrants, as in the cost–benefit approach of Todaro (1969), to the collective decision-making process of the family or household, as developed by Stark (1991), in what is referred to as the 'New Economics of Migration'. This has shown how families, even in the absence of appreciable wage differentials, may actively encourage emigration by some of their members to diversify risk: having emigrant relatives is a way of developing a safety net of remittances, which may guard against a future downturn in the local economy. It has also been found that families generally assess their economic position in relation to their local community. If they find their place in the local hierarchy to be one of 'relative deprivation', they may use migration as a strategy to improve their position. Douglas Massey has argued for a risk-averse, family-based migration decision-making process that is designed not to maximise individual opportunity but to minimise potential collective loss (1990, 69; 1998). Such a coping strategy helps to explain why, for example, it was more likely in 2007 for Poles to arrive in Ireland, where there were plenty of relatively poorly paid jobs, than in other countries, where the wages might be higher but the chances of finding work not as high (P. Mac Éinrí, pers. comm.).

An important contribution to migration theory from the discipline of geography, already hinted at above, has been Zelinsky's 'Mobility Transition' theory (1971), which seeks to account for migration within all human movement by distinguishing it from 'circulation' (including seasonal movements, journeys to work, holidays). Also from geography has come a focus on the importance of geographical proximity in determining migration destinations based on the idea of the 'friction of distance' – that overcoming distance usually requires effort and money. According to Zipf's 'Inverse Distance Law' (1949), 'the volume of migration is inversely proportional to the distance travelled by the migrants'. So, for example, Finns tend to emigrate to Sweden, whereas Mexicans and Canadians tend to emigrate to the United States, and Italians to Switzerland. Of course, not all cases fit this model, as, for example, the Irish in the second half of the nineteenth century who had a stronger tendency to emigrate to the United States than to Britain.

Into migration theory from the discipline of sociology has come a new focus on migration as an important component of social change and a general recognition that 'the social structure and cultural system both of places of origin and of destination are affected by migration and in turn affect the migrant' (Jansen 1969, 60). If a particular household, local community or region has a 'tradition' of emigration and a well-established network, this will affect future emigration, as will a change in the social or economic structure of the community, such as agricultural mechanisation reducing the demand for labour. Who goes and who stays will be determined differently according to age, sex, social class and education. In this regard network theory has proved very productive in analysing migration flows as to what determined them and what, at least, determined the initial place of settlement of migrants (Boyd 1989; see also Collyer 2005). Also important has been the world systems theory and analysis of Wallerstein (1974; 1975; Hopkins and Wallerstein 1982), based on distinguishing between two types of world-systems: 'world-economies', which are systems of polities or states integrated within a single economy, and 'world-empires', where a single polity or state dominates and integrates an economy'.

Explaining migration also involves explaining non-migration or 'staying' and why the majority did not leave (Hammar et al. 1997; Delaney 2000, 18, 14). Here we may recall

Ravenstein's fifth 'law': that 'the natives of towns are less migratory than those of rural areas'. We are also reminded to be wary of exaggerating the importance of migration because in general 'the departure of large numbers of people is not likely to produce sweeping social change' (Scott 1960, 167). For example, emigration may act in conservative interests as a safety-valve by enabling a large numbers of dissatisfied, unemployed people to leave, so helping to reduce radical unrest at home. In the case of Ireland, it has been argued that the continuous high-level flow of emigration to Britain after 1945 resulted in the country remaining conservative in outlook (Delaney 2000, 15). However, it is generally recognised that socio-cultural change *can* be brought about if contact is 'maintained with the emigrants in their new environment' (Scott 1960, 167). In the case of Ireland, as we shall see, the development of homeland–diaspora relations has resulted in significant change in the homeland in the late twentieth century, especially with the emergence of the Celtic Tiger economy and the Northern Ireland peace process.

As much as by its emigrants, the homeland may be affected by its immigrants. Much work has been done recently on the effects that migrants have had on the receiving society in terms of their 'reception', 'settlement', 'absorption', 'assimilation' and 'integration'. Generally, these are regarded as positive processes. However, there has also been a focus on the 'resistance' of migrant groups to adaptation to the receiving society. This has been investigated in terms of their 'ethnic identity' and 'marginalisation', 'exclusion' and 'alienation', as for example in the case of Turkish migrants in post-war Germany (Rex and Mason 1986; Alexander 2003). In the European Union at present the two-way processs of integration is generally preferred to the one-way process of assimilation (Lucassen 2005; Mac Éinrí 2007). The question of adjustment to immigration is an important theme in Part II.

Into migration theory from the discipline of psychology has come Stouffer's 'Theory of Intervening Opportunities' (1940), which was refined by Everett Lee in his 'Origin – Intervening Obstacles – Destination' theory (1966). According to this, the number of migrants moving from place A to place B is directly proportional to the number of opportunities in B, and inversely proportional to the number of 'intervening opportunities' between A and B (for example, housing and employment vacancies). So altogether four sets of factors or forces are seen as influencing the decision to migrate: those associated with the place of origin (push); those associated with the place of destination (pull); the intervening opportunities and obstacles which lie between origin and destination, such as method and cost of transport, immigration laws, language, political ties or their absence; and the individuality of migrants, who may judge differently the relative strengths of push factors, intervening opportunities and obstacles, and pull factors.

Into migration theory from the discipline of political science has come a focus on migration policy – the control which the state has exercised over the flow of people across its borders since the creation of the modern passport system during the First World War gave states 'monopoly of the legitimate means of movement' (Torpey 2000; 2001; also Brubaker 1989; Joppke 1998). In most European countries since the Second World War, the trend has been to increasing restriction of entry, as in the case of Britain's move away from a tradition of 'free entry' after 1962 (Collinson 1993). The question of state control of migration in the Irish case is addressed in more detail below.

The final theoretical framework in migration studies to which Delaney (2000) draws attention is that derived from the organisational 'Exit-Voice Polarity' theory of Hirschman (1970). If a firm, organisation or state is in decline, Hirschman argues, its employees, members or citizens alike have three options: the 'exit' option is to leave; the 'loyalty' option is to stay put; the 'voice' option is stay but negotiate with the 'managers' to reverse the decline by complaining, protesting or organising internal opposition. The decision to leave (emigrate) or stay is affected by the degree of loyalty of the individual: the more loyal they are, the more likely they are to choose the 'voice' rather than the 'exit' option. Interestingly, Hirschman derived his theory from the 'Fight or Flight' theory developed by the physiologist Walter Cannon (1915), whose 'exit' (migration) option corresponds with 'flight' and 'voice' (non-migration) option corresponds with 'fight'. To these insights may be added others, such as those from the analysis of the role of gender in migration (Boyle and Halfacree 1999; Sharpe 2001; Andall 2003) and from structuration theory, including the idea that although social life is not the sum of all *micro*-level activity, social activity cannot be fully explained from a *macro* perspective (Giddens 1984). As Karl Marx put it,

> People make their own history, but not just as they please. They do not choose the circumstances for themselves, but have to work upon circumstances as they find them, have to fashion the material handed down by the past. That is to say, we make our own history, but not under circumstances of our own choosing.
>
> (*The Eighteenth Brumaire of Louis Bonaparte*, 1852)

The benefit accruing from the application of insights from this wide range of disciplines is increasingly evident in Irish historiography where, for example, 'some of the most illuminating accounts of migration incorporate elements of individual decision-making and the economic and social process at work' (Delaney 2000 7, 20). The one theoretical framework not referred to by Delaney in *Demography, State and Society* is that based on the concept of diaspora – the idea that it is important to study the changing relationship between homelands and their 'scatterings' of migrants and their descendants (however, see Delaney's entry on 'diaspora' in Lalor (2003, 294–6), an indicator of how the concept has become central).

Appendix III
Individual Migrants

The migrants named in this book make up a minute fraction of the millions who migrated in the course of these four centuries. For convenience of recalling them, they are set out below chronologically and grouped as immigrants, internal migrants and emigrants. Following the prosopographical approach (see chapter 15), where possible they have been further grouped according to other common aspects, such as occupation. Groups of migrants mentioned in the text, whose members are mostly if not all anonymous, are also included.

Immigrants

1607–1650

At the top of the social scale, Richard Boyle, arriving in Munster from Kent to become the first Earl of Cork; Charles Blount arriving in Ulster to become Lord Deputy Mountjoy; Arthur Chichester arriving in Ulster from Devon to become Lord Deputy; James Hamilton and Hugh Montgomery arriving in Co. Down from Scotland to settle in Bangor and Greyabbey; Toby Caulfield arriving in Tyrone from Oxfordshire to build Castlecaulfied; and members of the Catholic family of Hamilton arriving in Tyrone from Scotland to establish the Abercorn estate.

In the middle of the social scale, the step migrant Matthew de Renzy, arriving in Londonderry from London having moved there from Germany; and Sir Robert McCelland, arriving on the Haberdasher's proportion in Co. Londonderry from his home in Bomby, near Kirkcudbright, Galloway.

At the bottom of the social scale, the Native American, John Fortune, who arrived in Ulster in time to be caught up in the 1641 Rising.

1650–1700

Members of the Welsh community in Dublin in 1671 gathering in St Werbergh's church; Samuel Hayman arriving in Youghal, Cork, from Minehead, Somerset, to become in the 1670s a successful trader; the antiquary Thomas Dineley in 1680 arriving in Staplestown, Carlow from England to visit the model settlement; John Bufton arriving in Dublin from Coggeshall, Essex and moving north to Drogheda to become a port official; and the Quaker George Bewley, in 1698 arriving in Dublin from Cumberland to become an apprentice to the draper Edward Webb.

1700–1750

John Evelyn Jr, Francis Robartes and Thomas Meddlycott arriving in Dublin from England to take up successively the post of Revenue Commissioner; Richard Musgrave from the north-west of England arriving as land agent on an estate in Blackwater valley, Cork, and Mr (first name unknown) Hume arriving on the Malton estate on the Wicklow/Wexford border, also as a land agent; Samuel Bagshawe and Adolphus Oughton, British army officers arriving in Ireland from England and both staying after leaving the army to settle in Ireland; Daniel Burgess arriving in Charleville, Cork, from England to become head teacher of the Earl of Orrery's endowed school; two anonymous youths arriving in Dublin from Wales, both to become apprentices; an anonymous woman from Wales arriving in the 1730s in Roscommon to be married; Rev. William Preston arriving in 1738 in Carlow from England to take up a well-endowed living.

As well as these there were artists and craftsmen. Among those arriving from England were Giles King and Andrew Miller (engravers), Peter Lens, John Simpson, Benjamin Wilson and James Worsdale (painters); from France came James Mannin; from the Hague came Johann Van der Hagen; and from Amsterdam came Isaac Vogelsang; the 70 Huguenot workers who arrived with Louis Crommelin in Lisburn, Antrim, to help establish in 1701 the first large-scale bleaching works; and the French Huguenots who were settled by the Huguenot immigrant Henry de Ruvigny, Earl of Galway, in the model village of Portarlington, Queen's County (Laois).

1750–1800

Samuel Bagshawe, an army officer originally from Derbyshire, well settled and elected to the Irish House of Commons in 1761; a number of British-born artists and craftsmen of all kinds working in Dublin and elsewhere in Ireland, including William Ashford from Birmingham, Samuel Collins from Bristol, Horace Hone from London, Faithful Pack from Norwich, Thomas Snagg from London, James Tassie from Glasgow and Francis Wheatley from London; the step migrant painter Chevalier Manini, originally from Milan, arriving in Dublin from London; the step migrant merchant John Anderson, originally from near Dumfries, arriving in Cork city from Glasgow eventually to acquire an estate near Fermoy; and the freed slave Tony Small, arriving in Dublin from America in 1782 with Lord Edward Fitzgerald; and 60 skilled men who arrived in Tipperary from Scotland to work on the construction of Damer Court; and those of the members of the Jewish and Palatine communities.

1800–1845

The engineer Alexander Nimmo, arriving in 1810 in Connemara from Kirkcaldy, Scotland, eventually to design the Wellesley (later Sarsfield) Bridge, Limerick; James Shaw Kennedy, arriving from Scotland, to become eventually the first Inspector-General of the Royal Irish Constabulary; John Lynch and William Blacker, arriving on the Palmerston and Gosford estates in Sligo and Armagh respectively as 'improving' agriculturalists; Carlo Bianconi, arriving in Dublin in 1810 from Tregolo, Lombardy, to become an apprentice and eventually proprietor of the 'big house' at Longfield, Tipperary; and the evangelical missionary, Asenath Nicholson, arriving in Ireland in 1844 from Vermont, USA; the three Jewish families reported as being resident in Dublin in 1805; and the 60 men brought to Ireland from Scotland by Blacker as 'peasant chasers'.

1845–1855

In 1846 and 1847, the philanthropist Vere Foster and Frederick Blackwood, first Marquess of Dufferin and Ava, arriving from England in Co. Louth and Co. Down respectively to take up residence on their family estates; the French chef Alexis Soyer, arriving in Dublin from London to supervise the soup kitchen in Merrion Square; the Galway-born Robert Burke in 1848 arriving back in Ireland from Europe to take up a post in the Royal Irish Constabulary, before eventually re-emigrating; the few arriving in Dublin from Europe, to join the Jewish community.

1855–1900

Louis Goldberg in 1882, arriving in Queenstown from Lithuania and being met by a fellow Lithuanian Jew, Isaac Marcus; and Guiseppe Cervi and James Pearse arriving in Dublin from Italy and England respectively and both settling in Great Brunswick Street.

1900–1950

Isaac Black arriving in Belfast from Poland, via Hamburg and London, eventually to establish a house furnishing business; and Victor Fiorentini and his wife and father-in-law, arriving in Derry from Italy, to set up in the restaurant business; and the Germans, Italians, Austrians and Czechs, who were interned in 1940 on the Isle of Man.

1950–2007

In 1953 and 1966, Johnnie Chada and Diljit Rana arriving from India to become entrepreneurs in Sligo and Belfast respectively; and in 1957 a group of 350 refugees arriving from Hungary at Knockalisheen, near Limerick.

Internal migrants

1607–1650

James Hoole, originally from Thornton, Lancashire, probably moving between Dublin, where he was based, and Kilrea, Co. Londonderry, where he owned timber.

1650–1700

General Ireton moving through Munster in the 1650s, reporting on the desolation; and the frustrated land agent, E. Richardson in Donegal who in 1665 found the mobile native tenantry 'snail-like'.

1700–1750

The step migrant Jane McDaniel arriving in Dublin from Newtownards, Down, to work as a servant before marrying a tailor and moving to London; Primate Boulter, Archbishop of Armagh, travelling in 1727 on visitation through Ulster. We may also wonder at the migration stories of the gentlemen of Ulster origin concentrated in Dublin in the northside parish of St Michan's; and likewise those northerners tempted in the 1730s and 1740s to move south to the Temple estate in Sligo, the Smythe estate in Westmeath and Sir Maurice Crosby's estate in Kerry.

1750–1800

Robert Bell, from Ulster, travelling throughout the island in the 1780s; the niece of the Bishop of Elphin's housekeeper arriving in Dublin from Roscommon to become the bishop's housekeeper; Margaret Leeson (*née* Plunkett) arriving in Dublin from Westmeath to become a fashionable brothel-keeper; and Lady Arabella Denny arriving in Dublin from Kerry eventually to found the first Magdalen Asylum. We might also wonder about the migration stories of the 61 families who were settled in Armagh city in 1664, but a century later were all gone; and likewise of those in the 1790s named in the admissions journal of the Limerick House of Industry; and of the Presbyterian weavers arriving in Mayo from Ulster to settle in the Earl of Arran's linen-producing estate village of Mullifarragh; and the refugee Catholic weavers arriving in Tipperary from Ulster in order to resettle, becoming known by the locals as the 'Oultachs'.

1800–1845

The 24-year-old William Carleton, arriving on foot in Dublin in 1810 from the Clogher valley, Tyrone; John Foster, an elderly itinerant beggar from Connacht, giving evidence to the Poor Law Inquiry in 1836; William Waters and Robert Dunlop arriving in Dublin in 1810 and 1843 from Wicklow and Down respectively, the former serving successively in Galway, Mayo and Down and the latter at various places in Leinster and finally in Longford. We may also wonder about the migration stories of the thousands of beggars persuaded by members of the Association for the Suppression of Mendicity in Dublin to leave the city limits; or those of the 3,000 workers in the 1810s arriving in the Kilcock district of Kildare from Roscommon for harvest work.

1845–1855

Husband and wife John and Ellen Mullherin arriving in the winter of 1846–7 in Dublin from Leitrim to live for a few weeks in squalid conditions in the yard of a house in Hendrick Street. We may also wonder about the stories of those arriving in the spring of 1847 in Cork to find the north and south gates of the city barred; those in the winter of 1847 who set out but never arrived in Dublin from Ballykilcline, Roscommon; and those arriving in the spring of 1850 in Dublin from all over Ireland to become patients in the Cork Street Fever Hospital.

1855–1900

The tobacco businessman Thomas Gallaher and the versatile clergyman Richard Rutledge Kane arriving in the 1850s in Derry city and Belturbet, Cavan, from Templemoyle, near Limavady, and Omagh, Tyrone, respectively, and both ending up in Belfast.

1900–1950

The 23-year old Muiris Ó Súilebháin, the 16-year-old Tom Lynam and the 14-year-old Maura Murphy, in 1927, 1935 and 1942 respectively, arriving in Dublin from the Great Blasket Island, Kerry, Marlinstown, Westmeath, and Clonmore, Offaly, to take up their first waged employment. Also the migration stories of the 'New Dubliners', arriving from the western counties, studied in the 1940s by the anthropologist Humphreys (1966); those who took part in the reverse 'transplatation' from Connacht to establish new Irish-speaking settlements close to Dublin; and those who were refugees from 'Troubles' north and south, such as those northerners given shelter in the Workhouse, Dublin in 1922.

1950–2007

Polly Devlin in the 1950s arriving in Belfast from the 'remote' parish of Ardboe, Tyrone, to be surprised by the poverty of both Protestant and Catholic children; and the Rocks family in the early 1970s being forced out their home, nextdoor to Geoffrey Beattie, to a 'safer' part of Ligoniel, Belfast.

Emigrants

1607–1650

The anonymous individuals on board four emigrant ships: the 40 or so who were on board the anonymous ship that took the Earls Hugh O'Neill and Hugh O'Donnell to Europe in 1607; the 80 emigrants who sailed in 1621 with Daniel Gookin from Cork to Virginia; the 40 or more emigrants in 1630 who were on board the people trafficker Maurice Keyson's barque *Peter*, sailing from Dungarvan, when it was intercepted by the authorities near Bristol; and intending emigrants who were on board the *Eagle Wing* from Groomsport, Down, in 1636 when it turned back halfway across the Atlantic. In England, the widow Alice Stonier who in 1642 had returned there with her five children from Dublin to her home parish of Leek, Staffordshire; in Spain, Robert Comerford, a leading merchant in La Coruna, Galicia, who was originally from Waterford; and in various parts of the New World, the Ireland-based adventurers Walter Raleigh, Humphrey Gilbert, Richard Grenville and Ralph Lane.

1650–1700

Luke Quirke, a sailor in St Malo, writing to his cousin, John Kearney, also in France, asking 'how all our poor friends in Clonmel do?'; Francis Makemie from Ramelton, Donegal helping to establish Presbyterianism in the Chesapeake tidewater during the 1690s; Charles Carroll in 1688 arriving in Maryland from Tipperary via London to become Lord Baltimore's attorney general; John Barnwell in 1700 leaving Dublin for Carolina because he had 'a humour to go to travel'.

1700–1750

The young men leaving Ireland for good in 1726, allegedly on the pretence of going to England for temporary work; Andrew MacManus arriving in 1741 in Newgate gaol, London, from Dublin, having walked from Parkgate via Manchester and Staffordshire; Patrick Rice, an Irish-born shoemaker, being questioned in 1745 in London about possible involvement in a Jacobite conspiracy; the Irish-born Thomas Reynolds being arrested in 1750 in London for recruiting for the French army; the three nabobs in the East India Company originally from Londonderry; Sir Arthur Dobbs arriving in North Carolina from Antrim to become Governor; the Irish-born Daniel Fagan, Jerry Corker, John Coffin, William Kane and Edward Murphy being arrested in 1741 in Hughson's tavern, New York, accused of involvement in a plot to destroy the Fort St George garrison on St Patrick's Day; the anonymous unskilled Irishmen that were proving a problem in 1726 in London for the members of the Tin Plate Workers Company; and the 171 Irish men and women executed in the course of the eighteenth century at Tyburn, London.

1750–1800

The ten-year-old chain migrant, John Dunlap arriving with his uncle in Philadelphia in 1757 from Strabane, Tyrone, eventually to become the printer of the Declaration of Independence; Henry Joy McCracken attempting in 1798 to escape to the United States from Larne; Ambrose O'Higgins arriving successively in Spain, Argentina, Peru and Chile from Co. Meath, eventually to become Viceroy of Peru; and the merchant Thomas O'Gorman arriving in Spain and South America from Co. Clare.

1800–1845

The family of Thomas Mellon in 1818 arriving in Baltimore, Maryland, via St John, New Brunswick, from near Omagh, Tyrone; and Maurice Shea in 1815 arriving at Waterloo from near Tralee, Kerry, to go on to serve with the British army in Ceylon and after, having returned to Ireland, to emigrate eventually with his wife, Mary O'Connor from Cahirciveen, Kerry, and six children to Montreal. Those anonymous individuals in 1806 who responded to seeing the Irish-language army recruitment poster printed by Dublin Castle (Plate 7) and ended up, like Maurice Shea (Plate 19), being posted abroad.

1845–1855

The Young Ireland political exiles Mitchel, Smith O'Brien, Meagher and McGee; and two resourceful Donegal emigrants, James Morrow and William McIlhinney, arriving in America from Derry having worked their passage; the 40 Irish paupers arriving illegally in 1847 on the south Wales coast on board the *Lady Ann of Kinsale*; those sailing from Derry to Philadelphia who perished on board the *Exmouth* off the west coast of Scotland; those who on arriving in America opened savings accounts in the New York Emigrant Savings Bank or ended up being named in the 'Missing Friends' section of the *Boston Pilot*; and the 15-year-old Owen Peter Mangan and three friends taking the boat to Liverpool in 1853.

1855–1900

The Ballygoghlan-born Herbert Kitchener leaving with his family for Switzerland in 1862; those who were assisted to emigrate to Australia and were remembered in the 1930s by the Tipperary blacksmith Thomas Magner; Charles Mullen and A. B. McMillan arriving in Brooklyn and Pittsburgh respectively and writing home in the 1880s and 1890s to relations in Sligo and Newtownards about how they wished they could return; and the individuals in the large numbers of family and other group photographs that survive from this period.

1900–1950

Three passengers in 1912 in steerage on the *Titanic*, crossing to New York from Queenstown: the 17-year-old Ellen Corr from Corglass, Longford, the 23-year-old Andy Keane from Derrydonnell near Athenry, Galway, and the 31-year-old Thomas Morrow from Drumlough near Rathfriland, Down; James Smyth, arriving in Canada from Castledamph near Plumbridge, Tyrone, returning frequently to Ireland as an emigration agent, acting on behalf of the Canadian government; and Charles Fitzgerald and Douglas Lambkin, arriving in 1918 in Salford, Lancashire and Golders Green, London, from Dublin after service in France on the Western Front.

1950–2007

Edna O'Brien recalling her arrival at Euston Station in 1952; John B. Keane recalling the 'Many Young Men of Twenty' who emigrated in the 1950s; Hugo MacNeill recalling the attitudes in the 1980s of those who stayed to those who emigrated; Joseph O'Connor recalling the pressure on young people to consider emigration in the early 1990s; and Lucy Caldwell recalling her migration from Belfast to England in 1999.

Bibliography

Aalen, F. H. A., Whelan, K. and Stout, M. (1997), *Atlas of the Irish Rural Landscape*, Cork University Press, Cork

Adair, A. S., Berry, J. N., McGreal, W. S. J., Murtagh, B. and Paris, C. (2000), 'The Local Housing System in Craigavon, N. Ireland: Ethno-religious Residential Segregation, Socio-tenurial Polarisation and Sub-markets', *Urban Studies*, 37(7), 1079–1092

Adams, I. and Somerville, M. (1993), *Cargoes of Despair and Hope: Scottish Emigration to North America, 1603–1803*, John Donald, Edinburgh

Adams, W. F. (1932), *Ireland and Irish Emigration to the New World from 1815 to the Famine*, Genealogical Publishing, Baltimore, MD

Agnew, J. (1996), *Belfast Merchant Families in the Seventeenth Century*, Four Courts Press, Dublin

Akenson, D. H. (1973), *Education and Enmity: The Control of Schooling in Northern Ireland, 1920–50*, David & Charles, Newton Abbot

Akenson, D. H. (1984), *The Irish in Ontario: A Study in Rural History*, McGill-Queen's University Press, Montreal, Kingston

Akenson, D. H. (1988; 1991), *Small Differences: Irish Catholics and Irish Protestants, 1815–1922*, McGill-Queen's University Press, Montreal, London

Akenson, D. H. (1993; 1996), *The Irish Diaspora: A Primer*, Institute of Irish Studies, Queen's University, Belfast

Akenson, D. H. (1997a), *If the Irish Ran the World: Montserrat, 1630–1730*, Liverpool University Press, Liverpool

Akenson, D. H. (1997b), 'A Midrash on "Galut", "Exile" and "Diaspora" Rhetoric', in E. M. Crawford, (ed.), *The Hungry Stream: Essays on Emigration and Famine*, Queen's University Belfast Institute of Irish Studies, Belfast, 5–16

Akenson, D. H. (2000), 'No Petty People: Pakeha History and the Historiography of the Irish Diaspora', in L. Fraser (ed.), *A Distant Shore: Irish Migration and New Zealand Settlement*, University of Otago Press, Dunedin, 13–24

Akenson, D. H. (2005a), *An Irish History of Civilization, Volume One*, Granta, London

Akenson, D. H. (2005b), *An Irish History of Civilization, Volume Two*, Granta, London

Alexander, M, (2003), 'Local Policies toward Migrants as an Expression of Host–Stranger Relations: a Proposed Typology, *Journal of Ethnic and Migration Studies*, 29(3), 411–430

Allen, S. (*c*.1982), *To Ulster's Credit*, Plantation Press, Lisburn

Almeida, L. D. (1992), '"And they still haven't found what they're looking for": A Survey of the New Irish in New York City', in P. O'Sullivan (ed.), *The Irish World Wide*, vol. 1, *Patterns of Migration*, Leicester University Press, Leicester, 196–221

Almeida, L. D. (2001), *Irish Immigrants in New York City, 1945–1995*, Indiana University Press, Bloomington, IN

Anbinder, T. (2002), 'From Famine to Five Points: Lord Landsdowne's Tenants Encounter North America's Most Notorious Slum', *American Historical Review*, 107, 351–387

Andall, J. (ed.) (2003), *Gender and Ethnicity in Contemporary Europe*, Berg, London, New York

Anderson, B. (1983), *Imagined Communities: Reflections on the Origin and Spread of Nationalism*, Verso, London

Anderson, J. and Shuttleworth, I. (1994), 'Sectarian Readings of Sectarianism: Interpreting the Northern Ireland Census', *Irish Review*, 16, 74–93

Anderson, J. and Shuttleworth, I. (1998), 'Sectarian Demography, Territoriality and Political Development in Northern Ireland', *Political Geography*, 17(2), 187–208

Anderson, M. and Bort, E. (eds) (1999), *The Irish Border: History, Politics, Culture*, Liverpool University Press, Liverpool

Andrews, J. H. (1975; 1993; 2001), *A Paper Landscape: The Ordnance Survey in Nineteenth-Century Ireland*, Oxford University Press, Oxford

Andrews J. H. (1985), *Plantation Acres: An Historical Study of the Irish Land Surveyor*, Ulster Historical Foundation, Belfast

Andrews, J. H. (1997), *Shapes of Ireland: Maps and Their Makers, 1564–1839*, Geography Publications, Dublin

Anwar, M. (1979), *The Myth of Return: Pakistanis in Britain*, Heinemann, London

Appleby, J. (1989–90), 'Settlers and Pirates in Early Seventeenth-century Ireland: a Profile of Sir William Hull', *Studia Hibernica*, 25, 76–104

Arnold, B. (1997), *A Concise History of Irish Art*, revised edition, Thames & Hudson, Norwich

Arensberg, C. M. and Kimball, S. T. (1940; 1968 edn), *Family and Community in Ireland*, Harvard University Press, Cambridge, MA

Arrowsmith, A. (2000), 'Plastic Paddy: Negotiating Identity in Second Generation Irish-English Writing', *Irish Studies Review*, 8(1), 35–44

Aspinwall, B. (1991), 'The Catholic Irish and Wealth in Glasgow', in T. M. Devine (ed.), *Irish Immigrants and Scottish Society in the Nineteenth and Twentieth Century*, Proceedings of the Scottish Historical Studies Seminar, University of Strathclyde, John Donald, Edinburgh, 91–115

Aughey, A. (2005), *The Politics of Northern Ireland: Beyond the Belfast Agreement*, Routledge, London, New York

Aughton, P. (2003), *Liverpool: A People's History*, Carnegie, Lancaster

Austin, R. et al. (1993), *Plantations: Experiences of Colonisation in the 17th Century*, Northern Ireland Centre for Learning Resources, Belfast

Bade, K. (2003), *Migration in European History*, trans. Allison Brown, Blackwell, Oxford

Bade, K. J., Emmer, P. C., Lucassen, L. and Oltmer, J. (eds) (2007), *Enzyclopädie Migration in Europa: vom 17. Jahrhundert bis zur Gegenwart*, Verlag Ferdinand Schönigh, Paderborn

Bade, K. J. and Weiner, Myron (1997), *Migration Past, Migration Future: Germany and the United States*, Berghahn Books, Providence, RI, Oxford

Bailyn, B. (1986; 1987), *Voyagers to the West: Emigration from Britain to America on the Eve of the Revolution*, Taurus, London

Baines, D. (1985), *Migration in a Mature Economy: Emigration and Internal Migration in England and Wales, 1861–1900*, Cambridge University Press, Cambridge

Baines, D. (1991), *Emigration from Europe, 1815–1930*, Macmillan, Basingstoke

Bairner, A. and Shirlow, P. (2003), 'When Leisure Turns to Fear: Fear, Mobility and Ethno-sectarianism in Belfast', *Leisure Studies*, 22(3), 203–221

Baldassar, L. (2001), *Visits Home: Migration Experiences between Italy and Australia*, Melbourne University Press, Melbourne

Barber, M. (2005),'"Two homes now": the Return Migration of the Fellowship of the Maple Leaf', in M. Harper (ed.), *Emigrant Homecomings: the Return Movement of Emigrants, 1600–2000*, Manchester University Press, Manchester, 197–214

Barber, S. (2005), 'Settlement, Transplantation and Expulsion: a Comparative Study of the Placement of Peoples', in C. Brady and J. Ohlmeyer (eds), *British Interventions in Early Modern Ireland*, Cambridge University Press, Cambridge, 280–298

Bardon, J. (1992), *A History of Ulster*, Blackstaff Press, Belfast

Barnard, T. (1975), *Cromwellian Ireland: English Government and Reform in Ireland 1649–1660*, Oxford University Press, Oxford

Barnard, T. (1993), 'The Political, Material and Mental Culture of the Cork Settlers, c. 1650–1700', in P. O'Flanagan and C. B. Buttimer (eds), *Cork: History & Society*, Geography Publications, Dublin, 1993, 209–266

Barnard, T. (2001), '"Grand metropolis" or "The anus of the world"? The Cultural Life of Eighteenth-century Dublin', in P. Clark and R. Gillespie (eds), *Two Capitals: London and Dublin, 1500–1800*, Oxford University Press, Oxford, 185–210

Barnard, T. (2003), *A New Anatomy of Ireland: The Irish Protestants, 1649–1770*, Yale University Press, New Haven, CT

Barnard, T. C. and Neely, W. G. (eds) (2006), *The Clergy of the Church of Ireland, 1000–2000: Messengers, Watchmen and Stewards*, Four Courts Press, Dublin

Barry, J. (ed.) (1990), *The Tudor and Stuart Town: A Reader in Urban History, 1530–1688*, Longman, Harlow

Bartlett, T. (1990) 'Army and Society in Eighteenth-Century Ireland', in W. A. Maguire (ed.), *Kings in Conflict: The Revolutionary War in Ireland and its Aftermath, 1689–1750*, Blackstaff Press, Belfast, 173–184

Bartlett, T. (2001) 'Britishness, Irishness and the Act of Union', in D. Keogh and K. Whelan (eds), *Acts of Union: The Causes, Contexts, and Consequences of the Act of Union*, Four Courts Press, Dublin, 243–258

Bartlett, T. (2002), '"The Academy of Warre": Military Affairs in Ireland, 1660–1800', *O'Donnell Lecture*, National University of Ireland, Dublin

Bartlett, T. (2004), 'Ireland, Empire and Union, 1690–1801', in K. Kenny (ed.), *Ireland and the British Empire*, Oxford University Press, Oxford, 61–89

Barton, B. (1995), *Northern Ireland and the Second World War*, Ulster Historical Foundation, Belfast

Barton, H. A. (1994), *A Folk Divided: Homeland Swedes and Swedish Americans, 1840–1940*, Southern Illinois University Press, Carbondale, IL

Basu, P. (2005), 'Roots Tourism as Return Movement: Semantics and the Scottish Diaspora', in M. Harper (ed.), *Emigrant Homecomings: the Return Movement of Emigrants, 1600–2000*, Manchester University Press, Manchester, 131–152

Bauder, H. (2006), *Labour Movement: How Migration Regulates Labour Markets*, Oxford University Press, Oxford

Bauer, E. and Thompson, P. (2004), '"She's always the person with a very global vision": the Gender Dynamics of Migration, Narrative Interpretation and the Case of Jamaican Transnational Families', *Gender & History* 16(2), 334–375

Bayly, C. A. (2004), *The Birth of the Modern World, 1780–1914: Global Connections and Comparisons*, Blackwell, Oxford

Beattie, G. (2004), *Protestant Boy*, Granta Books, London

Beckles, H. (1990), '"A Riotous and unruly lot": Irish Indentured Servants and Freemen in the English West Indies, 1644–1713', *William & Mary Quarterly*, 47, 503–522

Beesley, L. (1912; 2004 edn), *The Loss of the SS Titanic*, Kessinger

Beier, A. L. (1985) *Masterless Men: The Vagrancy Problem in England, 1560–1640*, Methuen, London

Belchem, J. (2007), *Irish, Catholic and Scouse: The History of the Liverpool-Irish, 1800–1939*, Liverpool University Press, Liverpool

Belchem, J. and MacRaild, D. M. (2006), 'Cosmopolitan Liverpool', in J. Belchem (ed.), *Liverpool 800: Culture, Character and History*, Liverpool University Press, Liverpool, 311–392

Bell, K., Jarman, N. and Lefebvre, T. (2004), *Migrant Workers in Northern Ireland*, Institute for Conflict Research, Belfast

Bennett, D. (1991; 2005), *The Encyclopaedia of Dublin: Revised and Expanded*, Gill and Macmillan, Dublin

Bertaux-Wiame, I. (1982), 'The Life History Approach to the Study of Internal Migration: How Women and Men came to Paris between the Wars', in P. Thompson, (ed.), *Our Common History: the Transformation of Europe*, Pluto, London

Best, E. J. (1997), *The Huguenots of Lisburn: The Story of the Lost Colony*, Lisburn Historical Society, Lisburn

Betts, J. and Hamilton, J. (2005), *New Migrant Communities in East Tyrone*, Institute for Conflict Research, Belfast

Bew, P. (2007), *Ireland: The Politics of Enmity, 1789–2006*, Oxford University Press, Oxford

Bhabha, H. K. (1994), *The Location of Culture*, Routledge, New York, London

Bianconi, M. O'C. and Watson, S. J. (1962), *Bianconi: King of the Irish Roads*, Allen Figgis, Dublin

Bielenberg, A. (ed.) (2000), *The Irish Diaspora*, Longman, Harlow

Billington, R. A. (1971), *The Genesis of the Frontier Thesis: a Study in Historical Creativity*, Huntingdon Library, San Marino, CA

Bishop, P. (1999), *The Irish Empire*, Boxtree, London

Black, E. (1983), *Paintings, Sculptures and Bronzes in the Collection of The Belfast Harbour Commissioners*, Belfast Harbour Commissioners, Belfast

Black, J. and MacRaild, D. M. (1997; 2000), *Studying History*, Palgrave Macmillan, Basingstoke

Black, R. and Saskia, G. (2006), 'Sustainable Return in Post-conflict Contexts', *International Migration*, 44(3), 15–38

Blethen, H. T. and Wood, C. W. (eds) (1997), *Ulster and North America: Transatlantic Perspectives on the Scotch-Irish*, University of Alabama Press, Tuscaloosa, AL

Boal, F. W. (1967), 'Contemporary Belfast and its Future Development', in J. C. Beckett and R. E. Glasscock (eds), *Belfast: Origin and Growth of an Industrial City*, BBC, London

Boal, F. W. (1987), 'Segregation', in M. Pacione (ed.), *Social Geography: Progress and Prospects*, London, Croom Helm

Boal, F. W. (1995), *Shaping a City: Belfast in the Late Twentieth Century*, Institute of Irish Studies, Queen's University, Belfast

Boal, F. W. (ed.) (2000), *Ethnicity and Housing: Accommodating Differences*, Ashgate, Aldershot

Boal, F. W. (2006), 'Big Processes and Little People: The Population of Metropolitan Belfast, 1901–2001', in F. W. Boal and S. A. Royle (eds), *Enduring City: Belfast in the Twentieth Century*, Blackstaff Press, Belfast, 56–83

Boal, F. W. and Douglas, J. N. (1982), *Integration and Division: Geographical Perspectives on the Northern Ireland Problem*, Academic Press, London

Booth, J. (1992), *A Vision of Ireland: Jack B. Yeats*, Thomas and Lochar, Nairn

Borsay, P. and Proudfoot, L. (eds) (2002), *Provincial Towns in Early Modern Ireland: Change, Convergence and Divergence*, Oxford University Press, Oxford

Böss, M. (2002), 'The Postmodern Nation: a Critical History of the "Fifth Province" Discourse', *Études Irlandaises*, 27(1), 139–159

Bottigheimer K. S. (1978), 'Kingdom and Colony: Ireland in the Westward Enterprise, 1536–1660', in K. R. Andrews, N. Canny and P. E. Hair (eds), *The Westward Enterprise: English Activities in Ireland, the Atlantic and America, 1480–1650*, Liverpool University Press, Liverpool, 45–66

Bourke, J. (1993), *Husbandry to Housewifery: Women, Economic Change, and Housework in Ireland, 1890–1914*, Oxford University Press, Oxford

Bowen, D. (1970), *Souperism: Myth or Reality? A Study of Catholics and Protestants during the Great Famine*, Mercier, Cork

Bowen, D. (1978), *The Protestant Crusade in Ireland, 1800–1870*, Gill and Macmillan, Dublin

Bowen, K. (1983), *Protestants in a Catholic State: Ireland's Privileged Minority*, Gill and Macmillan, Dublin/McGill-Queen University Press, Kingston, Ontario

Boyd, G. A. (2006), *Dublin 1745–1922: Hospitals, Spectacle and Vice*, Four Courts Press, Dublin

Boyd, M. (1989), 'Family and Personal Networks in International Migration: Recent Developments and New Agendas', *International Migration Review*, 23, 638–670

Boyle, K. and Hadden, T. (1994), *Northern Ireland: The Choice*, London, Penguin

Boyle, P. and Halfacree, K. (1999), *Migration and Gender in the Developed World*, Routledge, London

Bracken, D. (2001), 'Piracy and Poverty: Aspects of the Irish Jacobite Experience in France, 1691–1720', in T. O'Connor (ed.), *The Irish in Europe 1580–1815*, Four Courts Press, Dublin, 127–142

Bradley, W. J. (2000), *Gallon: the History of Three Townlands in County Tyrone from the Earliest Times to the Present Day*, Guildhall Press, Derry

Brady, B., Faul, D. and Murray, R. (1975) *Internment, 1971–1975*, The Authors, Dungannon

Brady, C. (1994), *Interpreting Irish History: the Debate on Historical Revisionism, 1938–1994*, Irish Academic Press, Dublin

Brady, C. (1995), 'Comparable Histories? Tudor Reform in Wales and Ireland', in S. G. Ellis and S. Barber (eds), *Conquest & Union: Fashioning a British State, 1485–1725*, Longman, London

Brady, C. (1996), 'The Captains' Game: Army and Society in Elizabethan Ireland', in T. Bartlett and K. Jeffrey (eds), *A Military History of Ireland*, Cambridge University Press, Cambridge, 136–159

Brady, J. (2001), 'Dublin at the Turn of the Century', in J. Brady and A. Simms (eds), *Dublin Through Space and Time*, Four Courts Press, Dublin, 221–282

Brah, A. (1996), *Cartographies of Diaspora: Contesting Identities*, Routledge, London

Braziel, J. E. and Mannur, A. (eds) (2003), *Theorizing Diaspora: A Reader*, Blackwell, Oxford

Breathnach, C. (2005), *The Congested Districts Board of Ireland, 1891–1923: Poverty and Development in the West of Ireland*, Four Courts Press, Dublin

Brendon, P. (2007), *The Decline and Fall of the British Empire, 1781–1997*, Jonathan Cape, London

Brett, C. E. B. (1986), *Housing a Divided Society*, Institute of Public Administration, Belfast, Dublin

Brettell, C. B. and Hollifield, J. F. (eds) (2000), *Migration Theory: Talking across Disciplines*, Routledge, New York

Brewer, J. (1989), *The Sinews of Power: War, Money and the English State, 1688–1783*, Routledge, New York

Bridge, C. and Fedorowich, K. (2003), *The British World: Diaspora, Culture and Identity*, Frank Cass, London

Briscoe, M. L. (ed.) (1994), *Thomas Mellon and His Times*, Centre for Emigration Studies, Ulster American Folk Park, Omagh

Broderick, M. (1994), *History of Cobh (Queenstown), Ireland*, Carraig, Cobh

Brown, M. E. (1991), 'The Adoption of the Tactics of the Enemy: The Care of Italian Immigrant Youth in the Archdiocese of New York during the Progressive Era', in W. Pencak, W. Berrol and S. and R. M. Miller (eds), *Immigration to New York*, Balch Institute, Philadelphia, 109–125

Brubaker, W. R. (1989), *Immigration and the Politics of Citizenship in Europe and America*, University Press of America, Lanham, MD

Brunicardi, N. (1987), *John Anderson Entrepreneur*, Eigse Books, Fermoy

Bryan, D. (2003), 'Rituals of Irish Protestantism and Orangeism: The Transnational Grand Orange Lodge of Ireland', *European Studies: A Journal of European Culture, History and Politics*, 19, 105–123

Buchanan, R. H. and Wilson, A. (1977), *Downpatrick: Irish Historic Towns Atlas*, 8, Royal Irish Academy, Dublin

Buckely, A. D. and Anderson, T. K. (1988), *Brotherhoods in Ireland*, Ulster Folk and Transport Museum, Cultra

Budge, I. and O'Leary, C. (1973), *Belfast: Approach to Crisis. A Study of Belfast Politics, 1613–1970*, Macmillan, London

Burke, H. (1987), *The People and the Poor Law in 19th-Century Ireland*, Women's Education Bureau, Littlehampton

Burke, K. (2005), 'Canada in Britain: Returned Migrants and the Canada Club', in M. Harper (ed.), *Emigrant Homecomings: the Return Movement of Emigrants, 1600–2000*, Manchester University Press, Manchester, 184–196

Burton, F. (1978), *The Politics of Legitimacy: Struggles in a Belfast Community*, Routledge & Kegan Paul, London

Butler, D. J. (2006), *South Tipperary, 1570–1841: Religion, Land and Rivalry*, Four Courts Press, Dublin

Butlin, R. A. (1965), 'The Population of Dublin in the late Seventeenth Century', *Irish Geography*, V(2), 51–66

Butlin, R. A. (1976), 'Land and People c. 1600', in T. W. Moody, F. X. Martin and F. J. Byrne (eds), *A New History of Ireland*, vol. III, *Early Modern Ireland, 1536–1691*, Oxford University Press, Oxford, 587–633

Butlin, R. A. (1977), *The Development of the Irish Town*, Croom Helm, London

Byrne, J. (2004), *Out of Sight: Young People and Paramilitary Exiling in Northern Ireland*, Institute for Conflict Research, Belfast

Byrne, J. (1997), *War and Peace: The Survival of the Talbots of Malahide, 1641–1671*, Irish Academic Press, Dublin

Byron, R. (1999), *Irish America*, Clarendon, Oxford

Caldicott, C. E. J., Gough, H. and Pitman, J.–P. (1987), *The Huguenots and Ireland: Anatomy of an Emigration*, Glendale Press, Dún Laoghaire

Campbell, M. (2000), 'Immigrants on the Land: a Comparative Study of Irish Rural Settlement in Nineteenth-Century Minnesota and New South Wales', in A. Bielenberg, (ed.), *The Irish Diaspora*, Pearson Education, Harlow, 176–194

Campbell, M. (2008), *Ireland's New Worlds: Immigrants, Politics, and Society in the United States and Australia, 1815-1922*, University of Wisconsin Press, Madison

Campey, L. H. (2002), *Fast Sailing and Copper-Bottomed: Aberdeen Sailing Ships and the Emigrant Scots They Carried to Canada, 1774–1855*, Natural Heritage Books, Toronto

Canny, N. (1970), 'Hugh O'Neill, Earl of Tyrone, and the Changing Face of Gaelic Ulster', *Studia Hibernica*, X, 27–35

Canny, N. (1982), *The Upstart Earl: A Study of the Social and Mental World of Richard Boyle, First Earl of Cork, 1566–1643*, Cambridge University Press, Cambridge

Canny, N. (1985), 'Migration and Opportunity: Britain, Ireland and the New World', *Irish Economic and Social History*, XII, 7–33

Canny, N. (1986), 'Debate Reply', *Irish Economic and Social History*, XIII, 96–100

Canny, N. (1988), *Kingdom and Colony: Ireland in the Atlantic World, 1500–1800*, Johns Hopkins University Press, Baltimore, MD

Canny, N. (1991), 'The Marginal Kingdom: Ireland as a Problem in the First British Empire', in B. Bailyn and P. D. Morgan (eds), *Strangers within the Realm*, University of North Carolina Press, Chapel Hill, NC, 35–67

Canny, N. (1994a), 'English Migration into and across the Atlantic during the Seventeenth and Eighteenth Centuries', in N. Canny (ed.), *Europeans on the Move: Studies on European Migration, 1500–1800*, Oxford University Press, Oxford, 39–76

Canny, N. (1994b), 'In Search of a Better Home? European Overseas Migration, 1500–1800', in N. Canny (ed.), *Europeans on the Move: Studies on European Migration, 1500–1800*, Oxford University Press, Oxford, 263–283

Canny, N. (1998), 'England's New World and the Old, 1480s–1630s', in N. Canny (ed.), *The Oxford History of the British Empire, I: The Origins of Empire to 1689*, Oxford University Press, Oxford, 148–170

Canny, N. (2001), *Making Ireland British, 1580–1650*, Oxford University Press, Oxford

Carleton, W. and O'Donoghue, D. J. (1896; 1996 edn), *The Life of William Carleton*, Downey, London

Carolan, N. (1997), *A Harvest Saved: Francis O'Neill and Irish Music in Chicago*, Ossian, Cork

Carr, P. (2003; 2005), *Portavo: An Irish Townland and its Peoples, Part One; Part Two*, Whiterow Press, Belfast

Carroll, F. M. (1978), *American Opinion and the Irish Question, 1910–1923*, Gill and Macmillan, Dublin

Carroll-Burke, P. (2000), *Colonial Discipline: The Making of the Irish Convict System*, Four Courts Press, Dublin

Carter, T. (2005), 'The migration of sporting labour into Ireland', in A. Bairner (ed), *Sport and the Irish: Histories, Identities, Issues*, University College Dublin Press, Dublin, 191–205

Carty, J. (1949; 1951), *Ireland from the Flight of the Earls to Grattan's Parliament (1607–1782): A Documentary Record*, Fallon, Dublin

Carty, T. J. (2004), *A Catholic in the White House? Religion, Politics and John F. Kennedy's Presidential Campaign*, Palgrave Macmillan, Basingstoke

Casey, M. R. (2002), 'Refractive History: Memory and the Founders of the Emigrant Savings Bank', *Radharc*, 3, 74–107; rept. (2006), in J. J. Lee and Marion R. Casey (eds), *Making the Irish American: History and Heritage of the Irish in the United States*, New York University Press, New York, 302–331

Casserley, H. C. (1974), *Outline of Irish Railway History*, David & Charles, Newton Abbot

Castles, S. and Miller, M. J. (1998; 2003), *The Age of Migration*, Palgrave Macmillan, Basingstoke

Casway, J. (1991), 'Irish Women Overseas, 1500–1800', in M. MacCurtain and M. O'Dowd (eds), *Women in Early Modern Ireland*, Wolfhound Press, Dublin, 112–132

Chadwick, O. (1995), *A History of Christianity*, Weidenfeld & Nicolson, London

Chaliand, G. and Rageau, J. P. (1995), *Penguin Atlas of Diasporas*, Penguin, Harmondsworth

Chambers, I. (1994), *Migrancy, Culture, Identity*, Routledge, London, New York

Chan, S. (2006), '"God's Little Acre" and "Belfast Chinatown": Cultural Politics and Agencies of Anti-Racist Spatial Inscription', *Translocations: The Irish Migration, Race and Social Transformation Review*, 1(1), 56–75

Christopher, A. J. (1995), 'The Apartheid City: its Development and Future', *Geographical Viewpoint*, 23(1), 76–87

Church, R. (ed.) (2000), *A Miscellany of British and Irish Vagrants Passing through Wiltshire 1790 to 1796*, 2, Wiltshire Family History Society, Devizes

Clark, D. J. (1977), *Irish Blood: Northern Ireland and the American Conscience*, Kennikat Press, Port Washington, NY

Clark, D. (1995), 'Irish Women Workers and American Labor Patterns: the Philadelphia Story', in P. O'Sullivan (ed.), *The Irish World Wide: History, Heritage, Identity*, vol. 4, *Irish Women and Irish Migration*, Leicester University Press, Leicester, 113–130

Clark, P. and Slack, P. (1976), *English Towns in Transition, 1500–1700*, Oxford University Press, Oxford

Clark, P. (1983), *The English Alehouse: A Social History 1200–1830*, Longman, London

Clark, P. (1987), 'Migrants in the City: the Process of Social Adaptation in English Towns, 1500–1800', in P. Clark and D. Souden (eds), *Migration and Society in Early Modern England*, Hutchinson, London, 267–291

Clark, P. and Gillespie, R. (2001), *Two Capitals: London and Dublin, 1500–1840*, Oxford University Press, Oxford

Clark, P. and Souden, D. (eds) (1987), *Migration and Society in Early Modern England*, Hutchinson, London

Clarke, D. (1957), *Arthur Dobbs Esquire, 1689–1765: Surveyor-General of Ireland, Prospector and Governor of North Carolina*, University of North Carolina Press, Chapel Hill, NC

Clarkson, L. A. (1997), 'Population Change in County Down 1841–1911', in L. Proudfoot and W. Nolan (eds), *Down History and Society*, Geography Publications, Dublin, 383–404

Clarkson, L. A. (2005), 'Armagh Town in the Eighteenth Century', in B. Collins, P. Ollerenshaw and T. Parkhill (eds), *Industry, Trade and People in Ireland, 1650–1950*, Ulster Historical Foundation, Belfast, 51–68

Clarkson, L. A. and Crawford, E. M. (1985), *Ways to Wealth: The Cust Family of Eighteenth-century Armagh*, Ulster Society for Irish Historical Studies, Belfast

Clear, C. (1987), *Nuns in Nineteenth-century Ireland*, Gill and Macmillan, Dublin

Clear, C. (2007), *Social Change and Everyday Life in Ireland, 1850–1922*, Manchester University Press, Manchester

Clinch, P., Convery, F. and Walsh, B. (eds) (2002), *After the Celtic Tiger: Challenges Ahead*, O'Brien Press, Dublin

CMS IED, Centre for Migration Studies Irish Emigration database, www.qub.ac.uk/cms

Coakley, J. (2004), *Ethnic Conflict and the Two-state Solution: the Irish Experience of Partition* (42), Institute for British-Irish Studies, University College Dublin

Coakley, J. and O'Dowd, L. (2005), *The Irish Border and North–South Co-operation: an Overview* (47), Institute for British–Irish Studies, University College Dublin

Coakley, J. and O'Dowd, L. (2007), 'Partition and the Reconfiguration of the Irish Border', *Political Geography*, 26(8), 877–885

Coffey, L-A. (2006), *The Planters of Luggacurran, County Laois: A Protestant Community, 1879–1927*, Maynooth Studies in Local History 68, Four Courts Press, Dublin

Cohen, A. (1985), *The Symbolic Construction of Community*, Routledge, London

Cohen, M. (1995), 'The Migration Experience of Female-headed Households: Gilford, Co. Down to Greenwich, New York, 1880–1910', in P. O'Sullivan (ed.), *The Irish World*

Wide: History, Heritage, Identity, vol. 4, *Irish Women and Irish Migration,* Leicester University Press, Leicester, 131–145

Cohen, M. (1997), *Linen, Family and Community in Tullylish, County Down, 1690–1914,* Four Courts Press, Dublin

Cohen, R. (1997), *Global Diasporas: an Introduction,* UCL Press, London

Cole, J. (ed.) (2000), *A Miscellany of British and Irish Vagrants Passing through Wiltshire: Vagrants' Passes in the Wiltshire County Treasurers' Finance Papers, 1702–05; 1708–12; 1740–42; 1774–76,* 3, Wiltshire Family History Society, Devizes

Coleman, D. A. (1999), 'Demography and Migration in Ireland, North and South', in A. F. Heath, R. Breen and C. T. Whelan (eds), *Ireland North and South: Perspectives from Social Science,* Oxford University Press, Oxford, 69–116

Coleman, T. (1972), *Passage to America: a History of Emigrants from Great Britain and Ireland to America in the mid-Nineteenth Century,* Hutchinson, London

Collins, B. (1993), 'The Irish in Britain, 1780–1921', in B. J. Graham and L. J. Proudfoot (eds), *An Historical Geography of Ireland,* Academic Press, London, 366–398

Collins, B. (1994), *Flax to Fabric: the Story of Irish Linen,* Irish Linen Centre, Lisburn

Collins, B. (1997), 'The Linen Industry and Emigration to Britain during the mid-Nineteenth Century', in E. M. Crawford, (ed.), *The Hungry Stream,* Institute of Irish Studies, Belfast, 151–160

Collinson, S. (1993), *Europe and International Migration,* Royal Institute of International Affairs, London

Collyer, M. (2005), 'When Do Social Networks Fail to Explain Migration? Accounting for the Movement of Algerian Asylum Seekers to the UK', *Journal of Ethnic and Migration Studies,* 31(4), 699–718

Comerford, R. V. (1998), *The Fenians in Context: Irish Politics and Society, 1848–82,* Wolfhound Press, Dublin

Compton, P. A. (1995), *Demographic Review Northern Ireland,* Northern Ireland Economic Development Office, Belfast

Compton, P. and Power, J. (1986), 'Estimates of the Religious Composition of Northern Ireland Local Government Districts in 1981 and Change in the Geographical Pattern of Religious Composition between 1971 and 1981', *Economic and Social Review,* 17, 87–105

Connolly, S. J. (1982), *Priests and People in Pre-Famine Ireland, 1780–1845,* Gill and Macmillan, Dublin/St Martin's Press, New York

Connolly, S. J. (1992), *Religion, Law and Power: The Making of Protestant Ireland, 1660–1760,* Oxford University Press, Oxford

Connolly, S. J. (ed.) (1998), *The Oxford Companion to Irish History,* Oxford University Press, Oxford

Connolly, S. J. (2007), *Contested Island: Ireland, 1460–1630,* Oxford University Press, Oxford

Connolly, T. (2000), 'Irish Workers in Britain during World War Two', in B. Girvan and G. Roberts (eds), *Ireland and the Second World War: Politics, Society and Remembrance,* Four Courts Press, Dublin, 121–132

Conroy, P., McKearney, T. and Oliver, Q. (2005), *All over the Place: People Displaced to and from the Southern Border Counties as a Result of the Conflict 1969–1994,* European Union House, Monaghan

Conway, M. and Byrne, J. (2005), *Interface Issues: An Annotated Bibliography,* Institute for Conflict Research, Belfast

Coogan, T. P. (2000), *Wherever Green is Worn: the Story of the Irish Diaspora,* Random, London

Cookson, J. E. (1997), *The British Armed Nation, 1793–1815*, Oxford University Press, Oxford

Corcoran, M. P. (1993), *Irish Illegals: Transients between Two Societies*, Greenwood Press, Westport, CT

Corcoran, M. P. (1999), 'Emigration: the End of the Irish Wake', in M. Glazier (ed.), *The Encyclopedia of the Irish in America*, University of Notre Dame Press, South Bend, IN, 266–268

Corcoran, M. P. (2003), 'The Process of Migration and the Reinvention of Self: the Experiences of Returning Irish Emigrants', in K. Kenny (ed.), *New Directions in Irish-American History*, University of Wisconsin Press, Madison, WI, 302–318

Corcoran, M. P, Keaveney, K. and Duffy, P. J. (2007), 'Transformations in Housing', in B. Bartley and R. Kitichin (eds), *Understanding Contemporary Ireland*, Pluto, London, Dublin, Ann Arbor, MI, 249–263

Corfield, P. J. (1982), *The Impact of English Towns, 1700–1800*, Oxford University Press, Oxford

Coughlan, P. (1999), 'An Léiriú ar Shaol na mBan i dTéacsanna Dírbheathaisnéise Pheig Sayers', in M. Ní Chéileachair (eag), *Peig Sayers Scéalai 1873–1958* , Ceiliúradh an Bhlascaoid 3, Coiscéim, Baile Átha Cliath, 20–57

Coughlan, P. (2003), 'Sayers, Peig', in B. Lalor (ed.), *Encyclopaedia of Ireland*, Gill and Macmillan, Dublin, 963–964

Courtney, D. (2000), 'A Quantification of Irish Migration with Particular Emphasis on the 1980s and 1990s', in A. Bielenberg (ed.), *The Irish Diaspora*, Pearson Education, Harlow, 287–316

Cousens, S. H. (1960), 'The Regional Pattern of Emigration during the Great Irish Famine, 1846–1851', *Institute of British Geographers Transactions and Papers*, 28, 119–134

Cousens, S. H. (1965), 'The Regional Variation in Emigration from Ireland between 1821 and 1841', *Institute of British Geographers Transactions and Papers*, 37, 15–30

Cowan, A. (1998), *Urban Europe, 1500–1700*, Arnold, London

Cowan, P. C. (1918), *Report on Dublin Housing*, Cahill, Dublin

Cowley, U. (2001), *The Men Who Built Britain: A History of the Irish Navvy*, Wolfhound Press, Dublin

Craig, M. (1969), *Dublin, 1660–1860*, Allen Figgis, Dublin

Crawford, E. M. (1997), 'Migrant Melodies: Unseen Lethal Baggage', in E. M. Crawford (ed.), *The Hungry Stream: Essays on Emigration and Famine*, Institute of Irish Studies, Queen's University, Belfast and Centre for Emigration Studies, Ulster-American Folk Park, Omagh, 137–150

Crawford, E. M. (ed.) (1997), *The Hungry Stream: Essays on Emigration and Famine*, Queen's University, Belfast Institute of Irish Studies, Belfast and Centre for Migration Studies, Ulster-American Folk Park, Omagh

Crawford, E. M. (1999), 'Typhus in Nineteenth-Century Ireland', in G. Jones and E. Malcolm (eds), *Medicine, Disease and the State in Ireland, 1650–1940*, Cork University Press, Cork, 121–137

Crawford, E. M. (2003), *Counting the People: A Survey of Irish Censuses, 1813–1911*, Maynooth Research Guides for Irish Local History, 6, Four Courts Press, Dublin

Crawford, W. H. (1975), 'Landlord–Tenant Relations in Ulster, 1609–1820', *Irish Economic and Social History*, II, 5–21

Crawford, W. H. (1994), *The Handloom Weavers and the Ulster Linen Industry*, Ulster Historical Foundation, Belfast

Crawford, W. H. (2001), 'Evolution of Towns in County Armagh', in A. J. Hughes and W. Nolan (eds), *Armagh: History & Society*, Geography Publications, Dublin, 851–880

Crawford, W. H. (2002), 'The Creation and Evolution of Small Towns in Ulster in the Seventeenth and Eighteenth Centuries', in P. Borsay and L. Proudfoot (eds), *Provincial Towns in Early Modern England and Ireland: Change, Convergence and Divergence*, Oxford University Press, Oxford, 97–120

Crawford, W. H. (2005), *The Impact of the Domestic Linen Industry in Ulster*, Ulster Historical Foundation, Belfast

Crawford, W. H. and Foy, R. H. (eds) (1998), *Townlands in Ulster: Local History Studies*, Ulster Historical Foundation, Belfast

Crawley, H. (2006), 'Forced Migration and the Politics of Asylum: the Missing Pieces of the International Migration Puzzle?', *International Migration*, 44(1), 21–26

Cregan, D. F. (1970), 'Irish Recusant Lawyers in Politics in the Reign of James I', *Irish Jurist*, ns v, 306–320

Cromie, H. (1976; 1984), *Ulster Settlers in America*, Universities Press, Belfast

Cronin, M. and Adair, D. (2002), *The Wearing of the Green: A History of St Patrick's Day*, Routledge, London, New York

Cronin, S. (1987), *Washington's Irish Policy, 1916–1986: Independence, Partition, Neutrality*, Anvil Books, Dublin

Crookshank, A. and the Knight of Glin (2002), *Ireland's Painters, 1600–1940*, Yale University Press, London

Crossman, V. (2006), *The Poor Law in Ireland, 1838–1948*, Studies in Irish Economic and Social History 10, Dundalgan Press, Dublin

Crowley, J., Devoy, R., Linehan, D. and O'Flanagan, P. (eds) (2005), *Atlas of Cork City*, Cork University Press, Cork

Crowley, U. M. (2005) 'Liberal Rule through non-Liberal Means: the Attempted Settlement of Irish Travellers, 1955–1975', *Irish Geography* 38(2), 128–150

Cullen, F. and Foster, R. F. (2005), '*Conquering England': Ireland in Victorian London*, National Portrait Gallery, London

Cullen, K. J., Whatley, C. A. and Young, M. (2006), 'King William III's Years: New Evidence on the Impact of Scarcity and Harvest Failure during the Crisis of the 1690s on Tayside', *Scottish Historical Review*, 85(2), 250–276

Cullen, L. M (1968), *Anglo-Irish Trade, 1660–1800*, Manchester University Press, Manchester

Cullen, L. M. (1975), 'Population Trends in Seventeenth-Century Ireland', *Economic and Social Review*, 6, 149–165

Cullen, L. M. (1981), *The Emergence of Modern Ireland, 1600–1900*, Gill and Macmillan, Dublin

Cullen, L. M. (1986a), 'Economic Development, 1691–1750', in T. W. Moody and W. E. Vaughan (eds), *A New History of Ireland, IV: Eighteenth Century Ireland*, Oxford University Press, Oxford, 123–195

Cullen, L. M. (1986b), 'Man, Landscape and Roads: The Changing Eighteenth Century', in W. Nolan (ed.), *The Shaping of Ireland: The Geographical Perspective*, Mercier Press, Dublin, 123–136

Cullen, L. M. (1992), 'The Growth of Dublin 1600–1900: Character and Heritage', in F. H. A. Allen and K. Whelan (eds), *Dublin, City and County: From Prehistory to Present*, Geography Publications, Dublin, 251–278

Cullen, L. M. (1994), 'The Irish Diaspora of the Seventeenth and Eighteenth Centuries', in N. Canny (ed.), *Europeans on the Move: Studies on European Migration 1500–1800*, Oxford University Press, Oxford, 113–149

Cullen, P. (2000), *Refugees and Asylum Seekers in Ireland*, Cork University Press, Cork

Cullen Owens, R. (2005), *A Social History of Women in Ireland, 1870–1970*, Gill and Macmillan, Dublin

Cunningham, J. B. (2006), 'The Lost English Plantation of Fermanagh', in B. S. Turner (ed.), *Migration and Myth: Ulster's Revolving Door*, Ulster Local History Trust, Downpatrick, 92–96

Curl, S. (1986), *The Londonderry Plantation, 1609–1914*, Phillimore, Chichester

Curry, P. (2000), '"… she never let them in": Popular Reactions to Refugees Arriving in Dublin', in M. MacLachlan and M. O'Connell (eds), *Cultivating Pluralism: Psychological, Social and Cultural Perspectives on a Changing Ireland*, Oak Tree Press, Dublin, 137–152

Curtin, C., Donnan, H. and Wilson, T. M. (eds) (1993), *Irish Urban Cultures*, Institute of Irish Studies, The Queen's University, Belfast

Cutler, D. M., Glaeser, E. L. and Vigdor, J. L. (2007), *When are Ghettos Bad? Lessons from Immigrant Segregation in the United States*, National Bureau of Economic Research, Cambridge, MA

Cwerner, S. B. (2001), 'The Times of Migration', *Journal of Ethnic and Migration Studies*, 27(1), 7–36

Daly, M. (1981), *Social and Economic History of Ireland since 1800*, Educational Company of Ireland, Dublin

Daly, M. (1997), *Women and Work in Ireland*, Dundalgan Press, Dublin

Daly, M. (2006a), 'Forty Shades of Grey? Irish Historiography and the Challenges of Multidisciplinarity', in L. Harte and Y. Whelan (eds), *Ireland Beyond Boundaries: Mapping Irish Studies in the Twenty-first Century*, Pluto, London, 92–110

Daly, M. (2006b), *The Slow Failure: Population Decline and Independent Ireland, 1920–1973*, University of Wisconsin Press, Madison, WI

Daniels, R. (1991), *Coming to America: A History of Immigration and Ethnicity in American Life*, HarperPerennial, New York

Darby, J. (1986), *Intimidation and the Control of the Conflict in Northern Ireland*, Gill and Macmillan, Dublin

Darby, J. (1988), 'Twentieth Century Settlers', in P. Loughrey (ed.), *The People of Ireland*, Appletree Press, Belfast

Davidson, N. (2003), *Discovering the Scottish Revolution, 1692–1746*, Pluto, London

Davies, N. (1996; 1997), *Europe: A History*, Oxford University Press, Oxford/Pimlico, London

Davis, E. (1889), *Souvenirs of Irish Footprints over Europe*, Freeman's Journal, Dublin

Davis, G. (1991), *The Irish in Britain, 1815–1914*, Gill and Macmillan, Dublin

Dawe, G. (2007), *My Mother-City*, Lagan Press, Belfast

Dawson, G. (2007), *Making peace with the past? Memory, trauma and the Irish Troubles*, Manchester University Press, Manchester

Day, A. and McWilliams, P. (eds) (1994), *Ordnance Survey Memoirs of Ireland*, vol. 25, *Parishes of County Londonderry vii, Tamlaght Finlagan*, Institute of Irish Studies, Queen's University, Belfast

Day, A. and McWilliams, P. (eds) (1995), *Ordnance Survey Memoirs of Ireland*, vol. 28, *Parishes of County Londonderry ix, West Londonderry*, Institute of Irish Studies, Queen's University, Belfast

Day, A. and McWilliams, P. (eds) (1996a), *Ordnance Survey Memoirs of Ireland*, vol. 36, *Parishes of County Londonderry xiv, Faughanvale*, Institute of Irish Studies, Queen's University, Belfast

Day, A. and McWilliams, P. (eds) (1996b), *Ordnance Survey Memoirs of Ireland*, vol. 34, *Parishes of County Londonderry xiii, Clondermot and The Waterside*, Institute of Irish Studies, Queen's University, Belfast

De Crevecoeur, H. St J. (1782), *Letters from an American Farmer*, London

De Fréine, S. (1956), *The Great Silence*, Foilseacháin Náisiúnta Teoranta, Dublin

Delaney, E. (2000), *Demography, State and Society: Irish Migration to Britain, 1921–1971*, Liverpool University Press, Liverpool

Delaney, E. (2002), *Irish Emigration Since 1921*, Economic and Social History Society of Ireland, Dublin

Delaney, E. (2005a), 'Emigration, Political Cultures and the Evolution of Post-war Irish Society', in B. Girvin and G. Murphy (eds), *The Lemass Era: Politics and Society in the Ireland of Seán Lemass*, University College Dublin Press, Dublin

Delaney, E. (2005b), 'Transnationalism, Networks and Emigration from Post-war Ireland', *Immigrants & Minorities*, 23(2/3), 425–446

Delaney, E. (2006), 'The Irish Diaspora', *Irish Economic and Social History*, XXXIII, 35–45

Delaney, E. (2007), *The Irish in Post-War Britain*, Oxford University Press, Oxford

Delaney, E. and MacRaild, D. M. (eds) (2007), *Irish Migration, Networks and Ethnic Identities Since 1750*, Routledge, Abingdon

Dennehy, Archdeacon (1923), *History of the Great Island, Ancient Cove and Modern Queenstown*, Guy, Cork

Department of the Environment and Local Government (2002), *The National Spatial Strategy: 2002–2020 People, Places, Potential*, Stationery Office, Dublin

Department of Regional Development (2001), *Shaping Our Future: Regional Development Strategy for Northern Ireland 2005*, Corporate Document Services, Belfast

Devine, T. M. (ed.) (1991), *Irish Immigrants and Scottish Society in the Nineteenth and Twentieth Centuries: Proceedings of the Scottish Historical Studies Seminar, University of Strathclyde, 1989/90*, John Donald, Edinburgh

Devine, T. M. (1992), 'Introduction: The Paradox of Scottish Emigration', in T. M. Devine (ed.), *Scottish Emigration and Scottish Society*, John Donald, Edinburgh, 1–15

Devine, T. M. (1999), *The Scottish Nation: A History, 1700–2000*, Penguin, London

Devine, T. M. (2003), *Scotland's Empire, 1600–1815*, Penguin, London

Devlin, P. (1983; 2003), *All of Us There*, Virago, London

De Vries, J. (1984), *European Urbanisation, 1500–1800*, Methuen, London

Dezell, M. (2000), *Irish America, Coming into Clover: The Evolution of a People and a Culture*, Doubleday, New York

Dickson, D. (1983) 'The Place of Dublin in the Eighteenth-century Irish Economy', in T. M. Devine and D. Dickson (eds), *Ireland and Scotland 1600–1850: Parallels and Contrasts in Economic and Social Development*, John Donald, Edinburgh

Dickson, D. (1989), 'The Gap in Famines: A Useful Myth?', in E. M. Crawford (ed.), *Famine: The Irish Experience: 900–1900*, John Donald, Edinburgh, 96–111

Dickson, D. (1991), '"No Scythians Here": Women and Marriage in Seventeenth-century Ireland', in M. MacCurtain and M. O'Dowd (eds), *Women in Early Modern Ireland*, Wolfhound Press, Dublin, 223–233

Dickson, D. (1997), *Arctic Ireland: The Extraordinary Story of the Great Frost and Forgotten Famine of 1740–41*, White Row Press, Belfast

Dickson, D. (2000), *New Foundations: Ireland 1660–1800*, Irish Academic Press, Dublin

Dickson, D. (2005), *Old World Colony: Cork and South Munster 1630–1830*, Cork University Press, Cork

Dickson, R. J. (1966; 1988), *Ulster Emigration to Colonial America, 1718–1775*, Routledge and Kegan Paul, London; Ulster Historical Foundation, Belfast

Diner, H. (1983), *Erin's Daughters in America: Irish Immigrant Women in the Nineteenth Century*, Johns Hopkins University Press, Baltimore, MD, London

Doan, J. E. (2000), 'The Eagle Wing Expedition (1636) and the Settlement of Londonderry, New Hampshire (1719)', *Journal of Scotch-Irish Studies*, 1(1), 1–17

Docherty, R. (2000), 'Irish Heroes of the Second World War', in B. Girvan and G. Roberts (eds), *Ireland and the Second World War: Politics, Society and Remembrance*, Four Courts Press, Dublin

Doherty, G. and Keogh, D. (2003), *De Valera's Ireland*, Mercier, Dublin

Doherty, P. and Poole, M. A. (2000), 'Living Apart in Belfast: Residential Segregation in a Context of Ethnic Conflict', in F. W. Boal (ed.), *Ethnicity and Housing: Accommodating Differences*, Ashgate, Aldershot, 179–189

Donnelly, J. S. Jr (2001), *The Great Irish Potato Famine*, Sutton, Stroud

Dooley, T. (2000), *The Plight of the Monaghan Protestants, 1912–26*, Four Courts Press, Dublin

Dooley, T. (2004), *'The Land for the People': The Land Question in Independent Ireland*, UCD Press, Dublin

Dougherty, J. E. (2001), 'Mr and Mrs England: the Act of Union as National Marriage', in D. Keogh and K. Whelan (eds), *Acts of Union: The Causes, Contexts and Consequences of the Act of Union*, Four Courts Press, Dublin, 202–215

Dowling, M. (1999), *Tenant Right and Agrarian Society in Ulster, 1600–1850*, Irish Academic Press, Dublin

Downey, D. (2002), 'Wild Geese and the Double-Headed Eagle: Irish Integration in Austria, c. 1630–c.1918, in P. Leifer and E. Sagarra (eds), *Austro-Irish Links Through the Centuries*, Diplomatic Academy, Favorita Papers, Vienna

Downey, D. and MacLennan, J. C. (2006), *Spanish–Irish Relations through the Ages: New Historical Perspectives*, Four Courts Press, Dublin

Doyle, D. (1981), *Ireland, Irishmen and Revolutionary America, 1760–1820*, Mercier Press, Dublin

Doyle, D. N. (1989), 'The Irish in Australia and the United States: Some Comparisons, 1800–1939, *Irish Economic and Social History*, XVI, 73–94

Doyle, D. N. (1994), Small Differences? The Study of the Irish in the United States and Britain', *Irish Historical Studies*, XXIX, 114–119

Doyle, D. N. (2006a), 'Scots Irish or Scotch-Irish', in J. J. Lee and M. R. Casey (eds), *Making The Irish American: History and Heritage of the Irish in the United States*, New York University Press, New York, 151–170

Doyle, D. N. (2006b), 'The Irish in North America, 1776–1845', in J. J. Lee and M. R. Casey (eds), *Making The Irish American: History and Heritage of the Irish in the United States*, New York University Press, New York, 171–212

Doyle, D. N. (2006c), 'The Remaking of Irish-America, 1845–1880', in J. J. Lee and M. R. Casey (eds), *Making The Irish American: History and Heritage of the Irish in the United States*, New York University Press, New York, 213–254

Doyle, N., Hughes, G. and Wadensjö, E. (2006), *Freedom of Movement for Workers from Central and Eastern Europe: Experiences in Ireland and Sweden,* 5, Swedish Institute for European Policy Studies, Stockholm

Drudy, P. J. and McAleese, D. (eds) (1984), *Ireland and the European Community*, Cambridge University Press, Cambridge

Dudley Edwards, R. (1977; 2006), *Patrick Pearse: The Triumph of Failure*, Gollancz, London

Dufferin and Ava, Lord and Boyle, G. F. (1847), *Narrative of a Journey from Oxford to Skibbereen during the Year of the Irish Famine*, John Henry Parker

Duffy, P. J. (1997), 'Management Problems on a Large Estate in mid-Nineteenth-century Ireland: William Steuart Trench's Report of the Shirley Estate in 1843', *Clogher Record*, 16, 101–123

Duffy, P. J. and Moran, G. (eds) (2004), *To and from Ireland: Planned Migration Schemes, c. 1600–2000*, Geography Publications, Dublin

Duffy, P. J. (2004), '"Disencumbering our crowded places": Theory and Practice of Estate Emigration Schemes in mid-Nineteenth-century Ireland', in P. J. Duffy and G. Moran (eds), *To and from Ireland: Planned Migration Schemes, c. 1600–2000*, Geography Publications, Dublin, 79–104

Duffy, P. (2006), 'Placing Migration in History: Geographies of Irish Population Movements', in B. Turner (ed.), *Migration and Myth: Ulster's Revolving Door*, Ulster Local History Trust, Downpatrick, 22–37

Duffy, P. J., Edwards, D. and Fitzpatrick, E. (eds) (2001), *Gaelic Ireland c. 1250–c.1650: Land, Lordship and Settlement*, Four Courts Press, Dublin

Duffy, S. (ed.) (2007), *The World of the Galloglass: Kings, Warlords and Warriors in Ireland and Scotland, 1200–1600*, Four Courts Press, Dublin

Dumbrell, J. (2000), 'Hope and History: the US and Peace in Northern Ireland', in M. Cox, A. Guelke, A. and F. Stephen (eds), *A Farewell to Arms? From 'Long War' to Long Peace in Northern Ireland*, Manchester University Press, Manchester

Dunnigan, D. (2007), *A South Roscommon Emigrant: Emigration and Return, 1890–1920*, Maynooth Studies in Local History, 73, Four Courts Press, Dublin

Earle, P. (1994), *A City Full of People: Men and Women of London 1650–1750*, Methuen, London

Earner-Byrne, L. (2004), '"Moral Repatriation': the Response to Irish Unmarried Mothers in Britain, 1920s–1960s', in P.Duffy (ed.), *To and from Ireland: Planned Migration Schemes, c. 1600–2000*, Geography Publications, Dublin, 155–173

Ebbenwhite, F. A. (1896), *The Tin Plate Workers Company*, London

Edwards, D. (2004), 'Legacy of Defeat: the Reduction of Gaelic Ireland after Kinsale', in H. Morgan (ed.), *The Battle of Kinsale*, Wordwell, Dublin, 279–299

Ekirch, R. A. (1987), *Bound for America: The Transportation of British Convicts to the Colonies, 1718–1775*, Clarendon, Oxford

Elliott, B. (1987), 'Emigration from South Leinster to Eastern Upper Canada', in K. Whelan (ed.), *Wexford: History and Society*, Geography Publications, Dublin, 422–446

Elliott, B. S. (1998; 2002), *Irish Migrants in the Canadas: a New Approach*, McGill-Queen's University Press, Montreal, London

Elliott, B. S. (2005), '"Settling down": Masculinity, Class and the Rite of Return in a Transnational Community', in M. Harper (ed.), *Emigrant Homecomings: the Return Movement of Emigrants, 1600–2000*, Manchester University Press, Manchester, 153–183

Elliott, M. (1982), *Partners in Revolution: United Irishmen and France*, Yale University Press, New Haven, CT

Elliott, M. (2000), *The Catholics of Ulster: A History*, Penguin, London

Ellis, S. G. (1985), *Tudor Ireland: Crown, Community and the Conflict of Cultures, 1470–1603*, Longman, London

Ellmann, R. (1959), *James Joyce*, Oxford University Press, Oxford

Eltis, D. (2002), *Coerced and Free Migration: Global Perspectives*, Stanford University Press, Stanford, CA

Emmer, P. C. and Mörner, M. (eds) (1992), *European Expansion and Migration: Essays on the Intercontinental Migration from Africa, Asia and Europe*, Berg, Oxford

Emmons, D. (1989), *The Butte Irish: Class and Ethnicity in an American Mining Town*, University of Illinois Press, Urbana, IL

Engerman, S. L. (2002), 'Changing Laws and Regulations and Their Impact on Migration', in D. Eltis (ed.), *Coerced and Free Migration: Global Perspectives*, Stanford University Press, Stanford, CA, 75–93

English, R. (2006), *Irish Freedom: The History of Nationalism in Ireland*, Macmillan, Basingstoke, Oxford

Errington, E. J. (2007), *Emigrant Worlds and Transatlantic Communities: Migration to Upper Canada in the First Half of the Nineteenth Century*, McGill-Queen's University Press, Montreal & Kingston, London, Ithaca

Eversley, D. (1991), ' Demography and Unemployment in Northern Ireland', in R. J. Cormack and R. D. Osborne (eds), *Discrimination and Public Policy in Northern Ireland*, Clarendon, Oxford, 72–92

Fagan, P. (1998), *Catholics in a Protestant City: The Papist Constituency in Eighteenth-century Dublin*, Four Courts Press, Dublin

Fahey, T. (2007), 'Population', in S. O'Sullivan (ed.), *Contemporary Ireland: A Sociological Map*, University College Dublin Press, Dublin, 13–29

Fallon, B. (1998), *An Age of Innocence: Irish Culture, 1930–1960*, Gill and Macmillan, Dublin

Fannin, S. (2003), 'The Irish Community in Eighteenth-century Cadiz', in T. O'Connor and M. A. Lyons (eds), *Irish Migrants in Europe after Kinsale, 1602–1820*, Four Courts Press, Dublin, 135–148

Fanning, B. (2001), 'Reluctant Hosts: Refugee Policy in Twentieth-century Ireland', *Administration*, Institute for the Study of Social Change, Dublin, 48.4

Fanning, B. (2002) *Racism and Social Change in the Republic of Ireland*, Manchester University Press, Manchester

Fanning, B. (ed.) (2007), *Immigration and Social Change in the Republic of Ireland*, Manchester University Press, Manchester

Farrar, C. F. (1926), *Old Bedford: the Town of Sir William Harper, John Bunyan and John Howard the Philanthropist*, F. R. Hockliffe, Bedford

Fender, S. (1992), *Sea Changes: British Emigration and American Literature*, Cambridge University Press, Cambridge

Ferriter, D. (2004), *The Transformation of Ireland, 1900–2000*, Profile, London

Ferriter, D. (2006), *What If? Alternative Views of Twentieth-Century Ireland*, Gill & Macmillan, Dublin

Figorito, M. (2006), *Ellis Island: Welcome to America*, Rosen Publishing, New York

Fischer, D. H. (1989) *Albion's Seed: Four British Folkways in America*, Oxford University Press, Oxford

Fisk, R. (1983), *In Time of War: Ireland, Ulster and the Price of Neutrality, 1939–45*, Gill and Macmillan, Dublin

FitzGerald, G. (1972; 1973), *Towards a New Ireland*, Torc Books, Dublin

FitzGerald, G. (2003), *Reflections on the Irish State*, Irish Academic Press, Dublin

Fitzgerald, P. (1994) 'Poverty and Vagrancy in Early-Modern Ireland, 1530–1770', unpublished PhD thesis, Queen's University, Belfast

Fitzgerald, P. (1997), 'Famine in Ireland: Changing Patterns of Crisis', in E. M. Crawford (ed.), *The Hungry Stream: Essays on Famine and Emigration*, Institute of Irish Studies, Queen's University, Belfast and Centre for Migration Studies, Ulster-American Folk Park, Omagh, 101–122

Fitzgerald, P. (2000), 'From the Flight of the Earls to the Famine: Tyrone's Migration History', in C. Dillon and H. A. Jefferies (eds), *Tyrone: History and Society*, 461–88

Fitzgerald, P. (2001), '"A Sentence to Sail": The Transportation of Irish Convicts and Vagrants to Colonial America in the Eighteenth Century', in P. Fitzgerald and S. Ickringill (eds), *Atlantic Crossroads: Historical Connections between Scotland, Ulster and North America*, Colourpoint, Newtownards, 114–132

Fitzgerald, P. (2004a), '"Black '97": Reconsidering Scottish Migration to Ireland in the Seventeenth Century and the Scotch-Irish in America', in W. Kelly and J. R. Young (eds), *Ulster and Scotland 1600–2000: History, Language and Identity*, Four Courts Press, Dublin, 71–84

Fitzgerald, P. (2004b), '"Farewell to Fermanagh": Aspects of Emigration from County Fermanagh', in E. M. Murphy and W. J. Roulston (eds), *Fermanagh: History and Society*, 479–500

Fitzgerald, P. (2005a), '"Come back Paddy Reilly": Aspects of Irish Return Migration, 1600–1845', in M. Harper (ed.), *Emigrant Homecomings: the Return Movement of Emigrants, 1600–2000*, Manchester University Press, Manchester, 32–54

Fitzgerald, P. (2005b), 'Scottish Migration to Ireland in the Seventeenth Century', in S. Murdoch and A. Grosjean (eds), *Scottish Communities Abroad in the Early Modern Period*, Brill, Leiden, Boston, 27–52

Fitzgerald, P. (2006a), 'Exploring a Shared Migration Heritage', in B. S. Turner (ed.), *Migration and Myth: Ulster's Revolving Door*, Ulster Local History Trust, Downpatrick, 38–43

Fitzgerald, P. (2006b), 'Mapping the Ulster Diaspora 1607–1960', *Familia*, 22, 1–17

Fitzgerald, P. (2007), '"The Departure of O'Neill out of Ireland" by Thomas Ryan RHA', *History Ireland*, 15(4), 14–15

Fitzgerald, P. (2008), 'Ireland as Part of the Italian Diaspora', in B. Borza (ed.), *Italians in Ireland: A Photo-History*, Ulster Historical Foundation, Belfast

Fitzgerald, P. and Ickringill, S. (eds) (2001), *Atlantic Crossroads: Historical Connections Between Scotland, Ulster and North America*, Colourpoint, Newtownards

Fitzgerald, P. and Lambkin, B. (2004), 'Townland Diasporas', in B. S. Turner (ed.), *The Heart's Townland: Marking Boundaries in Ulster*, Ulster History Trust, Downpatrick, 88–92

Fitzpatrick, D. (1984), *Irish Emigration, 1801–1921*, Dundalgan Press, Dublin

Fitzpatrick, D. (1989) 'Irish Emigration, 1801–70', in W. E. Vaughan (ed.), *A New History of Ireland, vol. V, Ireland under the Union, I, 1801–70*, Oxford University Press, Oxford, 562–622

Fitzpatrick, D. (1994), *Oceans of Consolation: Personal Accounts of Irish Migration to Australia*, Cork University Press, Cork

Fitzpatrick, D. (1996a) 'Irish Emigration, 1871–1921', in W. E. Vaughan (ed.), *A New History of Ireland, vol. VI, Ireland under the Union, II, 1870–1921*, Oxford University Press, Oxford, 606–647

Fitzpatrick, D. (1996b), 'Militarism in Ireland, 1900–22', in T. Bartlett and K. Jeffrey (eds), *A Military History of Ireland*, Cambridge University Press, Cambridge, 379–406

Fitzpatrick, D. (1997a), 'The Failure: Representations of the Irish Famine in Letters to Australia', in E. M. Crawford (ed.), *The Hungry Stream: Essays on Emigration and Famine*, Institute of Irish Studies, Queen's University, Belfast and Centre for Emigration Studies, Ulster-American Folk Park, Omagh, 161–174

Fitzpatrick, D. (1997b), 'Women and the Great Famine', in M. Kelleher and J. H. Murphy (eds), *Gender Perspectives in 19th-century Ireland: Public and Private Spheres*, Irish Academic Press, Dublin, 50–69

Fitzpatrick, D. (1998), *The Two Irelands, 1912–1939*, Oxford University Press, Oxford

Fitzpatrick, D. (1999), 'Ireland and Empire', in A. Porter (ed.), *The Oxford History of the British Empire, vol. III, The Nineteenth Century*, Oxford University Press, Oxford, 494–521

Fitzpatrick, D. (2000), 'Emigration: 1801–1921', in M. Glazier (ed.), *The Encyclopedia of the Irish in America*, University of Notre Dame Press, Bloomington, IN, 254–262

Flackes, W. D. and Elliott, S. (1994), *Northern Ireland: A Political Directory, 1968–1993*, Blackstaff Press, Belfast

Flanagan, W. (2007), *Ireland Now: Tales of Change from the Global Island*, University of Notre Dame, Notre Dame, Indiana

Fleming, N. C. and O'Day, A. (2005), *The Longman Handbook of Modern Irish History Since 1800*, Pearson Education, Harlow

Flinn, M. W. (ed.) (1977), *Scottish Population History*, Cambridge University Press, Cambridge

Fogleman, A. S. (1992), 'Migrations to the Thirteen British North American Colonies, 1700–1775', *Journal of Interdisciplinary History*, XXII(4), 691–709

Fogleman, A. S. (1998), 'From Slaves and Servants to Free Passengers', *Journal of American History*, 85(1), 43–76

Foley, M. C. and Guinnane, T. W. (1999), 'Did Irish Marriage Patterns Survive the Emigrant Voyage? Irish-American Nuptiality, 1880–1920', in *Irish Economic and Social History*, 26, 15–34

Foley, T. and O'Connor, M. (2006), *Ireland and India: Colonies, Culture and Empire*, Irish Academic Press, Dublin

Forrest, G. A. (1995), 'Religious Controversy within the French Protestant Community in Dublin, 1692–1716: An Historiographical Critique', in K. Herlihy (ed.), *The Irish Dissenting Tradition, 1650–1750*, Four Courts Press, Dublin, 96–110

Foster, R. F. (1988), *Modern Ireland, 1600–1972*, Penguin, London

Foster, R.F. (2007), *Luck & the Irish: A Brief History of Change c. 1970–2000*, Penguin, London

Fox, S. (2003), *The Ocean Railway: Isambard Kingdom Brunel, Samuel Cunard and the Revolutionary World of the Great Atlantic Steamships*, HarperCollins, London

Fraser, L. (ed.) (2000), *A Distant Shore: Irish Migration and New Zealand Settlement*, University of Otago Press, Dunedin

Fraser, L. (2007), *Castles of Gold: A History of New Zealand's West Coast Irish*, Otago University Press, Dunedin

Fraser, T. G. (1996), 'Ireland and India', in K. Jeffery (ed.), *An Irish Empire? Aspects of Ireland and the British Empire*, Manchester University Press, Manchester, 77–93

Friedrichs, C. R. (1995), *The Early Modern City, 1450–1750*, Longman, London

Froggatt, P. (1989), 'The Response of the Medical Profession to the Great Famine', in E. M. Crawford (ed.), *Famine: The Irish Experience, 900–1900*, John Donald, Edinburgh, 134–156

Fumerton, P. (2006), *Unsettled: The Culture of Mobility and the Working Poor in Early Modern England*, University of Chicago Press, Chicago, London

Gabaccia, D. (1996), 'Women of the Mass Migrations: From Minority to Majority, 1820–1930', in D. Hoerder and L. P. Moch (eds), *European Migrants: Global and Local Perspectives*, Northeastern University Press, Boston, MA, 90–111

Gabaccia, D. (2000), *Italy's Many Diasporas*, UCL Press, London

Gailey, A. (1975), 'The Scots Element in North Irish Folk Culture: Some Problems in the Interpretation of an Historical Acculturation', *Ethnologia Europaea*, 8(1), 2–22

Gallagher, E. (2007), 'Racism and Citizenship Education in Northern Ireland', *Irish Educational Studies* 26(3), 253–269

Gallagher, R. (2004), *Violence and Politics in Derry, 1920–1923*, Four Courts Press, Dublin

Gallmann, J. M. (2000), *Receiving Erin's Children: Philadelphia, Liverpool and the Irish Famine Migration, 1845–1855*, University of North Carolina Press, Chapel Hill, NC, London

Galvin, T. (2000), 'Refugee Status in Exile: The Case of African Asylum-seekers in Ireland', in M. MacLachlan and M. O'Connell (eds), *Cultivating Pluralism: Psychological, Social and Cultural Perspectives on a Changing Ireland*, Oak Tree Press, Dublin, 199–218

Games, A. (2002), 'Migration', in D. Armitage and M. J. Braddick (eds), *The British Atlantic World, 1500–1800*, Palgrave Macmillan, Basingstoke, 31–50

Garnham, N. (1996), *The Courts, Crime and the Criminal Law in Ireland, 1692–1760*, Irish Academic Press, Dublin

Garner, S. (2004), *Racism in the Irish Experience*, Pluto Press, London, Dublin, Sterling, VA

Garvin, T. (2004), *Preventing the Future: Why was Ireland so Poor for so Long?*, Gill and Macmillan, Dublin

Geary, L. M. (1995), 'Famine, Fever and the Bloody Flux', in C. Póirtéir (ed.), *The Great Irish Famine*, Mercier, Dublin, 74–85

Geary, L. M. (1999), "The whole country was in motion": Mendicancy and Vagrancy in pre-Famine Ireland', in J. Hill and C. Lennon (eds), *Luxury and Austerity: Historical Studies*, XXI, University College Dublin Press, Dublin, 121–136

Geary, L. M. (2004), *Medicine and Charity in Ireland, 1718–1851*, University College Dublin Press, Dublin

Geary, L. M. and Kelleher, M. (eds) (2005), *Nineteenth-century Ireland: A Guide to Recent Research*, University College Dublin Press, Dublin

Geary, L.M. and McCarthy, A.J. (eds) (2008), *Ireland, Australia and New Zealand: History, Politics and Culture*, Irish Academic Press, Dublin

Gerber, D. A. (2000), 'Theories and Lives: Transnationalism and the Conceptualization of International Migrations to the United States', *IMIS-Beiträge*, 15(1), 15–34

Gerber, D. A. (2006), *Authors of Their Lives: The Personal Correspondence of British Immigrants to North America in the Nineteenth Century*, New York University Press, New York, London

Gibbon, J. (1938), *Canadian Mosaic: The Making of a Northern Nation*, McClelland & Stewart, Toronto

Giddens, Anthony (1984), *The Constitution of Society: Outline of the Theory of Structuration*, Polity, Cambridge

Gilbert, J. T. (ed.) (1889), *Calendar of Ancient Records of Dublin, in the Possession of the Municipal Corporation of that City*, 22 vols, Dollard, Dublin

Gillespie, R. (1984), 'Harvest Crises in Early Seventeenth-century Ireland', *Irish Economic and Social History*, XI, 5–18

Gillespie, R. (1986), 'Migration and Opportunity: A Comment', *Irish Economic and Social History*, XIII, 90–96

Gillespie, R. (1988) *Settlement and Survival on an Ulster Estate: The Brownlow Leasebook, 1667–1711*, Public Record Office of Northern Ireland, Belfast

Gillespie, R. (1989), 'Meal and Money: The Harvest Crisis of 1621–4 and the Irish Economy', in E. M Crawford (ed.), *Famine: The Irish Experience, 900–1900*, John Donald, Edinburgh, 75–95

Gillespie, R. (1991), *The Transformation of the Irish Economy, 1550–1700*, Studies in Irish Economic and Social History, VI, Dundalk

Gillespie, R. (1993) 'Destabilizing Ulster, 1641–2', in B. Mac Cuarta (ed.), *Ulster 1641: Aspects of the Rising*, Institute for Irish Studies, Queen's University, Belfast, 107–122

Gillespie, R. (1995) 'Dissenters and Nonconformists, 1661–1700', in K. Herlihy (ed.), *The Irish Dissenting Tradition, 1650–1750*, Four Courts Press, Dublin, 11–28

Gillespie, R. (2001) 'Religion and Urban Society: The Case of Early Modern Dublin', in P. Clark and R. Gillespie (eds), *Two Capitals: London and Dublin, 1500–1840*, Oxford University Press for the British Academy, Oxford, 223–238

Gillespie, R. (2006), *Seventeenth-century Ireland: Making Ireland Modern*, Gill and Macmillan, Dublin

Gillespie, R. (2007), *Early Belfast: The Origins and Growth of an Ulster Town to 1750*, Ulster Historical Foundation, Belfast

Gillespie, R. and Richmond, A. H. (1984), 'Explaining Return Migration', in D. Kubát (ed.), *The Politics of Return: International Return Migration in Europe*. Proceedings of the First European Conference on International Return Migration, Rome and New York: Centre for Migration Studies, 269–275

Gillespie, R. and Richmond, A. H. (1985), *Colonial Ulster: The Settlement of East Ulster, 1600–1641*, Cork University Press, Cork

Gillespie, R. and Royle, S. A. (2007), *Belfast c. 1600 to c. 1900*, Royal Irish Academy, Dublin

Gilmore, P. (2005), '"If they would come to America": Inheritance as a Form of Chain Migration', *Familia: Ulster Genealogical Review*, 21, 1–4

Gilzean, N. and McAuley, J. (2002), 'Strangers in a Strange Land? (Re)constructing "Irishness" in a Northern English Town', *Irish Journal of Sociology*, 11(2), 54–76

Gladwell, M. (2000), *The Tipping Point: How Little Things Can Make a Big Difference*, Little, Brown, London

Glasgow, M. (1936), *The Scotch-Irish in Northern Ireland and the American Colonies*, G. P. Putnam, New York

Glassie, H. (1982), *Passing the Time: Folklore and History of an Ulster Community*, O'Brien Press, Dublin

Glazer, N. and Moynihan, D. P. (1970), *Beyond the Melting Pot: the Negroes, Puerto Ricans, Jews, Italians and Irish of New York City*, MIT Press, Cambridge, MA

Glazier, M. (ed.) (1999), *The Encyclopedia of the Irish in America*, University of Notre Dame Press, Notre Dame, IN

Gleeson, D. T. (2001), *The Irish in the South, 1815–1877*, University of North Carolina Press, Chapel Hill, NC

Gmelch, S., Langan, P. and Gmelch, G. (1975), *Tinkers and Travellers: Ireland's Nomads*, O'Brien Press, Dublin

Gould, G. D. (1980), 'European Inter-continental Emigration. The Road Home: Return Migration from the USA', *Journal of European Economic History*, IX(I), 41–111

Gray, B. (2002a), '"Breaking the Silence" – Questions of Staying and Going in 1950s Ireland', *Irish Journal of Psychology*, 23, 158–183; http://migration.ucc.ie/oralarchive

Gray, B. (2002b), 'The Irish Diaspora: Globalised Belonging(s)', *Irish Journal of Sociology*, 11(2), 123–144

Gray, B. (2004), *Women and the Irish Diaspora*, Routledge, London, New York

Gray, J. (2006), interview, *A Tale of Two Cities*, BBC 1 Northern Ireland, 9 October

Gray, P. (1995), *The Irish Famine*, Thames & Hudson, London

Gray, P. (1999), *Famine, Land and Politics: British Government and Irish Society, 1843–50*, Irish Academic Press, Dublin, Portland, OR

Gray, P. (ed.) (2004), *Victoria's Ireland? Irishness and Britishness, 1837–1901*, Four Courts Press, Dublin

Greaves, R. L. (1997), *God's Other Children: Protestant Nonconformists and the Emergence of Denominational Churches in Ireland, 1660–1700*, Stanford University Press, Stanford, CA

Greig, W. (1976), *General Report on the Gosford Estates in County Armagh in 1821*, HMSO, Belfast

Griffin, B. (2006), *Cycling in Victorian Ireland*, Nonsuch Publishing, Dublin

Griffin, P. (2001), *The People with no Name: Ireland's Ulster-Scots, America's Scots-Irish and the Creation of a British Atlantic World, 1689–1764*, Princeton University Press, Princeton, NJ

Griffin, W. D. (1981), *A Portrait of the Irish in America*, Academy Press, Dublin

Griffin, W. D. (1998), *The Irish American: the Immigrant Experience*, Hugh Lauter Levin Associates, Fairefield, CT

Grigg, D. B. (1977), 'E.G. Ravenstein and the "Laws of Migration"', *Journal of Historical Geography*, 3, 41–54

Grimes, S. (1992), 'Friendship Patterns and Social Networks among Post-war Irish Migrants in Sydney', in P. O'Sullivan (ed.), *Patterns of Migration, The Irish World-Wide: History, Heritage and Identity*, vol. 1, *The Irish in the New Communities*, Leicester University Press, Leicester, 164–182

Grosjean, A. (2005), 'Returning to Belhelvie, 1593–1875: the Impact of Return Migration on an Aberdeenshire Parish', in M. Harper (ed.), *Emigrant Homecomings: the Return Movement of Emigrants, 1600–2000*, Manchester University Press, Manchester, 216–232

Guinnane, T. (1997), *The Vanishing Irish: Households, Migration, and the Rural Economy in Ireland, 1850–1914*, Princeton University Press, Princeton, NJ

Guinness, P. (2002), *Migration*, Hodder & Stoughton, London

Gunnar, M. (1944), *An American Dilemma: The Negro Problem and Modern Democracy*, Harper and Brothers, New York

Gurrin, B. (2002), *Pre-Census Sources for Irish Demography*, Maynooth Research Guides for Irish Local History, 5, Four Courts Press, Dublin

Gwynn, A. (1932), 'Documents Relating to the Irish in the West Indies', *Analecta Hibernica*, 4, 139–286

Hadfield, A. and McVeigh, J. (1994), *Strangers to that Land: British Perceptions of Ireland from the Reformation to the Famine*, Colin Smythe, Gerrards Cross, Bucks

Haines, R. F. (1997), *Emigration and the Labouring Poor: Australian Recruitment in Britain and Ireland, 1831–60*, Macmillan, Basingstoke

Hainsworth, P. (1998), 'Politics, Racism and Ethnicity in Northern Ireland', in P. Hainsworth (ed.), *Divided Society: Ethnic Minorities and Racism in Northern Ireland*, Pluto, London, 33–51

Hainsworth, P. (ed.) (1998), *Divided Society: Ethnic Minorities and Racism in Northern Ireland*, Pluto, London

Halfacree, K. and Boyle, P. (1993), 'The Challenge Facing Migration Research: the Case for a Biographical Approach', *Progress in Human Geography*, 17, 333–348

Halpin, B. (2000), 'Who are the Irish in Britain? Evidence from Large-scale Surveys', in A. Bielenberg (ed.), *The Irish Diaspora*, Longman, London, 89–108

Hamilton, J. (2006), 'Northern Ireland Research Findings', in P. Watt and F. McGaughey (eds) *Improving Government Service Delivery to Minority Ethnic Groups: Northern Ireland, Republic of Ireland, Scotland*, National Consultative Committee on Racism and Interculturalism; www.ofmdfmni.gov.uk/nccrireport2.pdf, 38–45

Hammar, T., Brochmann, G., Tamas, K. and Faist, T. (eds) (1997), *International Migration, Immobility and Development: Multidisciplinary Perspectives*, Berg, Oxford

Hand, G. J. (intro.) (1969), *Report of the Irish Boundary Commission: first publication of the 1925 document*, Irish University Press, Shannon

Hanna, C. A. (1902), *The Scotch Irish: or, the Scot in North Britain, North Ireland and North America*, 2 vols, New York

Hannan, D. F. (1970), *Rural Exodus: a Study of the Forces Influencing Large-scale Migration of Irish Youth*, Geoffrey Chapman, London

Hansen, M. L. (1940), *The Immigrant in American History*, Harper & Row, New York

Harper, M. (2003), *Adventurers and Exiles: The Great Scottish Exodus*, Profile, London

Harper, M. (2004), 'Enticing the Emigrant: Canadian Agents in Ireland and Scotland, c.1870–c.1920', *Scottish Historical Review*, 83(215), 41–58

Harper, M. (ed.) (2005), *Emigrant Homecomings: the Return Movement of Emigrants, 1600–2000*, Manchester University Press, Manchester

Harrington J. P. (ed.) (1991), *The English Traveller in Ireland: Accounts of Ireland and the Irish through Five Centuries*, Wolfhound Press, Dublin

Harris, R-A. (2000), 'Searching for Missing Friends in the *Boston Pilot* Newspaper, 1831–1863', in A. Bielenberg (ed.), *The Irish Diaspora*, Pearson Education, Harlow, 158–175

Harris, R-A. and Jacobs, D. M. (eds) (1989–93), *The Search for Missing Friends: Irish Immigrant Advertisements Placed in the Boston Pilot, 1831–56*, 3 vols, New England Historic Genealogical Society, Boston, MA

Harrison, R. S. (1995), '"As a Garden Enclosed": The Emergence of Irish Quakers, 1650–1750', in K. Herlihy (ed.), *The Irish Dissenting Tradition, 1650–1750*, Four Courts Press, Dublin, 81–95

Hart, P. (1998), *The IRA and its Enemies: Violence and Community in Cork, 1916–1923*, Oxford University Press, Oxford

Harte, L. (2003), 'Immigrant Self-fashioning: the Autobiographies of the Irish in Britain, 1856–1934', in O. Walsh (ed.), *Ireland Abroad: Politics and Professions in the Nineteenth Century*, Four Courts Press, Dublin, 47–61

Harte, L. (ed.) (2004), *Modern Irish Autobiography: Self, Nation and Society*, Palgrave Macmillan, Basingstoke

Harte, L. (2007), *The Irish Migrant Experience in Britain: an Anthology of Autobiography*, Palgrave Macmillan, Basingstoke

Hartley, T. (2006), *Written in Stone: The History of Belfast City Cemetery*, Brehon Press, Belfast

Harvey, B., Kelly, A., McGearty, S. and Murray, S. (2005), *The Emerald Curtain: The Social Impact of the Irish Border*, Triskele Community Training and Development, Carrickmacross

Harvey, C. J. and Ward, M. (eds) (2001), *No Welcome Here? Asylum Seekers and Refugees in Ireland and Britain. An Attempt to Inform the Debate on Asylum and Advance Practical Proposals for the Creation of a Truly Multi-cultural Society*, Democratic Dialogue, Belfast

Harvey, D. and White, G. (1997), *The Barracks: A History of Victoria/Collins Barracks, Cork*, Mercier Press, Dublin

Hatton, T. J. and Williamson, J. G. (2005), *Global Migration and the World Economy: Two Centuries of Policy and Performance*, MIT Press, Cambridge, MA, London

Hay, D. and Rogers, N. (1997), *Eighteenth-century English Society*, Oxford University Press, Oxford

Hayes, M. (2006), *Irish Travellers: Representations and Realities*, Liffey Press, Dublin

Hayes-McCoy, G. A. (1937; 1996), *Scots Mercenary Forces in Ireland, 1565–1603*, de Burca, Dublin

Hayton, D. (1976), 'Introduction', *Ireland after the Glorious Revolution, 1692–1715: Education Facsimiles*, 221–240, PRONI, Belfast

Hayward, K. and Howard, K. (2007), 'Cherry-picking the Diaspora', in Bryan Fanning (ed.), *Immigration and Social Change in the Republic of Ireland*, Manchester University Press, Manchester, 47–62

Healy, J. (1978), *Nineteen Acres*, Kennys, Galway

Heaney, S. (2002), 'Through-Other Places, Through-Other Times: The Irish Poet in Britain', in *Finders Keepers: Selected Prose*, Faber, New York, 365–382

Hearn, T. (2000a), 'Irish Migration to New Zealand to 1915', in L. Frazer (ed.), *A Distant Shore: Irish Migration and Settlement in New Zealand*, University of Otago Press, Dunedin, 55–74

Hearn, T. (2000b), 'The Irish on the Otago Goldfields, 1861–71', in L. Frazer (ed.), *A Distant Shore: Irish Migration and Settlement in New Zealand*, University of Otago Press, Dunedin, 75–85

Hegarty, N. (2007), *Dublin: A View from the Ground*, Portrait, London

Helleiner, J. (1993), 'Traveller Settlement in Galway City: Politics, Class and Culture', in C. Curtin, H. Donnan and T. M. Wilson (eds), *Irish Urban Cultures*, Institute of Irish Studies, The Queen's University of Belfast, 181–202

Hempton, D. (1988), 'Religious Minorities', in P. Loughrey (ed.), *The People of Ireland*, Appletree Press, Belfast, 155–168

Hennessy, T. (2005), *Northern Ireland: The Origins of the Troubles*, Gill and Macmillan, Dublin

Henry, B. (1996), *Dublin Hanged: Crime, Law Enforcement and Punishment in late 18th-century Dublin*, Irish Academic Press, Dublin

Henry, G. (1992), *The Irish Military Community in Spanish Flanders*, Irish Academic Press, Dublin

Henry, G. (1993), 'Ulster Exiles in Europe, 1610–1641', in B. Mac Cuarta (ed.), *Ulster 1641: Aspects of the Rising*, Institute of Irish Studies, Queen's University, Belfast, 37–60

Henry, G. (1995), 'Women "Wild Geese", 1585–1625: Irish Women and Migration to European Armies in the Late Sixteenth and Early Twentieth Centuries', in P. O'Sullivan (ed.), *The Irish World Wide: History, Heritage, Identity*, vol. 4, *Irish Women and Irish Migration*, Leicester University Press, Leicester, 23–40

Henry, W. (1997), *The Shimmering Waste: the Life and Times of Robert O'Hara Burke*, W. Henry, Galway

Hepburn, A. C. (1996), *A Past Apart: Studies in the History of Catholic Belfast, 1850–1960*, Ulster Historical Foundation, Belfast

Herlihy, J. (2005), *Royal Irish Constabulary Officers: A Bibliographical Guide and Genealogical Guide, 1816–1922*, Four Courts Press, Dublin

Herlihy, K. (1995), '"The Faithful Remnant": Irish Baptists, 1650–1750', in K. Herlihy (ed.), *The Irish Dissenting Tradition, 1650–1750*, Four Courts Press, Dublin, 65–80

Hershkowitz, L. (1996), 'The Irish and the Emerging City: Settlement to 1844', in R. H. Bayor and T. J. Meagher (eds), *The New York Irish*, Johns Hopkins University Press, Baltimore, MD, 11–34

Heslinga, M. W. (1979), *The Irish Border as a Cultural Divide: A Contribution to the Study of Regionalism in the British Isles*, Van Gorcum, Assen

Hewson, E. (2004), *The Forgotten Irish: Memorials of the Raj*, Kabristan Archives, Wembley

Hickey, P. (2002), *Famine in West Cork: The Mizzen Peninsula Land and People 1800–1852*, Mercier Press, Dublin

Hickman, M. (1995), *Religion, Class and Identity: the State, the Catholic Church and the Education of the Irish in Britain*, Avebury, Aldershot

Hickman, M. (1996), 'Incorporating and Denationalizing the Irish in England: the Role of the Catholic Church', in P. O'Sullivan (ed.), *The Irish World-Wide, History, Heritage, Identity*, vol. 5, *Religion and Identity*, Leicester University Press, Leicester 196–216

Hickman, M. (1999), 'Alternative Historiographies of the Irish in Britain: a Critique of the Segregation/Assimilation Model', in R. Swift and S. Gilley (eds), *The Irish in Victoria Britain: The Local Dimension*, Four Courts Press, Dublin, 236–253

Hickman, M. (2002), '"Locating" the Irish Diaspora', *Irish Journal of Sociology*, 11(2), 8–26

Hickman, M. (2005), 'Migration and Diasporas', in J. Cleary and C. Connolly (eds), *The Cambridge Companion to Modern Irish Culture*, Cambridge University Press, Cambridge, 117–136

Hill, J. (1997), *From Patriots to Unionists: Dublin Civic Politics and Irish Protestant Patriotism, 1660–1840*, Clarendon, Oxford

Hill, J. M. (1993), 'The Origins of the Scottish Plantations in Ulster to 1625: a Reinterpretation', *Journal of British Studies*, 32, 24–43

Hill, M. (2003), *Women in Ireland, 1900–2000*, Blackstaff Press, Belfast

Hillan, S. (2005), 'Wintered into Wisdom: Michael McLaverty, Seamus Heaney, and the Northern Word-Hoard', *New Hibernia Review*, 19(3), 86–106

Hillyard, P. (1983), 'Law and Order', in J. Darby, *Northern Ireland: The Background to the Conflict*, Appletree Press, Belfast

Hillyard, P. (1993), *Suspect Community: People's Experiences of the Prevention of Terrorism Acts in Britain*, Pluto Press/Liberty, London

Hillyard, P. (1997), 'Security Strategies in Northern Ireland: Consolidation or Reform?', in C. Gilligan and J. Tonge, (eds), *Peace or War?: Understanding the Peace Process in Northern Ireland*, Ashgate, Aldershot

Hirschman, A. O. (1970), *Exit, Voice and Loyalty: Responses to Decline in Firms, Organizations and States*, Harvard University Press, Cambridge, MA

Hitchens, D. M. W. N., Birnie, J. E. and Wagner, K. (1993), 'Economic Performance in Northern Ireland: A Comparative Perspective', in P. Teague (ed.), *The Economy of Northern Ireland: Perspectives for Structural Change*, Lawrence & Wishart, London, 24–59

Hoerder, D. (2002), *Cultures in Contact: World Migrations in the Second Millennium*, Duke University Press, Durham, NC

Hoerder, D. and Knauf, D. (1992), *Fame, Fortune and Sweet Liberty: The Great European Emigration*, Edition Temmen, Bremen

Hoerder, D. and Page Moch, L. (eds) (1996), *European Migrants: Global and Local Perspectives*, Northeastern University Press, Boston, MA

Hoffman, E. (1989), *Lost in Translation: a Life in a New Language*, E. P. Dutton, New York

Hoffman, R. (2000), *Princes of Ireland, Planters of Maryland: A Carroll Saga, 1500–1782*, University of North Carolina Press, Chapel Hill, NC

Holmes, J. (2005), 'Irish Evangelicals and the British Evangelical Community, 1820s–1870s', in J. H. Murphy (ed.), *Evangelicals and Catholics in Nineteenth-century Ireland*, Four Courts Press, Dublin, 209–222

Holton, K., Clare, L. and Ó Dálaigh, B. (eds) (2004), *Irish Villages*, Four Courts Press, Dublin

Hood, A. D. (2003), 'Flax Seed, Fibre, and Cloth: Pennsylvania's Domestic Linen Manufacture and its Irish Connections, 1700–1830', in B. Collins and P. Ollerenshaw (eds), *The European Linen Industry in Historical Perspective*, Oxford University Press, Oxford, 139–158

Hooper, G. (2001), *The Tourist's Gaze*, Cork University Press, Cork

Hopkins, T. and Wallerstein, I. (1982), *World Systems Analysis: Theory and Methodology*, Sage, London, Beverly Hills, CA

Horn, J. (1998a), 'Tobacco Colonies: The Shaping of English Society in Seventeenth-century Chesapeake', in N. Canny (ed.), *The Oxford History of the British Empire, vol. I: The Origins of Empire to 1689*, Oxford University Press, Oxford, 170–193

Horn, J. (1998b), 'British Diaspora: Emigration from Britain, 1680–1815', in P. J. Marshall (ed.), *The Oxford History of the British Empire, vol. II, The Eighteenth Century*, Oxford University Press, Oxford, 28–52

Horning, A. (2001), '"Dwelling houses in the old barbarous manner": Archaeological Evidence for Gaelic Architecture in an Ulster Plantation Village', in P. Duffy, D. Edwards and E. FitzPatrick (eds), *Gaelic Ireland: Land, Lordship & Settlement, c. 1250–c. 1650*, Four Courts Press, Dublin, 375–396

Horning, A. (2004), 'Archaeological Explorations of Cultural Identity and Rural Economy in the North of Ireland: Goodland, County Antrim', *International Journal of Historical Archaeology*, 8(3), 199–215

Hotten-Somers, D. M. (2003), 'Relinquishing and Reclaiming Independence: Irish Domestic Servants, American Middle-class Mistresses, and Assimilation, 1850–1920', in K. Kenny (ed.), *New Directions in Irish-American History*, University of Wisconsin Press, Madison, WI, 227–242

Houston, C. J. and Smyth W. J. (1990), *Irish Emigration and Canadian Settlement: Patterns, Links & Letters*, University of Toronto Press, Buffalo/Ulster Historical Foundation, Belfast

Houston, R. A. (1992), *The Population History of Britain and Ireland, 1500–1750*, Macmillan, Basingstoke

Hout, M. (1989), *Following in Father's Footsteps: Social Mobility in Ireland*, Harvard University Press, London

Howe, S. (2000), *Ireland and Empire*, Oxford University Press, Oxford

Hughes, A. J. (1989), 'An Account of a Sea-Voyage from Derry to America, 1818', *Ulster Folklife*, 35, 18–41

Hughes, J. and Donnelly, C. (2001), 'Integrate or Segregate? Ten Years of Social Attitudes to Community Relations in Northern Ireland', *ARK*, Belfast

Hughes, J. G. and Walsh, B. M. (1980), *Internal Migration Flows in Ireland and their Determinants*, Economic and Social Research Institute, Dublin

Hume, D. (2005), *Far from the Green Fields of Erin: Ulster Emigrants and Their Stories*, Colourpoint Books, Newtownards

Hume, J. (2002), *Derry beyond the Walls: Social and Economic Aspects of the Growth of Derry*, Ulster Historical Foundation, Belfast

Humphreys, A. J. (1966), *New Dubliners: Urbanization and the Irish Family*, Routledge & Kegan Paul, London

Hunter, R. (1999), 'The Fishmongers' Company of Londonderry and the Londonderry Plantation, 1609–41', in G. O'Brien (ed.), *Derry & Londonderry: History & Society*, Geography Publications, Dublin, 205–258

Hyland, Á. (2003), 'Education', in B. Lalor (ed.), *The Encyclopedia of Ireland*, Gill and MacMillan, Dublin, 342–343

Hylton, R. (1999), 'Portarlington and the Huguenots in Laois', in P. Lane and W. Nolan (eds), *Laois: History & Society*, Geography Publications, Dublin, 415–434

Hyman, L. (1972), *The Jews of Ireland*, Israel University Press, London

Ignatiev, N. (1996), *How the Irish Became White*, Routledge, London, New York

Inglis, B. (1962), *West Briton*, Faber and Faber, London

Inglis, T. (2008), *Global Ireland: Same Difference*, Routledge, New York, London

International Organisation for Migration (2003), *World Migration 2003. Managing Migration: Challenges and Responses for People on the Move*, IOM, Geneva

Irish Empire, The (1999), Programme 3: 'A World Apart', Littlebird Productions, Dublin

Irwin, G. and Dunn, S. (1997), *Ethnic Minorities in Northern Ireland*, Centre for the Study of Conflict, University of Ulster, Coleraine

Jackson, D. (1970), *Intermarriage in Ireland, 1550–1650*, Cultural and Educational Productions, Montreal

Jackson, J. A. (ed.) (1969; 1986), *Migration*, Sociological Studies, 2, Cambridge University Press, Cambridge/Longman, London, New York

Jackson, J. H. Jr and Page Moch, L. (1994), 'Migration and the Social History of Modern Europe', in M. Drake (ed.), *Time, Family and Community: Perspectives on Family and Community History* Open University, Milton Keynes/Blackwell, Oxford, 181–198

Jansen, C. (1969), 'Some Sociological Aspects of Migration', in J. A. Jackson (ed.), *Migration*, Cambridge University Press, Cambridge

Jarman, N. (2004), 'From War to Peace? Changing Patterns of Violence in Northern Ireland', *Terrorism and Political Violence*, 16(3) (Autumn), 420–438

Jarman, N. (2005), *Demography, Development and Disorder: Changing Patterns of Interface Areas*, Community Relations Council, Belfast

Jarman, N. and O'Halloran, C. (2000), *Peacelines or Battlefields: Responding to Violence in Interface Areas*, Community Development Centre North Belfast, Belfast

Jarman, N. and Monaghan, R. (2004), *Racist Harassment in Northern Ireland*, Institute for Conflict Research, Belfast

Jeffrey, K. (2000), *Ireland and the Great War*, Cambridge University Press, Cambridge

Jenkins, W. (2003), '"In the Shadow of a Grain Elevator": A Portrait of an Irish Neighborhood in Buffalo, New York, in the Nineteenth and Twentieth Centuries', in K. Kenny (ed.), *New Directions in Irish-American History*, University of Wisconsin Press, Madison, WI, 162–184

Jenkins, W. (2007a), 'Identity, Place, and the Political Mobilization of Urban Minorities: Comparative Perspectives on Irish Catholics in Buffalo and Toronto, 1880–1910', *Environment and Planning D: Society and Space*, 25(1), 160–186

Jenkins, W. (2007b), 'Deconstructing Diasporas: Networks and Identities among the Irish in Buffalo and Toronto, 1870–1910', in E. Delaney and D. M. MacRaild (eds), *Irish Migration, Networks and Ethnic Identities Since 1750*, Routledge, Abingdon, 210–249

Johnson, D. S. and Kennedy, L. (2003), 'Two Economies in Ireland in the Twentieth Century', in J. R. Hill (ed.), *A New History of Ireland, Vol. VII, Ireland, 1921–1984*, Oxford University Press, Oxford, 452–486

Jones, M. (1969), 'Ulster Emigration, 1783–1815', in E. R. R. Green (ed.), *Essays in Scotch-Irish History*, Routledge & Kegan Paul, London, 46–68

Jones, M. (1976), *Destination America*, Weidenfeld & Nicolson, London

Jones, R. C. (2003), 'Multinational Investment and Return Migration in Ireland in the 1990s: a County-level Analysis', *Irish Geography*, 36(2), 153–169

Joppke, C. (ed.) (1998), *Challenge to the Nation State: Immigration in Western Europe and the United States*, Oxford University Press, Oxford

Jordan, D. E. (1994), *Land and Popular Politics in Ireland: County Mayo from the Plantation to the Land War*, Cambridge University Press, Cambridge

Joyce, J. (1922; 1975), *Ulysses*, Penguin, London

Jüte, R. (1994) *Poverty and Deviance in Early Modern Europe*, Cambridge University Press, Cambridge

Kapur, N. (1997), *The Irish Raj: Illustrated Stories about Irish in India and Indians in Ireland*, Greystone Press, Antrim

Kearney, H. F. (2007), *Ireland: Contested Ideas of Nationalism and History*, Cork University Press, Cork

Kearney, R. (ed.) (1988), *Across the Frontiers: Ireland in the 1990s*, Wolfhound Press, Dublin

Kearney, R. (ed.) (1990), *Migrations: The Irish at Home and Abroad*, Wolfhound Press, Dublin

Keenan, D. (1983), *The Catholic Church in Nineteenth-Century Ireland*, Gill and Macmillan, Dublin

Kelleher, M. (ed.), *Nineteenth-century Ireland: A Guide to Recent Research*, University College Dublin Press, Dublin

Kells, M. (1995), '"I'm myself and nobody else": Gender and Ethnicity among Young Middle-class Irish Women in London', in P. O'Sullivan (ed.), *The Irish World Wide: History, Heritage, Identity*, vol. 4, *Irish Women and Irish Migration*, Leicester University Press, Leicester, 201–234

Kelly, F. (1988), *A Guide to Early Irish Law*, Dublin Institute for Advanced Studies, Dublin

Kelly, J. (1992a), 'Harvests and Hardship: Famine and Scarcity in Ireland in the Late 1720s', *Studia Hibernica*, 26, 65–105

Kelly, J. (1992b), 'Scarcity and Poor Relief in Eighteenth-century Ireland: the Subsistence Crisis of 1782–4', *Irish Historical Studies*, 28(109), 38–62

Kelly, J. (1992/3), 'The Resumption of Emigration from Ireland after the American War of Independence: 1783–1787', *Studia Hibernica*, 61–88

Kelly, J. (2003), 'Transportation from Ireland to North America, 1703–1789', in D. Dickson and C. Ó Gráda (eds), *Refiguring Ireland: Essays in Honour of L. M. Cullen*, Lilliput Press, Dublin, 112–135

Kelly, J. (2005), *The Liberty and Ormond Boys: Factional Riot in Eighteenth-century Dublin*, Four Courts Press, Dublin

Kelly, K. and Nic Giolla Choille, T. (1995), 'Listening and Learning: Experiences in an Emigrant Advice Agency', in P. O'Sullivan (ed.), *The Irish World Wide: History, Heritage, Identity*, vol. 4, *Irish Women and Irish Migration*, Leicester University Press, Leicester, 168–191

Kelly, M. P. (1994), *Home Away From Home: The Yanks in Ireland*, Appletree Press, Belfast

Kennedy, L. (1986), *Two Ulsters: A Case for Repartition*, Queen's University, Belfast

Kennedy, L. (1994), *People and Population Change*, Co-operation North, Dublin, Belfast

Kennedy, L. (1996), *Colonialism, Religion, and Nationalism in Ireland*, Institute of Irish Studies, Queen's University, Belfast

Kennedy, L. and Clarkson, L. (1993), 'Birth, Death and Exile: Irish Population History, 1700–1921', in B. J. Graham and L. J. Proudfoot (eds), *An Historical Geography of Ireland*, Academic Press, London, 158–178

Kennedy, L., Ell, P. S., Crawford E. M. and Clarkson, L. A. (1999), *Mapping the Great Irish Famine*, Four Courts Press, Dublin

Kennedy, L., Miller, K. and Graham, M. (1991), 'The Long Retreat: Protestants, Economy and Society, 1660–1926', in R. Gillespie and G. Moran (eds), *Longford: Essays in County History*, Lilliput Press, Dublin, 31–61

Kenny, K. (2000), *The American Irish: A History*, Pearson Education, London

Kenny, K. (2003a), 'Diaspora and Comparison: The Global Irish as a Case Study', *Journal of American History*, 90(1) (June), 134–162

Kenny, K. (2003b), 'Writing the History of the Irish Diaspora', in R. Savage (ed.), *Ireland in the New Century*, Four Courts Press, Dublin, 206–226

Kenny, K. (2004), 'The Irish in the Empire', in K. Kenny (ed.), *Ireland and the British Empire*, Oxford University Press, Oxford, 90–122

Kenny, K. (2006), 'Diaspora and Irish Migration History', *Irish Economic and Social History*, XXXIII, 46–50

Keogh, D. (1998), *Jews in Twentieth-century Ireland: Refugees, Anti-Semitism and the Holocaust*, Cork University Press, Cork

Keogh, D. and McCarthy, A. (2005), *Limerick Boycott 1904: Anti-Semitism in Ireland*, Mercier Press, Cork

Keogh, D., O'Shea, F. and Quinlan, C. (eds) (2003), *Ireland in the 1950s: the Lost Decade?*, Cork University Press, Cork

Kiely, B. (1947), *Poor Scholar: a study of William Carleton*, Sheed & Ward, London

Kilroy, P. (1994), *Protestant Dissent and Controversy in Ireland, 1660–1714*, Cork University Press, Cork

Kinealy, C. (1994), *This Great Calamity: The Great Irish Famine, 1845–52*, Gill and Macmillan, Dublin

Kinealy, C. and Parkhill, T. (1997), *The Famine in Ulster: the regional impact*, Ulster Historical Foundation, Belfast

Kinealy, C. and MacAtasney, G. (2000), *The Hidden Famine: Hunger, Poverty and Sectarianism in Belfast*, Pluto, London

King, T. (1997), *Carlow: The Manor and Town, 1674–1721*, Maynooth Studies in Local History, Irish Academic Press, Dublin

Kirk, J. M. and Ó Baoill, D. P. (2002), *Travellers and their Language*, Cló Ollscoil na Banríona, Queen's University, Belfast

Kirk, T. (1993), 'The Polarisation of Protestants and Roman Catholics in Rural Northern Ireland: A Case Study of the Glenravel Ward, Co. Antrim, 1956–1998', unpublished PhD thesis, School of Geosciences, Queen's University, Belfast

Kirkham, G. (1988), 'Introduction', in R. J. Dickson, *Ulster Emigration to Colonial America, 1715–1775*, Ulster Historical Foundation, Belfast, vii–xviii

Kirkham, G. (1990), 'Literacy in North-West Ulster, 1680–1860', in M. Daly and D. Dickson (eds), *The Origins of Popular Literacy in Ireland: Language Change and Educational Development, 1700–1920*, Departments of History, TCD and UCD, Dublin, 73–96

Kirkham, G. (1997), 'Ulster Emigration to North America', in H. T. Blethen and C. W. Wood (eds), *Ulster and North America: Transatlantic Perspectives on the Scotch-Irish*, University of Alabama Press, Tuscaloosa, AL, 76–117

Kissane, N. (ed.) (1994), *Treasures from the National Library of Ireland*, Boyne Valley Honey, Drogheda

Klier, J. D. and Lambroza, S. (1998; 2004), *Pogroms, Anti-Jewish Violence in Modern Russian History*, Cambridge University Press, Cambridge

Knox, Andrea (2007), '"Women of the Wild Geese": Irish Women, Exile and Identity in Spain, 1750-1775' in E. Delaney and D.M. MacRaild (eds), *Irish Migration Networks and Ethnic Identities Since 1750*, Routledge, London and New York, 1-17

Koch, C. (2002), *The Many-Coloured Land: A Return to Ireland*, Picador, London

Kofman, E. (2004), 'Gendered Global Migrations', *International Feminist Journal of Politics*, 6(4), 643–665

Koivukangas, O. (2005), 'Connecting Contemporary Migration with the Past', *Journal of the Association of European Migration Institutions*, 3, 61–65

Koser, K. (2007), *International Migration: A Very Short Introduction*, Oxford University Press, Oxford

Kuhling, C. and Keohane, K. (2007), *Cosmopolitan Ireland: Globalisation and Quality of Life*, Pluto, London, Dublin, Ann Arbor, MI

Lagden, A. and Sly, J. (eds), *The 2 / 73rd At Waterloo with Biographical Notes*, Brightlingsea, Essex

Lalor, B. (ed.) (2003), *The Encyclopedia of Ireland*, Gill and Macmillan, Dublin

Lambert, S. (2001), *Irish Women in Lancashire, 1922–1960: Their Story*, University of Lancaster, Lancaster

Lambkin, B. (1985–6), 'The Structure of the Blathmac Poems', *Studia Celtica*, 20–21, 67–77

Lambkin, B. (1998), 'Taking Townland Studies into the New Millennium', *Familia: Ulster Genealogical Review*, 14, Belfast, 96–107

Lambkin, B. (2001), 'Segregation, Integration and the Third Way', in J. Gardner and R. Leitch (eds), *Education 2020: A Millennium Vision*, Blackstaff Press, Belfast, 32–40

Lambkin, B. (2002), 'The Return to Ulster of Thomas Mellon: A Pilgrimage', *Journal of Scotch-Irish Studies*, 1(3), 37–53

Lambkin, B. (2005a), 'Charles Gavan Duffy's "The Irish Chiefs": Diasporic Trajectories of a Young Ireland Text in the United States and Australia', *Canadian Journal of Irish Studies*, 31(1), 98–107

Lambkin, B. (2005b), 'Moving Titles of a Young Ireland Text: Davis, Duffy and McGee and the Origins of *Tiocfaidh Ár Lá*', in L. Harte (ed.), *Ireland: Space, Text and Time*, Manchester University Press, Manchester, 103–111

Lambkin, B. (2006), 'Representing "Migrant Objects" in Cinema and Museum: a Recent Case Study from Northern Ireland', *Journal of the Association of European Migration Institutions*, 4, 22–35

Lambkin, B. (2007a), 'The Art of European Migration Virtual Archive: Comparing "Rituals" of Departure', *Journal of the Association of European Migration Institutions*, 5, 153–161

Lambkin, B. (2007b), '"Emigrants" and "Exiles": Migration in the Early Irish and Scottish Church', *Innes Review: Journal of the Scottish Catholic Historical Association*, 58(2), 133–155

Lambkin, B. (2008a), 'The Emotional Function of the Migrant's "Birthplace" in Transnational Belonging: Thomas Mellon (1813–1908) and Andrew Carnegie (1835–1919)', *Journal of Intercultural Studies*, 29(3), 315–329

Lambkin, B. (2008b), 'Islay, North-West Ulster and the Emigrant Trade: remembering the 1847 *Exmouth* Disaster', in J. D. McClure, J. Kirk and M. Storrie (eds), *Proceedings of the Eighth International Conference on the Languages of Scotland and Ulster*

Lambkin, B. and Meegan, J. (2005), 'The Fabric of Memory, Identity and Diaspora: an Irish Needlework Sampler in Australia with United States and Canadian Connections', *Folklife: Journal of Ethnological Studies*, 42(2003–2004), 7–31

Lambkin, R. (1992), *My Time in the War: An Irishwoman's Diary*, Wolfhound Press, Dublin

Lansdowne, Marquess of (ed.) (1927; repr 1967), *The Petty Papers: Some Unpublished writings of Sir William Petty in Two Volumes*, Augustus M. Kelley, New York

Laoide, S. (eag.) (1904), *Seachrán Chairn tSiadháil: Amhrán Ilcheardaidheachta agus Seanchas Síor-chuartaidheachta*, Connradh na Gaedhilge, Baile Átha Cliath

Larcom, T. A. (ed.) (1851; repr 1967), *The History of the Survey of Ireland Commonly Called The Down Survey by Doctor William Petty*, Augustus M. Kelley, New York

Lee, E. S. (1966; 1969), 'A Theory of Migration', *Demography*, 3(1), 47–57; reprinted in J. A. Jackson (ed.), *Migration*, Cambridge University Press, Cambridge, 282–297

Lee, J. J. (1989), *Ireland 1912–1985: Politics and Society*, Cambridge University Press, Cambridge

Lee, J. J. (1992), 'The Twentieth Century: "We can't all live on a small island"', *The Irish Abroad*, supplement to *Ireland of the Welcomes*, Bord Fáilte-Irish Tourist Board, Dublin, 18–20

Lee, J. J. (2005), 'The Irish Diaspora in the Nineteenth Century', in L. Geary and M. Kelleher, (eds), *Nineteenth-Century Ireland: A Guide to Recent Research*, University College Dublin Press, Dublin, 182–222

Lees, L. H. (1979), *Exiles of Erin: Irish Migrants in Victorian London*, Manchester University Press, Manchester

Legg, M-L. (2004), *The Census of Elphin 1749*, Irish Manuscripts Commission, Dublin

Lenihan, P. (1997), 'War and Population, 1649–52', *Irish Economic and Social History*, XXIV(21), 1–21

Lenihan, P. (2008), *Consolidating Conquest: Ireland 1603–1727*, Pearson Longman, Harlow

Lennon, C. (1989), *The Lords of Dublin in the Age of R eformation*, Irish Academic Press, Dublin

Lennon, C. (1994), *Sixteenth-century Ireland: The Incomplete Conquest*, Gill and Macmillan Press, Dublin

Lentin, R. and McVeigh, R. (2006), *After Optimism? Ireland, Racism and Globalisation*, Metro Éireann Publications, Dublin

Letford, L. and Pooley, C. G. (1995), 'Geographies of Migration and Religion: Irish Women in mid-Nineteenth-century Liverpool', in P. O'Sullivan (ed.), *The Irish World Wide, History, Heritage, Identity: Irish Women and Irish Migration*, vol. 4, Leicester University Press, London, 89–112

Le Roux, L. N. (1932), *Patrick H. Pearse*, trans. D. Ryan, Talbot Press, Dublin

Levi, C. (1965), *Cristo si è fermato a Eboli* [1946], trans. Peter M. Brown, Harrap, London

Levy, A. (2005), 'A Community that is both a Center and a Diaspora: Jews in late Twentieth-century Morocco', in A. Levy and A. Weingrod (eds), *Homelands and Diasporas: Holy Lands and Other Places*, Stanford University Press, Stanford, CA, 68–96

Lewis, Geoffrey (2005), *Carson: The Man Who Divided Ireland*, Hambledon Continuum, London

Leyburn, J. (1962), *The Scotch-Irish: A Social History*, University of North Carolina Press, Chapel Hill, NC

Lindley, K. (1972), 'The Impact of the 1641 Rebellion upon England and Wales, 1641–5', *Irish Historical Studies*, 70, 143–76

Linebaugh, P. (1991), *The London Hanged: Crime and Civil Society in the Eighteenth Century*, Penguin, London

Linebaugh, P. and Redicker, M. (2000), *The Many-Headed Hydra: Sailors, Slaves, Commoners, and the Hidden History of the Revolutionary Atlantic*, Beacon Press, Boston, MA

Little, A. (2003),' Multiculturalism, Diversity and Liberal Egalitarianism in Northern Ireland', *Irish Political Studies* 18(2), 23–39

Litvak, L. B. (1996), 'The Psychology of Song: the Theology of Hymn. Songs and Hymns of the Irish Migration', in P. O'Sullivan (ed.), *The Irish World Wide, History, Heritage, Identity*, vol. 5, *Religion and Identity*, Leicester University Press, London, New York, 70–89

Livi Bacci, M. (1999), *The Population of Europe*, Blackwell, London

Lloyd, D. (1994), 'Making Sense of the Dispersal', *The Irish Reporter*, 13 (first quarter), 3–4

Lockhart, A. (1975), *Some Aspects of Irish Emigration from Ireland to the North American Colonies between 1660 and 1775*, Arno Press, New York

Long, L. D. and Oxfeld, E. (eds) (2004), *Coming Home? Refugees, Migrants, and Those who Stayed Behind*, University of Pennsylvania Press, Philadelphia

Lorimer, J. (1989), *English and Irish Settlement on the River Amazon, 1550–1646*, Haklyut Society, London

Loshitzky, Y. (ed.) (2006), *Fortress Europe: Migration, Culture and Representation*, Routledge, London

Loughlin, J. (2003), *The Ulster Question Since 1945*, Palgrave Macmillan, Basingstoke

Loyal, S. (2003), '"Welcome to the Celtic Tiger": Racism, Immigration and the State', in C. Coulter and S. Coleman (eds), *The End of Irish History: Critical Reflections on the Celtic Tiger*, Manchester University Press, Manchester, 74–94

Loyal, S. (2007), 'Immigration', in S. Sullivan (ed.), *Contemporary Ireland: A Sociological Map*, University College Dublin Press, Dublin, 30–47

Lowenthal, D. (1985), *The Past is a Foreign Country*, Cambridge University Press, Cambridge

Lucassen, J. and Lucassen L. (eds) (1999), *Migration, Migration History, History: Old Paradigms and New Perspectives*, Peter Lang, Bern, Berlin, Frankfurt/M., New York

Lucassen, L. (1999), 'Eternal Vagrants? State Formation, Migration and Travelling Groups in Western Europe, 1350–1914', in J. Lucassen and L. Lucassen (eds), *Migration, Migration History, History: Old Paradigms and New Perspectives*, Peter Lang, Bern, Berlin, Frankfurt/M., New York, 225–252

Lucassen, L. (2005), *The Immigrant Threat: The Integration of Old and New Migrants in Western Europe since 1850*, University of Illinois Press, Urbana, IL

Luddy, M. (2000), 'Women and Work in Nineteenth- and Early Twentieth-century Ireland: an Overview', in B. Whelan (ed.), *Women and Paid Work in Ireland, 1500–1930*, Four Courts Press, Dublin, 44–56

Lunny, L. (1991), 'Knowledge and Enlightenment: Attitudes to Education in Early Nineteenth-Century East Ulster', in M. Daly and D. Dickson (eds), *The Origins of Popular Literacy in Ireland: Language Change and Educational Development 1700–1920*, Departments of History, TCD and UCD, Dublin, 97–112

Luu, L. B. (2005), *Immigrants and the Industries of London, 1500–1700*, Ashgate, Aldershot

Lynam, T. (2004), *A Country Boy: Stories and Reminiscences of a Young Man's Journey from Mullingar to 1930s Dublin*, Siobhán Lynam, Dublin

Lynch, J. (1998), *A Tale of Three Cities: Comparative Studies in Working-class Life*, Macmillan, Basingstoke

Lynch, J. (2001), *An Unlikely Success Story: the Belfast Shipbuilding Industry, 1880–1935*, The Belfast Society in association with the Ulster Historical Foundation, Belfast

Lynch, T. J. (2004), *Turf War: The Clinton Administration and Northern Ireland*, Ashgate, Aldershot

Lyons, M. (ed.) (1995), *The Memoirs of Mrs. Leeson, Madam, 1727–1797*, Lilliput Press, Dublin

Lyons, M. A. (2000), '"Vagabonds", "Mendicants", "Guex": French Reaction to Irish Immigration in the Early Seventeenth Century', *French History*, 14(4), 363–382

Lyons, M. A. (2001), 'The Emergence of an Irish Community in Saint-Malo, 1550–1710', in T. O'Connor (ed.), *The Irish in Europe, 1580–1815*, Four Courts Press, Dublin, 107–126

Macafee, C. I. (ed.) (1996), *A Concise Ulster Dictionary*, Oxford University Press, Oxford

MacAfee, W. (2000), 'The Population of County Tyrone, 1600–1991', in C. Dillon and H. A. Jefferies (eds), *Tyrone: History & Society*, Geography Publications, Dublin, 433–460

Macafee, W. (2005), 'The pre-Famine population of Ireland: a Reconsideration', in B. Collins, P. Ollerenshaw and T. Parkhill (eds), *Industry, Trade and People in Ireland, 1650–1950, Essays in Honour of W.H. Crawford*, Ulster Historical Foundation, Belfast, 69–86

Macafee, W. and Morgan, V. (1981), 'Population in Ulster, 1660–1760', in P. Roebuck (ed.), *Plantation to Partition: Essays in Ulster History in honour of J. L. McCracken*, Blackstaff Press, Belfast, 46–63

MacArthur, Sir W. P. (1956), 'Medical History of the Famine', in R. Dudley-Edwards and T. D. Williams (eds), *The Great Famine: Studies in Irish History, 1845–52*, Browne and Nolan, Dublin, 263–315

McAuley White, J. (1996), 'Under an Orange Banner: Reflections on the Northern Protestant Experiences of Emigration', in P. O'Sullivan (ed.), *The Irish World Wide: History, Heritage, Identity*, vol. 5, *Religion and Identity*, Leicester University Press, Leicester, 43–69

McBride, I. (1997), *The Siege of Derry in Ulster Protestant Mythology*, Four Courts Press, Dublin

McCann, M., Ó Siocháin, S. and Ruane, J. (1994), *Irish Travellers: Culture and Ethnicity*, Institute of Irish Studies for the Anthropological Association of Ireland, Queen's University, Belfast

McCaffrey, L. (1992), *Textures of Irish America*, Syracuse University Press, New York

McCaffrey, L. J. (1997), *The Irish-Catholic Diaspora in America*, Catholic University of America Press, Washington, DC

McCarthy, A. (2005), *Irish Migrants in New Zealand, 1840–1937: 'The Desired Haven'*, Boydell Press, Woodbridge

McCarthy, A. (2007), *Personal Narratives of Irish and Scottish Migration, 1921–65: 'For Spirit and Adventure'*, Manchester University Press, Manchester

MacCarthy-Morrogh, M. (1986), *The Munster Plantation: English Migration to Southern Ireland, 1583–1641*, Oxford University Press, Oxford

MacCarthy Morrogh, M. (1998), *The Irish Century*, Weidenfeld & Nicolson, London

McCavitt, J. (1998), *Sir Arthur Chichester: Lord Deputy of Ireland, 1605–16*, Institute of Irish Studies, Queen's University, Belfast

McCavitt, J. (2002), *The Flight of the Earls*, Gill and Macmillan, Dublin

McCone, K. (1990), *Pagan Past and Christian Present*, An Sagart, Maynooth

McCourt, D. (1999), 'County Derry and New England: The Scotch-Irish Migration of 1718, in G. O'Brien (ed.), *Derry & Londonderry: History and Society*, Geography Publications, 303–320

McCracken, D. P. (1997), 'The Land the Famine Irish Forgot', in E. M. Crawford (ed.), *The Hungry Stream: Essays on Emigration and Famine*, Institute of Irish Studies, Queen's University, Belfast and Centre for Emigration Studies, Ulster-American Folk Park, Omagh, 41–48

McCracken, D. P. (2000), 'Odd Man Out: The South African Experience', in A. Bielenberg (ed.), *The Irish Diaspora*, Longman, London, 251–271

McCracken, E. (1971), *The Irish Woods since Tudor Times: Their Distribution and Exploitation*, Institute of Irish Studies, Queen's University, Belfast

Mac Cuarta, B. (1993), *Ulster 1641: Aspects of the Rising*, Institute of Irish Studies, Queen's University, Belfast

Mac Cuarta, B. (2007), 'Religious Violence against Settlers in South Ulster, 1641–2', in D. Edwards, P. Lenihan and C. Tait (eds), *Age of Atrocity: Violence and Political Conflict in Early Modern Ireland*, Four Courts Press, Dublin, 154–175

McCullagh, C. (1991), 'A Tie that Binds: Family and Ideology in Ireland', *Economic and Social Review*, 22(3), 199–211

McDannell, C. and Lang, B. (1988), *Heaven: A History*, Yale University Press, New Haven, CT, London

MacDonagh, O. (1956), 'Irish Emigration to the United States of America and the British Colonies during the Famine', in R. Dudley Edwards and T. Desmond Williams (eds), *The Great Famine: Studies in Irish History, 1845–52*, Brown and Nolan, Dublin, 319–387

MacDonagh, O. (1961), *A Pattern of Government Growth, 1800–1860: The Passenger Acts and Their Enforcement*, MacGibbon and Kee, London

MacDonagh, O. (1986), 'The Irish in Australia: A General View', in O. MacDonagh and W. F. Mandle (eds), *Ireland and Irish-Australia: Studies in Cultural and Political History*, Croom Helm, London, Sydney, Woleboro, NH, 155–174

MacDonald, P. T. (2005), *Exiles and Emigrants: Epic Journeys to Australia in the Victorian Era*, National Gallery of Victoria, Melbourne

McDonough, T. (2005), *Was Ireland A Colony? Economics, Politics and Culture in Nineteenth-Century Ireland*, Irish Academic Press, Dublin

McDowell, R. B. (1964), *The Irish Administration, 1801–1914*, Routledge & Kegan Paul, London

McDowell, R. B. (1979), *Ireland in the Age of Imperialism and Revolution, 1760–1801*, Oxford University Press, Oxford

McDowell, R. B. (1997), *Crisis and Decline: The Fate of Southern Unionists*, Lilliput Press, Dublin

Mac Éinrí, P. (2000), 'Introduction', in A. Bielenberg (ed.), *The Irish Diaspora*, Pearson Education, London, 1–15

Mac Éinrí, P. (2001), 'Immigration Policy in Ireland', in F. Farrell and P. Watt (eds), *Responding to Racism in Ireland*, Veritas, Dublin, 46–87

Mac Éinrí, P. (2005), 'Migration', in J. S Crowley et al. (eds), *Atlas of Cork City*, Cork University Press, Cork, 419–423

Mac Éinrí, P. (2006), 'Ireland: Research Findings', in P. Watt and F. McGaughey (eds), *Improving Government Service Delivery to Minority Ethnic Groups: Northern Ireland, Republic of Ireland, Scotland*, National Consultative Committee on Racism and Interculturalism, www.ofmdfmni.gov.uk/nccrireport2.pdf, 106–115

Mac Éinrí, P. (2007a), 'Integration Models and Choices', in B. Fanning (ed.), *Immigration and Social Change in the Republic of Ireland*, Manchester University Press, Manchester, 214–236

Mac Éinrí, P. (2007b), 'Immigration: Labour Migrants, Asylum Seekers and Refugees', in B. Bartley and R. Kitchin (eds), *Understanding Contemporary Ireland*, Pluto, London, Dublin, Ann Arbor, MI, 236–248

Mac Éinrí, P. and Lambkin, B. (2002), 'Whose Diaspora? Whose Migration? Whose Identity? Some Current Issues in Irish Migration Studies', *Irish Journal of Psychology*, 23(3–4), 125–157

Mac Éinrí, P. and Walley, P. (eds) (2003), *Labour Migration into Ireland*, Immigration Council of Ireland, Dublin

MacFarlane, A. (1994), *The British in the Americas, 1480–1815*, Longman, London

Mac Gabhann, M. (1959; 1996 edn), *Rotha Mór An tSaoil*, Cló Iar-Chonnachta, Indreabhán, Conamara

MacGill, P. (1914), *Children of the Dead End: The Autobiography of a Navvy*, Herbert Jenkins, London

MacGowan, M. (1962), *The Hard Road to Klondike*, trans. V. Iremonger, Routledge & Kegan Paul, London

McGowan, M. G. (1999), *The Waning of the Green: Catholics, the Irish, and Identity in Toronto, 1887–1922*, McGill-Queen's University Press, Montreal, Kingston

McGrath, B. (2004), 'Ireland and the Third University: Attendance at the Inns of Court, 1603–1649', in D. Edwards (ed.), *Regions and Rulers in Ireland, 1100–1650*, Four Courts Press, Dublin, 217–236

McGrath, G. (2007), *Hidden Connections: Ulster and Slavery, 1807–2007*, Linen Hall Library, Belfast

McGurk, J. (1992), 'Wild Geese: The Irish in European Armies (Sixteenth to Eighteenth Centuries)', in P. O'Sullivan (ed.), *The Irish World Wide: History, Heritage, Identity*, vol. 1, *Patterns of Migration*, Leicester University Press, Leicester, 36–62

McHugh, N. (1999), *Drogheda before the Famine: Urban Poverty in the Shadow of Privilege, 1826–45*, Four Courts Press, Dublin

McIlvanney, L. and Ryan, R. (2005), *Ireland and Scotland: Culture and Society, 1700–2000*, Four Courts Press, Dublin

Macinnes, A. I. (2007), *Union and Empire: The Making of the United Kingdom in 1707*, Cambridge University Press, Cambridge

McKay, P. (1999; 2007), *A Dictionary of Ulster Place-Names*, Institute of Irish Studies, Queen's University, Belfast

McKenna, P. (2000), 'Irish Emigration to Argentina: a Different Model', in A. Bielenberg (ed.), *The Irish Diaspora*, Longman, London, 195–212

McKenna, P. (2003), 'The Irish in Argentina', in B. Lalor (ed.), *The Encyclopedia of Ireland*, Gill and MacMillan, Dublin

McKenny, K. (1995), 'The Seventeenth-century Land Settlement in Ireland: Towards a Statistical Interpretation', in J. H. Ohlmeyer (ed.), *Ireland: From Independence to Occupation, 1641–1660*, Cambridge University Press, Cambridge

McKenna, P. (1992), 'Irish Migration to Argentina', in P. O'Sullivan (ed.), *The Irish World Wide: History, Heritage, Identity*, vol. I, *Patterns of Migration*, Leicester University Press, Leicester, 63–83

McKittrick, D. and McVea, D. (2000), *Making Sense of the Troubles*, Blackstaff Press, Belfast

McLeod, M. (1996), *Leaving Scotland*, National Museum of Scotland, Edinburgh

Mac Laughlin, J. (1994), *Ireland: The Emigrant Nursery and the World Economy*, Cork University Press, Cork

McLeod, W. (2004), *Divided Gaels: Gaelic Cultural Identities in Scotland and Ireland, c. 1200–c.1650*, Oxford University Press, Oxford

Mac Laughlin, J. (1997), 'The Devaluation of "Nation" as "Home" and the Depoliticisation of Recent Irish Emigration', in J. Mac Laughlin (ed.), *Location and Dislocation in Contemporary Irish Society*, Cork University Press, Cork, 179–208

McLoughlin, D. (1995), 'Superfluous and Unwanted Deadweight: the Emigration of Nineteenth-century Irish Pauper Women', in P. O'Sullivan (ed.), *The Irish World Wide: History, Heritage, Identity*, vol. 4, *Irish Women and Irish Migration*, Leicester University Press, Leicester, 66–88

McManus, R. (2002), *Dublin, 1910–1940: Shaping the City and Suburbs*, Four Courts Press, Dublin

MacMaster, R. (2005), 'Flaxseed and Emigrants: Origins of Philadelphia's Trade with Ulster', *Journal of Scotch-Irish Studies*, 2(2), 23–39

McNeill, M. (1971), *Vere Foster, 1819–1900*, David & Charles, Newton Abbott

McNiffe, L. (1997), *A History of the Garda Síochána: a Social History of the Force 1922–52 with an Overview for the Years 1952–97*, Wolfhound Press, Dublin

McPeake, J. (1998), 'Religion and Residential Search Behaviour in the Belfast Urban Area', *Housing Studies*, 13(4), 527–548

MacPherson, C. (1997), *The Weir*, Nick Hearn Books, London

MacRaild, D. M. (1998), *Culture, Conflict and Migration: The Irish in Victorian Cumbria*, Liverpool University Press, Liverpool

MacRaild, D. M. (1999), *Irish Migrants in Modern Britain, 1750–1922*, Macmillan, Basingstoke

MacRaild, D. M. (ed.) (2000), *The Great Famine and Beyond: Irish Migrants in Britain in the Nineteenth and Twentieth Centuries*, Irish Academic Press, Dublin

MacRaild, D. M. (2000), 'Crossing Migrant Frontiers: Comparative Reflections on Irish Migrants in Britain and the United States during the Nineteenth Century', in

D. M. MacRaild (ed.), *The Great Famine and Beyond: Irish Migrants in Britain in the Nineteenth and Twentieth Centuries*, Irish Academic Press, Dublin, 40–70

MacRaild, D. M. (2002/3), 'Wherever Orange is worn: Orangeism and Irish migration in the 19th and 20th Centuries', *Canadian Journal of Irish Studies*, 28(2) and 29(1), 98–116

MacRaild, D. M. (2005a), *Faith, Fraternity and Fighting: The Orange Order and Irish Migrants in Northern England, c. 1860–1914*, Liverpool University Press, Liverpool

MacRaild, D. M. (2005b), 'Networks, Communication and the Irish Protestant Diaspora in Northern England, c.1860–1914', *Immigrants and Minorities*, 23(2/3), 311–337

MacRaild, D. M. (2006a), '"Diaspora" and "Transnationalism": Theory and Evidence in Explanation of the Irish World-wide', *Irish Economic and Social History*, 33, 51–58

MacRaild, D. M. (2006b), *The Irish in Britain, 1800–1914*, Studies in Irish Economic and Social History 9, Dundalgan Press, Dublin

MacRaild, D. M. and MacPherson, D. A. F. (2006), 'Sisters of the Brotherhood: Female Orangeism on Tyneside in the Late Nineteenth and Early Twentieth Centuries', *Irish Historical Studies*, 137(35), 40–60

McRonald, M. (2005), *The Irish Boats, Vol. 1, Liverpool to Dublin*, Tempus, Stroud

McVeigh, R. (1998), '"There's no Racism Because There's no Black People Here": Racism and Anti-racism in Northern Ireland', in P. Hainsworth, *Divided Society: Ethnic Minorities and Racism in Northern Ireland*, Pluto, London, 11–32

McWilliams, D. (2007), *The Generation Game*, Gill and Macmillan, Dublin

Mackey, B. (2003), 'Overseeing the Foundation of the Irish Linen Industry: The Rise and Fall of the Crommelin Legend', in B. Collins and P. Ollerenshaw (eds), *The European Linen Industry in Historical Perspective*, Oxford University Press, Oxford, 99–122

Madden, K. (2005; 2006), *Forkhill Protestants and Forkhill Catholics, 1787–1858*, McGill-Queen's University Press, Montreal/Liverpool University Press, Liverpool

Madden, R. R. (1846, 1998 edn.), *The Autobiography of James (Jemmy) Hope as Published in The United Irishmen: Their Lives and Times*, Farset, Belfast

Maguire, J. F. (1868), *The Irish in America*, London

Maguire, W. A. (1993), *Belfast*, Keele University Press, Keele, Staffs

Maher, J. P. (ed.) (2004), *Returning Home: Transatlantic Migration from North America to Britain & Ireland, 1858–1870*, Irish Records Index, vol. 5, National Archives of Ireland, Eneclann

Malcolmson, A. (1974), 'Absenteeism in Eighteenth Century Ireland', *Irish Economic and Social History*, I, 15–35

Mann-Kler, D. (1997), *Out of the Shadows: an Action Research Report into Families, Racism and Exclusion in Northern Ireland*, Barnardos et al., Belfast

Manning, P. (2005), *Migration in World History*, Routledge, New York, London

Mannion, J. J. (1974), *Irish Settlements in Eastern Canada: A Study of Cultural Transfer and Adaptation*, University of Toronto Press, Toronto

Mannion, J. (2001), 'Irish Migration and Settlement in Newfoundland: the Formative Phase, 1697–1732', *Newfoundland Studies*, 17(2), 257–293

Mannion, J. and Maddock, F. (1990), 'Old World Antecedents, New World Adaptations: Inistioge Immigrants in Newfoundland', in W. Noland and K. Whelan (eds), *Kilkenny: History and Society*, Geography Publications, Dublin, 345–404

Marley, L. (2007), *Michael Davitt: Freelance Radical and Frondeur*, Four Courts Press, Dublin

Marranci, G. (2003), '"We speak English": Language and Identity Processes in Northern Ireland's Muslim Community', *Ethnologies* 25(2), 59–75

Marshall, W. F. (1943), *Ulster Sails West*, np, Belfast

Marx, K. (1867; 1906), *Capital: A Critique of Political Economy*, vol. I, *The Process of Capitalist Production*, Charles H. Kerr and Co., Chicago

Massey, D. (1998), *Worlds in Motion: Understanding International Migration at the End of the Millennium*, Clarendon, Oxford

Massey, D. (1990), 'The Social and Economic Origins of Immigration', *Annals of the American Academy of Political and Social Science*, 510, 60–72

Maume, P. (ed.) (2005), *The Last Conquest of Ireland (Perhaps) by John Mitchel*, University College Dublin Press, Dublin

Maxwell, C. (1936), *Dublin under the Georges*, Tempest, Dundalk

Maxwell, C. (1954, 1979 edn.), *The Stranger in Ireland*, Gill and Macmillan, Dublin

Meagher, T. J. (2001), *Inventing Irish America*, University of Notre Dame Press, South Bend, IN, 14–15

Meinhof, U. H. (ed.) (2002), *Living (with) Borders: Identity Discourses on East–West Borders in Europe*, Ashgate, Aldershot

Melucci, A. (1989), *Nomads of the Present: Social Movements and Individual Needs in Contemporary Society*, Hutchinson Radius, London

Mellon, T. (1885; 1994 edn.), *Thomas Mellon and His Times*, M. Briscoe (ed.), Centre for Emigration Studies, Ulster American Folk Park, Omagh

Meredith, D. (2006), 'Changing Distribution of Ireland's Population 1996–2006: Urban/Rural Analysis', www.teagasc.ie/publications/2006/06-wp-rels.pdf

Miller, D. W. (1999), 'Irish Presbyterians and the Great Famine', in J. Hill and C. Lennon (eds), *Luxury and Austerity, Historical Studies XXI*, University College Dublin Press, Dublin, 165–181

Miller, K.A. (1985), *Emigrants and Exiles: Ireland and the Irish Exodus to North America*, Oxford University Press, Oxford

Miller, K. A., Boling, B. and Doyle, D. N. (1980), 'Emigration and Exiles: Irish Cultures and Irish Emigration to North America, 1790–1922', *Irish Historical Studies*, XXII (September), 92–125

Miller, K. A. with Doyle, D. N. and Kelleher, P. (1995), '"For love and liberty": Irish Women, Migration and Domesticity in Ireland and America, 1815–1920', in P. O'Sullivan (ed.), *The Irish World Wide, History, Heritage, Identity*, vol. 4, *Irish Women and Irish Migration*, Leicester University Press, Leicester, 41–65

Miller, K. A., Doyle, D. N., Boling, B. and Schrier, A. (2003), *Irish Immigrants in the Land of Canaan: Letters and Memoirs from Colonial and Revolutionary America, 1675–1815*, Oxford University Press, New York

Miller, K. A., Boling, B. D. and Kennedy, L. (2003), 'The Famine's Scars: William Murphy's Ulster and American Odyssey', in K. Kenny (ed), *New Directions in Irish-American History*, University of Wisconsin Press, Madison, 36–60

Miller, K. A. and Kennedy, L. (2003), 'Irish Migration and Demography, 1659–1831', in K. A. Miller et al. (eds), *Irish Immigrants in the Land of Canaan: Letters and Memoirs from Colonial and Revolutionary America, 1675–1815*, Oxford University Press, Oxford, 656–659

Millsop, S. A. (1998), 'Ballymagee, County Down', in W. H. Crawford and R. H. Foy (eds), *Townlands in Ulster: Local History Studies*, Ulster Historical Foundation, Belfast, 95–110

Mokyr, J. (2006), 'Famine Disease and Famine Mortality', in C. Ó Gráda (ed.), *Ireland's Great Famine: Interdisciplinary Perspectives*, University College Dublin Press, Dublin, 63–85

Molloy, C. (2002), *The Story of the Irish Pub*, Liffey Press, Dublin

Moloney, M. (2002), *Far from the Shamrock Shore: the Story of Irish-American Immigration through Song*, Collins Press, Cork

Molony, S. (2000), *Irish Aboard the 'Titanic'*, Wolfhound Press, Dublin

Montgomery, M. (2006), *From Ulster to America: the Scotch-Irish Heritage of American English*, Ulster Historical Foundation, Belfast

Moody, T. W. (ed.) (1938), 'Ulster Plantation Papers, 1608–13', *Analecta Hibernica*, 8, 179–298

Moody, T. W. (1939), *The Londonderry Plantation*, William Mullan, Belfast

Moran, G. (1996), 'From Connacht to North America: State-aided Emigration from County Galway in the 1880s', in G. Moran (ed.), *Galway: History and Society*, Geography Publications, Dublin, 487–521

Morash, C. (1995), *Writing the Irish Famine*, Clarendon, Oxford

Moreton, C. (2000), *Hungry for Home. Leaving the Blaskets: a Journey from the Edge of Ireland*, Viking, London

Morgan, K. (2000), *Slavery and Servitude in North America, 1607–1800*, Edinburgh University Press, Edinburgh

Morgan, V. (1976), 'A Case Study of Population Change over Two Centuries: Blaris, Lisburn 1661–1848', *Irish Economic and Social History*, III, 5–16

Morgan, V., Smyth, M., Robinson, G. and Fraser, G. (1996), *Mixed Marriages in Northern Ireland*, Centre for the Study of Conflict, University of Ulster, Coleraine

Moroney, A. (2006), *Exploring the Lives of the Non-Irish National Population of Co. Cavan*, Cavan County Development Board and Cavan County Community and Voluntary Forum

Moulden, J. (1994), *Thousands are Sailing: a Brief Song History of Irish Emigration*, Ulstersongs, Portrush

Moulden, J. (2001), '"The Blooming Bright Star of Belle Isle": American Native or Irish Immigrant', in P. Fitzgerald and S. Ickringill (eds), *Atlantic Crossroads: Historical Connections between Scotland, Ulster and North America*, Colourpoint, Newtownards, 55–66

Muhr, K. (1996), *Place-Names of Northern Ireland, Volume Six, County Down IV North-West Down, Iveagh*, Northern Ireland Place-Name Project, Department of Celtic, The Queen's University of Belfast

Muhr, M. K. (1999), *Celebrating Ulster's Townlands*, Ulster Place-Name Society, Belfast

Mulligan, W. H. (2001a), 'From the Beara to the Keweenaw: the Migration of Irish Miners from Allihies, County Cork to the Keweenaw Peninsula, Michigan, USA, 1845–1880', *Journal of the Mining Heritage Trust of Ireland*, 1, 19–24

Mulligan, W. H. (2001b), 'Irish Immigrants in Michigan's Copper Country: Assimilation on a Northern Frontier', *New Hibernia Review*, 5(4), 109–122

Mulligan, W. H. (2004), '"The Merchant Prince" of the Copper Country: One Immigrant's American Success Story', *Tipperary Historical Journal*, 151–160

Murdoch, S. (2000), *Britain, Denmark–Norway and the House of Stuart, 1603–1660*, Tuckwell Press, East Linton

Murdoch, S. (2005), 'Children of the Diaspora: the "Homecoming" of the Second-generation Scot in the Seventeenth Century', in M. Harper (ed.), *Emigrant Homecomings: the Return Movement of Emigrants, 1600–2000*, Manchester University Press, Manchester, 55–76

Murnane, J. H. and Murnane, P. (1999), *At the Ford of the Birches: the History of Ballybay, its People and Vicinity*, Murnane Brothers, Monaghan

Murphy, M. (1997), 'The Fionnuala Factor: Irish Sibling Emigration at the Turn of the Century', in A. Bradley and M. Valiulis (eds), *Gender and Sexuality in Modern Ireland*, University of Massachusetts Press, Amherst, MA, 85–101

Murphy, M. (ed.) (2002), *Ireland's Welcome to the Stranger: Asenath Nicholson*, Lillput Press, Dublin

Murphy, M. (2004), *Don't Wake Me at Doyles: A Memoir*, Hodder Headline, London

Murray, T. (1919), *Story of the Irish in Argentina*, P. J. Kenedy, New York

Murtagh, B. (2002), *The Politics of Territory: Policy and Segregation in Northern Ireland*, Palgrave Macmillan, Basingstoke

Murtagh, H. (1996), 'Irish Soldiers Abroad, 1600–1800', in T. Bartlett and K. Jeffery (eds), *A Military History of Ireland*, Cambridge University Press, Cambridge, 294–314

Myers, A. C. (1969), *Immigration of the Irish Quakers into Pennsylvania, 1682–1750*, Heritage, Baltimore, MD

Neal, F. (1988), *Sectarian Violence, The Liverpool Experience, 1819–1914: An Aspect of Anglo-Irish history*, Manchester University Press, Manchester

Neal, F. (1997), '"Black '47": Liverpool and the Irish Famine', in E. M. Crawford (ed.), *The Hungry Stream*, Institute of Irish Studies, Belfast, 123–136

Neal, F. (1998), *Black '47: Britain and the Famine Irish*, Macmillan, Basingstoke

Neal, F. (2000), 'The Foundations of the Irish Settlement in Newcastle upon Tyne: the Evidence of the 1851 Census', in D. MacRaild (ed.), *The Great Famine and Beyond: Irish Migrants in Britain in the Nineteenth and Twentieth Centuries*, Irish Academic Press, Dublin, 71–93

Neeson, E. (1991), *A History of Irish Forestry*, Lilliput Press, Dublin

Neidhardt, W. S. (1975), *Fenianism in North America*, Penn State University Press, University Park, PA

Neill, W. J. V. (2004), 'Cosmopolis Postponed: Planning and Management of Cultural Conflict in the British and/or Irish City of Belfast', in W. J. V. Neill, *Urban Planning and Cultural Identity*, Routledge, London

Neville, G. (1992), '"She never then after that forgot him": Irishwomen and Emigration to North America in Irish Folklore', *Mid-America: An Historical Review*, 74(iii), 271–289

Neville, G. (2000), '*Rites de passage*: Rituals of Separation in Irish Oral Tradition', in C. Fanning (ed.), *New Perspectives on the Irish Diaspora*, Illinois University Press, Carbondale, IL, 117–130

Newman, K. (1993), *Dictionary of Ulster Biography*, Institute of Irish Studies, Queen's University, Belfast

Nicholas, S. and Shergold, P. R. (1990), 'Irish Inter-county Mobility before 1840' *Irish Economic and Social History*, XVII, 22–43

Nicholls, K. (2001), 'Woodland Cover in pre-Modern Ireland', in P. Duffy, D. Edwards and E. Fitzpatrick (eds), *Gaelic Ireland: Land, Lordship and Settlement c. 1250–c. 1650*, Four Courts Press, Dublin, 181–206

Ní Laoire, C. (2000), 'Conceptualising Irish Rural Youth Migration: a Biographical Approach', *International Journal of Population Geography*, 6, 229–243

Ní Laoire, C. (2003), 'Discourses of Nation among Migrants from Northern Ireland: Irishness, Britishness and the Spaces in-Between', *Scottish Geographical Journal*, 118(3), 183–199

Ní Laoire, C. (2007a), '"Settling Back"? A Biographical and Life-course Perspective on Ireland's Recent Return Migration', *Public Geography Research Papers*, Department of Geography, University College, Cork, http://www.ucc.ie/academic/geography/public/NiLaoire0701.pdf

Ní Laoire, C. (2007b), 'The "green green grass of home"? Return Migration to Rural Ireland', *Journal of Rural Studies*, 23, 332–344

Ní Laoire, C. (2007c), 'To Name or not to Name: Reflections on the Use of Anonymity in an Oral Archive of Migrant Life Narratives', *Social and Cultural Geography*, 8(3), 373–390

Ní Mhurchadha, M. (2005), *Fingal, 1603–60: Contending Neighbours in North Dublin*, Four Courts Press, Dublin

Ní Shuinéar, S. (2003), 'Travellers, or the Travelling People', in B. Lalor (ed.), *Encyclopedia of Ireland*, Gill and Macmillan, Dublin, 1071–1072

Ní Shuinéar, S. (2006), 'Travellers and their Travels', in B. S. Turner (ed.), *Migration and Myth: Ulster's Revolving Door*, Ulster History Trust, Downpatrick, 81–84

Nolan, J. (1989), *Ourselves Alone: Women's Emigration from Ireland 1885–1920*, University Press of Kentucky, Lexington, KY

Nolan, J. (2004), *Servants of the Poor: Teachers and Mobility in Ireland and Irish America*, University of Notre Dame Press, South Bend, IN

Nolan, W. (2006), 'The Land of Kildare: Valuation, Ownership and Occupation, 1850–1906', in W. Nolan and T. McGrath (eds), *Kildare: History and Society, Geography Publications*, Dublin, 549–584

Northern Ireland Housing Executive (1987), *Coping with Conflict*, NIHE, Belfast

Northern Ireland Museums Council (2005), *Our People Our Times: a History of Northern Ireland's Cultural Diversity*, Belfast

Northern Ireland Office (1998), *The Agreement*, NIO, Belfast

Novick, P. (1999), *The Holocaust and Collective Memory: The American Experience*, Bloomsbury, London

Nowlan, K. B. (1973), *Travel and Transport in Ireland*, Gill and Macmillan, Dublin

O'Brien, D. (1970), *W. R. Rodgers, 1909–1969*, Bucknell University Press, Lewisburg, PA

O'Brien, E. (1976), *Mother Ireland: a memoir*, Plume, London

O'Brien, G. A. T. (1918, 1977 edn.), *Economic History of Ireland in the Eighteenth Century*, Porcupine Press, Philadelphia

O'Brien, J. A. (ed.) (1954), *The Vanishing Irish: the Enigma of the Modern World*, W. H. Allen, London

O'Brien, M. J. (2003), 'Transatlantic Connections and the Sharp Edge of the Great Depression', in K. Kenny (ed.), *New Directions in Irish-American History*, University of Wisconsin Press, Madison, WI, 78–98

Ó Buachalla, B. (1996), *Aisling ghéar: na Stíobhartaigh agus an taos léinn, 1603–1788*, Clochomhar, Baile Átha Cliath

O'Callaghan, Sean (2000), *To Hell or Barbados: The Ethnic Cleansing of Ireland*, Brandon, Dingle

O'Carroll, Í. B. (1995), 'Breaking the Silence from a Distance: Irish Women Speak on Sexual Abuse', in P. O'Sullivan, P. (ed.), *The Irish World Wide: History, Heritage, Identity*, vol. 4, *Irish Women and Irish Migration*, Leicester University Press, Leicester, 192–200

Ó Ciardha, É. (2001), *Ireland and the Jacobite Cause, 1685–1766: a Fatal Attachment*, Four Courts Press, Dublin

Ó Cinnéide, B. (2002), *Riverdance: The Phenomenon*, Blackhall Publishing, Blackrock

Ó Ciosáin, É. (2001), 'A Hundred Years of Irish Migration to France, 1590–1688', in T. O'Connor (ed.), *The Irish in Europe, 1580–1815*, Four Courts Press, Dublin, 93–106

O'Clery, C. (1996), *The Greening of the White House: the Inside Story of How America Tried to Bring Peace to Ireland*, Gill and Macmillan, Dublin

O'Connell, P. (2001), 'The Early-modern Irish College Network in Iberia, 1590–1800', in T. O'Connor (ed.), *The Irish in Europe, 1580–1815*, Four Courts Press, Dublin, 49–64

O Connor, F. (1993), *In Search of a State: Catholics in Northern Ireland*, Blackstaff Press, Belfast

O'Connor, J. (1994), *The Secret World of the Irish Male*, New Island, Dublin

O'Connor, M. (2006), 'Fearful Symmetry: an Emigrant's Return to Celtic Tiger Ireland', *New Hibernia Review*, 10(1), 9–16

O'Connor, P. (1989) *People Make Places: the Story of the Irish Palatines*, Oireacht na Mumhan Books, Newcastle West

O'Connor, P. (1996), *All Ireland is in and about Rathkeale*, Oireacht na Mumhan Books, Newcastle West

O'Connor, P. J. (2006), *Seeing Through Counties: Geography and Identity in Ireland*, Oireacht na Mumhan Books, Newcastle West

O'Connor, T. (ed.) (2001), *The Irish in Europe, 1580–1815*, Four Courts Press, Dublin

O'Connor, T. and Lyons, M. A. (eds) (2003), *Irish Migrants in Europe after Kinsale, 1602–1820*, Four Courts Press, Dublin

O'Connor, T. and Lyons, M. A. (eds) (2006), *Irish Communities in Early Modern Europe*, Four Courts Press, Dublin

Ó Dálaigh, B. (1995), *Ennis in the Eighteenth Century: Portrait of an Urban Community*, Irish Academic Press, Dublin

Ó Dálaigh, B., Cronin, D. A. and Connell, P. (eds) (1998), *Irish Townlands: Studies in Local History*, Four Courts Press, Dublin

O'Day, A. (1996), 'Revising the Diaspora', in Boyce, G. and O'Day, A. (eds), *The Making of Irish History: Revisionism and the Revisionist Controversy*, Routledge, London, 188–215

O'Donnell, R. (1998), *The Rebellion in Wicklow, 1798*, Irish Academic Press, Dublin

O'Donnell, R. and Teague, P. (1993), 'The Potential and Limits of North–South Economic Co-operation', in P. Teague (ed.), *The Northern Ireland Economy: Perspectives for Structural Change*, Lawrence & Wishart, London, 340–372

O'Dowd, A. (1991), *Spalpeens and Tattie Hokers: History and Folklore of the Irish Migratory Agricultural Workers in Ireland and Britain*, Irish Academic Press, Dublin

O'Dowd, L. (1993), 'Craigavon: Locality, Economy and the State in a Failed "New City"', in C. Curtin, H. Donnan and T. M. Wilson (eds), *Irish Urban Cultures*, Institute of Irish Studies, Queen's University, Belfast

O'Dowd, M. (1986), 'Gaelic Society and Economy', in C. Brady and R. Gillespie (eds), *Natives and Newcomers: The Making of Early Colonial Society*, Irish Academic Press, Dublin, 120–147

O'Dowd, M. (1991a), 'Women and War in Ireland in the 1640s', in M. MacCurtain and M. O'Dowd (eds), *Women in Early Modern Ireland*, Wolfhound Press, Dublin, 91–111

O'Dowd, M. (1991b), *Power, Politics and Land: Early Modern Sligo, 1568–1688*, Institute of Irish Studies, Queen's University, Belfast

O'Dowd, M. (2005), *A History of Women in Ireland, 1500–1800*, Longman, Harlow

O'Farrell, P. (1986; 2001), *The Irish in Australia, 1788 to the Present*, New South Wales University Press, Kensington/Cork University Press, Cork

O'Farrell, P. (2000), 'Varieties of New Zealand Irishness: A Meditation', in L. Fraser (ed.), *A Distant Shore: Irish Migration and New Zealand Settlement*, University of Otago Press, Dunedin, 25–35

Office of the First Minister and Deputy First Minister (2005), *A Shared Future: Policy and Strategic Framework for Good Relations in Northern Ireland*, Belfast

Ó Fiaich, T. (1971), 'Filíocht Uladh mar Fhoinse don Stair Shóisialta', *Studia Hibernica*, 11, 80–129

Ó Fiaich, T. (1990), 'Migration from Ulster to County Mayo in 1795–96', *Ulster Local Studies*, 7–19

O'Flanagan, P. (1988), 'Urban Minorities and Majorities: Catholics and Protestants in Munster Towns c. 1659–1850', in W. J. Smyth and K. Whelan (eds), *Common Ground: Essays on the Historical Geography of Ireland Presented to T. Jones Hughes*, Cork University Press, Cork, 124–148

O'Flanagan, P. et al. (eds) (2005), *Atlas of Cork City*, Cork University Press, Cork

O'Gallagher, M. (1984), *Grosse Île: Gateway to Canada, 1832–1937*, Livres Carraig Books, Quebec

O'Gallagher, M. (1995), *Eyewitness Grosse Isle, 1847*, Livres Carraig Books, Quebec

Ó Gráda, C. (1989), *The Great Irish Famine*, Macmillan, London

Ó Gráda, C. (1995) *Ireland: A New Economic History, 1780–1939*, Oxford University Press, Oxford

Ó Gráda, C. (1997a), *A Rocky Road: The Irish Economy Since the 1920s*, Manchester University Press, Manchester

Ó Gráda, C. (1997b), 'The Great Famine and Other Famines', in C. Ó Gráda (ed.), *Famine 150: Commemorative Lecture Series*, University College Dublin Press, 129–158

Ó Gráda, C. (1998), *Immigrants, Savers and Runners: the Emigrant Industrial Savings Bank in the 1850s*, Department of Economics, UCD, Dublin

Ó Gráda, C. (1999), *Black '47 and Beyond: The Great Irish Famine in History, Economy and Memory*, Princeton University Press, Princeton, NJ

Ó Gráda, C. (2006), *Jewish Ireland in the Age of Joyce: A Socioeconomic History*, Princeton University Press, Princeton, NJ

Ó Gráda, C. and Walsh, B. M. (1995), 'Fertility and Population in Ireland, North and South', *Population Studies*, 49(2), 259–279

Ó Gráda, Cormac and O'Rourke, Kevin H. (2006), 'Mass Migration as Disaster Relief', in C. Ó Gráda (ed.), *Ireland's Great Famine: Interdisciplinary Perspectives*, University College Dublin Press, Dublin, 121–142

O' Hara, D. (2006), *English Newsbooks and Irish Rebellion 1641–1649*, Four Courts Press, Dublin

Ohlmeyer, J. (1998), '"Civilizing of Those Rude Parts": Colonization within Britain and Ireland, 1580s–1640s', in N. Canny (ed.), *The Oxford History of the British Empire, vol. I: The Origins of Empire to 1689*, Oxford University Press, Oxford, 124–147

Ohlmeyer, J. (1995), *Ireland from Independence to Occupation, 1641–1660*, Cambridge University Press, Cambridge

O'Leary, P. (2000), *Immigration and Integration: The Irish in Wales, 1798–1922*, University of Wales Press, Cardiff

Ollerenshaw, P. (1985), 'Industry', in L. Kennedy and P. Ollerenshaw (eds), *An Economic History of Ulster, 1820–1939*, Manchester University Press, Manchester, 62–108

Olson, S. (2003), *Mapping Human History: Genes, Race and Our Common Origins*, Houghton Mifflin, Boston, New York

O'Mahoney S. C. (2000), 'Cromwellian Transplantation from Limerick', *North Munster Antiquarian Journal*, 42, 29–52

O Mahony, C. (1997), *In the Shadows: Life in Cork 1750–1930*, Tower Books, Cork

Ó Maitiú, S. (2003), *Dublin's Suburban Towns 1834–1930: Governing Clontarf, Drumcondra, Dalkey, Killiney, Kilmainham, Pembroke, Kingstown, Blackrock, Rathmines and Rathgar*, Four Courts Press, Dublin

Ó Muraíle, N. (ed.) (2007), *Turas na dTaoiseach nUltach as Érinn: from Ráth Maoláin to Rome: Tadhg Ó Cianáin's Contemporary Narrative of the Journey into Exile of the Ulster Chieftains and Their Followers, 1607–8 (The so-called 'Flight of the Earls')*, Pontifical Irish College, Rome

Ó Murchada, C. (1998), *Sable Wings over the Land: Ennis, County Clare, and its Wider Community during the Great Famine*, Clasp Press, Ennis

O'Riordan, M. (1905), *Catholicity and Progress in Ireland*, Herder, Dublin

Osborne, R. D. (1982), 'The Lockwood Report And The Location of a Second University In Northern Ireland', in F. W. Boal and J. N. H. Douglas (eds), *Integration and Division: Perspectives on the Northern Ireland Problem*, Academic Press, London

Osborne, R., Cormack, R. and Gallagher, A. (1991), 'Educational Qualifications and the Labour Market', in R. Osborne and R. Cormack (eds), *Discrimination and Public Policy in Northern Ireland*, Clarendon, Oxford, 93–119

Osborne, R. and Smith, A. with Hayes, A. (2006), *Higher Education in Northern Ireland: A Report on Factors Associated with Participation and Migration*, Office of First Minister and Deputy First Minister, Equality Directorate Research Branch, Belfast

O'Scea, C. (2001), 'The Devotional World of the Irish Catholic Exile in Early-modern Galicia, 1598–1666', in T. O'Connor (ed.), *The Irish in Europe, 1580–1815*, Four Courts Press, Dublin, 27–48

O'Scea, C. (2004), 'Irish Emigration to Castille in the Opening Years of the Seventeenth Century', in P. J. Duffy (ed), *To and from Ireland: Planned Migration Schemes c. 1600–2000*, Geography Publications, Dublin, 17–38

Ó Súileabháin, M. (1933; 1976 edn.), *Fiche Blian Ag Fás*, An Sagart, Má Nuad

O'Sullivan, M. (1933; 1953 edn.), *Twenty Years A-Growing*, trans. M. L. Davies and G. Thomson, Oxford University Press, Oxford

O'Sullivan, M. J. (2006), *Ireland and the Global Question*, Cork University Press, Cork

O'Sullivan, P. (ed.) (1992–97), *The Irish World Wide: History, Heritage, Identity*, 6 vols, Leicester University Press, Leicester

O'Sullivan, P. (ed.) (1992), *Patterns of Migration, The Irish World-Wide: History, Heritage and Identity*, vol. 1, *The Irish in the New Communities*, Leicester University Press, Leicester

O'Sullivan, P. (1992a), 'General Introduction', in P. O'Sullivan (ed.), *The Irish World-Wide: History, Heritage and Identity*, vol. 1, *Patterns of Migration*, Leicester University Press, Leicester, xiii–xxiv

O'Sullivan, P. (1994), 'Introduction', in P. O'Sullivan (ed.), *The Irish World-Wide: History, Heritage and Identity*, vol. 3, *The Creative Migrant*, Leicester University Press, London and New York, 1–27

O'Sullivan, P. (ed.) (1995), *The Irish World Wide: History, Heritage, Identity*, vol. 4, *Irish Women and Irish Migration*, Leicester University Press, Leicester

O'Sullivan, P. (2003), 'Developing Irish Diaspora Studies: A Personal View', *New Hibernia Review*, 7(1), 130–148

O'Toole, F. (1997), *The Ex-Isle of Erin: Images of Global Ireland*, New Island Books, Dublin

Owens, G. (2005), 'Social History', in L. M. Geary and M. Kelleher (eds), *Nineteenth-century Ireland: A Guide to Recent Research*, University College Dublin Press, Dublin, 27–42

Page Moch, L. (1992; 2003), *Moving Europeans: Migration in Western Europe since 1650*, Indiana University Press, Bloomington, IN

Page Moch, L. (1999), 'Dividing Time: Analytical Framework for Migration History Periodization', in J. Lucassen and L. Lucassen (eds), *Migration, Migration History, History*, Peter Lang, Bern, 41–56

Paisley, Ian R. K. (1976), *America's Debt to Ulster: Bicentenary of the United States, 1776–1976*, Martyrs Memorial Publications, Belfast

Palmer, S. H. (1988), *Police and Protest in England and Ireland, 1780–1850*, Cambridge University Press, Cambridge

Panayi, P. (ed.) (1996), *Germans in Britain since 1500*, Hambledon Press, London

Papastergiadis, N. (1999), *The Turbulence of Migration: Globalization, Deterritorialization and Hybridity*, Polity Press, Cambridge

Park, R. E., Burgess, E. W. and McKenzie, R. D. (1967), *The City*, University of Chicago Press, Chicago

Parkhill, T. (1997), '"Permanent Deadweight": Emigration from Ulster Workhouses during the Famine', in E. M. Crawford (ed.), *The Hungry Stream*, Institute of Irish Studies, Belfast, 87–100

Parkhill, T. (2001), '"God help them, what is to become of them?" Famine Emigration from Ulster', in P. Fitzgerald and S. Ickringill (eds), *Atlantic Crossroads: Historical Connections between Scotland, Ulster and North America*, Colourpoint, Newtownards, 41–54

Parkhill, T. (2003), 'The Wild Geese of '98: Émigrés of the Rebellion', *Seanchas Ard Mhaca*, 19(2), 18–35

Parkhill, T. (2004), '"With a little help from their friends": Assisted Emigration Schemes, 1700–1845', in P. J. Duffy and G. Moran (eds), *To and from Ireland: Planned Migration Schemes, c. 1600–2000*, Geography Publications, Dublin, 57–78

Parkinson, A. (2004), *Belfast's Unholy War: The Troubles of the 1920s*, Four Courts Press, Dublin

Paris, C., Adair, A., Berry, J., McGreal, S., Murtagh, B. and O'Hanlon, C. (1997), *Local Housing Market Analysis and Perceptions of Local Housing Markets within the Craigavon District Council Area, Final Report to the Northern Ireland Housing Executive*, University of Ulster, Londonderry

Patterson, B. (ed.) (2002), *The Irish in New Zealand: Historical Contexts and Perspectives*, Stout Research Centre for New Zealand Studies, Victoria University of Wellington

Patterson, B. (ed.) (2006), *Ulster–New Zealand Migration and Cultural Transfers*, Four Courts Press, Dublin

Pearsall, A. W. H. (1989), 'Steam in the Irish Sea', in M. McCaughan and J. Appleby (eds), *The Irish Sea: Aspects of Maritime History*, Institute of Irish Studies, Queen's University, Belfast, 111–120

Pelly, P. and Tod, A. (2005), *The Highland Lady in Dublin, 1851–1856: Elizabeth Grant of Rothiemurchus*, New Island, Dublin

Pender, S. (ed.) (2002), *A Census of Ireland circa 1659 with Essential Materials from the Poll Money Ordinances 1660–1661*, new introduction by W. J. Smyth, Irish Manuscripts Commission, Dublin

Perceval Maxell, M. (1973; 1990; 1999), *The Scottish Migration to Ulster in the Reign of James I*, Ulster Historical Foundation, Belfast

Perceval-Maxwell, M. (1987), 'Debate Reply', *Irish Economic and Social History*, XIV, 59–61

Petty, W. (1972, 1970 edn), *Political Anatomy of Ireland*, Irish University Press, Shannon

Place, G. (1994), *The Rise and Fall of Parkgate: Passenger Port for Ireland, 1686–1815*, Chetham Society, Manchester

Póirtéir, C. (1995), *Famine Echoes*, Gill and Macmillan, Dublin

Pollock, J. (2002), *Kitchener*, Constable and Robinson, London

Poole, M. A. (1982). 'Religious Residential Segregation in Northern Ireland', in F. Boal and J. Douglas (eds), *Integration and Division: Geographical Perspectives on the Northern Ireland Problem*, Academic Press, London, 281–308

Poole, M. A. (1999), 'Religious Residential Segregation in Urban County Derry, 1831–1991: A Study of Variation in Space and Time', in G. O'Brien (ed.), *Derry & Londonderry: History & Society*, Geography Publications, Dublin, 557–572

Poole, M. A. (2004), 'Has it Made Any Difference? The Geographical Impact of the 1994 Cease-fire in Northern Ireland', *Terrorism and Political Violence*, 16(3), 401–419

Poole, M. A. and Doherty, P. (1996a), *Ethnic Residential Segregation in Belfast*, University of Ulster, Coleraine

Poole, M. A. and Doherty, P. (1996b), *Ethnic Residential Segregation in Northern Ireland*, University of Ulster, Coleraine

Pooley, C. G. (1989), 'Segregation or Integration? The Residential Experience of the Irish in mid-Victorian Britain', in R. Swift and S. Gilley (eds), *The Irish in Britain, 1815–1939*, Barnes & Noble, Savage, MD

Pooley, C. G. (2000), 'From Londonderry to London: Identity and Sense of Place for a Protestant Northern Irish Woman in the 1930s', in D. MacRaild (ed.), *The Great Famine and Beyond: Irish Migrants in Britain in the Nineteenth and Twentieth Centuries*, Irish Academic Press, Dublin, 189–213

Pooley, C. G. (2006), 'Living in Liverpool: the Modern City', in J. Belchem (ed.), *Liverpool 800: Culture, Character and History*, Liverpool University Press, Liverpool, 171–256

Pope, P. E. (2004), *Fish into Wine: the Newfoundland Plantation in the Seventeenth Century*, University of North Carolina Press, Chapel Hill and London

Porter, J. (1965), *The Vertical Mosaic: An Analysis of Social Class and Power in Canada*, University of Toronto Press, Toronto

Powell, J. S. (1994), *Huguenots, Planters, Portarlington*, Frenchchurch Press, Dublin

Power, T. (2004), 'The Palmerston Estate in County Sligo: Improvement and Assisted Emigration before 1850', in P. J. Duffy and G. Moran (eds), *To and from Ireland: Planned Migration Schemes c. 1600–2000*, Geography Publications, Dublin, 105–136

Power, U. (1988), *Terra Straniera: The Story of the Italians in Ireland*, np, Dublin

Prunty, J. (1998), *Dublin Slums, 1800–1925: A Study in Urban Geography*, Irish Academic, Dublin

Prunty, J. (2004), *Maps and Map-Making in Local History*, Four Courts Press, Dublin

Purdie, B. (1990), *Politics in the Streets: The Origins of the Civil Rights Movement in Northern Ireland*, Blackstaff Press, Belfast

Pyle, H. (1993), *Jack B. Yeats: His Watercolours, Drawings and Pastels*, Irish Academic Press, Dublin

Quine, M. S. (1996), *Population Politics in Twentieth-century Europe: Fascist Dictatorships and Liberal Democracies*, Routledge, London

Quinn, D. B. (1985), *The Image of Irelande with a Discoverie of Woodkarne by John Derricke 1581: With an Introduction, Transliteration and Glossary by David B. Quin*, Blackstaff Press, Belfast

Quinn, D. B. (1991), *Ireland and America: Their Early Associations, 1500–1640*, Liverpool University Press, Liverpool

Rankin, K. J. (2001), 'County Armagh and the Boundary Commission', in A. J. Hughes and W. Nolan (eds), *Armagh: History and Society*, Geography Publications, Dublin, 947–990

Raughter, R. (1992), 'A Natural Tenderness: Women's Philanthropy in Eighteenth Century Ireland', unpublished MA thesis, University College, Dublin

Ravenstein, E. G. (1885; 1889), 'The Laws of Migration', *Journal of the Royal Statistical Society*, 48, 167–227; 52, 214–301

Ray, C. (2001), *Highland Heritage: Scottish Americans in the American South*, University of North Carolina Press, Chapel Hill, NC, London

Redmond, A. (ed.) (2000), *That was Then, This is Now: Change in Ireland, 1949–1999*, Central Statistics Office, An Príomh-Oifig Staidrimh, Dublin

Reece, B. (2001), *The Origins of Irish Convict Transportation to New South Wales*, Palgrave Macmillan, Basingstoke

Rees, J. (2000), *Surplus People: The Fitzwilliam Clearances, 1847–1856*, Collins Press, Cork

Reimers, D. M. (1998), *Unwelcome Strangers: American Identity and the Turn Against Immigration*, Columbia University Press, New York

Rex, J. and Mason, D. (eds) (1986), *Theories of Race and Ethnic Relations*, Cambridge University Press, Cambridge

Richards, E. (2002), *Britannia's Children: Emigration from England, Scotland, Wales and Ireland since 1600*, Hambledon Press, London

Richards, E. (2005), 'Running Home from Australia: Intercontinental Mobility and Migrant Expectations in the Nineteenth Century', in M. Harper (ed.), *Emigrant Homecomings: the Return Movement of Emigrants, 1600–2000*, Manchester University Press, Manchester, 77–104

Richmond, A. H. (1984), 'Explaining Return Migration', in D. Kubát (ed.), *The Politics of Return: International Return Migration in Europe*. Proceedings of the First European Conference on International Return Migration, Rome and New York: Centre for Migration Studies, 269–275

Ridge, J. T. (1996), 'Irish County Societies in New York, 1880–1914', in R. H. Bayor and T. J. Meagher (eds), *The New York Irish*, Johns Hopkins University Press, Baltimore, MD

Rivlin, R. (2003) *Shalom Ireland: A Social History of Jews in Modern Ireland*, Gill and MacMillan, Dublin

Roberts, G. (2004), 'Neutrality, Identity and the Challenge of the Irish Volunteers', in D. Keogh and M. O'Driscoll (eds), *Ireland in World War Two: Neutrality and Survival*, Mercier Press, Dublin, 274–284

Robertson, R. (1992), *Globalization: Social Theory and Global Culture*, Sage, London

Robins, J. (1995), *The Miasma: Epidemic and Panic in Nineteenth Century Ireland*, Institute of Public Administration, Dublin

Robinson, P. (1984), *The Plantation of Ulster: British Settlement in an Irish Landscape, 1600–1670*, Gill and Macmillan, Dublin

Rodgers, N. (2000), *Equiano and Anti-Slavery in Eighteenth Century Belfast*, Linenhall Library, Belfast

Rodgers, N. (2004), *Ireland, Slavery and Anti-Slavery, 1645–1865*, Macmillan, London

Rodriguez, M. S. and Grafton, A. T. (2007), *Migration in History: Human Migration in Comparative Perspective*, University of Rochester Press, Rochester, NY

Roediger, D. R. (1999), *The Wages of Whiteness: Race and the Making of the American Working Class*, Verso, New York/Haymarket, London

Rogers, N. (1975), 'Popular Disaffection in London during the '45', *London Journal*, 1(1), 5–27

Rose, M. E. (1976), 'Settlement, Removal and the New Poor Law', in D. Fraser (ed.), *The New Poor Law in the Nineteenth Century*, Macmillan, London, 25–44

Rowland, K. T. (1970), *Steam at Sea: A History of Steam Navigation*, David & Charles, Newton Abbot

Royle, S. (1993), 'Industrialization, Urbanization and Urban Society in Post-Famine Ireland c. 1850–1921', in B. J. Graham and L. J. Proudfoot (eds), *An Historical Geography of Ireland*, Academic Press, London, 258–288

Royle, S. (2003), 'Blasket Islands', in B. Lalor (ed.), *Encyclopaedia of Ireland*, Gill and Macmillan, Dublin, 97

Rudé, G. (1959), 'Mother Gin and the London Riots of 1736', *Guildhall Miscellany*, I, pt. 10, 53–62

Ruhs, M. (2004), 'Ireland: A Crash Course in Immigration Policy', Centre on Migration, Policy and Society, Oxford University, http://www.migrationinformation.org

Ryan, D. (1997), 'Jewish Immigrants in Limerick – a Divided Community', in D. Lee (ed.), *Limerick Remembered*, Limerick Civic Trust, Limerick, 167–170

Ryan, L. (1990), 'Irish Emigration to Britain since World War II', in R. Kearney (ed.), *Migrations: The Irish at Home & Abroad*, Wolfhound Press, Dublin, 45–68

Ryan, L. (2003), 'Moving Spaces and Changing Places: Irish Women's Memories of Emigration to Britain in the 1930s', *Journal of Ethnic and Migration Studies*, 29(1), 67–83

Ryan, L. (2004), 'Family Matters: (E)migration, Familial Networks and Irish Women in Britain', *The Sociological Review*, 52(3), 351–370

Ryan, L. (2007a), 'Who Do You Think You Are? Irish Nurses Encountering Ethnicity and Constructing Identity in Britain', *Ethnic and Racial Studies*, 30(3), 416–438

Ryan, L. (2007b), 'Migrant Women, Social Networks and Motherhood: the Experiences of Irish Nurses in Britain', *Sociology*, 41(2), 295–312

Savage, R. J. Jr (2003), 'Constructing/Deconstructing the Image of Sean Lemass' Ireland', in R. J. Savage (ed.), *Ireland in the New Century: Politics, Culture and Identity*, Four Courts Press, Dublin, 151–162

Scally, R. (1984), 'Liverpool Ships and Irish Emigrants in the Age of Sail', *Journal of Social History*, 17, 5–30

Scally, R. (1995), *The End of Hidden Ireland: Rebellion, Famine and Emigration*, Oxford University Press, Oxford

Schellekens, J. (1996), 'Irish Famines and English Mortality in the Eighteenth Century', *Journal of Interdisciplinary History*, XXVII, 29–42

Schepin, O. P. and Yermakov, W. V. (1991), *International Quarantine*, International Universities Press, Madison, WI

Schrier, A. (1958), *Ireland and the American Emigration 1850–1900*, University of Minnesota Press, Minneapolis, MN

Scott, F. D. (1960), 'The Study of the Effects of Migration', *Scandinavian Economic History Review*, 3, 161–174

Seaver, G. (1963), *John Allen Fitzgerald Gregg, Archbishop*, Faith Press, London

Senior, H. (1972), *Orangeism: the Canadian Phase*, McGraw-Hill Ryerson, Toronto

Senior, H. (1991), *The Last Invasion of Canada: The Fenian Raids, 1866–1870*, Dundurn Press, Toronto, Oxford

Sexton, J. J. (2003) 'Emigration and Immigration in the Twentieth Century: an Overview', in J. R. Hill (ed.), *A New History of Ireland, Vol. VII, Ireland, 1921–1984*, Oxford University Press, Oxford, 796–824

Sexton J. J. and O'Leary, R. (1996), 'Factors Affecting Population Decline in Minority Religious Communities in the Republic of Ireland', in *Building Trust in Ireland: Studies Commissioned by the Forum for Peace and Reconciliation*, Blackstaff Press, Belfast, 255–332

Sharpe, J. A. (1987), *Early Modern England: A Social History, 1550–1760*, Edward Arnold, London

Sharpe, P. (ed.) (2001), *Women, Gender and Labour Migration*, Routledge, London

Shearman, H. (1955), *Northern Ireland: Its History Resources and People*, Belfast, Her Majesty's Stationery Office

Sheffer, G. (2003), *Diaspora Politics at Home and Abroad*, Cambridge University Press, Cambridge

Sheridan, V. (2007), 'Tuyen Pham: Caught between Two Cultures', in B. Fanning (ed.), *Immigration and Social Change in the Republic of Ireland*, Manchester University Press, Manchester, 129–152

Sheridan, E. (2001a), 'Designing the Capital City: Dublin, c. 1660–1810', in J. Brady and A. Simms (eds), *Dublin Through Space and Time*, Four Courts Press, Dublin, 66–135

Sheridan, E. (2001b) 'Living in the Capital City: Dublin in the Eighteenth Century', in J. Brady and A. Simms (eds), *Dublin Through Space and Time*, Four Courts Press, Dublin, 136–158

Sheridan-Quantz, E. (2001), 'The Multi-Centred Metropolis: The Social Topography of Eighteenth-century Dublin', in P. Clark and R. Gillespie (eds), *Two Capitals: London and Dublin 1500–1840*, Oxford University Press, Oxford, 265–295

Shields, S. (1984), 'Population Decline in Inishatieve-Altanagh, 1841–1951', *An Tearmann*, 4, 74–79

Shirlow, P. (2003), 'Who Fears to Speak: Fear, Mobility and Ethno-sectarianism in the Two "Ardoynes"', *The Global Review of Ethnopolitics*, 3(1), 76–91

Shirlow, P., Graham, B., McMullan, A., Murtagh, B., Robinson, G. and Southern, N. (2005), *Population Change and Social Inclusion Study, Derry/Londonderry*, St Columb's Park House, Derry/Londonderry

Shirlow, P. and Murtagh, B. (2006), *Belfast: Segregation, Violence and the City*, Pluto, London

Shuttleworth, I. and Green, A. (2004), 'Labour Market Change in Northern Ireland: Unemployment, Employment and Policy', in I. Shuttleworth and R. Osborne (eds), *Fair Employment in Northern Ireland: a Generation On*, Blackstaff Press, Belfast, 100–121

Shyllon, F. O. (1977), *Black People in Britain, 1555–1833*, Oxford University Press, Oxford

Sigona, N. (2003), 'How can a "Nomad" be a "Refugee"? Kosovo Roma and Labelling Policy in Italy', *Sociology*, 37(1), 69–79

Silke, J. J. (1976), 'The Irish Abroad, 1534–1691', in T. W. Moody, F. X. Martin and F. J. Byrne (eds), *A New History of Ireland, vol. III, Early Modern Ireland, 1534–1691*, Oxford University Press, Oxford, 587–632

Silverman, M. (2006), *An Irish Working Class: Explorations in Political Economy and Hegemony, 1800–1950*, University of Toronto Press, Toronto

Silvey, Rachel (2004), 'Power, Difference and Mobility: Feminist Advances in Migration Studies', *Progress in Human Geography*, 28(4), 490–506

Simmington, R. C. (1970), *The Transplantation to Connacht 1654–58*, Irish University Press, Dublin

Simms, A. (2001), 'Origins and Early Growth', in J. Brady and A. Simms (eds), *Dublin Through Space & Time*, Four Courts Press, Dublin, 15–65

Simms, A. and Andrews, J. H. (1994), *Irish Country Towns*, Mercier Press, Dublin

Simms, A. and Andrews, J. H. (1995), *More Irish Country Towns*, Mercier Press, Dublin

Simms, H. (1993), 'Violence in County Armagh, 1641', in B. Mac Cuarta (ed.), *Ulster 1641: Aspects of the Rising*, Institute of Irish Studies, Queen's University, Belfast, 123–138

Simms, J. G. (1969), *Jacobite Ireland, 1685–91*, Routledge & Kegan Paul, London

Skinner, E. P. (1982), 'The Dialectic between Diasporas and Homelands', in J. E. Harris (ed.), *Global Dimensions of the African Diaspora*, Howard University Press, Washington, DC

Slack, P. (1988), *Poverty and Policy in Tudor & Stuart England*, Longman, London

Sloan, R. (2000), *William Smith O'Brien and the Young Ireland Rebellion of 1848*, Four Courts Press, Dublin

Smith, A. E. (1947), *Colonists in Bondage: White Servitude and Convict Labor in America, 1607–1776*, University of North Carolina Press, Chapel Hill, NC

Smith, B. G. (1990) *The 'Lower Sort': Philadelphia's Labouring People, 1750–1800*, Cornell University Press, Ithaca, NY

Smout, T. C., Landsman, N. C. and Devine, T. M. (1994), 'Scottish Emigration in the Seventeenth and Eighteenth Centuries', in N. Canny (ed.), *Europeans on the Move: Studies on European Migration, 1500–1800*, Oxford University Press, Oxford, 76–112

Smyth, M. (1995), *Borders within Borders: Material and Ideological Aspects of Segregation*, Templegrove Action Research, Derry/Londonderry

Smyth, W. J. (1992), 'Irish Emigration, 1700–1920', in P. C. Emmer and M. Mörner (eds), *European Expansion and Migration: Essays on the Intercontinental Migration from Africa, Asia, and Europe*, Berg, New York, Oxford, 49–78

Smyth, W. J. (1997), 'A Plurality of Irelands: Regions, Societies and Mentalities', in B. Graham (ed.), *In Search of Ireland: A Cultural Geography*, Routledge, London, New York, 19–42

Smyth, W. J. (2000), 'Ireland a Colony: Settlement Implications of the Revolution in Military-administrative, Urban and Ecclesiastical Structures, c.1550 to c. 1730', in T. Barry (ed.), *A History of Settlement in Ireland*, Routledge, London, 158–186

Smyth, W. J. (2006) *Map-making, Landscapes and Memory: A Geography of Colonial and Early Modern Ireland, c. 1530–1750*, Cork University Press, Cork

Soja, E. W. (1996), *Thirdspace: Journeys to Los Angeles and other Real-and-Imagined Places*, Blackwell, Oxford, Cambridge, MA

Solar, P. (1983), 'Agricultural Productivity and Economic Development in Ireland and Scotland in the Early Nineteenth Century', in T. M. Devine and D. Dickson (eds), *Ireland and Scotland, 1600–1850: Parallels and Contrasts in Economic and Social Development*, John Donald, Edinburgh, 70–88

Spiers, E. M. (1996), 'Army Organisation and Society in the Nineteenth Century', in T. Bartlett and K. Jeffery (eds), *A Military History of Ireland*, Cambridge University Press, Cambridge, 335–357

Spjut, R J. (1986), 'Internment and Detention without Trial in Northern Ireland 1971–1975: Ministerial Policy and Practice', *Modern Law Review* (November), 712–739

Stark, O. (1991), *The Migration of Labour*, Blackwell, Oxford

Stewart, A. T. Q. (1995), *The Summer Soldiers: The 1798 Rebellion in Antrim and Down*, Blackstaff Press, Belfast

Stevenson, J. (1920; 1990 edn.), *Two Centuries of Life in Down, 1600–1800*, White Row Press, Belfast

Stock, J. and Freyer, G. (eds) (1800, 1988 edn.), *Narrative of the Year of the French, 1798*, Irish Humanities Centre, Dublin

Stockdale, A. (1992), 'State Intervention and the Impact on Rural Mobility Flows in Northern Ireland', *Journal of Rural Studies*, 8(4), 411–421

Stockdale, A. (1993), 'Residential Mobility Patterns in Rural Northern Ireland: Clean Break or More of the Same?', *Scottish Geographical Magazine*, 109(1), 32–36

Stradling, R. A. (1994), *The Spanish Monarchy and Irish Mercenaries: The Wild Geese in Spain, 1618–68*, Irish Academic Press, Dublin

Strickland, W. G. (1913; 1989) *A Dictionary of Irish Artists*, 2 vols, Irish Academic Press, Dublin

Sullivan, A. M. (1867; 1898), *The Story of Ireland*, Gill, Dublin

Sullivan, M. (2005), 'Who was Thomas Kittle? Aspects of Emigration from County Cavan', unpublished MSSc thesis, Queen's University of Belfast, Centre for Migration Studies at the Ulster-American Folk Park

Sullivan, M. (2006), 'The Cavan Diaspora', in B. S. Turner (ed.), *Migration and Myth: Ulster's Revolving Door*, Ulster Local History Trust, Downpatrick, 69–80

Swift, R. and Gilley, S. (eds) (1999), *The Irish in Britain: The Local Dimension*, Four Courts Press, Dublin

Swords, L. (2007), *The Flight of the Earls: A Popular History*, Columba Press, Dublin

Takaki, R. T. (1979; 1980), *Iron Cages: Race and Culture in Nineteenth-Century America*, Athlone, London

Tansey, P. (1998), *Ireland at Work: Economic Growth and the Labour Market, 1987–1997*, Oak Tree Press, Dublin

Taylor, A. (2001), *American Colonies: The Settlement of North America to 1800*, Penguin, London

Templegrove Action Research (1995), *Survey of Two Enclave Communities in Derry/ Londonderry*, TAR, Derry/Londonderry

Tennant, V. (2003), *Sanctuary in a Cell: The Detention of Asylum Seekers in Northern Ireland*, Law Centre (NI), Belfast

't Hart, M. (1982), 'Heading for Paddy's Green Shamrock Shore: The Returned Emigrants in Nineteenth Century Ireland', unpublished MA, Rijks Unversiteit, Groningen, summarised by M. Hart (1983), in *Irish Economic and Social History*, X, 96–97

't Hart, M. (1985), 'Irish Return Migration in the Nineteenth Century', *Tijdschrift voor Economische en Sociale Geografie*, LXXVI(3), 223–231

Thébaud, A. J. (1879), *The Irish Race in the Past and the Present*, Peter F. Collier, New York

Thomas, A. (1992), *The Walled Towns of Ireland*, Vol. 1, Irish Academic Press, Blackrock

Thomas, C. (1999), 'The City of Londonderry: Demographic Trends and Socio-economic Characteristics, 1650–1900', in G. O'Brien (ed.), *Derry and Londonderry: History & Society*, Geography Publications, Dublin, 359–378

Thomas, W. I. and Znaniecki, F. (1918–20; 1974), *The Polish Peasant in Europe and America*, Octagon Books, Chicago, New York

Thompson, J. E. (2001) *American Policy and Northern Ireland: A Saga of Peacebuilding*, Praeger, London

Thomson, A. (2005), '"My wayward heart": Homesickness, Longing and the Return of British Post-war immigrants from Australia', in M. Harper (ed.), *Emigrant Homecomings: the Return Movement of Emigrants, 1600–2000*, Manchester University Press, Manchester, 105–131

Tillyard, S. K. (1998), *Citizen Lord: Edward Fitzgerald, 1763–98*, Vintage, London

Todaro, M. P. (1969), 'A Model of Labor Migration and Urban Unemployment in Less Developed Countries', *American Economic Review*, 59, 138–148

Tölyan, K. (1991), 'Commentary', *Diaspora*, 1(2), 225–228

Toner, G. (1996), *Place-names of Northern Ireland, vol. 5, County Derry I, The Moyola Valley*, Institute of Irish Studies, Queen's University, Belfast

Toner, P. M. (ed.) (1988), *New Ireland Remembered: Historical Essays on the Irish in New Brunswick*, New Ireland Press, Fredericton

Tonge, J. (2005), *The New Northern Ireland Politics?*, Palgrave Macmillan, Basingstoke

Torpey, J. (2000), *The Invention of the Passport: Surveillance, Citizenship and the State*, Cambridge University Press, Cambridge

Torpey, J. (2001), 'The Great War and the Birth of the Modern Passport System', in J. Caplan and J. Torpey (eds), *Documenting Individual Identity: The Development of State Practices in the Modern World*, Princeton University Press, Princeton, NJ, 256–270

Travers, P. (1988), *Settlements and Divisions: Ireland, 1870–1922*, Helicon, Dublin

Travers, P. (1995a), '"There was nothing for me there": Irish Female Emigration, 1922–71', in P. O'Sullivan (ed.), *The Irish World Wide: History, Heritage, Identity*, vol. 4, *Irish Women and Irish Migration*, Leicester University Press, Leicester, 146–167

Travers, P. (1995b), 'Emigration and Gender: The Case of Ireland, 1922–60', in M. O'Dowd and S. Wichert (eds), *Chattel, Servant, or Citizen? Women's Status in Church, State, and Society*, Institute of Irish Studies, Queen's University, Belfast, 187–199

Travers, P. (2003), 'Emigration, Commission on', in B. Lalor (ed.), *Encyclopedia of Ireland*, Gill and Macmillan, Dublin, 351

Treadwell, V. (1998), *Buckingham in Ireland, 1616–1628: a Study in Anglo-Irish Politics*, Four Courts Press, Dublin

Trew, J. D. (2000), 'Treasures from the Attic: Viva Voce Records', *Journal of American Folklore*, 113, 305–313

Trew, J. D. (2005a), 'The Forgotten Irish? Contested Sites and Narratives of Nation in Newfoundland', *Ethnologies*, 27(2), 43–77

Trew, J. D. (2005b), 'Challenging Utopia: Irish Migrant Narratives of Canada', *Canadian Journal of Irish Studies*, 31(1), 108–116; 31(2), 5

Trew, J. D. (2007), 'Negotiating Identity and Belonging: Migration Narratives of Protestants from Northern Ireland', *Immigrants & Minorities*, 25(1), 22–48

Trew, J. D. (2008) 'Reluctant Diasporas of Northern Ireland: Narratives of Home, Conflict, Difference', *Journal of Ethnic and Migration Studies*

Truxes, T. M. (1988), *Irish-American Trade, 1660–1783*, Cambridge University Press, Cambridge

Turner, F. J. (1920), *The Frontier in American History*, H. Holt, New York

Turton , J. (1999), 'Mayhew's Irish: the Irish Poor in mid-Nineteenth-century London', in R. Swift and S. Gilley (eds), *The Irish in Victorian Britain: The Local Dimension*, Four Courts Press, Dublin, 122–155

Twiss, R. (1776), *A Tour in Ireland in 1775*, London

Twomey, B. (2005), *Smithfield and the Parish of St. Paul, Dublin, 1698–1750*, Four Courts Press, Dublin

Tyson, R. E. (1986), 'Famine in Aberdeenshire, 1695–9: Anatomy of a Crisis', in D. Stevenson (ed.), *From Lairds to Louns: County and Burgh Life in Aberdeen, 1600–1800*, Aberdeen University Press, Aberdeen, 32–52

Ugba, A. (2007), 'African Pentecostals in Twenty-first-century Ireland: Identity and Integration', in B. Fanning (ed.), *Immigration and Social Change in the Republic of Ireland*, Manchester University Press, Manchester, 168–184

Usherwood, P. and Spencer-Smith, J. (1987), *Lady Butler Battle Artist, 1846–1933*, National Army Museum, London

Vallely, F. (ed.), *The Companion to Irish Traditional Music*, Cork University Press, Cork

Van Amersfoort, H. (2004), 'The Waxing and Waning of a Diaspora: Moluccans in the Netherlands, 1950–2002', *Journal of Ethnic and Migration Studies*, 30(1), 151–174

Vaughan. W. E. (1994), *Landlords and Tenants in Mid-Victorian Ireland*, Oxford University Press, Oxford

Vaughan, W. E. and Fitzpatrick, A. J. (1978), *Irish Historical Statistics: Population, 1821–1971*, Royal Irish Academy, Dublin

Vertovec, S. and Cohen, R. (1999), *Migration, Diasporas and Transnationalism*, Edward Elgar, Cheltenham

Villiers-Tuthill, K. (2006), *Alexander Nimmo and the Western District: Emerging Infrastructure in Pre-Famine Ireland*, Connemara Girl Publications, Galway

Wallerstein, I. (1974), *Capitalist Agriculture and the Origins of the European World-economy in the Sixteenth Century*, Studies in Social Discontinuity, Academic Press, New York, London

Wallerstein, I. (ed.) (1975), *World Inequality: Origins and Perspectives on the World System*, Spokesman, Nottingham

Walsh, B. (2002), *Roman Catholic Nuns in England and Wales, 1800–1937: A Social History*, Irish Academic Press, Dublin

Walsh, B. M. (1974), 'Expectations, Information and Human Migration: Specifying an Econometric Model of Irish Migration to Britain', *Journal of Regional Science*, 14, 107–120

Walsh, B. M. (1989), *Ireland's Changing Demographic Structure*, Gill and Macmillan, Dublin

Walsh, J. P. (1979), *The San Francisco Irish 1850–1976*, Irish Literary and Historical Society, San Francisco

Walsh, P. (ed.) (1916), *The Flight of the Earls: Edited from the Author's Manuscript with Translation and Notes*, Maynooth Record Society, Gill, Dublin

Walsh, P. (ed.) (1948), *Beatha Aodha Ruaidh Uí Dhomhnaill: The Life of Aodh Ruadh O Domhnaill, Transcribed from the Book of Lughaidh Ó Clérigh*, Irish Texts Society, 42(1)

Walter, B. (2001), *Outsiders Inside: Whiteness, Place and Irish Women*, Routledge, London

Walter, B. (2003), 'Women, Emigration', in B. Lalor (ed.), *Encyclopedia of Ireland*, Gill and Macmillan, Dublin, 1147–1148

Walter, B. with Gray, B., Almeida, L. D. and Morgan, S. (2002), *Irish Emigrants and Irish Communities Abroad: a Study of the Existing Sources of Information and Analysis for the Task Force on Policy Regarding Emigrants*, Department of Foreign Affairs, Dublin; www.gov.ie/iveagh

Ward, E. (1996), '"A big show-off to show what we could do": Ireland and the Hungarian Refugee Crisis of 1956', *Irish Studies in International Affairs*, 8, 131–141

Ward, E. (1998), 'Ireland and Refugees/Asylum-seekers: 1922–1996', in *The Expanding Nation: Towards a Multi-ethnic Ireland*. Proceedings of a conference held in Trinity College, Dublin, 41–48

Ward, E. (2000), 'Ireland's Refugee Policies: A Critical Historical Overview', in D. Driscoll (ed.), *Irish Human Rights Review 2000*, Round Hall, Dublin, 157–175

Ward, P. (2002), *Exile, Emigration and Irish Writing*, Irish Academic Press, Dublin

Warm, D. (1998), 'The Jews of Northern Ireland', in P. Hainsworth (ed.), *Divided Society: Ethnic Minorities and Racism in Northern Ireland*, Pluto, London

Waters, M. C (1990), *Ethnic Options: Choosing Identities in America*, University of California Press, Berkeley, CA, Oxford

Watt, P. and McCaughey, F. (eds) (2006), *Service Delivery to Minority Ethnic Groups, Northern Ireland, Republic of Ireland*, Scotland, Office of First Minister and Deputy First Minister, Belfast

Weber, P. (1997), *On the Road to Rebellion: The United Irishmen and Hamburg, 1796–1803*, Four Courts Press, Dublin

Weiner, G. (2001), 'Irish Jewry in the 17th and 18th Centuries', in R. Vigne and C. Littleton (eds), *From Strangers to Citizens: The Integration of Immigrant Communities in Britain, Ireland and Colonial America, 1550–1750*, Sussex Academic Press, Eastbourne, 276–284

Weir, R. M. (1983), *Colonial South Carolina: A History*, KTO Press, New York

Weldon, N. G. (2002), *Pioneers in Flight: Aer Lingus and the Story of Aviation in Ireland*, Liffey Press, Dublin

Wells, R. (1996), 'The Irish Famine of 1799–1801: Market Culture, Moral Economies and Social Protest', in A. Randall and A. Charlesworth (eds), *Markets, Market Culture and Popular Protest in Eighteenth-century Britain and Ireland*, Liverpool University Press, Liverpool, 163–194

Wells, R. A. (2004), 'The Nameless Dead Migrants and the Historian's Task', paper given at the Fifteenth Ulster American Heritage Symposium, Magee College, University of Ulster, Derry, June

Wheeler, J. S. (2002), 'Sense of Identity in the Army of the English Republic, 1645–51', in A. I. Macinnes and J. Ohlmeyer (eds), *The Stuart Kingdoms in the Seventeenth Century: Awkward Neighbours*, Four Courts Press, Dublin, 151–168

Whelan, K. (1990), 'The Catholic Community in Eighteenth-century County Wexford', in T. P. Power and K. Whelan (eds), *Endurance and Emergence: Catholicism in the Eighteenth Century*, Irish Academic Press, Dublin, 129–170

Whelan, K. (1991) 'Settlement and Society in Eighteenth-century Ireland', in G. Dawe and J. W. Foster (eds), *The Poet's Place: Ulster Literature and Society*, Institute of Irish Studies, Queen's University, Belfast, 45–62

Whelan, M., Nolan, W. and Duffy, P. J. (2004), 'State-sponsored Migrations to the East Midlands in the Twentieth Century', in J. Duffy (ed.), *To and from Ireland: Planned Migration Schemes, c. 1600–2000*, Geography Publications, Dublin, 175–196

Whelan, T. (1987), 'The New Emigrants', *Newsweek*, 10 October

White, P. and Woods, R. (eds) (1980), *The Geographical Impact of Migration*, Longman, London

White, R. (1998; 1999), *Remembering Ahanagran: Storytelling in a Family's Past*, Cork University Press, Cork

Whyte, I. D. (1995), *Scotland before the Industrial Revolution: An Economic and Social History, c. 1050–1750*, Longman, London

Whyte, I. D. (1995) 'Scottish and Irish Urbanisation in the Seventeenth and Eighteenth Centuries: a Comparative Perspective', in S. J. Connolly, R. A. Houston and R. J. Morris (eds), *Conflict, Identity and Economic Development: Ireland and Scotland, 1600–1939*, Carnegie, Preston, 14–28

Whyte, I. D. (2000), *Migration and Society in Britain, 1550–1830*, Macmillan, Basingstoke

Whyte, J. (1983), 'The Permeability of the United Kingdom/Irish Border: A Preliminary Reconnaissance', *Administration*, 31(3), 300–315

Wigfall-Williams, W. and Robinson, G. (2001), 'A World Apart: Mixed Marriage in Northern Ireland', *ARK*, Belfast

Wiggins, J. (nd), *The Exmouth of Newcastle, 1811–1847: the Story of an Irish Emigrant Ship Wrecked on the Scottish Isle of Islay*, Bowmore, Islay

Williams, R. (1988), *Keywords: a Vocabulary of Culture and Society*, Fontana, London

Wilson, A. J. (1995), *Irish America and the Ulster Conflict 1968–1995*, Blackstaff, London

Wilson, A. J. (2005), 'Maintaining the Cause in the Land of the Free: Ulster Unionists and US Involvement in the Northern Ireland Conflict, 1968–72', *Éire–Ireland*, 40(3/4), 212–239

Wilson, D. A. (1998), *United Irishmen, United States: Immigrant Radicals in the Early Republic*, Four Courts Press, Dublin

Wilson, D. A. (2008), *Thomas D'Arcy McGee: Passion, Reason and Politics, 1825–57*, McGill-Queen's, Montreal and Kingston

Wilson, T. M. and Donnan, H. (2006), *The Anthropology of Ireland*, Berg, Oxford, New York

Winder, R. (2004), *Bloody Foreigners: The Story of Immigration to Britain*, Little, Brown, London

Wokeck, M. S. (1989) 'German and Irish Immigration to Colonial Philadelphia', *Proceedings of the American Philosophical Society*, 133(2), 128–143

Wokeck, M. (1999), *Trade in Strangers: The Beginnings of Mass Migration to North America*, Penn State University Press, University Park, PA

Wokeck, M. (2002), 'Irish and German Migration to Eighteenth-century North America', in D. Eltis (ed.), *Coerced and Free Migration: Global Perspectives*, Stanford University Press, Stanford, CA, 152–175

Woodham-Smith, C. (1962), *The Great Hunger: Ireland 1845–9*, Hamish Hamilton, London

Wright, L. B. and Fowler, E. W. (1968), *English Colonization of North America*, Edward Arnold, London

Wright, R. L. (1975), *Irish Emigrant Ballads and Songs*, Bowling Green University Popular Press, Bowling Green, OH

Wrightson, K. (1982), *English Society, 1580–1690*, Hutchinson, London

Wrightson, Keith (2002), *Earthly Necessities: Economic Lives in Early Modern Britain, 1470–1750*, Penguin, London

Wrigley, E. A. and Schofield, R. S. (1981), *A Population History of England, 1541–1871*, Arnold, London

Wyman, M. (1993), *Round-Trip to America: The Immigrants Return to Europe, 1880–1930*, Cornell University Press, Ithaca, NY

Wyman, M. (2005), 'Emigrants Returning: the Evolution of a Tradition', in M. Harper (ed.), *Emigrant Homecomings: the Return Movement of Emigrants, 1600–2000*, Manchester University Press, Manchester, 16–31

Yiftachel, O. (1992), *Planning a Mixed Region in Israel*, Avebury, Aldershot

Young, Arthur (1780; repr 1970), *A Tour in Ireland, 1776–1779*, ed. A. W. Hutton with a new introduction by J. B, Ruane, 2 vols, Irish University Press, Shannon

Young, J. R. (2004), 'Scotland and Ulster in the Seventeenth Century: the Movement of Peoples over the North Channel', in W. Kelly and J. R. Young (eds), *Ulster and Scotland, 1600–2000*, Four Courts Press, Dublin, 11–32

Young, J. R. (2007), 'Escaping Massacre: Refugees in Scotland in the Aftermath of the 1641 Ulster Rebellion', in D. Edwards, P. Lenihan and C. Tait (eds), *Age of Atrocity: Violence and Political Conflict in Early Modern Ireland*, Four Courts Press, Dublin, 219–241

Yuzyk, P. (1967), *Ukrainian Canadians: Their Place and Role in Canadian Life*, Ukrainian Canadian Business and Professional Federation, Toronto

Zelinsky, W. (1971), 'The Hypothesis of the Mobility Transition', *Geographical Review*, 61, 219–249

Zipf, G. K. (1949; 1965), *Human Behaviour and the Principle of Least Effort: an Introduction to Human Ecology*, Haffner, New York

Zolberg, A. and Benda, P. (eds) (2001), *Global Migrants, Global Refugees: Problems and Solutions*, Berghahn, Oxford

Index of Subjects

Index of Personal Names

Index of Place Names

Place names in the text are listed here alphabetically. They are also grouped in relation to the homeland of Ireland/Northern Ireland (by county) and the main regions of its global diaspora (Africa, Asia, Australasia, Britain, Europe, North America, South America).